W9-BKH-685

# The Past Speaks TO 1688

## SOURCES AND PROBLEMS IN ENGLISH HISTORY

# the
# PAST
# SPEAKS *to 1688*

*Sources and Problems in English History*

INTRODUCED AND EDITED BY

*Lacey Baldwin Smith*

*and*

*Jean Reeder Smith*

Northwestern University

D. C. HEATH AND COMPANY
Lexington, Massachusetts   Toronto

Cover: *A View of London Bridge ca. 1616*. John Freeman & Company.

ILLUSTRATION CREDITS

p. 284: From W. C. Sellar and R. J. Yeatman, *1066 And All That*, illus. John
Reynolds (London: Methuen & Co., Ltd., 1930). Reprinted by permission
of Associated Book Publishers, Ltd.

*Copyright © 1981 by D. C. Heath and Company.*

All rights reserved. No part of this publication
may be reproduced or transmitted in any form or
by any means, electronic or mechanical, including
photocopy, recording, or any information storage
or retrieval system, without permission in writing
from the publisher.

Published simultaneously in Canada.

Printed in the United States of America.

International Standard Book Number: 0–669–02920–3

Library of Congress Catalog Card Number: 80–81773

# pREFACE

There are no substitutes for original documents; they are the voice of the past that not even the most immaculate and imaginative historians can recreate in their own words. It is not enough that tomorrow's students be told that an absolutely new and unprecedented fear has entered into the modern world which affects, directly or indirectly, every human being on earth: the knowledge that the human species has the power to exterminate itself. To savor and to comprehend the full impact of that horror, it is necessary to read the words of those who helped create the specter and of those who must live with it. Similarly, the nightmares of the past — the dread of disease and plague that could wipe out a family and strike down the young and healthy without warning; the fear of starvation; the knowledge that storm, pestilence, and crop failure could leave a family destitute — are dead memories that no amount of demographic information can resurrect unless the past is allowed to speak for itself.

The dead speak, but they rarely do so in a fashion understandable to the living. What our forefathers did can readily be extracted from the sources. Even on the basis of the most haphazard and accidental documentation, the picture of their deeds and actions is relatively clear and precise. But why they did what they did is infinitely more obscure; for self-analysis, the desire to dissect the social organism and assign functional explanations to human behavior, is a relatively recent phenomenon. The distant past was content to describe, to command, to condemn, and to praise, but rarely did it seek to explain in a manner intelligible to the modern mind. It is easy enough to record the power and position of the Catholic Church in medieval society; it is infinitely more difficult to demonstrate the religious orientation of those who worshipped, prayed, and obeyed the will of God. Thirteenth-century sources portray feudalism in action, but only indirectly do they reveal the feudal mind at work — the concept of lordship, the acceptance of hierarchy, the love of display, the ideal of personal honor, and the military ethos that pervaded feudal society.

The temptation in compiling a book of readings is to stick to descriptions and avoid explanations, to record in a series of documentary snippets the panorama of the past — its vagaries and varieties, its richness and poverty, its political successes and human achievements, as well as its social blunders and individual suffering. Such an anthology assures coverage and satisfies every historical taste; however, it also ignores the mind and motive behind economic, social, and political activity. The doorway to history is via the primary sources; the path to comprehending actions that seem incomprehensible is to listen to the voice of the past. Understanding can be achieved only by reading the entire document, noting what is said and what is not said, then asking what are the assumptions about man, society, and God that are implied but not necessarily stated. The story of the "Palfrey" in Chapter 5 of this book, for example, is a delightful romance, and it conjures up the happy picture of baronial halls lit with torches, of lords and ladies sitting about the banquet table, and of troubadours and professional storytellers enthralling their audiences with tales of good and evil. But read in its entirety with a critical and historical mind, the story becomes a wellspring of information about the mentality of the age — how the medieval author organized a story, why the characterization seems deficient to the modern reader, what feudal society regarded as normal and acceptable behavior, what it viewed as the ideal social code, and what it thought about the purpose of society and man's proper role in life.

Unfortunately, documents given in their entirety or presented in an abbreviated form, which does not emasculate their historical usefulness, means selection, and selection in turn means omission. It is, however, the underlying principle of this collection of readings that a few well-chosen documents* directed to a select number of central themes are more valuable than a myriad of tidbits covering all aspects of the past. Accordingly, the sources have been organized into sixteen chapters, each representing approximately one week of discussion and speculation. Tastes vary; for some readers the emphasis may seem too cultural, too political, too social, and the themes selected for each chapter may appear arbitrary. But this anthology has been compiled around a single thesis: the basic biological and psychological drives of men and women — hunger, sex, love, fear, and the need to socialize — remain constant, yet what makes a society distinctive and what gives explanation to a particular style of human behavior is society's views on the purpose of life and the meaning of the universe, and its aspirations for humanity.

L. B. S.

J. R. S.

---

* In most of the selections, the spelling, punctuation, and word usage have been modernized in order to make the readings more intelligible to the twentieth-century reader.

# CONTENTS

# 7 The Old Church  131

# 8 Society Gone Wrong?  151

# 9 The Utopia  173

# 10 The Structure of Tudor Society  189

## 11 Renaissance England

## 12 Protestant–Catholic: Good Christian–Good Subject

## 13 Political Styles and Constitutional Conflict

# 14 *The Great Rebellion*    283

# 15 *Changing Perceptions of Society*    305

# 16 *New Horizons*    331

# *The Past Speaks* TO 1688

SOURCES AND PROBLEMS IN ENGLISH HISTORY

# 1

# Anglo-Saxon England:
# The Structure of "Primitive" Society

There are many questions that might be asked about Anglo-Saxon England: How extensive was the destruction of Roman Britain, and how rapid was the so-called "barbarization" of the island? How was Anglo-Saxon tribal society organized, and how swiftly did tribal groups develop into larger, if not necessarily more complex, political units? What the following six documents emphasize are three important but interrelated problems: the social and psychological conditions that delimited and conditioned the process of state and kingdom building; the virtues and behavior patterns upon which society attempted to build; and, finally, the role and function of religion in this "civilizing" process. In a sense this chapter is central to the entire volume, for the remaining fifteen chapters are all extensions upon and contrasts to the political, social, and religious mentality that prevailed from the seventh to the tenth centuries.

The first document, the *Anglo-Saxon Chronicle*, is probably the most important single source we possess on Anglo-Saxon England, for it covers the entire span from the Germanic invasions to one hundred years after the Norman Conquest, a period of over seven centuries. The *Chronicle* appears in a number of different versions, is the work of several authors, draws heavily on other documents, and is probably not complete. Nevertheless, it represents an invaluable picture not only of Anglo-Saxon and early Norman England but also of the mentality of the various authors who wrote it. The reader should pay special attention to the organizational principle (or lack thereof) underlying the *Chronicle* and the kinds of events that are recorded, for both reveal the chroniclers' views of history as well as the strengths and weaknesses of Anglo-Saxon society.

THE LANDING OF HENGIST AND HORSA

The song or poem of "The Battle of Maldon" is a composition that even in prose translation possesses considerable literary merit. It describes an episode in the Danish invasion of England that took place in August of 991 and was probably composed by one of the participants. Better than almost any other source, it dramatizes the ethical strengths and weaknesses that underlay Anglo-Saxon society. The third selection, King Edmund II's Code (939–946), is one of many efforts on the part of Anglo-Saxon kings to impose a degree of rationality on human relations. It is interesting to note the avowed purpose of the regulations and how they attempted to control and, at the same time, build upon the basic instincts and behavior patterns of a society that as yet had very little experience with or taste for a centralized royal authority.

The remaining four documents focus on the conversion of England to Christianity, the message that the Church sought to convey to Christians and pagans alike, and the view of God and religion that prevailed throughout most of Anglo-Saxon society. The story of the conversion of Edwin, King of Northumbria, in 625 is from the Venerable Bede's *Ecclesiastical History of the English Nation*. It shows the nature of the competition between Christianity and paganism and describes what influenced individuals to accept one faith over the other. The letter of advice written by Bishop Daniel of Winchester (705–744) to St. Boniface is a considerably more sophisticated discussion of the problem of how best to appeal to the pagans; and the warning by Alcuin of York (735–804) to King Ethelred of Northumbria describes not only the realities of eighth-century Anglo-Saxon political life but also the Church's efforts to introduce a bare minimum of ethical and social standards.

Alcuin was the most thoughtful and influential schoolmaster of his age and eventually became head of Charlemagne's palace school at Aachen. He felt that he had cause for alarm because, ever since Aelfwald had seized the throne of Northumbria in 758, the history of that kingdom had been little more than a series of royal assassinations and atrocities. Ethelred himself survived as king for five years; he was then deposed, but regained his throne in 788, and was finally murdered in 796, three years after Alcuin's letter of warning. The occasion for Alcuin's epistle was the sack in June of 793 of the monastery of Lindisfarne by the Norsemen, and the schoolmaster was at pains to point out the lesson to Ethelred. The final selection describing the miracle of a Northumbrian "called Cuningham" is found in Bede's *Ecclesiastical History* and gives an idea of the intensity and quality of the popular religion that was believed in by all people — the mighty and the humble alike.

## The Anglo-Saxon Chronicle

The Anglo-Saxon Chronicle was written in the late ninth century and is associated with the reign of King Alfred. Around 892, a Wessex chronicler, using earlier and now lost sources, wrote a year-by-year narrative of English history starting with the birth of Christ. Copies were sent to various religious centers where they were kept up to date. Consequently, there are four different chronicles, three ending between 1066 and 1079 and the fourth continuing to 1154. The excerpts from the years 446 to 1042 give a grim picture of the life expectancy of Anglo-Saxon kings, but chronicles, like newspapers today, give more space to disasters than to the humdrum of daily life.

**446** In this year the Britons sent across the sea to Rome and begged for help against the Picts,[1] but they got none there, for the Romans were engaged in a campaign against Attila, king of the Huns. And they then sent to the Angles, and made the same request of the chieftains of the English.

. . .

**449** Vortigern[2] invited the English hither, and they then came in three ships to Britain at the place Ebbsfleet. King Vortigern gave them land in the south-east of this land on condition that they should fight against the Picts. They fought against the Picts and had the victory wherever they came. They then sent to Angeln, bidding them more help, and had them informed of the cowardice of the Britons and the excellence of the land. They then immediately sent hither a greater force to help of the others. Those men came from three tribes of Germany; from the Old Saxons, from the Angles, from the Jutes. From the Jutes came the people of Kent and of the Isle of Wight, namely the tribe which now inhabits the Isle of Wight and that race in Wessex which is still called the race of the Jutes. From the Old Saxons came the East Saxons, the South Saxons, and the West Saxons. From Angeln, which ever after remained waste, between the Jutes and the Saxons, came the East Angles, the Middle Angles, the Mercians, and all the Northumbrians. Their leaders were two brothers, Hengest and Horsa, who

SOURCE: From Dorothy Whitelock with David C. Douglas and Susie I. Tucker, trans. and eds., *The Anglo-Saxon Chronicle* (London: Eyre & Spottiswoode, Ltd., publishers, 1961), pp. 9–11, 30–1, 37, 40, 102–6. By permission of the publishers.

[1] from Scotland   [2] King of the Britons

were sons of Wihtgils. Wihtgils was the son of Witta, the son of Wecta, the son of Woden. From that Woden has descended all our royal family, and that of the Southumbrians also.

**455** In this year Hengest and Horsa fought against King Vortigern at the place which is called Ægelesthrep, and his brother Horsa was killed there; and after that Hengest and his son Æsc succeeded to the kingdom.

**456** In this year Hengest and his son Æsc fought against the Britons in the place which is called Creacanford and killed 4,000 men; and the Britons then deserted Kent and fled with great fear to London.

**465** In this year Hengest and Æsc fought against the Britons near Wippedesfleet, and there slew twelve British chiefs, and a thegn[3] of theirs was slain there whose name was Wipped.

**473** In this year Hengest and Æsc fought against the Britons and captured countless spoils and the Britons fled from the English as from fire.

. . .

**491** In this year Ælle and Cissa besieged Andredesceaster, and killed all who were inside, and there was not even a single Briton left alive.

**495** In this year two chieftains, Cerdic and his son Cynric, came with five ships to Britain at the place which is called Cerdicesora, and they fought against the Britons on the same day.

**501** In this year Port and his two sons Bieda and Maegla came to Britain with two ships at the place which is called Portsmouth; and there they killed a British man of very high rank.

**508** In this year Cerdic and Cynric killed a British king, whose name was Natanleod, and 5,000 men with him; and the land right up to Charford was called Netley after him.

**514** In this year the West Saxons came into Britain with three ships at the place which is called Cerdicesora; and Stuf and Wihtgar fought against the Britons and put them to flight.

**519** In this year Cerdic and Cynric succeeded to the kingdom [of the West Saxons]; and in the same year they fought against the Britons at a place called Charford.

. . .

**757** In this year Cynewulf and the councillors of the West Saxons deprived [King] Sigeberht of his kingdom because of his unjust acts, except for Hampshire; and he retained that until he killed the ealdorman[4] who stood by him longest; and then Cynewulf drove him into the Weald,[5] and he lived there until a swineherd stabbed him to death by the stream at Privett, and he was avenging Ealdorman Cumbra. And Cynewulf often fought with great battles against the Britons. And when he had held the kingdom 31 years, he wished to drive out an atheling[6] who was called Cyneheard, who was brother of the aforesaid Sigeberht. And Cyneheard discovered that the king was at Meretun visiting his mistress with a small following, and he overtook him there and surrounded the chamber before the men who were with the king became aware of him.

Then the king perceived this and went to the doorway, and nobly defended himself until he caught sight of the atheling (and thereupon he rushed out against him and wounded him severely). Then they all fought against the king until they had slain him. Then by the woman's outcry, the king's thegns became aware of the disturbance and ran to the spot, each as he got ready (and as quickly as possible). And the atheling made an offer to each of money and life; and not one of them would accept it. But they continued to fight until they all lay dead except for one British hostage, and he was severely wounded.

Then in the morning the king's thegns who had been left behind heard that the king had been slain. Then they rode thither

---

[3] warrior    [4] chief    [5] forests of Southeast England    [6] a prince

— his ealdorman Osric and his thegn Wigfrith and the men he had left behind him — and discovered the atheling in the stronghold where the king lay slain — and they had locked the gates against them — and they went thither. And then the atheling offered them money and land on their own terms, if they would allow him the kingdom, and told them that kinsmen of theirs, who would not desert him, were with him. Then they replied that no kinsman was dearer to them than their lord, and they would never serve his slayer; and they offered their kinsmen that they might go away unharmed. Their kinsmen said that the same offer had been made to their comrades who had been with the king. Moreover they said that they would pay no regard to it, "any more than did your comrades who were slain along with the king." And they proceeded to fight around the gates until they broke their way in, and killed the atheling and the men who were with him, all except one, who was the ealdorman's godson. And he saved his life, though he was often wounded. And Cynewulf reigned 31 years, and his body is buried at Winchester and the atheling's at Axminster; and their true paternal ancestry goes back to Cerdic.

And in the same year Æthelbald, king of the Mercians, was slain at Seckington, and his body is buried at Repton. And Beornred succeeded to the kingdom and held it for but a little space and unhappily. And that same year Offa succeeded to the kingdom and held it for 39 years, and his son Ecgfrith held it for 141 days. Offa was son of Thingfrith, the son of Eanwulf, the son of Osmod, the son of Eawa, the son of Pybba, the son of Creoda, the son of Cynewold, the son of Cnebba, the son of Icel, the son of Eomaer, the son of Angeltheow, the son of Offa, the son of Waermund, the son of Wihtlaeg, the son of Woden.

• • •

**798** In this year Cenwulf, king of the Mercians, ravaged the people of Kent and

of the Marsh, and they seized Praen their king and brought him in fetters into Mercia, and they had his eyes put out and his hands cut off. And Æthelheard, archbishop of Canterbury, arranged a synod, and established and confirmed at the command of Pope Leo all the things relating to God's monasteries which were appointed in the days of King Wihtred and of other kings.

**799** In this year the Romans cut out Pope Leo's tongue and put out his eyes and banished him from his see; and then immediately afterwards he could, with God's help, see and speak and was again pope as he had been before.

• • •

**821** In this year Cenwulf, king of the Mercians, died, and Ceolwulf succeeded to the kingdom. And Ealdorman Eadberht died.

**823** In this year Ceolwulf was deprived of his kingdom.

**824** In this year two ealdormen, Burghelm and Muca, were killed. And there was a synod at Clofesho.

**825** In this year there was a battle between the Britons and the men of Devon at Galford. And the same year Egbert[7] and Beornwulf, king of the Mercians, fought at Wroughton, and Egbert had the victory and a great slaughter was made there. Then he sent from the army his son Æthelwulf and his bishop Ealhstan and his ealdorman Wulfheard to Kent, with a large force, and they drove King Bealdred north across the Thames; and the people of Kent and of Surrey and the South Saxons and the East Saxons submitted to him because they had been wrongfully forced away from his kinsmen. And the same year the king of the East Angles and the people appealed to King Egbert for peace and protection, because of their fear of the Mercians. And that same year the East Angles killed Beornwulf, king of the Mercians.

**827** In this year Ludeca, king of the Mercians, was killed, and his five ealdormen

---

[7] King of the West Saxons

with him; and Wiglaf succeeded to the king-dom.

829  In this year there was an eclipse of the moon on Christmas eve. And that year King Egbert conquered the kingdom of the Mercians, and everything south of the Humber; and he was the eighth king who was "Bretwalda."[8]

·  ·  ·

The following portion of the *Chronicle* deals with the political and dynastic confusion following the death of Cnut in 1035, and a genealogy may be helpful in getting the relationships straight.

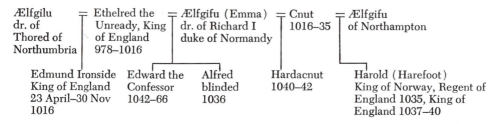

| Ælfgilu dr. of Thored of Northumbria | = | Ethelred the Unready, King of England 978–1016 | = | Ælfgifu (Emma) dr. of Richard I duke of Normandy | = | Cnut 1016–35 | = | Ælfgifu of Northampton |
|---|---|---|---|---|---|---|---|---|

| Edmund Ironside King of England 23 April–30 Nov 1016 | Edward the Confessor 1042–66 | Alfred blinded 1036 | Hardacnut 1040–42 | Harold (Harefoot) King of Norway, Regent of England 1035, King of England 1037–40 |
|---|---|---|---|---|

1035  In this year King Cnut died at Shaftesbury and he is buried in Winchester in the Old Minster; and he was king over all England for very nearly 20 years. And immediately after his death there was an assembly of all the councillors at Oxford. And Earl Leofric and almost all the thegns north of the Thames and the shipmen in London chose Harold to the regency of all England, for himself and for his brother Hardacnut, who was then in Denmark. And Earl Godwine[9] and all the chief men in Wessex opposed it as long as they could, but they could not contrive anything against it. And it was then determined that Ælfgifu, Hardacnut's mother, should stay in Winchester with the housecarls[10] of her son the king, and they should keep all Wessex in his possession; and Earl Godwine was their most loyal man. Some men said about Harold that he was the son of King Cnut and of Ælfgifu, the daughter of Ealdorman Ælfhelm, but it seemed incredible to many men; and yet he was full king over all England.

1036  In this year the innocent atheling Alfred, the son of King Ethelred, came into this country, wishing to go to his mother who was in Winchester, but Earl Godwine did not allow him, nor did the other men who had great power, because feeling was veering much towards Harold, although this was not right.

But Godwine then stopped him and put him in captivity, and he dispersed his companions and killed some in various ways; some were sold for money, some were cruelly killed, some were put in fetters, some were blinded, some were mutilated, some were scalped. No more horrible deed was done in this land since the Danes came and peace was made here. Now we must trust to the beloved God that they rejoice happily with Christ who were without guilt so miserably slain. The atheling still lived. He was threatened with every evil, until it was decided to take him thus in bonds to Ely. As soon as he arrived, he was blinded on the ship, and thus blind was brought to the monks, and he dwelt there as long as he lived. Then he was buried as well befitted him, very honourably, as he deserved, in the south chapel at the west end, full close to the steeple. His soul is with Christ.

1037  In this year Harold was chosen as king everywhere, and Hardacnut was deserted because he was too long in Denmark; and then his mother, Queen Ælfgifu, was

---

[8] ruler of Britain   [9] Father of Harold Godwine, King of England, 1066   [10] body guards

driven out without any mercy to face the raging winter. And she then went across the sea to Bruges, and Earl Baldwin received her well there and maintained her there as long as she had need. And previously in this year, Æfic, the noble dean of Evesham, died.

**1040** In this year King Harold died. Then they sent to Bruges for Hardacnut, thinking that they were acting wisely, and he then came here with 60 ships before midsummer, and then imposed a very severe tax, which was endured with difficulty, namely eight marks to the rowlock.[11] And all who had wanted him before were then ill-disposed towards him. And also he did nothing worthy of a king as long as he ruled. He had the dead Harold dug up and thrown into the fen.

**1041** In this year Hardacnut had all Worcestershire ravaged for the sake of his two housecarls, who had exacted that severe tax. The people had then killed them within the town in the minster.[12] And soon in that year there came from beyond the sea Edward, his brother on the mother's side, the son of King Ethelred, who had been driven from his country many years before — and yet he was sworn in as king; and he thus stayed at his brother's court as long as he lived. And in this year also Hardacnut betrayed Earl Eadwulf under his safe-conduct and he was then a pledge-breaker. (And in this year Æthelric was consecrated bishop in York on 11 January.)

**1042** In this year Hardacnut died in this way: he was standing at his drink and he suddenly fell to the ground with fearful convulsions, and those who were near caught him, and he spoke no word afterwards. He died on 8 June. And all the people then received Edward as King, as was his natural right.

## The Battle of Maldon (991)

The Battle of Maldon was fought in 991 near the coastal town of Maldon, in Essex, between the Anglo-Saxons and the invading Danes. The Saxon leader, Byrhtnoth, ealdorman of Essex, scorns the Viking demand for tribute and leads his thanes into battle where he is "cut down, the hero in the dust." There is no better description of the Anglo-Saxon warrior's sense of honor and loyalty.

---

Then he bade each warrior leave his horse, drive it afar and go forth on foot, and trust to his hands and to his good intent.

Then Offa's kinsman first perceived that the earl would suffer no faintness of heart; he let his loved hawk fly from his hand to the wood and advanced to the fight. By this it might be seen that the lad would not waver in the strife now that he had taken up his arms.

With him Eadric would help his lord, his chief in the fray. He advanced to war with spear in hand; as long as he might grasp his shield and broad sword, he kept his purpose firm. He made good his vow, now that the time had come for him to fight before his lord.

Then Byrhtnoth began to array his men; he rode and gave counsel and taught his warriors how they should stand and keep their ground, bade them hold their shields aright, firm with their hands and fear not at all. When he had meetly[13] arrayed his host, he alighted among the people where it pleased him best, where he knew his body-guard to be most loyal.

---

SOURCE: Reprinted from *English and Norse Documents Relating to the Reign of Ethelred the Unready* by Margaret Ashdown, by permission of Cambridge University Press, London, 1930, alternate pp. 23–37.

[11] tax on shipping    [12] church    [13] suitably

Then the messenger of the Vikings stood on the bank; he called sternly, uttered words, boastfully speaking the seafarers' message to the earl, as he stood on the shore. "Bold seamen have sent me to you, and bade me say, that it is for you to send treasure quickly in return for peace, and it will be better for you all that you buy off an attack with tribute, rather than that men so fierce as we should give you battle. There is no need that we destroy each other, if you are rich enough for this. In return for the gold we are ready to make a truce with you. If you who are richest determine to redeem your people, and to give to the seamen on their own terms wealth to win their friendship and make peace with us, we will betake us to our ships with the treasure, put to sea and keep faith with you."

Byrhtnoth lifted up his voice, grasped his shield and shook his supple spear, gave forth words, angry and resolute, and made him answer: "Hear you, searover, what this folk says? For tribute they will give you spears, poisoned point and ancient sword, such war gear as will profit you little in the battle. Messenger of the seamen, take back a message, say to your people a far less pleasing tale, how that there stands here with his troop an earl of unstained renown, who is ready to guard this realm, the home of Ethelred my lord, people and land; it is the heathen that shall fall in the battle. It seems to me too poor a thing that you should go with our treasure unfought to your ships, now that you have made your way thus far into our land. Not so easily shall you win tribute; peace must be made with point and edge, with grim battle-play, before we give tribute." . . .

There, ready to meet the foe, stood Byrhtnoth and his men. He bade them form the war-hedge with their shields, and hold their ranks stoutly against the foe. The battle was now at hand, and the glory that comes in strife. Now was the time when those who were doomed should fall. Clamour arose; ravens went circling, the eagle greedy for carrion. There was a cry upon earth.

They let the spears, hard as files, fly from their hands, well ground javelins. Bows were busy, point pierced shield; fierce was the rush of battle, warriors fell on either hand, men lay dead. Wulfmær was wounded, he took his place among the slain; Byrhtnoth's kinsman, his sister's son, was cruelly cut down with swords. Then was payment given to the Vikings; I heard that Edward smote one fiercely with his blade, and spared not his stroke, so that the doomed warrior fell at his feet. For this his lord gave his chamberlain thanks when time allowed.

Thus the stout-hearted warriors held their ground in the fray. Eagerly they strove, those men at arms, who might be the first to take with his spear the life of some doomed man. The slain fell to the earth.

The men stood firm; Byrhtnoth exhorted them, bade each warrior, who would win glory in fight against the Danes, to give his mind to war.

Then came one, strong in battle; he raised his weapon, his shield to defend him and bore down upon the man; the earl, no less resolute, advanced against the "churl." Each had evil intent toward the other. Then the pirate sent a southern spear, so that the lord of warriors was stricken. He pushed with his shield so that the shaft was splintered, and shivered the spear so that it sprang back again. The warrior was enraged; he pierced with his lance the proud Viking who had given him the wound. The warrior was deft; he drove his spear through the young man's neck; his hand guided it so that it took the life of his deadly foe. Quickly he shot down another, so that his corselet burst asunder; he was wounded through his mail in the breast, a poisoned point pierced his heart. The earl was the more content; then the proud man laughed, and gave thanks to his Creator for the day's work that the Lord had granted him.

Then one of the warriors let a dart fly from his hand, so that it pierced all too deeply Ethelred's noble thane. By his side stood a warrior not yet full grown, a boy in war. Right boldly he drew from the warrior the bloodly spear, Wulfstan's son, Wulfmær the young, and let the weapon, wondrous strong, speed back again; the point drove in so that he who had so cruelly pierced his lord lay dead on the ground. Then a man, all armed, approached the earl, with intent to bear off the warrior's treasure, his raiment and his rings and his well-decked sword. Then Byrhtnoth drew his blade, broad and of burnished edge, and smote upon his mail. All too quickly one of the seamen checked his hand, crippling the arm of the earl. Then his golden-hilted sword fell to the earth; he could not use his hard blade nor wield a weapon. Yet still the white-haired warrior spoke as before, emboldened his men and bade the heroes press on. He could no longer now stand firm on his feet. The earl looked up to heaven and cried aloud: "I thank thee, Ruler of Nations, for all the joys that I have met with in this world. Now I have most need, gracious Creator, that thou grant my spirit grace, that my soul may fare to thee, into thy keeping, Lord of Angels, and pass in peace. It is my prayer to thee that fiends of hell may not entreat it shamefully."

Then the heathen wretches cut him down, and both the warriors who stood near by, Ælfnoth and Wulfmær, lay overthrown; they yielded their lives at their lord's side.

Then those who had no wish to be there turned from the battle. Odda's sons were first in the flight, Godric for one turned his back on war, forsook the hero who had given him many a steed. He leapt upon the horse that had been his lord's, on the trappings to which he had no right. With him his brothers both galloped away, Godwin and Godwig, they had no taste for war, but turned from the battle and made for the wood, fled to the fastness and saved their lives, and more men than was fitting at all, if they had but remembered all the favours that he had done them for their good. It was as Offa had told them on the field when he held a council, that many were speaking proudly there, who later would not stand firm in time of need.

Now was fallen the people's chief, Ethelred's earl. All the retainers saw how their lord lay dead. Then the proud thanes pressed on, hastened eagerly, those undaunted men. All desired one of two things, to lose their lives or to avenge the one they loved.

With these words Ælfric's son urged them to go forth, a warrior young in years, he lifted up his voice and spoke with courage. Ælfwine said: "Remember the words that we uttered many a time over the mead, when on the bench, heroes in hall, we made our boast about hard strife. Now it may be proved which of us is bold! I will make known my lineage to all, how I was born in Mercia of a great race. Ealhelm was my grandfather called, a wise ealdorman, happy in this world's goods. Thanes shall have no cause to reproach me among my people that I was ready to forsake this action, and seek my home, now that my lord lies low, cut down in battle. This is no common grief to me, he was both my kinsman and my lord."

Then he advanced (his mind was set on revenge), till he pierced with his lance a seaman from among the host, so that the man lay on the earth, borne down with his weapon.

Then Offa began to exhort his comrades, his friends and companions, that they should press on. He lifted up his voice and shook his ash-wood spear: "Lo! Ælfwine, you have exhorted all us thanes in time of need. Now that our lord lies low, the earl on the ground, it is needful for us all that each warrior embolden the other to war, as long as he can keep and hold his weapon, hard blade, spear and trusty sword. Godric, Odda's cowardly son, has betrayed us all. Too many a man, when he rode on that horse, on that proud steed, deemed that it was our lord. So was our host divided on the field, the shield-wall broken. A curse upon his deed, in that he has put so many a man to flight!"

Leofsunu lifted up his voice and raised his shield, his buckler to defend him, and gave him answer: "This I avow, that I will not flee a foot-space hence, but will press on and avenge my liegelord in the fight. About Sturmer the steadfast heroes will have no need to reproach me now that my lord has fallen, that I made my way home, and turned from the battle, a lordless man. Rather shall weapon, spear-point and iron blade, be my end." He pressed on wrathful and fought sternly, despising flight.

Dunhere spoke and shook his lance; a simple churl, he cried above them all, and bade each warrior avenge Byrhtnoth: "He that thinks to avenge his lord, his chief in the press, may not waver nor reck for his life." Then they went forth, and took no thought for life; the retainers began to fight hardily, those fierce warriors. They prayed God that they might take vengeance for their lord, and work slaughter among their foes. . . .

Then Offa smote a seaman in the fight, so that he fell to the earth. Gadd's kinsman too was brought to the ground, Offa himself was quickly cut to pieces in the fray. Yet he had compassed what he had promised his chief, as he bandied vows with his generous lord in days gone by, that they should both ride home to the town unhurt or fall among the host, perish of wounds on the field. He lay, as befits a thane, at his lord's side.

Then came a crashing of shields; seamen pressed on, enraged by war; the spear oft pierced the life-house of the doomed. Wistan went forth, Thurstan's son and fought against the men. Wighelm's child was the death of three in the press, before he himself lay among the slain.

That was a fierce encounter; warriors stood firm in the strife. Men were falling, worn out with their wounds; the slain fell to the earth.

Oswold and Eadwold all the while, that pair of brothers, urged on the men, prayed their dear kinsmen to stand firm in the hour of need, and use their weapons in no weak fashion.

Byrhtwold spoke and grasped his shield (he was an old companion); he shook his ash-wood spear and exhorted the men right boldly: "Thoughts must be the braver, heart more valiant, courage the greater as our strength grows less. Here lies our lord, all cut down, the hero in the dust. Long may he mourn who thinks now to turn from the battle-play. I am old in years; I will not leave the field, but think to lie by my lord's side, by the man I held so dear." . . .

## Edmund II's Code (939–946)

King Edmund's Code is one of a number of statements by Anglo-Saxon kings aimed at controlling violence, especially family and kin vengeance.

---

I, King Edmund, inform all people, both high and low, who are under my authority, that I have been considering, with the advice of my councillors both ecclesiastical and lay, first of all how I could best promote Christianity.

Now, it has seemed to us first of all especially needful that we steadfastly maintain peace and concord among ourselves throughout all my dominion. I myself and all of us are greatly distressed by the manifold illegal deeds of violence which are in our midst. We have therefore decreed:

1. Henceforth, if anyone slay a man, he shall himself [alone] bear the vendetta, unless with the help of his friends he pay composition for it, within twelve months, to the full amount of the slain man's wergeld,[14] according to his inherited rank.

If, however, his kindred abandon him and will not pay compensation on his behalf, it is my will that, if afterwards they give him neither food nor shelter, all the kindred, except the delinquent, shall be free from vendetta.

SOURCE: Reprinted from *The Laws of the Kings of England from Edmund to Henry* I by A. J. Robertson, by permission of Cambridge University Press, London, 1925, alternate pp. 9–11.

[14] price set upon a man, according to rank, paid by way of compensation in case of homicide

If, however, any of his kinsmen harbour him thereafter, then, inasmuch as they had previously disclaimed him, that kinsman shall forfeit all his property to the king, and shall incur vendetta with the kin [of the slain man].

If, however, anyone from the other kindred take vengeance on any man other than the actual delinquent, he shall incur the hostility of the king and all of his friends, and shall suffer the loss of all that he possesses.

2. If anyone flees [for sanctuary] to a church or to my premises, and anyone attacks or injures him there, those who do so shall incur the penalty which has already been stated.

3. My will is that no fine for fighting or compensation for a slain dependent be remitted.

4. Further, I declare that I forbid anyone [who commits homicide] to have right of access to my household, until he has undertaken to make amends as the church requires, and has made — or set about making — reparation to the kin, and has submitted to every legal penalty prescribed by the bishop in whose diocese it is.

5. Further, I thank God and all of you, who have given me full support, for the immunity from thefts which we now enjoy. I therefore confidently expect of you, that you will be all the more willing to give your support towards this [maintenance of the public peace] in proportion as its observance is a more urgent matter for us all.

6. Further, with respect to violation of [the king's] mund[15] and attacks on a man's house, we have ordained that he who commits either of these after this shall forfeit all that he possesses, and it shall be for the king to decide whether his life shall be preserved.

7. The authorities must put a stop to vendettas. First, according to public law, the slayer shall give security to his advocate, and the advocate to the kinsmen [of the slain man], that he (the slayer) will make reparation to the kindred.

After that it is incumbent upon the kin of the slain man to give security to the slayer's advocate, that he (the slayer) may approach under safe-conduct and pledge himself to pay the wergeld.

When he has pledged himself to this, he shall find a surety for the payment of the wergeld.

When that is done, the king's "mund" shall be established. In twenty-one days from that time healsfang[16] shall be paid; in twenty-one days after that manbot[17] and twenty-one days after that the first instalment of the wergeld.

## The Conversion of Northumbria (625)

King Edwin of Northumbria (616–632) was one of the most able and successful rulers of his era, and his conversion to Roman-Benedictine Christianity was an important step in the Christianization of Anglo-Saxon England, a step which the Venerable Bede (673–735) described in detail in his *Ecclesiastical History of the English Nation.*

At this time the nation of the Northumbrians, that is, the nation of the Angles, that live on the north side of the river Humber, with their king, Edwin, received the faith, through the preaching of Paulinus, above mentioned. This Edwin, as a reward of his receiving the faith, and as an earnest of his share in the heavenly kingdom, received an

SOURCE: From J. A. Giles, trans., *The Historical Works of Venerable Bede,* 2 vols. (London, 1843), *The Ecclesiastical History of the English Nation,* Vol. I, pp. 91–94.

[15] protection  [16] part of the wergeld that went to the nearest kin  [17] the compensation due to the slain man's lord

increase of that which he enjoyed on earth, for he reduced under his dominion all the borders of Britain that were provinces either of the aforesaid nation, or of the Britons, a thing which no British king had ever done before; and he in like manner subjected to the English the Mevanian islands, as has been said above. The first whereof, which is to the southward, is the largest in extent, and most fruitful, containing nine hundred and sixty families, according to the English computation; the other above three hundred.

The occasion of this nation's embracing the faith was, their aforesaid king being allied to the kings of Kent, having taken to wife Ethelberga, otherwise called Tate, daughter to King Ethelbert. He having by his ambassadors asked her in marriage of her brother Eadbald, who then reigned in Kent, was answered, "That it was not lawful to marry a Christian virgin to a pagan husband, lest the faith and the mysteries of the heavenly King should be profaned by her cohabiting with a king that was altogether a stranger to the worship of the true God." This answer being brought to Edwin by his messengers, he promised in no manner to act in opposition to the Christian faith, which the virgin professed; but would give leave to her, and all that went with her, men or women, priests or ministers, to follow their faith and worship after the custom of the Christians. Nor did he deny, but that he would embrace the same religion, if, being examined by wise persons, it should be found more holy and more worthy of God.

Hereupon the virgin was promised, and sent to Edwin, and pursuant to what had been agreed on, Paulinus, a man beloved of God, was ordained bishop, to go with her, and by daily exhortations, and celebrating the heavenly mysteries, to confirm her, and her company, lest they should be corrupted by the company of the pagans. Paulinus was ordained bishop by the Archbishop Justus, on the 21st day of July, in the year of our Lord 625, and so he came to King Edwin with the aforesaid virgin, as a companion of their union in the flesh. But his mind was wholly bent upon reducing the nation to which he was sent to the knowledge of truth; according to the words of the apostle, "To espouse her to one husband, that he might present her as a chaste virgin to Christ." Being come into that province, he laboured much, not only to retain those that went with him, by the help of God, that they should not revolt from the faith, but, if he could, to convert some of the pagans to a state of grace by his preaching. But, as the apostle says, though he laboured long in the word, "The god of this world blinded the minds of them that believed not, lest the light of the glorious Gospel of Christ should shine unto them."

The next year, there came into the province a certain assassin, called Eumer, sent by the king of the West Saxons, whose name was Quichelm, in hopes at once to deprive King Edwin of his kingdom and his life. He had a two-edged dagger, dipped in poison, to the end, that if the wound were not sufficient to kill the king, it might be performed by the venom. He came to the king on the first day of Easter, at the river Derwent, where then stood the regal city, and being admitted as if to deliver a message from his master, whilst he was in an artful manner delivering his pretended embassy, he started on a sudden, and drawing the dagger under his garment, assaulted the king; which Lilla, the king's most beloved minister, observing, having no buckler at hand to secure the king from death, he interposed his own body to receive the stroke; but the wretch struck so home, that he wounded the king through the knight's body. Being then attacked on all sides with swords, he in that confusion also slew another soldier, whose name was Forthhere.

On that same holy night of Easter Sunday, the queen had brought forth to the king a daughter, called Eanfled. The king, in the presence of Bishop Paulinus, gave thanks to his gods for the birth of his daughter; and the bishop, on the other hand, returned thanks to Christ, and endeavoured to persuade the king, that by his prayers to him he had obtained, that the queen should bring forth the child in safety, and without much pain. The king, delighted with his words, promised, that in case God would grant him life and victory over the king by whom the assassin had been sent, he would cast off his idols, and serve Christ; and in earnest that he would perform his promise, he delivered up that same daughter to Paulinus, to be consecrated to Christ. She was the first baptized of the nation of the Northumbrians, on Whitsunday, with twelve others of her family. At that time, the king being recovered of the wound which he had received, marched with his army against the nation of the West Saxons; and having begun the war, either slew or subdued all those that he had been informed had conspired to murder him. Returning thus victorious into his own country, he would not immediately and unadvisedly embrace the mysteries of the Christian faith, though he no longer worshipped idols, ever since he made the promise that he would serve Christ; but thought fit first at leisure to be instructed, by the venerable Paulinus, in the knowledge of faith, and to confer with such as he knew to be the wisest of his prime men, to advise what they thought was fittest to be done in that case. And being a man of extraordinary sagacity, he often sat alone by himself a long time, silent as to his tongue, but deliberating in his heart how he should proceed, and which religion he should adhere to.

## Bishop Daniel of Winchester's Advice to Boniface (723–724)

One hundred years after the conversion of Northumbria, Anglo-Saxon England was exporting Roman-Benedictine Christianity back to the continent. The greatest of these missionaries, who sought to spread the gospel among the Germans east of the Rhine River, was the Wessex monk St. Boniface (d. 754). In this letter, Bishop Daniel of Winchester gives Boniface advice on how to convert the heathens.

To the venarable and beloved prelate Boniface, Daniel, servant of the people of God.

I rejoice, beloved brother and fellow priest, that you are deserving of the highest prize of virtue. You have approached the hitherto stony and barren hearts of the pagans, trusting in the plenitude of your faith, and have labored untiringly with the plowshare of Gospel preaching, striving by your daily toil to change them into fertile fields. To you may well be applied the Gospel saying: "The voice of one crying in the wilderness," etc. Yet a part of the second prize shall be given, not unfittingly, to those who support so pious and useful a work with what help they can give and supplement the poverty of those laborers with means sufficient to carry on zealously the work of preaching which has already begun and to raise up new sons to Christ.

And so I have with affectionate good will taken pains to suggest to your prudence a few things that may show you how, according to my ideas, you may most readily overcome the resistance of those uncivilized people. Do not begin by arguing with them about the origin of their gods, false as those are, but let them affirm that some of them were begotten by others through the intercourse of male with female, so that you may at least prove that gods and goddesses born after the manner of men are men and not gods and, since they did not exist before, must have had a beginning.

Then, when they have been compelled to learn that their gods had a beginning since

SOURCE: From Ephraim Emerton, trans., *The Letters of Saint Boniface* (New York: Columbia University Press, 1940), Letter XV, pp. 48–50.

some were begotten by others, they must be asked in the same way whether they believe that the world had a beginning or was always in existence without beginning. If it had a beginning, who created it? Certainly they can find no place where begotten gods could dwell before the universe was made. I mean by "universe" not merely this visible earth and sky, but the whole vast extent of space, and this the heathen too can imagine in their thoughts. But if they argue that the world existed without beginning, you should strive to refute this and to convince them by many documents and arguments. Ask your opponents who governed the world before the gods were born, who was the ruler? How could they bring under their dominion or subject to their law a universe that had always existed before them? And whence, or from whom or when, was the first god or goddess set up or begotten? Now, do they imagine that gods and goddesses still go on begetting others? Or, if they are no longer begetting, when or why did they cease from intercourse and births? And if they are still producing offspring, then the number of gods must already be infinite. Among so many and different gods, mortal men cannot know which is the most powerful, and one should be extremely careful not to offend that most powerful one.

Do they think the gods are to be worshiped for the sake of temporal and immediate good or for future eternal blessedness? If for temporal things, let them tell in what respect the heathen are better off than Christians. What gain do the heathen suppose accrues to their gods from their sacrifices, since the gods already possess everything? Or why do the gods leave it in the power of their subjects to say what kind of tribute shall be paid? If they are lacking in such things, why do they not themselves choose more valuable ones? If they have plenty, then there is no need to suppose that the gods can be pleased with such offerings of victims.

These and many similar things which it would take long to enumerate you ought to put before them, not offensively or so as to anger them, but calmly and with great moderation. At intervals you should compare their superstitions with our Christian doctrines, touching upon them from the flank, as it were, so that the pagans, thrown into confusion rather than angered, may be ashamed of their absurd ideas and may understand that their infamous ceremonies and fables are well known to us.

This point is also to be made: if the gods are all-powerful, beneficent, and just, they not only reward their worshipers but punish those who reject them. If, then, they do this in temporal matters, how is it that they spare us Christians who are turning almost the whole earth away from their worship and overthrowing their idols? And while these, that is, the Christians, possess lands rich in oil and wine and abounding in other resources, they have left to those, that is, the pagans, lands stiff with cold where their gods, driven out of the world, are falsely supposed to rule. They are also frequently to be reminded of the supremacy of the Christian world, in comparison with which they themselves, very few in number, are still involved in their ancient errors.

If they boast that the rule of the gods over those peoples has been, as it were, lawful from the beginning, show them that the whole world was once given over to idol-worship, until by the grace of Christ and through the knowledge of one God, its Almighty Founder and Ruler, it was enlightened, brought to life, and reconciled to God. For what is the daily baptism of the children of believing Christians but purification of each one from the uncleanness and guilt in which the whole world was once involved?

I have been glad to call these matters to your attention, my brother, out of my affection for you, . . .

I pray for your welfare in Christ, my very dear colleague, and beg you to bear me in mind.

## Alcuin of York's Letter of Warning to King Ethelred of Northumbria (793)

Alcuin of York (735–804) was a scholar in the Bede tradition and the leading intellectual at the Court of Charlemagne (768–814) at Aachen. He lived during a time when the prosperity and ecclesiastical learning of Bede's era (the seventh and early eighth centuries) were being systematically destroyed by the Norse invaders. His letter of warning to King Ethelred of Northumbria is perfectly clear: divine punishment for the sins of kings was at hand.

To his beloved lord, King Ethelred, and all his nobles, Alcuin, a humble deacon, sends greetings.

It is because I remember your tender affection, my brothers, fathers and Christian lords, and desire that divine mercy may long keep prosperous this country of ours, which by his grace he generously gave us long ago, that I constantly give you my counsel, dear comrades, either personally by word of mouth, or, if separated from you, by writing as the spirit directs, and repeatedly bringing to your ears as my fellow-countrymen what we know is important for the safety of our earthly homeland and for happiness in the everlasting kingdom, that by constant reiteration it may become fixed in your minds for your good. What sort of love is it that will not speak for a friend's good? To what does a man owe loyalty if not to his country, or prosperity, if not to its citizens? We are doubly related as fellow-citizens — of one city in Christ, as sons of mother church, and as natives of one fatherland. So do not shrink from accepting graciously what I offer in my concern for the good of my country; and do not think I am finding fault with you but rather wishing to save you from punishment.

We and our fathers have now lived in this fair land for nearly three hundred and fifty years, and never before has such an atrocity been seen in Britain as we have now suffered at the hands of a pagan people.[18] Such a voyage was not thought possible. The church of St. Cuthbert is spattered with the blood of the priests of God, stripped of all its furnishings, exposed to the plundering of pagans — a place more sacred than any in Britain. Suffering and disaster have started in the very place where, after the departure of St. Paulinus from York [633], the Christian religion began in our nation. Who is not afraid at this? Who does not grieve for this, as if his own fatherland were taken? The foxes have despoiled the chosen vineyard; the inheritance of the Lord has been given to a people not his own. Pagans play where God was praised. The holy feast is turned to mourning.

Consider closely and carefully, brothers, in case this unprecedented, unheard-of disaster is due to some unheard-of evil practice. I do not say that the sin of fornication has not existed among our people in the past. But since the days of King Aelfwald, fornication, adultery and incest have flooded the land to such an extent that these sins are committed without any shame even among nuns. Why should I mention greed, robbery and judicial violence when it is as clear as day how these crimes have increased everywhere. A plundered people is proof of it. He who reads Holy Scripture and studies

---

SOURCE: Extract from S. Allott, *Alcuin of York, ca. A.D. 732 to 804, His Life and Letters* (York, England: William Sessions Ltd., The Ebor Press, 1974), pp. 18–20. By permission of Mr. Allott and the publishers.

[18] *atrocity* . . . the sack of the monastery of Lindisfarne by the Norsemen in 793

ancient history and considers the way the world develops will find that kings have lost kingdoms and peoples their lands for sins of this kind, and when powerful men have wrongly seized the property of others, they have rightly lost their own.

There were warnings of this calamity in unusual happenings or strange conduct. What is the meaning of the bloody rain which we saw in Lent in the city of York in the church of St. Peter, the chief apostle, in the chief church of the kingdom, falling in a clear sky menacingly from the top of the roof at the north end of the building? Does it not mean that punishment by blood was coming from the north upon the people? Its beginning may be seen in the blow which recently fell upon the house of God? . . .

A terrifying judgment has begun at the house of God where rest some of the brightest lights of all Britain. What must we think of other places, when divine judgment has not spared this most holy place? I do not think this is only for the sins of those who live there.

I wish their punishment would reform others, that many would fear what a few have suffered and each one would say in his heart in fear and trembling: "If so many men and such holy fathers could not protect their home and resting-place, who will protect mine?" Protect your country by regular prayer to God and by works of justice and mercy to men. Be moderate in dress and food. A country has no better protection than the justice and goodness of its leaders and the prayers of the servants of God. Remember that the good and just King Hezekiah obtained from God by a single prayer the destruction of a hundred and eighty-five thousand of the enemy by an angel in a single night. Similarly he averted imminent death by bitter tears and won fifteen years more of life from God by such prayer (Isa. 37.36 and 38.5).

In conduct be upright, pleasing God and winning praise from men. Be rulers, not ravagers, of the people, pastors, not predators. You received your honours at God's hand: keep his commandments that he who has been your benefactor may be your saviour. Obey God's priests. They must give account to God for their advice to you, and you for your obedience to them. Let there be united peace and love between you. They pray for you; you protect them. Above all, have the love of God in your hearts, and show this love in keeping his commandments. Love him as father, that he may protect you as sons. He will be your judge, whether you will or no. Be constant in good works, that you may have his favour. "For the fashion of this world passes" and all things are fleeting which are seen or possessed here. All a man can take with him of his labours is his alms and good works. We all have to stand before the judgment-seat of Christ, that each may show what he has done, good or bad. Beware of the torments of hell while they can be avoided, and win for yourselves the kingdom of God and everlasting joy with Christ and his saints for all eternity.

My dear lords, fathers, brothers and sons, may God make you happy in this earthly kingdom and grant you an eternal fatherland with his saints.

## The Miracle of Cuningham (696)

The Venerable Bede (673–735), who has been described as "the first articulate Englishman," spent his life at the Benedictine monastery at Jarrow in Northumbria. There he wrote his magnificent *Ecclesiastical History*, which he conceived as the

SOURCE: From J. A. Giles, trans., *The Historical Works of Venerable Bede*, 2 vols. (London, 1843), *The Ecclesiastical History of the English Nation*, Vol. I, pp. 287–292.

chronicle of the miraculous triumph of the Christian faith in England and Christianity's role in transforming the chaos of meaningless events into the order of divinely inspired history. Bede never doubted that miracles happened, for God could interfere at will in the affairs of men and women, and He did so for good and sufficient reasons. Bede also had his own good and sufficient reasons for relating the miracle of a man called Cuningham.

---

At this time a memorable miracle, and like to those of former days, was wrought in Britain; for, to the end that the living might be saved from the death of the soul, a certain person, who had been some time dead, rose again to life, and related many remarkable things he had seen; some of which I have thought fit here briefly to take notice of. There was a master of a family in that district of the Northumbrians, which is called Cuningham, who led a religious life, as did also all that belonged to him. This man fell sick, and his distemper daily increasing, being brought to extremity, he died in the beginning of the night; but in the morning early, he suddenly came to life again, and sat up, upon which all those that sat about the body weeping, fled away in a great fright; only his wife, who loved him best, though in a great consternation and trembling, remained with him. He, comforting her, said, "Fear not, for I am now truly risen from death, and permitted again to live among men; however, I am not to live hereafter as I was wont, but from henceforward after a very different manner." Then rising immediately, he repaired to the oratory of the little town, and continuing in prayer till day, immediately divided all his substance into three parts: one whereof he gave to his wife, another to his children, and the third, belonging to himself, he instantly distributed among the poor. Not long after he repaired to the monastery of Melros, which is almost enclosed by the winding of the river Twede, and having been shaven, went into a private dwelling, which the abbot had provided, where he continued till the day of his death, in such extraordinary contrition of mind and body, that though his tongue had been silent, his life declared that he had seen many things either to be

dreaded or coveted, which others knew nothing of.

Thus he related what he had seen. "He that led me had a shining countenance and a bright garment, and we went on silently, as I thought, towards the north-east. Walking on, we came to a vale of great breadth and depth, but of infinite length; on the left it appeared full of dreadful flames, the other side was no less horrid for violent hail and cold snow flying in all directions; both places were full of men's souls, which seemed by turns to be tossed from one side to the other, as it were by a violent storm; for when the wretches could no longer endure the excess of heat, they leaped into the middle of the cutting cold; and finding no rest there, they leaped back again into the middle of the unquenchable flames. Now whereas an innumerable multitude of deformed spirits were thus alternately tormented far and near, as far as could be seen, without any intermission, I began to think that this perhaps might be hell, of whose intolerable flames I had often heard talk. My guide, who went before me, answered to my thought, saying, 'Do not believe so, for this is not the hell you imagine.'

"When he had conducted me, much frightened with that horrid spectacle, by degrees, to the farther end, on a sudden I saw the place begin to grow dusk and filled with darkness. When I came into it, the darkness, by degrees, grew so thick, that I could see nothing besides it and the shape and garment of him that led me. As we went on through the shades of night, on a sudden there appeared before us frequent globes of black flames, rising as it were out of a great pit, and falling back again into the same. When I had been conducted thither, my leader suddenly vanished, and left me alone in the midst of darkness and this horrid vision, whilst those same globes of fire, without intermission, at one time flew up and at another fell back into the bottom of the abyss; and I observed that all the flames, as they ascended, were full of human souls, which, like sparks flying up with smoke, were sometimes thrown on high, and again, when the vapour of the fire ceased, dropped down into the depth below. Moreover, an insufferable stench came forth with the vapours, and filled all those dark places.

"Having stood there a long time in much dread, not knowing what to do, which way to turn, or what end I might expect, on a sudden I heard behind me the noise of a most hideous and wretched lamentation, and at the same time a loud laughing, as of a rude multitude insulting captured enemies. When that noise, growing plainer, came up to me, I observed a gang of evil spirits dragging the howling and lamenting souls of men into the midst of the darkness, whilst they themselves laughed and rejoiced. Among those men, as I could discern, there was one shorn like a clergyman, a layman, and a woman. The evil spirits that dragged them went down into the midst of the burning pit; and as they went down deeper, I could no longer distinguish between the lamentation of the men and the laughing of the devils, yet I still had a confused sound in my ears. In the meantime, some of the dark spirits ascended from that flaming abyss, and running forward, beset me on all sides, and much perplexed me with their glaring eyes and the stinking fire which proceeded from their mouths and nostrils; and threatened to lay hold on me with burning tongs, which they had in their hands, yet they durst not touch me, though they frightened me. Being thus on all sides enclosed with enemies and darkness, and looking about on every side for assistance, there appeared behind me, on the way that I came, as it were, the brightness of a star shining amidst the darkness, which increased by degrees, and came rapidly towards me. When it drew near, all those evil spirits, that sought to carry me away with their tongs, dispersed and fled.

"He, whose approach put them to flight, was the same that had led me before; who, then turning towards the right, began to lead me, as it were, towards the south-east, and having soon brought me out of the darkness, conducted me into an atmosphere of clear light. While he thus led me in open light, I saw a vast wall before us, the length and height of which, in every direction, seemed to be altogether boundless. I began to wonder why we went up to the wall, seeing no door, window, or path through it. When we came to the wall, we were presently, I know not by what means, on the top of it, and within it was a vast and delightful field, so full of fragrant flowers that the odour of its delightful sweetness immediately dispelled the stink of the dark furnace, which had pierced me through and through. So great was the light in this place, that it seemed to exceed the brightness of the day, or the sun in its meridian height. In this field were innumerable assemblies of men in white, and many companies seated together rejoicing. As he led me through the midst of those happy inhabitants, I began to think that this might, perhaps, be the kingdom of heaven, of which I had often heard so much. He answered to my thought, saying, 'This is not the kingdom of heaven, as you imagine.'

"When we had passed those mansions of blessed souls and gone farther on, I discovered before me a much more beautiful light, and therein heard sweet voices of persons singing, and so wonderful a fragrancy proceeded from the place, that the other which I had before thought most delicious, then seemed to me but very indifferent; even as that extraordinary brightness of the flowery field, compared with this, appeared mean and inconsiderable. When I began to hope we should enter that delightful place, my guide, on a sudden, stood still; and then turning back, led me back by the way we came.

"When we returned to those joyful mansions of the souls in white, he said to me, 'Do you know what all these things are which you have seen?' I answered, I did not; and then he replied, "That vale you saw, so dreadful for consuming flames and cutting cold, is the place in which the souls of those are tried and punished, who, delaying to confess and amend their crimes, at length have recourse to repentance at the point of death, and so depart this life; but nevertheless because they, even at their death, confessed and repented, they shall all be received into the kingdom of heaven at the day of judgment. But many are relieved before the day of judgment, by the prayers, alms, and fasting, of the living, and more especially by masses. That fiery and stinking pit, which you saw, is the mouth of hell, into which whosoever falls shall never be delivered to all eternity. This flowery place, in which you see these most beautiful young people, so bright and merry, is that into which the souls of those are received who depart the body in good works, but who are not so perfect as to deserve to be immediately admitted into the kingdom of heaven; yet they shall all, at the day of judgment, see Christ, and partake of the joys of his kingdom. For whoever are perfect in thought, word and deed, as soon as they depart the body, immediately enter into the kingdom of heaven; in the neighbourhood whereof that place is, where you heard the sound of sweet singing, with the fragrant odour and bright light. As for you, who are now to return to your body, and live among men again, if you will endeavour nicely to examine your actions, and direct your speech and behaviour in righteousness and simplicity, you shall, after death, have a place of residence among these joyful troops of blessed souls; for when I left you for a while, it was to know how you were to be disposed of.' When he had said this to me, I much abhorred returning to my body, being delighted with the sweetness and beauty of the place I beheld, and with the company of those I saw in it. However, I durst not ask him any questions; but in the meantime, on a sudden, I found myself alive among men."

Now these and other things which this man of God saw, he would not relate to slothful persons and such as lived negligently; but only to those who, being terrified with the dread of torments, or delighted with the hopes of heavenly joys, would make use of his words to advance in piety. . . .

## FURTHER DISCUSSION QUESTIONS

### The Anglo-Saxon Chronicle

1. What subjects interested the authors of the *Chronicle*?
2. How did the authors view the course of human events?
3. What virtues and qualities did they praise the most?
4. On what basis did they select the events to be recorded?

### The Battle of Maldon

1. What virtues are extolled in the account?
2. What were the strengths and weaknesses of the Anglo-Saxon warrior?
3. What, according to the author, was the cause of the defeat, and what was the importance of the battle?
4. If you were writing a description of the battle, what, if anything, would you have added to the account and what would you have deleted?

### Edmund II's Code

1. What aspects of Anglo-Saxon life was Edmund seeking to curb and regulate?
2. How did Edmund expect to control violence, and what was the basis of his concept of justice?
3. Is the king concerned with the moral implications of murder or its political consequences?
4. What principles voiced by the king might an Anglo-Saxon nobleman or freeman have objected to and why?

### The Conversion of Northumbria

1. What did the conversion to Christianity mean to King Edwin?

### Bishop Daniel of Winchester's Advice to Boniface

1. Of the two approaches for converting the pagans, which do you think was more effective — Bishop Paulinus' or Bishop Daniel's?

### Alcuin of York's Letter of Warning to King Ethelred

1. What social and ethical ideals was Alcuin trying to demonstrate, and what were the lessons to be learned from the sack of Lindisfarne?
2. Compare and contrast King Edmund's and Alcuin's approach to the ills of society.

### The Miracle of Cuningham

1. What is the picture of heaven and hell given in Cuningham's miracle? Why would the pagans have found it attractive? What, if any, might the social consequences of such a picture have been?
2. What is the level of religion and its appeal presented in these six sources?
3. What is the explanation for human success or failure and the nature of historical causation suggested in these documents?

# 2

# Reconstruction Norman Style

The debate over what was old and what was new in Norman England, the extent to which the invaders built on Saxon institutions and social habits, and whether feudalism was an imported and essentially French political organization or was indigenous to the island dominates early English history. The documents selected for this chapter, however, have less to do with origins than with operations. How successfully did Anglo-Norman feudalism function? To what extent did Anglo-Norman kings enforce feudalism or distort it? Was England, as a consequence of the conquest, the most feudal or least feudal kingdom in Europe? What were the human qualities that made feudalism function "properly"? What were the problems inherent in the system? What were the social and political aims of feudalism? And, finally, what was feudal reality? In short, the sources present a picture of Anglo-Norman feudalism in action.

Central to this picture is the conquest itself and the man who led it and triumphed. The first three selections give a clear picture of the invasion, its human consequences, and above all the qualities of William himself. William of Poitiers' description of the duke in "The Life of William, the Conqueror," was written about 1071, or some five years after the invasion. Although Poitiers, a Norman soldier-churchman, did not accompany the Conqueror on his military adventure, he knew his master well, for he had long served as William's chaplain. The *Anglo-Saxon Chronicle* for the year 1087 gives a view of the entire reign and is an important counterbalance to William of Poitiers' bias. Despite its own built-in prejudices, the *Chronicle* presents a surprisingly fair portrait of the new ruler. The final source from the *Abingdon Chronicle* is a fascinating account of the affairs of the abbey and the Abbot of Abingdon in the years following the invasion. It not only dramatizes the consequences of the conquest for the defeated Saxons but also presents the problems that the new monarch had to face and resolve during the early years of the reign.

THE LANDING OF WILLIAM THE CONQUEROR

The next set of readings — William I's Statute, Henry I's Coronation Charter (1101), Glanville's "Treatise on the Laws and Customs" of England (1190?), and Roger Archbishop of York's knight-service owed to Henry II (1166) — presents facets of Anglo-Norman feudalism and government in action. The richest selection is Ranulph de Glanville's discussion of feudal homage, as it functioned during the closing years of Henry II's reign. Glanville (1130–1190) was an extremely important and loyal crown official who eventually became chief justiciar of England in 1180 and was known as the "king's eye." His description of the feudal laws of the kingdom, as well as his administrative career, symbolizes the achievements and aspirations of Henry II's reign.

The concluding selection is taken from the *Anglo-Saxon Chronicle* for the year 1137. It stands in stark contrast to the readings that have preceded it and might be described as a picture of feudalism gone wrong.

## WILLIAM OF POITIERS, *The Life of William the Conqueror* (ca. 1071)

William of Poitiers' life of William the Conqueror is one of the major sources for the Duke's personality and the history of the invasion of England. The author describes the sailing of the fleet from Normandy, the rival claims of William and Harold, the Battle of Hastings, and the crowning of William.

At last the long awaited wind blew. Soldiers lifted their voices and hands to heaven in thanks; and in great mutual excitement, they embarked with the greatest speed, and

SOURCE: Translated from M. Guizot, *Collection des Mémoires relatifs à l'histoire de France* (Paris, 1826), Vol. XXIX, pp. 392–415.

with intense eagerness began the dangerous voyage. The commotion that prevailed was such that the one shouted for his guard, the other for his companion, but most, disregarding vassals, companions and baggage, and fearing that they might be left behind, rushed to get on board. The Duke's very eagerness shamed and urged on those vassals who were slow. However, out of fear that, arriving before day break on the English coast, the army would run the risk of landing at an enemy or unknown port, he ordered a herald to announce that, when all the troops were sea-borne, the fleet was to heave to for the night, and drop anchor not far from his ship until they saw a lamp at its masthead; then forthwith the sound of a trumpet would be the signal for departure. . . .

During the night, after a short rest, the fleet weighed anchor. The vessel which carried the Duke, rowing with the greatest ardor towards victory, and sustained by the determination of the Conqueror, shortly left the rest of the fleet behind. At dawn an oarsman, being ordered to look out from the main-mast and see if the main fleet was following, announced that he could see nothing but sea and sky. At once the Duke dropped anchor, and concerned that his company might lose courage from fear and grief, he ordered, with memorable gaity and as if they were all in a dining room, a splendid feast which lacked nothing, not even spiced wine, and he assured his men that the others would soon arrive, helped by the grace of God under whose protection he stood. . . . The oarsman, having looked for the fleet a second time, cried out that he could see four vessels on the horizon; when he looked a third time there seemed to be so many ships that their masts, crowded together, looked like a forest. The reader can readily guess what joy sustained the expectations of the Duke and how much he praised divine mercy from the depth of his heart. Driven on by a favorable wind, he entered unopposed into the port of Pévensey. . . .

One day as the Duke inspected the posts guarding the fleet and was strolling nearby some ships, a monk, who was a messenger from Harold, was brought into his presence. He [Duke William] immediately approached the man and ingenuously said: "I am the steward of William, Duke of Normandy, and it is I who serve him his food. Only through me will you be able to speak to him. Tell me the message you bring; I will readily make it known to him, because no one is more dear to him than I. Later through my efforts you will be able freely to speak to him in person as you wish." The monk having revealed the message, the Duke at once had him housed and treated with great kindness. During this interval, he thought over what answer he should make and discussed the matter with his followers.

Next day, seated in the midst of his nobles, he called the monk before him and said to him: "It is I who am William, Prince of the Normans by the grace of God. Repeat now in the presence of this group what you told me yesterday." The messenger spoke thus: "This is what King Harold would have you know. You have entered his land; he does not know with what self-conceit and by what rashness. He remembers well that King Edward at first named you heir to the kingdom of England, and that he [Harold] brought to Normandy the insurance of that succession. But he also knows that, according to the right he possessed, the same king, his overlord, at the last moment presented him with the gift of the crown; and since that time when St. Augustine entered England, it has been an enduring custom of this country to regard as inviolable bequests made by dying men. This is why with every right he demands that you return with your followers to your country. Otherwise, he renounces the friendship and all agreements which have been concluded with you in Normandy; and he leaves the choice entirely to you."

After having heard Harold's message, the Duke asked the monk if he would be willing to safely escort his envoy into Harold's presence. The monk promised that he would take as much care of the messenger's safety as of his own. Thereupon the Duke charged a monk of Fécamp to promptly report these words to Harold. "It is not with rashness and injustice but deliberately and motivated by equity that I have come into this land, of which my overlord and relative, King Edward, has named me his heir, on account of the high honors and numerous favors that I and my nobles have done him, as well as to his son and servants, as Harold himself avows. He also believed that of all those who were related to him, I was the best and most capable, the greatest help to him while he lived, the best ruler of the kingdom after he was dead; and the choice was not made without the consent of his nobles, but with the counsel of Archbishop Stigand, Earl Godwine, Earl Leofric and Earl Sigard, who took an oath to accept me as king after Edward's death, and swore not to take over the country during his lifetime in order to prevent it falling to me. He gave me as hostage the son and nephew of Godwine. Finally, he sent Harold himself to Normandy to take in my presence the oath to support me which his father and other afore-named nobles had sworn in my absence. While Harold was on this commission he fell into captivity from which he was rescued only by my wisdom and power. He did me homage on his own behalf and with his hands in mine he guaranteed me the kingdom of England. I am ready to plead my cause in judgment against him on the basis of Norman laws, or better yet those of England, as it pleases him. If the Normans or the English pronounce according to justice and truth that the possession of the crown legitimately belongs to him, then he may have it in peace; but if they agree that by right it belongs to me, then he must suffer me to have it. If he refuses this proposal, I do not believe it proper that my men and his should die in a quarrel in which they are in no way involved. Therefore, I am ready to maintain at the risk of my life against him that the Kingdom of England by right belongs to me rather than to him.". . .

Upon hearing this message from the monk, Harold, whose men were advancing, went pale, and kept silent for a long while,

as if rendered speechless. The messenger requested a reply of him several times, and at first he answered: "We shall march without delay"; and the second time: "We shall march off to combat." The messenger pressed him to give another response, and repeated that the Duke of Normandy wanted to fight him alone, rather than destroy both their armies, for this brave and generous man preferred to give up a just and pleasing endeavour to prevent the death of a great number of soldiers. He hoped to strike off the head of Harold whose strength would not stand him in good stead since justice was not on his side. Then Harold lifted his eyes to heaven and said: "Let the Lord choose between William and myself, and show us who is in the right." Blinded by his thirst for power, and forgetting, in his fright, the injustice he had perpetrated, he rushed headlong to his destruction, guided by some inner voice.

Meanwhile several tried and true knights whom the Duke had sent off to reconnoiter, returned promptly and announced the arrival of the enemy. . . . The Duke immediately ordered all of those present in the camp to take up arms, for most of his companions had gone off to forage that day; and he then took part in the mystery of the mass with the utmost piety, and strengthened his body and soul by communing with the body and blood of the Lord. With great humility he hung around his neck those very relics whose protection Harold could no longer invoke, for he had violated the oath he had taken upon them. With the Duke were two bishops who had escorted him from Normandy, Eudes, bishop of Bayeux, and Geoffroi Constantin, besides numerous members of the clergy and several monks. This congregation readied itself to wage war by means of prayers. A lesser man than the Duke would have taken fright upon seeing his armour slip to the left as he was being clad in it; but he laughed it off as if it were a mishap, rather than taking fright at so gloomy an omen.

The beauty of the brief exhortation with which he whipped up the courage of his warriors cannot be doubted, though it has not been recorded in all of its majesty. He reminded the Normans that under his banners they had always emerged victorious from great and numerous perils. He reminded them all of their fatherland, of their noble deeds and their illustrious reputation. "Now is the time," he told them, "to show what strength flows through your arms, and what courage through your souls. It is no longer a matter of living as masters, but of staying alive through the peril that threatens us. Fight like men, and you shall attain victory, honor, and wealth. Otherwise you shall be slaughtered on the spot, or as captives will become playthings to the most cruel of foes. What is more, you will be shrouded in eternal infamy. There is no path open for retreat; one side is barred off by a foreign country and by force of arms, the other by sea and other weapons. It behooves no man to take fright at greater numbers. The English have often fallen victim to the blows of their enemies; they fell under a foreign yoke the many times they were vanquished, and never gained glory through their feats of arms. The courage of a small number of warriors can easily strike down troops unskilled in warfare, especially when the cause of justice is strengthened by divine assistance. You need only dare; let nothing stop you, and soon victory will set your hearts aglow."

His troops set forth in perfect order, carrying the banner that had been sent by the Pope. In the front lines he placed foot-soldiers, carrying arrows and cross-bows, and behind them the more trustworthy infantrymen, carrying armour. The last row was made up of battalions of knights in the midst of whom he rode, unshakeable in his strength, and whence he could give orders on all sides by word or action. . . .

Undaunted by the difficulty of the climb, the Duke and his men made their way up the steep hill. The terrible sound of the trumpets signaled the start of the battle, and the Normans, burning to display their valor, charged into battle from all sides, just as, in a trial for theft, the man who has been

wronged will be the first to speak. Thus the Norman foot-soldiers came forward and challenged the English with shafts that brought injury and death. The enemy put up a brave resistance, each one according to his strength. They responded with spears and different sorts of shafts, frightful hatchets and stones bound to pieces of wood. One might expect to see our men overcome, as if crushed under a deadly weight. But the knights followed up, leaving the rear to position themselves along the front line. They were shameful of fighting from afar, and their courage spurred them into drawing their swords. The shrill cries of the Normans and their barbarian enemies were drowned by the clash of weapons and the groans of dying men. The fighting went on this way for some time with both sides displaying great vigor. The English, however, enjoyed the advantage of an elevated site on which they could gather in serried ranks, and they had the advantage of a defensive position. They were also favored by their great numbers of men who formed an unshakeable mass, and by their weapons which penetrated easily the shields and other defensive arms [of the Normans]. For these reasons they defended themselves and drove back with great vigor those who dared to attack them sword in hand. They also injured those who sent spears flying from afar. Behold then how the foot soldiers and Breton knights, frightened by such ferocity, turned and fled as did also the auxilary troops on the left flank; nearly the entire army of the Duke was in retreat. This can be said without offending the Normans, a race quite invincible . . . [for] the Normans believed that their Duke and leader had fallen. They did not retreat in shameful flight but with sadness because their chief was for them a great support.

The Prince, seeing that a great part of the enemy was rushing after his retreating army, jumped into the front ranks of his troops, and stopped their flight by his striking appearance and menacing spear. Head bare and without his helmet, he shouted: "Everyone look at me! I am alive and by God's grace I shall conquer. What madness leads you to flight? What path can you find for your retreat? You are allowing yourselves to be driven back and killed by those whom you could butcher as if they were a herd [of cattle]. You forsake victory and eternal glory; you are running to your ruin and to perpetual disgrace. If you fly, no one will escape death." These words restored their courage. Brandishing his terrible sword, he stationed himself at their head and defied the enemy who deserved death for their rebellion against him, their King. The Normans, inflamed with ardor, turned and surrounded many thousand of those who had pursued them and quickly cut them to pieces so that none escaped. Immensely encouraged by this success, they attacked the main Saxon army which, even having sustained such a heavy loss, did not appear diminished. The English fought with courage and with all their strength, trying in particular to prevent an opening from being cut in their ranks which were so tight that not even the dead could fall. However, the steel of the most intrepid soldiers soon hewed an opening in various places. . . .

The Normans and their allies, perceiving that they could not achieve victory against an army so tightly massed without heavy loses, retreated, cleverly pretending that they were in full flight, for they recalled how, shortly before, their earlier retreat had been the occasion for their victory. The barbarians, jubilant that final triumph was in their grasp, with shouts of joy, and showering the Normans with insults, threatened to burst upon them. Several thousand dared, as before, to open ranks and, as if they were a flock of birds, to follow those whom they thought to be in flight. Then suddenly the Normans turned their horses, surrounded their pursuers and cut them to pieces without anyone escaping. Being twice served by this ruse, the Normans attacked the rest of the Saxon forces with the greatest impetuousness. That army was still formidable and very difficult to overwhelm. The two sides were engaged in a battle of a new kind in which one side attacked with every

means available, and the other, as if fixed to the ground, suffered the blows. The English began to falter, and as if avowing their crime by their defeat, they endured their punishment. The Normans shot arrows, striking and piercing. The movement of the dead who fell seemed more alive than that of the living. Those who were wounded slightly could not escape because of the great number of their companions, [and] they perished smothered in the multitude. Thus fortune intervened in the triumph of William.

The victory near at hand, the Duke returned to the main field of battle where he could not look upon the carnage without pity, although the victims were godless men and it is good, glorious and beneficial to kill a tyrant. The ground was covered with the flower of English nobility and manhood, stained in blood. The two brothers of Harold were found next to him, and the fallen king, stripped of all badges of honor, was recognized, not by his face but by certain marks [on his body]. His corpse was carried to the Duke's camp where William gave it for burial to William, surnamed Malet, and not to Harold's mother who offered for her dear son's body its weight in gold. The Duke knew that he could not properly receive gold for such a transaction, and he judged it scandalous that the corpse be buried according to the wish of the mother when Harold's excessive greed was the cause that so many men now lay dead without burial. Someone in jest said that he should inter Harold in a place where he could watch over the sea and shoreline to which in his fury he had sought to prevent access.

[After the battle and death of Harold], Stigand, archbishop of Canterbury who, elevated by his wealth and office, had the greatest influence among the English, joined with the son of Aelfgar and other magnates to continue the fight against William. They established as king Edgar the Atheling, a young boy but descended from the noble race of King Edward, because their principal desire was not to have a stranger as king. But the one who ought to be their master advanced fearlessly, stopping outside London in a spot where he had been informed they often gathered. This city [London] is watered by the Thames River which makes a harbor into which the riches of foreign countries pour. The citizens of London could by themselves supply a large and formidable military force, and they were now reinforced by such a multitude of armed men that despite its large size, the city could scarcely house them. Five hundred Norman knights, sent as an advance force, bravely forced a party of Saxons to retreat back into the walls of the city. This heavy carnage was followed by fire, whereby all the buildings on this side of the river were burnt in order to inflict a double blow upon the inordinate pride of the enemy. Then the Duke advanced without opposition, and having

crossed the Thames by a ford and across a bridge, he arrived at Wallingford.

The metropolitan bishop, Stigand, came to him and put himself in his hands, swearing fidelity and renouncing the Atheling whom he had thoughtlessly acclaimed king. Having followed his destiny, the Duke, as soon as he came in sight of London, was met by the important people of the city who put themselves and the entire city under his authority, like the people of Canterbury had done before them, and brought him hostages in great numbers and of such quality as he demanded. Then the bishops and the other magnates begged him to accept the crown, saying that they were used to obeying a king and that they wished to have a king as their lord.

## The Anglo-Saxon Chronicle of 1087

This portion of the *Anglo-Saxon Chronicle* gives a detailed description of the new Norman King of England, William I.

If anyone wishes to know what sort of a man he was, or what dignity he had, or of how many lands he was lord — then we will write of him even as we, who have looked upon him, and once lived at his court, have perceived him to be.

This King William of whom we speak was a very wise man, and very powerful and more worshipful and stronger than any predecessor of his had been. He was gentle to the good men who loved God, and stern beyond all measure to those people who resisted his will. In the same place where God permitted him to conquer England, he set up a famous monastery and appointed monks for it, and endowed it well. In his days the famous church at Canterbury was built, and also many another over all England. Also, this country was very full of

monks, and they lived their life under the rule of St. Benedict, and Christianity was such in his day that each man who wished followed out whatever concerned his order. Also, he was very dignified: three times every year he wore his crown, as often as he was in England. At Easter he wore it at Winchester, at Whitsuntide at Westminster, and at Christmas at Gloucester, and then there were with him all the powerful men over all England, archbishops and bishops, abbots and earls, thegns[1] and knights. Also, he was a very stern and violent man, so that no one dared do anything contrary to his will. He had earls in his fetters, who acted against his will. He expelled bishops from their sees, and abbots from their abbacies, and put thegns in prison, and finally he did not spare his own brother, who was called

SOURCE: From Dorothy Whitelock with David C. Douglas and Susie I. Tucker, trans. and eds., *The Anglo-Saxon Chronicle* (London: Eyre & Spottiswoode, Ltd., Publishers, 1961), pp. 163–165. By permission of the publishers.

[1] warriors

Odo; he was a very powerful bishop in Normandy (his cathedral church was at Bayeux) and was the foremost man next the king, and had an earldom in England. And when the king was in Normandy, then he was master in this country; and he [the king] put *him* in prison. Amongst other things the good security he made in this country is not to be forgotten — so that any honest man could travel over his kingdom without injury with his bosom full of gold; and no one dared strike another, however much wrong he had done him. And if any man had intercourse with a woman against her will, he was forthwith castrated.

He ruled over England, and by his cunning it was so investigated that there was not one hide of land in England that he did not know who owned it, and what it was worth, and then set it down in his record. Wales was in his power, and he built castles there, and he entirely controlled that race. In the same way, he also subdued Scotland to himself, because of his great strength. The land of Normandy was his by natural inheritance, and he ruled over the county called Maine; and if he could have lived two years more, he would have conquered Ireland by his prudence and without any weapons. Certainly in his time people had much oppression and very many injuries:

> He had castles built
> And poor men hard oppressed.
> The king was so very stark
> And deprived his underlings of many a mark
> Of gold and more hundreds of pounds of silver,
> That he took by weight and with great injustice
> From his people with little need for such a deed.
> Into avarice did he fall
> And loved greediness above all.
> He made great protection for the game
> And imposed laws for the same,
> That who so slew hart or hind
> Should be made blind.

> He preserved the harts and boars
> And loved the stags as much
> As if he were their father.
> Moreover, for the hares did he decree that they should go free.
> Powerful men complained of it and poor men lamented it,
> But so fierce was he that he cared not for the rancour of them all,
> But they had to follow out the king's will entirely
> If they wished to live or hold their land,
> Property or estate, or his favour great.
> Alas! woe, that any man so proud should go,
> And exalt himself and reckon himself above all men!
> May Almighty God show mercy to his soul
> And grant unto him forgiveness for his sins.

These things we have written about him, both good and bad, that good men may imitate their good points, and entirely avoid the bad, and travel on the road that leads us to the kingdom of heaven.

## The Abingdon Chronicle (ca. 1066)

*The Abingdon Chronicle* records the consequences of being on the losing side: the unavailing efforts of the monastery of Abingdon to defend itself, its lands and rights, from the encroachment of the victorious Normans.

William obtained the crown of England. Some submitted to him and swore fealty, but not a few departed into exile, hoping that they might find for themselves homes in other lands. Abbot Ealdred[2] at first joined the former of these parties and swore fealty to the king. But when many, including the mother of the slain king, changed over and joined the latter party, the abbot also left England taking with him among others a priest named Blacheman. This priest, as has earlier been mentioned in connection with Abbot Ordric, was a man of the church of Abingdon and held from the monastery Sandford and Chilton and Leverton. When he left England, everything which he possessed was taken into the hands of the king since he was held to be a renegade, and it was with the greatest difficulty that the abbot secured the restoration of his lands to the church.

As the abbot was successful in this instance, so also in other cases where lands had been alienated from the church he might perhaps have vindicated his right if he had not to his own loss and to the loss of the church incurred the enmity of the king. Of this we shall learn more later. A certain rich man, Turchill by name, with the witness and consent of Earl Harold, had performed homage to the church and to Abbot Ordric for his land which was called Kingston. For then a freeman was allowed so to act that the lordship of the aforesaid village might ever after pertain to the church. When this man fell in the famous battle [of Hastings] Henry of Ferrières

seized his land for himself despite the protests of the abbot, and despite the fact that the lordship of this land had been vested in the church a long time before this battle. A similar usurpation took place at Fyfield. There, a certain Godric, who was sheriff, had held from the church on a lease for three lives, on the understanding that whatever mischance might befall the tenants, the church should suffer no loss therefrom. But when Godric likewise was killed in the same battle, Henry of Ferrières added this village also to his possessions.

In these days not only was the abbey thus robbed of its estates, but the ornaments of the sanctuary itself were stolen. An order came that the most precious of these should be sent to the queen. The abbot and the monks took counsel what should be done in this matter, and planned to send to the queen certain ornaments. But she declined those which were offered and demanded more precious treasures. Wherefore the abbot and monks, oppressed by fear of their new rulers from overseas, decided that their orders must in some measure be obeyed. To meet the wishes of the queen they therefore made a compromise, and sent a chasuble wonderfully embroidered throughout with gold and the best ceremonial cope, and an alb with a stole, and a gospel book decorated with gold and precious gems.

Meanwhile many plots were hatched in the kingdom of England by those who resented the unaccustomed yoke of a foreign rule. Some of them hid in woods and islands, living like outlaws and plundering and at-

SOURCE: From David C. Douglas and George W. Greenaway, eds., *English Historical Documents* (London: Eyre Methuen, Ltd., publishers, 1953), Vol. II, pp. 900–901. By permission of the publishers.

[2] of Abingdon

tacking those who came their way. Others besought the Danes to come to England. And when the Danes came in answer to this call, they in their turn plundered the land and laid it waste by fire, and took away many into captivity. But they were not strong enough to wage a pitched battle or to subdue the kingdom, and so with their task unaccomplished they returned to their own land.

Men of all ranks and classes took part in these attempts. Æthelwine, bishop of Durham, for instance, was found amongst those who were taken prisoner, and having been brought to Abingdon he ended his days there in captivity. The men of the abbey of Abingdon, although they ought to have sustained the cause of King William, listened to the opposite advice and went armed to join a gathering of the enemies of the king. Being intercepted on their journey, they were captured and imprisoned and grievously punished. For this reason the king was incensed against their lord, that is to say, Abbot Ealdred, also named Brichwin, who was therefore thrown into prison immediately in Wallingford Castle. After

being kept for some time in that place, he was at length taken thence and given into the charge of Walkelin, bishop of Winchester, with whom he remained for the rest of his life.

At this time, owing to the changed state of the kingdom, many treasures were deposited in the monastery of Abingdon in the hope that, being protected by the custody of the abbey, they might escape plunder. But when the officers of the court obtained knowledge of this through informers, everything that had been secretly sent, and everything that was found so stored, was taken away. Besides this, whatever was found in the treasure chests of the monks was removed. Thus much of what had been contributed for the honour and use of the church was removed, gold and silver, vestments, books and vessels. No respect was paid to the threshold of the holy places, and no pity was shown to the afflicted monks. Outside, with a similar lack of respect, the villages were widely devastated. How much of the property of the abbey was lost at this time it would be hard to reckon. . . .

## Statute of William the Conqueror

The new King of England attempts to impose his law impartially on all his subjects, great and small, Norman and Saxon.

1. Firstly that, above all things, he wishes one God to be venerated throughout his whole kingdom, one faith of Christ always to be kept inviolate, peace and security to be observed between the English and the Normans.

2. We decree also that every free man shall affirm by a compact and an oath that, within and without England, he desires to be faithful to king William, to preserve with him his lands and his honour with all fidelity, and first to defend him against his enemies.

3. I will, moreover, that all the men whom I have brought with me, or who have come after me, shall be in my peace and quiet. And if one of them shall be slain, the lord of his murderer shall seize him within five days, if he can; but if not, he shall begin to pay to me forty-six marks of silver as long as his possessions shall hold out. But when the possessions of the lord of that man are at an end, the whole hundred[3] in which the slaying took place shall pay in common what remains.

SOURCE: From Ernest F. Henderson, trans. and ed., *Select Historical Documents of the Middle Ages* (London: George Bell and Sons, 1910), pp. 7–8.
[3] division of land

4. And every Frenchman who, in the time of my relative king Edward, was a sharer in England of the customs of the English, shall pay according to the law of the English what they themselves call "onhlote" and "anscote." This decree has been confirmed in the city of Gloucester.

5. We forbid also that any live cattle be sold or bought for money except within the cities, and this before three faithful witnesses; nor even anything old without a surety and warrant. But if he do otherwise he shall pay, and shall afterwards pay a fine.

6. It was also decreed there that if a Frenchman summon an Englishman for perjury or murder, theft, homicide, or "ran" — as the English call evident rape which cannot be denied — the Englishman shall defend himself as he prefers, either through the ordeal of iron, or through wager of battle. But if the Englishman be infirm he shall find another who will do it for him. If one of them shall be vanquished he shall pay a fine of forty shillings to the king. If an Englishman summons a Frenchman, and be unwilling to prove his charge by judgment or by wager of battle, I will, nevertheless, that the Frenchman purge himself by an informal oath.

7. This also I command and will, that all shall hold and keep the law of Edward the king with regard to their lands, and with regard to all their possessions, those provisions being added which I have made for the utility of the English people.

8. Every man who wishes to be considered a freeman shall have a surety, that his surety may hold him and hand him over to justice if he offend in any way. And if any such one escape, his sureties shall see to it that, without making difficulties, they pay what is charged against him, and that they clear themselves of having known of any fraud in the matter of his escape. The hundred and county shall be made to answer as our predecessors decreed. And those that ought of right to come, and are unwilling to appear, shall be summoned once; and if a second time they are unwilling to appear, one ox shall be taken from them and they shall be summoned a third time. And if they do not come the third time, another ox shall be taken: but if they do not come the fourth time there shall be forfeited from the goods of that man who was unwilling to come, the extent of the charge against him, — "ceapgeld" as it is called, — and besides this a fine to the king.

9. I forbid any one to sell a man beyond the limits of the country, under penalty of a fine in full to me.

10. I forbid that any one be killed or hung for any fault, but his eyes shall be torn out or his testicles cut off. And this command shall not be violated under penalty of a fine in full to me.

## *The Coronation Charter of Henry I* (1101)

Henry I's Coronation Charter was not a real charter of liberties but an effort to win popular support in his struggle to keep the throne away from his brother Robert, Duke of Normandy, by swearing on his coronation oath to stop the abuses and governmental encroachments of William II. Although Henry failed to abide by his charter, those promises embodied what his feudal subjects thought were the proper actions of a feudal king, and years later, during the crisis of Magna Carta (1215), Henry I's charter became an important precedent for curbing the actions of King John.

SOURCE: From Edward P. Cheyney, ed., *Translations and Reprints from Original Sources of European History* (Philadelphia: University of Pennsylvania, 1900), "English Constitutional Documents," Vol. I, No. 5, pp. 3–5.

In the year of the incarnation of the Lord, 1101, Henry, son of King William, after the death of his brother William, by the grace of God, king of the English, to all faithful, greeting:

1. Know that by the mercy of God, and by the common counsel of the barons of the whole kingdom of England, I have been crowned king of the same kingdom; and because the kingdom has been oppressed by unjust exactions, I, from regard to God, and from the love which I have toward you, in the first place make the holy church of God free, so that I will neither sell nor place at rent, nor, when archbishop, or bishop, or abbot is dead, will I take anything from the domain of the church, or from its men, until a successor is installed into it. And all the evil customs by which the realm of England was unjustly oppressed will I take away, which evil customs I partly set down here.

2. If any one of my barons, or earls, or others who hold from me shall have died, his heir shall not redeem his land, as he did in the time of my brother, but shall relieve it by a just and legitimate relief.[4] Similarly also the men of my barons shall relieve their lands from their lords by a just and legitimate relief.

3. And if any one of the barons or other men of mine wishes to give his daughter in marriage, or his sister or niece or [female] relation, he must speak with me about it, but I will neither take anything from him for this permission, nor forbid him to give her in marriage, unless he should wish to join her to my enemy. And if when a baron or other man of mine is dead a daughter remains as his heir, I will give her in marriage according to the judgment of my barons, along with her land. And if when a man is dead his wife remains and is without children, she shall have her dowry and right of marriage, and I will not give her to a husband except according to her will.

4. And if a wife survived with children, she shall have her dowry and right of marriage, so long as she shall have kept her body legitimately, and I will not give her in marriage, except according to her will. And the guardian of the land and children shall be either the wife or another one of the relatives as shall seem to be most just. And I require that my barons should deal similarly with the sons and daughters or wives of their men.

5. The common tax on money[5] which used to be taken through the cities and counties, which was not taken in the time of King Edward, I now forbid altogether henceforth to be taken. If any one shall have been seized, whether a moneyer or any other, with false money, strict justice shall be done for it.

6. All fines and all debts which were owed to my brother, I remit, except my rightful rents, and except those payments which had been agreed upon for the inheritances of others or for those things which more justly affected others. And if any one for his own inheritance has stipulated anything, this I remit, and all reliefs which had been agreed upon for rightful inheritances.

7. And if any one of my barons or men shall become feeble, however he himself shall give or arrange to give his money, I grant that it shall be so given. Moreover, if he himself, prevented by arms, or by weakness, shall not have bestowed his money, or arranged to bestow it, his wife or his children or his parents, and his legitimate men shall divide it for his soul, as to them shall seem best.

8. If any of my barons or men shall have committed an offence he shall not give security to the extent of forfeiture of his money, as he did in the time of my father, or of my brother, but according to the measure of the offense so shall he pay, as he would have paid from the time of my father backward, in the time of my other predecessors; so that if he shall have been convicted of treachery or of crime, he shall pay as is just.

9. All murders, moreover, before that day in which I was crowned king, I pardon; and those which shall be done henceforth shall be punished justly according to the law of King Edward.

---

[4] inheritance fee   [5] form of sales

10. The forests, by the common agreement of my barons, I have retained in my own hand, as my father held them.

11. To those knights who hold their land by the cuirass,[6] I yield of my own gift the lands of their demesne[7] ploughs free from all payments and from all labor, so that as they have thus been favored by such a great alleviation, so they may readily provide themselves with horses and arms for my service and for the defence of the kingdom.

12. A firm peace in my whole kingdom I establish and require to be kept from henceforth.

13. The law of King Edward I give to you again with those changes with which my father changed it by the counsel of his barons.

14. If any one has taken anything from my possessions since the death of King William, my brother, or from the possessions of any one, let the whole be immediately returned without alteration, and if any one shall have retained anything thence, he upon whom it is found will pay it heavily to me. Witnesses Maurice, bishop of London, and Gundulf, bishop, and William, bishop-elect, and Henry, earl, and Simon, earl, and Walter Giffard, and Robert de Montfort, and Roger Bigod, and Henry de Port, at London, when I was crowned.

RANULPH DE GLANVILLE, *A Treatise on the Laws and Customs of the Kingdom of England, Composed in the Time of King Henry the Second* (1190?)

According to Warren Hollister, Ranulph de Glanville's "Treatise on the Laws and Customs of the Kingdom" is "England's first systematic legal treatise," representing "an intellectual landmark in the rise of a coherent body of royal law." It is an extremely practical manual on feudal homage.

## Chapter I

It remains to resume the subject of performing Homages,[8] and receiving Reliefs. Upon the death of the Father, or any other Ancestor, the Lord of the Fee is bound, from the first, to receive the Homage of the Right Heir, whether the Heir has attained his full age, or not, if he be a Male. For, Females cannot by Law perform any Homage, although, generally speaking, they are to do Fealty to their Lords.

But, if they are married, their Husbands ought to do Homage to their Lords for their Fees; I mean, if Homage be due in respect of such Fees. If, however, the Heir be a Male and a Minor, the Lord of the Fee is not entitled by Law to the Custody, either of the Heir, or his Inheritance, until he has received the Homage of the Heir; because, it is a general principle, that no one can exact from an Heir, whether he is of age, or not, any service, consisting in a Relief or otherwise, until he has received the Homage of the Heir, in respect of that Tenement, for which the service is claimed. But a person may perform Homage to several Lords on account of different Fees; but, of these Homages, one should be the chief, and accompanied with allegiance,[9] and this must be made to the Lord, from whom the person performing Homage, holds his Chief Estate. Homage ought to be done in this form, namely, the party performing it shall so become the Man of his Lord, that he shall bear faith to him for the Tenement in respect of which he does Homage, and shall preserve

---

SOURCE: From John Beames, trans., *A Translation of Glanville*, to which are added notes with an introduction by Henry Beale (Washington, D.C., John Byrne and Co., 1900), pp. 175–192.

[6] military service  [7] free land  [8] semi-religious ritual by which a tenant becomes "the man" of his lord  [9] liege homage

the Lord's terrene[10] Honor in all things, saving the faith due to the King, and his Heirs.

From this it is evident, that a Vassal cannot injure his Lord, consistently with the Faith implied in Homage; unless, possibly, in his own defence, or unless, in compliance with the King's precept, he join his Army when it proceeds against his Lord; and, generally speaking, no one can by Law, consistently with the Faith implied in Homage, do any thing which tends to deprive his Lord of his Inheritance, or to affix a personal stain upon him. If, then, a Tenant has in respect of several Fees done Homage to different Lords, who afterwards make war on each other; and the Chief Lord should command the Tenant to accompany him in person against another of his Lords, he ought to yield obedience to this Mandate, saving however the service due to the other Lord for the Fee held of him.

From what has gone before it is evident, that if a Tenant should do any thing to the disinherison[11] of his Lord, and should be convicted of it, he and his Heirs shall according to the Law for ever lose the Fee held of such Lord. The same consequence will follow, if the Tenant lay violent hands on his Lord to hurt him, or to commit any atrocious injury upon him, and this be lawfully proved in Court against the Tenant. But, it may be asked, whether any one can be compelled in the Lord's Court, to defend himself against the Lord from such charges; and whether his Lord can, by the Judgment of his own Court, distrain[12] the Tenant so to do, without the Precept of the King, or his Justices, or without the King's Writ, or that of his Chief Justice?

The Law, indeed, permits a Lord by the Judgment of his Court to call upon and distrain his Homager to appear in Court, and, unless he can purge himself against the charge of his Lord by three persons, or as many as the Court should award, he shall be amerced[13] to the Lord, to the extent of the whole Fee that he holds of him.

It may also be enquired, whether a Lord can distrain his Homager to appear in Court, and answer for a service, of which the former complains the Tenant has deforced him, or of which some part is unpaid?

The Lord, indeed, by Law may well do so, even without the precept of the King, or his Justices. And thus the Lord and his Homager may proceed to the Duel, or the Grand Assise,[14] by means of one of the Peers, who choses to make himself a Witness[15] of the fact, as having seen the Tenant himself, or his Ancestors, perform such service for the Fee in dispute to the Lord or his Ancestors, and is prepared to prove the fact. But, if the Tenant be convicted of this charge, he shall by Law be disinherited of the whole Fee, which he holds of his Lord. If, however, any one is unable to constrain his Tenants, it then becomes necessary to have recourse to the Court.[16] Every free Male person may perform Homage, whether of full age, or otherwise, whether a Clergyman or Layman. But consecrated Bishops are not in the habit of doing Homage to the King, even for their Baronies; but merely Fealty, accompanied with an oath. But Bishops-elect are accustomed to do Homage, previous to their Consecration.

## Chapter II

But Homage is due only for Lands, free Tenements, Services, Rents in certain, whether in Money, or in other things. But, in respect of Dominion[17] alone, Homage ought not to be rendered to any one, except to the King. Yet Homage is not always performed for every species of Land. Thus, it is not due for Land in Dower, nor for free Marriage-hood, nor from the Fee of Younger Sisters holding of the Eldest, within the third descent on both sides; nor is it due from a Fee given in Free-Alms, nor for any Tenement given in any way in Marriagehood, as far as concerns the person of the Husband of the Woman to whom the property belongs as her Marriagehood.

---

10 earthly   11 disinheritance   12 force   13 fined   14 trial by jury   15 one of the Tenants equals
16 i.e., the King's court   17 free property and authority over it; also lordship

## Chapter III

But Homage may be done to any free person, whether Male or Female, whether of full age or otherwise, whether Clergy or Lay. Yet should it be understood, that if a person has done Homage for a Tenement to a Woman who afterwards marries any man, he shall be compelled to repeat it to her Husband for the same Tenement. But, if any one has by Concord[18] made in Court recovered a Tenement against another who had previously paid a Relief for it to the Chief Lord, it may be questioned, whether the person so recovering the Tenement ought to pay any Relief for it.

## Chapter IV

Reciprocal, indeed, ought to be the Relation of Fidelity between Dominion,[19] and Homage. Nor does the Tenant owe more to his Lord, in respect of Homage, than the Lord owes to the Tenant on account of Dominion, Reverence [to the lord] alone excepted. Hence, if one person give to another any Land in return for Service and Homage, which is afterwards recovered against the Tenant by a third person, the Lord shall be bound to warrant such Land to him, or to return him an adequate equivalent. It is different, however, with respect to him who holds a Fee of another, as his Inheritance, and, in this character, has done Homage; because although he lose the Land, the Lord shall not be bound to give him an equivalent. In the case we have formerly mentioned, of the death of the Father or Ancestor, leaving an Heir, a Minor, the Lord of the Fee has no right to the Custody of the Heir, or his Inheritance, unless he has first received the Homage of the Heir. But the Homage having been received, the Heir, with his Inheritance, shall continue in the manner before mentioned, in the Custody of his Lord, until he has attained his full age. Having at last arrived at such age, and received restitution of his Inheritance, he

shall, by reason of his having been in Custody, be exempt from the payment of any Relief. But a Female Heir, whether she has attained her full age, or not, shall remain in the Custody of her Lord, until, with his advice, she is married. If, however, she was within age, when the Lord received her into Custody, then, upon her marriage, the Inheritance shall be discharged from the Relief, so far as respects herself and her Husband. But, if she was of full age at that time, although she continue some time in her Lord's custody before she is married, her Husband shall pay a Relief. When, however, the Relief has been once paid by the Husband of a Woman, it shall exempt both the Husband and the Wife during their several lives from payment of another Relief, on account of such Inheritance; because, neither the Woman herself, nor her second Husband, if she should espouse a second upon the death of the former, nor her first Husband, should he survive her, shall again pay a Relief for the same Land. But when a Male Heir is left of full age, and known to be the Heir, he shall hold himself in his Inheritance, as we have formerly observed, even though his Lord be unwilling, provided he make a Tender to his Lord, as he ought to do, of his Homage, and reasonable Relief, in the presence of creditable persons. A person's Relief is said to be reasonable, with reference to the Custom of the Realm, according to which the Relief of a Knight's Fee is one hundred Shillings, wilst that of Land in Socage[20] is one Year's Value. But as to Baronies nothing certain is enacted, because Barons holding of the King *in Capite*[21] are accustomed to pay their Reliefs to the King, according to his pleasure, and indulgence. The same Rule prevails as to Serjeanties.[22] If, however, the Lord will neither receive the Homage nor reasonable Relief of the Heir, then, the latter should safely keep the Relief, and frequently tender it to his Lord, by the hands of respectable persons. If the Lord will by no means

---

[18] agreement  [19] lordship: the right to rule  [20] free land  [21] in chief  [22] form of feudal tenure on condition of rendering specified personal service to the king

receive it, then, the Heir should make complaint of him to the King, or his Justices; and shall have the following Writ.

## Chapter V

The King to the Sheriff, Health. "Command N. that, justly and without delay, he receive the Homage, and reasonable Relief of R. concerning the free Tenement which he holds, in such a Vill,[23] and that he claims to hold of him; and, unless he does so, summon him by good Summoners, that he be before me or my Justices on such a day, to shew why he has not done it. And have there the Summoners, and this Writ. Witness &c."

## Chapter VI

As to the proceedings which are to be resorted to, in case the Lord should not obey this Summons, and the means by which he shall be distrained to appear in Court, they may be collected from the former part of this Treatise. When, at last, he appears in Court, he will either acknowledge that the Tenant is the right Heir, or deny that he is the Heir, or he will doubt, whether he is the right Heir or not. If he should acknowledge him to be the Heir, he will, then, either deny that the Tenant has tendered him the Homage and reasonable Relief, or he will admit it. If he confess both the one and the other, he shall either immediately receive the Tenant's Homage and reasonable Relief in Court, or he shall appoint him a fit day for doing it. The same observation may be made, although he deny that the Tenant has proffered to him his Homage or Relief, provided he admit the Tenant to be the Heir. But if in decided terms he denies the Tenant to be the Heir, then, indeed, may the latter, if out of possession, require against his Lord an Assise *de morte Antecessoris sui*.[24] Should the Tenant, however, happen to be in possession, he may hold himself in it, and patiently await, until it pleases his Lord to accept his Homage; because, no one is previously bound to answer his Lord

as to the Relief, until the latter has received his Homage for the Fee, on account of which Homage is due to him. But if the Lord doubts, whether the person tendering the Homage be the right Heir or not, being for example unknown to the Lord himself, or even to the Vicinage[25] in the character of Heir, then the Lord of the Fee may take the Land into his own hands, and retain it, until the point be fully cleared up, a course of proceeding, which the King generally adopts with respect to all his Barons holding of him *in Capite.*

For, upon the death of a Baron holding of him in chief, the King immediately retains the Barony in his own hands, until the the Heir has given security for the Relief, although the Heir should be of full age. But Lords, for a reasonable cause, may sometimes postpone receiving Homage and Relief for their Fees. Suppose, for Example, another person, than the one who asserts himself to be the Heir, should claim a right in the Inheritance. During the pendency of this Suit, Homage ought not to be received, nor a Relief given. Or, if the Lord think that he himself has a right to hold the Inheritance in his own Demesne. And if in such case he should, by force of the King's Writ or that of his Justices, implead[26] the person in possession, the Tenant may put himself upon the King's Grand Assise, . . .

## Chapter VIII

But after it has been settled between the Lord and the Heir of the Tenant concerning the giving and receiving of the reasonable Relief, the latter may exact reasonable Aids[27] from his Homagers. This, however, must be done with moderation, keeping in view the extent of their Fees, and the circumstances of the Tenants, least they should be too much oppressed, or lose their Contenement.[28] But nothing certain is fixed, concerning the giving or exacting Aids of this description, unless that the form we have mentioned should be inviolably ob-

---

[23] village   [24] trial by jury   [25] neighborhood   [26] sue   [27] financial obligation of a tenant to his lord
[28] ability to live in one's accustomed style of life

served. There are also other cases, in which a Lord can exact from his Homagers similar Aids, observing, however, the principle we have laid down: as if his Son and Heir should be made a Knight, or if he should marry off his Eldest Daughter. But, whether Lords can exact these Aids to maintain their own Wars, is doubtful. The opinion that prevails is, that they cannot by right distrain[29] their Tenants for such purpose, unless so far as the Tenants may feel disposed. But, with respect to the rendering of reasonable Aids, Lords may of right, without the King's precept, or that of his Justices, but by the Judgment of their own Court, distrain their Tenants by such of their chattels as may be found within their Fees, or by their Fees, if necessary; provided the Tenants are dealt with according to the Judgment of the Court, and consistently with the reasonable Custom of it. If, therefore, a Lord may thus distrain his Tenants to render such reasonable Aids, much stronger is the argument in favor of its being lawful for him to distrain in the same manner for a Relief, as also for any other service necessarily due to him, in respect of the Fee. But if a Lord is unable to compel his Tenant to render his services or Customs, then recourse must he had to the Assistance of the King, or his Chief Justice, and he shall obtain the following Writ —

**Chapter IX**

The King to the Sheriff, Health. "I command you that you adjudge N. that, justly and without delay, he render to R. the Customs and right Services which he ought to render him, for the Tenement that he holds of him, in such a Vill, as can be reasonably shewn to be due to him, least he again complains for want of right.    Witness, &c."

## Knight-Service Owed by Roger, Archbishop of York, to Henry II (1166)

In an era of few written records and obligations going back generations, a feudal king had great difficulty discovering exactly who owed him what kind of service, either financial or military. In this document, Henry II has demanded that one of his tenants-in-chief, Roger Archbishop of York, report on the number of his lesser tenants or sub-vassals and how many knight's fees or fiefs each possesses. Henry was probably as interested in the financial implications of his survey as the military. The document comes from the *Cartae Baeronum*, or written statements required from all the king's tenants-in-chief.

To his dearest lord, Henry, by the grace of God, king of the English, duke of the Normans and of the men of Aquitaine, count of the Angevins, his man Roger, by the same grace, archbishop of York, and legate of the apostolic see, gives greeting. Your dignity has ordered all your liegemen, both clerks and lay, who hold of you in chief in Yorkshire to send to you, by letters carrying their seals outside, answers to the following questions: how many knights does each possess by the old enfeoffment[30] of the time of the king, your grandfather, that is to say, in the year and on the day in which that king was alive and dead; and how many knights has he of the new enfeoffment, that is to say, enfeoffed after the death of your grandfather of good memory; and how many knights are on the demesne[31] of each? And there is also to be included in the return the names of

SOURCE: From David C. Douglas and George W. Greenaway, eds., *English Historical Documents* (London: Eyre Methuen, Ltd., publishers, 1953), Vol. II, pp. 906–908. By permission of the publishers.

[29] force    [30] the investment of a fief    [31] land directly controlled by the lord

all those, both of the old and new enfeoffments, because you wish to know if there are any who have not yet done you allegiance and whose names are not written in your roll, so that they may do you allegiance before the first Sunday in Lent. Wherefore I, being one of those subjected in all things to your orders, have made as thorough an investigation in my holdings as the short time permitted, and in this return I am declaring all these things to you as my Lord.

Know therefore, in the first place, my lord, that there is no knight's fee on the demesne of the archbishopric of York, since we have sufficient enfeoffed knights to discharge all the service which we owe you, and which our predecessors have performed. We have indeed more knights enfeoffed than are necessary for that service as you may learn from what follows. For our predecessors enfeoffed more knights than they owed to the king, and they did this, not for the necessities of the royal service, but because they wished to provide for their relatives and servants.

Here follow the names of those who were enfeoffed in the time of King Henry:

William, count of Aumale, holds a fee of 3 knights.
Henry of Lassy, 2 knights.
Roger of Montbrai [Mowbray], a quarter of a knight's fee.
Herbert, son of Herbert, 3 knights.
Gilbert, son of Nigel, 2 knights.
Payn 'de Landa', 3 knights.
Mauger, son of Hugh, 1 knight.
Richard, son of Hugh, 1 knight.
William of Bellewe, 1 knight.
Robert Morin, 2 knights.
Gilbert, son of Herbert, 2 knights.
Hugh 'de Muschamp', 2 knights.
Walter of Ancourt, 2 knights.
Robert Mansel, 1 knight.
Robert, son of Wiard, half a knight's fee.
Peter 'de Perintone', half a knight's fee.
Hugh of Vesly, 4 knights.
William Cokerel, 1 knight.
Thomas of Everingham, 2½ knights' fees.
Simon Wahart, 1 knight.
Ralph 'de Nowewica', half a knight's fee.
Robert Poer, half a knight's fee.
Walter of Denton, half a knight's fee.
Robert, son of Hugh, a quarter of a knight's fee.
William of Lubbenham, half a knight's fee.
Alexander of Newby, 4 parts of half a knight's fee.
Herbert of Markington, a quarter of a knight's fee.
Peter 'de Belingee', 1 knight.
Oliver the Angevin, 1 knight.
William 'de Pantone', 1 knight.
Thomas, son of Aubert, a quarter of a knight's fee.
Alice of Molescroft, a quarter of a knight's fee.
Thomas, son of Hervey, 1 knight.
Benedict of Sculcoates, the eighth part of a knight's fee.
Bernard of Cottingham, a quarter of a knight's fee.

Leofred, a thirteenth of a knight's fee.
John of Meaux, an eighth of a knight's fee.
Ivo, a quarter of a knight's fee.
Serlo of Poole, a third of a knight's fee.

After the death of King Henry there were enfeoffed:

Peter the butler, with half a knight's fee.
Peter the chamberlain, with the twentieth part of a knight's fee.
Geoffrey of Burton, with a twelfth of a knight's fee.
Gervase of Bretton, with a third of a knight's fee.

And since, my lord, I claim from some of these men more service than they are now performing, whereas others are keeping back services which are said to be due, not to themselves, but to the table and the demesne of the archbishop, I humbly beg that this my return may not be allowed to do harm to me or to my successors by preventing the Church from recovering or preserving its legal rights. Farewell, my lord.
And besides the aforesaid knights:

Thurstan 'de Lechamtone' [holds] half a knight's fee.
Gilbert 'de Miners', a third of a knight's fee.
Werri 'de Marinis', a third of a knight's fee.
William of Escures, a half of a knight's fee.
William Pallefrei, 1 knight.
William of Bellewe and Richard 'de Crochetone' hold a quarter of a knight's fee.

## The Anglo-Saxon Chronicle of 1137

In this selection from *The Anglo-Saxon Chronicle*, the author is reporting on what is wrong with the kingdom and its sovereign, King Stephen.

This year [1137] King Stephen went overseas to Normandy, and was received there because they expected that he would be just as his uncle had been, and because he still had his treasure; but he distributed it and squandered it like a fool. King Henry had gathered a great amount — gold and silver — and no good to his soul was done with it.

When King Stephen came to England he held his council at Oxford, and there he took Roger, bishop of Salisbury, and Alexander, bishop of Lincoln, and the chancellor Roger, his [Roger's] nephews, and put them all in prison till they surrendered their castles. When the traitors understood that he was a mild man, and gentle and good, and did not exact the full penalties of the law, they perpetrated every enormity. They had done him homage, and sworn oaths, but they kept no pledge; all of them were perjured and their pledges nullified, for every powerful man built his castles and held them against him and they filled the country full of castles. They oppressed the wretched people of the country severely with castle-building. When the castles were built, they filled them with devils and wicked men. Then, both by night and day they took those people that they thought had any goods — men and women — and put them in prison and tor-

SOURCE: From Dorothy Whitelock with David C. Douglas and Susie I. Tucker, trans. and eds., *The Anglo-Saxon Chronicle* (London: Eyre and Spottiswoode, Ltd., publishers, 1961), pp. 198–200. By permission of the publishers.

tured them with indescribable torture to extort gold and silver — for no martyrs were ever so tortured as they were. They were hung by the thumbs or by the head, and corselets were hung on their feet. Knotted ropes were put round their heads and twisted till they penetrated to the brains. They put them in prisons where there were adders and snakes and toads, and killed them like that. Some they put in a 'torture-chamber' — that is in a chest that was short, narrow and shallow, and they put sharp stones in it and pressed the man in it so that he had all his limbs broken. In many of the castles was a 'noose-and-trap' — consisting of chains of such a kind that two or three men had enough to do to carry one. It was so made that it was fastened to a beam, and they used to put sharp iron around the man's throat and his neck, so that he could not in any direction either sit or lie or sleep, but had to carry all that iron. Many thousands they killed by starvation.

I have neither the ability nor the power to tell all the horrors nor all the torments they inflicted upon wretched people in this country; and that lasted the nineteen years while Stephen was king, and it was always going from bad to worse. They levied taxes on the villages every so often, and called it 'protection money.' When the wretched people had no more to give, they robbed and burned the villages, so that you could easily go a whole day's journey and never find anyone occupying a village, nor land tilled. Then corn was dear, and meat and butter and cheese, because there was none in the country. Wretched people died of starvation; some lived by begging for alms, who had once been rich men; some fled the country.

There had never been till then greater misery in the country, nor had heathens ever done worse than they did. For contrary to custom, they respected neither church nor churchyard, but took all the property that was inside, and then burnt the church and everything together. Neither did they respect bishops' land nor abbots' nor priests', but robbed monks and clerics, and everyone robbed somebody else if he had the greater power. If two or three men came riding to a village, all the villagers fled from them; they expected they would be robbers. The bishops and learned men were always excommunicating them, but they thought nothing of it, because they were all utterly accursed and perjured and doomed to perdition.

Wherever cultivation was done, the ground produced no corn, because the land was all ruined by such doings, and they said openly that Christ and his saints were asleep. Such things, too much for us to describe, we suffered nineteen years for our sins. . . .

## FURTHER DISCUSSION QUESTIONS

### William of Poitiers, The Life of William the Conqueror

1. What qualities of leadership did Duke William display during the invasion?
2. How did William seek to turn the invasion into a crusade?
3. How do you explain the English defeat at Hastings?
4. How truthful and accurate a recorder of the events of the invasion would you judge William of Poitiers to be?
5. What qualities did Duke William possess that might have helped to make feudalism work?

### The Anglo-Saxon Chronicle of 1087

1. What aspect of King William's rule does the *Chronicle* approve or deplore?
2. In what ways does the portrait of the Conqueror in the *Chronicle* agree or disagree with that given by William of Poitiers?

### The Abingdon Chronicle

1. What is the picture of England given in *The Abingdon Chronicle?* Compare it with that presented in *The Anglo-Saxon Chronicle* of 1087.
2. If William of Poitiers described the invasion as a crusade, how would you say *The Abington Chronicle* described it?

### Statute of William the Conqueror

1. Judging from the statute, what can be deduced about the character of the man who enacted and enforced it?
2. What was William attempting to do by the statute?
3. Did William by his statute strengthen or weaken feudalism?

### The Coronation Charter of Henry I

1. What kind of promises was Henry I making to his barons, and why were they interested in exacting such promises? (Keep in mind Magna Carta — see Chapter 3.)
2. What abuses are suggested in the charter and why were they so prevalent?
3. What are the realities of the feudal relationships and the operation of feudalism implied in the charter?

### Ranulph de Glanville, Treatise on the Laws and Customs . . . of England

1. How did homage attempt to hold society together?
2. To what extent did feudalism (homage, etc.) resolve the social and political problems of the age?
3. Glanville speaks of the importance of exacting aids in moderation. What kept aids moderate, and who determined what constituted moderation?
4. What aspects of the feudal relationship would you expect to cause the greatest trouble and conflict?

### Knight-Service Owed by Roger, Archbishop of York to Henry II

1. Why was it difficult for Archbishop Roger to know the exact extent of the military service in his archbishopric owed to the king?
2. What problems inherent in feudalism do you detect in the document?

### The Anglo-Saxon Chronicle of 1137

1. What went wrong with Anglo-Norman feudal society under Stephen?
2. What attributes of kingship did Stephen lack?

# 3

# The Governmental Crisis of the Thirteenth Century: King, Barons, Church

It is a cliché to state that a particular century is a period of crisis. The human political experience is such that when two or more people are gathered together, it is almost a certainty that someone will be odd fellow out, and that is the making of a crisis. In the thirteenth century, political, social, and economic power rested with the three divisions of feudal society — kings, barons, church — and the feudal ideal entailed an exquisite but unattainable balance among the three. Unfortunately, each element had its own definition of its proper function in society. Each, on quite legitimate grounds, sought to extend its particular sphere of interest, thereby distorting the "true" feudal relationship and creating strains within society. In the name of effective government and of law, which should be common to all subjects, the crown developed one view of society; in the name of the spiritual welfare of Christendom, the church advocated yet another; and in the name of custom, kin, and the rights of individuals, the barons demanded still another. The clash between the three resulted in a governmental crisis that produced Magna Carta and the baronial wars and unrest of the reign of Henry III.

The crown's position, its economic and jurisdictional claims as well as its political ideals, are embodied in the Constitutions of Clarendon (1164), which sought to curtail the authority and independent status of the church, and in the Assize of Clarendon (1166), which established the jury of presentment or grand jury and encroached upon an older and largely baronial concept of justice. Both documents could easily have been placed in Chapter 4, dealing with the rationalization of society. The reader should keep in mind that Magna

Carta and the demands of the barons were only in part a reaction to royal abuse and corruption of government; they were also an answer to the "distortion" of feudal government implied in the developing bureaucratic and centralized concepts of administration explicit in the readings in Chapter 4.

Magna Carta (1215) is a declaration of political concessions, imposed by the baronage but never totally accepted by the crown, which eventually evolved into an enduring constitutional formula. "The Song of Lewes" (1264–65), written some fifty years later, is a statement of political philosophy — the baronial interpretation of how and what feudal government was all about. The author of the song was undoubtedly a cleric, probably a Franciscan friar and clearly a strong advocate of Simon de Montfort, and he may even have been present at the battle and attached to the Earl's household. This document, like Magna Carta, is a fascinating medley of contemporary complaints, selfish power politics, and lasting constitutional principles, for "The Song of Lewes" raises important issues regarding the nature of royal authority, the source of law, the process of governmental decision making, and the responsibility of royal councillors.

The next set of readings reflect the ecclesiastical point of view. They deal with the rivalry between a feudal crown and a centralized cosmopolitan church, which grew out of the medieval formula of a dual authority: "Render therefore unto Caesar the things which are Caesar's; and to God the things that are God's." The genesis of King John's struggle with Pope Innocent III was rooted in the investiture controversy that was inherent in feudal society: To whom were bishops (indeed, all clerics) responsible in a world where ecclesiastics were both shepherds of souls and important feudal-political personages? Under the circumstances, the right of appointment to ecclesiastical offices was central, and King John and Pope Innocent clashed over the elevation of Stephen Langton in 1207 to the archbishopric of Canterbury. Innocent's spiritual and political claims in the ensuing conflict, his placing of England under an interdict, and his successful demand that the kingdom become a papal fief represents the zenith of papal power both in fact and in theory, for as God's viceregent on earth, Innocent regarded himself as "the Lord's anointed...set in the midst between God and man...less than God but greater than man, judge of all men and judged by none." The consequences of Innocent's style of politics and jurisdictional claims and his use of spiritual weapons in the political arena bear careful scrutiny, especially as the reader moves to the documents in Chapters 6, "The Religious Structure of Life," and 7, "The Old Church."

The concluding selection is a return to human reality, for constitutional issues are historically, if not philosophically, meaningless without the human component. The governmental crisis of the late twelfth and thirteenth centuries had far more to do with the personalities of rulers and their styles of government than with abstract political theories. Of the four kings — Henry II, Richard I, John, and Henry III — Henry II was the most important. Although Gerald of Wales (1147–1220) heartily disliked Henry II (the King had turned down his suit to be appointed Bishop of St. David), the strength of that monarch's character graphically emerges from Gerald's analysis and description.

A final question should be kept in mind in reading these documents: Given the arguments and the regal personalities involved, was it ever possible for the social ideal — king, barons, church living in perfect accord with one another — to be achieved?

## The Constitutions of Clarendon (1164)

The Constitutions of Clarendon, the product of a special and enlarged meeting of the King's Great Council at his hunting lodge at Clarendon, attempted to codify the historic practices governing the relationship between state and church. The customs discovered and written down by the council were heavily pro-state and led directly to the Henry II–Thomas à Becket controversy and the eventual murder of the Archbishop. After Becket's death, the Constitutions were withdrawn, but most of the provisions continued to be quietly enforced by King Henry.

In the year of the incarnation of the Lord, 1164, of the papacy of Alexander, the fourth year, of the most illustrious king of the English, Henry II, the tenth year, in the presence of the same king, has been made this memorial or acknowledgment of a certain part of the customs and franchises and dignities of his predecessors, that is to say of King Henry, his grandfather, and of other kings, which ought to be observed and held in the kingdom. And on account of the discussions and disputes which have arisen

SOURCE: From Edward P. Cheyney, ed., *Translations and Reprints from Original Sources of European History*, (Philadelphia, University of Pennsylvania, 1900), "English Constitutional Documents" Vol. I, No. 6, pp. 26–30.

between the clergy and the justices of our lord the king and the barons of the kingdom concerning the customs and dignities, this acknowledgment is made in the presence of the archbishops and bishops and clergy and earls and barons and principal men of the kingdom. And these customs, acknowledged by the archbishops and bishops and earls and barons, and by the most noble and ancient of the kingdom, Thomas, archbishop of Canterbury, and Roger, archbishop of York, . . . [plus 12 bishops and 38 named barons] and many others of the principal men and nobles of the kingdom, as well clergy as laity.

Of these acknowledged customs and dignities of the realm, a certain part is contained in the present writing. Of this part the heads are as follows:

1. If any controversy has arisen concerning the advowson[1] and presentation of churches between laymen and ecclesiastics, or between ecclesiastics, it is to be considered or settled in the courts of the lord king.

2. Churches of the fee of the lord king cannot be given perpetually without his assent and grant.

3. Clergymen charged and accused of anything, when they have been summoned by a justice of the king shall come into his court, to respond there to that which it shall seem good to the court of the king for them to respond to, and in the ecclesiastical court to what it shall seem good should be responded to there; so that the justice of the king shall send into the court of holy church to see how the matter shall be treated there. And if a clergyman shall have been convicted or has confessed, the church ought not to protect him otherwise.

4. It is not lawful for archbishops, bishops, and persons of the realm to go out of the realm without the permission of the lord king. And if they go out, if it please the lord king, they shall give security that neither in going nor in making a stay nor in returning will they seek evil or loss to the king or the kingdom. . . .

7. No one who holds from the king in chief, nor any one of the officers of his demesnes shall be excommunicated, nor the lands of any one of them placed under an interdict, unless the lord king, if he is in the land, first agrees, or his justice, if he is out of the realm, in order that he may do right concerning him; . . .

8. Concerning appeals, if they should occur, they ought to proceed from the archdeacon to the bishop, from the bishop to the archbishop. And if the archbishop should fail to show justice, it must come to the lord king last, in order that by his command the controversy should be finally terminated in the court of the archbishop, so that it ought not to proceed further without the assent of the lord king. . . .

10. If any one who is of a city or a castle or a borough or a demesne manor of the lord king has been summoned by the archdeacon or the bishop for any offence for which he ought to respond to them, and is unwilling to make answer to their summons, it is fully lawful to place him under an interdict, but he ought not to be excommunicated before the principal officer of the lord king for that place agrees, in order that he may adjudge him to come to the answer. And if the officer of the king is negligent in this, he himself will be at the mercy of the lord king, and afterward the bishop shall be able to coerce the accused man by ecclesiastical justice.

11. Archbishops, bishops, and all persons of the realm, who hold from the king in chief, have their possessions from the lord king as a barony, and are responsible for them to the justices and officers of the king, and follow and perform all royal rules and customs; and just as the rest of the barons ought to be present at the judgment of the court of the lord king along with the barons, at least till the judgment reaches to loss of limbs or to death.

12. When an archbishopric or bishopric or abbacy or priorate of the demesne of the king has become vacant, it ought to be in his hands, and he shall take thence all its rights and products just as demesnes. And when

---

[1] living

it has come to providing for the church, the lord king ought to summon the more powerful persons of the church, and the election ought to be made in the chapel of the lord king himself, with the assent of the lord king and with the agreement of the persons of the realm whom he has called to do this. And there the person elected shall do homage and fealty to the lord king as to his liege lord, concerning his life and his limbs and his earthly honor, saving his order, before he shall be consecrated. . . .

This acknowledgment of the aforesaid royal customs and dignities has been made by the aforesaid archbishops, and bishops, and earls, and barons, and the more noble and ancient of the realm, at Clarendon, on the fourth day before the Purification of the Blessed Mary, perpetual Virgin, Lord Henry being there present with his father, the lord king. There are, however, many other and great customs and dignities of holy mother church and of the lord king, and of the barons of the realm, which are not contained in this writing. These are preserved to holy church and to the lord king and to his heirs and to the barons of the realm, and shall be observed inviolably forever.

## The Assize of Clarendon (1166)

In the Assize of Clarendon (issued at the King's hunting lodge at Clarendon), Henry II took what has been called a crucial step toward the "extension of royal jurisdiction into areas traditionally reserved for the local courts." He established inquest juries of twelve men from each hundred (or subdivision of the shire) to meet regularly and report to the king's sheriff the names of all persons suspected of having committed a crime.

Here begins the Assize of Clarendon, made by King Henry II, with the assent of the archbishops, bishops, abbots, earls and barons of all England.

1. In the first place, the aforesaid King Henry, with the consent of all his barons, for the preservation of the peace and the keeping of justice, has enacted that inquiry should be made through the several counties and through the several hundreds, by twelve of the most legal men of the hundred and by four of the most legal men of each manor, upon their oath that they will tell the truth, whether there is in their hundred or in their manor, any man who has been accused or publicly suspected of himself being a robber, or murderer, or thief, or of being a receiver of robbers, or murderers, or thieves, since the lord king has been king. And let the justices make this inquiry before themselves, and the sheriffs before themselves.

2. And let any one who has been found by the oath of the aforesaid to have been accused or publicly suspected of having been a robber, or murderer, or thief, or a receiver of them, since the lord king has been king, be arrested and go to the ordeal of water and let him swear that he has not been a robber, or murderer, or thief, or receiver of them since the lord king has been king, to the value of five shillings, so far as he knows. . . .

4. And when a robber, or murderer, or thief, or receiver of them shall have been seized through the above-mentioned oath, if the justices are not to come very soon into that county where they have been arrested, let the sheriffs send word to the nearest justice by some intelligent man that they have arrested such men, and the justices will send back word to the sheriffs where they wish that these should be brought before them;

SOURCE: From Edward P. Cheyney, ed., *Translations and Reprints from Original Sources of European History* (Philadelphia: University of Pennsylvania, 1900), "English Constitutional Documents" Vol. I, No. 6, pp. 22–25.

and the sheriffs shall bring them before the justices; and along with these they shall bring from the hundred and the manor where they have been arrested, two legal men to carry the record of the county and of the hundred as to why they were seized, and there before the justice let them make their law.

5. And in the case of those who have been arrested through the aforesaid oath of this assize, no one shall have court, or judgment, or chattels, except the lord king in his court before his justices, and the lord king shall have all their chattels. In the case of those, however, who have been arrested, otherwise than through this oath, let it be as it has been accustomed and ought to be. . . .

11. And let there be none within a city or borough or within a castle or without, or even in the honor of Wallingford, who shall forbid the sheriffs to enter into his land or his jurisdiction to arrest those who have been charged or publicly suspected of being robbers or murderers or thiefs or receivers of them, or outlaws, or persons charged concerning the forest; but he requires that they should aid them to capture these.

12. And if any one is captured who has in his possession the fruits of robbery or theft, if he is of bad reputation and has an evil testimony from the public, and has not a warrant, let him not have law. . . .

13. And if any one shall have acknowledged robbery or murder or theft or the reception of them in the presence of legal men or of the hundred, and afterwards shall wish to deny it, he shall not have law. . . .

15. And the lord king forbids any vaga-bond, that is a wandering or an unknown man, to be sheltered anywhere except in a borough, and even there he shall be sheltered only one night, unless he shall be sick there, or his horse, so that he is able to show an evident excuse.

16. And if he shall have been there more than one night, let him be arrested and held until his lord shall come to give securities for him, or until he himself shall have secured pledges; and let him likewise be arrested who has sheltered him.

17. And if any sheriff shall have sent word to any other sheriff that men have fled from his county into another county, on account of robbery or murder or theft, or the reception of them, or for outlawry or for a charge concerning the forest of the king, let him arrest them. And even if he knows of himself or through others that such men have fled into his county, let him arrest them and hold them until he shall have secured pledges from them.

18. And let all sheriffs cause a list to be made of all fugitives who have fled from their counties; and let them do this in the presence of their county courts, and they will carry the written names of these before the justices when they come first before these, so that they may be sought through all England, and their chattels may be seized for the use of the king. . . .

20. The lord king, moreover, prohibits monks and canons and all religious houses from receiving any one of the lesser people as a monk or canon or brother, until it is known of what reputation he is, unless he shall be sick unto death.

## Magna Carta (15 June, 1215)

Magna Carta was the climax to a revolt in the spring of 1215 against King John by barons who had been badly hurt financially by administrative extortions. By June, after the King, Archbishop Stephen Langton, loyal barons, and disloyal barons

SOURCE: From Edward P. Cheyney, ed., *Translations and Reprints from Original Sources of European History* (Philadelphia: University of Pennsylvania, 1900), "English Constitutional Documents" Vol. I, No. 6, pp. 6–17.

had haggled bitterly over terms, John finally affixed his seal to a document that encompassed the full gamut of feudal complaints against the crown. Magna Carta represents the transformation of unwritten, timeless customs and private feudal contractual rights into the modern concept of government ruled by written and public law.

---

John, by the grace of God, king of England, lord of Ireland, duke of Normandy and Aquitaine, count of Anjou, to the archbishops, bishops, abbots, earls, barons, justiciars, foresters, sheriffs, reeves, servants, and all bailiffs and his faithful people greeting. Know that by the inspiration of God and for the good of our soul and those of all our predecessors and of their heirs, to the honor of God and the exaltation of holy church, and the improvement of our kingdom, by the advice of ... [one archbishop, eight bishops, four barons, twelve advisors and "others of our faithful"].

1. In the first place, we have granted to God, and by this our present charter confirmed, for us and for our heirs forever, that the English church shall be free, and shall hold its rights entire and its liberties uninjured; and we will that it be thus observed; which is shown by this, that the freedom of elections, which is considered to be most important and especially necessary to the English church, we, of our pure and spontaneous will, granted, and by our charter confirmed, . . .

We have granted moreover to all free men of our kingdom for us and our heirs forever all the liberties written below, to be had and holden by themselves and their heirs from us and our heirs.

2. If any of our earls or barons, or others holding from us in chief by military service shall have died, and when he has died his heir shall be of full age and owe relief,[2] he shall have his inheritance by the ancient relief; that is to say, the heir or heirs of an earl for the whole barony of an earl a hundred pounds; the heir or heirs of a baron for a whole barony a hundred pounds; the heir or heirs of a knight for a whole knight's fee a hundred shillings at most; and who owes

less let him give less according to the ancient custom of fiefs.

3. If moreover the heir of any one of such shall be under age, and shall be in wardship, when he comes of age he shall have his inheritance without relief and without a fine. . . .

6. Heirs shall be married without disparity, so nevertheless that before the marriage is contracted, it shall be announced to the relatives by blood of the heir himself.

7. A widow, after the death of her husband, shall have her marriage portion and her inheritance immediately and without obstruction, nor shall she give anything for her dowry or for her marriage portion, or for her inheritance, which inheritance her husband and she held on the day of the death of her husband; and she may remain in the house of her husband for forty days after his death, within which time her dowry shall be assigned to her.

8. No widow shall be compelled to marry so long as she prefers to live without a husband, provided she gives security that she will not marry without our consent, if she holds from us, or without the consent of her lord from whom she holds, if she holds from another. . . .

12. No scutage or aid shall be imposed in our kingdom except by the common council of our kingdom, except for the ransoming of our body, for the making of our oldest son a knight, and for once marrying our oldest daughter, and for these purposes it shall be only a reasonable aid; in the same way it shall be done concerning the aids of the city of London. . . .

14. And for holding a common council of the kingdom concerning the assessment of an aid otherwise than in the three cases mentioned above, or concerning the assessment

---

[2] payment made by tenant to his lord upon inheritance, usually first year's rent

of a scutage, we shall cause to be summoned the archbishops, bishops, abbots, earls, and greater barons by our letters under seal; and besides we ·shall cause to be summoned generally, by our sheriffs and bailiffs all those who hold from us in chief, for a certain day, that is at the end of forty days at least, and for a certain place; and in all the letters of that summons, we will express the cause of the summons, and when the summons has thus been given the business shall proceed on the appointed day, on the advice of those who shall be present, even if not all of those who were summoned have come. . . .

16. No one shall be compelled to perform any greater service for a knight's fee, or for any other free tenement than is owed from it.

17. The common pleas shall not follow our court, but shall be held in some certain place.

18. The recognitions of *novel disseisin, mort d'ancestor,* and *darrein presentment*³ shall be held only in their own counties and in this manner: we, or if we are outside of the kingdom our principal justiciar, will send two justiciars through each county four times a year, who with four knights of each county, elected by the county, shall hold in the county and on the day and in the place of the county court the aforesaid assizes of the county. . . .

28. No constable or other bailiff of ours shall take anyone's grain or other chattels, without immediately paying for them in money, unless he is able to obtain a postponement at the good will of the seller.

29. No constable shall require any knight to give money in place of his ward of a castle if he is willing to furnish that ward in his own person or through another honest man, if he himself is not able to do it for a reasonable cause; and if we shall lead or send him into the army he shall be free from ward in proportion to the amount of time by which he has been in the army through us.

30. No sheriff or bailiff of ours or any one else shall take horses or wagons of any free man for carrying purposes except on the permission of that free man.

31. Neither we nor our bailiffs will take the wood of another man for castles, or for anything else which we are doing, except by the permission of him to whom the wood belongs.

32. We will not hold the lands of those convicted of a felony for more than a year and a day, after which the lands shall be returned to the lords of the fiefs. . . .

39. No free man shall be taken or imprisoned or dispossessed, or outlawed, or banished, or in any way destroyed, nor will we go upon him, nor send upon him, except by the legal judgment of his peers or by the law of the land.

40. To no one will we sell, to no one will we deny, or delay right or justice. . . .

52. If any one shall have been dispossessed or removed by us without legal judgment of his peers, from his lands, castles, franchises, or his right, we will restore them to him immediately; and if contention arises about this, then it shall be done according to the judgment of the twenty-five barons, of whom mention is made below concerning the security of the peace. . . .

54. No one shall be seized nor imprisoned on the appeal of a woman concerning the death of any one except her husband.

55. All fines which have been imposed unjustly and against the law of the land, and all penalties imposed unjustly and against the law of the land are altogether excused, or will be on the judgment of the twenty-five barons of whom mention is made below. . . .

61. Since, moreover, for the sake of God, and for the improvement of our kingdom, and for the better quieting of the hostility sprung up lately between us and our barons, we have made all these concessions; wishing them to enjoy these in a complete and firm stability forever, we make and concede to them the security described below; that is to say, that they shall elect twenty-five barons of the kingdom, whom they will, who ought

---

³ *novel disseisin* . . . all forms of trial by jury

with all their power to observe, hold, and cause to be observed, the peace and liberties which we have conceded to them, and by this our present charter confirmed to them; in this manner, that if we or our justiciar, or our bailiffs, or any of our servants shall have done wrong in any way toward any one, or shall have transgressed any of the articles of peace or security; and the wrong shall have been shown to four barons of the aforesaid twenty-five barons, let those four barons come to us or to our justiciar, if we are out of the kingdom, laying before us the transgression, and let them ask that we cause that transgression to be corrected without delay. And if we shall not have corrected the transgression or, if we shall be out of the kingdom, if our justiciar shall not have corrected it within a period of forty days, counting from the time in which it has been shown to us or to our justiciar, if we are out of the kingdom; the aforesaid barons shall refer the matter to the remainder of the twenty-five barons, and let these twenty-five barons with the whole community of the country distress and injure us in every way they can; that it to say by the seizure of our castles, lands, possessions, and in such other ways as they can until it shall have been corrected according to their judgment, saving our person and that of our queen, and those of our children; and when the correction has been made, let them devote themselves to us as they did before. . . .

62. And all ill-will, grudges, and anger sprung up between us and our men, clergy and laymen, from the time of the dispute, we have fully renounced and pardoned to all. . . .

63. Wherefore we will and firmly command that the Church of England shall be free, and that the men in our kingdom shall have and hold all the aforesaid liberties, rights and concessions, well and peacefully, freely and quietly, fully and completely, for themselves and their heirs, from us and our heirs, in all things and places, forever, as before said. It has been sworn, moreover, as well on our part as on the part of the barons, that all these things spoken of above shall be observed in good faith and without any evil intent. Witness the above named and many others. Given by our hand in the meadow which is called Runnymede, between Windsor and Staines, on the fifteenth day of June, in the seventeenth year of our reign.

## The Song of Lewes (1264)

The Song of Lewes was written to celebrate the baronial victory of Simon de Monfort, Earl of Leicester, over Henry III at the Battle of Lewes (May, 1264). The reign of Henry III has been described as "a commentary upon the Great Charter," for during this period the kingdom sought (not very successfully) to put into effect the governmental ideal of a feudal king ruling with the cooperation of the "community of the realm." The Song of Lewes is a political statement by the baronial faction of what was meant by the "community of the realm."

See! we touch the root of the disturbance of the kingdom about which we are writing, and of the dissension of the parties who fought the said battle; to different objects did they turn their aim. The King with his party wished to be thus free, and urged that he ought to be so, and was of necessity, or that deprived of a king's right he would cease to be king, unless he should do whatever he might wish; that the magnates of the realm had not to heed, whom he set over his own counties, or on whom he conferred the wardenship of castles, or whom he would have to show justice to his people;

SOURCE: From *The Song of Lewes*, C. L. Kingsford, ed. (Oxford, England: Clarendon Press, 1890), pp. 43–52.

and he would have as chancellor and treasurer of his realm anyone soever at his own will, and counsellors of whatever nation, and various ministers at his own discretion, without the barons of England interfering in the King's acts, as "the command of the prince has the force of law"; and that what he might command of his own will would bind each. For every earl also is thus his own master, giving aught of his own in what measure and to whom he will — castles, lands, and revenues, he entrusts to whom he will, and although he be a subject, the King permits it all. Wherein if he shall have done well, it is of profit to the doer, if not, he himself shall see to it; the King will not oppose him whilst injuring himself. Why is the prince made of worse condition, if the affairs of a baron, a knight, and a freeman are so managed? Wherefore they intrigue for the King to be made a servant, who wish to lessen his power, and to take away his dignity of prince; they wish to thrust down into wardship and subjection the royal power made captive through sedition, and to disinherit the King, that he may not have power to rule so fully as hitherto have done the kings who preceded him, who were in no wise subject to their own people, but managed their own affairs at their will, and conferred their own at their own pleasure. This is the King's pleading which seems true, and this allegation protects the right of the realm.

But now let my pen be turned to the opposite side. Let the proposal of the barons be subjoined to what has already been said; and when the parties have been heard let the statements be compared, and after comparison let them be closed by a definite termination, so that the truer part may be clear; the people are more prone to obey the more true. Therefore let the party of the barons now speak on its behalf, and let it duly follow whither it is led by zeal. Which party in the first place openly makes protestation, that it devices naught against the royal honour, or seeks anything contrary to it; nay, is zealous to reform and magnify the kingly state; just as, if the kingdom were

devastated by enemies, it would not then be reformed without the barons, to whom this would be proper and suitable; and he who should then falsify himself, him the law would punish as guilty of perjury, as a betrayer of the king. He who can contribute aught of aid to the king's honour, owes it to his lord when he is in peril, when the kingdom is deformed as it were in extremity.

The king's adversaries are enemies who make war, and counsellors who flatter the king, who by deceitful words mislead the prince, and with double tongues lead him into error; these are worse adversaries than the perverse, they make themselves out to be good, when they are misleaders, and they are procurers of their own honour; they deceive the unwary whom they render more careless through pleasant words, whence they are not guarded against but are looked on as speaking useful things. These can deceive more than can the open, as they know how to feign themselves as not hostile. What, if such wretches and such liars should cleave to the side of the prince, full of all malice, fraud and falsehood, pricked with the stings of envy they would devise a deed of wickedness, through which they might bend to their own ostentation the rights of the realm; and should fashion some hard arguments, which would gradually confound the community, crush and impoverish the commonalty of the people, and subvert and infatuate the kingdom, so that no one might be able to obtain justice unless he were willing to foster the pride of such men by means of money amply bestowed? Who would endure so great a wrong to be imagined? And if such men by their aims were to alter the realm, so as to supplant right by unright; and after trampling on the natives were to call in strangers, and were to subdue the kingdom to foreigners; were not to regard the magnates and nobles of the land, and were to put mean men in the highest place, and were to cast down and humble the great, were to pervert order and turn it upside down; were to abandon the best, be urgent on the worst; would not those who should do thus, lay waste the kingdom? Although they might not be fighting with weapons of war from abroad, yet would they be contending with the devil's weapons, and pitifully violating the state of the realm, although their manner was different (lit. differently) they would do no less damage. Whether the king consenting through misguidance, or not perceiving such deceit, were to approve such measures destructive to the kingdom; or whether the king out of malice were to do harm, by preferring his own power to the laws, or by abusing his strength on account of his opportunity; or if thus or otherwise the kingdom be wasted, or the kingdom be made utterly destitute, then ought the magnates of the kingdom to take care, that the land be purged of all errors. And if to them belongs the purging of error, and to them, belongs provision [for] the governess of customs, how would it not be lawful for them to take foresight lest any evil happen which might be harmful; which, after it may have happened, they ought to remove, lest of a sudden it make the unweary to grieve. . . .

Since it is agreed that all this is lawful for the barons, it remains to reply to the reasonings of the king. The king wishes, by the removal of his guardians, to be free, and wishes not to be subject to his inferiors, but to be over them, to command his subjects and not to be commanded; nor does he wish to be humbled to those set in authority, for those, who are set in authority, are not set over the king, nay rather are men of distinction who support the right of the one; otherwise the king would not be without a rival (lit. unique) but they, whom the king was under, would reign equally. Yet this incongruity which seems so great, may, with God's assistance, be easily solved. For we believe that God, through Whom we thus dissolve this doubt, desires the truth. One alone is called, and is King in truth, through Whom the world is ruled by pure majesty, Who needs not assistance whereby He may be able to reign, nay nor counsel, Who cannot err. Therefore all-powerful and knowing He excels in infinite glory all, to whom He has granted to rule His people under Him

and as it were to reign, who are able to fail and able to err, and who cannot stand by their own strength and overcome their enemies by their own valour, nor govern kingdoms by their own understanding, but go badly astray in the pathlessness of error; they need assistance that supports them, yea and counsel that keeps them right. The king says: "I agree to thy reasoning, but the election of these men falls under my choice; I will associate with me whom I will, by whose defence I will govern all things; and if my own men be insufficient, have not understanding, or be not powerful, or if they be evil-wishers, and be not faithful, but may perchance be treacherous, I wish thee to make clear, why I ought to be constrained to certain persons, and from whom I have power to get better assistance." The reasoning on which matter is quickly declared, if it be considered what the constraining of the king is. All constraint does not deprive of liberty, nor does all restriction take away power. Those that are princes wish for free power, those that are lords wish not for wretched slavery. To what purpose does free law wish kings to be bound? That they may not be able to be stained by an adulterine law. And this constraining is not of slavery, but is the enlarging of kingly virtue. So is the king's child preserved that he may not be hurt, yet he becomes not a slave when he is so constrained. . . . Yea thus also are the angel spirits constrained, who are confirmed that they be not apostate. For that the Author of all is not able to err, that the Beginning of all is not able to sin, is not impotence but the highest power, the great glory of God and His great majesty. Thus he who is able to fall, if he be guraded that he fall not, is aided by such guardianship to live freely; neither is such sustenance of slavery, but is the protectress of virtue. Therefore let the king like everything that is good, but let him not dare evil; this is, the gift of God. They who guard the king, that he sin not when tempted, are themselves the servants of the king, to whom let him be truly grateful, because they free him from being made a slave, because they do not surpass him, by whom he is led. But whoever is truly king is truly free, if he rule himself and his kingdom rightly; let him know that all things are lawful for him which are fitted for ruling the kingdom, but not for destroying it. It is one thing to rule, which is the duty of a king, another to destroy by resisting the law. . . .

Let every king understand that he is the servant of God; let him love that only which is pleasing to Him; and let him seek His glory in ruling, not his own pride by despising his equals. Let the king, who wishes the kingdom which is put under him to obey him, render his duty to God, otherwise let him truly know that obedience is not due to him, who denies the service by which it is held of God. Again, let him know that the people is not his own but God's, and let him be profitable to it as a help. . . . And thus the wise prince will never reject his own men, but the foolish one will disturb the kingdom. Whence if the king be less wise than he ought, what service is he for ruling the kingdom? Shall he of his own proper understanding seek by whom he may be supported, by whom his own lack may be supplied? If he alone choose, he will be easily deceived, who has no knowledge who may be useful. Therefore let the community of the realm take counsel, and let that be decreed which is the opinion of the commonalty, to whom their own laws are most known; nor are all the men of the province such fools as not to know better than others their own realm's customs, which those who are before bequeath to those who come after. Those, who are ruled by the laws, have more knowledge of them; those, in whose use they are, become more experienced. And because it is their own affair which is at stake, they will care more and will procure for themselves the means whereby peace is acquired. They can know little who are not experienced, they will profit the kingdom little except they are stedfast. From this it can be gathered that the kind of men, who ought rightly to be chosen for the service of the kingdom, touches the community; namely those who

have the will and knowledge and power to be of profit, let such men be made counsellors and coadjutors of the king; . . .

If therefore the king has not the knowledge to choose by himself men who know how to counsel him, it is hence clear what ought then to be done; for it concerns the community that wretched men be not made guides of the royal dignity, but the best and chosen men, and the most approved who can be found. For since the governance of the realm is the safety or ruin of all, it matters much whose is the guardianship of the realm; just as it is on the sea, all things are confounded if fools are in command. . . .

We say also that law rules the dignity of the king; for we believe that law is a light, without which we infer that the guide goes astray. Law, whereby is ruled the world and the kingdoms of the world, is described as fiery, because it contains a mystery of deep meaning; it shines, burns, glows; fire by shining prevents wandering, it avails against cold, purifies, and reduces to ashes, some hard things it softens, and cooks what was raw, takes away numbness, and does many other good things. Sacred law supplies like gifts to the king. This wisdom Solomon asked for; its friendship he sought for with all his might. If the king be without this law, he will go astray; if he hold it not, he will err shamefully. Its presence gives right reigning, and its absence the disturbance of the realm. That law speaks thus: "By me kings reign, by me is justice shown to those who make laws." That stable law shall no king alter, but through it shall he strengthen his changing self. It he conform to this law he shall stand, and if he disagree with it he will stagger. It is commonly said, "As the king wills, the law goes"; truth wills otherwise, for the law stands, the king falls. Truth and charity and the zeal of salvation are the integrity of law, the rule of virtue; truth is light, charity warmth, zeal burns: this variety of the law takes away all crime. Whatever the king determines, let it be consonant with these; for if he do otherwise the commons will be rendered sorrowful. . . .

## The Letters of Pope Innocent III (1207–1215)

The first five letters deal with the controversy over the election of Stephen Langton as Archbishop of Canterbury. In the first letter (May, 1207), Innocent chastizes King John for his failure to consent to the election. In his second letter (August, 1207), he orders the bishops of London, Ely and Worcester, to publish the Pope's sentence of Interdict since John continues to be obstinate, and in the third letter (November, 1207), he reinforces this step by urging the nobles of the kingdom to defy their sovereign. In the fourth and fifth letters (February, 1213, and April, 1214), Innocent informs John of the surrender terms and announces the superior authority of popes over mere secular figures. The sixth and final letter (March, 1215) to the nobles of England refers to the Magna Carta crisis and the baronial revolt against King John. Innocent's message in this case is very different from the one found in his November, 1207, letter to the nobles of the kingdom.

---

### To King John

Innocent, bishop, servant of the servants of God to his well-beloved son in Christ, John, illustrious king of the English, greeting and apostolic benediction.

On the matter of the church of Canterbury we wrote to you meekly and kindly, requesting and exhorting: but you (with respect be it said) wrote back to us insolently and impudently as though threatening and expostulating ... [and] offering, as you do, certain paltry reasons which, you aver, prevent you from granting your consent to the election (recently celebrated by the monks of Canterbury) of our beloved son Stephen, cardinal priest of the title of St Chrysogonus, — such paltry reasons as that he has lived among your enemies and that his person is entirely unknown. . . .

Your envoys told us another reason for your not granting your consent to the election — namely, that your consent had never been sought by those who should have asked for it. . . . [Innocent denies this and adds:] We also, who have plenary authority over the church of Canterbury, deigned in a letter to entreat your royal favour in this matter: and our courier who delivered to you this apostolic letter also delivered to your Majesty a letter requesting your assent from the prior and monks who by mandate from the whole chapter of Canterbury had celebrated the aforesaid election.

Wherefore, we do not think it necessary to ask again for the king's consent after all these approaches; but swerving neither to the right hand nor to the left, we have resolved to follow the course appointed by the canonical decrees of the holy fathers — namely, that no delay or difficulty should be allowed to thwart good arrangements, lest the Lord's flock should for a long time be without pastoral care. . . .

So therefore, well-beloved son, to whose honour we have been careful to defer beyond what is required by law, be zealous in deferring to our honour as the law requires, that you may richly merit both the divine favour and ours; lest perchance, if you act otherwise, you may involve yourself in a difficulty from which you could not easily be freed, for in the end He must win "to whom every knee bows, of things in heaven, and things in earth, and things under the earth," whose power, however unworthily, we as Vicar exercise on earth. . . .

*The Lateran, the 26th of May,*
*in the tenth year of our Pontificate* [1207].

SOURCE: From C. R. Cheney and W. H. Semple, eds., *Selected Letters of Pope Innocent III Concerning England* (Oxford, England: Oxford University Press, 1953), Letters 29, 30, 32, 45, 67, 74, pp. 86–95, 97–99, 130–136, 177–182, 194–195. By permission of the publisher.

*To the Bishops of London, Ely, and Worcester*

We believe, therefore, that no more useful provision can at this time be made for the king's honour and salvation than that the church of Canterbury should have a prelate who, being renowned in reputation, knowledge and life, should be able by proofs and instances to summon him to the things which are of God and, cleaving to him with the whole affection of his mind, should give him sound advice on spiritual and temporal benefits; and since we know these qualities to reside in our venerable brother, Stephen, archbishop of Canterbury, cardinal of the Holy Roman Church, ... yet because we desire to promote the king's benefit and salvation and also intend to provide for Stephen's advancement, we have with our hands consecrated him archbishop, canonically postulated and elected as he was by the community of the church of Canterbury: and, giving him a pall from the body of St Peter as a symbol of the plenitude of his episcopal office, we have thought fit to send him to the government of the church committed to his care.

Therefore, although we unfeignedly love the king (with God as our witness we say it) and desire to defer to his honour, yet because it becomes us to defer to God rather than to men, and because in the execution of justice there ought not to be respect or choice of persons, we earnestly warn and exhort you as our brethren, strictly directing and charging you by apostolic letter, that ... you should together approach the king and in the spirit of freedom should respectfully exhort him as king, and diligently persuade him as a son, to submit to wise counsels, thus providing salvation for souls, peace for the peoples, honour to God and liberty to the Church. ...

[If John refuse this wise counsel] then laying aside all earthly fear and forbidding any opposition or appeal, you are to publish throughout England the general sentence of Interdict, permitting no ecclesiastical office except the baptism of infants and the confession of the dying to be celebrated there. ...

*Viterbo, the 27th of August, in the tenth year of our Pontificate* [1207].

*To all the nobles of England*

If to our well-beloved son in Christ, John, illustrious king of the English, you pay the loyalty that is his due, be assured that this is pleasing both to God and to us. But because you should regulate your loyal attachment to the earthly king so as never to offend the Heavenly King, being upright and loyal men you ought to be on guard to save the king by your faithful advice from a policy which he has seemingly planned in enmity to God — that of persecuting our venerable brother, Stephen, archbishop of Canterbury and, through him, the church committed to his charge. So, with all your strength, save him from rejecting the counsel of good men and from walking in the counsel of the ungodly, whose thoughts will all perish in one day whereas the counsel of the Lord which they attempt to bring to nought standeth for ever. Indeed, since "ye cannot serve two masters" (as the Truth puts it in the Gospel), it is undoubtedly in your interests, in view of the king's opposition to God, not to support him and, putting the fear of God above that of man, not to caress him in company with those who "sew pillows under his elbow" with their flattering hand, and not to fear displeasing him temporarily in the cause of justice — for conduct so upright will not injure you by exciting him to hatred, but will in time benefit you by winning his love. ...

Do you, therefore, whose loyalty and wisdom should make themselves powerfully felt in the difficulties of the king and kingdom, now at this time of misfortune begin loyally and wisely to combat the king's purpose so as not to let yourselves and the kingdom be drawn into a turmoil from which (and may God avert the danger!) there could be no easy escape. For we, who would not shrink, if occasion demanded, from fighting to the death for the justice of this cause, do not intend to withdraw our apostolic hand from the defence of ecclesiastical liberty. Assuredly, our hand is not shortened: indeed by God's grace it is so extended that, if any man's sins make it heavy against him, it will be able to bring upon him, spiritually and temporally, a crushing weight of punishment.

*St. Peter's, Rome, the 21st of November, in the tenth year of our Pontificate* [1207].

### To King John

To John, illustrious king of the English, a spirit of sounder understanding.

We have heard the statement of your envoys who presented themselves before us: and although on your behalf they did not adequately offer terms sufficient for reparation in respect of the many great wrongs and losses you have for a long time inflicted on the English church, contrary to the glory of the Divine Name and the honour of the Apostolic See, and to the peril of your soul and the loss of your reputation, yet still wishing to try whether we can recall you from error to truth, behold! we set before you a blessing and a curse after the example of Him who by His servant Moses set before the children of Israel blessings and curses, that you may choose which you prefer, either a blessing leading to salvation if you make reparation, or a curse leading to ruin if you show contempt. . . .

But that we may overcome evil with good and deprive you of all ground of excuse, we are still ready to keep those terms if before the 1st of June next ensuing, on the oaths of four of your barons swearing on your soul in your presence and at your command, and by your own letters patent[4] you renew your promise, faithfully and effectively to implement those terms according to the interpretations and explanations we have thought fit to append for the removal of every shade of misunderstanding, and if within this time-limit you have by your letters patent made all this known to our venerable brother Stephen archbishop of Canterbury and to his bishops who are with him. Otherwise, by the example of Him who with a strong hand freed His people from the bondage of Pharaoh, we intend with a mighty arm to free the English church from your bondage: and we now truthfully and firmly forewarn you that, if you will not accept peace when you may, you may not when you will, and repentance will be useless after your downfall — as you may learn from the instances of those who in your own time have acted with a similar presumption.

The terms with which we charged our aforenamed envoys, we send to you enclosed in the present letter. The interpretations and explanations are as follows:

First, in the presence of our legate or delegate you will solemnly and unreservedly swear to abide by our commands in respect of all matters for which you are excommunicated by us. . . .

At the same time you will publicly take an oath in the presence of our legate or delegate that you will not injure the said individuals or their people nor cause or permit them to be injured in person or property, and will forgo all your anger against them and receive them into your favour and in good faith maintain them there, and that you will not hinder the said archbishop and bishops, nor cause or permit them to be hindered, from freely exercising their office and using as they should the full authority of their jurisdiction. On these matters you will give both to us and to the archbishop and to the individual bishops your own letters patent, and you will cause your bishops, earls, and barons (as many of them and whichever of them the said archbishop and bishops shall require) to give oaths and letters patent that they will work in good faith to ensure that this agreement and guarantee be firmly kept; and that, if you contravene

---

[4] written grant from a government to a person in a form readily open for inspection

it (which God forbid!) either personally or through agents, they will stand fast by the apostolic commands on the Church's side against the violators of the guarantee and the peace, and you will for ever lose the custody of vacant churches. If you cannot persuade them to accept this final part of the oath, namely that, if personally or by agents you contravene the agreement, they will stand fast by the apostolic commands on the Church's side against the violators of the guarantee and the peace, you will on this account make over by your letters patent to us and the Roman Church all right of patronage that you have in English churches. . . .

No compact, promise, or concession shall prevent compensation for losses and the return of things seized, and this applies alike to the property of the living and of persons now dead. You shall not retain any of the seized property on the score of feudal service which ought to have been paid to you: but afterwards due compensation will be paid to you in lieu of service. You will immediately cause all clergy whom you detain to be unconditionally released and restored to their personal liberty and similarly all laymen who are detained because of this business. . . . When all these conditions have been duly fulfilled, the sentence of interdict will be relaxed. . . .

*The Lateran, the 27th of February,*
*in the sixteenth year of our Pontificate*
*[1213].*

*To King John*

Innocent, bishop, servant of the servants of God, to his well-beloved son in Christ, John illustrious king of the English, and to his legitimate free-born heirs for ever.

The King of kings and Lord of lords, Jesus Christ, a priest for ever after the order of Melchisedech, has so established in the Church His kingdom and His priesthood that the one is a kingdom of priests and the other a royal priesthood, as is testified by Moses in the Law and by Peter in his Epis-

tle; and over all He has set one whom He has appointed as His Vicar on earth [the Pope], so that, as every knee is bowed to Jesus, of things in heaven, and things in earth, and things under the earth, so all men should obey His Vicar and strive that there may be one fold and one shepherd. All secular kings for the sake of God so venerate this Vicar, that unless they seek to serve him devotedly they doubt if they are reigning properly. To this, dearly beloved son, you have paid wise attention; and by the merciful inspiration of Him in whose hand are the hearts of kings which He turns whithersoever He wills, you have decided to submit in a temporal sense yourself and your kingdom to him to whom you knew them to be spiritually subject, so that kingdom and priesthood, like body and soul, for the great good and profit of each, might be united in the single person of Christ's Vicar. He has deigned to work this wonder, who being alpha and omega has caused the end to fulfil the beginning and the beginning to anticipate the end, so that those provinces which from of old have had the Holy Roman Church as their proper teacher in spiritual matters should now in temporal things also have her as their peculiar sovereign. You, whom God has chosen as suitable minister to effect this, by a devout and spontaneous act of will and on the general advice of your barons have offered and yielded, in the form of an annual payment of a thousand marks, yourself and your kingdoms of England and Ireland, with all their rights and appurtenances, to God and to SS Peter and Paul His apostles and to the Holy Roman Church and to us and our successors, to be our right and our property — as is stated in your official letter attested by a golden seal, the literal tenor of which is as follows:

"John, by the grace of God king of England, lord of Ireland, duke of Normandy and Aquitaine, count of Anjou, to all the faithful of Christ who may see this charter, greeting in the Lord.

"By this charter attested by our golden seal we wish it to be known to you all that, having in many things offended God and

Holy Church our mother and being there-fore in the utmost need of divine mercy and possessing nothing but ourselves and our kingdoms that we can worthily offer as due amends to God and the Church, we desire to humble ourselves for the sake of Him who for us humbled Himself even unto death; and inspired by the grace of the Holy Spirit — not induced by force nor compelled by fear, but of our own good and spon-taneous will and on the general advice of our barons — we offer and freely yield to God, and to SS Peter and Paul His apostles, and to the Holy Roman Church our mother, and to our lord Pope Innocent III and his catholic successors, the whole kingdom of England and the whole kingdom of Ireland with all their rights and appurtenances for the remission of our sins and the sins of our whole family, both the living and the dead. And now, receiving back these king-doms from God and the Roman Church and holding them as feudatory vassal, in the presence of our venerable father, lord Nich-olas, bishop of Tusculum, legate of the Apos-tolic See, and of Pandulf, subdeacon and member of household to our lord the Pope, we have pledged and sworn our fealty henceforth to our lord aforesaid, Pope Inno-cent, and to his catholic successors, and to the Roman Church, in the terms herein-under stated; and we have publicly paid liege homage for the said kingdoms to God, and to the Holy Apostles Peter and Paul, and to the Roman Church, and to our lord aforesaid, Pope Innocent III, at the hands of the said legate who accepts our homage in place and instead of our said lord, the Pope; and we bind in perpetuity our suc-cessors and legitimate heirs that without question they must similarly render fealty and acknowledge homage to the Supreme Pontiff holding office at the time and to the Roman Church. As a token of this our per-petual offering and concession we will and decree that out of the proper and special revenues of our said kingdoms, in lieu of all service and payment which we should ren-der for them, the Roman Church is to re-ceive annually, without prejudice to the

payment of Peter's pence, one thousand marks sterling. . . ."

This offer and concession so piously and wisely made we regard as acceptable and valid, and we take under the protection of Saint Peter and of ourselves your person and the persons of your heirs together with the said kingdoms and their appurtenances and all other goods which are now reason-ably held or may in future be so held: to you and to your heirs, according to the terms set out above and by the general advice of our brethren, we grant the said kingdoms in fief and confirm them by this privilege, on condition that any of your heirs on receiving the crown will publicly acknowledge this as a fief held of the Su-preme Pontiff and of the Roman Church, and will take an oath of fealty to them. Let no man, therefore, have power to in-fringe this document of our concession and confirmation, or presume to oppose it. If any man dare to do so, let him know that he will incur the anger of Almighty God and of SS Peter and Paul, His apostles. AMEN, amen, AMEN.

. . . I, Innocent, bishop of the Catholic Church, have signed. Farewell. [21 April, 1214]

## To the Nobles of England

It is a grievous trouble to us that, as we have heard, a difference between some of you and our well-beloved son in Christ, John, illustrious king of the English, has arisen over certain matters recently in dis-pute — a difference which will cause serious loss, unless the matters are quickly settled by wise counsel and earnest attention. We utterly condemn it, if (as alleged by many) you have dared to form leagues or con-spiracies against him and presumed arro-gantly and disloyally by force of arms to make claims which, if necessary, you ought to have made in humility and loyal de-votion. Lest, therefore, the king's good in-tention should be thwarted for reasons of this kind, by apostolic authority we de-nounce as null and void all leagues and con-spiracies set on foot since the outbreak of dissension between the kingdom and the priesthood, and under sentence of excommunication we forbid the hatching of such plots in [the] future — prudently admonishing and strongly urging you to appease and reconcile the king by manifest proofs of your loyalty and submission, rendering him the customary services which you and your predecessors paid to him and his predecessors; and then, if you should decide to make a demand of him, you are to implore it respectfully and not arrogantly, maintaining his royal honour, so that you may the more easily gain your object....

*The Lateran, the 19the of March,*
*in the eighteenth year of our Pontificate*
[1215].

GERALD OF WALES, *Description of Henry II*

Gerald of Wales is better known to historians as Giraldus Cambreusis. His description of Henry II is extremely modern in its psychological flavor and is one of the best we possess for any medieval English king.

It were not amiss in this place to draw the portrait of the king, that so his person as well as his character may be familiar to posterity; and those who in future ages shall hear and read of his great achievements, may be able to picture him to themselves as he was. For the history on which I am employed must not suffer so noble an ornament of our times to pass away with only a slight notice....

Henry II, king of England, had a reddish complexion, rather dark, and a large round head. His eyes were grey, bloodshot, and flashed in anger. He had a fiery countenance, his voice was tremulous, and his neck a little bent forward; but his chest was broad, and his arms were muscular. His body was fleshy, and he had an enormous paunch, rather by the fault of nature than from gross feeding. For his diet was temperate, and indeed in all things, considering he was a prince, he was moderate, and even parsimonious. In order to reduce and cure, as far as possible, this natural tendency and defect, he waged a continual war, so to speak, with his own belly by taking immoderate exercise. For in time of war, in which he was almost always engaged, he took little rest, even during the intervals of business and action. Times of peace were no seasons of repose and indulgence to him, for he was immoderately fond of the chase, and devoted himself to it with excessive ardour. At the first dawn of day he would mount a fleet horse, and indefatigably spend the day in riding through the woods, penetrating the depths of forests, and crossing the ridges of hills. On his return home in the evening he was seldom seen to sit down, either before he took his supper or after; for, notwithstanding his own great fatigue, he would weary all his court by being constantly on his legs. But it is one of the most useful rules in life, not to have too much of any one thing, and even medicine is not in itself perfect and always to be used; even so it befell this king. For he had frequent swellings in his legs and feet, increased much by his violent exercise on horseback, which added to his other complaints, and if they did not bring on serious disorders, at least hastened that which is the source of all, old age. In stature he may be reckoned among men of moderate height, which was not the case with either of his sons; the two eldest being

SOURCE: From Thomas Forester, trans., *The Historical Works of Giraldus Cambreusis Containing the Topography of Ireland*, rev. and ed. by Thomas Wright (London: George Bell & Sons, 1913), pp. 249–253.

somewhat above the middle height, and the two youngest somewhat below.

When his mind was undisturbed, and he was not in an angry mood, he spoke with great eloquence, and, what was remarkable in those days, he was well learned. He was also affable, flexible, and facetious, and, however he smothered his inward feelings, second to no one in courtesy. Withal, he was so clement a prince, that when he had subdued his enemies, he was overcome himself by his pity for them. Resolute in war, and provident in peace, he so much feared the doubtful fortune of the former, that, as the comic poet writes, he tried all courses before he resorted to arms. Those whom he lost in battle he lamented with more than a prince's sorrow, having a more humane feeling for the soldiers who had fallen than for the survivors; and bewailing the dead more than he cared for the living. In troublesome times no man was more courteous, and when all things were safe, no man more harsh. Severe to the unruly, but clement to the humble; hard towards his own household, but liberal to strangers; profuse abroad, but sparing at home; those whom he once hated, he would scarcely ever love, and from those he loved, he seldom withdrew his regard. He was inordinately fond of hawking and hunting, whether his falcons stooped on their prey, or his sagacious hounds, quick of scent and swift of foot, pursued the chase. Would to God he had been as zealous in his devotions as he was in his sports.

It is said that after the grievous dissensions between him and his sons, raised by their mother, he had no respect for the obligations of the most solemn treaties. True it is that from a certain natural inconstancy he often broke his word, preferring rather, when driven to straits, to forfeit his promise than depart from his purpose. In all his doings he was provident and circumspect, and on this account he was sometimes slack in the administration of justice, and, to his people's great cost, his decisions on all proceedings were dilatory. Both God and right demand that justice should be administered

gratuitously, yet all things were set to sale and brought great wealth both to the clergy and laity; but their end was like Gehazi's gains.

He was a great maker of peace, and kept it himself; a liberal alms-giver, and an especial benefactor to the Holy Land. He loved the humble, curbed the nobility, and trod down the proud; filling the hungry with good things, and sending the rich empty away; exalting the meek, and putting down the mighty from their seat. He ventured on many detestable usurpations in things belonging to God, and through a zeal for justice (but not according to knowledge), he joined the rights of the church to those of the crown, and therein confused them, in order to centre all in himself. Although he was the son of the church, and received his crown from her hands, he either dissembled or forgot the sacramental unction. He could scarcely spare an hour to hear mass, and then he was more occupied in counsels and conversation about affairs of state than in his devotions. The revenues of the churches during their avoidance, he drew into his own treasury, laying hands on that which belonged to Christ; and as he was always in fresh troubles and engaged in mighty wars, he expended all the money he could get, and lavished upon unrighteous soldiers what was due to the priests. In his great prudence he devised many plans, which, however, did not all turn out according to his expectations; but no great mishap ever occurred, which did not originate in some trifling circumstance.

He was the kindest of fathers to his legitimate children during their childhood and youth, but as they advanced in years looked on them with an evil eye, treating them worse than a step-father; and although he had such distinguished and illustrious sons, whether it was that he would not have them prosper too fast, or whether they were ill-deserving, he could never bear to think of them as his successors. And as human prosperity can neither be permanent nor perfect, such was the exquisite malice of fortune against this king, that where he should have received comfort he met with opposition; where security, danger; where peace, turmoil; where support, ingratitude; where quiet and tranquillity, disquiet and disturbance. Whether it happened from unhappy marriages, or for the punishment of the father's sins, there was never any good agreement either of the father with his sons, or of the sons with their parent, or between themselves. . . .

I had almost forgotten to mention that his memory was so good, that, notwithstanding the multitudes who continually surrounded him, he never failed of recog-nizing any one he had ever seen before, nor did he forget any thing important which he had ever heard. He was also master of nearly the whole course of history, and well versed in almost all matters of experience. To conclude in few words: if this king had been finally chosen of God, and had turned himself to obey his commands, such were his natural endowments that he would have been, beyond all comparison, the noblest of all the princes of the earth in his times. But enough: let what I have written, briefly and imperfectly indeed, but not altogether foreign to my subject, content the reader. . . .

## FURTHER DISCUSSION QUESTIONS

### The Constitutions of Clarendon

1. What advantage was it to the crown to have conflicts involving ecclesiastic lands resolved in the king's courts? Why would the king want to prevent clerics from leaving the kingdom? Why would the king wish to prevent the excommunication of his servants and vassals?
2. Why would the church have resisted so vigorously article eight dealing with judicial appeals?
3. What was the "legal" basis on which the king made his claims and sought to establish the "proper" relationship between church and state?

### The Assize of Clarendon

1. To what extent does the Assize of Clarendon represent an improvement over the older system of justice? (Compare with documents in Chapter 1.)
2. Why might the great barons have been unhappy with some of the implications of the Assize?
3. What concept of law is being voiced by the royal government?

### Magna Carta

1. Is there any evidence that Magna Carta sought to extend royal government as well as limit it?
2. To what extent was Magna Carta a victory for customary law as opposed to royal law?
3. What view of aids and scutage is being voiced that ran counter to royal action and theory?
4. Why was it so important that the language of Magna Carta was so free from coercion?
5. What if any enduring human rights and constitutional principles are explicit in Magna Carta? To what extent are they implicit?

### The Song of Lewes

1. What view of kingship is being voiced in the song, and what, according to the author, is the proper role and behavior of a king?

2. What is the "true" source of law within the kingdom? What gives it credibility and makes it enforceable?
3. What enduring constitutional principles are present in the song?
4. Is there any truth in the assertion that the barons wanted to turn the king into a puppet and deprive him of his "royal dignity"?
5. Are there any inconsistencies in the baronial constitutional argument as presented in the song?

## The Letters of Pope Innocent III

1. On what grounds did Innocent claim authority? Why wouldn't John accept the election of Stephen Langton?
2. What kind of picture of Innocent and John emerges from these letters?
3. Is it possible to reconcile Innocent's advice to the nobles in 1207 and in 1215?
4. What was Innocent's view of the ideal feudal society? What did John gain by making England a papal fief and himself a vassal of the pope?

## Gerald of Wales' Description of Henry II

1. What qualities made Henry an effective feudal monarch? What qualities might be considered detrimental, and by whom?
2. Why did Henry have so much trouble with his children?

# 4

# *The Rationalization of Society*

The bureaucratic and administrative mind that instinctively prefers to define, categorize, and record, that seeks to organize institutional procedure on the basis of rational principles, and that abhors the ad hoc, random, and emotional actions of primitive societies is probably the most important single characteristic of modern society. The bureaucratic mind began to emerge in England under the early Norman and Plantagenet monarchs as the king's perambulating household, staffed by private servants, slowly transformed itself into the permanent centralized, professionalized, and specialized governmental administration of modern times. What was gained by this transformation, what was lost, what was changed and distorted, not to mention what new principles of government were being voiced — these questions are the themes of this chapter. The documents in Chapter 4 stand in contrast to the picture of society that appears in Chapter 1.

The first four documents present baronial and royal justice in action, and the grounds and rationale on which justice for both the great and small was based. The first selection, "The Trial Held on Pinnenden Hill" in 1075, is important not only because it involves the great personages of the realm — Stephen Lanfranc, Archbishop of Canterbury; Odo, Bishop of Bayeux and Earl of Kent, who was also the king's bastard half brother; and William the Conqueror himself — but also because it demonstrates early Anglo-Norman efforts to establish justice on the basis of something other than might making its own right by redressing Bishop Odo's seizure of many of the archdiocesan lands and privileges in Kent. Two centuries later the chronicler Walter of Hemingburgh was recording a similar situation when he described baronial reaction to Edward I's efforts to introduce a degree of rational order into feudal landholding by his famous statute of *Quo Warranto* (1278). This statute required the possessors of feudal franchises and privileges to prove their historic right

Earl de Warenne producing his title to the Commissioners.

or warrant. Walter of Hemingburgh's chronicle is followed by the trial of the Earl of Surrey in 1279, which displays the new law at work and indicates that it could protect as well as endanger the historic privileges of the great barons. The Earl was, incidentally, the same nobleman who appears in Walter of Hemingburgh's chronicle. The fourth selection, an inquest taken at the city of Leicester in 1253, is a delightful picture of primitive justice in action and reveals the need for a better method for settling disputes.

The next two documents — "The Establishment of the Royal Household" (ca. 1136) and *The Course of the Exchequer* (ca. 1177) — give a vivid account of the king's government. Despite the fact that they were written within two generations of each other, the differences between the two accounts — the minds of the men who wrote them and the kinds of governments described — is startling. "The Establishment of the Household" presents the household-administrative structure that existed under Henry I and his predecessors. Except for its size, the organization and operation of the royal household were probably no different from that of any great feudal personage, clerical or secular. In contrast, *The Course of the Exchequer* is profoundly modern in its approach and organization. Written by Richard [Fitz]Nigel, Bishop of London, Treasurer of England under Henry II and Richard I, and a third generation royal servant, it is a model of the organizational and rational mind in operation. As F. W. Maitland said, "That such a book should be written is one of the most wonderful things of Henry's wonderful reign."

The last document, "How to Hold a Parliament," was written probably between 1316 and 1324, and demonstrates how far representative government had come since it had emerged out of the king's Great Council in the twelfth and thirteenth centuries and had begun to develop rational and written procedures sanctified by usage. As the kingdom slowly changed from a feudal association held together by common allegiance to the king into a state that operated upon fixed legal principles and whose members possessed established rights, less and less was left to the will of the sovereign. The king's government had always had to work within the limitations laid down by mindless historic custom and local privilege, but now those limitations were becoming increasingly rational and standardized.

## The Trial Held on Pinnenden Hill (ca. 1075)

The trial on Pinnenden Hill involved the clash between two strong-minded and politically powerful men — Lanfranc, the reforming Archbishop of Canterbury, and Odo, Bishop of Bayeux, Earl of Kent and bastard brother of King William — and the efforts of the Conqueror to resolve the dispute by law.

In the time of the great King William, who conquered England by his arms and subjected it to his sway, it happened that Odo, bishop of Bayeux, who was the brother of that king, came to England some time before Lanfranc, archbishop of Canterbury. He established himself in the country of Kent very strongly and exercised great power therein. Moreover, because in those days there was no one in that shire who could resist so powerful a magnate, he attached to himself many men of the archbishopric of Canterbury, and seized many of the customary rights which pertained to it. These he annexed wrongfully to his own lordship. Not long afterwards, the aforesaid Lanfranc, who was then abbot of Caen, himself came to England by the command of the king, and by the grace of God was made archbishop of Canterbury and primate of the realm of England. When the archbishop had resided here for some time he discovered that his church lacked many of its ancient possessions and that these had

been dissipated or alienated through the negligence of his predecessors. He therefore diligently collected accurate information, and then, hastening to the king, he energetically stated his case. The king thereupon gave orders that the whole shire court should meet without delay, and that there should be brought together not only all the Frenchmen in the county, but also and more especially those English who were well acquainted with the traditional laws and customs of the land. This assembly met in due course at Pinnenden. At this trial very many questions were raised between the archbishop and the bishop of Bayeux relating both to the ownership of particular estates and also to the legal customs of the country; and at the same time many points were mooted concerning the customary rights to which the king and the archbishop were respectively entitled. So numerous indeed were the matters in dispute that all the business could not be transacted in one day, and for that reason the court of the

SOURCE: From David C. Douglas and George W. Greenaway, eds., *English Historical Documents* (London, Eyre Methuen, Ltd., Publishers, 1953), Vol. II, Doc. 50, pp. 449–451. By permission of the publishers.

shire was held in continuous session for three whole days at this place. During these three days Lanfranc, the archbishop, proved his title to many lands which were then held by men of the bishop, to wit: Herbert, son of Ivo, Thorold of Rochester, Ralph of Courbépine, and others of his vassals. He vindicated his rights in these lands and in the customs which went with them against the bishop of Bayeux himself, and against the aforesaid men of the bishops and against others also. These were the lands in question: Detling; Stoke; Preston; Denton; and many other smaller estates. And against Hugh of Montfort-sur-Risle, he vindicated his rights in Ruckinge and Brook; and against Ralph of Courbépine, 60 solidates in the island of "Grean." Over all these lands and others the archbishop vindicated his rights so completely that on the day on which the trial ended there was not a man in the whole kingdom of England who could claim any jot or tittle of them.

In this plea the archbishop not only proved his right to these and other lands; he also vindicated afresh the liberties of his church and the customary jurisdiction which he was entitled to exercise, to wit: sake and soke, toll and team, flymenafyrrmth, grithbryce, forsteal, hamfare and infangenthef,[1] with all other customs like to these and less than these, on land and water, in woods and ways and meadows, within city and without, within borough and without, and everywhere in the land. And verdict was passed in his favour by all the worthy and wise men who were present, and by the whole court of the shire, who all gave judgment that just as the king himself held his lands in every way freely and quit from tribute, so also did the archbishop of Canterbury.

At this plea there were present: Geoffrey, bishop of Coutances, who was there representing the king, and who presided over this trial; Lanfranc, the archbishop, who pleaded and justified his plea; the earl of Kent,

that is to say, the aforesaid Odo, bishop of Bayeux; Ernost, bishop of Rochester; Ægelric, bishop of Chichester, a man of great age and very wise in the law of the land, who, by the command of the king, was brought to the trial in a wagon in order that he might declare and expound the ancient practice of the laws; Richard of Tonbridge; Hugh of Montfort-sur-Risle; William of Arques; Haimo the sheriff; and many other barons both of the king and the archbishop; and many men of the aforesaid bishops; and other men of other shires; and many men both French and English of great authority from the county of Kent.

In the presence of all these men, it was further fully proved that the king of the English could claim in all the lands of the church of Canterbury no customary dues save only three. If any men of the archbishop are arrested in the act either of digging up the royal roads which lead from city to city, or of felling trees so close to those roads that an obstruction is caused, then shall they fall under the jurisdiction of the king's officer, whether they had previously given surety or not, and they shall be fined by him according to justice. The third custom concerns any man who commits homicide or any felonious act on the king's highway: if caught in the act and arrested forthwith, he shall be punished by the king; if however he is not caught in the act but, being suspected, absconds without giving any surety, the king shall have no jurisdiction over him. In the same trial it was shown that the archbishop justly exercises many customary rights over certain lands both of the king and the earl. From the beginning of Lent to the Octave of Easter, anyone who sheds blood shall be punished by the archbishop; and at all times, both during Lent and otherwise, anyone who commits adultery shall pay either the whole or half the penalty to the archbishop, to wit, during Lent the whole, and outside Lent either the whole or half. The archbishop

---

[1] *sake* . . . various types of jurisdictions

shall also have in the same lands whatever pertains to the care of souls.

When the king heard the judgment given in this plea, and had been made aware of those who ratified it, and when he had learnt the many reasons which could be adduced in support of it, he gave thanks, and joyfully confirmed the judgment with the assent of all his magnates, and ordered that it should be steadfastly and completely upheld. Wherefore this has been written down so that it may in the future be kept in perpetual remembrance, and so that those who shall hereafter succeed to the Church of Christ in Canterbury may know of it; and may be aware of the rights they hold from God in the same church; and may have knowledge of what things the kings and magnates of the realm may exact from them.

## *The Chronicle of Walter of Hemingburgh* (ca. 1204–1215)

Walter of Hemingburgh in telling his story has lumped together the Statute of Gloucester (1278) and the Statute Quo Warranto (1290). Both statutes deal with the same subject: Edward I's determination that all "who claim rights of jurisdiction by charters of the king's predecessors . . . or by any other title, shall come before the king . . . to show what sorts of franchises they claim to have and by what warrant. . . . And if [they] . . . fail to come . . . those franchises shall be taken into the king's hand. . . ." Edward was endeavoring to maintain the supremacy of royal jurisdiction and the principle that a baron exercised justice only though royal authority.

In the year of our Lord 1278, a fortnight after the feast of St. John the Baptist, the King held his Parliament at Gloucester and . . . he made the statute of quo warranto. . . .

Soon after he disquieted some of the magnates of the land by means of his justices, who sought to know by what warrant they held their lands. If they had no good warrant, he took possession of their lands. Among the rest Earl Warenne was summoned before the King's justices and asked by what warrant he held. He produced an ancient and rusty sword, and cried, "Here, my lords, here is my warrant! My ancestors came over with William the bastard and conquered their lands by the sword, and I will defend those same lands by the sword against any, whosoever he may be, who seeks to occupy them. For the King did not conquer and subdue the land by himself, but my ancestors were his partners and helpers." Other magnates adhered to him and his argument, and went off angry and in disorder. When the King heard of this he feared for himself, and ceased from his mistaken policy. Besides, soon after the Welsh rose in rebellion, and the King had great need of his magnates. So when the King was holding a certain Parliament, and the sons of the magnates were standing in his presence at vespers, he said to them, "What were you talking about while I was in consultation with your fathers?" And one answered, "You will not be angry if we tell you the truth?" "No," said the King. "Sire, we were saying this: —

> The King desires our money,
> The Queen our manors too,
> The writ of 'By what warrant'
> Will make a sad to-do."

SOURCE: From H. Johnstone, *A Hundred Years of History* (Essex, England: Longman Group Ltd., 1912), pp. 152–153.

## The Trial of John Warenne, Earl of Surrey (June, 1279)

Not every case of Quo Warranto went in favor of the King.

John of Warenne, Earl of Surrey, was summoned to be here on this day to show by what warrant he claimed to have free warren and chase[2] in the following manors of ... [64 are named] in the county [of Sussex]. And William of Giselham, who conducted the case for the King, said that William of Warenne, father of the present Earl, had seized the rights of warren and chase in these manors from lord King Henry, father of the present King, and the rights which the present Earl holds he has merely seized to the loss of the lord King.

And the Earl came and denied both the force and the injury. He said that William of Warenne, his father (whose heir he was) held the barony and honor of Lewes with the feudal rights and the rights of warren, etc., and that all of the liberties aforementioned were added and joined to that barony and honor which William held from the lord King Henry as a tenant-in-chief, and without premeditation King Henry, by reason of this, had received his homage. And in this homage William had died seized of the rights of warren and chase as well as all the liberties added and joined to the aforesaid barony and honor [of Lewes]. After William's death the barony and honor (with the liberties) came into the hands of King Henry by reason of the wardship of John [the present Earl] who was under age. And during the whole time of this wardship, which was seventeen years and more, King Henry was in possession of the rights of warren and chase, in as much as these belonged to the aforesaid barony and honor.

And Earl John said that when he came of age, King Henry restored to him this barony and honor together with all the liberties including rights of chase, and all of them were restored to him in the same state as his father William had held them when he died. And the Earl said that King Henry accepted his homage for the barony and the things pertaining to it, and gave it to him in seizin[3] on his own account. And in like manner the present lord King [Edward] had received his homage for the barony and for all things pertaining to it.

By that warrant he claims to have warren and chase in the aforementioned manors. ... And though the present King seeks judgment for the said barony and honor, the Earl asks whether King Edward should not be the warrant against himself for the reasons mentioned before. And if the court considered that this [claim] was not sufficient he was prepared to reply, etc.

Later, in the octave of St. Martin [Dec. 18], the Earl came to Chichester and said that in [the manors in question] he himself had his own parks, and asked whether the King had any claim on these parks. And William of Giselham, the King's attorney, said that these parks had nothing to do with the present case.

The Earl said that all his ancestors had adhered strictly to the Kings of England. And he said that because at the time of departure from Normandy his ancestors, who had been Counts of Warenne there, were unwilling to adhere to the King of France and for this reason had lost their Norman lands in consequence, King John of England, by way of recompense, gave to the Earl's ancestors more land [in England] and granted that they and their heirs should hold all those lands, thus given, from

SOURCE: From *Crises in English History 1066–1945: Select Problems in Historical Interpretation* by Basil Duke Henning, Archibald S. Foord, and Barbara L. Mathias. Copyright, 1949, Henry Holt and Company, Inc. Reprinted by permission of Holt, Rinehart and Winston.

[2] hunting rights    [3] to be held as a freehold

the King himself, and also any lands which they might obtain. And they were to have the right of warren because their name was Warenne.

And the Earl said that his father had held all those rights of chase and warren in the manors in which he claimed to have them even before King Henry had assumed the governance of the realm.

Therefore the Earl said that his father had made no seizure from King Henry nor from the present King. And he asked that an inquest be made that it were so. And William of Giselham, who conducted the case for the King, similarly asked that an inquest be made.

Accordingly the case went to the jury, and the sheriff was ordered to have a jury elected in his presence. And [twelve jurors, the first six being listed as "knights," the remainder as "lords of manors"] were selected with the consent of William of Heure,

the King's attorney, and with the consent of the Earl.

And these jurors declared upon their oath that even before King Henry was crowned King, William of Warenne, Earl of Surrey, the father of the present Earl, had possessed all the said liberties of chase and warren belonging to the honor and barony of Lewes. And they held that Earl William had not seized or usurped anything either from King Henry or from the present King. . . .

And because it was agreed by the jury that Earl William had made use of these rights of chase and warren in the aforementioned manors before the coronation of King Henry; and because Earl William had not seized or usurped anything from King Henry or the present King, it was decided that the King could not seize by his writ.

And Earl John of Warenne was confirmed in possession of these rights indefinitely.

## The Inquest Taken at Leicester (1253)

Violence was endemic to medieval society, but there were limits to how far that violence could be allowed to go.

The jury say upon their oath that, in the days of Robert de Meulan, then Earl of Leicester, it befell that two kinsmen, Nicholas son of Hacon and Geoffrey son of Nicholas of Leicester, waged battle for a certain piece of land which was disputed between them; and they fought from the hour of prime[4] till past noon. And, as they thus strove together, one drove the other up to a certain small ditch and, as he stood over it and should have fallen therein, his kinsman cried to him, "have a care of that ditch which is behind thee, lest thou fall therein"; whereupon there arose such a shout and tumult from those who stood and

sat around, that the lord Earl heard their shout even in the castle where he sat, and enquired of his men what might be the cause thereof; and they told him how these two kinsmen fought for the land, and how one drove the other to the ditch and warned him when he stood over it and should have fallen therein. Then the burgesses, moved with pity, made a covenant with the said Earl, that they should give him three pence yearly from each house which had a gable on the High Street, on condition that he would allow them to dispute and determine all pleas concerning the citizens by means of 24 jurats.[5]

SOURCE: Reprinted from *Social Life in Britain from the Conquest to the Reformation*, G. G. Coulton, ed., by permission of Cambridge University Press, Cambridge. 1918, #15, pp. 513–514.

[4] sunrise or six o'clock    [5] sworn men

# The Establishment of the Royal Household (ca. 1136)

It was out of this simple domestic household organization that the complex administration and judicial divisions of state eventually emerged.

*This is the establishment of the King's Household Pay and Allowances*

## Chancery and Chapel

*Chancellor:* 5s[6] a day, and one superior and two salt simnels,[7] one sextary[8] of dessert wine, and one of *vin ordinaire*, one large wax candle and forty candle-ends.

*Master of the Writing-Chamber:* Originally 10d.[9] a day, and one salt simnel, and half a sextary of *vin ordinaire*, and one large candle and twenty-four candle-ends. But King Henry so increased Robert de Sigillo, that on the day of the King's death he had 2s., and one sextary of *vin ordinaire*, and one salt simnel, and one small wax candle and twenty-four candle-ends.

*Chaplain — in charge of the chapel and relics:* Diet for two men. And four serjeants of the chapel, each double rations. And two sumpter-horses of the chapel, each 1d. a day, and a penny a month for shoeing them. For the chapel service, two wax candles on Wednesday and two on Saturday, and every night one wax candle before the relics, and thirty candle-ends, and one gallon of dessert wine for mass, and one gallon of *vin ordinaire* on Holy Thursday to wash the altar. On Easter day at communion, one sextary of dessert wine and one of *vin ordinaire*.

## Steward's Department

*Sewers:*[10] Sewers as the Chancellor, if they eat out. If indoors, 3s. 6d., two salt simnels, one sextary of *vin ordinaire* and candles at discretion.

*Clerk of the Spence*[11] *of bread and wine:* 2s. a day, and a salt simnel, and one sextary of *vin ordinaire*, and one small wax candle and twenty-four candle-ends.

PANTRY

*Dispensers of bread:* The master-dispenser of bread, a permanent officer, if he eats out-of-doors, 2s. 10d. a day, and one salt simnel, one sextary of *vin ordinaire*, one small wax candle and twenty-four candle-ends. But if indoors, 2s. a day, half a sextary of *vin ordinaire* and candles at discretion. . . .

*Napiers:*[12] The Napier has the customary diet. His man three halfpence a day, 1d. for the sumpter-horse and 1d. a month for shoeing.

*Usher of the Spence:* The same except for the sumpter-horse.

*Accountant of the Pantry:* The customary diet.

*Four Bakers serving together:* The two who serve indoors shall eat there. The two who go in advance shall have 40d. to buy a Rouen *muid*[13] from which they are to produce forty superior simnels and 150 salt, and 260 baker's loaves. A superior simnel for four men, a salt simnel for two, a loaf for one man.

*Waferer:*[14] The waferer has the customary diet, and three halfpence for his man.

*Keeper of the tables:* The same; and besides a sumpter-horse with its livery.

*Bearer of the alms-bowl:* Shall eat in the house.

SOURCE: From Charles Johnson, trans., *The Course of the Exchequer by Richard, Son of Nigel, Treasurer of England and Bishop of London* (Oxford, England: Oxford University Press, 1950), alternate pp. 129–135. By permission of the publisher.

[6] 5 shillings   [7] kind of cake or bread   [8] gallon   [9] 10 pence   [10] officers in charge of waiting on table   [11] cupboard or room   [12] officers in charge of table linen   [13] a measure of corn   [14] baker of biscuits

LARDER AND KITCHEN

*Dispensers of the Larder:* The Master-Dispenser of the Larder, permanent, as the Master-Dispenser of bread and wine, and in the same manner. Likewise the dispensers of the larder serving in turn as the dispensers of bread and wine serving in turn. The Lardiners who serve in turn have the customary diet, and three halfpence a day for a man.

*Ushers of the Larder:* The same.

*Slaughtermen:* The customary diet only.

*Cooks:* The Cook of the upper kitchen shall eat in the house, and have three halfpence for his man. The *Usher* of the same kitchen, the customary diet and three halfpence for his man. The *Scullion* shall eat in the house and have three halfpence for his man, and have a sumpter-horse with its livery. The *Sumpterman* of the same kitchen, the like. The *Serjeant of the Kitchen,* the customary diet only. The *Cook of the King's personal servants and of the Dispensers,* the like. . . .

*Great Kitchen:* Owen Polcheard has the customary diet and three halfpence a day for his man. Two *Cooks,* each the customary diet and three halfpence a day for his man. *Serjeants* of the same Kitchen: The customary diet only. *Usher of the Roasting House:* The customary diet and three halfpence for his man. *Roaster:* The like. *Scullion:* The like, and a sumpter-horse besides with its livery. *Carter of the Great Kitchen:* Double diet, and the due livery for his horse.

*Carter of the Larder:* The like.

The *Serjeant who receives the Venison:* Shall eat indoors, and have three halfpence for his man.

## Buttery

*Master-Butler:* As a sewer; the same livery and in like manner.

*Master-Dispenser of the Buttery:* As the Master-Dispenser of bread and wine. *Dispensers of the Buttery* serving in turn. As

the dispensers of the Spence serving in turn; but they have more candles, because they have a small wax candle and twenty-four candle-ends. *Usher of the Buttery:* The customary diet, and three halfpence for his man. The *Cellarmen* shall eat in the house, and have three halfpence each for their men.

The *Cooper:*[15] The customary diet, and 3d. for his men, and half a sextary of *vin ordinaire,* and twelve candle-ends. *Labourers in the Buttery:* The customary diet only; but its *Serjeant* has besides, three halfpence for his man, and two sumpter-horses with their liveries.

*Cupbearers:* Only four should serve together in turn; of whom two shall eat in the house, and each have three halfpence for his man. The other two shall have the customary diet, and likewise three halfpence for their men. The *Mazerkeeper*[16] has double diet only.

*Fruiterers:* The fruiterer shall eat in the house, and have 3d. for his men.

The *Carter* has the customary diet, and livery for his horses.

## Chamber

The *Master-Chamberlain's* livery is the same as that of a sewer. The *Treasurer* as the Master-Chamberlain, if he is at Court and serves in the Treasury. William Mauduit[17] 14d. a day; and shall eat permanently in the house, and have one large candle and fourteen ends, and two sumpter-horses with their liveries.

The *Bearer of the King's Bed* shall eat in the house, and have three halfpence a day for his man, and one sumpter-horse with its livery. A *Chamberlain* serving in his turn, 2s. a day, one salt simnel, and sextary of *vin ordinaire,* one small wax candle and twenty-four candle-ends. The *Chamberlain of the Chandlery:* 8d. a day, and half a sextary of *vin ordinaire.* The *King's Tailor* shall eat in his own house, and have three halfpence a day for his man. A *Chamberlain* without livery [i.e., not on duty] shall eat

---

15 barrel maker   16 wooden bowl and cup keeper   17 treasurer of the chamber

in the house, if he wishes. The *Ewer*[18] has double diet; and when the King goes on a journey, 1*d.* for drying the King's clothes; and when the King bathes, 4*d.* except on the three great feasts of the year. The wages of the *Laundress* are in doubt.

**Constabulary and Marshalsea** [19]

The *Constables* have liveries as the Sewers, and in like manner. . . .

*Marshalsea:* The *Master-Marshal,* . . . the like. And besides this he ought to have tallies of the gifts and liveries from the King's Treasury and Chamber; . . . Four *Marshals* who serve the King's Household, . . . on a day when they are finding lodgings or [otherwise] out of court on the King's business, 8*d.* a day, one gallon of *vin ordinaire* and twelve candle-ends. If indoors, 3*d.* a day for their men, and candles at discretion. But if any of the Marshals is sent on the King's business, 8*d.* only. The *Marshal's serjeants,* if sent on the King's business, 3*d.* a day each; if not, they shall eat in the King's house. The *Ushers,* knights, shall eat in the house themselves, and have three halfpence a day for their men and eight candleends. . . . *Watchmen:* Double diet, three halfpence a day for their men, and four candles. And besides, in the morning, two loaves each, one mess[20] of meat and one gallon of ale. *Stoker:* Shall always eat in the house, and have 4*d.* a day for the fire, from Michaelmas to Easter.

*Usher of the Chamber:* Every day when the King is on a journey, 4*d.* for the King's bed. *Tent-Keeper:* Shall eat in the house; when he had the tents moved, he had livery for one man and one sumpter-horse.

[HUNTING STAFF]

Each of four *Hornblowers* 3*d.* a day. Twenty *Serjeants:* Each 1*d.* a day. *Fewterers:*[21] Each 3*d.* a day, and 2*d.* for their men; and for each greyhound a halfpenny a day. *The King's Pack of Hounds:* 8*d.* a day. *Knight-Huntsmen:* Each 8*d.* a day. *Huntsmen:* Each 5*d.* *Leader of the Lime-Hound:*[22] 1*d.* and the lime-hound a halfpenny. *Berner*[23] 3*d.* a day. *Huntsmen of the Hounds on the Leash:* Each 3*d.* a day. Of the great leash four [hounds] 1*d.* And of the small leashes six should have 1*d.* For the great leashes two men, each 1*d.* a day; and for the small, two men, each 1*d.* a day. . . . *Wolf-Hunters:* 20*d.* a day for horses, men and hounds; and they should have twenty-four running hounds and eight greyhounds, and £6 a year to buy horses; but they say "eight." Each of the *Archers* who carried the King's bow 5*d.* a day; and the other archers as much.

---

RICHARD NIGEL, *The Course [dialogue] of the Exchequer* (ca. 1177)

*The Course of the Exchequer* is in the form of a dialogue between an experienced Exchequer official, the master, and a novice, the scholar. Organizationally and analytically it is a remarkable piece of work, for it describes in detail the function and organization of the Exchequer and the duties of each Exchequer official.

---

**[Dedication]**

To the powers ordained of God we must be subject and obedient with all fear. For there is no power but of God. There is clearly, therefore, nothing incongruous, or incon-

SOURCE: From Charles Johnson, trans., *The Course of the Exchequer by Richard, Son of Nigel, Treasurer of England and Bishop of London* (Oxford, England: Oxford University Press, 1950), alternate pp. 1–32, 52–53, 126. By permission of the publisher.

[18] water carrier  [19] domestic household court  [20] measurement of food set on a table at one time  [21] keeper of the greyhounds  [22] bloodhound  [23] feeder of hounds

sistent with the clerical character in keeping God's laws by serving kings as supreme and other powers, especially in those affairs which involve neither falsehood nor dishonour. And we ought to serve them by upholding not only those excellencies in which the glory of kingship displays itself but also the worldly wealth which accrues to kings by virtue of their position. Those confer distinction, this gives power. Their power indeed rises and falls as their portable wealth flows or ebbs. Those who lack it are a prey to their enemies, those who have it prey upon them. . . . We are, of course, aware that kingdoms are governed and laws maintained primarily by prudence, fortitude, temperance and justice, and the other virtues, for which reason the rulers of the world must practise them with all their might. But there are occasions on which sound and wise schemes take effect earlier through the agency of money, and apparent difficulties are smoothed away by it, as though by skilful negotiation. Money is no less indispensable in peace than in war. . . . Therefore, greatest of earthly princes, because I have often witnessed your Majesty's glory in peace and war alike, not hoarding treasure but spending it as it should be spent, in due place and time and on fit persons, I dedicate to Your Excellency this little book, on no lofty subject nor in eloquent language but written with an unskilful pen, about the procedure necessary in your Exchequer.

## [Prologue]

In the twenty-third year of the reign of King Henry II, as I was sitting at a turret window overlooking the Thames, I was addressed by someone who said, very earnestly, "Master! . . . [why] do you not teach others that knowledge of the Exchequer for which you are famous, and put it in writing lest it should die with you?" . . . "Be of good comfort; [I said] I shall take your advice. Get up, and sit down opposite me, and ask any questions which occur to you." . . .

---

24 chess-board

## [Dialogue]

SCHOLAR. What is the Exchequer?

MASTER. The exchequer[24] is an oblong board measuring about ten feet by five, used as a table by those who sit at it, and a rim round it about four finger-breadths in height, to prevent anything set on it from falling off. Over the [upper] exchequer is spread a cloth, bought in Easter term, of a special pattern, black, ruled with lines a foot, or a full span, apart. In the spaces between them are placed the counters, in their ranks, as will be explained in another place. But though such a board is called "exchequer," the name is transferred to the Court in session at it; so that if a litigant wins his case, or a decision on any point is taken by common consent, it is said to have happened "at the Exchequer" of such a year. But where we now say "at the Exchequer," they used to say "at the Tallies."

SCHOLAR. Why is the Court so called?

MASTER. I can think, for the moment, of no better reason than that it resembles a chess-board.

SCHOLAR. Was its shape the only reason why our wise forefathers gave it that name? For they might equally well have called it a draught-board.

MASTER. I was justified in calling you "precise." There is another less obvious reason. For as on the chess-board the men are arranged in ranks, and move or stand by definite rules and restrictions, some pieces in the foremost rank and others in the foremost positions; here, too, some [the barons] preside, others assist ex officio, and nobody is free to overstep the appointed laws, as will appear later. Again, just as on a chess-board, battle is joined between the kings; here too the struggle takes place, and battle is joined, mainly between two persons, to wit, the Treasurer and the Sheriff who sits at his account, while the rest sit by as judges to see and decide.

SCHOLAR. Does the Treasurer really take the account when there are many present who appear by reason of their power to be more important?

MASTER. It is obvious that the Treasurer takes the account from the Sheriff, because it is from him that an account is required when the King so pleases. Nor would that be demanded of him unless he had received it. Some say, however, that the Treasurer and Chamberlains are only accountable for those sums which are entered in the Roll as "in the Treasury." But the more correct view is that they are answerable for all that is written in the Roll,[25] as will appear later.

SCHOLAR. Is the Exchequer where this conflict takes place the only Exchequer?

MASTER. No. For there is a Lower Exchequer, also called the Receipt, where the money received is counted and entered on rolls and tallies, in order that the account may be made up from them in the Upper Exchequer. But both spring from the same root, because whatever is found in the Upper Exchequer to be due, is paid in the Lower, and what is paid in the Lower is credited in the Upper.

SCHOLAR. What is the plan or constitution of the Lower Exchequer? . . .

MASTER. In the Lower Exchequer are the Treasurer's Clerk, with his seal, and the two knights of the Chamberlains. There is also a knight[26] whom we may call the Knight Silversmith, since it is his duty to preside over the assay.[27] There is also the Melter, who assays the silver. There are four Tellers to count the money. And there are the Usher of the Treasury, and the Watchman. Their duties are as follows.

The Treasurer's Clerk seals up the money when it has been counted and packed in forels[28] of a hundred pounds each, and records in writing how much he has received, from what person and on what account. He also inscribes the tallies made by the Chamberlains for the money received. He may also, if he chooses, seal up not only the sacks of money, but also the chests or forels containing rolls or tallies. He supervises the work of all his subordinates, and nothing escapes his eye.

The duty of the Knights (who are also called Chamberlains because they act for them) is as follows. They bear the keys of the chests, for each chest has two locks of different patterns such that the key of one lock will not open the other—and they have the keys. But each chest has also a strap round it, and fastened to it, which is sealed with the Treasurer's seal after the chests have been locked, in order that none of the three can open the chest without the consent of the others. It is also their duty to weigh the money when it has been counted and placed in wooden bowls holding a hundred shillings each, lest there should have been an error in the counting, and afterwards to pack it, as we have said, in forels holding a hundred pounds each. . . . They also make tallies of the receipts, and are jointly responsible with the Treasurer's Clerk for all payments out of the treasure received; either by the King's Writ or by order of the Barons, not however, without reference to their masters. These three are sent, all together or by turns, with treasure when necessary. And theirs is the principal charge in all business done in the Lower Exchequer. . . .

SCHOLAR. I think you have answered all my questions. Now, pray, proceed to the greater Exchequer.

MASTER. Although the functions of those who sit at the greater Exchequer are different, the duty and aim of all is the same: to secure the King's advantage, without injustice, according to the appointed laws of the Exchequer. Its plan or constitution is warranted both by antiquity and by the authority of the magnates who sit at it. For it is said to have begun with King William's Conquest and to have borrowed its constitution from the Exchequer of Normandy. . . .

But whenever the Exchequer came into use it is certain that it is so potent owing to the authority of its Barons that no man may break its laws or be bold enough to resist them. For it shares with the King's

---

[25] record  [26] the *Pesour*  [27] weighing or testing of silver  [28] leather cases or bags

Court in which he administers justice in person the privilege that its records and judgments may not be impugned. The Exchequer has this eminent authority both on account of the excellence of the King's image which is an essential to his seal preserved in the Treasury, and on account of those who sit at its board as we have said, by whose wisdom the whole state of the realm is kept secure. For at it there sits the King's Chief Justiciar, second only to the King by virtue of his jurisdiction, and all the Barons of the realm who are the King's Privy Councillors, in order that the decrees made in such an important assembly may be inviolable. But some sit *ex officio*, others by the King's command alone.

Sitting *ex officio*, in the chief place, and presiding, is the first subject in the realm, the Chief Justiciar. His assessors, appointed merely by the King's command and with a temporary and revocable authority, are among the greatest and most prudent in the realm, whether clerks or courtiers. Their function, I may say, is to declare the law, and to resolve the doubtful points which arise constantly in the matters under discussion. For the highest skill at the Exchequer does not lie in calculations, but in judgments of all kinds. It is easy enough to set down the sum due, and to set underneath for comparison the sums paid, and find by subtraction whether the debt has been paid or what is the balance due. But when complicated questions arise about payments which reach the Treasury in different ways, are due on different accounts and are demanded of the Sheriffs in different fashions, some people find it a difficult matter to decide whether the Sheriffs have acted wrongly: and for that reason knowledge of these things is regarded as the more important at the Exchequer. . . .

SCHOLAR. What is the duty of this most eminent member of the court?

MASTER. The best way of describing it is to say that he supervises everything that is done either in the Lower or in the Upper Exchequer, and that all the inferior offices are at his entire disposal; provided always,

however, that the King's advantage is duly consulted. But the most exalted of all his privileges is that he can cause writs to be issued, either of *liberate*, for the payment of money out of the Treasury, or of *computate*, for the allowance of expenditure to accountants, in the King's name with his own as witness, or, should he so prefer, in his own name with other witnesses, to the same effect. . . . To understand the arrangement of the seats, you must know that four settles or benches are set at the four sides of the Exchequer Board. At the head of the Board, that is the narrow way, in the middle not of the bench but of the Board, is the place of that chief personage whom we have mentioned. Next [to] him, on his left, sits the Chancellor, if present, by virtue of his office; next [to] him the Knight-Commander, whom we call the Constable; after him the two Chamberlains, the elder first, out of respect for his years; and after them the Knight, whom we commonly call the Marshal. . . .

At the head of the second bench, which runs the long way of the board, sits the Clerk or other servant of the Chamberlains with the foils, that is, the counter-tallies of receipt. After him, but separated from him by some persons who do not sit *ex officio* but are sent by the King, is the place, almost in the middle of the long side of the board, for the Accountant with his counters. Then come some who do not sit *ex officio*, but are nevertheless needed; and at the end of the bench sits, *ex officio*, the Master of the Writing-Office. That completes the second bench.

Immediately on the right of the President, the Justiciar, sits the present Bishop of Winchester, formerly Archdeacon of Poitiers, *ex officio*, but by a recent ordinance, so that he may be next the Treasurer and keep a careful watch on the writing of the Roll. Next him, on his right, sits the Treasurer, at the head of the third bench, who must have especial care of all that is done in the Exchequer, being bound to give account of it all if needed. Next sits the Scribe of the Treasury Roll, then the Scribe of the Chancery Roll, and next again the Chancellor's Clerk, who watches with a careful eye to see that his Roll corresponds exactly with the other, so that not a single "jot" is missing and the order of the words is the same. Then, at the end of the bench, sits the Clerk of the Constabulary, a great and important person in the King's Court, and with duties here also, which he performs in person, or, if the King requires his presence elsewhere, by a discreet clerk. That completes the third bench.

On the fourth bench, opposite the Justiciar, and at its head, sits Master Thomas Brown, with a third Roll, which was added by a recent ordinance, that is by our Lord the King. For it is written, "A threefold cord is not quickly broken." Next him come the Sheriff and his clerks who sit to account with tallies and other vouchers. And that is the arrangement of the fourth bench.

SCHOLAR. Does Master Thomas's scribe sit with the other scribes?

MASTER. His seat is not with them but above them.

SCHOLAR. Why so?

MASTER. Since the original arrangement was that the Treasurer's Scribe should sit beside the Treasurer, lest anything that should be written should escape his eye; and the Chancellor's Scribe beside the Treasurer's, so that he might faithfully copy what the other was writing; and the Chancellor's Clerk must needs be next to his Scribe to see that he made no mistakes; there was no place left in the row on the bench for Master Thomas's Scribe to sit in; but a place has been given him up above so that he can overlook the Treasurer's Scribe who is the original writer, and copy what is necessary from him.

SCHOLAR. He must be "lynx eyed" to avoid mistakes; and in these matters, I am told, a mistake is serious.

MASTER. He may make some mistake in copying from being so far away; but when the Rolls are corrected all three are compared, and any error is easily amended.

SCHOLAR. That is enough about the ar-rangement of the seats. Now, please, continue with the duties of the sitters, beginning on the President's left.

MASTER. On that side the first is the Chancellor. In the Exchequer, as in the Court, he is so great a man that nothing important is or should be done without his consent and advice. But his duty when sitting at the Exchequer is as follows. He is the official custodian of the King's Seal, which is in the Treasury, but is only taken out when, by order of the Justiciar, it is brought by the Treasurer or one of the Chamberlains from the Lower to the Upper Exchequer, and then only for Exchequer business. When this is completed, it is put in a purse, which is sealed by the Chancellor, and handed to the Treasurer to keep. When it is required again, it is handed to the Chancellor under seal, in view of everybody and may never be taken out of the Treasury by him or any other on any other occasion. He is also the keeper, by his deputy, of the Chancellor's Roll. And it has been held by the Barons that he is equally responsible with the Treasurer for everything which is written in the Roll except for the receipts "in the Treasury." For, though he is not, as the Treasurer is [by his scribe] the original writer, he copies it as it is written; and if the Treasurer makes a mistake, he or his clerk may, with due modesty, check the Treasurer and suggest what ought to be written. But if the Treasurer persists and refuses to make an alteration, he may, if he feels sure enough, argue the point before the Barons, and let them decide what ought to be done. . . .

The Constable's duty at the Exchequer is to witness, with the President, all writs of *Liberate* and *Computate*. For in all such writs, by ancient custom, the names of two witnesses must be given. It is also his duty, when the King's mercenaries come to the Exchequer for their wages, whether they dwell in the King's castles or not, to take with him the Clerk of the Constabulary, whose business it is to know their terms of service, and the Marshal of the Exchequer, and to credit them with their wages, take their *affidavits* as to arrears of pay and cause what remains owing to them to be paid. For all wages, whether of ostringers,[29] falconers or keepers of hounds are his affair. . . .

The duty of the Chamberlains is closely connected with that of the Treasurer, whose dignity and responsibility they share, and their will to do the King service is so blended into one that the act of any one of them cannot be disowned by either of the others. For the Treasurer receives the accounts on behalf of them all, and dictates what is to be written in the Roll according to the nature of the debts; in all which, by the law of partnership, the others are equally bound. And the same rule applies throughout to everything done by him or by them (saving the King's credit), whether in writing the Roll, receiving the money, cutting the tallies or paying out the treasure.

The Marshal's task is to set apart in the Sheriff's forel the tallies of debts which he has put in (though these are noted in the Roll), and also the King's writs of allowance, pardon or payment out of the sums demanded of the Sheriff in the summons. The forel is inscribed with the name of the county to which its contents relate, and a forel for each county ought to be supplied to the Marshal by the Sherriff accounting. . . .

At the head of the second bench is, first, the servant of the Chamberlains, whether clerk or layman, whose work is easier to describe than to perform. He produces the tallies from the Treasury against the Sheriff or other accountant, and as the process of the account demands, alters, reduces or adds to the tally, to which the Sheriff's "stock" or countertally has been joined. . . .

Since we have mentioned tallies, let me briefly explain how tallies are made. There is one kind which we call simply, a tally, and another which we call a memoranda tally. The length of a lawful tally is from the tip of the index finger to the tip of the outstretched thumb. At that distance it has a small hole bored in it. But the memoranda tally, which is always made for Blanch Farm,[30] is somewhat shorter because, after the assay by which the farm is blanched, that first tally is broken, and a tally of full length is only issued when the combustion tally is attached to it.

The method of cutting is as follows. A thousand pounds are shown by a cut at the top [or end] of the tally wide enough to hold the thickness of the palm of the hand, a hundred that of the thumb, twenty pounds that of the little finger, a pound that of a swelling barley-corn, a shilling smaller, but enough for the two cuts to make a small notch. A penny is indicated by a single cut without removing any of the wood. On the edge of the tally on which a thousand is cut you may put no other number save the half of a thousand, which is done by halving the cut in like manner and putting it lower [i.e., nearer the butt of the stock and the left-hand end of the foil]. The same rule holds for a hundred, if there is no thousand, and likewise for a score and for twenty shillings which make a pound. But if several thousands, hundreds, or scores of pounds are to be cut, the same rule must be observed, that the largest number is to be cut on the more open edge of the tally, that is to say that which is directly before you when the note is made, the smaller on the other. But the larger number is always on the obverse of the tally, and the smaller on the reverse. There is no single cut signifying a mark of silver: it is shown in shillings [and pence]. But you should cut a mark of gold, as you do a pound, in the middle of the tally. A gold penny[31] is not cut like a silver one; but the notch is cut in the middle of the tally with the knife perpendicular, and not sloping as with a silver one. Thus the position of the cut on the tally and the difference in the

---

[29] keeper of goshawks   [30] rent paid in silver, not in service or produce   [31] i.e., *a besant*

cutting settles what is gold and what is silver.

But the system of this is according to the usual course of the Exchequer, not by the rules of Arabian arithmetic. You remember my saying, I imagine, that a cloth is laid on the Exchequer table ruled with lines, and that the coins used as counters are placed in the spaces between them. The Accountant sits in the middle of his side of the table, so that everybody can see him, and so that his hand can move freely at its work. In the lowest space, on the right, he places the heap of the pence, eleven or fewer. In the second the shillings, up to nineteen. In the third he puts the pounds; and this column should be directly in front of him, because it is the centre column in the Sheriffs usual accounts. In the fourth is the heap of the scores of pounds. In the fifth, hundreds, in the sixth, thousands, in the seventh, but rarely, tens of thousands. I say "rarely"; that is, when an account of the whole receipt of the realm is taken by the King, or by the magnates of the realm at his command from the Treasurer and Chamberlains. . . .

Next after the Accountant, *virtute officii*, sits the clerk who is Master of the Writing Office. It is his business to find suitable scribes for the Chancellor's Roll and for the King's Writs, which are drawn up in the Exchequer; and also for writing the summonses, and to see that they are properly written. These duties need but few words to explain, but demand almost endless labour, as those know who have learned by experience. That concludes the duties of those who sit on the second bench.

SCHOLAR. If I remember right, the Bishop of Winchester sits on the right of the President, and I should like to hear next what are his duties at the Exchequer. For he is a great personage, and his business should be equally important. . . .

MASTER. A place was given him beside the Treasurer, so that he should, jointly with him, attend to the writing of the Roll, and all such matters. The Treasurer, indeed, is so beset by so many constant great cares and anxieties, that he cannot be blamed if sleep sometimes overtakes him in the middle of it all. Moreover, in human affairs, scarcely anything is absolutely perfect.

SCHOLAR. . . . Well then, saving the Treasurer's reverence, this appointment seems to detract from his dignity, since his honour is not absolutely trusted.

MASTER. God forbid! Say rather that his labour is spared and his security assured. For it is not because either he or anyone else is not trusted that so many sit at the Exchequer; but because it is fitting that such great matters and the public affairs under so great a prince should be entrusted to many great personages, not merely for the King's profit, but to honour his excellence and royal state.

SCHOLAR. Pray proceed with the duties.

MASTER. The Treasurer's duty, or his care and anxieties, can hardly be expressed, even if I had the pen of a ready writer. For his careful attention is necessary in everything which is done in either the Upper or the Lower Exchequer. But it is pretty clear from what has been said, what are the main objects of his care, so important that he cannot be torn away from them while the Exchequer sits, viz. receiving the accounts of the Sheriffs, and writing the Roll. For he dictates the text of his own Roll as the nature of the business demands, and from it the text is copied, as we have said, on to the other Rolls. And he must be careful to make no mistake in the amount, the account or the person, lest he who is not quit should be acquitted, or he who has earned his quittance be resummoned. For the authority of the Roll is such that no man is allowed to dispute it or alter it, unless the mistake is so obvious that it is patent to all. Nor even then should it be changed except by the assent of all the Barons and in their presence, to wit, during the session of the Exchequer of that Roll. But the writing of the Roll of the previous year, or even of the same year, once the Exchequer has risen, can only be altered by the King, who, in these matters, "can do no wrong." It is also his right to be associated in all great matters with those of higher rank, and to be fully informed of everything. . . .

SCHOLAR. What is the formula used in the King's Writs for the issue of treasure?

MASTER. The Treasurer and Chamberlains do not pay out the money which they receive without the express order of the King or the presiding Justiciar. For they must have the authority of the King's Writ for the issue of the money when a general account shall be demanded of them. "H. King," etc. "to N. the Treasurer and so-and-so Chamberlains, greeting. Pay from my treasure to so-and-so such-and-such a sum. Witness the following at the place of N. at the Exchequer." . . .

SCHOLAR. . . . Now please, make haste to explain what are scuttage, murder-fine or danegeld.[32] They seem barbarous terms, but I am the more interested in them because you say that the officials of the Exchequer are free from them.

MASTER. It sometimes happens that when enemies threaten or attack the kingdom, the King decrees that a payment shall be made, say a mark or a pound from every knight's fee, to provide payment or rewards for soldiers. For the prince prefers to expose mercenaries to the hazards of war, rather than his own people. This sum, being paid according to the number of shields [of the knights], is called scutage. And from it those who sit at the Exchequer are quit.

Murder, strictly speaking, is the concealed death of a man at the hands of an unknown slayer. For "murder" means "hidden" or "secret." In the period immediately following the Conquest what were left of the conquered English lay in ambush for the suspected and hated Normans and murdered them secretly in woods and unfrequented places as opportunity offered. Now when the kings and their ministers had for some years inflicted the most severe penalties on the English without effect, it was finally decided that the hundred,[33] in which a Norman was found killed, without his slayer being known or revealing his identity by flight, should be mulcted[34] in a large sum of assayed [tested] silver, £ 30 or £ 44 according to the locality of the murder and the commonness of the crime. This is said to have been done for the security of travellers and to induce all men to make haste to punish such a crime or to deliver up to judgment the man by whose fault so great a loss injured the whole neighbourhood. You are aware that, as we said before, those who sit at the Exchequer table are quit of these fines.

SCHOLAR. Does the secret death of an Englishman, like that of a Norman, give rise to a murder-fine?

MASTER. It did not do so originally, as I have told you. But nowadays, when English and Normans live close together and marry and give in marriage to each other, the nations are so mixed that it can scarcely be decided (I mean in the case of the freemen) who is of English birth and who of Norman; except, of course, the villeins, who cannot alter their condition without the leave of their masters. For that reason whoever is found slain nowadays, the murder-fine is exacted, except in cases where there is definite proof of the servile condition of the victim. . . .

SCHOLAR. I can tell by the flagging of your pen that we are approaching the end of our discourse. . . .

---

[32] annual tax, originally to provide funds for protection against Danes, later became a land tax
[33] area of jurisdiction   [34] fined

# How to Hold a Parliament (1316–1324)

The description of parliament is tantalizingly modern. Clearly by the first decade of the fourteenth century, feudal society believed that parliament was a means through which the community spoke and kings were expected to listen.

### Chapter 1  The summoning of parliament

The summoning of a parliament ought to precede the first day of parliament by forty days.

### Chapter 2  Concerning the clergy

To parliament ought to be summoned and come archbishops, bishops, abbots, priors and other leading clergy who hold by earldom or barony by reason of such tenure, and no lower clergy unless their presence and attendance is required for reason other than their tenures, as for example if they are of the king's council or their presence is considered necessary or useful to parliament. . . .

### Chapter 3  Concerning the laity

Also, ought to be summoned and come every one of the earls and barons, and their peers,[35] that is those who have lands and rents to the value of a whole earldom, viz., twenty fees of one knight, each fee reckoned at twenty librates,[36] making four hundred librates in all, or to the value of one whole barony, that is, thirteen and one third fees of one knight, each fee reckoned at twenty librates, making in all four hundred marks;[37] and no lower laity ought to be summoned and come to parliament by reason of their tenure — they should be summoned and come only if their presence is useful or necessary to parliament on other grounds . . .

### Chapter 5  Concerning the knights of the shires

Also, the king used to send his writs to all the sheriffs of England for each to cause to be elected from his county by the county

two suitable honourable and experienced knights to come to his parliament, . . . but for the combined expenses of a shire's two knights it is not usual for more than one mark per day to be paid out.

### Chapter 6  Concerning the citizens

In the same way word used to be sent to the mayor and sheriffs of London, the mayor and bailiffs or mayor and citizens of York and other cities for them to elect on behalf of the community of their city two suitable, honourable and experienced citizens to come and be present at parliament . . . and the citizens used to be the peers of the knights of the shires on a level with them as to expenses while coming, staying and returning.

### Chapter 7  Concerning the burgesses

Also, in the same way word used to be, and ought to be, sent to the bailiffs and good men of boroughs for them to elect from themselves and in place of themselves two suitable, honourable and experienced burgesses to come and be present at the king's parliament, . . . but the two burgesses used not to receive more than ten shillings per day for their expenses. . . .

### Chapter 8  The custom of parliament

It having been shown first on what grounds, to whom, and how long in advance a summons of parliament ought to be issued and who ought to come by summons and who not, it must in the second place be said who they are who ought to come by reason of their offices and are bound to be present during the whole period of parlia-

source: From Harry Rothwell, ed., *English Historical Documents* (London: Eyre & Spottiswoode, Ltd., Publishers, 1975), Doc. 235, pp. 924–927, 930–933. By permission of the publishers.
[35] equals   [36] land and rent sufficient to provide yearly income of £20   [37] approximately £266

ment without a summons. In which connection it is to be observed that the two principal clerks of parliament chosen by the king and his council and the other secondary clerks, of whom and whose offices there will be more particular mention later, and the chief crier of England with his under-criers and the chief doorkeeper of England, which two offices, that is the office of crier and that of doorkeeper, used to belong to one and the same person, these two officials are bound to be present on the first day. The chancellor of England, the treasurer, the chamberlains and barons of the exchequer, the justices and all clerks and knights of the king, together with serjeants at the king's pleas, who are of the king's council are bound to be present on the second day, unless they have reasonable excuses for not being able to be present, and then they should send suitable excuses. . . .

### Chapter 16  Concerning the five clerks of parliament

The lord king shall assign five skilled and approved clerks, of whom the first shall minister to and serve the bishops, the second the proctors of the clergy, the third the earls and barons, the fourth the knights of the shires, the fifth the citizens and burgesses, and each of them, unless he is in the service of the king and receives from him a fee or wages that he can live suitably on, shall receive from the king two shillings a day if he does not eat at the king's table, and if he does eat at his table he shall get twelve pence a day. And these clerks shall write down their doubts and the answers they give to king and parliament [and] shall be present at their deliberations whenever they wish to have them there. And when they have nothing else to do they shall help the principal clerks with the enrolling.

### Chapter 17  Concerning difficult cases and judgments

When contention, doubt or a difficult matter of peace or war arises in the kingdom or outside it, the question shall be referred in writing to and recited in full parliament and considered and argued there between the peers of parliament and, if it be necessary, be it enjoined on each grade of the peers by the king, or on behalf of the king if he is not present, that each grade go on its own, that the question be delivered to its clerk in writing and that in a place prescribed they have it recited to them, in order that they may arrange and consider between themselves the best and justest possible way of proceeding in the matter as they, for the king and for themselves and for those they represent also, would wish to answer before God, and come back with their answers and observations in writing; and when all their answers, counsels and observations on either side have been heard, let the matter be dealt with according to the better and sounder counsel and when at least the greater part of parliament are of one mind. But if through discord between the king and some magnates, or perhaps among the magnates themselves, the peace of the realm is rendered insecure, or the people or the country afflicted, so that it appears to the king and his council that it would be expedient for the matter to be considered and corrected through the deliberations of all the peers of his kingdom, or if the king and his kingdom are afflicted with war, or if a difficult case comes before the chancellor of England or a difficult judgment has to be given before the justices, and such like, and if perchance in such deliberations all or even the greater part are unable to agree, then the earl steward, the earl constable and the earl marshal, or two of them, shall from all the peers of the kingdom select twenty-five, that is to say two bishops and three proctors for the whole body of clergy, two earls and three barons, five knights of the shires, five citizens and five burgesses, which makes twenty-five, and these twenty-five can if they wish choose twelve of themselves and stand down in their favour, and these twelve six and stand down in their favour, and these six yet again three and stand down in their favour, but these three cannot stand down in favour of a smaller number without getting permission from the lord king, though, if the king agrees, the three can submit to two and of the two one can submit to the other, so that at length what he ordains will stand above the whole parliament; and by thus coming down from twenty-five persons to a single one, if a greater number is not able to agree and ordain, in the end a single person as has been said will ordain for all who cannot disagree with himself, saving to the lord king and his council that after ordinances of this sort have been put into writing they, if they know how to and wish to, may examine and amend them, provided that this is done there and then in full parliament and with the agreement of parliament, and not after parliament is over. . . .

## Chapter 23 Concerning aids [38] for the king

The king used not to ask for an aid from his kingdom except when a war was imminent or for making his sons knights or marrying his daughters, and then aids of this sort ought to be asked for in full parliament, the request delivered to each grade of the peers of parliament in writing, and answered in writing. And be it known that for the granting of such aids all the peers of parliament ought to consent and it is to be understood that the two knights who come to parliament for the shire carry more weight in parliament in granting and refusing than the greatest earl of England, and in like manner the proctors of the clergy of a diocese carry more weight in parliament, if all are of the same mind, than the bishop

himself. And so too in all things which ought to be granted, refused or done by parliament: and this is clear from the fact that a king can hold a parliament with the community of his kingdom without the bishops, earls and barons, provided they have been summoned to parliament even if no bishop, earl or baron comes in accordance with their summonses, for there was once a time when there was neither bishop, nor earl, nor baron, yet kings then held their parliaments. But it is otherwise the other way round. Supposing the communities, clergy and laity, had been summoned to parliament (as of right they ought) but for certain reasons were not willing to come — for example if they alleged that the king was not rulinng them as he should and were to state specifically in what points he had misruled them — there would then be no parliament at all, even if all the archbishops, bishops, earls, barons and all their peers were present with the king. It is inescapable therefore that all things which ought to be affirmed or annulled, granted or refused, or done by parliament ought to be granted by the community of parliament, which is made up of three grades or kinds [of people] of parliament, that is to say, the proctors of the clergy, the knights of the shires, citizens and burgesses, who represent the whole community of England, and not of the magnates because each of them is at parliament for his own individual self and for no other person. . . .

## Chapter 26

. . . Here ends the custom of parliament.

---

## FURTHER DISCUSSION QUESTIONS

### The Trial Held on Pinnenden Hill

1. What was the basis on which rights to land were established, and how were these rights discovered? How would disputed land rights be settled today?
2. At what kind of disadvantage did King William find himself once he permitted the trial?

---

[38] form of feudal tax

3. Who made the decision at the trial?
4. What improvements in the operation and exercise of justice appear in the trial?

### The Chronicle of Walter of Hemingburgh

1. Why were the great magnates afraid of the statute of *Quo Warranto?* Why might they have argued that it was not "just"?
2. What clash of interpretation of historic land possession is implicit in Earl Warenne's defiance of Edward I?
3. Why did the king feel obliged to back down on the enforcement of this law?

### The Trial of John Warenne, Earl of Surrey

1. On what grounds and what kind of evidence was the verdict made?
2. How would the earl have had to defend his rights 150 years earlier?

### The Inquest Taken at Leicester

1. Why might the Lord Earl have been willing to administer justice for Leicester?
2. Why was it difficult for two kinsmen to settle their differences by the old method?

### The Establishment of the Royal Household

1. Were there any rational principles on which the household was organized?
2. Is it possible to distinguish between government (public) officials and household (private) servants?
3. If the records of a large domestic organization were being kept today, how would they compare and contrast with Henry I's household accounts?

### Richard Nigel, The Course of the Exchequer

1. On what does Nigel suggest power rests?
2. How does Nigel's approach to the description of the exchequer compare with that of the previous author's description of the household?
3. What organizational principles are inherent in the "dialogue"?
4. In what ways was the operation of the exchequer modern; in what ways was it still primitive?
5. Compare Nigel's sense of history and institutional change over time with that found in "The Establishment of the Household."
6. What was the relationship of the Exchequer to the king and to his private household?
7. How does the method of accounting described by Nigel compare with modern practices?

### How to Hold a Parliament

1. What parliamentary procedures have been standardized by the time of the writing of this document?
2. To what extent had the concept of majority rule developed by the fourteenth century?
3. How far had Parliament broken away from the king and his household?
4. What is the writer's definition of a parliament, and who must attend to make it a proper parliament?

# 5

# *The Good Life on Earth*

Chapters 5 and 6 are related and should be read as one, for both deal with the aspirations of a society that saw no distinction between the profane and the spiritual, the religious and the temporal, because both were viewed as the work of God. Body and soul, man and society, the smallest particle and the marvels of the firmament were exquisitely entwined into the fabric of divine creation in which Adam and Eve and their descendants played the central role: by choosing here on earth between good and evil, salvation and damnation, men and women fulfilled God's ultimate and divine purpose.

Societies should not be judged solely by their ideals, and the "good life" remained a dream in the midst of hypocrisy, meanness, avarice, and suffering. Yet the aspirations of a society in order to have any validity must be based on reality, both in the sense that they reflect the social, economic, and political power structure of the day, and that they endeavor to curb those human and social instincts endangering the welfare of society. The medieval world was masculine, feudal, and military. Violence, greed, private vengeance, filth, and bad manners prevailed, but medieval aspirations sought to limit and at the same time build upon these realities. Although the documents in this chapter give a highly idealized view of medieval society, possibly there is no better way of dramatizing the difference between our own world and the medieval past than to compare social ideals and aspirations.

The story of "The Palfrey" lends itself to such a comparison, and the reader might well ask how a modern author would portray the characters, assign the motives, and arrange the plot. The story itself is thirteenth century, probably French in origin, and versions of it were undoubtedly narrated all over Europe by professional storytellers or minstrels, and by the more aristocratic troubadours. "The Palfrey" represents the feudal knight at his best; but, under the delightful chivalric romance of an impecunious, boiler-plated young man clanking about the countryside in search of honor, adventure, and gain is hidden

ORIGIN OF THE ORDER OF THE GARTER

an ugly reality. Messire William in real life was a member of a group of bachelor knights — a very dangerous species, especially in the hands of damsels as intelligent and enterprising as William's "fair lady."

The next two selections — Richard of Devizes' *Chronicle of the Time of Richard I* and John of Salisbury's *Policraticus* (1159) — present different sides of the same ideal: the perfect king, a paragon who is difficult to imagine if only because his royal attributes were so hopelessly contradictory. Despite his manifest faults, Richard Coeur de Lion was for medieval society the military, kingly ideal. Though we today may shudder at his actions and wax cynical over his motives, Richard was for his namesake of Devizes and for succeeding generations a hero king. John of Salisbury's perfect prince is very different from the one pictured by Richard of Devizes, even though both authors were churchmen. Richard was a simple, if highly articulate, monk of St. Swithun's at Winchester, and John of Salisbury (1115–1180) was one of the major Latinists and political thinkers of his day and a career administrator within the church. Attached to the archdiocese of Canterbury and an expert on papal affairs, John was a champion of ecclesiastical independence and an admirer of Thomas à Becket. In fact, his *Policraticus* may have helped to persuade Becket to become an extreme supporter of the church when he became archbishop. John's ideal sovereign is the figment of a scholar's mind but embodies those human and institutional values and virtues that were regarded by the church as being essential to an efficiently administered society. Those ideals might well be compared and contrasted to the baronial concept of the ideal king described in the "Song of Lewes" in Chapter 3.

The final two selections are both more practical and mundane, dealing as they do with good manners and good advice. John Russell, who must have learned his courtesy under Edward III or Richard II, wrote his "Book of Nurture" (or what we would call today a manual of upbringing and education) as a practical lesson in how to master court etiquette and ceremony. That Russell thought it necessary to emphasize the rudimentary principles of good manners even on the level of the royal court is an appalling commentary upon the realities of life at every level of society. "How the Good Wife Taught Her Daughter" depicts the domestic ideal of the age and the proper role that a woman was expected to play. To what extent the good wife's "wise lore" for handling husbands, disciplining children and preserving one's wifely reputation corresponded to reality is anybody's guess.

## The Tale of the Palfrey

"The Palfrey" is a marvelous thirteenth-century romance about boy meets girl, boy gets girl after overcoming endless obstacles. It is also, however, a perceptive social commentary upon the period.

---

Once upon a time [there was] a certain knight, courteous and chivalrous, rich of heart, but poor in substance. . . . So stout of heart was this lord, so wise in counsel, and so compact of honour and all high qualities, that had his fortune been equal to his deserts he would have had no peer amongst his fellows. He was the very pattern of the fair and perfect knight, and his praise was ever in the mouth of men. In whatever land he came he was valued at his proper worth, since strangers esteemed him for the good that was told of him, and rumour but increased his renown. When he had laced the helmet on his head, and ridden within the lists, he did not court the glances of the dames, nor seek to joust with those who were of less fame than he, but there where the press was thickest he strove mightily

in the heart of the stout.[1] In the very depths of winter he rode upon his horse, attired in seemly fashion (since in dress may be perceived the inclinations of the heart) and this although his substance was but small. For the lands of this knight brought him of wealth but two hundred pounds of rent, and for this reason he rode to tourneys in hope of gain as well as in quest of honour.

This knight had set all his earthly hope and thoughts on gaining the love of a certain noble lady. The father of the damsel was a puissant Prince, lacking nought in the matter of wealth, and lord of a great house furnished richly as his coffers. His fief and domain were fully worth one thousand pounds a year, and many a one asked of him his fair daughter in marriage, because her exceeding beauty was parcel of

---

SOURCE: From Eugene Mason, trans., *Aucassin and Nicolette and Other Mediaeval Romances and Legends.* An Everyman's Library Series (New York and London: 1958), pp. 225–249. Reprinted by permission of E. P. Dutton and J. M. Dent & Sons Ltd., publishers.

[1] combat

the loveliness of the world. The Prince was old and frail; he had no other child than the maiden, and his wife had long been dead. . . .

The gentle knight who had set his heart on the love of the fair lady was named Messire William, and he lived within the forest in an ancient manor some two miles from the palace of the Prince. In their love they were as one, and ever they fondly dreamed one upon the other; but the Prince liked the matter but little, and had no mind that they should meet. So when the knight would gaze upon the face of his mistress, he went secretly by a path that he had worn through the profound forest, and which was known of none save him. By this path he rode privily on his palfrey, without gossip or noise, to visit the maiden, many a time. Yet never might these lovers see each other close, however great was their desire, for the wall of the courtyard was very high, and the damsel was not so hardy as to issue forth by the postern. So for their solace they spoke together through a little gap in the wall. . . .

Now the tale tells that in spite of his poverty the knight owned one thing that was marvellously rich. The palfrey on which he rode had not his like in all the world. It was grey and of a wonderful fair colour, so that no flower was so bright in semblance, nor did any man know of so beautiful a steed. . . . The knight loved his palfrey very dearly, and I tell you truly that in nowise would he part with him for any manner of wealth. . . . Upon this fair palfrey Messire William went often to his lady, along the beaten path through the solitary forest, known but to these two alone. Right careful was he to keep this matter from the father of the demoiselle, . . . for well they knew that should the old Prince know thereof, very swiftly would he marry his daughter to some rich lord.

Now the knight considered these things within himself, and . . . so at the end he summoned all his courage, and for weal or

woe resolved that he would go to the aged Prince and require of him his daughter for his wife, let that betide what may. . . . On a certain day he made himself ready, and repaired to the castle where the demoiselle dwelt with her father. He was welcomed very gladly by the Prince and his company, for he was esteemed a courteous and gentle knight. . . .

"Sire," said the knight, "I ask you of your grace to listen to my words. I enter in your house to crave of you such a gift as may God put it in your heart to bestow. . . . I pray — so it may please you, sire — your daughter as my wife. God grant that my prayer may not disturb your heart, and that my petition may not be refused to my shame. . . ."

The old man had no need for counsel in this matter, so without delay he made answer to the knight —

"I have heard with patience what you had to tell, Certes, and without doubt, my daughter is fair, and fresh, and pure, and a maiden of high descent. For myself, I am a rich vavasour,[2] and come of noble ancestry, having fief and land worth fully one thousand pounds each year in rent. Think you I am so besotted as to give my daughter to a knight who lives by play! I have no child but one, who is close and dear to my heart, and after I am gone all my wealth will be hers. She shall wed no naked man, but in her own degree. . . ."

The knight was all abashed at these proud words. He did not wait for further shame, but took his leave, and went as speedily as he might. But he knew not what to do, for Love, his guide, afflicted him very grievously, and bitterly he complained him thereof. When the maiden heard of this refusal, and was told the despiteful words her father had spoken, she was grieved in her very heart, for her love was no girl's light fancy, but was wholly given to the knight, far more than any one can tell. So when the knight — yet heavy and wrathful — came to the accustomed trysting place

---

[2] feudal tenant ranking immediately below a baron

to speak a little to the maiden, each said to the other what was in the mind. There he opened out to her the news of his access to her father, and of the disaccord between the twain.

"Sweet my demoiselle," said the knight, "what is there to do? It seems better to me to quit my home, and to dwell henceforth amongst strangers in a far land, for my last hope is gone. I may never be yours, neither know I how these things will end. . . ."

"Certes," answered she, "very gladly would I be no heiress, but only simple maid, if all things were according to my will. Sire, if my father took heed only to your good qualities, by my faith he would not pain himself to prevent your coming to me. . . . But age and youth walk not easily together, for in the heart is the difference between the old and young. Yet so you do according to my device, you shall not fail to gain what you would have."

"Yea, demoiselle, by my faith, I will not fail herein; so tell me now your will."

"I have determined on a thing to which I have given thought many a time and oft. Very surely you remember that you have an uncle who is right rich in houses and in goods. He is not less rich than my father; he has neither child, wife nor brother, nor any kindred of his blood nearer than you. Well is it known that all his wealth is yours when he is dead. . . . Now go to him without delay, for he is old and frail; tell him that between my father and yourself is such a business that it may not come to a good end unless he help therein. But that if he would promise you three hundred pounds of his land, and come to require grace of my father, very soon can the affair be ended. For my father loves him dearly, and each counts the other an honourable man. Your uncle holds my father as prudent and wise: they are two ancient gentlemen, of ripe years, and have faith and alliance the one in the other. . . . And when we are wedded together, then you can render again

to your uncle all the land that he has granted you. . . ."

"Fairest," cried the knight, "verily and truly there is nothing I crave in comparison with your love; so forthwith I will find my uncle, and tell him this thing. . . ."

[The knight] came without hindrance to Medet, where his uncle had his dwelling. . . . There he opened out his heart, and made plain to him all this business.

"Uncle," said he, "if you will do so much as to speak to her sire, and tell him that you have granted me three hundred pounds of your land, I will make this covenant with you, and plight you my faith, my hand in yours, that when I have wedded her who is now denied me, that I will render again and give you quittance for your land. Now I pray that you will do what is required of you."

"Nephew," answered the uncle, "this I will do willingly, since it pleases me right well. . . ."

So without further tarrying Messire William went his way, merry of heart because of his uncle's promise that without let[3] he should have as wife that maid whom so dearly he desired. . . .

On the morrow, very early in the morning, the uncle got to horse, and before the hour of prime[4] came to the rich mansion of that old Prince, and of her whose beauty had no peer. He was welcomed with high observance, for the ancient lord loved him very dearly, seeing that they were both of the same years, and were rich and puissant princes, near neighbours in that land. Therefore he rejoiced greatly that one so high in station did honour to his house, and spread before him a fair banquet, . . . But the uncle of the good knight would not forget his secret thought, and presently discovered it to the Prince in saying —

"What go I now to tell you? I love you very truly, as you may easily perceive. I am come to require a favour at your hand. . . . I am come to pray of you, fair sire, the hand of your virtuous maid in

---

[3] hindrance  [4] six o'clock or sunrise

marriage. When we once were wed I would endow her with my wealth to the utmost of my power. You know well that I have no heir of my body, which troubles me sorely; and I will keep good faith with you herein, for I am he who loves you dearly. When your daughter is bestowed upon me, it would not be my care to separate father and child, nor to withdraw my wealth from yours, but all our substance should be as one, and we would enjoy together in common that which God has given us."

When he whose heart was crafty heard these words, he rejoiced greatly, and made reply —

"Sire, I will give her to you right gladly, for you are a loyal and an honourable man. I am more content that you have required her of me than if the strongest castle of these parts had been rendered to my hand. . . ."

Then was promised and betrothed the damsel to a husband of whom she had little envy, for she was persuaded that another had asked her as his wife. When the maiden knew the truth thereof she was altogether amazed and sorrowful, and often she swore by St. Mary that never should she be wedded of him. Right heavy was she, and full of tears, and grievously she lamented her fate.

"Alas, unhappy wretch, for now I am dead. What foul treason has this old traitor done, for which he justly should be slain! How shamefully he has deceived that brave and courteous knight, whose honour is untouched by spot. By his wealth this aged, ancient man has bought me at a price. . . . Ah, God, what will become of me, and when shall he return who so foully is betrayed. If he but knew the trick his uncle has set on him, and how, too, I am taken in the snare, well I know that he would die of grief. . . . Fie on age! Fie upon riches! Never may bachelor wed with loving maid save he have money in his pouch. . . ."

Now he to whom the damsel was betrothed, because of his exceeding content, made haste to appoint some near day for

the wedding. For he knew little that she was as one distraught by reason of the great love she bore his nephew, as you have heard tell. So her father made all things ready, very richly, and when the third day was come he sent letters to the greybeards, and to those he deemed the wisest of that land, bidding them to the marriage of his daughter, who had bestowed her heart elsewhere. Since he was well known to all the country round, a great company of his friends came together to the number of thirty, to do honour to his house, since not one of them but owed him service for his lands. Then it was accorded between them that the demoiselle should be wedded early on the morrow, and her maidens were bidden to prepare their lady for the wedding on the appointed day and hour. But very wrathful and troubled in heart were the maidens by reason of this thing. . . .

Messire William, that brave and prudent knight, had little thought that his marriage was drawing so near its term. . . . Therefore he awaited in his manor, with what patience he might, the fair and pleasant tidings his uncle must presently send him, to hasten to the spousal of his bride. . . . At the time hope was growing sick a varlet came into the courtyard. When Messire William saw him the heart in his breast leaped and fluttered for joy.

"Sire," said the varlet, "God save you. My lord, your friend, whom well you know, has sent me to you in his need. You have a fair palfrey, than which none goes more softly in the world. My lord prays and requires of you that for love of him you will lend him this palfrey, and send it by my hand forthwith."

"Friend," answered the knight, "for what business?"

"Sire, to carry his lady daughter to the church, who is so dainty-sweet and fair."

"For what purpose rides she to church?"

"Fair sire, there to marry your uncle to whom she is betrothed. Early to-morrow morn my lady will be brought to the ancient chapel deep within the forest. Hasten, sire, for already I tarry too long. Lend your palfrey to your uncle and my lord. Well we know that it is the noblest horse within the realm, as many a time has been proved."

When Messire William heard these words —

"God," said he, "then I am betrayed by him in whom I put my trust; to whom I prayed so much to help me to my hope. May the Lord God assoil[5] him never for his treasonable deed. Yet scarcely can I believe that he has done this wrong. It is easier to hold that you are telling me lies."

"Well, you will find it truth to-morrow at the ringing of prime; for already is gathered together a company of the ancient lords of these parts."

"Alas," said he, "how, then, am I betrayed and tricked and deceived."

For a very little Messire William would have fallen swooning to the earth, had he not feared the blame of his household. But he was so filled with rage and grief that he knew not what to do, nor what to say. He did not cease lamenting his evil case till the varlet prayed him to control his wrath.

"Sire, cause the saddle to be set forthwith on your good palfrey, so that my lady may be carried softly to the church."

Then Messire William considered within himself to know whether he should send his grey palfrey to him whom he had cause to hate more than any man.

"Yea, without delay," said he, "since she who is the soul of honour has nothing to do with my trouble. My palfrey shall bear her gladly, in recompense of the favours she has granted me, for naught but kindness have I received of her. Never shall I have of her courtesies again, and all my joy and happiness are past. Now must I lend my palfrey to the man who has betrayed me to my death, since he has robbed me of that which I desired more than all the world. No man is bound to return love for treason. . . ."

In this manner the knight bewailed his heavy sorrow. Then he caused a saddle to be set upon the palfrey, and calling the

servitor delivered the horse to his keeping. So the varlet forthwith went upon his way.

Messire William, yet heavy and wrathful, shut himself fast within his chamber to brood upon his grief. . . . But whilst the knight was in this case, the servant in custody of the palfrey returned with all the speed he might to the castle of the old Prince, where all was merriment and noise.

The night was still and serene, and the house was filled with a great company of ancient lords. When they had eaten their full, the Prince commanded the watch that, without fail, all men should be roused and apparelled before the breaking of the day. He bade, too, that the palfrey and the horses should be saddled and made ready at the same hour, without confusion or disarray. Then they went to repose themselves and sleep. But one amongst them had no hope to sleep, because of the great unrest she suffered by reason of her love. All the night she could not close her eyes. Others might rest: she alone remained awake, for her heart knew no repose.

Now shortly after midnight the moon rose very bright, and shone clearly in the heavens. When the warder saw this thing, being yet giddy with the wine that he had drunken, he deemed that the dawn had broken.

"Pest take it," said he, "the lords should be about already."

He sounded his horn and summoned and cried —

"Arouse you, lords, for day is here."

Then those, yet drowsy with sleep, and heavy with last night's wine, got them from their beds all bewildered. The squires, too, made haste to set saddles upon the horses, believing that daybread had come, though before the dawn would rise very easily might the horses go five miles, ambling right pleasantly. So when the company which should bring this demoiselle to the chapel deep within the forest were got to horse, her father commended his maid to the most trusty of his friends. Then the saddle was

---

[5] pardon

put upon the grey palfrey; but when it was brought before the damsel her tears ran faster than they had fallen before. Her guardian recked[6] nothing of her weeping, for he knew little of maidens, and considered that she wept because of leaving her father and her father's house. So her tears and sadness were accounted as nought, and she mounted upon her steed, making great sorrow. They took their way through the forest, but the road was so narrow that two could not ride together side by side. Therefore the guardian put the maiden before, and he followed after, because of the straitness of the path. The road was long, and the company were tired and weary for want of sleep. They rode the more heavily, because they were no longer young, and had the greater need for rest. They nodded above the necks of their chargers, and up hill and down dale for the most part went sleeping. The surest of this company was in charge of the maiden, but this night he had taken so little sleep in his bed that he proved an untrusty warder, for he forgot everything, save his desire to sleep. The maiden rode, bridle in hand, thinking of nought except her love and her sorrow. Whilst she followed the narrow path the barons who went before had already come forth upon the high road. They dozed in their saddles, and the thoughts of those few who were awake were otherwhere, and gave no heed to the demoiselle. The maiden was as much alone as though she fared to London. The grey palfrey knew well this ancient narrow way, for many a time he had trodden it before. The palfrey and the maiden drew near a hillock within the forest, where the trees stood so close and thick that no moonlight fell within the shadow of the branches. The valley lay deeply below, and from the high road came the noise of the horses' iron shoes. Of all that company many slept, and those who were awake talked together, but none gave a thought to the maiden. The grey palfrey knew

nothing of the high road, so turning to the right he entered within a little path, which led directly to the house of Messire William. But the knight, in whose charge the damsel was placed had fallen into so heavy a slumber that his horse stood at his pleasure on the way. Therefore she was guarded of none — save of God — and dropping the rein upon the palfrey's neck, she let him have his will. The knights who preceded her rode a great while before they found that she was not behind them, and he who came after kept but a poor watch and ward. Nevertheless she had not escaped by her choice, for she recked nought of the path that she followed, nor of the home to which she would come. The palfrey followed the track without hesitation, for many a time he had journeyed therein, both winter and summer. The weeping maiden looked this way and that, but could see neither knight nor baron, and the forest was very perilous, and all was dark and obscure. . . . None regarded her safety, save God and the grey palfrey, so she commended herself to her Maker, whilst the horse ambled along the road. Nevertheless she had dropped the rein from her fingers, and kept her lips from uttering one single cry, lest she should be heard of her companions. For she chose rather to die in the woodlands than to endure such a marriage as this. The maiden was hid in thought, and the palfrey, in haste to reach his journey's end, and knowing well the path, ambled so swiftly. . . . A river ran there both dark and deep, but the horse went directly to the ford, and passed through as quickly as he was able. He had gone but little beyond when the maiden heard the sound of a horn, blown from that place where she was carried by the grey palfrey. The warder on his tower blew shrilly on his horn, and the demoiselle felt herself utterly undone, since she knew not where she had come, nor how to ask her way. But the palfrey stayed his steps on a bridge which led over the moat running

---

[6] cared

round the manor. When the watch heard the noise of the palfrey thereon, he ceased his winding, and coming from the tower demanded who it was who rode so hardily on the bridge at such an hour. Then the demoiselle made reply —

"Certes, it is the most unlucky maid of mother born. For the love of God give me leave to enter in your house to await the day, for I know not where to go."

"Demoiselle," answered he, "I dare not let you or any other in this place, save at the bidding of my lord, and he is the most dolorous knight in all the world, for very foully has he been betrayed."

Whilst the watch spoke of the matter he set his eye to a chink in the postern. He had neither torch nor lantern, but the moon shone very clear, and he spied the grey palfrey, which he knew right well. Much he marvelled whence he came, and long he gazed upon the fair lady who held the rein, and was so sweetly clad in her rich new garnishing. Forthwith he sought his lord, who tossed upon his bed with little delight.

"Sire," said he, "be not wrath with me. A piteous woman, tender of years and semblance, has come forth from the woodland, attired right richly. It seems to me that she is cloaked in a scarlet mantle, edged with costly fur. This sad and outworn lady is mounted on your own grey palfrey. Very enticing is her speech; very slim and gracious is her person. I know not, sire, if I am deceived, but I believe there is no maiden in all the country who is so dainty, sweet and fair. Well I deem that it is some fay whom God sends you, to bear away the trouble which is spoiling your life. Take now the gold in place of the silver you have lost."

Messire William hearkened to these words. He sprang forth from his bed without further speech, and with nothing but a surcoat[7] on his back hastened to the door. He caused it to be opened forthwith, and

the demoiselle cried to him pitifully in a loud voice —

". . . Sir Knight, be surety for the maid whom Fortune has guided to your door, for much am I sorrowful and perplexed."

When Messire William heard her voice he was like to swoon with joy. He knew again the palfrey which was so long his own. He gazed upon the lady, and knew her in his heart. I tell you truly that never could man be more happy than was he. He lifted her from the palfrey and brought her within his home. There he took her by the right hand, kissing her more than twenty times; and for her part the lady let him have his way, because she had looked upon his face. When the two sought each other's eyes, very great was the joy that fell between the twain and all their sorrow was as if it had never been. . . . Then the maiden told her bachelor this strange adventure, and said —

"Blessed be the hour in which God brought me to this place, and delivered me from him who sought to add my marriage chest to his own coffers."

When morning was come Messire William arrayed himself richly, and led the demoiselle within the chapel of his own house. Then, without delay, he called his chaplain to him, and was forthwith wedded to the fair lady by a rite that it was not lawful to call in question. So when the Mass was sung, blithe was the mirth of that household, squire and maiden and man-at-arms.

Now when that company which so lightly had lost the maiden came together at the ancient chapel, they were very weary by having ridden all the night, and were sore vexed and utterly cast down. . . .

The old Prince sought his daughter in every place, and inquired of her from every person, but he might not find her whereabouts, nor hear of any who had seen the maid. Yet all men marvelled at her loss, for none was able to bring him any news. The ancient bridegroom, that the demoiselle

---

[7] a tunic usually worn over armor

should have wed, grieved yet more at the loss of his bride, but to no purpose did he seek her, for the hind had left no slot. Now as the two lords were riding with their company in such fear as this, they saw upon the road a certain squire making towards them in all haste. When he was come to them he said —

"Sire, Messire William sends by me assurance of the great friendship he bears you. He bids me say that early this morning, at the dawn of day, he married your daughter, to his great happiness and content. Sire, he bids you welcome to his house. He also charged me to say to his uncle, who betrayed him so shamefully, that he pardons him the more easily for his treason, since your daughter has given him herself as a gift."

The old Prince hearkened to this wonder, but said no word in reply. He called together all his barons, and when they were assembled in hall, he took counsel as to whether he should go to the house of Sir William, and bring with him the lord to whom his daughter was betrothed. Yet since the marriage was done, nothing could make the bride again a maid. So, making the best of a bad bargain, he got to horse forthwith, and all his barons with him. When the company came to the manor they were welcomed with all fair observance, for right pleasing was this to Messire William, since he had all things to his own desire. Whether he would, or whether he would not, nought remained to the old Prince but to embrace his son-in-law; whilst as to that greybeard of a bridegroom, he consoled himself with what crumbs of comfort he could discover. Thus, since it was the will of God that these lovers should be wed, it pleased the Lord God also that the marriage should prove lasting. . . .

## RICHARD OF DEVIZES, *Description of King Richard Landing in Sicily While Enroute to the Third Crusade* (1190)

Richard of Devizes can find nothing whatever to criticize about the actions and methods of his hero king in Sicily.

People of all ages, a crowd beyond number, came to meet the king, marvelling and declaring how much more gloriously and impressively this king landed than did the king of France,[8] who had arrived with his troops a week before.

The king of England set up camp outside the city, because the king of France had already been received in the palace of Tancred, the king of Sicily, within the walls. On the same day the king of France, when he learned of the arrival of his companion and brother, flew to meet him, and gestures, between embraces and kisses, could not sufficiently express how much they delighted in each other. The armies refreshed themselves with mutual applause and conversation, just as if among so many thousands of men there were only one heart and one soul. The holiday was spent in such pleasures, and the kings, tired but still not satiated, separated, and everyone returned to his quarters.

The king of England immediately, on the next day, had gallows built outside the camp, on which to hang thieves and plunderers. The judges he designated spared neither sex nor age, and the law and the punishment were the same for the guilty, whether they were foreigners or natives.

SOURCE: From John T. Appleby, trans. and ed., *The Chronicle of Richard of Devizes of the Time of King Richard the First* (Oxford, England: Oxford University Press, 1963), alternate pp. 16–17, 19–25.

[8] Philip II

The king of France concealed whatever his men did or suffered, or kept silent about it. The king of England, giving no heed to the nationality of anyone involved in a crime, considered every man his subject and left no offence unpunished. For this reason the Griffons[9] called one king the Lamb and the other the Lion.

The king of England sent his ambassadors to the king of Sicily to demand his sister Joan, the former queen of Sicily,[10] and her dower, with a golden chair and all of King William's legacy that had been left to King Henry, Richard's father: that is, a golden table 12 feet long, a silken tent, a hundred first-class galleys with everything necessary for them for two years, 60,000 quarters of wheat, 60,000 of barley, 60,000 of wine, 24 golden cups, and 24 golden plates.

The king of Sicily, giving little weight to the commands of the king of the English and thinking even less of his demands, sent Richard's sister to him with the mere furniture of her bedchamber. Because of her royal station, however, he gave her a million terrini[11] for her expenses.

On the third day following, the king of England crossed the great river Del Far,[12] which separates Calabria from Sicily, . . . There he seized a very strongly fortified castle called La Bagnara, and, having thrown out the Griffons, he established his sister there and furnished the place with an armed guard.

Next the king seized a very strong castle called the Griffon's Monastery, situated on that same river Del Far between La Bagnara and Messina, and after he had captured it he fortified it. He mercilessly ground down with various punishments the Griffons who resisted him and made them a laughing-stock to his men. . . .

Before the arrival of King Richard in Sicily, the Griffons were stronger than all the other rulers of that region. While they had always hated the Ultramontanes,[13] now,

irritated by fresh injuries, they burned more fiercely than ever. They made peace with all who recognised the king of France as lord, and then they sought full revenge for their injuries from the king of the English and his tail-bearing men. (The paltry Greeks and Sicilians called all those who followed that king "Englishmen" and "tailed.") The English, therefore, were denied all trade with the country by edict, and they were slain both by day and by night by forties and fifties, wherever they were found unarmed. The slaughter increased every day, and it was planned to continue with this madness till every one of them was either killed or put to flight. The king of England, that fearful lion, was aroused by these tumults and roared horribly, burning with a rage worthy of such a beast. His raving fury terrified his dearest friends. The court drew together. The designated leaders of the army sat round the throne, each in his place; and one might very easily read in the ruler's face what he was silently considering in his mind, if anyone had dared lift his eyes to the king's face. After a long and profound silence, the king expressed his indignation thus: "O my soldiers, the strength and crown of my realm! You who have endured a thousand perils with me, you who by your bravery have conquered so many kings and cities for me, do you not see that the cowardly mob is now insulting us? Will we overcome Turks and Arabs, will we be the terror of the most invincible nations, will our right arms make a way for us to the ends of the earth after the Cross of Christ, will we restore the kingdom of Israel, if we show our backs to these vile and effeminate Griffons? If we are defeated here in the confines of our own country, will we go any farther? Shall the laziness of Englishmen be made a joke to the ends of the world? My men, is not this new cause of grief to me a very just one? It may be, I

---

[9] Sicilians who spoke Greek  [10] Joan was third daughter of Henry II and Eleanor. She married William II, who died in 1189 and was succeeded by his illegitimate cousin Tancred  [11] golden coins  [12] Straits of Messina  [13] Italians

think, that you are deliberately sparing your strength now, so that perhaps later on you may fight more boldly against Saladin.[14]

"I, your lord and your king, love you. I am solicitous for your good name. I tell you and I repeat that if by chance you go away from here without your revenge, the base repute of this flight will go ahead of you and accompany you. Old women and little children will rise up against you, and boldness will give a double strength to the enemies of men who have run away. I know that he who keeps a man against his will does the same as kill him. The king will keep no man against his will. I do not want to force anyone to stay with me, lest one man's fear in battle might destroy another's confidence. Let each man follow the course he chooses, but as for me, I will either die here or get revenge for my injuries, which are your injuries, too. If I go away from here alive, Saladin will not see me unless I am victorious. If you flee, you will leave me, your king, whom you will have deserted, to face the danger alone."

The king had scarcely finished his speech when all the brave men roared, disturbed only by the fact that their lord seemed not to trust his men. They promised from their hearts to be ready to do whatever he ordered, ready to scale mountains and to break through walls of bronze. Let him lay aside his frown; they would make all Sicily subject to him by their sweat, if he so ordered. They would all wade to the Pillars of Hercules in blood, if he so desired.

When the noise was hushed by the ruler's authority, "What I hear pleases me," he said. "You gladden my heart, you who are ready to cast away your disgrace. And, because it is always harmful to put things off when they are ready, there must be no delay, so that what we are going to do may be done quickly. First, you must capture Messina for me. Then the Griffons shall either ransom themselves or be sold into

slavery. If King Tancred does not make speedy satisfaction for my sister's dower and King William's legacy, which falls to me as my father's heir, after his kingdom has been depopulated he shall be compelled to pay everything four times over. Booty shall belong to whoever takes it in battle. Perfect peace is to be observed only towards my lord, the king of the French, who is taking his rest in the city, and all his men. Within two days let about 2,000 knights, chosen from the whole army, men whose hearts are not in their boots, and 1,000 archers on foot make ready. Let the law be observed without any exceptions. Whoever runs away on foot shall lose a foot. A knight shall be stripped of his belt. Let each man be in his proper place in the battle array according to military discipline, and on the third day, at the sound of the trumpet, let each man follow me into the city, and I will go first and show the way." The council broke up with great applause, and the king, his stern expression gone, seemed to thank them for their good-will by the very serenity of his countenance.

It wonderfully came to pass that even his enemies could not allege that the king's cause was unjust. On the third day, when the army was to have been led forth, early in the morning, Richard, archbishop of Messina, the archbishop of Monreale, the archbishop of Reggio, the Admiral Margarito, Jordan of Pin, and many other friends of King Tancred, taking with them Philip, king of the French, the bishop of Chartres, the duke of Burgundy, the counts of Nevers and Perche, and many followers of the king of France, as well as the archbishops of Rouen and Auch, the bishops of Évreux and Bayonne, and everyone who was thought to have some influence with the English, came respectfully to the king of England to make satisfaction to him for all his complaints, according to his pleasure. The king, after being long and earnestly entreated, yielded to the persistency of so

---

[14] sultan of Egypt and Syria

many men and left the terms of the peace to the suitors themselves. Let them consider what he had put up with, he said, and let them see to it that the terms of the treaty were no lighter than the wrongs he had suffered. He would be satisfied with whatever their deliberations should decide to be due, if only from that very moment none of the Griffons should lay hands on his men, now or in the future. Those who had come were greatly surprised and even more delighted at the unhoped-for mildness of his reply, and, agreeing to what he had last proposed, they sat down together to deal with the rest, away from the king's presence.

The king's army, numbered off the day before, had been waiting for the herald in solemn silence outside the camp since sunrise, and the peacemakers, proceeding in a dilatory fashion, had drawn out their negotiations till fully the third hour of the day, when behold! suddenly and unexpectedly a loud voice outside the gates cried: "To arms, to arms, men! Hugh the Brown has been seized and is being killed by the Griffons, his belongings are being plundered, and his men are being slain!" The cry that the peace had been broken threw the negotiators into confusion, and the king of France exclaimed: "I am convinced that God hates these men and has hardened their hearts, so that they may fall into the hands of the torturer!" He went quickly with all who were with him to the king's tent and found him already putting on his armour. He said to him in a few words: "I will be a witness before all men that, whatever may happen, you will be blameless if you now take up arms against the damned Griffons."

He spoke and withdrew. Those who had come with him followed him and were received with him into the city.

The king of England went forth armed; the terrible dragon standard was carried before him unfurled; and the army moved after him at the sound of a trumpet. The sun glistened on golden shields, and the mountains shone brightly with the reflection from them. They went forth carefully and in good order, and the business was done without any foolishness.

The Griffons, on the other side, locked the gates of the city and stood in arms at the ramparts of the walls and towers, fearing nothing as yet, and shot at the army incessantly. The king, who knew nothing better than storming cities and overthrowing castles, first let them empty their quivers. Then at length he made the first assault by his bowmen, who went in front of the army. The sky was hidden by a violent rain of arrows; a thousand darts pierced the shields extended along the ramparts; and nothing could save the rebels from the force of the javelins. The walls were left without guards, for no one could look out without getting an arrow in his eye immediately. In the meantime the king, with his army, came up to the gates of the city unopposed, freely, and, as it were, without restraint. When the battering ram was moved up, he broke down the gates more quickly than it takes to tell about it. He led the army into the city and captured all the fortified places up to Tancred's palace and the quarters of the French around their king's lodging, which he spared out of respect for his lord the king. The victors' banners were placed on the towers of the city in a circle. He turned over the captured fortifications to the leaders of the army, one to each, and he made his nobles take up quarters in the city. He took as hostages the sons of all the nobles of the city and the province, so that either they might be ransomed according to the king's valuation of them or else the remainder of the city might be given up to him without a struggle and his demands from its king, Tancred, might be satisfied. He began the assault of the city at the fifth hour of the day and took it on the tenth hour. Then he recalled his army and returned victorious to the camp. King Tancred, terrified when the news of the outcome of the engagement was brought to him, hastened to make a settlement with him. He sent him 20,000 ounces of gold for his sister's dower and another 20,000 ounces of gold as King William's legacy and to ensure the observance of a perpetual peace with him and his subjects. That small sum of money was received very reluctantly and indignantly; the hostages were returned, and a firm peace was sworn to by the great men on both sides.

The king of England, as yet trusting the natives very little, built a new stronghold of wood of great strength and height near the walls of Messina. As a taunt to the Griffons, he called it "The Griffon-Killer." The king's valour was greatly glorified, and "all the earth kept silent before him."

## JOHN OF SALISBURY, *Policraticus* (1159)

John of Salisbury (1115–1180) gives his idealized definition of the perfect prince. The real-life kings under whom John lived were Henry I, Stephen, and Henry II.

### CHAPTER I

#### Of the difference between a prince and a tyrant and of what is meant by a prince

Between a tyrant and a prince there is this single or chief difference, that the latter obeys the law and rules the people by its dictates, accounting himself as but their servant. It is by virtue of the law that he makes good his claim to the foremost and chief place in the management of the affairs of the commonwealth and in the bearing of its burdens; and his elevation over others consists in this, that whereas private men are held responsible only for their private affairs, on the prince fall the burdens of the whole community. Wherefore deservedly there is conferred on him, and gathered together in his hands, the power of all his subjects, to the end that he may be sufficient unto himself in seeking and bringing about the advantage of each individually, and of all; and to the end that the state of the human commonwealth may be ordered in the best possible manner, seeing that each and all are members one of another. Wherein we indeed but follow nature, the best guide of life; for nature has gathered together all the senses of her microcosm or little world, which is man, into the head, and has subjected all the members in obedience to it in such wise that they will all function properly so long as they follow the guidance of the head, and the head remains sane. Therefore the prince stands on a pinnacle which is exalted and made splendid with all the great and high privileges which he deems necessary for himself. And rightly so, because nothing is more advantageous to the people than that the needs of the prince should be fully satisfied; since it is impossible that his will should be found opposed to justice. Therefore, according to the usual definition, the prince is the public power, and a kind of likeness on earth of the divine majesty. Beyond doubt a large share of the divine power is shown to be in princes by the fact that at their nod men bow their necks and for the most part offer up their heads to the axe to be struck off, and, as by a divine impulse, the prince is feared by each of those over whom he is set as an object of fear. And this I do not think could be, except as a result of the will of God. For all power is from the

SOURCE: From John Dickinson, trans., *The Statesman's Book of John of Salisbury,* © 1963, pp. 3–5, 32–33, 37, 39–40, 43–44. Reprinted by permission of Prentice-Hall, Inc., Englewood Cliffs, New Jersey.

Lord God, and has been with Him always, and is from everlasting. The power which the prince has is therefore from God, for the power of God is never lost, nor severed from Him, but He merely exercises it through a subordinate hand, making all things teach His mercy or justice. "Who, therefore, resists the ruling power, resists the ordinance of God," in whose hand is the authority of conferring that power, and when He so desires, of withdrawing it again, or diminishing it. . . . To quote the words of the Emperor, "it is indeed a saying worthy of the majesty of royalty that the prince acknowledges himself bound by the Laws." For the authority of the prince depends upon the authority of justice and law; and truly it is a greater thing than imperial power for the prince to place his government under the laws, so as to deem himself entitled to do nought which is at variance with the equity of justice. . . .

## Chapter VII

**That he should be taught the fear of God, and should be humble, and so maintain his humility that the authority of the prince may not be diminished; and that some precepts are flexible, others inflexible**

The next commandment is that he [the prince] shall learn to fear the Lord his God, and to keep God's words which are prescribed in the law. The law itself adds the reason for keeping its precepts, — "To the end that he may learn," it says. For the diligent reader of the law is a pupil, not a master; he does not twist the law captive to his own inclination, but accommodates his inclinations to its intention and purity. But what does such a pupil learn? Above all, to fear the Lord his God. Rightly so, because it is wisdom which institutes and strengthens the government of a prince; and the beginning of wisdom is fear of the Lord. He therefore who does not begin with the first step of fear aspires in vain to the pinnacle

of legitimate princely rule. I say legitimate; for of certain rulers who are cast down while they are exalted, and are worthy of a yet·more miserable fate, it is written: "They have reigned, and not by me; princes have arisen and I knew it not"; and elsewhere, "They that handle the law have not known wisdom." Therefore let the prince fear God, and by prompt humility of mind and pious display of works show himself His servant. For a lord is the lord of a servant. And the prince is the Lord's servant, and performs his service by serving faithfully his fellow-servants, namely his subjects. But let him know also that his Lord is God, to whom is to be shown not alone fear of His majesty, but also pious love. For He is also a father, and one to whom as a result of His merits no creature of His can deny affection and love. "If I am Lord," He says, "where is my fear? If I am father, where is my love?" Also the words of the law are to be kept, which, commencing with the first timid step of fear, mounts upward through the virtues as upon a rising stair with happy ascent. "Love of Him," He says, "is the guardian of His laws" because all wisdom is fear of God. Further: "Who fears God will do good works, and who is faithful unto justice will apprehend her, and she will come forth to meet him as an honored mother." . . .

## Chapter VIII

**That the prince should effect a reconciliation of justice with mercy, and should so temper and combine the two as to promote the advantage of the commonwealth**

. . . This, however, is certain, that it is safer for the cords to be relaxed than to be stretched too tautly. For the tension of slack cords can be corrected by the skill of the artificer so that they will again give forth the proper sweetness of tone; but a string that has once been broken, no artificer can repair. Further, if a sound is asked of them which they do not have, they are stretched in vain, and more often come speedily to nought than to what is improperly asked. As the ethical writer says:

> The true prince is slow to punish, swift to reward,
> And grieves whenever he is compelled to be severe.

For while justice is one thing and godliness another, still both are so necessary to the prince that whoever without them attains, not necessarily to princely power, but even to any magistracy whatever, mocks himself in vain but will surely provoke against himself the mockery and scorn and hatred of others. "Let not kindness and truth," saith the Lord, "forsake thee, bind them about thy neck, and write them on the tablet of thy heart; so shalt thou find favor and obedience in the sight of God and men." For kindness deserves favor, justice deserves obedience. The favor and love of one's subjects, which are brought to pass by divine favor, are the most effective instrument of all accomplishments. But love without obedience is of no avail, because when the spur of justice ceases, then the people relax into unlawful courses. Therefore he must ceaselessly meditate wisdom, that by its aid he may do justice, without the law of mercy being ever absent from his tongue; and so temper mercy with the strictness of justice that his tongue speaks nought save judgment. For his office transmutes his justice into judgment continually and of necessity because he may never lawfully repose therefrom without thereby divesting himself of the honor that has been conferred on him. For the honor of a king delights in judgment and represses the faults of offenders with tranquil moderation of mind. . . .

## Chapter IX

### What the meaning is of inclining to the right hand or the left, which is forbidden to the prince

The next commandment is, "He shall not incline to the right hand nor to the left." To incline to the right hand signifies to insist too enthusiastically on the virtues themselves. To incline to the right is to exceed the bounds of moderation in the works of virtue, the essence of which is moderation. For truly all enthusiasm is the foe of salvation and all excess is a fault; nothing is worse than the immoderate practice of good works. Wherefore the heathen author says:

> The wise man will get the name of mad, the just man of being unjust,
> If he pursues virtue itself beyond the measure of what is sufficient.

And the philosopher warns us to avoid excess; for if a man depart from this caution and moderation, he will in his lack of caution forsake the path of virtue itself. Salomon, too, says, "Be not too just." What excess can then be of any profit, if justice herself, the queen of the virtues, is hurtful in excess? And elsewhere to the same effect: "Excessive humility is the highest degree of pride." To incline to the left means to slip or deviate from the way of virtue down the precipices of the vices. Therefore one turns aside to the left who is too ready to punish his subjects, and take revenge on them for their faults; on the other hand, he deviates to the right who is too indulgent to offenders out of excess of kindness. Both roads lead away from the true path; but that which inclines toward the left is the more harmful.

## JOHN RUSSELL, *Book of Nurture* (Late Fourteenth Century)

John Russell teaches the young man how to succeed at court and how to successfully carry out the duties of various offices in a noble or royal household.

"Now, good son, if I will teach, will you learn? Will you be a serving-man, a plough-man, a labourer, a courtier, a clerk, a merchant, a mason or an artificer, a chamberlain, a butler, a panter or a carver?"

"Teach me, sir, the duties of a butler, a panter or a chamberlain, and especially, the cunning of a carver. If you will make me to know all these, I will pray for your soul that it come never in pain!"

"Son, I will teach you with right good will. . . ."

### The Duties of a Panter or Butler

"The first year, my son, you shall be panter or butler. In the pantry, you must always keep three sharp knives, one to chop the loaves, another to pare them, and a third, sharp and keen, to smooth and square the trenchers[15] with.

"Always cut your lord's bread, and see that it be new; and all other bread at the table one day old ere you cut it, all household bread three days old, and trencher-bread four days old.

"Look that your salt be fine, white, fair, and dry; and have your salt-plane of ivory, two inches wide and three long; and see to it that the lid of the salt-cellar touch not the salt. . . ."

### The Buttery

"See that your cups and pots be clean, both within and without. Serve no ale till it is five days old, for new ale is wasteful.[16] And look that all things about you be sweet and clean.

"Be fair of answer, ready to serve, and gentle of cheer, and then men will say; 'There goes a gentle officer.'

"Beware that ye give no person stale drink, for fear that ye bring many a man into disease for many a year.[17] . . .

"Carry a towel about your neck when serving your lord, bow to him, uncover your bread and set it by the salt. Look that all have knives, spoons and napkins, and always when you pass your lord, see that you bow your knees. . . . Serve each according to his degree; and see that none lack bread, ale or wine.

"Be glad of cheer, courteous of knee, soft of speech; have clean hands and nails and be carefully dressed.

"Do not cough or spit or retch too loud, or put your fingers into the cups to seek bits of dust.

"Have an eye to all grumbling and fault-finding, and prevent backbiting of their fellows among the lords at meat, by serving all with bread, ale and wine; and so shall ye have of all men good love and praise."

### Simple Conditions

"I will that ye eschew forever the 'simple conditions' of a person that is not taught.

"Do not claw your head or your back as if you were after a flea, or stroke your hair as if you sought a louse.

"Be not glum, nor twinkle with your eyes, nor be heavy of cheer; and keep your eyes free from winking and watering.

"Do not pick your nose or let it drop

SOURCE: From Edith Rickert, ed., *The Babees' Book: Medieval Manners for the Young: Done into Modern English from Dr. Furnivall's Texts* (London: Chatto and Windus Ltd., 1908), pp. 49–52, 55–58, 69–76. By permission of the publisher.

[15] a plate made of stale bread on which meat was served. Later made of wood  [16] too much can be consumed because new ale is not intoxicating  [17] lead poisoning from pewter pots

clear pearls, or sniff, or blow it too loud, lest your lord hear.

"Twist not your neck askew like a jackdaw; wring not your hands with picking or trifling or shrugging, as if ye would saw [wood]; nor puff up your chest, nor pick your ears, nor be slow of hearing.

"Retch not, nor spit too far, nor laugh or speak too loud. Beware of making faces and scorning; and be no liar with your mouth. Nor yet lick your lips or drivel.

"Do not have the habit of squirting or spouting with your mouth, or gape, or yawn, or pout. And do not lick a dish with your tongue to get out dust.

"Be not rash or reckless — that is not worth a clout.

"Do not sigh with your breast, or cough, or breathe hard in the presence of your sovereign, or hiccough, or belch, or groan never the more. Do not trample with your feet, or straddle your legs, or scratch your body — there is no sense in showing off. Good son, do not pick your teeth, or grind, or gnash them, or with puffing and blowing cast foul breath upon your lord. . . . These gallants in their short coats — that is ungoodly guise. Other faults on this matter, I spare not to disapprove in my opinion, when [a servant] is waiting on his master at table. Every sober sovereign must despise all such things. . . ."

*The Office of Usher and Marshal*

"An usher or marshal, without fail, must know all the estates of the Church, and the excellent estate of a king with his honourable blood. This is a notable nurture, cunning, curious and commendable.

"The estate of the Pope has no peer, an emperor is next him everywhere and a King is correspondent, a high cardinal next in dignity, then a King's son (ye call him prince), an archbishop his equal; a duke of the blood royal; a bishop, marquis and earl coequal; a viscount, legate, baron, suffragan and mitred abbot; a baron of the exchequer, the three chief justices and the Mayor of London; a cathedral prior, unmitred abbot and knight bachelor; a prior, dean, archdeacon, knight and body esquire; the Master of the Rolls (as I reckon aright), and puisne[18] judge; clerk of the crown and the exchequer, and you may pleasantly prefer the Mayor of Calais.[19]

"A provincial, doctor of divinity and prothonotary[20] may dine together; and you may place the pope's legate or collector with a doctor of both laws. An ex-mayor of London ranks with a serjeant-at-law, next a Mastery of Chancery, and then a worshipful preacher of pardons, masters of arts, and religious orders, parsons and vicars, and parish priests with a cure, the bailiffs of a city, a yeoman of the crown, and serjeant-of-arms with his mace, with him a herald, the King's herald in the first place, worshipful merchants and rich artificers, gentlemen well-nurtured and of good manners, together with gentlewomen and lords' foster-mothers — all these may eat with squires.

"Lo, son, I have now told you, after my simple wit, the rank of every estate according to his degree, and now I will show you how they should be grouped at table in respect of their dignity, and how they should be served.

"The pope, an emperor, king, cardinal, prince with a golden royal rod,[21] archbishop in his pall — all these for their dignity ought not to dine in the hall.

"A bishop, viscount, marquis, goodly earl may sit at two messes if they be agreeable thereunto.

"The Mayor of London, a baron, a mitred abbot, the three chief justices, the Speaker of Parliament — all these estates are great and honourable, and they may sit together in chamber or hall, two or three at a mess, if it so please them; but in your office you must try to please every man.

"The other estates, three or four to a mess, equal to a knight's, are: unmitred abbot or prior, dean, archdeacon, Master of the Rolls, all the under judges and barons of the king's exchequer, a provincial, a

---

[18] inferior in rank    [19] head of a monastic order    [20] chief clerk    [21] sceptre

doctor of divinity or of both laws, a pro-thonotary, or the pope's collector, if he be there, and the Mayor of the Staple.

"Other ranks you may set four to a mess, of persons equal to a squire in dignity, serjeants-at-law and ex-mayors of London, the masters of Chancery, all preachers, resi-dencers, and parsons, apprentices of the law, merchants and franklins — these may sit properly at a squire's table.

"Each estate shall sit at meal by itself, not seeing the others, at meal-time or in the field or in the town; and each must sit alone in the chamber or in the pavilion.

"The Bishop of Canterbury shall be served apart from the Archbishop of York, and the Metropolitan shall be served alone. The Bishop of York must not be served in the presence of the Primate of England.

"Now, son, from divers causes, as equally from ignorance, a marshal is often puzzled how to rank lords of royal blood who are poor, and others not of royal blood who are rich, also ladies of royal blood wedded to knights, and poor ladies marrying those of royal blood. The lady of royal blood shall keep her rank, the lady of low blood and degree shall take her husband's rank. The substance of livelihood is not so digne[22] as royal blood, wherefore this prevails in chamber and hall, for some day blood royal might attain to the kingship.

"If the parents of a pope or cardinal be still alive, they must in no wise presume to be equal to their son, either sitting or standing. The estate of their son will not allow them either to sit or stand by him — nor should they desire it; wherefore they should have a separate chamber assigned to them.

"A marshal must look to the birth of each estate, and arrange officers such as chan-cellor, steward, chamberlain, treasurer, ac-cording to their degree.

"He must honour foreign visitors, and strangers to this land, even when they are resident here. A well-trained marshal should think beforehand how to place strangers

at the table, for if they show gentle cheer and good manners, he thereby doth honour his lord and bring praise to himself.

"If the king send any messenger to your lord, if he be a knight, squire, yeoman of the crown, groom, page or child, receive him honourably as a baron, knight, squire, yeoman or groom, and so forth, from the highest degree to the lowest, for a king's groom may dine with a knight or a marshal.

"A commendable marshal must also un-derstand the rank of all the worshipful officers of the commonalty of this land, of shires, cities and boroughs — such must be placed in due order, according to their rank.

"The estate of a knight of [good] blood and wealth is not the same as that of a simple and poor knight. Also, the Mayor of Queenborough[23] is not of like dignity with the Mayor of London — nothing like of degrees; and they must on no account sit at the same table.

"The Abbot of Westminster is the high-est in the land, and the Abbot of Tintern the poorest; both are abbots, yet Tintern shall neither sit nor stand with Westminster. Also, the Prior of Dudley may in no wise sit with the Prior of Canterbury. And re-member, as a general rule, that a prior who is a prelate of a cathedral church, shall sit above any abbot or prior of his own diocese, in church, chapel, chamber or hall.

"Reverend doctors of twelve years' stand-ing shall sit above those of nine years', al-though the latter may spend more largely of fine red gold. Likewise, the younger alderman shall sit or stand below their elders, and so in every craft, the master first, and then the ex-warden.

"All these points, with many more, be-long to the duty of a marshal; and so before every feast think what estates shall sit in the hall, and reason with yourself before your lord shall call upon you. If you are in any doubt, go either to your lord or to the chief officer, and then shall you do no wrong or prejudice to any state; but set all according to their birth, riches or dignity.

---

[22] worthy of respect   [23] small port town

"Now, good son, I have shown you the courtesy of the court, and how to manage in pantry, buttery, cellar or in carving, as a sewer or as a marshal. . . .

"All these divers offices may be filled by a single person, but the dignity of a prince requireth each office to have its officer and a servant waiting on him. Moreover, all must know their duties perfectly, for doubt and fear are a hindrance in serving a lord and pleasing his guests.

"Fear not to serve a prince — God be his speed! Take good heed to your duties, and be ever on the watch, and thus doing as ye should, there will be no need to doubt. . . ."

## How the Good Wife Taught Her Daughter (ca. 1430)

The good wife is at pains to educate her daughter in her own image. The reader may wish to compare this picture of thirteenth-century womanhood with the one found in the Paston Letters (Chapter 7).

The good wife taught her daughter,
    Full many a time and oft,
  A full good woman to be;
For said she: "Daughter to me dear,
Something good now must thou hear,
    If thou wilt prosper thee.

Daughter, if thou wilt be a wife,
    Look wisely that thou work;
Look lovely and in good life,
    Love God and Holy Kirk.[24]
Go to church whene'er thou may,
    Look thou spare for no rain,
For best thou farest on that day;
    To commune with God be fain.[25]
      He must needs well thrive,
      That liveth well all his life,
        My lief[26] child.    . . .

The man that shall thee wed before God with a ring,
Love thou him and honour most of earthly thing.
Meekly thou him answer and not as an atterling,[27]
So may'st thou slake his mood,[28] and be his dear darling.
      A fair word and a meek
      Doth anger slake,
        My lief child.
              . . .

SOURCE: From Edith Rickert, ed., *The Babees' Book: Medieval Manners for the Young: Done into Modern English from Dr. Furnivall's Texts* (London: Chatto and Windus Ltd., 1908), pp. 31–33, 35–37, 39–42. By permission of the publisher.

24 church   25 willing   26 dear   27 shrew   28 *slake* . . . quiet his wrath

And if thou be in any place where good ale is aloft,[29]
Whether that thou serve thereof or that thou sit soft,
Measurably thou take thereof, that thou fall in no blame,
For it thou be often drunk, it falleth to thy shame.
>           For those that be often drunk —
>           Thrift is from them sunk,
>                     My lief child.

Go not to the wrestling or shooting at the cock,
As it were a strumpet[30] or a gigggelot;[31]
Dwell at home, daughter, and love thy work much,
And so thou shalt, my lief child, wax the sooner rich.
>           A merry thing 'tis evermore,
>           A man to be served of his own store,
>                     My lief child.

Acquaint thee not with each man that goeth by the
>           street,
Though any man speak to thee, swiftly[32] thou him greet;
By him do not stand, but let him his way depart,
Lest he by his villainy should tempt thy heart.
>           For all men be not true
>           That fair words can shew,
>                     My lief child.

·  ·  ·

And wisely govern they house, and serving maids and men,
Be thou not too bitter or too debonaire with them;
But look well what most needs to be done,
And set thy people at it, both rathely[33] and soon.
>           For ready is at need
>           A foredone deed,
>                     My lief child.

And if thy husband be from home, let not thy folk do ill,
But look who doeth well and who doeth nil;
And he that doeth well, quit him well his while,
But he that doeth other, serve him as the vile.
>           A foredone deed
>           Will another speed,
>                     My lief child.

·  ·  ·

And if thy neighbour's wife hath on rich attire,
Therefore mock not, nor let scorn burn thee as a fire.
But thank thou God in heaven for what He may thee give,
And so shalt thou, my daughter dear, a good life live,
>           He hath ease in his power,
>           Who thanks the Lord every hour,
>                     My lief child.

·  ·  ·

---

[29] served   [30] prostitute   [31] giggling girl   [32] curtly   [33] quickly

And if thou art a rich wife, be not then too hard,
But welcome fair thy neighbours that come to-thee-ward
With meat, drink, and honest cheer, such as thou
    mayest bid,[34]
To each man after his degree, and help the poor at need.
    And also for hap that may betide,
      Please well thy neighbours that dwell thee beside,
        My lief child.

Daughter, look that thou beware, whatsoever thee
    betide,
Make not thy husband poor with spending or with pride.
A man must spend as he may that hath but easy good,[35]
For as a wren hath veins, men must let her blood.[36]
    His thrift waxeth thin
    That spendeth ere he win,
      My lief child.

        • • •

And if thy children be rebel and will not bow them low,
If any of them misdo, neither curse them nor blow;[37]
But take a smart rod and beat them in a row,
Till they cry mercy and their guilt well know.
    Dear child, by this lore
    They will love thee ever more,
      My lief child.

And look to thy daughters that none of them be lorn;[38]
From the very time that they are of thee born,
Busy thyself and gather fast for their marriage,
And give them to spousing, as soon as they be of age.
    Maidens be fair and amiable,
    But in their love full unstable,
      My lief child.

Now have I taught thee, daughter, as my mother did me;
Think thereon night and day, that forgotten it not be.
Have measure and lowness, as I have thee taught,
Then whatever man shall wed thee will regret it naught.
    Better you were a child unbore
    Than untaught in this wise lore,
      My lief child.

---

[34] offer   [35] small income   [36] *as* . . . i.e., you cannot squeeze blood out of a stone   [37] scold   [38] ruined

## FURTHER DISCUSSION QUESTIONS

### The Tale of the Palfrey

1. What chivalric and social ideals are apparent in the story? What prejudices appear in the story?
2. Why was it important to the proper operation of feudalism that the moral of the story be learned and accepted?
3. Why is Messire William potentially dangerous to medieval society?
4. Why is Messire William's conduct at tournament praised?
5. Who or what is the hero of the story?
6. What prevents Messire William from kidnapping his fair lady?
7. Why, according to the story, does Messire William want to marry the girl? Are there any other motives that come to mind?

### Richard of Devizes, Description of King Richard Landing in Sicily

1. What are the qualities that the author admired most in King Richard? Why is Richard regarded more highly than Philip?
2. What aspects of Richard's character and actions in no way shocked Richard of Devizes? Why?

### John of Salisbury, Policraticus

1. Salisbury speaks of "the law"; whose law was it and how was it made?
2. From whence does the prince's power stem? How does the ideal prince win the favor and obedience of his subjects?
3. Salisbury expounds a formula for perfect conduct which the medieval world would say applied not only to kings but to every individual in every walk of life and in every circumstance. What is it?
4. How close did Richard I come to the kingly ideal described by John of Salisbury. What English king, if any, approached this ideal?

### John Russell, Book of Nurture

1. What kind of society is depicted in Russell's advice? What social virtues were most esteemed?
2. If Russell presents what should be, what is your guess about reality?
3. Why were the office and duties of a marshal so difficult; why were they so important to a properly organized medieval society?

### How the Good Wife Taught Her Daughter

1. What, according to the "good wife," are the proper womanly virtues and aspirations?
2. How does the status of a wife in the fifteenth century compare with her status today?
3. What is the view of men expressed by the "good wife"?

# 6

## *The Religious Structure of Life*

Medieval society is often described as an age of faith, a generalization that does more to confuse than to clarify because it ignores the question: faith in what? The simplest answer is to say that medieval society had faith in two ideas: (1) God's universe is an interconnected totality in which all things — the leaf that falls to the ground or the comet that shoots across the August skies, the clash of human arms or the decisions of individual men and women — are part of a divine plan; and (2) existence is a spiritual and metaphysical problem. These two convictions are what is meant by "the religious structure of life," for medieval society sought to explain the unknowns of the universe in terms of a religious known, and to assign spiritual meaning to actions, events, institutions, and physical phenomena, which we today would maintain are solely social, economic, political, or material in their purpose, structure, and origin. Nothing sets the medieval world off from the modern as much as this built-in assumption that kingship and economics, crime and charity, heavenly movements and devastations of rain and wind are essentially spiritual matters that must be explained and analyzed in religious terms; they have as much to do with the next world as with earthly concerns. The documents in this chapter dramatize these points. The readings move from the general to the particular — from God's universe to man and his society — and then focus on the two ideal human types on earth — the parson and the plowman. The final four selections are episodes that either reveal the religious ideal in action or display society's preoccupation with man's soul and his spiritual welfare.

The first document is a tenth-century astronomical manual by an unknown writer who describes the universe, its movements and elements in terms that would be acceptable to the human mind and eye until the scientific revolution of the sixteenth and seventeenth centuries. The next two selections are by the greatest of the medieval schoolmen, the "angelic doctor" Thomas Aquinas (1225–1274). Postulating the essential compatibility of faith and reason in the

The Becket difficulty still kept Henry II awake at night.

ultimate contemplation and understanding of God, Aquinas endeavored to Christianize the physical and moral principles of Aristotle and to analyze and investigate the "true" meaning and purpose of man and his society. The result was one of the most extraordinary feats of learning and synthesis of Western history. In the selection from the *Summa Contra Gentiles*, he investigates man's true happiness; in his opus *On Kingship*, he relates the needs and end of man to the totality of society and its ultimate purpose. The final reading in this quartet of documents is from the prologue to Geoffrey Chaucer's (1340?– 1400) *Canterbury Tales*, where the parson and the plowman appear as the religious and the secular ideal in an assortment of very earthy and human pilgrims who are on their way to Thomas à Becket's shrine at Canterbury.

The concluding documents in the chapter reflect random facets of medieval society in which the spirituality of life predominates. "Our Lady's Tumbler" was to the religious world what "The Palfrey" was to the secular: an ideal rarely if ever attained but nevertheless deeply moving and compassionate in its presentation of what could be if only men and women had sufficient faith in God's grace. It is a tale that still has deep meaning and impact today. The story, recounted by William, monk of Malmesbury (1095?–1143?), of Stephen Harding's efforts in the early twelfth century to establish a new and better monastery, the Cistertian order, is part of society's age-old Odyssey to revitalize its institutions by bringing them into closer accord with social and moral ideals. Edward Grim's picture of Thomas à Becket's martyrdom (1170) is a near classic. By any standard, the archbishop's assassination is bloody and dramatic.

From the medieval perspective, it was one of the most heroic moments of history, and Grim's account has the added verisimilitude of participation. He was a visitor at Canterbury at the moment of the attack, and he was seriously wounded as a consequence of his efforts to defend the archbishop. The final selection is Thomas Aquinas' famous discussion of buying and selling, and the spiritual implications and limitations involved in economic enterprise.

An important comparison should be kept in mind while reading these documents: How does the quality and nature of religion portrayed compare with the kind of religion found in Chapter 1?

## Anglo-Saxon Manual of Astronomy (Tenth Century)

Although this description of the cosmos and of the physical principles upon which it operated is tenth-century, it remained essentially unchanged until the seventeenth century. No medieval or modern piece of literature should be read without an understanding of this view of the universe and how it functioned.

On the second day God made the heaven, which is called the firmament, which is visible and corporeal; and yet we may never see it, on account of its great elevation and the thickness of the clouds, and on account of the weakness of our eyes. The heaven incloses in its bosom all the world, and it ever turns about us, swifter than any mill-wheel, all as deep under this earth as it is above. It is all round and entire and studded with stars.... Truly the sun goes by God's command between heaven and earth by day above and by night under this earth, as far down under the earth in the night time as she rises above it by day. She is ever running about the earth, and so light shines under the earth by night as it does above our heads by day.... The sun is very great, as broad she is, from what books say, as the whole compass of the earth; but she appears to us very small, because she is very far from our sight. Everything the further it is, the less it seems.... The stars also, which seem to us little, are very broad, and on account of the great moisture that is between us they seem to our sight to be very small. Yet

they could not send any light to earth from the high heaven, if they were so small as they appear to our eyes. Truly the moon and all the stars receive light from the great sun, and none of them hath any rays but of the sun's rays.... The sun is typical of our Saviour Christ, who is the sun of righteousness, ... The moon that waxes and wanes is typical of the present congregation in which we are.... The bright stars are typical of the believers in God's congregation, who shine in good converse.... No one of us has any light of any goodness except by the grace of Christ, who is called the sun of true righteousness....

The moon has no light except from the sun's rays, and he is the lowest of all the planets, and therefore he enters the earth's shadow when he is full, yet not always on account of the broad circle which is called Zodiac, under which circle run the sun and moon and twelve celestial signs. Truly the moon's orb is always whole and perfect, although it does not shine always quite equally. Every day the moon's light is waxing or waning four points through the sun's light, and he goes daily either to the sun

SOURCE: From Thomas Wright, ed., *Popular Treatises on Science Written During the Middle Ages in Anglo-Saxon, Anglo-Norman, and English* (London: Historical Society of Science, 1841), pp. 1–19.

or from the sun so many points, not that he arrives at the sun, because the sun is much more elevated than the moon. Yet he comes before the sun, when he is heated by her. Always he turns his back to the sun, that is the round end which is there illuminated. We call it then new moon according to the custom of men, but he is always the same though his light often varies. The empty space above the atmosphere is ever shining with the heavenly stars. It happens sometimes when the moon runs on the same track that the sun runs, that his orb intercepts the sun's so much that she is all darkened, and the stars appear as by night. This happens seldom, and never but at new moon. By this is to be understood, that the moon is exceedingly large, since he can by his interposition darken the sun. . . .

All that is within the firmament is called the world. The firmament is the ethereal heaven, adorned with many stars; the heaven, and sea, and earth, are called the world. The firmament is always turning round about us, under this earth and above, and there is an incalculable space between it and the earth. Four and twenty hours have passed, that is one day and one night, before it is once turned round, and all the stars which are fixed in it turn round with it. The earth stands in the centre, by God's power so fixed that it never swerves either higher or lower than the Almighty Creator, who holds all things without labour, established it. . . .

Some men say that stars fall from heaven. But it is not stars that fall, but it is fire from the sky, which flies from the heavenly bodies as sparks do from fire. Certainly there are still as many stars in the heavens as there were at the beginning, when God made them. They are almost all fixed in the firmament, and will not fall thence while this world endures. The sun, and the moon, and the evening star, and the day star, and three other stars, are not fast in the firmament, but they have their own course severally. . . .

The atmosphere in which we live is one of the four elements in which every corporeal body dwells. There are four elements in which all earthly bodies dwell, which are, *aer, ignis, terra, aqua. Aer* is atmosphere; *ignis*, fire; *terra*, earth; *aqua*, water. Air is a very thin corporeal element; it goes over the whole world, and extends upwards nearly to the moon, in it fly fowls as fishes swim in the water. Not one of them could fly were it not for the air which bears them up; and no man or cattle has any breathing except by means of the air. The breath that we blow out and draw in is not our soul, but it is the air in which we live in this mortal life; as fishes die if they are out of the water, so also every earthly body dies if it be deprived of air. There is no corporeal thing which has not in it the four elements, that is, air, and fire, earth, and water. In every body are these four things. Take a stick, and rub on something, it becomes hot directly with the fire which lurks in it. Burn the one end, then goeth the moisture out at the other end with the smoke. So also our bodies have both heat and moisture, earth and air. The air of which we are speaking, rises up nearly to the moon, and supports all clouds and storms. The air when it is moved is wind. . . .

Rains come of the air through God's might. The atmosphere licks and draws up the moisture of all the earth, and of the sea, and gathers it into showers; and when it can bear no more, then it falls down loosed in rain, and dispersed sometimes by the winds in blasts, sometimes by the sun's heat. . . . It is, as we said before, that the atmosphere draws up from the earth and the sea all the moisture, which is turned to rain. The nature of the atmosphere is that she sucks all the water up to her. This may perceive he who will, how the moisture goes up similarly with smoke or with mist; and if it is salt from the sea, it is through the sun's heat and through the largeness of the atmosphere turned to fresh water. Truly God's might disposes all weathers, who regulates all things without difficulty. . . .

Thunder comes of heat and of moisture. The atmosphere draws the moisture to it from below, and the heat from above, and when they are gathered together, the heat and the moisture within the atmosphere strive with each other with fearful noise, and the fire bursts out through lightning, and injures the produce of the earth if it be greater than the moisture. If the moisture be greater than the fire, then it does good.

The hotter the summer, the more thunder and lightning in the year. . . . It is loud on account of the extent of the air, and dangerous on account of the shootings of the fire. Be this treatise here ended. God aid my hands!

## THOMAS AQUINAS, *Summa contra Gentiles* (1259–1264)

Thomas Aquinas defines the true nature of man's happiness and ultimate purpose.

Now the last end of man and of any intelligent substance is called happiness or beatitude; for it is this that every intelligent substance desires as its last end, and for its own sake alone. Therefore the last beatitude or happiness of any intelligent substance is to know God. . . .

[However] man's ultimate happiness does not consist in that knowledge of God whereby He is known by all or many in a vague kind of opinion, nor again in that knowledge of God whereby He is known in science through demonstration; nor in that knowledge whereby He is known through faith. . . . Seeing that it is not possible in this life to arrive at a higher knowledge of God in His essence, or at least so that we understand other separate substances, and thus know God through that which is nearest to Him, . . . and since we must place our ultimate happiness in some kind of knowledge of God, . . . it is impossible for man's happiness to be in this life.

Again. Man's last end is the term of his natural appetite, so that when he has obtained it, he desires nothing more: because if he still has a movement towards something, he has not yet reached an end wherein to be at rest. Now, this cannot happen in this life: since the more man understands, the more is the desire to understand increased in him — this being natural to men — unless perhaps someone

there be who understands all things: and in this life this never did nor can happen to anyone that was a mere man; seeing that in this life we are unable to know separate substances which in themselves are most intelligible. . . . Therefore man's ultimate happiness cannot possibly be in this life. . . .

Man cannot be wholly free from evils in this state of life; not only from evils of the body, such as hunger, thirst, heat, cold, and the like, but also from evils of the soul. For no one is there who at times is not disturbed by inordinate passion; who sometimes does not go beyond the mean, wherein virtue consists, either in excess or in deficiency; who is not deceived in some thing or another; or at least ignores what he would wish to know, or feels doubtful about an opinion of which he would like to be certain. Therefore no man is happy in this life. . . .

Again. The natural desire cannot be void; since *nature does nothing in vain*. But nature's desire would be void if it could never be fulfilled. Therefore man's natural desire can be fulfilled. But not in this life, as we have shown. Therefore it must be fulfilled after this life. Therefore man's ultimate happiness is after this life. . . . It is evident from what has been said, that in this happy state which results from the divine vision [a state of bliss], man's every desire is ful-

SOURCE: From Thomas Aquinas, *Summa contra Gentiles,* English Dominican Fathers, trans. (New York: Benziger Brothers, 1928), Vol. III, Pt. I, pp. 111–114, 148–150. By permission of Benziger Brothers.

filled . . . and his every end achieved. This is clear to anyone who considers man's various desires in kind.

There is a desire in man, as an intellectual being, to *know the truth*: and men pursue this desire by the study of the contemplative life. And this will be most clearly fulfilled in that vision, when the intellect by gazing on the First Truth will know all that it naturally desires to know, as we have proved above. . . .

Consequent to his life as a citizen, there are also certain goods that man needs for his civic actions. Such is *a position of honour*; through inordinate desire of which, men become proud and ambitious. Now by this [divine] vision men are raised to the highest position of honour, because in a way, they are united to God. . . .

There is another desirable thing consequent to the civic life, and this is *to be well known*; through inordinate desire of which men are said to be desirous of vain glory. Now by this vision the Blessed become well known, not in the opinion of men, who can both deceive and be deceived, but in the most true knowledge both of God and of all the Blessed. . . .

There is yet another desirable thing in the civic life, and this is *riches*; through inordinate desire of which men become illiberal and unjust. Now in that happy state there is a sufficiency of all goods: inasmuch as the Blessed enjoy him who contains the perfection of all goods. . . .

There is a third desire in man, common to him and other animals, namely the desire for *the enjoyment of pleasure*; and this men pursue especially by leading a voluptuous life, and through lack of moderation become intemperate and incontinent. Now in that vision there is the most perfect pleasure, all the more perfect than sensuous pleasure, as the intellect is above the senses; as the good in which we shall delight surpasses all sensible good, is more penetrating, and more continuously delightful; and as that pleasure is freer from all alloy of sorrow, or trouble of anxiety. . . . There is also the natural desire, common to all things, whereby all things seek to be preserved in their being, as far as possible; and through lack of moderation in this desire, men become timorous, and spare themselves overmuch in the matter of labour. This desire will be altogether fulfilled when the Blessed obtain perfect immortality, and security from all evil. . . . It is therefore evident that intellectual substances by seeing God attain to true beatitude, when their every desire is satisfied, and when there is a sufficiency of all good things, as is required for happiness. . . .

In this life there is nothing so like this ultimate and perfect happiness as the life of those who contemplate the truth, as far as possible here below. Hence the philosophers who were unable to obtain full knowledge of that final beatitude, placed man's ultimate happiness in that contemplation which is possible during this life. For this reason too, Holy Writ commends the contemplative rather than other forms of life. . . . For contemplation of truth begins in this life, but will be consummated in the life to come: while the active and civic life does not transcend the limits of this life.

## THOMAS AQUINAS, *On Kingship* (ca. 1260–1265)

Thomas Aquinas explains the purpose of society.

As long as man's mortal life endures there is an extrinsic good for him, namely, final beatitude which is looked for after death in the enjoyment of God, . . . Consequently the Christian man, for whom that beatitude has been purchased by the blood of Christ,

SOURCE: From Thomas Aquinas, *On Kingship: to the King of Cyprus*, Gerald R. Phelan, trans., revised by I. Th. Eschmann (Toronto, Canada: Pontifical Institute of Mediaeval Studies, 1949), pp. 59–60. By permission of the publisher.

and who, in order to attain it, has received the earnest[1] of the Holy Ghost, needs another and spiritual care to direct him to the harbour of eternal salvation, and this care is provided for the faithful by the ministers of the church of Christ.

Now the same judgment is to be formed about the end of society as a whole as about the end of one man. If, therefore, the ultimate end of man were some good that existed in himself, then the ultimate end of the multitude to be governed would likewise be for the multitude to acquire such good, and persevere in its possession. If such an ultimate end either of an individual man or a multitude were a corporeal one, namely, life and health of body, to govern would then be a physician's charge. If that ultimate end were an abundance of wealth, then knowledge of economics would have the last word in the community's government. If the good of the knowledge of truth were of such a kind that the multitude might attain to it, the king would have to be a teacher. It is, however, clear that the end of a multitude gathered together is to live virtuously. For men form a group for the purpose of living well together, a thing which the individual man living alone could not attain, and good life is virtuous life. Therefore, virtuous life is the end for which men gather together. The evidence for this lies in the fact that only those who render mutual assistance to one another in living well form a genuine part of an assembled multitude. If men assembled merely to live, then animals and slaves would form a part of the civil community. Or, if men assembled only to accrue wealth, then all those who traded together would belong to one city. Yet we see that only such are regarded as forming one multitude as are directed by the same laws and the same government to live well.

Yet through virtuous living man is further ordained to a higher end, which consists in the enjoyment of God, as we have said above. Consequently, since society must have the same end as the individual man, it is not the ultimate end of an assembled multitude to live virtuously, but through virtuous living to attain to the possession of God.

## *Chaucer's Parson and Plowman* (ca. 1387)

In the "Prologue" to the *Canterbury Tales*, Chaucer describes the ideal parson and ideal plowman.

**The Parson**

There was a Parson, too, that had his cure
In a small town, a good man and a poor;
But rich he was in holy thought and work.
Also he was a learned man, a clerk,
Seeking Christ's gospel faithfully to preach;
Most piously his people would he teach.
Benign and wondrous diligent was he,
And very patient in adversity —
Often had he been tried to desperation!
He would not make an excommunication
For tithes unpaid, but rather would
 he give —
Helping his poor parishioners to live —
From the offerings, or his own small
 property;
In little he would find sufficiency.
Broad was his parish, with houses far apart,
Yet come it rain or thunder he would start
Upon his rounds, in woe or sickness too,
And reach the farthest, poor or well-to-do,
Going on foot, his staff within his hand —

SOURCE: From *The Canterbury Tales: The Prologue and Four Tales with the Book of the Duchess and Six Lyrics by Geoffrey Chaucer* by Frank E. Hill, copyright by Frank E. Hill © 1935, published by Longman's Green and reprinted by permission of The David McKay Co., Inc.

[1] promise

Example that his sheep could understand —
Namely, that first he wrought and after
    taught.
These words from holy gospel he had
    brought,
And used to add this metaphor thereto —
That if gold rust, what then shall iron do?
For if the priest be bad, in whom we trust,
What wonder is it if a layman rust?
And shame to him — happy the priest who
    heeds it —
Whose flock is clean when he is soiled who
    leads it!
Surely a priest should good example give,
Showing by cleanness how his sheep
    should live.
He would not put his benefice to hire,
Leaving his sheep entangled in the mire,
While he ran off to London, to Saint Paul's,
To take an easy berth, chanting for souls,
Or with some guild a sinecure to hold,
But stayed at home and safely kept his fold
From wolves that else had sent it
    wandering;
He was a shepherd and no hireling.
And virtue though he loved, and holiness,
To sinful men he was not pitiless,
Nor was he stern or haughty in his speech,
But wisely and benignly would he teach.
To tempt folk unto heaven by high endeavor
And good example was his purpose ever.

But any person who was obstinate,
Whoever he was, of high or low estate,
Him on occasion would he sharply chide;
No better priest doth anywhere reside.
He had no thirst for pomp or reverence,
Nor bore too sensitive a consciënce,
But taught Christ's and his twelve apostles'
    creed,
And first in living of it took the lead.

**The Plowman**

With him his brother, a simple Plowman,
    rode,
That in his time had carted many a load
Of dung; true toiler and a good was he,
Living in peace and perfect charity.
First he loved God, with all his heart
    and will,
Always, and whether life went well or ill;
And next — and as himself — he loved his
    neighbor.
And always for the poor he loved to labor,
And he would thresh and ditch and dyke,
    and take
Nothing for pay, but do it for Christ's sake.
Fairly he paid his tithes when they
    were due,
Upon his goods and on his produce, too.
In plowman's gown he sat astride a mare.

## Our Lady's Tumbler

"Our Lady's Tumbler" is a tale, still told, about God's mercy and man's faith. It
concerns the story of an illiterate acrobat, surrounded by learned monks
ceaselessly working for God, who asks himself how he, a mere tumbler, can
do anything pleasing to God.

Amongst the lives of the ancient Fathers, wherein may be found much profitable matter, this story is told for a true example, I do not say that you may not often have heard a fairer story, but at least this is not to be despised, and is well worth the telling. Now therefore will I say and narrate what chanced to this minstrel.

He erred up and down, to and fro, so often and in so many places, that he took

SOURCE: From Eugene Mason, trans., *Aucassin and Nicolette and Other Mediaeval Romances and Legends*. An Everyman's Library Series (New York and London: 1958), pp. 59–73. Reprinted by permission of E. P. Dutton and J. M. Dent & Sons Ltd., publishers.

the whole world in despite,[2] and sought rest in a certain Holy Order. Horses and raiment and money, yea, all that he had, he straightway put from him, and seeking shelter from the world, was firmly set never to put foot within it more. For this cause he took refuge in this Holy Order, amongst the monks of Clairvaux. Now, though this dancer was comely of face and shapely of person, yet when he had once entered the monastery he found that he was master of no craft practised therein. In the world he had gained his bread by tumbling and dancing and feats of address. To leap, to spring, such matters he knew well, but of greater things he knew nothing, for he had never spelled from book — nor Paternoster, nor canticle, nor creed, nor Hail Mary, nor aught concerning his soul's salvation. . . .

The tumbler moved amongst his fellows like a man ashamed, for he had neither part nor lot in all the business of the monastery, and for this he was right sad and sorrowful. He saw the monks and the penitents about him, each serving God, in this place and that, according to his office and degree. He marked the priests at their ritual before the altars; the deacons at the gospels; the sub-deacons at the epistles; and the ministers about the vigils. . . . Yea, and the most ignorant amongst them yet can pray his Paternoster. . . . Then he said, "Holy Mary, . . . What do I here! Here there is none so mean or vile but who serves God in his office and degree, save only me, for I work not, neither can I preach. Caitif[3] and shamed was I when I thrust myself herein, seeing that I can do nothing well, either in labour or in prayer. I see my brothers upon their errands, one behind the other; but I do naught but fill my belly with the meat that they provide. If they perceive this thing, certainly shall I be in an evil case, for they will cast me out amongst the dogs, and none will take pity on the glutton and the idle man. . . ."

Driven mad with thoughts such as these, he wandered about the abbey until he found himself within the crypt, and took sanctuary by the altar, crouching close as he was able. Above the altar was carved the statue of Madame St. Mary. Truly his steps had not erred when he sought that refuge; nay, but rather, God who knows His own had led him thither by the hand. When he heard the bells ring for Mass he sprang to his feet all dismayed. "Ha!" said he; "now am I betrayed. Each adds his mite to the great offering, save only me. Like a tethered ox, naught I do but chew the cud, and waste good victuals on a useless man. Shall I speak my thought? Shall I work my will? By the Mother of God, thus am I set to do. None is here to blame. I will do that which I can, and honour with my craft the Mother of God in her monastery. Since others honour her with chant, then I will serve with tumbling."

He takes off his cowl, and removes his garments, placing them near the altar, but so that his body be not naked he dons a tunic, very thin and fine, of scarce more substance than a shirt. So, light and comely of body, with gown girt closely about his loins, he comes before the Image right humbly. Then raising his eyes, "Lady," said he, "to your fair charge I give my body and my soul. Sweet Queen, sweet Lady, scorn not the thing I know, for with the help of God I will essay[4] to serve you in good faith, even as I may. I cannot read your Hours nor chant your praise, but at the least I can set before you what art I have. Now will I be as the lamb that plays and skips before his mother. Oh, Lady, who art nowise bitter to those who serve you with a good intent, that which thy servant is, that he is for you."

Then commenced he his merry play, leaping low and small, tall and high, over and under. Then once more he knelt upon his knees before the statue, and meekly bowed his head. "Ha!" said he, "most gracious Queen, of your pity and your charity scorn not this my service." Again he leaped and played, and for holiday and festival, made

---

[2] contempt    [3] cowardly    [4] try

the somersault of Metz. Again he bowed before the Image, did reverence, and paid it all the honour that he might. Afterwards he did the French vault, then the vault of Champagne, then the Spanish vault, then the vaults they love in Brittany, then the vault of Lorraine, and all these feats he did as best he was able. Afterwards he did the Roman vault, and then, with hands before his brow, danced daintily before the altar, gazing with a humble heart at the statue of God's Mother. "Lady," said he, "I set before you a fair play. This travail I do for you alone; so help me God, for you, Lady, and your Son. Think not I tumble for my own delight; but I serve you, and look for no other guerdon[5] on my carpet. My brothers serve you, yea, and so do I. Lady, scorn not your villein, for he toils for your good pleasure; and, Lady, you are my delight and the sweetness of the world." Then he walked on his two hands, with his feet in the air, and his head near the ground. He twirled with his feet, and wept with his eyes. "Lady," said he, "I worship you with heart, with body, feet and hands, for this I can neither add to nor take away. Now am I your very minstrel. Others may chant your praises in the church but here in the crypt will I tumble for your delight. Lady, lead me truly in your way, and for the love of God hold me not in utter despite." . . . Then when the chants rose louder from the choir, he, too, forced the note, and put forward all his skill. So long as the priest was about that Mass, so long his flesh endured to dance, and leap and spring, till at the last, nigh fainting, he could stand no longer upon his feet, but fell for weariness on the ground. From head to heel sweat stood upon him, drop by drop, as blood falls from meat turning upon the hearth. "Lady," said he, "I can no more, but truly will I seek you again." . . .

In this fashion passed many days, for at every Hour he sought the crypt to do service, and pay homage before the Image. His service was so much to his mind that never once was he too weary to set out his most cunning feats to distract the Mother of God, nor did he ever wish for other play than this. Now, doubtless, the monks knew well enough that day by day he sought the crypt, but not a man on earth — save God alone — was aware of aught that passed there; neither would he, for all the wealth of the world, have let his goings in be seen, save by the Lord his God alone. For truly he believed that were his secret once espied he would be hunted from the cloister, and flung once more into the foul, sinful world, and for his part he was more fain to fall on death than to suffer any taint of sin. But God considering his simplicity, his sorrow for all he had wrought amiss, and the love which moved him to this deed, would that this toil should be known; and the Lord willed that the work of His friend should be made plain to men, for the glory of the Mother whom he worshipped, and so that all men should know and hear, and receive that God refuses none who seeks His face in love, however low his degree, save only he love God and strive to do His will. . . .

Thus things went well with this good man for a great space. For more years than I know the count of, he lived greatly at his ease, but the time came when the good man was sorely vexed, for a certain monk thought upon him, and blamed him in his heart that he was never set in choir for Matins. The monk marvelled much at his absence, and said within himself that he would never rest till it was clear what manner of man this was, and how he spent the Hours, and for what service the convent gave him bread. So he spied and pried and followed, till he marked him plainly, sweating at his craft in just such fashion as you have heard. "By my faith," said he, "this is a merry jest, and a fairer festival than we observe altogether. Whilst others are at prayers, and about the business of the House, this tumbler dances daintily, as though one had given him a hundred silver

---

[5] reward

marks. He prides himself on being so nimble of foot, and thus he repays us what he owes. Truly it is this for that; we chant for him, and he tumbles for us. We throw him largesse: he doles us alms. We weep his sins, and he dries our eyes. Would that the monastery could see him, as I do, with their very eyes; willingly therefore would I fast till Vespers. Not one could refrain from mirth at the sight of this simple fool doing himself to death with his tumbling, for on himself he has no pity. Since his folly is free from malice, may God grant it to him as penance. Certainly I will not impute it to him as sin, for in all simplicity and good faith, I firmly believe, he does this thing, so that he may deserve his bread." So the monk saw with his very eyes how the tumbler did service at all the Hours, without pause or rest, and he laughed with pure mirth and delight, for in his heart was joy and pity.

The monk went straight to the Abbot and told him the thing from beginning to end, just as you have heard. The Abbot got him on his feet, and said to the monk, "By holy obedience I bid you hold your peace, and tell not this tale abroad against your brother. I lay on you my strict command to speak of this matter to none, save me. Come now, we will go forthwith to see what this can be, and let us pray the Heavenly King, and His very sweet, dear Mother, so precious and so bright, that in her gentleness she will plead with her Son, her Father, and her Lord, that I may look on this work — if thus it pleases Him — so that the good man be not wrongly blamed, and that God may be the more beloved, yet so that thus is His good pleasure." Then they secretly sought the crypt, and found a privy place near the altar, where they could see and yet not be seen. From there the Abbot and his monk marked the business of the penitent. They saw the vaults he varied so cunningly, his nimble leaping and his dancing, his salutations of Our Lady, and his springing and his bounding, till he was nigh to faint. So weak was he that he sank on the ground, all outworn, and the sweat

fell from his body upon the pavement of the crypt. But presently, in this his need, came she, his refuge, to his aid. Well she knew that guileless heart.

Whilst the Abbot looked, forthwith there came down from the vault a Dame so glorious, that certainly no man had seen one so precious, nor so richly crowned. She was more beautiful than the daughters of men, and her vesture was heavy with gold and gleaming stones. In her train came the hosts of Heaven, angel and archangel also; and these pressed close about the minstrel, and solaced and refreshed him. When their shining ranks drew near, peace fell upon his heart; for they contended to do him service, and were the servants of the servitor of that Dame who is the rarest Jewel of God. Then the sweet and courteous Queen herself took a white napkin in her hand, and with it gently fanned her minstrel before the altar. Courteous and debonair, the Lady refreshed his neck, his body and his brow. Meekly she served him as a handmaid in his need. But these things were hidden from the good man, for he neither saw nor knew that about him stood so fair a company.

The holy angels honour him greatly, but they can no longer stay, for their Lady turns to go. She blesses her minstrel with the sign of God, and the holy angels throng about her, still gazing back with delight upon their companion, for they await the hour when God shall release him from the burden of the world, and they possess his soul.

This marvel the Abbot and his monk saw at least four times, and thus at each Hour came the Mother of God with aid and succour for her man. Never doth she fail her servants in their need. Great joy had the Abbot that this thing was made plain to him. But the monk was filled with shame, since God had shown His pleasure in the service of His poor fool. His confusion burnt him like fire. "Dominus," said he to the Abbot, "grant me grace. Certainly this is a holy man, and since I have judged him amiss, it is very right that my body should smart. Give me now fast or vigil or the scourge, for without question he is a saint. We are witnesses to the whole matter, nor is it possible that we can be deceived." But the Abbot replied, "You speak truly, for God has made us to know that He has bound him with the cords of love. So I lay my commandment upon you, in virtue of obedience, and under pain of your person, that you tell no word to any man of that you have seen, save to God alone and me." "Lord," said he, "thus I will do." On these words they turned them, and hastened from the crypt; and the good man, having brought his tumbling to an end, presently clothed himself in his habit, and joyously went his way to the monastery.

Thus time went and returned, till it chanced that in a little while the Abbot sent for him who was so filled with virtue. When he heard that he was bidden of the Abbot, his heart was sore with grief, for he could think of nothing profitable to say. "Alas!" said he, "I am undone; not a day of my days but I shall know misery and sorrow and shame, for well I trow[6] that my service is not pleasing to God. Alas! plainly doth He show that it displeases Him, since He causes the truth to be made clear. Could I believe that such work and play as mine could give delight to the mighty God! . . ." He came before the Abbot, with the tears yet wet upon his cheeks, and he was still weeping when he knelt upon the ground. "Lord," prayed he, "for the love of God deal not harshly with me. Would you send me from your door? Tell me what you would have me do, and thus it shall be done." Then replied the Abbot, "Answer me truly. Winter and summer have you lived here for a great space; now, tell me, what service have you given, and how have you deserved your bread?" "Alas!" said the tumbler, "well I knew that quickly I should be put upon the street when once this business was heard of you, and that you would keep me no more, Lord," said he, "I take my leave. Miserable I am, and miserable shall I ever be. Never yet have I made

a penny for all my juggling." But the Abbot answered, "Not so said I; but I ask and require of you — nay, more, by virtue of holy obedience I command you — to seek within your conscience and tell me truly by what craft you have furthered the business of our monastery." "Lord," cried he, "now have you slain me, for this commandment is a sword." Then he laid bare before the Abbot the story of his days, from the first thing to the last, whatsoever pain it cost him. . . .

The holy Abbot leaned above him, and, all in tears, raised him up, kissing both his eyes. "Brother," said he, "hold now your peace, for I make with you this true covenant, that you shall ever be of our monastery. God grant, rather, that we may be of yours, for all the worship you have brought to ours. I and you will call each other friend. Fair, sweet brother, pray you for me, and I for my part will pray for you. And now I pray you, my sweet friend, and lay this bidding upon you, without pretence, that you continue to do your service, even as you were wont heretofore — yea, and with greater craft yet, if so you may." "Lord," said he, "truly is this so?" "Yea," said the Abbot, "and verily." . . . Theretofore with a good heart he went about his service without rest, and Matins and Vespers, night and day, he missed no Hour till he became too sick to perform his office. So sore was his sickness upon him that he might not rise from his bed. Marvellous was the shame he proved when no more was he able to pay his rent. This was the grief that lay the heaviest upon him, for of his sickness he spake never a word, but he feared greatly lest he should fall from grace since he travailed no longer at his craft. He reckoned himself an idle man, and prayed God to take him to Himself before the sluggard might come to blame. . . . The holy Abbot does him all honour; he and his monks chant the Hours about his bed, . . .

---

[6] trust

The Abbot was in that cell with all his monks; there, too, was company of many a priest and many a canon. These all humbly watched the dying man, and saw with open eyes this wonder happen. Clear to their very sight, about that lowly bed, stood the Mother of God, with angel and archangel, to wait the passing of his soul. Over against them were set, like wild beasts, devils and the Adversary, so they might snatch his spirit. I speak not to you in parable. But little profit had they for all their coming, their waiting, and their straining on the leash. Never might they have part in such a soul as his. When the soul took leave of his body, it fell not in their hands at all, for the Mother of God gathered it to her bosom, and the holy angels thronging round, choired for joy, as the bright train swept to Heaven with its burthen, according to the will of God. . . .

Thus with great honour they laid him to his rest, and kept his holy body amongst them as a relic. At that time spake the Abbot plainly to their ears, telling them the story of this tumbler and of all his life, just as you have heard, and of all that he himself beheld within the crypt. No brother but kept awake during that sermon. . . .

Thus endeth the story of the minstrel. Fair was his tumbling, fair was his service, for thereby gained he such high honour as is above all earthly gain. . . . Now, therefore, let us pray to God — He Who is above all other — that He may grant us so to do such faithful service that we may win the guerdon of His love.

Here endeth the Tumbler of Our Lady.

## WILLIAM OF MALMESBURY's *Description of Stephen Harding and the Founding of the Cistertian Order* (ca. 1100)

Stephen Harding was what we today would describe as an alienated personality, a man who could find no spiritual solace in the existing monastic way of life. Therefore, he established his own foundation (the Cistertian) at Citeaux in Burgundy in 1098. When St. Bernard of Clairvaux joined the community in the early twelfth century, the Cistertians became the most advanced monastic order in Europe. By 1115 Citeaux had four sister houses; by 1200 the four had grown to nearly 500.

In his[7] time began the Cistertian order, which is now both believed and asserted to be the surest road to heaven. To speak of this does not seem irrelevant to the work I have undertaken, since it redounds to the glory of England to have produced the distinguished man who was the author and promoter of that rule. To us he belonged, and in our schools passed the earlier part of his life. . . . He was named Harding,[8] and [was] born in England of no very illustrious parents. From his early years, he was a monk at Sherborne; but when secular desires had captivated his youth, he grew disgusted with the monastic garb, and went first to Scotland, and afterwards to France. Here, after some years' exercise in the liberal arts, he became awakened to the love of God. . . . Returning into Burgundy, he was shorn at Molesmes, a new and magnificent monastery.[9] Here he readily admitted the first elements of the order, as he had formerly seen them; but when additional matters were proposed for his observance, such as he had neither read in the rule nor seen elsewhere, he began, modestly and as became a monk, to ask the reason of them, saying: "By reason the supreme

SOURCE: From J. A. Giles, ed., *William of Malmesbury's Chronicle of the Kings of England* (London: George Bell and Sons, 1911), pp. 347–351.

7 William II died in 1100   8 d. 1134   9 i.e., he entered the monastery

Creator has made all things; by reason he governs all things; by reason the fabric of the world revolves; by reason even the planets move; by reason the elements are directed; and by reason, and by due regulation, our nature ought to conduct itself. But since, through sloth, she too often departs from reason, many laws were, long ago, enacted for her use; and, latterly, a divine rule has been promulgated by St. Benedict, to bring back the deviations of nature to reason. In this, though some things are contained the design of which I cannot fathom, yet I deem it necessary to yield to authority. And though reason and the authority of the holy writers may seem at variance, yet still they are one and the same. For since God hath created and restored nothing without reason, how can I believe that the holy fathers, no doubt strict followers of God, could command anything but what was reasonable, as if we ought to give credit to their bare authority. See then that you bring reason, or at least authority, for what you devise. . . .

Sentiments of this kind, spreading as usual from one to another, justly moved the hearts of such as feared God, "lest haply they should or had run in vain." The subject, then, being canvassed in frequent chapters, ended by bringing over the abbat himself to the opinion that all superfluous matters should be passed by, and merely the essence of the rule be scrutinized. Two of the fraternity, therefore, of equal faith and learning, were elected, who, by vicarious examination, were to discover the intention of the founder's rule; and when they had discovered it, to propound it to the rest. The abbat diligently endeavored to induce the whole convent to give their concurrence, but "as it is difficult to eradicate from men's minds, what has early taken root, since they reluctantly relinquish the first notions they have imbibed," almost the whole of them refused to accept the new regulations, be-

cause they were attached to the old. Eighteen only, among whom was Harding, otherwise called Stephen, persevering in their holy determination, together with their abbat, left the monastery, declaring that the purity of the institution could not be preserved in a place where riches and gluttony warred against even the heart that was well inclined. They came therefore to Citeaux; a situation formerly covered with woods, but now so conspicuous from the abundant piety of its monks, that it is not undeservedly esteemed conscious of the Divinity himself. Here, by the countenance of the archbishop of Vienne, who is now pope, they entered on a labour worthy to be remembered and venerated to the end of time.

Certainly many of their regulations seem severe, and more particularly these: they wear nothing made with furs or linen, nor even that finely spun linen garment, which we call Staminium;[10] neither breeches, unless when sent on a journey, which at their return they wash and restore. They have two tunics with cowls, but no additional garment in winter, though, if they think fit, in summer they may lighten their garb. They sleep clad and girded, and never after matins return to their beds: but they so order the time of matins that it shall be light ere the lauds[11] begin; so intent are they on their rule, that they think no jot or tittle[12] of it should be disregarded. Directly after these hymns they sing the prime, after which they go out to work for stated hours. They complete whatever labour or service they have to perform by day without any other light. No one is ever absent from the daily services, or from complines,[13] except the sick. The cellarer[14] and hospitaller,[15] after complines, wait upon the guests, yet observing the strictest silence. The abbat allows himself no indulgence beyond the others, — everywhere present, — everywhere attending to his flock; except that he does not eat with the rest, because his table is

---

[10] woolen shirt   [11] the concluding psalms of the matin service   [12] the least bit   [13] prayers   [14] the keeper of provisions   [15] the person who is in charge of the sick and needy

with the strangers and the poor. Nevertheless, be he where he may, he is equally sparing of food and of speech; for never more than two dishes are served either to him or to his company; lard and meat never but to the sick. From the Ides of September till Easter, through regard for whatever festival, they do not take more than one meal a day, except on Sunday. They never leave the cloister but for the purpose of labour, nor do they ever speak, either there or elsewhere, save only to the abbat or prior. . . . While they bestow care on the stranger and the sick, they inflict intolerable mortifications on their own bodies, for the health of their souls.

The abbat, at first, both encountered these privations with much alacrity himself, and compelled the rest to do the same. In process of time, however, the man repented; he had been delicately brought up, and could not well bear such continued scantiness of diet. The monks, whom he had left at Molesmes, getting scent of this disposition, either by messages or letters, for it is uncertain which, drew him back to the monastery, . . . He left the narrow confines of poverty, and resought his former magnificence. All followed him from Citeaux, who had gone thither with him, except eight. These, few in number but great in virtue, appointed Alberic, one of their party, abbat, and Stephen prior. The former not surviving more than eight years was, at the will of heaven, happily called away. Then, doubtless by God's appointment, Stephen though absent was elected abbat, the original con-

triver of the whole scheme, the especial and celebrated ornament of our times. Sixteen abbeys which he has already completed, and seven which he has begun, are sufficient testimonies of his abundant merit. Thus, by the resounding trumpet of God, he directs the people around him, both by word and deed, to heaven; acting fully up to his own precepts; affable in speech, pleasant in look, and with a mind always rejoicing in the Lord. . . . He receives much, indeed, but expending little on his own wants, or those of his flock, he distributes the rest to the poor, or employs it immediately on the building of monasteries; for the purse of Stephen is the public treasury of the indigent. A proof of his abstinence is that you see nothing there, as in other monasteries, flaming with gold, blazing with jewels, or glittering with silver. For as a Gentile says, "Of what use is gold to a saint?" . . . Moreover, if at any time the laudable kindness of the abbat either desires, or feigns a desire, to modify aught from the strict letter of the rule, they are ready to oppose such indulgence, saying, that they have no long time to live, nor shall they continue to exist so long as they have already done; that they hope to remain stedfast in their purpose to the end, and to be an example to their successors, who will transgress if they should give way. . . . But to comprise, briefly, all things which are or can be said of them, — the Cistertian monks at the present day are a model for all monks, a mirror for the diligent, a spur to the indolent. . . .

EDWARD GRIM, *Account of the Martyrdom of Thomas à Becket* (1170)

Thomas à Becket (1118?–1170) was Henry II's friend, confidente, and Lord Chancellor when the King appointed him Archbishop of Canterbury in the expectation that he would bring the church to heel as successfully as he had brought the baronage under royal control when he was Lord Chancellor. Much to the King's surprise, however, Becket took an extreme pro-church stand and refused to accept the Constitutions of Clarendon. This led to a prolonged struggle between the two men, and Becket fled into exile for six years. The bitterness between the two was made worse by a further controversy over the coronation of Henry II's son as king of England. After a patched-up truce, Becket returned from exile in 1170 and promptly excommunicated the bishops who had attended upon that coronation; Henry II is said to have exclaimed on hearing the news: "Will no one rid me of this turbulent priest!" Four knights took him at his word and arrived at Canterbury on the evening of December 29, 1170. Edward Grim picks up the story from there.

---

When the holy archbishop entered the church the monks stopped vespers which they had begun and . . . they hastened, by bolting the doors of the church, to protect their shepherd from the slaughter. But the champion, turning to them, ordered the church doors to be thrown open, saying: "It is not meet to make a fortress of the house of prayer, the church of Christ: though it be not shut up it is able to protect its own; and we shall triumph over the enemy rather in suffering than in fighting, for we came to suffer, not to resist." And straightway they [the four knights and a clerk] entered the house of peace and reconciliation with swords sacrilegiously drawn, causing horror to the beholders by their very looks and the clanging of their arms.

All who were present were in tumult and fright, for those who had been singing vespers now ran hither to the dreadful spectacle.

Inspired by fury the knights called out, "Where is Thomas Becket, traitor to the king and realm?" As he answered not, they cried out the more furiously, "Where is the archbishop?" At this, intrepid and fearless, . . . he descended from the stair where he had been dragged by the monks in fear of the knights, and in a clear voice answered: "I am here, no traitor to the king, but a priest. Why do ye seek me?" And whereas he had already said that he feared them not, he added, "So I am ready to suffer in His name, who redeemed me by His blood; be it far from me to flee from your swords or to depart from justice." Having thus said, he turned to the right, under a pillar, having on one side the altar of the Blessed Mother of God and ever Virgin Mary, on the other that of St. Benedict the Confessor, by whose example and prayers, having crucified the world with its lusts, he bore all that the murderers could do, with such constancy of soul as if he had been no longer in the flesh.

The murderers followed him. "Absolve," they cried, "and restore to communion those whom you have excommunicated, and restore their powers to those whom you have suspended." He answered, "There has been no satisfaction, and I will not absolve them." "Then you shall die," they cried, "and receive what you deserve." "I am ready," he replied, "to die for my Lord, that in my blood the church may obtain liberty and peace. But in the name of Almighty God I forbid you to hurt my people, whether clerk or lay." Thus piously and thoughtfully did the noble martyr provide that no one near him should be hurt or the innocent be brought to death, whereby his glory should be dimmed as he hastened to Christ. Thus did it become the martyr knight to follow in the footsteps of his Captain and Saviour, who, when the wicked sought Him, said, "If ye seek me, let these go their way."

Then they laid sacrilegious hands on him, pulling and dragging him that they might kill him outside the church, or carry him away a prisoner, as they afterwards confessed. But when he would not be forced away from the pillar, one of them pressed on him and clung to him more closely. Him he pushed off, calling him "pander,[16]" and saying, "Touch me not, Reginald; you owe me fealty and subjection; you and your

---

SOURCE: From Edward P. Cheyney, *Readings in English History Drawn from the Original Sources* (New York: Ginn & Co., 1908), pp., 155–158.

[16] a pimp

accomplices act like madmen." The knight, fired with terrible rage at this severe rebuke, waved his sword over the sacred head. "No faith," he cried, "nor subjection do I owe you against my fealty to my lord the king." Then the unconquered martyr, seeing the hour at hand which should put an end to this miserable life, and give him straightway the crown of immortality promised by the Lord, inclined his head as one who prays, and, joining his hands, lifted them up and commended his cause and that of the church to God, to St. Mary, and to the blessed martyr Denys. Scarce had he said the words when the wicked knight, fearing lest the archbishop should be rescued by the people and escape alive, leapt upon him suddenly and wounded this lamb who was sacrificed to God, on the head, cutting off the top of the crown which the sacred unction of the chrism[17] had dedicated to God; and by the same blow he wounded the arm of him who tells this. For he, when the others, both monks and clerks, fled, stuck close to the sainted archbishop and held him in his arms till the arm he interposed was almost severed. . . .

Then he received a second blow on the head, but still stood firm. At the third blow he fell on his knees and elbows, offering himself a living victim, and saying in a low voice, "For the name of Jesus and the protection of the church I am ready to embrace death." Then the third knight inflicted a terrible wound as he lay, by which the sword was broken against the pavement, and the crown, which was large, was separated from the head; so that the blood white with the brain, and the brain red with blood, dyed the surface of the virgin mother church with the life and death of the confessor and martyr in the colors of the lily and the rose.

The fourth knight prevented any from interfering, so that the others might freely perpetrate the murder. In order that a fifth blow might not be wanting to the martyr who was in other things like to Christ, the fifth (no knight, but that clerk who had entered with the knights) put his foot on the neck of the holy priest and precious martyr, and, horrible to say, scattered his brains and blood over the pavement, calling out to the others, "Let us away, knights; he will rise no more."

THOMAS AQUINAS, *Of Cheating, Which Is Committed in Buying and Selling* ( 1266–1273 )

Thomas Aquinas discusses the spiritual risk involved in buying and selling.

### First Article: Whether It Is Lawful to Sell a Thing for More Than Its Worth?

*We proceed thus to the First Article.*

It would seem that it is lawful to sell a thing for more than its worth. In the commutations of human life, civil laws determine that which is just. Now according to these laws it is just for buyer and seller to deceive one another; and this occurs by the seller selling a thing for more than its worth, and the buyer buying a thing for less than its worth.

Therefore, it is lawful to sell a thing for more than its worth.

Further, that which is common to all would seem to be natural and not sinful. Now Augustine relates that the saying of a certain jester was accepted by all. "You wish to buy for a song and to sell at a premium." . . .

Further, it does not seem unlawful if that which honesty demands be done by mutual agreement. Now, according to the philosopher [Aristotle] in the friendship which is

---

SOURCE: From Thomas Aquinas, *Summa Theologica*, English Dominican Fathers, trans. ( New York: Benziger Brothers, 1948), Vol. II, Pt. II, Question 77, Articles 1 and 4, pp. 317–328.

17 anointing with a consecrated oil

based on utility, the amount of recompense for a favor received should depend on the utility accruing to the receiver; and this utility sometimes is worth more than the thing given, for instance if the receiver be in great need of that thing, whether for the purpose of avoiding a danger, or of deriving some particular benefit. Therefore, in contracts of buying and selling, it is lawful to give a thing in return for more than its worth.

On the contrary, it is written: "All things . . . whatsoever you would that men should do to you, do you also to them." But no man wishes to buy a thing for more than its worth. Therefore, no man should sell a thing to another man for more than its worth.

I answer that, it is altogether sinful to have recourse to deceit in order to sell a thing for more than its just price, because this is to deceive one's neighbor so as to injure him. . . .

But, apart from fraud, we may speak of buying and selling in two ways. First, as considered in themselves and from this point of view, buying and selling seem to be established for the common advantage of both parties, one of whom requires that which belongs to the other, and vice versa, as the Philosopher states. Now whatever is established for the common advantage should not be more of a burden to one party than to another, and consequently all contracts between them should observe equality of thing and thing. . . . Therefore, if either the price exceed the quantity of the thing's worth or, conversely, the thing exceed the price, there is no longer the equality of justice; and consequently, to sell a thing for more than its worth, or to buy it for less than its worth, is in itself unjust and unlawful.

Secondly, we may speak of buying and selling, considered as accidentally tending to the advantage of one party and to the disadvantage of the other: for instance, when a man has great need of a certain thing, while another man will suffer if he

be without it. In such a case the just price will depend not only on the thing sold but on the loss which the sale brings on the seller. And thus, it will be lawful to sell a thing for more than it is worth in itself, though the price paid be not more than it is worth to the owner. Yet if the one man derive a great advantage by becoming possessed of the other man's property, and the seller be not at a loss through being without that thing, the latter ought not to raise the price, because the advantage accruing to the buyer is not due to the seller, but to a circumstance affecting the buyer. Now no man should sell what is not his, though he may charge for the loss he suffers.

On the other hand, if a man find that he derives great advantage from something he has bought, he may, of his own accord, pay the seller something over and above; and this pertains to his honesty.

Human law is given to the people among whom there are many lacking virtue, and it is not given to the virtuous alone. Hence human law was unable to forbid all that is contrary to virtue, and it suffices for it to prohibit whatever is destructive of human intercourse, while it treats other matters as though they were lawful, not by approving of them but by not punishing them. Accordingly, if without employing deceit the seller disposes of his goods for more than their worth, or the buyer obtain them for less than their worth, the law looks upon this as licit,[18] and provides no punishment for so doing, unless the excess be too great, because then even human law demands restitution to be made: for instance, if a man be deceived in regard of more than half the amount of the just price of a thing.

On the other hand, the Divine law leaves nothing unpunished that is contrary to virtue. Hence, according to the Divine law, it is reckoned unlawful if the equality of justice be not observed in buying and selling, and he who has received more than he ought must make compensation to him that has suffered loss, if the loss be considerable.

---

[18] legal

I add this condition because the just price of things is not fixed with mathematical precision, but depends on a kind of estimate, so that a slight addition or subtraction would not seem to destroy the equality of justice. . . .

**Fourth Article: Whether, in Trading, It Is Lawful to Sell a Thing at a Higher Price Than What Was Paid for It?**

*We proceed thus to the Fourth Article.*

It would seem that it is not lawful, in trading, to sell a thing for a higher price than we paid for it. . . . Further, it is contrary to justice to sell goods at a higher price than their worth, or to buy them for less than their value. Now if you sell a thing for a higher price than you paid for it, you must either have bought it for less than its value or sell it for more than its value. Therefore, this cannot be done without sin. . . .

I answer that a tradesman is one whose business consists in the exchange of things. According to the Philosopher exchange of things is twofold: one, natural as it were, and necessary, whereby one commodity is exchanged for another, or money taken in exchange for a commodity, in order to satisfy the needs of life. Such like trading, properly speaking, does not belong to tradesmen but rather to housekeepers or civil servants who have to provide the household or the state with the necessaries of life. The other kind of exchange is either that of money for money, or of any commodity for money, not on account of the necessities of life but for profit, and this kind of exchange, properly speaking, regards tradesmen, according to the Philosopher. The former kind of exchange is commendable because it supplies a natural need; but the latter is justly deserving of blame because, considered in itself, it satisfies the greed for gain, which knows no limit and tends to infinity. Hence, trading, considered in itself, has a certain debasement attaching thereto, in so far as, by its very nature, it does not imply a virtuous or necessary end. Nevertheless, gain which is the end of trading, though not implying, by its nature, anything virtuous or necessary, does not, in itself, connote anything sinful or contrary to virtue. Wherefore nothing prevents gain from being directed to some necessary or even virtuous end and thus trading becomes lawful. Thus, for instance, a man may intend the moderate gain which he seeks to acquire by trading for the upkeep of his household, or for the assistance of the needy; or again, a man may take to trade for some public advantage — for instance, lest his country lack the necessaries of life — and seek gain, not as an end, but as payment for his labor. . . .

## FURTHER DISCUSSION QUESTIONS

### An Anglo-Saxon Manual of Astronomy

1. To what extent is this description of the universe anthropomorphic?
2. It is sometimes said that the trouble with medieval science and astronomy is that they were too empirical: scientists believed what they saw. Is there any evidence for this assertion in the manual?
3. What astronomical movements did the author clearly understand? What did he confuse and why?

### Thomas Aquinas, Summa contra Gentiles

1. What is man's final end? Why is it impossible for man's ultimate happiness to be here on earth?
2. What is the ideal life on earth?

3. How does Aquinas' view of religion compare and contrast with that found in Chapter 1.

### Thomas Aquinas, On Kingship

1. What is the end of society? Has that end changed since the medieval period?
2. What is Aquinas' definition of the "good life"?

### Geoffrey Chaucer, The Canterbury Tales

1. What characteristics of the parson and the plowman make them so remarkable?

### Our Lady's Tumbler

1. What is the vocation most pleasing to the Virgin?
2. What was the message for the average medieval person in this story?
3. What does the story show about the position of the monastic ideal in medieval society?
4. How does the approach to religion compare with that found in Chapter 1?

### William of Malmesbury's Description of the Cistertian Order

1. What was it that Harding objected to about the monastic order he initially joined?
2. Why was the Cistertian order "asserted to be the surest road to heaven"?

### Edward Grim's Account of the Martyrdom of Thomas à Becket

1. Is there any evidence in this account that Becket may have sought and worked for martyrdom? If he did, would this have been acceptable to the church?
2. Based on Grim's description of Becket, what is your view of the archbishop's character?

### Thomas Aquinas, Of Cheating, Which Is Committed in Buying and Selling

1. What, according to Aquinas, is the just price and how is it determined?
2. How does he differ from a modern economist in his approach to trade and commercial activity?

# 7
# The Old Church

The great danger of history is that it is lived forwards but narrated backwards. The historian knows how the plot turns out, and in analyzing the institutional vitality of the old church, there is an overwhelming temptation to see the fourteenth- and fifteenth-century ecclesia in terms of what happened in the sixteenth century — the Protestant Reformation. It is far too easy to forget that there are two sets of questions — not one — that must be asked about the documents in this chapter. (1) What were the institutional ills and psychological failures afflicting the old church that helped produce the Protestant Reformation? (2) Even more important, what psychological strengths and social functions made the old church attractive to so many people for so many years? Possibly there is still a third set of questions that ought to be posed: Were the obvious flaws and defects that beset the church all that important? Were they peculiar to the fifteenth-century church, or are they universal to all religious institutions in all centuries? And, finally, what other factors and forces, to which the church was either oblivious or unable to respond, may have helped produce the Protestant Reformation?

If the documents in the previous chapter present the religious ideal, those in this chapter portray reality, which on occasion could be brutal and scandalous, but which was always marvelously human. Of all of the selections in the chapter, the first, Jocelin of Brakelond's *Chronicle*, is the most delightful. Filled with wry humor, it gives comic details and human intimacy that go far to counterbalance the picture of monastic life presented in the previous chapter by William of Malmesbury. Jocelin joined the rich Norfolk monastery of St. Edmund's in 1173 and probably wrote his description of the election and career of Abbot Samson a generation later, around 1200. Clearly an admirer of the abbot (he was Samson's chaplain) Jocelin never loses either his sense of humor or his sense of accuracy.

Edward III pawning the Crown with the Archibishop of Treves.

If Abbot Samson in the midst of his busy life represents one kind of reality, the confession of the Lollard heretic, Edmund Archer, in 1430 represents another. Two hundred years after the death of Abbot Samson, some very alarming and dangerous religious-social ideas were being spread about the Norfolk countryside by the likes of Edmund Archer. The existence of those beliefs, their social implications, and the church's institutional response to them are all important pieces of evidence in determining the strengths and weaknesses of the established church of the fifteeenth century.

Reality is not simply a matter of men and institutions; it also involves the quality of thought of those who seek to explain the mysteries of existence. The "Master of Oxford's Catechism" (ca. 1420) gives a vivid picture of what every schoolboy was expected to know, the education process by which he learned, and the depth of his understanding of the wonders of heaven and earth.

The remaining documents are all fiction, and they suffer from the disadvantages of their genre. Nevertheless, they present a strong, intimate, and highly revealing picture of the old church in action. The first, Chaucer's *Canterbury Tales*, has already been encountered, and the descriptions of the prioress, monk, friar, and pardoner are very different from those of the parson and the plowman. The second, William Langland's *Vision of Piers Plowman*, is almost as well known as the *Canterbury Tales*. While Chaucer (1340?–1400) belonged at the royal court and associated with the great and mighty, his contemporary Langland (1332?–1400?) was an unknown clerk in minor orders, a man of the people. Thus, the level of his criticism and the social content of his satire are very different from those of Geoffrey Chaucer, who was an esquire to the king, a justice of the peace, a member of parliament, an ambassador to foreign parts, and a relation by marriage to the Duke of Lancaster.

The last three selections are typical of the droll stories told at the expense of the old church. The first was recounted by the humanist martyr Sir Thomas More (1478–1535), whose *Utopia* can be read in Chapter 10. The remaining tales appeared in an early sixteenth-century edition of *One Hundred Merry Tales*. All three reveal the kind of criticism that was directed at the church long before the Protestant Reformation.

It has already been suggested that Chapters 6 and 7 should be read as a study in contrasts; the reader may also wish to skip to Chapter 12 ("Protestant — Catholic: Good Christian — Good Subject"), for many of the subjects and problems raised in connection with the medieval church and its relationship to society will be similar to those confronted by the Protestants and Catholics in the sixteenth century.

## JOCELIN OF BRAKELOND, *Chronicle* (ca. 1190)

Jocelin of Brakelond, a lifetime member of the monastery of St. Edmund's in Norfolk, gives an intimate and revealing description of the operation of a large and wealthy monastery, the political and worldly life of its abbot, and the personality clashes involved in such a closed and restricted environment.

I have been at pains to set down the things that I have seen and heard, which came to pass in the Church of St. Edmund in our days, from the year in which the Flemings were taken prisoner outside the town, that being the year in which I assumed the religious habit, and Prior Hugh was deposed and his office given to Robert; and I have included certain evil things for a warning, and certain good as an example to others. At that time Abbot Hugh was grown old and his eyes waxed somewhat dim. Pious he was and kindly, a strict monk and good, but in the business of this world neither good nor wise. For he trusted those about him overmuch and gave them too ready credence, relying always on the wisdom of others rather than his own. Discipline and religion and all things pertaining to the Rule were zealously observed within the cloister; but outside all things were badly handled, and every man did, not what he ought, but what he would, since his lord was simple and growing old. The townships of the Abbot and all the hundreds were given out to farm; the woods were destroyed, the houses of the manors threatened to fall in ruin, and day by day all things went from bad to worse. The Abbot found but one remedy and one consolation — to borrow money, that thus at least he might be able to maintain the honour of his house. . . .

In the twenty-third year of his abbacy it came into Abbot Hugh's mind to go to the shrine of St. Thomas to pray; and on his way thither upon the day after the Nativity of the Virgin he had a grievous fall near Rochester, so that his knee-cap was put out and

SOURCE: From H. E. Butler, trans., *The Chronicle of Jocelin of Brakelond Concerning the Acts of Samson Abbot of the Monastery of St. Edmund* (Oxford, England: Oxford University Press, 1949), alternate pp. 1, 7–9, 11–14, 16, 22–23, 28–30, 33–35, 39–42, 55–58, 65–66, 71–72.

lodged in the ham of his leg. Physicians hastened to him and tortured him in many ways, but healed him not; and he was carried back to us in a horse litter and devoutly received as was his due. To cut a long story short, his leg mortified and the pain ascended even to his heart, and by reason of the pain a tertian fever laid hold on him, in the fourth fit of which he died and gave up his soul to God on the morrow of the day of St. Brice. Before he died, everything was pillaged by his servants so that nothing was left in his house but three-legged stools and tables which they were unable to carry off. The Abbot himself was scarce left with his coverlet and two old torn blankets which someone had placed over him after removing those that were whole. There was nothing worth a single penny that could be distributed to the poor for the benefit of his soul. . . .

While the abbacy was vacant, the Prior was above all things zealous for the maintenance of peace in the Convent and the preservation of the honour of our Church in the entertainment of guests, desiring neither to disturb anyone or provoke any to anger, so that he might keep all men and all things in peace. Yet none the less he shut his eyes to certain things that deserved correction in the conduct of our obedientiaries, above all of the Sacrist who, during the vacancy, as though he did not care what he did with the sacristy, paid not a single debt nor built anything at all, but oblations and chance incomings were foolishly squandered. Wherefore the Prior who was the head of the Convent was thought blameworthy and called remiss. And our brethren spoke of this among themselves, when the time came for the election of an Abbot.

Our Cellarer[1] received all guests of whatever rank at the expense of the Convent. William the Sacrist gave and spent as he pleased, a kindly man, giving away both that which should be given and that which should not, and "blinding the eyes of all

with gifts." Samson the sub-sacrist, being master over the workmen, left nothing broken or cracked or split or unrepaired to the best of his power: wherefore he won the favour of the Convent and above all of the cloister monks. . . .

While the abbacy was vacant, we often besought God and his holy martyr, St. Edmund, as was meet and right, to give us a fitting shepherd for our Church, thrice every week prostrating ourselves in the choir after leaving the chapter house, and singing the seven penitential psalms; and some there were who, if they had known who was to be our Abbot, would not have prayed so devoutly. As to the choice of an Abbot, should the King grant us a free election, divers persons spoke in divers manners, some in public, some in private, and every man had his own opinion. And one said of another, "That brother is a good monk, a person worthy of approval: he knows much concerning the Rule and the customs of the Church; though he be not so perfect a philosopher as certain others he might well fill the office of Abbot. Abbot Ording was an illiterate man, and yet he was a good Abbot and ruled this house wisely; moreover, we read in the Fables that it proved better for the frogs to choose a log for their king, in whom they could trust, than a serpent who hissed venomously and after hissing devoured his subjects." To this another made answer, "How may that be? How can he, a man who has no knowledge of letters, preach a sermon in Chapter, or on feast days to the people? How shall he who does not understand the Scriptures, have knowledge how to bind and how to loose? seeing that 'the rule of souls is the art of arts and the science of sciences.' " . . . Again another said of yet another, "That brother is literate, eloquent and prudent, strict in his observance of the Rule; he has greatly loved the Convent, and has endured many ills for the possessions of the Church; he is worthy to be made Abbot." And another replied,

---

[1] officer in charge of provisions

"From all good clerks, O Lord deliver us; ..." Again one said of a certain brother, "That brother is a good manager, as is proved by the performance of his tasks and by the offices that he has filled so well, and the buildings and repairs that he has made. He knows how to work hard and to defend our house, and he is something of a clerk, though 'much learning maketh him not mad.' He is worthy to be Abbot." The other made answer, "God forbid that a man who cannot read or sing or celebrate the holy offices, a wicked man and unjust, a flayer of the poor — God forbid that such an one should be made Abbot!" Again a certain brother said of someone, "that brother is a kindly man, affable and amiable, peaceful and composed, bountiful and generous, a literate man and eloquent, a very proper man in aspect and bearing, who is loved by many both within and without. And such a man, God willing, might be made Abbot to the great honour of the Church.". . . Again another, who thought himself wise, said, "May God Almighty give us for our shepherd one who is a fool and ignorant, so that he will have to ask us to help him!" And I heard indeed that a certain man who was industrious and literate and of noble birth, was condemned by certain of our seniors because he was a novice, while the novices said of the seniors that they were decrepit old men, unfit to rule the Abbey. And so, many men said many things, and each of them "was fully persuaded in his own mind." I once saw Samson the sub-sacrist sitting by at gatherings of this kind at the time of blood-letting, when the cloister monks are wont to reveal the secrets of their hearts, each to each, and to confer with one another — I saw him sitting by and smiling, without a word, and noting words of each. . . .

After the death of Abbot Hugh, when a year and three months were gone, our lord the King sent letters to us, commanding that our Prior and twelve of the Convent, unanimously chosen by our whole body, should appear before him on an appointed day to elect an Abbot. On the day after we had received these letters we assembled in the chapterhouse to deal with the matter. First of all the King's letters were read before the Convent: after this we asked the Prior and charged him on the peril of his soul to nominate according to his conscience the twelve whom he should take with him, men whose life and character made it clear that they would refuse to stray from the right way. And he, granting our petition and inspired by the Holy Spirit, chose six from one side of the choir and six from the other, and satisfied us, not a voice being raised against his choice. . . .

The twelve came before the king, and after much discussion, the choice came down to the Prior and Samson.

Denys, speaking for us all, began to commend the persons of the Prior and Samson, saying that both were literate, both good, both of praiseworthy life and of unblemished reputation; but always in the corner of his speech thrusting Samson forward, multiplying the words he uttered in his praise and saying that he was a man strict in his behaviour, stern in chastising transgressions, a hard worker, prudent in worldly business, and proved in divers offices. The Bishop of Winchester replied, "We understand clearly what you mean; from your words we gather that your Prior seems to you to be somewhat slack and that you desire him whom you call Samson." Denys replied, "Both of them are good, but we should like, God willing, to have the better." The Bishop made answer, "Of two good men you must choose the better. Tell me openly, do you wish to have Samson?" And a number, making a majority, answered clearly, "We want Samson," not a voice being raised against them, though some of set purpose said nothing, because they wished to offend neither the one or the other. Samson then having been nominated in the presence of the King, and the latter having taken brief counsel with his Advisers, all the rest were summoned, and the King said, "You have presented Samson to me: I do not know him. If you had presented your Prior, I should have accepted him; for I have seen him and know him. But, as it is, I will do what you desire. . . .

Samson returned home to be installed as abbot.

After he had received homage, the [new] Abbot demanded an aid from his knights, who promised him twenty shillings each; but they had no sooner done so than they took counsel together and withdrew twelve pounds in respect of twelve knights, saying that those twelve ought to help the other forty in respect of castleward and scutages[2] and likewise of aids to the Abbot. When the Abbot heard this, he was angry and said to his friends that, if he lived, he would render them like for like, and trouble for trouble. After this the Abbot caused an inquiry to be made as to the annual rents due from the free men in each manor and as to the names of the peasants and their holdings and the services due from each; and he had them all set down in writing. But he restored old halls and ruinous houses, through which kites and crows were flying; he built new chapels and lodgings and chambers in many places, where there had never before been buildings save only barns. He also made a number of parks which he filled with beasts, and kept a huntsman and hounds; and when any distinguished guest came to him, he would sit at times with his monks in some woodland glade and watch the hounds run; but I never saw him taste venison. He also cleared many lands and brought them back into cultivation. . . . At his bidding a general inventory was made, in each hundred, of leets[3] and suits, hidages[4] and corn-dues, payments of hens, and other customs, revenues and expenses, which had hitherto been largely concealed by the tenants: and he had all these things set down in writing, so that within four years from his election there was not one who could deceive him concerning the revenues of the Abbey to a single pennyworth, and this although he had not received anything in writing from his predecessors concerning the administration of the Abbey, save for one small sheet containing the names of the knights of St. Edmund, the names of the manors and the rent due from each tenancy. Now this book, in which were also recorded the debts which he had paid off, he called his Kalendar, and consulted it almost every day, as though he could see therein the image of his own efficiency as in a mirror. . . .

He issued an edict that henceforth no man should pledge any of the ornaments of the church without consent of the Convent, as was commonly done, and that no charter should be sealed with the seal of the Convent save in Chapter in the presence of the Convent. And he made Hugh sub-sacrist, giving orders that William the Sacrist should do nothing in the sacristy in respect either of revenues or expenses, save with his assent. After this, but not on the same day, he transferred the former guardians of the oblations to other offices. And last of all he deposed William himself; whereat some who loved William said, "Behold the Abbot! Behold the wolf of the dream! Behold how he ravens!". . .

Seven months had not passed since his election, when lo and behold! letters of the Lord Pope were brought to him, offering to appoint him judge delegate for the hearing of causes, a task of which he had neither knowledge nor experience, though he was learned in the liberal arts and in the Holy Scriptures, being a literate man, brought up in the schools and once a schoolmaster, well known and approved in his country. He forthwith called to him two clerks skilled in the law and associated them with himself, making use of their counsel in ecclesiastical

---

[2] *castleward* . . . feudal taxes    [3] manor court    [4] feudal tax

business, and studying the decrees and decretal letters, whenever he had time, so that within a short time by reading of books and practice in causes he came to be regarded as a wise judge, proceeding in court according to the form of law. Wherefore one said, "A curse upon the court of this Abbot, where neither gold or silver may help me for the confounding of my adversary!" In process of time when he had acquired some practice in secular cases, being guided by his native power of reasoning, he showed himself so subtle of understanding, that all marvelled, and the Undersheriff Osbert Fitz-Hervey said of him, "This Abbot is a fine disputer: if he goes on as he has begun, he will blind us all, every one." And having approved himself in causes of this kind, he was made a justice errant, though he erred not, but was careful not to wander from the right way. But "Envy assails earth's highest!" When his men complained to him in the court of St. Edmund, because he would not give judgment hastily nor "believe every spirit," but proceeded in the order prescribed by law, knowing that the merits of causes are revealed by the statements of the parties, it was said that he was unwilling to do justice to any complainant, unless money were first given or promised; and because his glance was sharp and penetrating, and his brow worthy of Cato and rarely relaxed into a smile, he was said to be more inclined to severity than kindness. And when he took amercements[5] for any offence, he was said to exalt justice above mercy, because, as it seemed to many, when it was a matter of getting money, he rarely remitted what he might justly receive. As his wisdom grew, so also did his prudence in managing his property and increasing it, and in all honourable expenditure. . . .

Abbot Samson was of middle height, and almost entirely bald; his face was neither round nor long, his nose prominent, his lips thick, his eyes clear as crystal and of penetrating glance; his hearing of the sharpest; his eyebrows grew long and were often

clipped; a slight cold made him soon grow hoarse. On the day of his election he was forty-seven years old, and had been a monk for seventeen. He had a few white hairs in a red beard and a very few in the hair of his head, which was black and rather curly; but within fourteen years of his election he was white as snow. He was a man of extreme sobriety, never given to sloth, extremely strong and ever ready to go either on horseback or on foot, until old age prevailed and tempered his eagerness. When he heard of the capture of the Cross and the fall of Jerusalem, he began to wear drawers of haircloth, and a shirt of hair instead of wool, and to abstain from flesh and meat. . . .

He read English perfectly, and used to preach in English to the people, but in the speech of Norfolk, where he was born and bred, and to this end he ordered a pulpit to be set up in the church for the benefit of his hearers and as an ornament to the church. The Abbot seemed also to love the active life better than the contemplative; he had more praise for good obedientiaries than for good cloister monks; and rarely did he approve of any man solely for his knowledge of literature, unless he were also wise in worldly affairs. And when he heard of any prelate that grew faint beneath the burden of his pastoral cares and turned anchorite,[6] he did not praise him for so doing. He was loth to bestow much praise on kindly men, for he said, "He that seeks to please everyone, ought to please nobody." So in the first year of his abbacy he regarded all flatterers with hatred, especially if they were monks. But in process of time he seemed more ready to give ear to them and to be more friendly toward them. Wherefore it came to pass that, when a certain brother skilled in this art kneeled before him, and under pretence of giving him some advice had poured the oil of flattery into his ears, I laughed softly as I stood afar off: but when the monk retired, he called me and asked me why I laughed, and I replied that it was because the world was full of flatterers. To which

---

[5] fines    [6] one who lives in seclusion

the Abbot made answer. "My son, it is long since I have been acquainted with flatterers, and it is therefore that I cannot help listening to them. In many things I must feign, and in many I must dissemble, to maintain peace in the Convent. I shall not cease to listen to their words, but they will not deceive me, as they deceived my predecessor who was so foolish as to put faith in their counsels, so that long before his death neither he nor his household had aught to eat save what was borrowed from their creditors. . . ."

As for the monks who had been his comrades before he succeeded to the abbacy, and had stood high in his love and regard, he rarely promoted them to office on the strength of his former affection, unless they were fit; wherefore some of our brethren, who had favoured his election as Abbot, said that he showed less regard than was seemly toward those who had loved him before he was Abbot, and that he loved those better who had both openly and in secret disparaged him, and had publicly and even in the hearing of many called him an angry and unsociable man, a haughty fellow and a barrator[7] from Norfolk. But as after his succession to the abbacy he vouchsafed no indiscreet affection or honour to those who had once been his friends, even so he showed no sign or rancour or hatred to others, such as their conduct might seem to deserve, sometimes rendering good for evil and doing good to those who had persecuted him. . . .

After the return of King Richard to England, licenses for tournaments were granted to knights. And a number gathered for this purpose between Thetford and St. Edmund's. The Abbot forbade them, but they resisted his authority and fulfilled their desire. On another occasion fourscore young men, the sons of nobles, came with their followers to the same place fully armed for a return match. This accomplished, they came to this town to find lodging. But the Abbot, hearing this, gave orders that the gates should be barred and all of them shut in. The next day was the vigil of the Feast of St. Peter and St. Paul. So, when they had promised him that they would not go forth without his leave, they all ate with the Abbot that day; but after dinner, when the Abbot retired to his lodgings, they all arose and began to dance and sing, and sending into the town to fetch wine, they drank, and after that they yelled, robbing the Abbot and the whole Convent of their sleep, and doing everything they could to make a mockery of the Abbot; and they continued thus till evening and refused to obey the Abbot when he ordered them to desist. But when evening was come, they broke the gates of the town and forced their way out. But the Abbot solemnly excommunicated them all, by the advice of Hubert, Archbishop of Canterbury, who was then Justiciar. And many of them came to make amends, and begged for absolution. . . .

A general summons was made in the hundred[8] of Risbridge that the complaint and claim of the Earl of Clare might be heard at Wickhambrook. He himself came surrounded by a throng of barons and knights, Earl Aubrey and many others supporting him; and he said that his bailiffs gave him to understand that they used formerly to receive five shillings a year on his behalf from the hundred and its bailiffs, but that now this sum was unjustly denied them; and he alleged that his predecessors at the time of the conquest of England had been enfeoffed[9] of the land of Alfric the son of Withar, who was once the lord of that hundred. But the Abbot, consulting his own good and yielding no ground, made answer, "My Lord Earl, I marvel at your words. Your claim fails! King Edward gave this hundred to St. Edmund in its entirety and confirmed his gift by charter; and there is no mention therein of those five shillings. You must tell me for what service or cause you demand these five shillings." And the Earl, after consulting his friends, replied that it was his duty to carry the standard of St.

---

[7] a seller of offices   [8] a division of a shire, having its own court   [9] invested with a fief

Edmund in the army, and that it was for this that the five shillings were due to him. And the Abbot made answer, "In truth five shillings is but a paltry sum for a man so great as the Earl of Clare to receive for such service: but it is no great burden for the Abbot of St. Edmund to give five shillings. Earl Roger Bigot maintains and asserts that he is seized of the duty of carrying the standard of St. Edmund; for he carried it when the Earl of Leicester was taken and the Flemings destroyed. Thomas of Mendham also says this is his right. When you have made good your claim against these two, I will gladly pay you the five shillings which you demand." The Earl replied that he would talk over the matter with his kinsman Earl Roger, and thus the affair was put off even to this day. . . .

Abbot Samson entered on a dispute with his knights, himself against all, and all against him. He put to them that they ought to do him full service of fifty knights in respect of scutages, aids and the like, since, as he said, they held so many knights' fees; why should ten of those fifty knights do no service, or for what reason and by whose authority should those forty receive the service of ten knights. They all replied with one voice that it had always been the custom for ten of them to help the forty, and they neither would nor ought to be answerable nor to be called into court on this matter. So when they had been summoned to answer for this in the King's court, some of them deliberately excused themselves, while others appeared out of guile, saying that they would not answer in the absence of their peers. On another occasion those presented themselves who had previously been absent, and they likewise said that they ought not to answer in the absence of their peers, who were concerned in the same dispute. And when they had thus many times baffled the Abbot and had vexed him with great and heavy expenses, he complained to Archbishop Hubert who was then justiciar; and he answered in full council that every knight ought to speak for himself and for his own holding. And he said openly that

the Abbot had both the knowledge and the power to make good the claim of his Church against each and all. Therefore Earl Roger Bigot, first of them all, of his free will acknowledged in court that he owed his lord the Abbot full service of three knights in reliefs, scutages and aids; but he was silent about the performance of castleward at Norwich. After him there came first two knights, and then three, more later, and finally almost all, and following the example of the Earl they acknowledged that they owed the same service; and because their acknowledgement of this in the court of St. Edmund was not sufficient, the Abbot took them all to London at his own expense, and their wives as well and such women as were heiresses of lands, that they might make their acknowledgement in the King's court; and each of them received separate records of the fine. . . .

Geoffrey Ridell, Bishop of Ely, asked the Abbot to give him timber for the making of certain great buildings at Glemsford, and this request the Abbot, not wishing to offend him, granted though sore against his will. Now while the Abbot was making a stay at Melford, there came to him a clerk of the Bishop's, who asked on behalf of his lord that the promised timber might be taken from a part of his domain at Elmswell; and he made a slip of the tongue, saying Elmswell, when he should have said Elmset, which is the name of a certain great wood of Melford. And the Abbot wondered at his message, since such timber was not to be found at Elmswell. But when Richard, the forester of the same township, heard this, he said in secret to the Abbot that the Bishop had, during the past week, sent his carpenters to explore the woods of Elmset, and that they had chosen the best trees in the whole wood and placed their marks upon them. Hearing this the Abbot suddenly perceived that the messenger of the Bishop had made a mistake in delivering his errand, and said to him in answer that he would gladly do as the Bishop desired. On the next day the messenger set off on his return, and the Abbot, after hearing mass, went at once with his carpenters to the aforesaid wood and caused all the oaks already marked together with more than a hundred others to be marked with his mark for the use of St. Edmund and for the top of the great tower; and he gave orders that they should be cut down as soon as possible. But the Bishop when he learned from his messenger's reply that the aforesaid timber was to be taken at Elmswell, after roundly abusing that same messenger, sent him back to the Abbot to correct his mistake by saying Elmset, not Elmswell; but before he reached the Abbot, all the trees that the Bishop had desired and his carpenters had marked were already cut down, and so he would have to find other timber elsewhere, if he wanted any. But I, when I beheld this, laughed and said in my heart, "Thus guile is tricked by guile."

## *Lollard Heresy Trial, The Case of Edmund Archer* (1430)

Lollardy stemmed from the teachings of John Wycliffe (1320?–1384) who advocated a return to the poverty of the primitive church and argued that ecclesiastical property should be confiscated by the crown and redistributed. He also denied the efficacy of the sacramental system and the miraculous powers of the priesthood, maintaining that the existing church hierarchy was nothing but a human contrivance and that the true church consisted of the brotherhood of all believers. Every Christian was guided solely by his or her own faith and by the Holy Scripture and confronted God directly without clerical intercession. Wycliffe's beliefs immediately became popular with the poorer elements and were spread about the countryside by disciples called Lollards (mumblers). After the Peasants' Revolt of 1381, the social implications of Lollardy were sensed by the upper classes, and crown and church joined forces to exterminate the heresy.

In the name of God, before you, the worshipful father in Christ, William, by the grace of God bishop of Norwich, I, Edmund Archer of London of your diocese, cord maker, sometime apprentice and servant with Thomas Moone of the same town, your subject, feeling and understanding that I have by right familiar conversation and homily with many notorious and [in]famous heretics ... whose schools I have kept and continued long time, and of whom I have heard, learned and reported the false doctrine and untrue opinions which be written and contained in these articles underwritten, which I confess heretical and erroneous and which I have held, believed and affirmed; that is to say:

First that the sacrament of baptism, done in water as the common form is used in the church, is of little effect . . . if the father and mother of the person which should be baptized be of Christ's belief.

Also that the sacrament of confirmation, done by a bishop as the common use is had in the church, is neither expedient nor necessary unto the salvation of man's souls.

Also that confession oweth to be made only to God, and to no earthly priest, for no earthly priest hath power to absolve a man of sin.

Also that no priest hath power to make Christ's very body at mass in the sacrament of the alter, but that after the sacramental words said of any priest at mass there re-

SOURCE: From Norman P. Tanner, ed., *Heresy Trials in the Diocese of Norwich, 1428–1431* (London: Royal Historical Society, 1977), Camden Society, 4th Series, Vol. 20, pp. 164–167. By permission of the Royal Historical Society and the Archbishop of Westminster.

maineth nothing else but only a cake of material bread.[10]

Also that only consent of love betwixt man and woman sufficeth for the sacrament of matrimony, without contract of words or solemnization in church.

Also that no person is bound to fast in Lent, . . . Fridays, vigils of saints nor other days and times which be commanded of the church to be fasted, but that it is lawful to all Christ's people such days and times at all hours to eat flesh and all manner of meats at their own lust . . . .

Also I have held, believed and affirmed that God's people is not bound to keep the holydays which be commanded of the church to be had holy, but it is lawful [for] all Christ's people to do all bodily works [on] all festival and holy days except only the Sundays.

Also I have held, believed and affirmed that all Christ's people may lawfully withhold and withdraw all manner of tithes and offerings from churches and curates, so it be done prudently.

Also I have held, believed and affirmed that every good Christian man is a good priest, and hath as much power as any priest ordered, be he a bishop or a pope.

Also I have held, believed and affirmed that chastity of monks, cannons, friars, nuns, priests and of any other persons is not commendable nor meritorious, but it is more commendable and more pleasing unto God [that] all such persons to be wedded and bring forth fruit of their bodies.

Also I have held, believed and affirmed that it is no sin to do the contrary of the precepts of holy church.

Also that censures of holy church done by a bishop or any other ordinary [prelate] be but trifles and not to be dreaded.

Also I have held, believed and affirmed that all prayers ought to be made only to God, and to no other saint.

Also I have held, believed and affirmed that it is not lawful to swear in any case. . . .

Also I have held, believed and affirmed that no manner of worship ought to be done or made to any images of the crucifix, of Our Lady Saint Mary or none other saints, and especially to no image of Christ's cross, for every such cross is the sign and token of Anti-Christ.

Also I have held, believed and affirmed that is is not lawful to put any man to death for any cause.

Because of which and many other errors and heresies, I am called before you, worshipful father, which have cure of my soul. And be you fully informed that mine affirming, believing and holding be open errors and heresies and contrary to the determination of the church, wherefore I willingly follow and pursue the doctrines of holy church, and depart from all manner of error and heresy, and turn with good will and heart to the one head of the church. Considering the holy church turns not her bosom to him that will turn again, and God wills not the death of a sinner but rather that he be turned and live with a pure heart, I confess, detest and despise my said errors and heresies, and these said opinons I confess heretical and erroneous and to the faith of the church of Rome and all universal church repugnant. . . .

I shall never after this time be a receiver, favorer, councillor or defender of heretics or of any persons suspect of heresy. . . . If I know any heretics or of heresy any persons suspect or of them favorers, comforters, or defenders, or of any persons making private conventicles[11] or assembles, or holding any divers or singular opinions from the common doctrine of the church, I shall let you, worshipful father, or your vicar general in your absence or the diocesans[12] [know] of such persons. . . . So help me God at holy doom and these holy gospels. . . .

---

[10] *material* . . . i.e., ordinary bread  [11] secret meetings  [12] bishops

## *The Master of Oxford's Catechism* (ca. 1420)

Like many catechisms, the Master of Oxford's is in the form of a classroom recitation. The master possesses a vast fund of marvelously precise information about a wide variety of religious and secular matters.

THE CLERK'S QUESTION: Say me where was God when he made heaven and earth?

THE MASTER'S ANSWER: I say, in the further end of the wind.

CLERK: Tell me what word God first spake?

MASTER: Be thou made light, and light was made.

CLERK: What is God?

MASTER: He is God, that all things made, and all things hath in His power.

CLERK: In how many days made God all things?

MASTER: In six days. . . .

CLERK: Whereof was Adam made?

MASTER: Of eight things: the first of earth, the second of fire, the third of wind, the fourth of clouds, the fifth of air wherethrough he speaketh and thinketh, the sixth of dew whereby he sweateth, the seventh is salt whereof Adam hath salt tears.

CLERK: Whereof was found the name of Adam?

MASTER: Of four stars, this be the names, Arcax, Dux, Arostolym, and Momfumbres.

CLERK: Of what state was Adam when he was made?

MASTER: A man of thirty winter of age.

CLERK: And of what length was Adam?

MASTER: Of four score and six inches.

CLERK: How long lived Adam in this world?

MASTER: 900 and 30 winter, and afterward in hell till the passion of our Lord God.

CLERK: Of what age was Adam when he begat his first child?

MASTER: An 100 and 30 winter, and had a son that hight[13] Seth. . . .

CLERK: What was he that never was born, and was buried in his mother's womb, and since was christened and saved?

MASTER: That was our father Adam.

CLERK: How long was Adam in Paradise?

MASTER: Seven years, and at seven years' end he trespassed against God for the apple that he ate on a Friday, and an angel drove him out.

CLERK: How many winters was Adam when our Lord was done on the cross?

MASTER: That was 5,200 and 32 years.

CLERK: What hight Noes [Noah's] wife?

MASTER: Dalida, . . .

CLERK: Whereof was made Noes ship?

MASTER: Of a tree that was cleped[14] Chy.

CLERK: And what length was Noes ship?

MASTER: Fifty fathom of breadth, and 200 fathom of length, and 30 fathom of height.

CLERK: How many winter was Noes ship in making?

MASTER: Four score years.

CLERK: How long dured Noes flood?

MASTER: Forty days and forty nights.

CLERK: How many children had Adam and Eve?

MASTER: Thirty men children and thirty women children.

CLERK: What city is there where the sun goeth to rest?

MASTER: A city that is called Sarica.

CLERK: What be the best herbs that God loved?

MASTER: The rose and the lily.

CLERK: What fowl loved God best?

MASTER: The dove, for God sent His Spirit from heaven in likeness of a dove.

CLERK: Which is the best water that ever was?

SOURCE: From Thomas Wright and James Orchard Halliwell, ed., *Reliquiae Antiquae: Scraps from Ancient Manuscripts illustrating chiefly Early English Literature and the English Language* (London: William Pickering, 1841), Vol. I, pp. 230–232.

[13] named  [14] called

MASTER: River Jordan, for God was baptised therein.

CLERK: Where be the angels that God put out of heaven and became devils?

MASTER: Some into hell, and some reigned in the sky, and some in the earth, and some in waters and in woods.

CLERK: How many waters be there?

MASTER: Two salt waters, and two fresh waters.

CLERK: Who made first ploughs?

MASTER: Cam [Cain], that was Noes son.

CLERK: Why beareth not stones fruit as trees?

MASTER: For Cayme [Cain] slew his brother Abell with the bone of an ass's cheek.

CLERK: What is the best thing and the worst among men?

MASTER: Word is best and worst.

CLERK: Of what thing be men most afraid?

MASTER: Men be most afraid of death.

CLERK: What are the four things that men may not live without?

[MASTER]: Wind, fire, water, and earth.

CLERK: Where resteth a man's soul, when he shall sleep?

MASTER: In the brain, or in the blood, or in the heart.

CLERK: Where lieth Moises' [Moses'] body?

MASTER: Beside the house that hight Enfegor.

CLERK: Why is the earth cursed, and the sea blessed?

MASTER: For Noe and Abraham, and for christening that God commanded.

CLERK: Who set first vines?

MASTER: Noe set the first vines.

CLERK: Who cleped first God?

MASTER: The devil.

CLERK: Which is the heaviest thing bearing?

MASTER: Sin is the heaviest.

CLERK: Which thing is it that some loveth, and some hateth?

MASTER: That is judgment.

CLERK: Which be the four things that never was full nor never shall be?

MASTER: The first is earth, the second is fire, the third is hell, the fourth is a covetous man.

CLERK: How many of birds be there, and how many of fishes?

MASTER: Fifty-four of fowls and twenty-six of fishes.

CLERK: Which was the first clerk that ever was?

MASTER: Elias was the first.

CLERK: What hight the four waters that runneth through paradise?

MASTER: The one hight Eyson, the other Egeon, the third hight Tygrys, and the fourth Effraton. These be milk, honey, oil, and wine.

CLERK: Wherefore is the sun red at even?

MASTER: For he goeth toward hell.

CLERK: Who made first cities?

MASTER: Marcurius the giant.

CLERK: How many languages be there?

MASTER: Sixty-two, and so many disciples has God without his apostles.

## *Chaucer's Prioress, Monk, Friar, and Pardoner* (ca. 1387)

Geoffrey Chaucer in the "Prologue" to the *Canterbury Tales* gives a vivid and unflattering picture of common medieval clerical types.

### The Prioress

Also there was a nun, a PRIORESS,
And she went smiling, innocent and coy;

The greatest oath she swore was by Saint Loy;
And she was known as Madame Eglentine.

SOURCE: From *The Canterbury Tales: The Prologue and Four Tales with the Book of the Duchess and Six Lyrics by Geoffrey Chaucer* by Frank E. Hill, copyright by Frank E. Hill © 1935, published by Longman's Green and reprinted by permission of The David McKay Co., Inc.

Full well she sang the services divine,
Intoning through her nose right prettily,
And fair she spoke her French and fluently
After the school of Stratford-at-the-Bow;
(The French that Paris spoke she didn't
   know).
Well-taught she was at table; she would let
No food fall from her lips; she never wet
Her fingers deeply in the sauce; with care
She raised each morsel; well would she
   beware
Lest any drop upon her breast should fall;
In manners she delighted above all.
Always she wiped her upper lip so clean
That never a fleck of grease was to be seen
Within her cup when she had drunk. When she ·
Reached for her food, she did it daintily.
Pleasant she was, and loved a jest as well,
And in demeanor she was amiable.
Ever to use the ways of court she tried,
And sought to keep her manner dignified,
That all folk should be reverent of her.
But, speaking of her heart and character,
Such pity had she, and such charity
That if she saw a trapp'd mouse she would
   cry —
If it had died, or even if it bled;
And she had little dogs to which she fed
Fine roasted meat, or milk, or dainty bread;
How would she weep if one of them were
   dead,
Or any one should strike it viciously:
She was all heart and sensibility!
Her face was fair in pleated wimple draped,
Her eyes were gray as glass, her nose
   well-shaped,
Her mouth full small and thereto soft and
   red,
But of a truth she had a fair forehead,
A span in breadth or I should be surprised,
For certainly she was not undersized.
Handsome her cloak, as I was well aware;
And wrought of coral round her arm she
   bare
A bracelet all of beads and green gauds[15]
   strung,
And down from this a golden pendant
   hung —

A brooch on which was written a crown'd *A*
Followed by *Amor Vincit Omnia.*

## The Monk

A MONK was there, of much authority;
A hunter and a rider-out was he,
A manly man, to be an abbot able.
Full many a dainty horse he had in stable,
And when he rode ye might his bridle hear
Jingle upon the whistling wind as clear
And all as loud as sounds the chapel bell
Where this same lord was keeper of the
   cell.
The rules of Maurice and of Benedict,
These being ancient now, and rather strict,
This monk ignored, and let them go their
   ways,
And laid a course by rules of newer days.
He held that text worth less than a
   plucked hen
Which said that hunters were not holy men,
Or that a monk who follows not the rule
Is like a fish when it is out of pool —
That is to say, a monk out of his cloister.
Indeed, he held that text not worth an
   oyster;
And his opinion here was good, I say.
For why go mad with studying all day,
Poring over a book in some dark cell,
And with one's hands go laboring as well,
As Austin[16] bids? How shall the world be
   served?
Let Austin's work for Austin be reserved!
Therefore he hunted hard and with delight;
Greyhounds he had as swift as birds in
   flight;
To gallop with the hounds and hunt
   the hare
He made his joy, and no expense would
   spare.
I saw his sleeves trimmed just above the
   hand
With soft gray fur, the finest in the land;
And fastening his hood beneath his chin,
Wrought out of gold, he wore a curious
   pin —
A love-knot at the larger end there was!

---

[15] rosary beads   [16] St. Augustine

His head was wholly bald and shone like
    glass,
As did his face, as though with ointment
    greased
He was full fat and sleek, this lordly priest.
His fierce bright eyes that in his head
    were turning
Like flames beneath a copper cauldron
    burning,
His supple boots, the trappings of his steed,
Showed him a prelate fine and fair indeed!
He was not pale like some tormented ghost.
He loved a fat swan best of any roast.
His palfrey was as brown as is a berry.

## The Friar

There was a FRIAR, a wanton and a merry,
Licensed to beg — a gay, important fellow.
In all four orders no man was so mellow
With talk and dalliance. He had brought
    to pass
The marrying of many a buxom lass,
Paying himself the priest and the recorder:
He was a noble pillar to his order!
He was familiar too and well-beloved
By all the franklins everywhere he moved
And by good women of the town withal,
For he had special powers confessional
As he himself would let folk understand:
He had been licensed by the Pope's own
    hand!
Full sweetly would he listen to confession,
And very pleasantly absolved transgression;
He could give easy penance if he knew
There would be recompense in revenue;
For he that to some humble order hath
    given —
Is he not by that token all but shriven?[17]
For if he gave, then of a certain, said he,
He knew the man was penitent already!
For many a man may be so hard of heart
He may not weep, though sore may be his
    smart,
Therefore his case no tears and prayers
    requires:
Let him give silver to the needy friars!

Always he kept his tippet[18] stuffed with
    knives
And pins, that he could give to comely
    wives.
And of a truth he had a merry note,
For he could sing and play upon the
    rote[19] —
There he would take the prize for certainty.
His neck was white as is the *fleur-de-lys*.
He was as strong as any champion.
As for the inns, he knew them every one,
Their hosts and barmaids too — much
    better than
He'd know a leper or a beggar-man;
For it was not for such a one as he
To seek acquaintance in the company
Of loathsome lepers — no, not for a minute!
There was no decency or profit in it.
One should avoid such trash and cultivate
Vendors of food and folk of rich estate.
And if a profit was to be expected
No courtesy or service he neglected.
There was no man so able anywhere —
As beggar he was quite beyond compare.
He paid a fee to get his hunting ground;
None of his brethren dared to come around;
For though a widow might not own a shoe,
So pleasant was his *In principio*[20]
That he would have a farthing ere he went;
His profits more than paid him back his
    rent!
And like a puppy could he romp; yet he
Could work on love days with authority,
For he was not a monk threadbare of collar,
Out of some cloister, like a half-starved
    scholar,
But rather like a master or a pope.
Of double worsted was his semi-cope,
That rounded upwards like a moulded bell.
He lisped a little, wantonly and well,
To make his words the sweeter on his
    tongue.
And in his harping, after he had sung,
Deep in his head his eyes would twinkle
    bright,
As do the stars upon a frosty night.
Hubert this begging friar was called
    by name.

---

[17] absolved   [18] cape   [19] stringed instrument   [20] greetings

### The Pardoner

The summoner brought a noble PARDONER[21],
Of Roncivalles, his fellow traveller
And crony, lately from the court at Rome,
Loudly he sang, "Come hither, love,
    O come!"
The summoner bore him bass — a mighty
    voice:
Never made trumpet half so loud a noise.
This pardoner had hair yellow as wax,
But smooth it hung, as hangs a hank of flax,
And down in strings about his neck it fell
And all about his shoulders spread as well;
Yet thin in wisps it lay there, one by one.
But hood, for jollity, the man would none,
Safe in his wallet it was packed away;
He thought he kept the fashion of the day;
Hair loose, save for his cap, his head was
    bared.
His bulging eyeballs like a rabbit's glared.
He had a vernicle sewed on his cap.
His wallet lay before him in his lap,
Brim full of pardons piping hot from Rome.
As small as any goat's his voice would come,
Yet no beard had he nor would ever have,
But all his face shone smooth as from
    a shave;
I think he was a gelding or a mare.
But at his trade, from Berwick unto Ware
There was no pardoner could go his pace.
For in his bag he kept a pillow-case
That was, he said, our Blessed Lady's veil;
He claimed to own the fragment of the sail
That Peter had the time he walked the sea
And Jesu saved him in his clemency.
He had a cross of latten[22] set with stones,
And in a glass a handful of pig's bones.
But with these relics when he had in hand
Some humble parson dwelling in the land,
In one day he could get more revenue
Than would the parson in a month or two.
And thus with tricks and artful flattery
He fooled both flock and parson thoroughly.
But let us say, to make the truth less drastic,
In church he was a fine ecclesiastic;
Well could he read a lesson or a story,
But best of all he sang an offertory;
For well he knew that when the song was
    sung
Then he must preach, and smoothly file
    his tongue
For silver, as he could full cunningly —
Therefore he sang so loud and merrily.

## WILLIAM LANGLAND, *Vision of Piers Plowman* (ca. 1362)

The plowman's dream of a church cleansed of sloth, greed, and profit and of a society filled with humble followers of Christ, all equal in the eyes of God, was a powerful and explosive social force in medieval society. It is only one of many examples of medieval anticlericalism and religious appeals to the social communism of a golden, bygone age before sin and pride had entered men's hearts.

In a summer season when the sun was warm, I clad me as a shepherd, in the habit of a hermit, an evil-doer, and I went far and wide through the world to hear the wonders.

But on a May morning on the Malvern Hills, a marvellous thing befell me; me-thought the fairies wrought it. I was out-wearied with wandering and went to rest down by a broad bank beside a burn,[23] and as I lay there leaning, and looked in the water, it sounded so merrily that I fell into a slumber.

SOURCE: From Kate M. Warren, trans., *Langland's Vision of Piers Plowman* (London: T. Fisher Unwin, 1895), pp. 1–5.

[21] a seller of pardons and indulgences    [22] an alloy that looks like brass    [23] stream

Then I dreamed a marvellous dream — that I was in a wilderness, I wist not where, and as I looked on high, into the East toward the sun, I beheld upon a hill a tower beautifully wrought. There was a deep dale below, and therein a dungeon with deep and dark ditches, and dreadful to look at. A fair field full of folk I found betwixt the dale and hill with all manner of men, working and wandering as the world requireth. Some put themselves to the plough and full seldom played. They laboured full hard in planting and in sowing, and won what wasters destroy with their gluttony. And some followed pride, and thereafter apparelled themselves and came tricked out[24] in fine clothing.

Many put themselves to prayers and penance; and all for our Lord's love, hoping to win the bliss of heaven, they lived full straitly; such as anchorites and hermits, who stay in their cells and covet not to wander through the land seeking dainty living to delight the flesh. And some choose trade, and these prosper the better, for it seemeth to us that such men thrive. And some as minstrels are skilled to make mirth and get gold by their glee; without sin, I grant. But jesters and janglers, the children of Judas, feign fancies and make fools of themselves, and yet have wit at will to work, if they needs must. I will not here prove what Paul preacheth of them, for *Qui turpiloquium loquitur*[25] is Lucifer's servant.

Bidders[26] and beggars moved quickly about with their bellies and their bags crammed full of bread, and told lying tales for their food and fought in the alehouse. God wot,[27] in gluttony those Robert[28] knaves go to bed, and rise up with ribaldry, and sleep, and sorry sloth ever pursue them. Pilgrims and palmers pledge themselves to seek St. James[29] and the saints in Rome. They went on their way with many wise[30] tales and had leave to lie all their life afterwards. I saw some who said they had sought saints, and in every tale they told it seemed from their speech that their tongues were more tuned to lying than to telling truth. A crowd of hermits with hooked staves went to Walsingham, and their wenches after them; [they were] great and long loobies[31] who were loath to labour, [and] clothed themselves in cloaks to be known from the others, and made hermits of themselves to have their ease.

There I found friars of all the four Orders[32] who preached to the people for their own profit, and interpreted the Gospel as it seemed good to them; for greed of clothing they explained it as they would. Many of these master friars may clothe them [selves] at their own liking, for their money and their merchandise go together; for since Charity hath turned chapman[33] and chief confessor of Lords,[34] many wonderful things have happened in a few years. Except[35] Holy Church and they hold together better, the greatest mischief on earth will speedily arise.

A Pardoner was preaching there as if he were a priest; he brought forth a bull with the bishop's seals, and said that he himself could absolve them all of broken fasts and broken vows. Laymen believed him, and liked his words, and they came up kneeling to kiss his [papal] bulls. He thrust his brevet[36] in their faces and bleared their eyes, and gained rings and brooches by his charter. Thus they give their gold to keep gluttons, and put their faith in such fellows, who follow lechery. If the bishop were holy and worth his two ears, his seal would never be sent to deceive the people thus. But it is not against the bishop that the youth preacheth, for the parish priest and he divide the silver which the poor folk of the parish ought to have, but for them.

Parsons and parish priests complained to the bishop that their parishes had been poor

---

[24] dressed    [25] *Qui . . .* who so speaketh filthy speech    [26] vagabonds    [27] knows    [28] outlawed    [29] His shrine was at Compostella in Galicia    [30] silly    [31] stupid fellows    [32] Augustines, Carmelites, Dominicans and Minorites    [33] gone into business    [34] received money for hearing confessions    [35] unless    [36] commission to sell indulgences

since the time of the pestilence,[37] [and asked] that they might get license and leave to dwell in London and sing for simony[38] the service there; for silver is sweet.

Bishops and novices, both masters and doctors, who hold their cures under Christ, and have the tonsure[39] in token and sign that they should shrive[40] their parishioners and preach and pray for them and feed the poor, live in London in Lent and at other times. Some serve the King and count out his silver; they claim his debts in Exchequer and Chancery . . . and also claim [the property of] waifs and strays. And some as servants serve lords and ladies, and sit as stewards giving judgment; their Mass and Matins and many of their Hours are done undevoutly. It is to be feared that Christ at the last will curse full many of them in His Court. . . .

## A Fifteenth-Century Con Man

Thoughtful men such as Sir Thomas More were deeply concerned by the fraud and quackery that was forever creeping into the church.

Some priest, to bring up a pilgrimage in his parish, may devise some false fellow faining[41] himself to come seek a saint in his church, and there suddenly say that he hath gotten his sight. Then shall ye have the bells rung for a miracle. And the fond folk of the country soon made fools. . . .

This is, quod I, very truth that such things may be, and sometime so be indeed. As I remember me that I have heard my father tell of a beggar that in King Henry, his days, the sixth, came with his wife to Saint Alban's, and there was walking about the town begging a five or six days before the King's coming thither, saying that he was born blind and never saw in his life. And was warned in his dream that he should come out of Berwyke, where he said he had ever dwelled, to seek saint Alban, and that he had been at his shrine and had not been holpen. And therefore he would go seek him at some other place. For he had heard some say since he came that saint Alban's body should be at Cologne, and indeed such a contention hath there been. . . . But to tell you forth when the king was come, and the town full, suddenly this blind man, at saint Alban's shrine, had his sight again, and a miracle solemnly rung and *Te Deum* sung, so that nothing was talked of in all the town, but this miracle.

So happened it, then, that Duke Humfrey of Gloucester, a great wise man and very well learned, having great joy to see such a miracle, called that poor man unto him. And first showing himself joyous of God's glory, so showed in the getting of his sight, and exhorting him to meekness, and to none ascribing of any part the worship to himself nor to be proud of the people's praise which would call him a good and a godly man thereby. At last he looked well upon his eye, and asked him whether he could never see nothing at all in all his life before. And when as well his wife as himself affirmed fastly no, then he looked advisedly upon his eye again, and said, "I believe you very well, for me thinketh that ye cannot see well yet."

"Yes, Sir," quod he, "I thank God and his holy martyr, I can see now as well as any man."

"Ye can," quod the Duke. "What colour is my gown?" Then anon the beggar told him.

SOURCE: From Sir Thomas More, *A Dialogue Concernyne Heresyes & Matters of Religion* (London, 1528), Chap. 14, p. 134.

[37] Black Death  [38] the buying and selling of church offices  [39] shaven head  [40] hear confession, impose penance, grant absolution  [41] pretending

"What colour," quod he, "is this man's gown?" He told him also, and so forth without any sticking, he told him the names of all the colours that could be showed him. And when my lord saw this, he ... made him be set openly in the stocks. For though he could have seen suddenly by miracle the difference between divers colours, yet could he not by the sight so suddenly tell the names of all these colours, but if he had known them before, no more than the names of all the men that he should suddenly see. ...

## Two Merry Tales (ca. 1526)

Although told at the expense of the church, these two "merry tales" go to the root of two fundamental failings within the medieval church.

---

In the time of Lent a Welchman came to be confessed of his curate — which in his confession said that he had killed a frair. To whom the curate said he could not absolve him. "Yes (quod the Welchman), if thou knewest all, thou wouldst absolve me well enough."

And when the curate had commanded him to show him all the case, he said thus: "Marry, there were two friars and I might have slain them both if I had list, but I let the one 'scape. Therefore, master curate, set the one against th' other and then the offence is not so great but ye may absolve me well enough."

By this, ye may see that divers men have so evil and large consciences that they think if they do one good deed, or refrain from the doing of one evil sin, that it is a satisfaction for other sins and offenses.

. . .

A certain confessor in the holy time of Lent enjoined his penitent to say daily for his penance this prayer: "Agnus dei miserere mei," which was as much to say in English as "The Lamb of God have mercy upon me." This penitent, accepting his penance, departed and that time twelve-month after, came again to be confessed of the same confessor, which demanded of him whether he had fulfilled his penance that he him enjoined the last year. And he said thus: "Ye, sir, I thank God, I have fulfilled it — for I have said thus today morning and so daily: 'The Sheep of God have mercy upon me.'"

To whom the confessor said: "Nay, I bad ye say — 'Agnus dei miserere mei' — that is, 'The Lamb of God have mercy upon me!'"

"Ye, sir," quod the penitent, "ye say truth. That was the last year, but now it is at twelve month sith and it is a sheep by this time. Therefore I must needs say now — 'The Sheep of God have mercy upon me.'"

By this tale ye may perceive that if holy scripture be expounded to rude lay people only in the literal sense, peradventure it shall do but little good.

### FURTHER DISCUSSION QUESTIONS

#### Jocelin of Brakelond, Chronicle

1. What kind of monk was Abbot Hugh?
2. Why was it difficult for Abbot Samson to lead the contemplative life?

SOURCE: Reprinted from *A Hundred Merry Tales and Other Jestbooks of the Fifteenth and Sixteenth Centuries*, Landmark Ed., by P. M. Zall by permission of University of Nebraska Press. Copyright © 1963 by the University of Nebraska Press. Tales #30, pp. 92–93, and #67, pp. 124–125.

3. How did the election of a new abbot work? (Keep in mind King John's conflict with Innocent III. See Chapter 3).
4. What were the qualities that made Samson a successful abbot?
5. On the basis of the *Chronicle*, what would you judge the strengths and weaknesses of the monastic system to have been?
6. What were the pressures and dangers from which the monastery had to defend itself? Was the monastery of St. Edmund's anything more than a "religious foundation"?
7. Compare and contrast the picture of monasticism given by Jocelin to the description given by William of Malmsbury in the previous chapter.

### Lollardy Heresy Trial, The Case of Edmund Archer

1. It is sometimes argued that what made Lollardy so dangerous was its socially revolutionary beliefs. On the basis of Archer's confession, would you say this to be true? Were they dangerous for other than social reasons?
2. In what ways did Lollard beliefs differ from the established faith of the old church; to what extent can it be said that Lollardy represented a "new" approach to religion and to society?

### The Master of Oxford's Catechism

1. Compare and contrast the kind and quality of religion found in the catechism with the religion expounded in Chapter 6.
2. On what kind of knowledge and on what methods of education was the catechism based?

### Chaucer's Prioress, Monk, Friar, and Pardoner

1. Of the four individuals described by Chaucer, who in your estimation was the most dangerous to the spiritual welfare of the church and why?
2. What qualities do the parson and the plowman (see Chapter 6) have that the prioress, monk, friar, and pardoner do not?
3. To what extent do Chaucer's descriptions of the four pilgrims constitute an attack on the church as an institution; as a body of faith; as a collection of individuals?

### William Langland, Vision of Piers Plowman

1. Compare and contrast the criticism directed at the church by Langland and Chaucer.
2. What, if any, are the social overtones implied in the vision?
3. Does Langland have any cures for what he feels to be wrong with the church and society?

### A Fifteenth-Century Con Man

1. Why was it dangerous for the church when educated and important people, such as Sir Thomas More, began telling droll tales about religion?

### Two Merry Tales

1. What aspects of the church are being criticized in these stories as well as in the "con man"? Is the criticism in any way different from that used by Chaucer or Langland?

# 8

## Society Gone Wrong?

The second half of the fourteenth century and most of the fifteenth century in England and throughout the continent (with the possible exception of Italy) have had a singularly bad press. As one jaundiced observer put it: the era produced only three individuals of real stature — Joan of Arc, John Huss, and Savonarola — and it burned all three of them. One of the period's most recent historians, Barbara Tuchman, is equally depressing. She turned to the calamities of the age in order to document her thesis that history is consoling: the horrors of today are nothing compared to the nightmares of the fourteenth century, "a violent, tormented, bewildered, suffering, and disintegrating age, a time, as many thought, of Satan triumphant." Like beauty or ugliness, the judgment that a society has gone wrong lies in the eyes of the beholder as much as in the realities of events. Indeed, whether the atrocities and misfortunes of one era can justifiably be compared or contrasted with those of another under any circumstances is an issue worth debating.

What in fact had gone wrong in England in the fourteenth and fifteenth centuries? How much had gone wrong? These are loaded questions, like when did you stop beating your wife. The cluster of letters in this chapter dealing with the Paston family has been selected to show that the answers one gets are dependent upon the questions one asks. The Paston correspondence, covering in its entirety the years 1422 to 1509, is unique, for it inaugurated a new era of historical documentation: the words of kings and statesmen, warriors and saints were for the first time being supplemented by the voices of somewhat lesser folk. In the fifteenth century the submerged nine-tenths of society still spoke only through the dead digits of statistics — wills, marriage licenses, baptismal records and the like — but with the Pastons historians finally have an intimate account of domestic, county, national, and international events as they affected and were recorded by the lesser elements of the ruling elite.

The Paston correspondence is preceded by five other documents dealing with those characteristics of English fourteenth- and fifteenth-century society that are most often presented as evidence that medieval society had in fact gone wrong and was in an economic, political, and psychological state of shock. Death existed on an unprecedented scale; morals and politics collapsed from within; class legislation was imposed from above; and social revolution erupted from below. Henry Knighton, who was a canon of St. Mary of the Meadows Abbey in Leicestershire in 1363, is our primary source for the social and bio-logical traumas of the century. His chronicle, which becomes more and more an eye-witness account as it moves from 1337 to its conclusion in 1395 (Knighton died in 1396), portrays one of the grimest pictures we possess of the Black Death, or bubonic plague, which first struck the island in 1348–1349, swept as many as one third of the population into mass graves, and finally settled down into a grizzly struggle between human fertility and bacterial mortality that lasted throughout most of the fifteenth century. Nowhere are the psychological malaise and economic-social consequences of the "Great Death" more effectively presented: "So few servants and laborers were left that no one knew where to turn for help." Alas, there was no help, spiritual or material.

Knighton is equally effective in his picture of the century's greatest social upheaval, the Peasants' Revolt of 1381. His information was clearly not first-hand, and it is interesting to note how he handled a vast and complex social movement and what events he elected to narrate. The two documents dealing with the palace revolution against Richard II and the king's abdication *hilari vultu* are from the *Parliamentary Rolls*, and though their baronial bias is transparent, they do more than present the Lancastrian case against Richard; they also raise basic constitutional and political issues about the relationship of the sovereign to the kingdom, and they might well be compared with the earlier baronial statement given in the *Song of Lewes* in Chapter 3. Finally, the Indenture of Ralph Longford to Lord Hastings in 1481 is a brief but cogent example of what historians call "bastard feudalism." Whether it was bastard or not, whether the contract entered into should be called feudal, whether the nature and condition of the services rendered by the contracting parties were different from what had existed two hundred years before are subjects of end-less and rather inconclusive debate. The Indenture should be read with care, for it is important to judge whether a new atmosphere and set of loyalties prevailed and to compare those loyalties and human relationships to those which appear in earlier documents. The troubles of the Paston family between 1449 and 1476 should also be read carefully. The reader should constantly ask what, if anything, is new in terms of motives and atmosphere and in terms of the political and social conditions that delimited human action. The England of the Pastons should be compared with both Anglo-Saxon society and the more immediate past of the twelfth and thirteenth centuries. Then and only then can the reader decide whether the accusation that fifteenth-century society had gone wrong is justified.

## *Henry Knighton's Description of the Black Death* (1349)

The Black Death was a combination of the bubonic plague carried by flea-infested animals — most often rats — and pneumonic plague transmitted by direct contact. Estimates of its fatality range from one fourth to one half of the population, but no one underestimates its impact, the social, economic, political, and psychological consequences of which can be read in Henry Knighton's account.

Then the dreadful pestilence made its way through the coast land by Southampton, and reached Bristol, and there perished al-most the whole strength of the town, as it were surprised by sudden death; for few kept their beds more than two or three days, or even half a day. Then this cruel death spread on all sides, following the course of the sun. And there died at Leicester, in the small parish of St. Leonard more than 380 persons, in the parish of Holy Cross, 400, in the parish of St. Margaret's, Leicester, 700; and so in every parish, in a great multitude. Then the Bishop of Lincoln sent notice throughout his whole diocese giving general power to all priests, as well regulars as seculars, of hearing confessions and giv-ing absolution to all persons with full epis-copal authority, except only in case of debt. And in this case, the debtor was to pay

SOURCE: From Dorothy Hughes, ed., *Illustrations of Chaucer's England* (Essex, England: Long-man Group Limited, 1918), Doc. 3, pp. 145–49. By permission of Longman Group Limited.

the debt, if he were able, while he lived, or others were to be appointed to do so from his property after his death. In the same way the Pope gave plenary remission of all offences to all receiving absolution at the point of death, and granted that this power should endure until Easter next following, and that every one might choose his own confessor at will.

In the same year there was a great murrain[1] of sheep everywhere in the kingdom, so that in one place more than 5000 sheep died in a single pasture; and they rotted so that neither bird nor beast would approach them. There was great cheapness of all things, owing to the general fear of death, since very few people took any account of riches or property of any kind. A horse that was formerly worth 40s.[2] could be had for half a mark, a fat ox for 4s., a cow for 12d.,[3] a heifer for 6d., a fat wether for 4d., a sheep for 3d., a lamb for 2d., a large pig for 5d.; a stone[4] of wool was worth 9d. Sheep and oxen strayed at large through the fields and among the crops, and there were none to drive them off or herd them, but they perished in remote by-ways and hedges in inestimable numbers throughout all districts, because that there was such great scarcity of servants that none knew what to do. For there was no recollection of such great and terrible mortality since the time of Vortigern, King of the Britons, in whose day, as Bede testifies, the living did not suffice to bury the dead.

In the following autumn a reaper was not to be had for less than 8d., with his food, a mower for less than 10d., with food. Wherefore many crops rotted in the fields for want of men to gather them. But in the year of the pestilence, as has been said above, of other things, there was so great an abundance of all kinds of corn that they were scarcely regarded.

The Scots, hearing of the dreadful pestilence in England, surmised that it had come about at the hand of an avenging God, and it became an oath among them, so that, according to the common report, they were accustomed to swear "be the foul deth of Engelond." Thus, believing that a terrible vengeance of God had overtaken the English, they came together in Selkirk forest with the intention of invading the realm of England, when the fierce mortality overtook them and their ranks were thinned by sudden and terrible death, so that in a short time some 5000 perished. And as the rest, the strong and the feeble, were making ready to return to their own country, they were pursued and surprised by the English, who killed a very great number of them.

Master Thomas Bradwardine was consecrated by the Pope as Archbishop of Canterbury, and when he returned to England, he came to London, and was dead within two days. He was renowned above all other clerks in Christendom, especially in theology and other liberal sciences. At this time there was everywhere so great a scarcity of priests that many churches were left destitute, without divine service, masses, matins, vespers or sacraments. A chaplain was scarcely to be had to serve any church for less than £10 or 10 marks, and whereas when there was an abundance of priests before the pestilence a chaplain could be had for 4, 5 or 11 marks, with his board, at this time there was scarcely one willing to accept any vicarage at £20 or 20 marks. Within a little time, however, vast numbers of men whose wives had died in the pestilence flocked to take orders, many of whom were illiterate, and as it were mere laymen, save so far as they could read a little, although without understanding.

In the meantime the King sent notice into all counties of the realm that reapers and other labourers should not receive more than they had been wont, under a penalty defined by statute; and he introduced a statute for this cause. But the labourers were so arrogant and hostile that they paid no

---

[1] pestilence    [2] shillings    [3] pence    [4] 14 pounds

heed to the King's mandate, but if anyone wanted to have them he was obliged to give them whatever they asked, and either to lose his fruits and crops, or satisfy their greed and arrogance. But the King levied heavy fines upon abbots, priors, knights of great and less degree, and others great and small throughout the countryside when it became known to him that they did not observe his ordinance, and gave higher wages to their labourers; taking 100s. from some, 40s. or 20s. from others, according as they were able to pay. Moreover he took 20s. from each plough-land throughout the kingdom, and notwithstanding this, he also took a "fifteenth."

Then the King caused many labourers to be arrested, and sent them to prison, many of whom escaped and went away to the forests and woods for a time, and those who were taken were heavily fined. Others swore that they would not take wages higher than had formerly been the custom, and so were set free from prison. The same thing was done in the case of other labourers in the towns. . . . After the pestilence many buildings both great and small in all cities, towns, and boroughs fell into ruins for want of inhabitants, and in the same way many villages and hamlets were de-populated, and there were no houses left in them, all who had lived therein being dead; and it seemed likely that many such hamlets would never again be inhabited. In the following winter there was such dearth of servants for all sorts of labour as it was believed had never been before. For the sheep and cattle strayed in all directions without herdsmen, and all things were left with none to care for them. Thus necessaries became so dear that what had previously been worth 1d. was now worth 4d. or 5d. Moreover, the great men of the land and other lesser lords who had tenants, remitted the payment of their rents, lest the tenants should go away, on account of the scarcity of servants and the high price of all things — some half their rents, some more, some less, some for one, two, or three years according as they could come to an agreement with them. Similarly, those who had let lands on labour-rents to tenants as is the custom in the case of villeins, were obliged to relieve and remit these services, either excusing them entirely, or taking them on easier terms, in the form of a small rent, lest their houses should be irreparably ruined and the land should remain uncultivated. And all sorts of food became excessively dear.

## Henry Knighton's Description of the Peasants' Revolt (1381)

The peasants' revolt was the product of many factors: the efforts of the ruling elite to keep down wages after the mortality of the Black Death had halved the labor supply, the hard times that followed in the wake of the plague, and the sense of grievance that expressed itself in William Langland's powerful social and political protest. It was triggered by the landowning element's efforts to push the cost of the unpopular and victoryless Hundred Years War onto the peasants. In 1381 the House of Commons passed a poll tax, and in late May much of southern England was in rebellion. The revolt lasted little more than a month. It began in Kent and spread to Essex and Surrey, and was led (very badly) by the Kentish Wat Tyler and the priest John Ball. The rebel bands converged on London, sacked the city for two days, and lynched the unpopular Archbishop of Canterbury. The climax came when

SOURCE: From Edward P. Cheyney, trans., *Readings in English History Drawn from the Original Sources* (New York: Ginn & Co., 1908), pp. 261–265.

young King Richard II, fronting for a badly frightened and disorganized aristocracy, met with Wat Tyler. During the second of these interviews Tyler was killed, and to the surprise of everyone, including all subsequent historians, the rebel forces hesitated and then dissolved. The revolt was, in effect, over, although violence continued in the countryside until the government could hunt down and execute the ringleaders. William Knighton's account of these events is important not only because it is a major source but also because of the way he handles the story.

---

In the year 1381, the second of the reign of King Richard Second, during the month of May, on Wednesday, the fourth day after the feast of Trinity, that impious band [of peasants] began to assemble from Kent, from Surrey, and from many other surrounding places. Apprentices also, leaving their masters, rushed to join these. And so they gathered on Blackheath, where, forgetting themselves in their multitude, and neither contented with their former cause nor appeased by smaller crimes, they unmercifully planned greater and worse evils and determined not to desist from their wicked undertaking until they should have entirely extirpated the nobles and great men of the kingdom.

So at first they directed their course of iniquity to a certain town of the archbishop of Canterbury called Maidstone, in which there was a jail of the said archbishop, and in the said jail was a certain John Ball, a chaplain who was considered among the laity to be a very famous preacher; many times in the past he had foolishly spread abroad the word of God, by mixing tares with wheat, too pleasing to the laity and extremely dangerous to the liberty of ecclesiastical law and order, execrably introducing into the church of Christ many errors among the clergy and laymen. For this reason he had been tried as a clerk and convicted in accordance with the law, being seized and assigned to this same jail for his permanent abiding place. On the Wednesday before the feast of the Consecration they came into Surrey to the jail of the king at Marshalsea, where they broke in the jail without delay, forcing all imprisoned there to come with

them to help them; and whomsoever they met, whether pilgrims or others of whatever condition, they forced to go with them.

On the Friday following the feast of the Consecration they came over the bridge to London; here no one resisted them, although, as was said, the citizens of London knew of their advance a long time before; and so they directed their way to the Tower where the king was surrounded by a great throng of knights, esquires, and others. It was said that there were in the Tower about one hundred and fifty knights together with one hundred and eighty others, with the mother of the king, the duchess of Britanny, and many other ladies; and there was present, also, Henry, earl of Derby, son of John, duke of Lancaster, who was still a youth;[5] so, too, Simon of Sudbury, archbishop of Canterbury and chancellor of England, and brother Robert de Hales, prior of the Hospital of England and treasurer of the king.

John Leg and a certain John, a Minorite, a man active in warlike deeds, skilled in natural sciences, an intimate friend of Lord John, duke of Lancaster, hastened with three others to the Tower for refuge, intending to hide themselves under the wings of the king. The people had determined to kill the archbishop and the others above mentioned with him; for this reason they came to this place, and afterwards they fulfilled their vows. The king, however, desired to free the archbishop and his friends from the jaws of the wolves, so he sent to the people a command to assemble outside the city, at a place called Mile End, in order to speak with the king and to treat with him

---

[5] the future Henry IV

concerning their designs. The [king's] soldiers who were to go forward, consumed with folly, lost heart, and gave up, on the way, their boldness of purpose. Nor did they dare to advance, but, unfortunately, struck as they were by fear, like women, kept themselves within the Tower.

But the king advanced to the assigned place, while many of the wicked mob kept following him. . . . More, however, remained where they were. When the others had come to the king they complained that they had been seriously oppressed by many hardships and that their condition of servitude was unbearable, and that they neither could nor would endure it longer. The king, for the sake of peace, and on account of the violence of the times, yielding to their petition, granted to them a charter with the great seal, to the effect that all men in the kingdom of England should be free and of free condition, and should remain both for themselves and their heirs free from all kinds of servitude and villeinage forever. This charter was rejected and decided to be null and void by the king and the great men of the kingdom in the parliament held at Westminster in the same year, after the feast of St. Michael.

While these things were going on, behold those degenerate sons, who still remained, summoned their father the archbishop with his above-mentioned friends without any force or attack, without sword or arrow, or any other form of compulsion, but only with force of threats and excited outcries, inviting those men to death. But they did not cry out against it for themselves, nor resist, but, as sheep before the shearers, going forth barefooted with uncovered heads, ungirt, they offered themselves freely to an undeserved death, just as if they had deserved this punishment for some murder or theft. And so, alas! before the king returned, seven were killed at Tower Hill, two of them lights of the kingdom, the worthy with the unworthy. John Leg and his three associates

were the cause of this irreparable loss. Their heads were fastened on spears and sticks in order that they might be told from the rest. . . .

Whatever representatives of the law they found or whatever men served the kingdom in a judicial capacity, these they slew without delay.

On the following day, which was Saturday, they gathered in Smithfield, where there came to them in the morning the king, who although only a youth in years yet was in wisdom already well versed. Their leader, whose real name was Wat Tyler, approached him; already they were calling him by the other name of Jack Straw. He kept close to the king, addressing him for the rest. He carried in his hand an unsheathed weapon which they call a dagger, and, as if in childish play, kept tossing it from one hand to the other in order that he might seize the opportunity, if the king should refuse his requests, to strike the king suddenly (as was commonly believed); and from this thing the greatest fear arose among those about the king as to what might be the outcome.

They begged from the king that all the warrens,[6] and as well waters as park and wood, should be common to all, so that a poor man as well as a rich should be able freely to hunt animals everywhere in the kingdom, — in the streams, in the fish ponds, in the woods, and in the forest; and that he might be free to chase the hare in the fields, and that he might do these things and others like them without objection. When the king hesitated about granting this concession Jack Straw came nearer, and, speaking threatening words, seized with his hand the bridle of the horse of the king very daringly. When John de Walworth, a citizen of London, saw this, thinking that death threatened the king, he seized a sword and pierced Jack Straw in the neck. Seeing this, another soldier, by name Radulf Standyche, pierced his side

---

[6] land enclosed for breeding game

with another sword. He sank back, slowly letting go with his hands and feet, and then died. A great cry and much mourning arose: "Our leader is slain." When this dead man had been meanly dragged along by the hands and feet into the church of St. Bartholomew, which was near by, many withdrew from the band, and, vanishing, betook themselves to flight, to the number it is believed of ten thousand. . . .

After these things had happened and quiet had been restored, the time came when the king caused the offenders to be punished. So Lord Robert Tresillian, one of the judges, was sent by order of the king to inquire into the uprisings against the peace and to punish the guilty. Wherever he came he spared no one, but caused great slaughter. And just as those evil doers plotted in hostile manner against the judges, Lord John de Candishe and any others they could find, by bringing them to capital punishment, and against all those skilled in the laws of the country whom they could reach, and not sparing any one of them, but punishing them by capital punishment, just so this judge spared no one, but demanded misfortune for misfortune. For whoever was accused before him in this said cause, whether justly or as a matter of spite, he immediately passed upon him the sentence of death. He ordered some to be beheaded, others to be hanged, still others to be dragged through the city and hanged in four different parts thereof; others to be disemboweled, and the entrails to be burned before them while they were still alive, and afterwards to be decapitated, quartered, and hanged in four parts of the city according to the greatness of the crime and its desert. John Ball was captured at Coventry and led to St. Alban's, where, by order of the king, he was drawn and hanged, then quartered, and his quarters sent to four different places.

## The Charges Against Richard II (1399)

Richard II was a victim of his own ineptly realized ambitions to be master in his own kingdom and the long constitutional tradition, which he vainly sought to reverse, that kings were expected to share power with the community. When he denied the right of his first cousin Henry Bolingbroke to inherit the lands and title of the King's uncle John of Gaunt, Duke of Lancaster, Richard triggered both a family and constitutional crisis that led to his overthrow, abdication, imprisonment, and death. The individual charges brought against him to justify his removal from office are in part real, in part window dressing, but collectively they constitute a powerful case against Richard.

Item, when the King asked and received many sums by way of loan from many lords and others of the realm, to be repaid at a certain term, notwithstanding that he had promised each individual from whom he received these loans, by his letters patent that he would repay them at the time appointed, he did not fulfill his promise, nor has satisfaction yet been made for the money, whence the creditors are greatly distressed. . . .

Item, whereas the King of England is able to live becomingly upon the issues of his realm and the estates belonging to the

SOURCE: From Dorothy Hughes, ed., *Illustrations of Chaucer's England* (Essex, England: Longman Group Limited, 1918), Doc. 53, pp. 290–292.

crown, without burdening his people, when that the realm be not charged with the expenses of war, the same King, although during almost the whole of his time there were truces between the realm of England and its enemies, not only gave away the greater part of his patrimony to unworthy persons, but on account of this every year charged his people with so many burdensome grants that they were sorely and excessively oppressed, to the impoverishment of his realm; not applying the money so raised to the common profit and advantage of his realm, but lavishly dissipating it upon his own pomp, display, and vain glory. And great sums of money are still owing for provisions for his household, and for his other purchases, although he had wealth and treasure more than any of his predecessors within memory.

Item, being unwilling to protect and preserve the just laws and customs of the realm ... frequently, from time to time, when the laws were declared and set forth to him by the Justices and others of his Council, and he should have done justice to those who sought it according to those laws — he said expressly, with harsh and insolent looks, that his laws were in his own mouth, and sometimes, within his breast; and that he alone could change or establish the laws of his realm. Deceived by which opinion, he would not allow justice to be done to many of his lieges, but compelled numbers of persons to desist from suing common right by threats and fear.

Item, after that certain statutes were established in his Parliament, which were binding until they should be especially repealed by the authority of another Parliament, the King, desiring to enjoy such liberty that no such statutes might restrain him . . . cunningly procured petition to be put forward in Parliament on behalf of the community of the realm, and to be granted him in general — that he might be as free as any of his predecessors; by colour of

which petition and concession the King frequently caused and commanded many things to be done contrary to such statutes then unrepealed.

Item, although by statute and custom of the realm, upon the summons of Parliament the people of each county ought to be free to choose and depute[7] knights for the county to be present in Parliament, set forth their grievances, and sue for remedy . . . yet, the more freely to carry out his rash designs, the King frequently commanded the sheriffs to cause certain persons nominated by himself to come to his Parliament; and the knights thus favourable to him he could, and frequently did, induce, sometimes by fear, and divers threats, sometimes by gifts, to consent to measures prejudicial to the realm and excessively burdensome to the people; and especially he induced them to grant him the subsidy of wools for the term of his life, and another subsidy for a term of years, greatly oppressing the people. . . .

Item, in many Great Councils, when the lords of the realm, Justices and others were charged faithfully to counsel the King in matters touching the estate of himself and the realm, the said lords, . . . when they gave counsel according to their discretion were often suddenly and so sharply rebuked and censured by him, that they dared not . . . speak the truth in giving their advice.

Item, the King was wont almost continually to be so variable and dissembling in his words and writings, and so utterly contradictory, especially in writing to the Pope and to Kings, and other lords within and without the realm, and to his other subjects, that scarcely any living man, being acquainted with his ways, could or would trust him. Indeed, he was held so faithless and inconstant that it gave ground for scandal not only as to his own person, but to the whole realm, and especially among foreigners throughout the world who became aware of it.

---

[7] appoint

## The Abdication of Richard II (1399)

Exactly how "freely, voluntarily, unequivocally" Richard abdicated may be doubted, but the wording of the abdication was crucial for the security of the Lancastrian dynasty.

In God's name, Amen. I, Richard, by the grace of God, king of England and France, and lord of Ireland, absolve all archbishops and bishops of the said kingdoms and lordships, and all other prelates whatsoever of secular or regular churches of whatsoever dignity, rank, state, or condition they may be, and dukes, marquises, earls, barons, knights, vassals, and vavassors[8] and all my liege men, clerical or secular by whatsoever name they are known, from the oath of fealty and homage and all others whatsoever made to me and from every bond of allegiance, royalty and lordship with which they have been or are bound by oath to me, or bound in any other way whatsoever; and these and their heirs and successors in perpetuity from these bonds and oaths and all other bonds whatsoever, I relieve, free, and excuse; absolved, excused and freed as far as pertains to my person, I release them from every performance of their oath which could follow from their promises or from any of them. . . . The name and honor and royal right and title of king, freely, voluntarily, unequivocally, and absolutely, and in the best fashion, wise, and form possible, in these writings I renounce, and resign as a whole, and release in word and deed, and yield my place in them, and retire from them forever.

Saving to my successors, kings of England, in the realms and lordships and all other premises in perpetuity, the rights belonging or to belong to them, in them or in any of them, I confess, acknowledge, consider, and truly judge from sure knowledge that I in the rule and government of the said realms and lordships and all pertaining to them have been and am wholly insufficient and useless, and because of my notorious deserts am not unworthy to be deposed. And I swear on these holy gospels touched bodily by me that I will never contravene these premises of renunciation, resignation, demise and surrender, nor will I impugn them in any way, in deed or in word by myself or by another or others, or as far as in me lies permit them to be contravened or impugned publicly or secretly, but I will hold this renunciation, resignation, demise, and surrender unalterable and acceptable and I will keep it firmly and observe it in whole and in every part; so may God help me and these holy scriptures of God. I, Richard, the aforesaid king, subscribe myself with my own hand.

---

SOURCE: From George Burton Adams and H. Morse Stephens, eds., *Select Documents of English Constitutional History* (New York: The Macmillan Co., 1904), Doc. 102, pp. 161–162.

[8] feudal tenant ranking immediately below a baron

## *The Indenture of Ralph Longford, Esquire* (25 April, 1481)

William Lord Hastings maintained ninety retainers who owed him service and wore his livery; twenty were gentlemen; fifty-nine, esquires; nine, knights; and two, barons. Twenty of these were sheriffs and thirty-three were justices of the peace. It would appear that Ralph Longford was among excellent and powerful company.

This indenture made the xxv day of April the xxi year of the reign of King Edward the IV between William Hastings, knight, Lord Hastings, on the one part, and Ralph Longford, esquire, on the other part, witnesseth that the said Ralph agreeth, granteth, and by these present indentures bindeth him to the said lord to be his retained servant during his life, and to him to do faithful and true service, and the part of the same lord take against all men in peace and war with as many persons defensibly arrayed as the same Ralph can or may make at all times that the said lord will command him, at the said lord's costs and charges, saving the allegiance which the same Ralph oweth to the king our sovereign lord and to the prince. And the said lord granteth to the said Ralph to be his good and favourable lord and him aid and support in his right according to the law. In witness hereof the foresaid parties to these present indentures have interchangeably set their seals and signs manual the day and year foresaid.

RALPH LONGFORD.

## *The Troubles of the Paston Family* (1449–1476)

The Pastons of Norfolk, like so many county families, were a highly ambitious and aggressive clan who were determined to convert their humble origins (Clement, the first Paston, was a husbandman and married a bondwoman) into a claim to gentle birth and Norman ancestry. By 1421 Clement's son William was well on his way up the social and economic ladder. Having been trained in the law, he became sergeant of the Court of Common Pleas and in 1429 a Justice. By the time of his death in 1444, the Pastons had become one of the substantial landowners of the county. The family's concern thereafter was to retain that position and, if possible, to improve on it by any means available — marriage, corruption, patronage, or the law. The following letters give a glimpse of the ordeal involved, for the higher the Pastons rose, the more predatory became the competition for land.

The first crisis emerged after Justice William Paston's death when in 1448–49 Robert Hungerford, Lord Molyns, claimed the Paston manor of Gresham and attempted to collect the rents.

*To my trusty and well beloved,*
*the Vicar and Tenants of*
*my Lordship of Gresham.*

Trusty and well beloved friends, I greet you well, and put you all out of doubt for all that ye have done for me; and the money that ye pay to my well beloved servant John Patrich, I will be your warrant as for

SOURCE: From William H. Dunham, *Lord Hastings' Indentured Retainers 1461–1483* (Middletown: Connecticut Academy of Arts and Sciences, 1955), Vol. 39, p. 132.

From James Gairdner, ed., *The Paston Letters 1422–1509* (Edinburgh: John Grant, 1910), 4 vols.: Vol. I, #65, p. 80, #67, pp. 82–83, #77, pp. 105–108, #159, pp. 213–216; Vol. II., #512, pp. 204–206, #513, pp. 207–208, #534, pp. 250–252, #576, pp. 307–309, #592, pp. 327–329, #620, pp. 371–373; Vol. III, #779, pp. 165–167.

your discharge, and save you harmless against all those that would grieve you, to my power. And, as heartily as I can, I thank you of the good will ye have had, and have towards me. And as to the title of right that I have to the Lordship of Gresham [it] shall within short time be known, and by the law so determined that ye shall all be glad that hath ought me your good will therein.

And Almighty God keep you, and by His grace, I shall be with you soon after the Parliament is ended.

Written at London, on Our Lady even last past.

R. H. [Robert Hungerford]
LORD MOLEYNS

[*March 24, 1449*]

The manor seems to have twice changed hands and a state of military seige developed as Margaret Paston's letter to her husband indicates.

#### To John Paston.

Right worshipful husband, I recommend me to you, and pray you to get some cross bows and wyndacs[9] to bind them with and quarrels,[10] for your house here be so low that there may none man shoot out with no long bow, though we had never so much need.

I suppose ye should have such things of Sir John Fastolf, if ye would send to him; and also I would ye should get two or three short pole-axes to keep with doors, and as many jacks, as ye may.

[John] Partrich and his fellowship[11] are sore afraid that ye would enter again upon them, and they have made great ordnance within the house, as it is told me. They have made bars to bar the doors cross wise, and they have made wickets on every quarter of the house to shoot out at, both with bows and with hand-guns; and the holes that be made for hand-guns they be scarce knee high from the plancher[12] and of such holes be made five. There can none man shoot out at them with no hand-bows.

Purry[13] fell in fellowship with William Hasard at Quarles's[14] and told him that he would come and drink with Partrich and

with him, and he said he should be welcome, and after noon he went thither for to espy what they did and what fellowship they had with them; and when he came thither the doors were fast sparred[15] and there were none folks with them but Mariott, and Capron and his wife, and Quarles's wife, . . . and the said Purry espied all these foresaid things. And Mariott and his fellowship had much great language that shall be told you when ye come home.

I pray you that ye will vouchsafe to do buy for me one pound of almonds and one pound of sugar, that ye will do buy some frieze[16] to make of your child his gowns, ye shall have best cheap, and best choice of Hay's wife, as it is told me. And that ye will buy a yard of broad cloth of black, for one hood for me of 44d.[17] or 4s.[18] a yard, for there is neither good cloth nor good frieze in this town. As for the child his gowns and I have them, I will do them maken.[19]

The Trinity have you in his keeping, and send you good speed in all your matters.

M. P. [Margaret Paston]

[*1449?*]

Then in late January of 1450 Lord Molyns attacked in force and committed an act of violence that induced John Paston to petition King Henry VI.

*To the King, our Sovereign Lord,*
*and to the right wise and*
*discreet Lords, assembled*
*in this present Parliament.*

Beseecheth meekly your humble liege man, John Paston, that where he . . . have been [im]peccably possessed of the manor of Gresham, within the county of Norfolk, 20

---

[9] device by which a crossbow is cocked  [10] metal bolts shot from a crossbow  [11] Lord Molyns' men  [12] floor  [13] a Paston servant  [14] an innkeeper  [15] fastened  [16] coarse wool  [17] pence  [18] shillings  [19] do . . . have them made

year and more, till the 17[th] day of February, the year of your noble reign 26 [1448], that Robert Hungerford, Knight, the Lord Molyns, entered into the said manor; and how be it that the said John Paston, after the said entry, sued to the said Lord Molyns and his council, in the most lowly manner that he could, daily from time of the said entry onto the fest of Michclmas then next following, during which time divers communications were had betwixt the council of the said Lord and the council of your beseecher. . . . And after suit made to the said Lord by your said beseecher, as well at Salisbury as in other places to his great cost, and none answer had but delays, which caused your said beseecher the 6[th] day of October last past to inhabit him in a mansion within the said town, keeping still there his possession, until the 28[th] day of January last past, the said Lord sent to the said mansion a riotous people, to the number of a thousand persons, . . . arrayed in manner of war, with curesse,[20] brigaunders,[21] jakks,[22] salettes,[23] gleyfes,[24] bows, arrows, pavises,[25] guns, . . . long cromes[26] to draw down houses, ladders, pikoys[27] with which they mined down the walls, and long trees with which they broke up gates and doors, and so came into the said mansion, the wife of your beseecher at the time being therein, and 12 persons with her; the which persons they drove out of the said mansion, and mined down the walls of the chamber wherein the wife of your said beseecher was, and bore her out at the gates, and cut asundry the posts of the houses and let them fall, and broke up all the chambers and coffers within the said mansion, and rifled, and in manner of robbery bore away all the stuff, array, and money that your said beseecher and his servants had there, on to the value of £200, . . . saying openly that if they might have found there your said beseecher . . . [he] should have died. And yet

divers of the said misdoers and riotous people unknown, contrary to your laws, daily keep the said manor with force and lie in wait of divers of the friends, tenants and servants of your said beseecher, and greviously vex and trouble him in divers wise, and seek him in her houses, ransaking and searching her sheaves and straw in her barns and other places with bare speers, swords, and gesernis,[28] as it seemeth, to slew him if they might have found him; and some have [been] beaten and left for dead, so that they, for doubt of their lives, dare not go home to their houses, nor occupy their husbandry, to the great hurt, fear and dread, as well of your said beseecher as of his said friends, tenants and servants. And also, they compel poor tenants of the said manor, now within their danger, again[st] their will, to take feigned [com]plaints in the courts of the hundred there again[st] the said friends, tenants and servants of your said beseecher, which dare not appear to answer for fear of bodily harm; nay can get no copies of the said [com]plaints to remedy them by the law, because he that keepth the said courts is of covyn[29] with the said misdoers, and was one of the said risers. . . .

Please it your highness, considering that if this great insurrection, riots and wrongs, and daily continuance thereof so heiniously done again[st] your crown, dignity and peace, should not . . . be duly punished, it shall give great boldness to them and all other misdoers to make congregations and conventicles riotously, . . . to the subversion and final destruction of your liege's people and laws. And also, how that your said beseecher is not able to sue the common law in redressing of this heinious wrong, for the great might and alliance of the said Lord: And also, that your said beseecher can have none action by your law again[st] the said riotous people for the goods and cattle by him so riotously and wrongfully taken and borne

---

[20] breast armour   [21] body armour   [22] jackets with armour   [23] helmets   [24] spears   [25] large shields
[26] scaling poles   [27] picks   [28] battle-axes   [29] collusion

away, because the said people be unknown.
. . . [I beg] that your said beseecher may be
restored to the said goods and cattle thus
riotously taken away; and that the said Lord
Molyns have such commandment that your
said beseecher be not thus with force, in
manner of war, held out of his said manor,
contrary to all your statutes made again[st]
such forcible entrees and holdings. . . .

John got nowhere at first in his efforts to evict Lord Molyns, but evidently he must
have received help from someone influential at court, for by 1451 he was back at
Gresham and had started legal proceedings against Lord Molyns and his retainers,
who had sacked his manor. John soon discovered from his friend John Osbern,
however, that he was no match for a nobleman who could call directly upon the
King for support.

*To my right reverend and*
*worshipful Master, John Paston,*
*be this delivered.*

Please it your mastership to weet[30] that I
have spoken with the Sheriff at his place,
moving to him, as for that,[31] that was left
with his Undersheriff; it is your will he
should send a man of his for it; for though
it were more ye would gladly he should take
it; he thanked you, and said his Undersheriff was at London, and himself had none
deserved,[32] and if he had he would have
taken it. And when I departed from him I
desired him again to send therefore, and
then he said it should abide till ye came
home, whereby I conceive he would have it,
and be glad to take it. Moreover I remembered[33] him of his promises made before to
you at London, . . . and then he said he would
do for you that he may, except for the ac-
quittal of the Lord Molyn's men, insomuch
as the King[34] hath written to him to show
favour in these indictments, he dare not
abide the jeopardy[35] of that, that he should
offend the King's commandments. He know
not how the King may be informed of him,
and what shall be said to him.

And then I said, as for any jeopardy that
he should abide in any thing that he doth
for you, or by your desire, you have offered
him, and will perform it, sufficient surety[36]
for to see him harmless, and therefore I
supposed there would none reasonable man
think but that he might do for you without
any jeopardy. And then he said, he might
none surety take that passed £100; and
the Lord Moleyns is a great Lord, he might
soon cause him to lose that and much more.
Then I said, by that mean[s] in default of a
Sheriff, every man may be put from his livelihood;[37] and then he said, . . . if the King
wrote again to him he will no longer abide
the jeopardy of the King's writing, but he
trusteth to God to impanel such men as
should to his knowledge be indifferent, and
none common jurors. As me seemeth, it
would do good and ye would get a commandment to the King to the Sheriff for to
show you favour, and to impanel gentlemen,
and not for to favour none such riots, &c.,
for he said that he sent you the letter that
the King sent him, and ye said a man should
get such one for a noble.[38]

Item, I remembered him of the promises
that he made to Timperley, and that if he
would make you very true promise, ye
would reward him as much as he would desire, or any other reasonable man for him,
and as much or more than any adversary ye
have would give him; then he said he took
never no money of none of them all. There
was proffered him at Walsingham for the
Lord Molyns 20 nobles,[39] he had not a
penny; moreover I proffered him, if he
would make you promise that ye might
verily trust upon him, ye would give him in
hand as he would desire, or to leave a sum
if he would have named it in a mean[40] man's

---

[30] know  [31] a sum of money  [32] *none* . . . i.e., no honest man to collect it  [33] reminded  [34] Henry
VI  [35] danger  [36] money  [37] property  [38] 6 shillings, 8 pence  [39] 6 pounds, 13 shillings, 4 pence
[40] middle

hand, and such as he hath trust to. And then he said, if he might do for you, or if he do any thing for you, then he will take your money with a good will; and other promise I could not have of him, but that he will do for you that he may, except for the indictments. I conceive verily he hath made promise to do his part that they shall be acquitted, but I suppose he hath made none other promise against you for the livelihood, but he looketh after a great bribe, but it is not for to trust him verily, without that he may not choose. I suppose he had no writing from my Lord of Norfolk as he said. . . .

Written at Norwich, the Thursday next after Saint Austin, &c.

By your servant,
JOHN OSBERN

[May 27, 1451]

The long and costly struggle to keep Gresham ended in negotiation, and John Paston in possession. As yet, however, the Pastons were relatively small landowners; this situation changed when in 1458 John inherited the estates of Sir John Fastolf and became one of the richest property holders in Norfolk and Suffolk. Feudal property rights — especially inherited land — were extremely difficult to establish in law, and almost immediately every nobleman who could maintain the flimsiest claim and had military and political power made a bid for the Fastolf inheritance, especially the richest plums: Caister Castle and the manors of Drayton, Hellesden, and Cotton. The Duke of Norfolk, who was the first to move, seized Caister Castle in 1461; but John Paston was a loyal Yorkist, and young Edward IV saw to it that the Duke returned the castle. Four years later the Duke of Suffolk attacked Drayton and Hellesdon manors, Paston possessions that were located directly across the river from the Duke's estates. The Pastons were harrassed at law and by armed retainers. Since John was in London at the time, the burden of defense was left to his wife, Margaret, and his bailiff, Richard Calle, whose letters give a vivid picture of the violence and destruction.

*To my Master John Paston,*
*in haste.*

Pleaseth it your mastership to weet of the rule and disposition of the Master Philip and the bailiff of Cossey, with others of my Lord of Suffolk's men. On Monday last past at afternoon [they] were at Hellesdon, with the number of 300 men for to have entered, notwithstanding they said they come not for to enter, but without doubt and [if] they had been strong enough for us, they would have entered, and that we understand enough but we knowing of their coming and purveyed so for them, that we were strong enough. We had 60 men within the place, and guns, and such ordnance so that, if they had set upon us, they had been destroyed. And there my Mistress[41] was within and my Master Sir John,[42] and [he] hath gotten him as great worship for that day as any gentle-man might do, and so is it reported of the party and in all Norwich. And my Lord of Norwich[43] sent thither Master John Salett and Master John Bulleman for to treat, and so they did, . . . and then appointment was taken that shall send home their men, and we should send home ours. And now my Lord of Suffolk's men come from Claxton to Norwich, and face us and fray upon us, this daily. There fell upon me before Swaine's door 12 of his men, 8 of them in harness, and there they would have mischieved me, and the Sheriff letted[44] them and other, and they made their avaunt where that I may be gotten, I should die; and so they lie in wait for to mischief me, Daubeney and Wykes; and so I dare not ride out alone without a man with me. And I understand there is coming an Oyer [and] Terminer[45] to enquire of all riots, and my Lord of Suffolk will be

---

41 Margaret Paston  42 John Paston's son  43 Bishop Lyhart  44 hindered  45 *Oyer* . . . a special commission

at Drayton on Lammas-day,[46] and keep the Court there, wherefore ye must seek a remedy for it, or el[se] it will not do well.

If my Lord of Norfolk would come, he should make all well, for they fear him above all things, for it is noised here that my Lord of Norfolk hath taken party in this matter, and all the country is glad of it, saying that if he come they will wholly go with him.

And me seemeth it were well done to move my Lord in it, though ye should give him the profits of Hellesdon and Drayton for the keeping, and some money beside; for ye must seek some other remedy than ye do, or el[se] in my conceit it shall go to the Devil, and be destroyed, and that in right short time. And therefore at the reverence of God take some appointment with Master Yelverton, such as ye think should most hurt.

I beseech you to pardon me of my writing, for I have pity to see the tribulation that my Mistress hath here, and all your friends, &c.

Almighty Jesu preserve and keep you. Written the Wednesday next Saint Thomas's day

Your poor Servant and Beadsman[47]<br>RIC[HARD] CALLE

[July 10, 1465]

*To my right worshipful Husband*
*John Paston, in haste.*

Right worshipful Husband, I recommend me to you, praying you heartily that ye will seek a mean[s] that your servants may be in peace, for they be daily in fear of their lives. The Duke of Suffolk's men threaten daily Daubeney, Wykes and Richard Calle, that wheresoever they may get them they should die, and affrays[48] have been made on Richard Calle this week, so that he was in great jeopardy at Norwich among them; and great affrays have been made upon me and

my fellowship here on Monday last past, of which Richard Calle telleth me that he hath sent you word of in writing, more plainly than I may do at this time, but I shall inform you more plainly hereafter.

I suppose there shall be great labour against you and your servants at the Assizes and Sessions[49] here; wherefore me seemeth, saving your better advice, it were well done that ye should speak with the Justices ere they come here; and if ye will that I complain to them or to any other, if God fortune me life and health, I will do as ye advise me to do, for in good faith, I have been simply[50] entreated among them; and what with sickness, and trouble that I have had, I am brought right low and weak, but to my power I will do as I can or may in your matters.

The Duke of Suffolk and both the Duchesses[51] shall come to Claxton this day, as I am informed, and this next week he shall be at Cossey whether he will come further hitherward or not, I wot[52] not yet. It is said that he should come hither, and yet his men said here on Monday that he claimed no title to this place; they said their coming was but to take out such riotous people as was here within this place, and such as were the King's felons, and endicted and outlawed men. Nevertheless they would show no warrants whereby to take none such, though there had [been] such here; I suppose, if they might have come in peaceably, they would have made another cause of their coming.

When all was done and they should depart, Harleston and other[s] desired me that I should come and see mine old Lady[53] and sue to my Lord, and if anything were amiss it should be amended. I said if I should sue for any remedy, that I should sue further, and let the King and all the Lords of this land to have knowledge what hath been done to us, if so were that the Duke would maintain that hath been done to us by his servants, if ye would give me leave.

---

[46] first of August  [47] one who prays for another  [48] attacks  [49] *Assizes* . . . law courts  [50] basely
[51] his wife and his mother  [52] know  [53] the dowager-duchess

I pray you send me word, if ye will that I make any complaint to the Duke or the Duchess, for it is told me, they know not the plainness[54] that hath been done in such things as hath been done in their names.

I should write much more to you but for lack of leisure. . . .

The Trinity have you in keeping. Written the Friday next after Saint Thomas,

By your

M. P. [Margaret Paston]

[July 12, 1465]

*To my right worshipful Husband*
*John Paston, be this*
*delivered in haste.*

Right worshipful Husband, I recommend me to you. Please it you to weet that I was at Hellesdon upon Thursday last past, and saw the place there, and in good faith there will no creature think how foully and horribly it is arrayed but if they saw it. There cometh much people daily to wonder thereupon, both of Norwich and of other places, and they speak shamefully thereof. The Duke had by better than £1000 that it had never been done, and ye have the more good will of the people that it is so foully done. And they made your tenants of Hellesdon and Drayton, with other[s], to help to break down the walls of the place and the lodge[55] both. God knoweth full evil against their wills, but that they durst no notherwise do for fear.[56] I have spoken with your tenants of Hellesdon and Drayton both, and put them in comfort as well as I can. The Duke's men ransacked the church, and bore away all the good[s] that was left there, both of ours and of the tenants, and left not so much but that they stood upon the high altar and ransacked the images, and took away such as they might find, and put away the parson out of the church till they had done; and ransacked every man's house in the town 5 or 6 times. And the chief masters of robbing

was the Bailiff of Eye, the Bailiff of Stradbrook, Thomas Slyford, and Porter; and Slyford was the chief robber of the church, and he hath most of the robbery next the Bailiff of Eye. And as for lead, brass, pewter, iron, doors, gates, and other stuff of the house, men of Cossey and Causton have it, and that they might not carry, they have hewn it asunder in the most dispiteous[57] wise. If it might be, I would some men of worship might be sent from the King to see how it is both there and at the lodge, ere then any snows come, that they may make report of the truth, else it shall not more be seen so plainly as it may now.

And at the reverence of God, speed your matters now, for it is too horrible a cost and trouble that we have now daily, and must have till it be otherwise; and your men dare not go about to gather up your livelihood, and we keep here daily more than 30 persons for salvation of us and the place, for in very truth, and the place had not been kept strong, the Duke had come hither. . . .

At the reverence of God, if any worshipful and profitable mean[s] may be taken in your matters, forsake it not in eschewing of our trouble and great costs and charges that we have, and may grow hereafter. It is thought here that if my Lord of Norfolk would take upon him for you, and that he may have a Commission for to enquire of such riots and robberies as hath been done to you and other[s] in this country, that then all the country will await upon him, and serve your intent; for the people loveth and dreadeth him more than any other lord, except the King and my Lord of Warwick, &c.

God have you in His keeping, and send us good tidings from you. Written in haste, upon the Sunday Saint Simon and Jude's Even.

By your

M. P. [Margaret Paston]

[October 27, 1465]

---

54 brutality   55 at Drayton   56 because of fear they could do nothing else   57 cruel

John Paston died in May, 1466, in the midst of defending his inheritance, and his son, Sir John, accepted what was tantamount to defeat. In order to buy off the Duke of Suffolk and others, he gave up all his rights to the Fastolf estates except one, the immense castle and rich manor of Caister, "the fairest flower in our garland." The retreat did him little good, for almost at once Fastolf's will was declared a forgery, and the Duke of Norfolk sent a small army of his men to seize the castle. Unfortunately for Sir John, the attack coincided with the overthrow of Edward IV and the reinstallation of Henry VI in 1469. Margaret Paston had been warning her son of the forthcoming assault and had been begging Sir John to find a patron at court in order to support his friends and well-wishers in the county.

*To Sir John Paston, Knight, be this delivered in haste.*

I greet you well, and send you God's blessing and mine; letting you weet that Blickling of Heylesdon came from London this week, and he is right merry, and maketh his boast that within this fortnight at Heylesdon should be both new lords and new officers. And also this day was brought me word from Caister that Rysing of Fretton should have heard said in divers places, there as he was in Suffolk, that Fastolf of Conghawe maketh all the strength that he may, and proposeth him to assault Caister, and to enter there if he may, insomuch that it is said that he hath a 5 score men ready, and sendeth daily spies to understand what fellowship keep the place. By whose power, or favour, or supportation that he will do this, I know not; but ye wot well that I have been afraid there before this time, when that I had other comfort than I have now; and I cannot well guide nor rule soldiers, and also they set not by a woman as they should set by a man. Therefore I would ye should send home your brothers or el[se] Daubeney to have a rule, and to take in such men as were necessary for the safeguard of the place, for if I were there without I had the more sadder[58] or worshipful persons about me, and there come a meny[59] of knaves and prevailed in their intent, it should be to me but a villainy. . . .

I have sent to Nicholas, and such as keep the place, that they should take in some fel-[lows] to assist and strength them till ye send home some other word, or some other man to govern them that be therein, &c.

I marvel greatly that ye send me no word how that ye do, for your elmyse[60] begin to wax right bold, and that putteth your friends both in great fear and doubt. Therefore purvey that they may have some comfort, that they be no more discouraged; for if we lose our friends it shall [be] hard in this troublous werd[61] to get them again.

The blessed Trinity speed you in your matters, and send you the victory of your elmyse, to your heart's ease and their confusion. Written at Norwich, the Saturday next before Relic Sunday, in haste. . . .

By your mother,
M. P. [Margaret Paston]

[July 11, 1467]

Sir John's efforts to defend Caister against such a powerful adversary were scarcely adequate, and his schemes at court to stop the Duke were just as unsuccessful as his letter to his brother (also called John) reveals.

*To my right well-beloved brother, John Paston, Esq., being at Caister, or to John Daubency there, be this letter delivered.*

Right well-beloved brother, I commend me to you; letting you weet that I have waged for to help you and Daubency to keep the place at Caister four well assured and true men to do all manner of thing what that

---

[58] graver   [59] group   [60] enemies   [61] troublesome world

they be desired to do in safeguard or inforcing of the said place; and moreover they be proved men, and cunning in the war and in feats of arms, and they can well shoot both guns and cross-bows, and amend and string them, and devise bulwarks, or anythings that should be a strength to the place; and they will, as need is, keep watch and ward. They be sad[62] and well-advised men, saving one of them, which is bald, and called William Peny, which is as good a man as goeth on the earth, saving a little, he will, as I understand, be a little copschotyn,[63] but yet he is no brawler but full of courtesty, much upon[64] James Halman; the other 3 be named Peryn Sale, John Chapman, Robert Jack's Son [Jackson], saving that as yet they have none harness come, but when it cometh it shall be sent to you, and in the mean while I pray you and Daubeney to purvey them some.

Also a couple of beds they must needs have, which I pray you by the help of my mother to purvey for them till that I come home to you. Ye shall find them gentlemanly, comfortable fellows, and that they will and dare abide by their tackling,[65] and if ye

understand that any assault should be towards, I send you these men, because that men of the country there about you should be afraid for fear of loss of their goods; wherefore if there were any such thing towards, I would ye took of men of the country but few, and that they were well assured men, for else they might discourage all the remanent.[66]

And as for any writing from the King, he hath promised that there shall come none, and if there do his unwarys,[67] your answer may be this, how the king hath said, and so delay them till I may have word, and I shall soon purvey a remedy.

I understand that ye have been with my Lord of Norfolk now of late. What ye have done I wot not; we see that he shall be here again this day. Moreover, I trow[68] John Alford shall not long abide with my Lord; I shall send you tidings of other things in haste, with the grace of God, who, &c. Written on Wednesday next before St. Martin.

JOHN PASTON

[*November, 9, 1468*]

By September, 1469, the situation, as Margaret Paston wrote, was desperate.

### To Sir John Paston

I greet you well, letting you weet that your brother and his fellowship stand in great jeopardy at Caister, and lack victuals, and Daubeney and Berney be dead, and divers other[s] greatly hurt, and they fail gunpowder and arrows, and the place [be] sore broken with guns of the other party, so that, but they have hasty help, they be like to lose both their lives and the place, to the greatest rebuke to you that ever came to any gentleman, for every man in this country marvelleth greatly that ye suffer them to be so long in so great jeopardy without help or other remedy.

The Duke [of Norfolk] hath been more fervently set thereupon, and more cruel, since that Writtill, my Lord of Clarence's

man, was there, than he was before, and he hath sent for all his tenants from every place, and other[s], to be there at Caister at Thursday next coming, that there is then like to be the greatest multitude of people that came there yet. And they purpose then to make a great assault — for they have sent for funds to Lyon and other place[s] by the sea's side — that, with their great multitude of guns, with other shot and ordnance, there shall no man dare appear in the place. They shall hold them so busy with their great people that it shall not lie in their power within to hold it against them without God help them or [they] have hasty succour from you.

Therefore, as ye will have my blessing, I charge you and require you that ye see

---

[62] sober   [63] high-crested   [64] like   [65] undertaking   [66] remainder   [67] without his knowledge
[68] trust

your brother be holpen[69] in haste. And if ye can have none mean[s], rather desire writing from my Lord of Clarence, if he be at London, or el[se] of my Lord Archbishop of York, to the Duke of Norfolk that he will grant them that be in the place their lives and their goods; and in eschewing of insurrections with other inconveniences that be like to grow within the shire of Norfolk, this troublous were because of such conventicles and gatherings within the said shire for cause of the said place, they shall suffer him to enter upon such appointment, or other like, taken by the advice of your council there at London, if ye think this be not good, till the law hath determined otherwise; and let him write another letter to your brother to deliver the place up on the same appointment. And if ye think, as I can suppose, that the Duke of Norfolk will not agree to this, because he granted this afore, and they in the place would not accept it, then I would the said messenger should with the said letters bring from the said Lord of Clarence, or el[se] my Lord Archbishop, to my Lord of Oxford other letters to rescue them forthwith, though the said Earl of Oxford should have the place during his life for his labour. Spare not this to be done in haste if ye will have their lives . . . though ye should lose the best manor of all for the rescue. I had lever[70] ye lost the livelihood than their lives. Ye must get a messenger of the Lords or some other notable man to bring their letters.

Do your devoir[71] now, and let me send you no more messengers for this matter, but send me by the bearer hereof more certain comfort than ye have done by all other[s] that I have sent before. . . . God keep you.

Written the Tuesday next before Holy Rood day,[72] in haste.

By your mother.
[Margaret Paston]

[*September 12, 1469*]

In the end the Duke's forces prevailed, and Caister Castle surrendered. Henceforth all of Sir John's efforts were directed at winning back his property. For almost seven years he begged, negotiated, and schemed, but it was not until May of 1476 that his case was brought before the King's council and his title was judged to be superior to that of the Duke's and he could later write his brother: "Blessed be God, I have Caister at my will." He was finally able to turn to more domestic concerns.

*To John Paston, esquire, being at the sign of the George, at Paul's wharf.*

. . . Item, where I told you that the gown cloth of old camblet,[73] I would have it home for my sister Anne, ye forgot it. I pray you send it home by the next messenger, and a letter with it of such tidings as ye know.

Item, blessed be God, I have Caister at my will. God hold it better than it [was] done heretofore. No more, but written the next day after Saint Peter, *anno* Edward IVth, 16th [year of reign]

J. PASTON, K.
[John Paston, Knight]

[*June 30, 1476*]

FURTHER DISCUSSION QUESTIONS

**Henry Knighton's Description of the Black Death**

1. What were the immediate economic consequences of the Black Death? What were the long-term consequences?

---

[69] helped    [70] rather    [71] duty    [72] September 14    [73] camel's hair fabric imported from the East

2. What was the impact of the Black Death on the church, both as an institution and in terms of its spiritual leadership? Could the Black Death have had anything to do with the rise of heresy?
3. What was the government's response to the economic-social problems that developed in the wake of the Black Death? Was that response realistic? Was any other response possible?

### Henry Knighton's Description of the Peasants' Revolt

1. Against what elements in society were the peasants most bitter?
2. What, according to Knighton, were the demands of the peasants? What were the implications of those demands if they had been granted?

### The Charges Against Richard II

1. What economic and constitutional sins are placed at Richard II's feet?
2. When the charges speak of "the people," to whom are they referring?
3. What is the picture of Richard as revealed in the charges?

### The Abdication of Richard II

1. What is the concept of kingship implicit in Richard's abdication? What are the constitutional problems that the abdication was meant to resolve?

### The Indenture of Ralph Longford

1. How does Longford's indenture differ from a "feudal" contract? What important element is missing from the indenture?
2. What do the contracting parties gain from the indenture?

### The Troubles of the Paston Family

1. What is the picture of upper-class life depicted in the letters?
2. How does John Paston endeavor to defend himself from the likes of Lord Molyns?
3. What is the picture of Henry VI that emerges in the Paston letters?
4. What is the position and character of Margaret Paston that emerges in the letters?
5. Why can the Duke of Suffolk and others like him get away with lawlessness?
6. Why in the end does John Paston retain Caister Castle?

# 9

# *The Utopia*

So far, the introduction to each chapter has attempted to pose and evaluate a general historical problem that the various readings seem to reflect. In contrast, this chapter contains a single selection — Sir Thomas More's *Utopia* — which documents social, economic, and political issues of the early sixteenth century but also constitutes a problem in its own right. Scholars have debated the *Utopia*'s worth for the past 450 years. What is its true social and intellectual message? Does it embody something more than traditional medieval ideas dressed up in the pleasing garb of Renaissance humanism? Equally baffling is the man who wrote the *Utopia*. How could Sir Thomas More, a humane Christian who advocated a high degree of religious toleration in the *Utopia*, have persecuted Protestant heretics when he became Lord Chancellor of England? How could a political theorist, who discarded the concept of divine-right kingship and aristocratic rule and advocated communal property in the *Utopia*, have served the interests of Henry VIII? How does one explain a scholar who seemed in his early career to have been on the "margins of modernity" yet who elected to die for a concept of medievalism that had long since ceased to exist in the sixteenth century? And, finally, how could the debonair, humanist, lawyer More have been the same man who wore a hair shirt beneath his secular robes? Under the circumstances it is not surprising that during the course of four centuries some one hundred full-length biographies and brief sketches have been written about Sir Thomas More.

More was born in 1474 just when the demographic, economic, and political configurations of England were establishing the conditions for the prosperity and relative stability of the Tudor age. Destined by his father, a well-to-do London lawyer and member of parliament, to follow in the family footsteps, young Thomas was sent to the household of John Cardinal Morton to learn the ways of a gentleman. Then, at the age of fourteen, he matriculated to

Henry the Eighth and his Queen "out a Maying."

Oxford, and, after two years of university life, he transferred to Lincoln's Inn for his legal training. For a short period it looked as if Thomas More would defy his father's wishes and enter a monastery; eventually, however, he decided on a public career. In 1504 More entered parliament. By 1523 he was speaker of the House of Commons, had been on extensive diplomatic and commercial missions to Europe, and had become Henry VIII's good friend and confidante. In 1529 he reached the top of the greasy political pole; on the disgrace of Cardinal Wolsey he was, somewhat surprisingly, appointed Lord Chancellor of England.

During the first decades of Henry VIII's reign, More became the focal point of English and international humanism. He wrote the *Utopia* in 1515 while on diplomatic service to Antwerp, and the following year he sent a completed manuscript for publication to Erasmus, who seven years previously had dedicated his own fantasy, *The Praise of Folly*, to his English friend. The *Utopia* appeared at a critical moment, for it followed Machiavelli's *Prince* by three years and was printed the same year as Erasmus' edition of the New Testament; all three books have shaped modern Western thought.

Partly because More was such an important humanistic figure, partly because he held the most important office at court, it was essential for Henry VIII to have his friend's support in the crisis of the "divorce" and ensuing break with Rome. This More would not or could not give. He resigned the chancellorship in 1532, refused the oath of supremacy, was imprisoned, was tried for high treason, and was executed on July 7, 1535. He died, as he said, "the King's good servant but God's first."

The *Utopia* is one of the great imaginative achievements of the sixteenth century. Whether it was written, as some scholars have maintained, as a casual piece of learned humor, a scholarly joke, or as a biting satire, a criticism of existing society, matters little. It has become a milestone in the evolution of political science and is regarded as a key document in the development of the "modern mind." Each reader must judge exactly how modern it is and where its modernity lies.

## THOMAS MORE, *Utopia* (1515)

The so-called first book of the *Utopia*, which is a dialogue between More and his alter ego, Raphael Hyphloday, over the ills of sixteenth-century society and whether the philosopher-scholar should go into politics in order to cure them, has been omitted. The present selection is limited to an abbreviated version of the second book in which Hyphloday describes the imaginary island and institutions of Utopia. While the first book of the Utopia is preoccupied with the sickness of society, the second lays down the conditions necessary for a sane society. The translation is taken from Ralph Robinson's original rendering from the Latin in 1551. The archaic spelling and phraseology have in part been modernized, but much of the sixteenth-century flavor of the work remains.

The island of Utopia contains in breadth in the middle part of it (for there it is broadest) two hundred miles. . . . There are in the island fifty-four large and fair cities, or shire towns, agreeing all together in one tongue, like manners, institutions, and laws. They are all set and situate alike, and in all points fashioned alike, as far as the place or plot allows. Of these cities they that are nearest together are twenty-four miles asunder. Again, there is none of them distant from the next above one day's journey afoot. There come yearly to Amaurote out of every city three old men, wise and well experienced, there to treat and debate of the common matters of the land. For this city (because it stands just in the midst of the island, and is therefore most meet[1] for the ambassadors of all parts of the realm) is taken for the chief and head city. The precincts and bounds of the shires be so conveniently appointed and set forth for the cities that never a one of them all has less than twenty miles of ground on every side, and in places also much more, as in that part where the cities are farthest distance asunder. . . .

These houses be inhabited by the citizens, who come thither to dwell in turn. No household or farm in the country has fewer than forty persons, men and women, besides two bondsmen, who be all under the rule and order of the goodman and goodwife of the house, being both very sage, discreet and ancient persons. And every thirty farms or families have one head ruler, who is called a philarch, being as it were a head bailiff. Out of every one of these families or farms come every year into the city twenty persons who have been two years

---

SOURCE: From Sir Thomas Moore, *Utopia*, "The Seconde boke . . . conteyninge the discription of Utopia . . ." Ralph Robinson, trans., 1556. *English Reprints*, Edward Arber, ed. (London: A. Constable & Co., Ltd., 1902).

[1] fit

in the country. In their place so many fresh be sent thither out of the city, to be instructed and taught by those who have been there a year already, and be therefore expert and skilled in the care and cultivation of the land. And they the next year shall teach the others. This order is used for fear that either scarceness of victuals, or some other like misfortune should result from lack of knowledge, if they should be altogether new, and fresh, and unexpert in farming. . . .

When their harvest day draws near and is at hand, then the philarchs, who be the head officers and bailiffs on the farms, send word to the magistrates of the city what number of harvest men is needful to be sent to them out of the city. This company of harvest men are there ready at the day appointed, and almost in one fair day despatch all the harvest work.

### Of the cities, and namely, of Amaurote

As for their cities, he that knows one of them knows them all, for they be as like one to another as the nature of the place permits. I will describe therefore to you one or another of them, for it matters not greatly which. But what one is better than Amaurote? Of them all this is the worthiest and of most dignity, for the rest acknowledge it as the head city, because there is the council house. . . .

The city is compassed about with a high thick stone wall full of turrets and bulwarks. A dry ditch, but deep and broad, and overgrown with bushes, briers, and thorns, surrounds three sides or quarters of the city. To the fourth side the river itself serves for a ditch. The streets be appointed and set forth very commodiously and handsomely, both for transport and also against the winds. The houses be of fair and gorgeous building, and on the street side they stand joined together in a long row through the whole street, without any partition or separation. The streets are twenty feet broad.

On the back side of the houses through the whole length of the street lie large gardens which are closed in round about by the back part of the streets. Every house has two doors, one into the street and a postern door on the back side into the garden. These doors are made with two leaves,[2] never locked or bolted, so easy to be opened that they will follow the least drawing of a finger, and shut again by themselves. Every man who wills may go in, for there is nothing within the houses that is private or any man's own. And every tenth year they change their houses by lot. . . .

The outsides of the walls be made either of hard flint, or of plaster, or else of brick, and the inner sides are well strengthened with timber work. The roofs are plain and flat, covered with a certain kind of plaster that is of no cost, and yet so tempered that no fire can hurt or destroy it, and it withstands the violence of the weather better than any lead. They keep the wind out of their windows with glass, for it is there much used, or in some places with fine linen cloth dipped in oil or resin of amber, a convenience in two ways; for by this means more light comes in, and the wind is better kept out.

### Of the magistrates

Every thirty families or farms choose yearly an officer, who in their old language is called the syphogrant, and by a newer name, the philarch. Every ten syphogrants, with all their thirty families be under an officer who was once called the tranibore, now the chief philarch. Moreover, as concerning the election of the prince, all the syphogrants, who be in number two hundred, first be sworn to choose him whom they think most fitting and expedient. Then by a secret election they name prince one of those four whom the people before named unto them. For out of the four quarters of the city there be four chosen, out

---

[2] parts

of every quarter one, to stand for the election, which is put up to the council. The prince's office continues all his lifetime, unless he is deposed or put down for suspicion of tyranny. They choose the tranibores yearly, but do not lightly change them. All the other offices be but for one year. The tranibores every third day, and sometimes, if need be, oftener, come into the council house with the prince. Their council is concerning the commonwealth. If there be any controversies among the commoners, which be very few, they despatch and end them speedily. They take always two syphogrants with them in counsel, and every day a new couple. And it is provided that nothing touching the commonwealth shall be confirmed and ratified unless it has been reasoned and debated three days in the council before it is decreed. It is death to have any consultation for the commonwealth outside the council, or the place of the common election. This statute, they say, was made to the intent that the prince and tranibores might not easily conspire together to oppress the people by tyranny, and to change the state of the commonwealth.

Therefore matters of great weight and importance are brought to the election house of the syphogrants, who explain the matter to their families. And afterward, when they have consulted among themselves, they report their plan to the council. Sometimes the matter is brought before the council of the whole island. Furthermore, this custom also the council uses: to dispute or reason of no matter the same day that it is first proposed or put forth, but to defer it to the next sitting of the council, in order that no man, when he has rashly there spoken what came first to his tongue's end, shall then afterward study rather for reasons wherewith to defend and maintain his first foolish sentence than for the good of the commonwealth: as one more willing to suffer harm or hindrance in the commonwealth than any loss or diminution of his own reputation; and as one that would not for shame (which is a very foolish shame)

appear to have been misled in the matter at the first, when at the first he ought to have spoken rather wisely, than hastily or rashly.

## Of sciences, crafts, and occupations

• • •

The chief and almost the only office of the syphogrants is to see and take heed that no man sit idle, but that everyone ply his own craft with earnest diligence. And yet for all that, not to be wearied from early in the morning to late in the evening with continual work, like laboring and toiling beasts. For this is worse than the miserable and wretched condition of bondsmen, but it is nevertheless almost everywhere the life of workmen and artisans, save in Utopia. For they, dividing the day and the night into twenty-four equal hours, appoint and assign only six of those hours to work, three before noon, after which they go straight to dinner; and after dinner, when they have rested two hours, then they work three, and upon that they go to supper. After eight of the clock in the evening (counting one of the clock as the first hour after noon), they go to bed; eight hours they give to sleep. All the spare time, that is, between the hours of work, sleep, and meat, they be permitted to spend every man as he likes best himself. Not to the intent that they should misspend this time in riot or slothfulness, but that being then freed from the labor of their own occupations, they should bestow the time well and thriftily upon some other good science, as shall please them. For it is a solemn custom there, to have lectures daily, early in the morning, where only those are constrained to be present that are chosen and appointed to learning. Howbeit a great multitude of every sort of people, both men and women, go to hear lectures, some to one and some to another, as every man's nature is inclined. Yet, this notwithstanding, if any man had rather bestow this time upon his own occupation (as it chances with many, whose minds rise not to the contemplation of any liberal science), he is not prevented or prohibited, but is also praised and commended, as being profitable to the commonwealth. After supper they spend one hour in play, in summer in their gardens, in winter in their common halls, where they dine and sup. There they exercise themselves in music, or else in honest and wholesome conversation. Dice-play, and such other foolish and pernicious games, they know not. . . .

But here, lest you be deceived, one thing you must look more narrowly upon. For seeing they bestow but six hours in work, perchance you may think that a lack of some necessary things may ensue therefrom. But this is not so. For that small time is not only enough but even too much for the store and abundance of all things that are requisite, either for the necessity or the comfort of life. And this you also shall perceive, if you weigh and consider with yourselves how great a part of the people in other countries live idle. First, almost all women, who be half of the whole number; or else if the women be anywhere occupied, there most commonly in their stead the men be idle. Besides this how great and how idle a company is there of priests and religious men, as they call them. Add thereto all rich men, especially all landed men, who be commonly called gentlemen and noblemen. Take into this number also their servants. I mean all that flock of stout bragging swashbucklers. Join to them also the sturdy and lusty beggars, cloaking their idle life under the color of some disease or sickness. And truly you shall find them much fewer than you thought, by whose labor all things are gotten that men use and live by. Next consider with yourself, of those few that do work, how few are occupied in necessary works. For where money is everything, there must needs be many vain and superfluous occupations, to serve only for riotous superfluity and unhonest pleasure. . . .

Now, sir, in their apparel, mark (I pray you) how few workmen they need. First of all, while they be at work they be plainly clad in leather or skins that will last seven years. When they go forth abroad they cast over them a cloak which hides the other plain apparel. These cloaks throughout the whole island be all of one color, and that is the natural color of the wool. They therefore do not only use much less woolen cloth than is used in other countries, but also the same stands them in much less cost. . . .

## Of their living and mutual intercourse together

But now will I declare how the citizens bear themselves one towards another, what familiar intercourse and entertainment there is among the people, and what fashion they employ in distributing everything. First, the city consists of families, the families most commonly composed of kindred. For the women, when they be married at a lawful age, go into their husbands' houses. But the male children with all the whole male offspring continue still in their own family and are governed by the eldest and ancientest father, unless he becomes a dotard; for then the next to him in age is put in his place. But to the intent the prescribed number of citizens should neither decrease, nor above measure increase, it is ordained that no city, including its outskirts, shall have more than 6,000 families, and that no family shall include fewer than ten or more than sixteen grown children, that is, of the age of fourteen or above. There is no rule for children under this age. This measure or number is easily observed and kept by putting those that in too full families are above the number into families of smaller increase. But if it chance that in the whole city the population increase above the just number, they fill up therewith the lack of other cities. But if it happen that the multitude throughout the whole island pass and exceed the due number, then they choose out of every city certain citizens, and build up a town under their own laws in the next land where the inhabitants have much waste and unoccupied ground, also some of the inhabitants among them, if they will join and dwell with them. . . .

But if the inhabitants of that land will not dwell with them, to be ordered by their laws, then they drive them out of those bounds which they have limited and defined for themselves. And if they resist and rebel, then they make war against them. For they count this the most just cause of war, when any people holds a piece of ground void and vacant, to no good or profitable use, keeping others from the use and possession of it, who, notwithstanding the law of nature, ought to be nourished and supported thereon. . . .

Moreover every street has certain great large halls set an equal distance one from another, every one known by its own name. In these halls dwell the syphogrants. And to every one of the same halls are appointed thirty families, fifteen on either side. The stewards of every hall at a certain hour come into the meat markets, where they receive meat according to the number of their halls. . . .

To these halls at the set hours of dinner and supper come all the whole syphogranty or ward, called by the noise of a brazen trumpet, except such as are sick in the hospitals, or else in their own houses. . . .

In this hall all menial service, all slavery, and drudgery, with all laborsome toil and base business, are done by bondmen. But the women of every family in turn have the office and charge of cookery for boiling and dressing the meat, and ordering all things belonging thereto. They sit at three tables or more, according to the number of their company. The men sit upon the bench next the wall, and the women opposite them on the other side of the table, so that if any sudden evil should chance to them, as many times happens to women with child, they may rise without trouble or disturb-

ance of anybody, and go thence to the nursery. . . .

### Of their journeying or traveling abroad, with divers other matters cleverly reasoned and wisely discussed

But if any are desirous to visit either their friends that dwell in another city, or to see the place itself, they easily obtain permission from their syphogrants and tranibores, unless there is some good reason. No man goes out alone, but a company is sent forth together with their prince's letters, which testify that they have licence to go [on] that journey, and prescribes also the day of their return. . . .

If any be desirous to walk abroad into the fields, or into the country that belongs to the same city that he dwells in, and obtains the good will of his father, and the consent of his wife, he is not prohibited. But into whatever part of the country he comes he has no meat given him until he has worked out his forenoon's task, or else despatched as much work as is wont to be done there before supper. Observing this law and condition, he may go whither he will, within the bounds of his own city. For he will be no less profitable to the city than if he remained within it. Now you see how little liberty they have to loiter, how they can have no cloak or pretense for idleness. There be neither wine taverns, nor ale houses, nor brothels, nor any opportunity for vice or wickedness, no lurking corners, no places of wicked counsels or unlawful assemblies; but they be in full view and under the eyes of every man. So that of necessity they must either ply their accustomed labors or else refresh themselves with honest and laudable pastimes. . . .

But when they have made sufficient store of provision for themselves (which they think not done until they have provided for the two years following, because of the uncertainty of the next year's crop) then from the things whereof they have abundance they carry forth into other countries great plenty, such as grain, honey, wool, flax, wood, madder,[3] purple dye, skins, wax, tallow, leather, and living beasts. And one-seventh part of all these things they give frankly and freely to the poor of that country. The remainder they sell at a reasonable and moderate price. By this trade or traffic of merchandise, they bring to their own country not only great plenty of gold and silver but also all such things as they lack at home, which is almost nothing, but iron. . . .

I mean in that they use no money themselves, but keep it for that chance, which either may happen, or may be, shall never come to pass. In the meantime, gold and silver, whereof money is made, they use as if none of them did esteem it more than the very nature of the thing deserved. And then who does not plainly see how far it is inferior to iron, without which men can no better live than without fire and water. . . .

Now if these metals among them were fast locked up in some tower, it might be suspected (as the people is ever foolishly imagining) that the prince and the council intended by some subtlety to deceive the commons, and to take some profit of them to themselves. Furthermore, if they made thereof plate and such other finely and cunningly wrought stuff, and if at any time they should have occasion to break it up and melt it again, and so therewith to pay their soldiers' wages, they see and perceive very well that men would be loath to part from those things that they had once begun to have pleasure and delight in. To remedy all this they have found a means, which, as it is agreeable to all their other laws and customs, so it is very different from ours, where gold is so much prized and so diligently kept, and is therefore incredible, except to them that are wise. For whereas they eat and drink in earthen and glass vessels, which be indeed elaborately and handsomely made, and yet of very small value, of gold and silver they commonly

make chamber pots, and other like vessels that serve for most vile uses, not only in their common halls, but in every man's private house. Furthermore, of the same metals they make the great chains, fetters and shackles wherein they tie their bondmen. Finally, whosoever for any offense be disgraced, in their ears they hang rings of gold, upon their fingers they wear rings of gold, and about their necks chains of gold, and, in conclusion, their heads are tied about with gold.

Thus by all means possible they contrive to have gold and silver among them held in reproach and infamy. And therefore these metals, which other nations do as grievously and sorrowfully give up, as in a manner from their own lives, if they should altogether be taken at once from the Utopians, no man there would think he had lost the worth of one farthing. They gather also pearls by the seaside, and diamonds and carbuncles upon certain rocks; and yet they seek not for them, but when by chance they find them, they cut and polish them. And therewith they deck their young infants, who in the first years of their childhood make much of and be fond and proud of such ornaments, but when they are a little more grown in years and discretion, perceiving that none but children do wear such toys and trifles, they lay them away even of their shamefacedness, without any bidding of their parents, even as our children, when they grow big, cast away nuts, trinkets and puppets. . . .

For though there be not many in every city who be exempt and discharged from all other labors, and appointed only to learning; that is to say, such in whom even from their very childhood they have perceived a singular forwardness, a fine wit, and a mind apt to good learning; yet all, in their childhood, be instructed in learning. And the better part of the people, both men and women, throughout all their whole life do bestow on learning those spare hours, which we said they have free from bodily labors.

---

[3] herb

They be taught learning in their own native tongue. For it is both copious in words, and also pleasant to the ear, and for the utterance of a man's mind very perfect and sure. . . .

## Of bondmen, sick persons, wedlock, and divers other matters

They neither make bondmen of prisoners taken in battle, unless it is in a battle they fought themselves, nor of bondmen's children, nor, to be brief, of any man whom they can get out of another country, even though he were there a bondman. But they take either such as among themselves for heinous offenses be punished with bondage, or else such as in the cities of other lands are condemned to death for great trespasses. And of this sort of bondmen they have most store.

Many of them they bring home, sometimes paying very little for them; yea most commonly getting them for thanks. These sorts of bondmen they keep not only in continual work and labor, but also in bonds. But their own men they handle hardest, for they judge them more desperate, and deserving of greater punishment, because after being so godly brought up to virtue in so excellent a commonwealth, they could not for all that be restrained from misdoing. Another kind of bondman they have: when a vile drudge, being a poor laborer in another country, chooses of his own free will to be a bondman among them. These they treat and order justly, and entertain almost as gently as their own free citizens, save that they put them to a little more labor, as being accustomed thereto. If any such is disposed to depart thence (which is seldom seen), they neither hold him against his will nor send him away with empty hands. . . .

The woman is not married before she is eighteen years old; the man four years older before he marries. If either the man or the woman is proved to have sexually offended before marriage with another, the party that so has trespassed is sharply punished. And

both the offenders are forbidden ever after in all their life to marry, unless the fault is forgiven by the prince's pardon. But both the good man and the good wife of the house where that offense was committed be in danger of great reproach and infamy, as being slack and negligent in looking to their charges. That offense is so sharply punished, because they perceive that unless the people are diligently kept from the liberty of this vice, few will join together in the love of marriage, wherein all the life must be led with one, and also all the griefs and displeasures that come therewith must be patiently taken and borne. Furthermore, in choosing wives and husbands they observe earnestly and strictly a custom which seemed to us very silly and foolish. For a grave and honest matron shows the woman, be she maid or widow, naked to the wooer. And likewise a sage and discreet man exhibits the wooer naked to the woman. At this custom we laughed and disallowed as foolish. But they on the other hand greatly do wonder at the folly of all other nations, which in buying a colt, whereas a little money is in hazard, be so chary and circumspect, that though he be almost all bare, yet they will not buy him unless the saddle and all the harness are taken off, lest under those coverings is hid some gall or sore. And yet in choosing a wife, who shall be either pleasure or displeasure to them all their life after, they are so reckless that while all the rest of the woman's body is covered with clothes, they judge her by scarcely one hand-breadth (for they can see no more than her face), and so join her to them not without great jeopardy of evil agreeing together, if anything in her body afterward offend and displease them. . . .

And matrimony is there never broken, but by death; except adultery break the bond, or else the intolerable, wayward manners of either party. If either of them find themselves for any such cause aggrieved, they may by the license of the council change and take another. . . . Breakers of wedlock[4]

---

[4] adulterers

be punished with most grievous bondage. And if both the offenders were married, then the parties which in that behalf have suffered wrong . . . , if they will, marry together, or else to whomsoever they like. But if either of them do still continue to love so unkind a bedfellow, the use of wedlock is not to them forbidden, if the party is disposed to follow in toiling and drudgery the person who for the offense is condemned to bondage. And very oft it chances that the repentance of the one, and the earnest diligence of the other, so moves the prince with pity and compassion, that he restores the bond person from servitude to liberty and freedom again. But if the same party is taken again in fault, there is no other way but death.

To other trespassers there is no prescribed punishment appointed by any law. But according to the heinousness of the offense or the contrary, so the punishment is moderated by the discretion of the council. The husbands chastise their wives, and the parents their children, unless they have committed so horrible an offense that the public punishment thereof does much to promote the advancement of honest manners. But most commonly the most heinous faults be punished with the hardship of bondage. For this they suppose is to the offenders no less painful and to the commonwealth more profitable than if they should hastily be put to death and removed out of the way. For there is more profit from their labor than from their death, and by their example they make others fear like punishments. But if when they are thus treated, they rebel and kick again, then forsooth they are slain as desperate wild beasts, whom neither prison nor chain could restrain and keep under. But they who take their bondage patiently be not left entirely hopeless. For after they have been broken and tamed with long miseries, if they then show such repentance that it may be perceived that they are sorrier for their offense than for their punishment, sometimes by the prince's prerogative, and sometimes by the voice and consent of the people, their bondage either is mitigated, or else clean remitted and forgiven. He that moves toward adultery is in no less danger and jeopardy than if he had committed the adultery in deed. For in all offenses they count the intention and alleged purpose as evil as the act or deed itself, for they think that no interference ought to excuse him that did his best to succeed. . . .

## Of warfare

They detest and abhor war or battle as a thing very beastly, although by no kind of beasts is it used so much as it is by man. And contrary to the custom of almost all other nations, they count nothing so inglorious as glory gotten in war. And therefore though they do daily practice and exercise themselves in the discipline of war, and not only the men, but also the women upon certain appointed days, lest they should be wanting skill of arms, if need should require; yet they never go to battle but either in defense of their own country, or to drive out of their friends' land the enemies that have invaded it, or by their power to deliver from the yoke and bondage of tyranny some people that be oppressed with tyranny. Which thing they do out of mere pity and compassion. . . .

They be not only sorry but also ashamed to achieve a victory with bloodshed, counting it great folly to buy precious wares too dear. They rejoice and boast if they vanquish and subdue their enemies by craft and deceit. And for that feat they hold a general triumph, and, as if the matter were manfully handled, they set up a pillar of stone in the place where they so vanquished their enemies, in token of the victory. For then they glory, then they boast and brag that they have played the man in deed, when they have so overcome as no other living creature but only man could; that is to say, by the might and power of wit. For with bodily strength (say they) bears, lions, boars, wolves, dogs, and other wild beasts do fight. And as most of them surpass us in strength and fierce courage, so in wit and reason we be much stronger than they all.

Their chief and principal purpose in war is to obtain that thing, which, if they had before obtained, they would not have waged battle. But if that be not possible, they take so cruel vengeance on those who be at fault that ever after they be afraid to do the like. This is their chief and principal purpose which they immediately and first of all prosecute and carry forward. But in such manner that they show themselves to be more circumspect in avoiding and eschewing dangers than desirous of praise and renown. Therefore, immediately after war is once solemnly declared, they procure many proclamations, signed with their own common seal to be set up secretly at one time in their enemies' land, in places most frequented. In these proclamations they promise great rewards to him who will kill their enemies' prince, and somewhat lesser gifts, but very great also, for every head of those whose names be contained in the said proclamations. They be those whom they count their chief adversaries, next to the prince. Whatsoever is promised to him who kills any of the proclaimed persons is doubled to him who brings any of the same to them alive; yea, and to the proclaimed persons themselves, if they will change their minds and come over to them and join them, they offer the same great rewards, with pardon and surety of their lives. . . .

The custom of buying and selling adversaries is disallowed among other people, as a cruel act of a base and cowardly mind. But the Utopians in this matter think themselves much praiseworthy, since like wise men they by this means despatch great wars without one battle or skirmish. Yea, they count it also a deed of pity and mercy, because by the death of a few offenders the lives of a great number of innocents, both of their own men, as also of their enemies be ransomed and saved, who in fighting would have been slain. For they do no less

pity the base and common sort of their enemies' people than they do their own; knowing that they are driven to war against their will by the furious madness of their princes and heads. But if by none of these means the affair proceeds as they would have it, then they contrive that causes of dispute and dissension be spread among their enemies, as by inciting the prince's brother, or some of the noblemen, to hope to obtain the kingdom. If in this way they prevail not, then they stir up the people that be next neighbors and borderers to their enemies, and them they set in their necks under color of some old title of right, such as kings do never lack. To them they promise help and aid in their war. And as for money they give them abundance. . . .

Yea, and besides their riches, which they keep at home, they have also an infinite treasure abroad, since, as I said before, many nations be in their debt. Therefore they hire soldiers out of all countries and send them to battle. . . . Next to these they use the soldiers of the people for whom they fight. And then the help of their other friends. And last of all they bring in their own citizens. . . .

But as none of the Utopians is thrust out of his country into war against his will, so women that be willing to accompany their husbands in times of war are not prohibited or stopped. Rather they provoke and exhort them to it with praises. And in battle array the wives do stand every one by her own husband's side. Also every man is surrounded with his own children, kinsfolk, and relatives by marriage; that they, whom nature chiefly moves to mutual succor, standing thus together, may help one another. It is a great reproach and dishonor for the husband to come home without his wife, or the wife without her husband, or the son without his father. And therefore, if the other side resists so hard that the battle comes to their hands, it is fought with great slaughter and bloodshed, even to the utter destruction of both parties. For as they employ all means and shifts to keep themselves from the necessity of fighting, and to despatch the battle with hired soldiers, so when there is no remedy but they must needs fight themselves, then they do fall to it courageously. . . .

But when the battle is finished and ended, they impose on their friends never a penny cost of all the charges they were at, but lay them upon the necks of the conquered. Them they burden with the whole charge of their expenses, which they demand of them partly in money, to be kept for like use in battle, and partly in lands bearing great revenues, to be paid unto them yearly for ever. Such revenues they have now from many countries, which little by little, starting from divers and sundry causes, be increased above seven hundred thousand ducats. . . .

### Of the religions in Utopia

There be divers kinds of religion not only in sundry parts of the island, but also in divers places of every city. Some worship for God the sun; some, the moon; some, others of the planets. There be those who worship a man, who was once of excellent virtue and famous glory, not only as God, but also as the chiefest and highest God. But the most and wisest number, rejecting all these, believe that there is a certain godly power, unknown, everlasting, incomprehensible, inexplicable, far above the capacity and reach of man's wit, dispersed throughout the world, not in bigness, but in virtue and power. Him they call the father of all. To him alone they attribute the beginnings, the increasings, the proceedings, the changes and the ends of all things. They give no divine honors to any other but to him. Yea, all the others also, though they be of divers opinions, yet on this point they agree all together with the wisest sort, in believing that there is one chief and principal God, the maker and ruler of the whole world, whom they commonly in their country call Mithra. But on this point they disagree: among some he is counted one thing,

and among some another. For every one of them, whatsoever it is which he takes for the chief God, thinks it to be the very same nature; to whose only divine might and majesty the sum and sovereignty of all things by the consent of all people is attributed and given.

Howbeit, they all begin little by little to forsake and abandon this variety of superstitions, and to agree together in that religion which seems by reason to surpass and excel the rest. And it is not to be doubted that all the others would long ago have been abolished, except that whatsoever unfortunate thing happened to any of them, as he was considering a change in his religion, the fearfulness of the people took it not as a thing coming by chance, but as sent from God out of heaven; as though the God whose honor he was forsaking would avenge that wicked purpose against him. But after they heard us speak of the name of Christ, of his doctrine, laws, miracles, and of the no less wonderful constancy of so many martyrs, whose blood willingly shed brought a great number of nations throughout all parts of the world into their sect, you will not believe with what glad minds they agreed to the same, whether it were by the secret inspiration of God, or else because they thought it nearest that opinion which among them is counted chief. Howbeit, I think this was no small help and furtherance in the matter that they heard us say that Christ instituted among his [followers] that all things be held in common; and that the same community of ownership does yet remain amongst the rightest Christian companies. . . .

For King Utopus, even at the first beginning, hearing that the inhabitants of the land were, before his coming thither, in continual dissension and strife among themselves over their religions; perceiving also that this general dissension (since every separate sect took a different side in fighting for their country) was the only cause of his conquest over them all; as soon as he had gotten the victory, first of all he made a decree that it should be lawful for every man to favor and follow whatever religion he would and that he might do the best he could to bring others to his opinion, so long as he did it peaceably, gently, quietly, and soberly, without haste and contentious rebuking and invoking against others. If he could not by fair and gentle speech induce them to accept his opinion, still he should use no kind of violence and should refrain from unpleasant and seditious words. For him who would vehemently and fervently strive and contend for this cause was decreed banishment or bondage.

This law did King Utopus make, not only for the maintenance of peace, which he saw through continual contention and mortal hatred would be utterly extinguished, but also because he thought this decree would make for the furtherance of religion. . . . And this surely he thought a very unmeet and foolish thing, and a sign of arrogant presumption, to compel all others by violence and threatenings to agree to the same that he believed to be true. Furthermore, though there be one religion which alone is true, and all others vain and superstitious, yet did he well foresee that if the matter were handled with reason and sober modesty, the truth of its own power would at the last issue forth and come to light. . . . Therefore, all this matter he left undiscussed and gave to every man free liberty and choice to believe what he would. Saving that he earnestly and strictly charged them that no man should conceive so vile and base an opinion of the dignity of man's nature as to think that souls die and perish with the body, or that the world runs by chance, governed by no divine providence. And therefore they believe that after this life vices be extremely punished and virtue bountifully rewarded. Him that is of a contrary opinion they count not in the number of mankind, but as one who has abased the high nature of his soul to the vileness of brute beasts' bodies; much less in the number of their citizens, whose laws and ordinances, if it were not for fear, he would

not at all respect. For you may be sure he would study either with craft privily to mock, or else violently to break the common laws of his country, in whom there remains no further fear but of the laws, nor no further hope beyond the body. Wherefore he that is thus minded is deprived of all honors and excluded from all public administration in the commonwealth. And thus he is despised by all sorts of people as an unprofitable and base and vile nature. Howbeit, they give him no punishment. . . . But they suffer him not to discuss his opinions among the common people. But among the priests and men of gravity, they do not only permit but also exhort him to dispute and argue, hoping that at last this madness will give place to reason. . . .

They utterly despise and mock soothsayings and divinations of things to come by the flight or the voices of birds, and all other divinations of vain superstition, which in other countries are given much attention. But they highly esteem and worship miracles that come by no help of nature, as works and witnesses of the present power of God. And these they say happen very often. And sometimes in great and doubtful matters, by common intercession and prayers, they procure and obtain them with a sure hope and confidence and steadfast belief. . . .

They have priests of exceeding holiness, and therefore very few. For there are but thirteen in every city according to the number of their churches, save when they go forth to battle. For then seven of them go forth with the army; in whose stead as many new are created at home. But the others at their return home again re-enter every one his own place, those that be above the number, until such time as they succeed to the places of the others at their dying, are in the meantime continually in the company of the bishops. For he is the chief head of them all. They be chosen by the people, as the other magistrates be, by secret voices, for the avoiding of strife.

After their election they are consecrated by their own company. They be overseers of all divine matters, orderers of religious ceremonies, and, as it were, judges and masters of manners. And it is a great dishonor and shame to be rebuked or spoken to by any of them for dissolute and incontinent living. But whereas it is their office to give good exhortations and counsel, so it is the duty of the prince and the other magistrates to correct and punish offenders, except that the priests excommunicate from having any part in divine matters those whom they find exceedingly vicious livers. . . .

They keep holy the first and the last day of every month and year, dividing the year into months, which they measure by the course of the moon, as they do the year by the course of the sun. . . .

Although religion is not there the same among all men, yet all the kinds and fashions of it, though they be sundry and manifold, agree together in the honor of the divine nature, going divers ways to one end. Therefore nothing is seen or heard in the churches, which seems not to agree impartially with them all. If there is a distinct kind of sacrament peculiar to any one sect, that they perform at home in their own houses. The public sacraments are so ordered that they be no derogation or prejudice to any of the private rites and religions. Therefore, no image of any god is seen in the church, to the intent it may be free for every man to conceive God by his religion after what likeness and similitude he will. . . .

Now I have declared and described unto you, as truly as I could, the form and order of that commonwealth, which verily in my judgment is not only the best, but also that which alone of good right may claim and take upon itself the name of commonwealth or public weal. For in other places they speak still of the commonwealth, but every man procures his own private gain. Here, where nothing is private, the common interests be earnestly looked to. And truly on both accounts they have good cause to do as they do. For in other countries, who knows that he will not starve for hunger, unless he makes some private provision for himself, even though[5] the commonwealth flourish never so much in riches? And, therefore, he is compelled even of very necessity to have regard to himself, rather than to the people, that is to say, to others. Contrariwise, here where all things are common to every man, it is not to be doubted that no man shall lack anything necessary for his private use, so long as the common storehouses and barns are sufficiently stored. For here nothing is distributed in a niggardly fashion, nor is there any poor man or beggar. And though no man owns anything, yet every man is rich. For what can be more rich than to live joyfully and merrily, without all grief and pensiveness, not concerned for his own living, nor vexed or troubled with his wife's importunate complaints, nor dreading poverty for his son, nor sorrowing for his daughter's dowry? . . .

Here now I would see, if any man dare be so bold as to compare with this equity the justice of other nations. Among whom, may I forsake God, if I can find any sign or token of equity and justice! For what justice is this, that a rich goldsmith, or usurer, or to be brief, any one of those who either do nothing at all, or else that which they do is not very necessary to the commonwealth, should have a pleasant and wealthy living, either in idleness, or in unnecessary business, when in the mean time poor laborers, carters, ironsmiths, carpenters, and plowmen, by such great and continual toil, . . . get so hard and poor a living and live so wretched and miserable a life that the state and condition of the laboring beasts may seem much better and more comfortable? For they[5] are not put to such continual labor, nor is their living much worse; yea, for them it is much pleasanter, for they take no thought in the meantime

---

[5] the beasts

for the future. But these silly, poor wretches be now tormented with barren and unfruitful labor, and the remembrance of their poor, indigent, and beggarly old age kills them off. For their daily wage is so little that it will not suffice for the same day, much less yield any overplus that may daily be laid up for the relief of old age. Is not this an unjust and an unkind commonwealth, which gives great fees and rewards to gentlemen, as they call them, and to goldsmiths, and to others who are either idle persons, or else only flatterers, and devisers of vain pleasures; and on the other hand, makes no considerate provision for poor plowmen, colliers, laborers, carters, ironsmiths and carpenters, without whom no commonwealth can continue? But when it has misused the labors of their lusty and flowering age, at the last when they are oppressed with old age, sickness, needy, poor, and indigent of all things, then forgetting their many painful watchings, not remembering their many and great benefits, it recompenses and requites them most unkindly with miserable death. . . .

Yet these most wicked and vicious men, when they have by their insatiable covertousness divided among themselves all the things which would have sufficed for all men, still how far are they from the wealth and felicity of the Utopian commonwealth! From which, in that all desire of money and use thereof are utterly excluded and banished, how great a heap of cares is cut away! How great a cause of wickedness and mischief is plucked up by the roots! For who does not know that fraud, theft, rapine, brawling, quarreling, brabling,[6] strife, chiding, contention, murder, treason, poisoning, which by daily punishments are rather avenged than restrained, die when money dies? And also that fear, grief, care, labors, and watchings perish even the very moment that money perishes? Yes, poverty itself, which only seemed to lack money, if money were gone, would also decrease and vanish

away. . . . And I doubt not that either the respect of every man's private comfort, or else the authority of our saviour Christ (which for his great wisdom could not but know what was best, and for his inestimable goodness could not but counsel that which he knew to be best) would have brought all the world long ago unto the laws of this commonwealth, if it were not that one single beast, the princess and mother of all mischief — pride — resists and hinders it. She measures not wealth and prosperity by her own well being, but by the miseries and discomforts of others; she would not by her own will be made a goddess, if there were no wretches left over whom she might, like a scornful lady, rule and triumph, over whose miseries her felicity might shine, and whose poverty she might vex, torment, and increase by gorgeously vaunting her riches. This hell-hound creeps into men's hearts, and plucks them back from entering the right path of life, and is so deeply rooted in men's breasts that she cannot be plucked out. . . .

This form and fashion of a publicwealth, which I would gladly wish for all nations, I am glad at least that it has chanced to the Utopians, who have followed those institutions of life whereby they have laid such foundations for the commonwealth as shall continue and last not only wealthily, but also, as far as man's wit may judge and conjecture, endure forever. For seeing that the chief causes of ambition and sedition with other vices are plucked up by the roots and abandoned at home, there can be no danger of civil strife, which alone has cast underfoot and brought to nought the well-fortified and strongly defended wealth and riches of many cities. And forasmuch as perfect concord remains, and wholesome laws are executed at home, the envy of all foreign princes be not able to shake or move the empire, though they have many times long ago gone about to do it, being evermore driven back.

---

[6] disputing

## FURTHER DISCUSSION QUESTIONS

### Thomas More, Utopia

1. What is the purpose of society in the *Utopia?* How did it differ from medieval society?
2. Who are the elite of the *Utopia?* How did this compare with More's own world?
3. How Utopian would you judge the *Utopia* to be: what ingredients does it lack in order to be, in your opinion, a "perfect society"? Why might More have omitted those ingredients?
4. What is More's view of human nature in the *Utopia?*
5. Compare and contrast the following in the *Utopia* with the real world of the sixteenth century: the organization of labor, political and social systems, urban life and organization, the role of women in society, the handling of crime, the organization of the church and its position in society, and finally, the purpose and methods of warfare.
6. Do you think the *Utopia* would work? What is it in the *Utopia* that explains why the book has been so influential for four hundred years?
7. Judging from the *Utopia*, what would you say More thought was most wrong about the world in which he lived?
8. Would you have liked to live in the *Utopia?*

# 10

# *The Structure of Tudor Society*

Societies consist of far more than political institutions, social divisions, economic organizations, and chains of command; they are composed of men and women who have a sense of participation and membership in an organism that exceeds the sum of its parts. Society has a spirit, a purpose, and a style of operation peculiar to itself. Except for the first document by Sir Thomas Smith, the selections in this chapter deal with Tudor society as an organic totality, in which the parts were subservient to the whole, in which theorists knew what constituted a healthy body politic, and in which individuals knew what it took to make the system work, generally to their own advantage. The discourse on *The Commonwealth of England*, penned by Sir Thomas Smith (1513–1577), while on diplomatic mission to France in 1565, is a scholarly description of the formal structure of English society, not an analysis of the realities of power, written by a man who was Principal Secretary of State under both Edward VI and Elizabeth I. It is Smith's most important treatise and is our primary source for the legal framework of Tudor government and society.

*England in the Reign of King Henry the Eighth* (1534) by Thomas Starkey (1499–1538) is quite different. It is written in the form of a dialogue between Thomas Lupset and Cardinal Pole, two humanist friends and patrons of Starkey when he was studying law in Padua during the 1520s. Comparing society to the human body and soul, it presents what contemporary theorists and public officials viewed as the well-formed, healthy commonwealth. "An Exhortation concerning Good Order and Obedience" is a far more polemical and political tract. Published in its original form as part of the Homilies of 1547, it was reissued thereafter almost every decade throughout the century. The "Exhortation" was written for popular consumption, and it sought not only to assure traitors a warm welcome in hell but also to dramatize to the unwashed multitude that society was religiously inspired and was a vital link in the divine

chain of being, reaching from God to the smallest particle of existence on earth. William Lambarde's *Eirenarcha: or, Of the Office of the Justices of Peace* (1581), unlike Smith's *Commonwealth*, is a study in the realities of power. Written by a practicing lawyer and Tudor antiquarian, the book focuses on an aspect of society about which the ruling elite felt strongly: law and justice in order to have any meaning must be enforced. (Possibly at this juncture the reader might think back on Sir Thomas More's handling of crime in the *Utopia* and his concept and organization of society.)

The next two documents display the relationship of the individual to society: these selections are the scaffold confessions of Queen Anne Boleyn and her brother, George Viscount Rochford, both of whom were executed in May, 1536. Anne's real sin was that she had been unable to bear her royal husband, Henry VIII, a male heir; her alleged crimes were adultery with a number of gentlemen of the court and incest with her brother. Given the improbable and trumped-up nature of the charges, their final words are not only extraordinary to modern ears but also deeply revealing of the social and religious mind of sixteenth-century England.

The remaining documents describe the style and organization of Tudor society. The first is an intimate and detailed picture of royalty at work: what a Tudor king did with his time and how he spent his money. The description comes from the privy purse expenses of Henry VII and covers the year 1497, with examples taken from the three years that followed. In order to appreciate the worth of the sums being spent, the reader should keep in mind that two pounds, ten shillings (120 pence or half a pound) was a living, if minimal, yearly wage. The accounts reveal much about the nature of early Tudor kingship, and they should be compared with the descriptions of Anglo-Saxon and medieval government in Chapters 1-4. The next two selections are royal speeches which, better than any portrait, depict the personalities of Henry VIII and his daughter Elizabeth, displaying their concept of royal office and style of royal government. Henry VIII's address — harangue is probably a better term — was directed at the Lords and Commons of parliament and was delivered in December of 1544, twenty-six months before he died. The King's message is clear: he was the nurse, pastor, and father of his subjects, who were displaying a deplorable tendency to indulge in discord and disagreement, and they had better change their ways and return to right-minded thinking. Elizabeth's address to parliament, her so-called "golden speech," was made in November of 1601, at a time when there was growing criticism of her government's economic policies, especially the granting of monopolies on such items as playing cards, wine, and soap. Monopolies were regarded by parliament as unfair and as the source of serious political and administrative corruption. Her words present the Queen at her oratorical and stylistic best. The question of political style will be discussed in Chapter 13, but it is important to note the role within Tudor society that Henry and Elizabeth cut out for themselves, how they regarded their royal charge, and how they managed the kingdom.

The concluding two selections are in the same vein, but are of a more pratical and didactic flavor: what to be on guard against in politics, how to behave at court, and how to manage the system. There is no better mirror of society than its textbooks and words of counsel. The first example is Sir Francis Bacon's advice to his friend and patron Robert Devereux, the flamboyant and ambitious Earl of Essex, who in 1596 was at the height of his popularity, was the Queen's fair-haired boy, and aspired to become her chief minister and sole political adviser. Bacon's purpose was to instruct the young Earl in how to achieve this end. The second example is Sir William Wentworth's (1562–1641) advice to his son Thomas, the future Earl of Strafford. Although Sir William wrote his precepts for success a year after Elizabeth's death, he had in fact formulated his principles throughout most of the years of her reign. His hard-nosed thoughts on how to manipulate justice, win political patronage, and avoid the wrath of the great and powerful give us an extraordinary window on the prevailing assumptions about acceptable political behavior, the nature of politics, and sixteenth-century attitudes toward human nature.

THOMAS SMITH, *The Commonwealth of England* (ca. 1565)

Thomas Smith defines the classes of people into which Tudor society was divided and describes the powers of parliament and the monarch.

## Classes of the people

### Of the first part of Gentlemen of England, called *nobilitas major*

. . . In England no man is created a baron, except he may dispend of yearly revenue one thousand pounds, or one thousand marks at the least . . .

### Of the second sort of Gentlemen, which may be called *nobilitas minor*, and first of knights

No man is a knight by succession, not the king or prince . . .: knights therefore be not born but made . . . In England whosoever may dispend of his free lands forty pounds sterling of yearly revenue . . . may be by the king compelled to take that order and honour, or to pay a fine . . .

### Of Esquires

Esquires (which we commonly call squires) be all those which bear arms (as we call them) or armories . . . these be taken for no distinct order of the commonwealth, but do go with the residue of the gentlemen . . .

### Of Gentlemen

Gentlemen be those whom their blood and race doth make noble and known . . . Ordinarily the king doth only make knights and create barons or higher degrees, for as for gentlemen they be made good cheap in England. For whosoever studieth the laws of the realm, who studieth in the Universities, who professeth liberal sciences, and to be short, who can live idly and without manual labour, and will bear the port, charge and countenance of a gentleman, he shall be called master, . . . and shall be taken for a gentleman . . .

### Of Yeomen

Those whom we call yeomen, next unto the nobility, knights and squires, have the greatest charge and doings in the commonwealth . . . I call him a yeoman whom our laws do call *legalem hominem* . . . which is a freeman born English, and may dispend of his own free land in yearly revenue to the sum of 40s. sterling . . . This sort of people confess themselves to be no gentlemen . . . and yet they have a certain preeminence and more estimation than labourers and artificers, and commonly live wealthily. . . . These be (for the most part) farmers unto gentlemen, . . . and by these means do come to such wealth, that they are able and daily do buy the lands of unthriftly gentlemen, and after setting their sons to the school at the Universities, to the laws of the realm, or otherwise leaving them sufficient lands whereon they may live without labour, do make their said sons by those means gentlemen . . .

### Of the fourth sort of men which do not rule

The fourth sort or class amongst us, is of those which the old Romans called *capite censi* . . . day labourers, poor husbandmen, yea merchants or retailers which have no free land, copyholders and all artificers . . . These have no voice nor authority in our commonwealth, and no account is made of them, but only to be ruled. . . .

SOURCE: From Thomas Smith, *The Commonwealth of England: and the manner and Governement thereof* (London, 1609; originally published 1583), Book I, pp. 21–42, Book II, pp. 44–50.

## Of Bondage and Bondmen

After that we have spoken of all the sorts of freemen, according to the diversity of their estates and persons, it resteth to say somewhat of bondmen . . . The Romans had two kinds of bondmen, the one which were called *servi* . . . all those kind of bondmen be called in our law villains in gross . . . Another they had . . . which they called *ad-scriptitii glebae* . . . and in our law are called villains regardant . . . Of the first I never knew any in the realm in my time; of the second, so few there be, that it is not almost worth the speaking, but our law doth acknowledge them in both those sorts. . . .

## Of the Parliament and the authority thereof

The most high and absolute power of the realm of England consisteth in the Parliament . . . The Parliament abrogateth old laws, maketh new, giveth order for things past and for things hereafter to be followed, changeth rights and possessions of private men, legitimateth bastards, establisheth forms of religion, altereth weights and measures, giveth forms of succession to the crown, defineth of doubtful rights whereof is no law already made, appointeth subsidies, tailles, taxes and impositions, giveth most free pardons and absolutions, restoreth in blood and name, as the highest court, condemneth or absolveth them whom the prince will put to that trial. And to be short, all that ever the people of Rome might do, either in *centuriatis comitiis* or *tributis*, the same may be done by the Parliament of England, which representeth and hath the power of the whole realm, both the head and the body. For every Englishman is intended to be there present, either in person or by procuration and attorney, . . . from the prince (be he king or queen) to the lowest person of England. And the consent of the parliament is taken to be every man's consent . . .

The Speaker . . . is commonly appointed by the king or queen, though accepted by the assent of the House.

. . . No bill is an Act of Parliament . . . until both the houses severally have agreed unto it . . . no, nor then neither. But the last day of that parliament or session the prince cometh in person in his parliament robes, and sitteth in his state . . . Then one reads the titles of every Act which hath passed at that session . . . : it is marked there what the prince doth allow, and to such he saith, *Le Roy* or *La Royne le veult* . . . To those which the prince liketh not, *Le Roy* or *La Royne s'advisera*, and those he accounted utterly dashed and of none effect . . .

## Of the monarch, King or Queen of England

The Prince . . . hath absolutely in his power the authority of war, and peace . . . His privy council be chosen also at the prince's pleasure . . . In war time and in the field the prince hath also absolute power . . . : he may put to death or to other bodily punishment whom he shall think so to deserve, without process of law or form of judgment. This hath been sometime used within the realm before any open war, in sudden insurrections and rebellions, but that not allowed of wise and grave men . . . This absolute power is called martial law . . . The prince useth also absolute power in crying and decreeing the money of the realm by his proclamation only . . . The prince useth also to dispense with laws made, whereas equity requireth a moderation to be had, and with pains for transgression of laws . . . The prince giveth all the chief and highest offices or magistracies of the realm . . . All writs, executions and commandments be done in the prince's name . . . The prince hath the wardship and first marriage of all those that hold land of him in chief . . . To be short, the prince is the life, the head and the authority of all things that be done in the realm of England.

## THOMAS STARKEY, *England in the Reign of King Henry the Eighth* (1534)

Thomas Starkey, in the guise of a conversation between Cardinal Pole and Thomas Lupset, analyzes the animate nature of the Tudor body politic.

POLE. First this is certain: that like as in every man there is a body and also a soul in whose flourishing and prosperous state both together standeth the weal and felicity of man, so likewise there is in every commonalty, city, and country, as it were, a politic body and another thing, also, resembling the soul of man, in whose flourishing both together resteth also the true commonweal. This body is nothing else but the multitude of people, the number of citizens in every commonalty, city, or country. The thing which is resembled to the soul is civil order and politic law administered by officers and rulers. For like as the body in every man receiveth his life by the virtue of the soul and is governed thereby, so doth the multitude of people in every country receive, as it were, civil life by laws well administered by good officers and wise rulers by whom they be governed and kept in politic order. Wherefore the one may, as me seemeth, right well be compared to the body, and the other to the soul.

LUPSET. This similitude liketh me well.

POLE. Then let us go forth with the same.... For this body [the state] hath his parts, which resemble also parts of the body of man, of which the most general to our purpose be these: the heart, head, hands, and feet. The heart thereof is the king, prince, and ruler of the state, whethersoever it be one or many, according to the governance of the commonalty and politic state; for some be governed by a prince alone, some by a council of certain wise men, and some by the whole people together.... But now to our purpose. He or they which have authority upon the whole state, right well may be resembled to the heart. For like as all wit, reason, and sense, feeling, life, and all other natural power, springeth out of the heart, so from the princes and rulers of the state cometh all laws, order and policy, all justice, virtue and honesty, to the rest of this politic body. To the head, with the eyes, ears, and other senses therein, resembled may be right well the under officers by princes appointed, for as much as they should ever observe and diligently wait for the weal of the rest of this body. To the hands are resembled both craftsmen and warriors which defend the rest of the body from injury of enemies outward, and work and make things necessary to the same. To the feet, the plowmen and tillers of the ground, because they, by their labour, sustain and support the rest of the body. These are the most general parts of this politic body which may justly be resembled after the manner declared to those chief parts in man's body. Now, as I said, the strength of these parts altogether is of necessity required, without the which the health of the whole cannot long be maintained.

And furthermore, yet though this politic body be healthy and strong, yet if it be not beautiful, but foul deformed, it lacketh a part of this weal and prosperous state. This beauty also standeth in the due proportion of the same parts together, so that one part ever be agreeable to another in form and fashion, quantity and number; as craftsmen and plowmen in due number and proportion with other parts, according to the place, city, or town. For if there be other too

SOURCE: From Thomas Starkey, *England in the Reign of King Henry the Eighth: A Dialogue between Cardinal Pole and Thomas Lupset,* J. M. Cowper, ed. (London: Early English Text Society, 1871), Extra Series Doc. XII, pp. 45–46, 48–54, 58–59.

many or too few of one or of the other, there is in the commonalty a great deformity, and so likewise of the other parts. Wherefore the due proportion of one part to another must be observed, and therein standeth the corporal beauty chiefly of this politic body. And so in these three things coupled together standeth, without fail, the weal and prosperous state of the multitude in every commonalty, which, as you now see, justly may be resembled to the body of every particular man. And yet further to proceed in this similitude. Like as the weal of the body, without riches and convenient abundance of things necessary, cannot continue nor be maintained, so this multitude which we call the politic body, without like abundance of all things necessary, cannot flourish in most perfect state. Wherefore these exterior things — friends, riches, and abundance of necessaries — are justly, in the second place, to be required to the maintenance of this true commonweal which we now search. For if a country be never so well replenished with people, healthy, strong, and beautiful, yet if there be lack of necessaries, it cannot long prosper; there will shortly grow in all kind of misery, for great poverty in any country hath ever coupled great misery. . . . Wherefore the friendship of other countries is no less required than riches and abundance of other things necessary. And so in these things joined together resteth the second point required to the weal of every commonalty.

The third — which is chief and principal of all — is the good order and policy by good laws established and set, and by heads and rulers put in effect; by the which the whole body, as by reason, is governed and ruled to the intent that this multitude of people and whole commonalty, so healthy and so wealthy, having convenient abundance of all things necessary for the maintenance thereof, may with due honour, reverence, and love, religiously worship God as fountain of all goodness, Maker and Governor of all this world, everyone also doing his duty to the other with brotherly love,

one loving one another as members and parts of one body. And that this is of the other points most chief and principal, it is evident and plain; for what availeth it in any country to have a multitude never so healthy, beautiful, and strong, which will follow no civil nor politic order, but everyone, like wild beasts drawn by foolish fantasy, is led by the same, without reason and rule? Or what availeth in any country to have never so great riches and abundance of all things both necessary and pleasant to man's life, whereas the people, rude without polity, cannot use that same to their own commodity? Without fail, nothing. But even like as every man having health, abundance of riches, friends, dignity, and authority, which lacketh reason and virtue to govern the same, ever abuseth them to his own destruction; so every country, city, and town, though they be never so replenished with people, having all abundance of things necessary and pleasant to the maintenance of the same, yet if they lack good order and politic rule, they shall abuse all such commodities to their own destruction and ruin, and never shall attain to any commonweal; which without civil order and politic rule can never be brought to purpose nor effect. . . .

For it is a certain rule whereby the people and whole commonalty, whether they be governed by a prince or common council, is ever directed in virtue and honesty. So that the end of all politic rule is to induce the multitude to virtuous living, according to the dignity of the nature of man. And so thus you have heard what thing it is that I so oft speak of and call politic rule, civil order, and just policy. You have heard also how diverse it is, for it may be other under a prince, common council of certain [wise men], or under the whole multitude; and as to dispute which of these rules is best and to be preferred above others, me seemeth superfluous, seeing that certain it is that all be good and to nature agreeable; and though the one be more convenient to the nature of some people than the other. . . .

And as to see and plainly to judge when

this commonweal most flourisheth, it is nothing hard but easy to perceive. For when all these parts, thus coupled together, exercise with diligence their office and duty, as the plowmen and labourers of the ground diligently till the same, for the getting of food and necessary sustenance to the rest of the body, and craftsmen work all things meet for maintenance of the same; yea, and the heads and rulers by just policy maintain the state established in the country, ever looking to the profit of the whole body; then that country must needs be in the most prosperous state. . . . So that of this you may be sure: wheresoever you see any country well garnished and set with cities and towns, well replenished with people, having all things necessary and pleasant to man, living together in civil life according to the excellent dignity of the nature of man, every part of this body agreeing to [the] other, doing his office and duty appointed thereto; there, I say, you may be sure is set a very and true commonweal; there it flourisheth as much as the nature of man will suffer.

And thus now, Master Lupset, shortly to conclude, after my mind you have heard rudely described, what is the things that I call the commonweal and just policy, wherein it standeth, and when it most flourisheth.

## An Exhortation Concerning Good Order and Obedience to Rulers and Magistrates (1574)

The Tudor pulpit was an important instrument in social control, and ministers were expected in government-sponsored sermons to preach the doctrine of obedience, the divinely inspired nature of social hierarchy and authority, and the holistic structure of the universe. "An Exhortation Concerning Good Order" was an often-delivered example of this kind of social indoctrination.

Almighty God hath created and appointed all things in heaven, earth, and waters, in a most excellent and perfect order. In heaven he hath appointed distinct and several orders and states of archangels and angels. In earth he hath assigned and appointed kings, princes, with other governors under them, in all good and necessary order. The water above is kept, and raineth down in due time and season. The sun, moon, stars, rainbow, thunder, lightning, clouds, and all birds of the air, do keep their order. The earth, trees, seeds, plants, herbs, corn, grass, and all manner of beasts, keep themselves in their order. All the parts of the whole year, as winter, summer, months, nights, and days, continue in their order. All kinds of fishes in the sea, rivers, and waters; with all fountains, springs; yea, the seas themselves, keep their comely course and order. And man himself also hath all his parts both within and without; as soul, heart, mind, memory, understanding, reason, speech, with all and singular corporal members of his body, in a profitable, necessary, and pleasant order. Every degree of people in their vocation, calling, and office, hath appointed to them their duty and order: some are in high degree, some in low; some kings and princes, some inferiors and subjects; priests and laymen, masters and servants, fathers and children, husbands and wives, rich and poor; and every one have need of other: so that in all things is

SOURCE: Reprinted from George E. Corrie, *Certain Sermons Appointed by the Queen's Majesty to be Declared and Read by all Parsons, Vicars and Curates, every Sunday and Holiday in their Churches . . . for the Better Understanding of the Simple People, 1574* (Cambridge, England: Cambridge University Press, 1850), pp. 104–105, 113.

to be lauded and praised the goodly order of God; without the which no house, no city, no commonwealth, can continue and endure, or last. For, where there is no right order, there reigneth all abuse, carnal liberty, enormity, sin, and Babylonical confusion. Take away kings, princes, rulers, magistrates, judges, and such estates of God's order; no man shall ride or go by the highway unrobbed; no man shall sleep in his own house or bed unkilled; no man shall keep his wife, children, and possessions in quietness: all things shall be common: and there must needs follow all mischief and utter destruction both of souls, bodies, goods, and commonwealth.

But blessed be God that we in this realm of England feel not the horrible calamities, miseries, and wretchedness, which all they undoubtedly feel and suffer, that lack this godly order: and praised be God that we know the great excellent benefit of God shewed towards us in this behalf. God hath sent us his high gift, our most dear sovereign lady Queen Elizabeth, with a godly, wise, and honourable council, with other superiors and inferiors, in a beautiful order, and goodly. Wherefore, let us subjects do our bounden duties; giving hearty thanks to God, and praying for the preservation of this godly order. Let us all obey, even from the bottom of our hearts, all their godly proceedings, laws, statutes, proclamations, and injunctions, with all other godly orders. Let us consider the Scriptures of the Holy Ghost, which persuade and command us all obediently to be subject, first and chiefly to the Queen's majesty, supreme governor over all; and next, to her honourable council, and to all other noblemen, magistrates, and officers, which by God's goodness be placed and ordered. For Almighty God is the only author and provider of this forenamed state and order: as it is written of God in the book of Proverbs, *Through me*

*kings do reign; through me counsellors make just laws; through me do princes bear rule, and all judges of the earth execute judgment: I am loving to them that love me. . . .*

Ye have heard before, in this Sermon of good Order and Obedience, manifestly proved both by scriptures and examples, that all subjects are bound to obey their magistrates, and for no cause to resist, or withstand, rebel, or make any sedition against them, yea, although they be wicked men. And let no man think that he can escape unpunished that committeth treason, conspiracy, or rebellion against his sovereign lord the king; though he commit the same never so secretly, either in thought, word, or deed; never so privily in his privy chamber by himself, or openly communicating and consulting with other. For treason will not be hid; treason will out at the length: God will have that most detestable vice both opened and punished; for that it is so directly against his ordinance, and against his high principal judge and anointed in earth. The violence and injury that is committed against authority is committed against God, the commonweal, and the whole realm; which God will have known, and condignly or worthily punished one way or other: for it is notably written of the wise man in scripture, in the book called Ecclesiastes, *Wish the king no evil in thy thought, nor speak no hurt of him in thy privy chamber; for the bird of the air shall betray thy voice, and with her feathers shall bewray thy words.*

These lessons and examples are written for our learning: therefore let us all fear the most detestable vice of rebellion; ever knowing and remembering, that he that resisteth or withstandeth common authority, resisteth or withstandeth God and his ordinance; as it may be proved by many other more places of holy scripture. . . .

## WILLIAM LAMBARDE, *Eirenarcha* (1581)

William Lambard explains the reasons for sixteenth-century punitive justice.

As justice cannot be administered without both a declaration of the law and an execution of the same, so, to the end that our justices of the peace may be able to deliver justice, they are accomplished with double power, the one of jurisdiction and the other of coercion; that is to say, with ample authority not only to convent[1] the persons but also (after the cause heard and adjudged) to constrain them to the obedience of their order and decree. . . .

But if the authority of these justices should cease when the fault is told, heard and adjudged, then should they be no better than half justices; and therefore the law hath also put coercion, execution or punishment (as I said) into their hands lest otherwise their judgements should be deluded for want of power to bring them to effect.

This punishment then is an orderly execution of a lawful judgement laid upon an offender by the minister of the law. And it is done for four causes: first, for the amendment of the offender; secondly, for example sake, that others may be thereby kept from offending; thirdly, for the maintenance of the authority and credit of the person that is offended; and these three reasons be common to all such punishments. Seneca rehearseth the fourth, final cause; that is to say that (wicked men being taken away) the good may live in better security; and this pertaineth not to all, but to capital punishments only. . . .

The punishments that be commonly put in execution at this day and wherewith the justices of the peace have to do, they be divided into corporal, pecuniary and infamous.

Corporal punishment is either capital or not capital. Capital (or deadly) punishment is done sundry ways as by hanging, burning, boiling or pressing. Not capital is of divers sorts also, as cutting off the hand or ear, burning (or marking) the hand or face, whipping, imprisoning, stocking, setting on the pillory, or cuckingstool, which in old time was called the tumbrel. This kind of punishment our old law (making precious estimation of the lives of men) had more sorts than we now have as pulling out the tongue for false rumours, cutting off the nose for adultery, taking away the privy parts for counterfeiting of money, etc.

Under the name of pecuniary punishment I comprehend all issues, fines, amercements[2] and forfeitures of offices, goods or lands.

And if the justices of the peace may by virtue of their commission . . . cause any person to be indicted of felony whereof afterward he is acquitted . . . then there is a special punishment in that case appointed by law which . . . is termed . . . infamous because the judgement in such case shall be . . . that their oaths shall not be of any credit after; nor [shall it be] lawful for them in person to approach the Queen's courts; and that their lands and goods [shall] be seized into the Queen's hands; their trees rooted up; and their bodies imprisoned, etc. And at this day, the punishment appointed for perjury (having somewhat more in it than corporal or pecuniary pain) stretching to the discrediting of the testimony of the offender for ever after, may be partaker of this name.[3]

SOURCE: From William Lambarde, *Eirenarcha: or, of the Office of the Justices of Peace, 1581* (London, 1591), pp. 65–68.

[1] i.e., summon them to meet  [2] punishments  [3] i.e., kind of punishment

# The Scaffold Speeches of Anne and George Boleyn (1536)

Anne Boleyn was Henry VIII's second wife, and her marriage to the King led to the break with Rome and the English Reformation. In order to understand both Anne's and George's confessions, when they were about to be executed for high treason on the grounds of adultery and incest, it is necessary to realize that the government did not have to prove the overt act, only the thought.

## Anne Boleyn's words (May, 1536)

Good friends, I am not come here to excuse or to justify myself, for as much as I know full well that aught that I could say in my defense doth not appertain unto you, and that I could draw no hope of life from the same. But I come here only to die, and thus to yield myself humbly to the will of the King my lord. And if in my life I did ever offend the King's grace, surely with my death I do now atone for the same. And I blame not my judges, nor any other manner of person, nor anything save the cruel law of the land by which I die. But be this, and be my faults as they may, I beseech you all, good friends, to pray for the life of the King my sovereign lord and yours, who is one of the best princes on the face of the earth, and who hath always treated me so well that better could not be; wherefore I submit to death with a good will, humbly asking pardon of the world.

## George Boleyn's words (May, 1536)

O ye gentlemen and Christians, I was born under the law and I die under the law, for as much as it is the law which hath condemned me. Ye gentlemen here present, I come not hither to preach unto you, but to die. Nor do I now seek for anything, in the sorrowful plight in which I here stand, save that I may soon bathe my dry and parched lips in the living fountain of God's everlasting and infinite mercy. And I beseech you all, in his holy name, to pray unto him for me, confessing truly that I deserve death, even though I had a thousand lives — yea even to die with far more and worse shame and dishonour than hath ever been heard of before. For I am a miserable sinner, who have grievously and oftentimes offended; nay and in very truth, I know not of any more perverse or wicked sinner than I have been up until now. Nevertheless, I mean not openly now to relate what my many sins may have been, since in sooth it can yield you no profit, nor me any pleasure here to reckon them up; enough be it that God knoweth them all. And ye, gentlemen of the court, mine especial and ancient familiars, I beseech you, of all love, that ye take heed not to fall into the errors of my ways, and that ye be warned by my example; and I pray to the Father, Son and Holy Ghost, three persons in one God, that ye may wisely profit by the same, and that from my mishap ye may learn not to set your thoughts upon the vanities of this world, and least of all, upon the flatteries of the court and the favors and treacheries of fortune, which only raiseth men aloft that with so much the greater force she may dash them again upon the ground. She in truth it is who is the cause that, as ye all witness, my miserable head is now to be dissevered from my neck; or rather, in greater truth, the fault is mine, and it is I who ought to be blamed for having adventured to learn on fortune, who hath proved herself fickle and false unto me, and who now maketh me as an example to

SOURCE: From Francisque Michel, *Lettre d'un gentilhomme portugais à un de ses amis de Lisbonne sur l'execution d'Anne Boleyn, Lord Rochford, Brereton, Norris, Smeton, et Weston . . .* (Paris, 1832), pp. 10–13.

you all and to the whole world. And do ye all, sirs, take notice, that in this my sorrowful condition, I pray for the mercy of God Almighty, and that I do moreover forgive all men, with all my heart and mind, even as truly as I hope that the Lord God will forgive me. And if so be that I should in aught have offended any man not now here present, do ye entreat him, when ye chance to meet him, that he also may of his charity forgive me; for, having lived the life of a sinner, I would fain die the death of a Christian man.

## The Privy Purse Expenses of Henry VII (1491–1505)

In the sixteenth century, there was no clear distinction between what was private and what was public. As the privy purse expenses of Henry VII reveal, although expenses were carefully recorded, there was no notion of modern auditing.

*January* 2. For christening of Winslow child, £3 6s 8d. To Hugh Denes for a musk ball, 6s 8d.

*January* 6. To Hugh Vaughan for two harpers, 13s 4d. To Graunt Pier, the founder, in reward, £1. To Courtevild, the ambassador of Flaunders, £33 6s 8d.

*January* 7. For two new great gests,[4] £1 13s 4d. To a little maiden that danceth, £12. To a Welshman that maketh rhymes, 6s 8d.

*January* 20. To John Flee for a case for the cape and sword of maintenance, £1 2s.

*February* 1. Delivered to the Queen's grace for to pay her debts, which is to be repaid, £2,000. Delivered to the Sergeant of the Poultry to meet the archduke's sisters, £40. To Sir Thomas Lovell for cost made about the Lord Fitzwater, £5 5s 8d.

*February* 17. Delivered to William Fisher, treasurer, for my Lord of York's expenses, £166 8s. To the Queen's fiddler in reward, £1 6s 8d. To the gardener at Shene for grafts, £2.

*February* 19. To the great Welsh child, 6s 8d.

*March* 17. At Shene. To Baily for watching the crows, 13s 4d. Delivered to my Lady Fitzwater, £33 6s 6d. Delivered and sent by the King's commandment to York, Durham and Newcastle, £4,000.

*March* 31. Delivered to the Greek in reward, £4. To the friar that preached in French, £2.

*April* 3. To a Welsh rhymer in reward, 13s 4d.

*April* 17. At London. [April] 21. At Greenwich. To Dr. Mydelton going ambassador, £2. To Dr. Ruthall going with him, £23 6s 8d.

*May* 1. For redeeming of prisoners out of the King's Bench, £7 14s 8d.

*May* 13. Delivered and sent by the King's commandment to Berwick towards the wars, £6,300.

*May* 24. For redeeming of certain persons out of the Marchalsie [prison] by bill, £3 17s 4d. Delivered to the Cofferer for as much money paid by Master Hugh Oldeham for 100 pieces of Cornish tin, £250.

*May* 31. Delivered to the Queen's grace for jewels, £31 10s. To a woman for aqua vita,[5] 5s.

*June* 5. Delivered to the ambassador of Naples, £66 13s 4d. To Sir John Cheyne by M. Esterfeld, £100.

*June* 9. At Alesbury. [June] 11. At Bucks. [June] 12. At Banbury.

SOURCE: From Samuel Bentley, *Excerpta Historica* (London, 1833), pp. 85–133.

[4] histories   [5] pure water

*June 12.* Paid for a pair of carving knives, £1 6s 8d.

*June 13.* At Woodstock. [June] 14. At Abindon. [June] 15. At Walingford. [June] 16. At Reding and Windsor. [June] 17. At Kingston. [June] 18. At St. Georgefeld. [June] 19. At Blackheath.

*June 23.* At the Tower. To Burley for keeping of Sir Th. Turnbull, £4 4s 9d. Paid upon a bill for the wars, £40 13s 4d. To one that took the Lord Audeley, £1. To my Lord Dacre's servant that took the Lord Audeley, for his costs, £1 6s 8d.

*June 24.* Midsummer Day. For making of the bonfire, 10s.

*June 30.* To two ambassadors of France, £40. To three other Frenchmen in reward, £10. To one that took the Lord Audeley, £2. To the Prior of the Charterhouse servant for a table of imagery, 6s 8d. To the Queen's grace for garnishing of a salet,[6] £10.

*July 1.* At Shene. Delivered and sent by the King's commandment northward for the King's wars, £12,000. For paling[7] of Eltham park, £1.

*July 21.* To my Lord of Dudley's bastard brother, £66 8s.

*July 26.* To Quintin Paulet for a book, £23.

*July 29.* At Netley. [July] 30. At Woodstock. For sixteen pair of gloves, 5s. 4d.

*August 9.* To John Vandelf for garnishing of a salet, £38 1s 4d. For twenty jackets of the best sort, £19 6s 4d. For embroidering of the same jackets, £18. For garnishing of the King's sword, £6 10s 7d.

*August 10.* To him that found the new isle [Newfoundland],[8] £10.

*August 19.* At Cornbury. [August] 21. At Minst. Lovell. [August] 22. At Woodstock. To two friars of Inde in reward, 3s 4d.

*August 30.* Delivered to Robert Court for to be delivered to the King's commissioners in the west parts, £333 6s 8d. To Jacques Haute for the tennis play, £10.

For making of the King's standing[9] in the park upon a bill, £1 17s 6d.

*September 1.* To Piers Lloyd for convening of St. Mary's men to the Tower of London, 13s 4d.

*September 10.* To John Myklow for the ambassadors' expenses at Oxford, upon a bill, £2 11s 2d. Delivered to Richard Empson for to carry to Exeter for the business there, £666 13s 4d.

*September 20.* Delivered for the retinue of Sir John Cheyne, £500. To Robert Whitlock, Thomas Bromfeld, John Sharp, Richard Pitt, lying as posts,[10] £2.

*September 22.* Delivered to Doctor Middleton, to convey to my Lord Chamberlain, £666 13s 4d. To four carts for carriage of money three days from London to Woodstock, £4.

*September 25.* To a man that come from Perkin [Warbeck], £1.

*September 27.* At Chichester. [September] 28. At Malmesbury. [September] 29. At Bath. [September] 30. At Wells. To carry to my Lord Chamberlain at Excester, £500.

*September 30.* Paid and delivered to diverse captains for their wages with their retinue, £4,000.

*October 1.* At Wells. For a guide to Bath in reward, 1s 8d.

*October 2.* At Glastonbury. [October] 3. At Bridgewater. [October] 4. At Taunton. For the King's loss at cards at Taunton, £9.

*October 5.* This day came Perkin Warbeck. [October] 6. At Tiverton. [October] 7. At Excester.

*October 15.* To Garter [one of the heralds] for two coats armour bought for the Lord Audeley, 13s 4d. To Robert Suthwell for horses, saddles and other necessarys bought for the conveying of my Lady Katheryn Huntley, £7 13s 4d.

*November 3.* At Otery. [November] 4. At Newnham. [November] 10. At Bridport. [November] 11. At Dorchester. [November] 12. At Blanford. [November] 13. At

---

[6] helmet   [7] enclosing   [8] i.e., John Cabot   [9] hunting station   [10] messengers

Salisbury. [November] 14. At Andover. [November] 15. At Freefold. [November] 18. At Basingstok. [November] 19. At Esthamsted. [November] 20. At Windsor. [November] 21. At Shene. [November] 27. At Westminster.

December 1. To my Lady Katheryn Huntley, £2.

December 3. To my Lady, the King's mother's poet, £3 6s 8d.

December 8. To a surgeon that healed my Lord Kildare's son, in reward, £2.

December 10. To Piers Barbor for spices for ipocras,[11] 6s 8d. To Hugh Denes for the King's play at dice upon Friday last passed, £7 15s. To Courtevild ambassador of Flanders, £20.

December 18. Delivered by the King's commandment in repayment of diverse loans, £3,364. To blind Cunningham, 13s 4d. To the ambassador of Spain in reward, £66 15s. To Hugh Denes for Perkin's costs, £2.

December 24. To my Lord of Landaff for belding[12] at Shene, over and besides £40 to him delivered in prest,[13] £101 4s 2d.

For rewards given to them that found the King's jewels at Shene, £20. To the gardiner for sope hashs,[14] 10s. For two pairs of bellows, 10d. To my Lord Prince's poet in reward, £3 6s 8d. For the wages of the King's scholar, John Taylor, at Oxenford, £2 10s. To Robert Jones upon a bill for Perkin's horsemeat unto the first day of February, £1 8s 6d. To John Atkinson for a paper book, 3s 4d. To Story the carpenter for making a gallery at Greenwich, £2. To one that tumbled at Eltham, £1. To the secretary of Venes in reward, £20.

Delivered to Launcelot Thirkill going towards the new isle in prest, £20. To Thomas Bradley and Launcelot Thirkill going to the new isle, £30. To Arnold player

at recorders, £1. To John Carter going to the new isle in reward, £2. To Sir Pieter for a mass book, 8s. To the Queen's grace, £6 13s 4d. To Robert Taylor the Queen's surgeon, £3 6s 8d.

Delivered by the King's commandment for to repay the loan money, £10,000. For a coat and a pair of hoses bought and made for the King's fool, 15s 2d. For making of a bonfire, 10s. To the binding of the Keeper's daughter of Westminster to prentassode,[15] £4. To Arnold Jeffrey, organ player, for a quarter wages unto Midsummer last, 10s. To Master Coningesby servant and Master Frowick servant for writing of certain books for the King, £3 6s 8d. To one that found a Stock dove, 1s. To a fool at Master Knyvett's, 3s. 4d. To a piper at Huntingdon, 2s. To my Lord Prince's organ players for a quarter wages ended at Michellmas, 10s.

To Oliver Tonor for relics, in reward, £2 13s 4d. To Master William Paronus, an astronomer, £1. To one that went to the Holy land, £1.

Delivered and paid by the King's commandment upon a bill signed, £4820. To the May game at Greenwich, 4s. For the King's loss at tennis, 8s. To the players with marvels,[16] £4. To the printers at Westminster, £1. To a woman for a red rose, 2s. To the King's piper in reward, 10s. To the Pope's collect servant for hawks, 10s. To the ambassador of Spain in reward, £66 15s. To a Frenchman for certain books, £56 4s. Delivered by the King's commandment for his works in sundry and diverse places, £7640. To Quintin for 3 books, £1. To one that brought the King date trees, 6s 8d. To an astronomer for a prognostication, £3 6s 8d. To a fellow for eating of coles,[17] 6s 8d. Delivered to John Myklow for the expense of the ambassador of Flanders to London, £6 3s 3d. To Thomas Blakall the King's fool, 6s 8d.

---

[11] a cordial wine   [12] protection   [13] ready money   [14] chopped-up wet grass, mulch   [15] apprentice-ship?   [16] magicians?   [17] cabbages?

## Henry VIII's Last Speech to Parliament (24 December, 1545)

Henry VIII was in no mood to trifle when he delivered his final address to parliament. The Reformation had unleashed controversy and dissension upon his kingdom, and his subjects had strayed from that charity and fraternal love which he expected of them.

Although my Chancellor for the time being hath before this time used very eloquently and substantially to make answer to such orations as hath been set forth in this high court of Parliament, yet is he not so able to open and set forth my mind and meaning, and the secrets of my heart, in so plain and ample manner as I myself am and can do: wherefore I taking upon me to answer your eloquent oration, master Speaker, say that where you, in the name of our well beloved commons, hath both praised and extolled me for the notable qualities that you have conceived to be in me, I most heartily thank you all that you have put me in remembrance of my duty, which is to endeavour myself to obtain and get such excellent qualities and necessary virtues, as a Prince or governor should or ought to have, . . . Surely if I, contrary to your expectation, should suffer the ministers of the Church to decay, or learning (which is great a jewel) to be [di]minished, or poor and miserable people to be unrelieved, you might say that I being put in so special a trust, as I am in this case, were no trusty friend to you, no charitable man to mine even Christian, neither a lover of the public wealth, nor yet one that feared God, to whom account must be rendered of all our doings. Doubt not, I pray you, but your expectations shall be served, more godly and goodly than you will wish or desire, as hereafter you shall plainly perceive.

Now sithence I find such kindness on your part toward me, I cannot chose but love and favour you, affirming that no prince in the world more favoureth his subjects than I do you, nor no subjects or commons more love and obey their sovereign lord than I perceive you do me, for whose defence my treasure shall not be hidden, nor, if necessity require, my person shall not be unadventured: yet although I with you, and you with me, be in this perfect love and concord, this friendly amity cannot continue, except both you, my lords temporal, and you, my lords spiritual, and you, my loving subjects, study and take pain to amend one thing which surely is amiss, and far out of order, to the which I most heartily require you; which is, that charity and concord is not amongst you, but discord and dissension beareth rule in every place. St. Paul sayeth to the Corinthians, in the xiii Chapter, Charity is gentle, charity is not envious, charity is not proud and so forth in the said chapter: behold then, what love and charity is amongst you, when the one calleth the other, heretic and Anabaptist, and he calleth him again Papist, hypocrite, and Pharisee. Be these tokens of charity amongst you? are these the signs of fraternal love between you? No, no, I assure you that this lack of charity amongst yourselves will be the hindrance and assuaging of the fervent love between us, as I said before, except this would be salved and clearly made whole. I must needs judge the fault and occasion of this discord to be partly by negligence of you the fathers and preachers of the spirituality. For if I know a man which liveth in adultery, I must judge him a lecherous and a carnal person:

SOURCE: From Edward Hall, *The Union of the Two noble and illustre families of Lancastre & Yorke* (London, 1548), ff. cclxi–cclxii.

if I see a man boast and brag himself, I cannot but deem him a proud man. I see and hear daily that you of the clergy preach one against another, teach one contrary to another, inveigh one against another without charity or discretion. Some be too stiff in their old Mumpsimus, other be too busy and curious in their new Sumpsimus. Thus all men almost be in variety and discord, and few or none preach truly and sincerely the word of God, according as they ought to do. Shall I now judge you charitable persons doing this? No, no, I cannot so do. Alas how can the poor souls live in concord when you preachers sow amongst them in your sermons, debate and discord: of you they look for light, and you bring them darkness. Amend these crimes, I exhort you, and set forth God's word, both by true preaching and good example giving, or else I whom God hath appointed his Vicar and high minister here, will see these divisions extinct, and these enormities corrected, according to my very duty, or else I am an unprofitable servant and untrue officer.

Although, as I say, the spiritual men be in some fault, that charity is not kept amongst you, yet you of the temporality be not clean and unspotted of malice and envy, for you rail on Bishops, speak slanderously of priests, and rebuke and taunt preachers, both contrary to good order and Christian fraternity. If you know surely that a bishop or preacher erreth or teacheth perverse doctrine, come and declare it to some of our Council or to us, to whom is committed by God the high authority to reform and order such causes and behaviours: and be not judges yourselves of your own phantastical opinions and vain expositions, for in such high causes ye may lightly err. And although you be permitted to read holy scripture, and to have the word of God in your mother tongue, you must understand that it is licensed you so to do, only to inform your own conscience, and to instruct your children and family, and not to dispute and make scripture, a railing and a taunting stock against priests and preachers (as many light persons do). I am very sorry to know and hear how unreverently that most precious jewel the word of God is disputed, rimed, sung and jangled in every alehouse and tavern, contrary to the true meaning and doctrine of the same. And yet I am even as much sorry that the readers of the same follow it in doing so faintly and coldly. for of this I am sure, that charity was never so faint amongst you, and virtuous and godly living was never less used, nor God himself amongst Christians was never less reverenced, honoured or served. Therefore, as I said before, be in charity one with another, like brother and brother; love, dread and serve God (to the which I, as your supreme head and sovereign lord, exhort and require you) and then I doubt not but that love and league that I spake of in the beginning shall never be dissolved or broken between us. . . .

## Elizabeth's "Golden Speech" to Parliament (30 November, 1601)

The kingdom was in the midst of a serious depression, and criticism of the Queen's economic policies was growing, but Elizabeth set out to win even the most aggrieved heart in this her "golden speech" to parliament.

Mr. Speaker,

We have heard your declaration and perceive your care of our state, by falling into the consideration of a grateful acknowledgment of such benefits as you have received; and that your coming is to present thanks unto us, which I accept with no less joy than your loves can have desire to offer such a present.

I do assure you, there is no prince that

source: From Hayward Townshend, *Historical Collections* (London, 1680), pp. 263–266.

loveth his subjects better, or whose love can countervail our love. There is no jewel, be it of never so rich a price, which I set before this jewel; I mean your love. For I do more esteem of it than of any treasure or riches, for that we know how to prize, but love and thanks I count invaluable.

And, though God hath raised me high, yet this I count the glory of my crown, that I have reigned with your loves. This makes me that I do not so much rejoice that God hath made me to be a queen, as to be a queen over so thankful a people.

Therefore, I have cause to wish nothing more than to content the subjects, and that is a duty which I owe. Neither do I desire to live longer days than I may see your prosperity; and that's my only desire.

And as I am that person that still (yet under God) hath delivered you, so I trust (by the Almighty Power of God) that I still shall be His instrument to preserve you from envy, peril, dishonor, shame, tyranny and oppression; partly by means of your intended helps, which we take very acceptably, because it manifests the largeness of your loves and loyalty to your sovereign.

Of myself I must say this: I was never any greedy scraping grasper, nor a straight, fast-holding prince, nor yet a waster. My heart was never set on worldly goods, but only for my subjects' good. What you do bestow on me, I will not hoard it up, but receive it to bestow on you again. Yea, my own properties I count yours, and to be expended for your good; and your eyes shall see the bestowing of all for your good. Therefore, render unto them from me, I beseech you, Mr. Speaker, such thanks as you imagine my heart yieldeth but my tongue cannot express.

*Note, all this while we kneeled. Whereupon her majesty said: Mr. Speaker, I would wish you and the rest to stand up, for I shall yet trouble you with longer speech. So we all stood up, and she went on with her speech, saying:*

Mr. Speaker,

You give me thanks, but I doubt me that I have more cause to thank you all than you me. And I charge you to thank them of the Lower House from me. For had I not received a knowledge from you, I might have fallen into the lapse of an error, only for lack of true information.

Since I was Queen, yet did I never put my pen unto any grant[18] but that, upon pretext and semblance made unto me, it was both good and beneficial to the subject in general, though a private profit to some of my ancient servants who had deserved well at my hands. But the contrary being found by experience, I am exceedingly beholding to such subjects as would move the same at the first. And I am not so simple to suppose but that there are some of the Lower House whom these grievances never touched. And for them, I think they spake out of zeal for their countries, and not out of spleen or malevolent affection as being parties grieved. And I take it exceeding gratefully from them, because it gives us to know that no respects or interests had moved them other than the minds they bear to suffer no diminution of our honour and our subjects' loves unto us. The zeal of which affection, tending to ease my people and knit their hearts unto me, I embrace with a princely care, for (above all earthly treasure) I esteem my people's love more than which I desire not to merit.

That my grants should be grievous to my people and oppressions privileged under color of our patents, our kingly dignity shall not suffer it. Yea, when I heard it I could give no rest unto my thoughts until I had reformed it.

Shall they think to escape unpunished, that have thus oppressed you and have been respectless of their duty and regardless of our honor? No, Mr. Speaker, I assure you, were it not more for conscience sake than for any glory or increase of love that I desire these errors, troubles, vexations and oppressions done by these varlets and lewd

---

18 i.e., monopoly

persons, not worthy the name of subjects, should not escape without condign punishment. But I perceive they deal with me like physicians who, administering a drug, make it more acceptable by giving it a good aromatical savor, or when they give pills do gild them all over.

I have ever used to set the last Judgment Day before my eyes, as so to rule as I shall be judged to answer before a higher Judge, to whose judgment seat I do appeal: that never thought was cherished in my heart that tended not to my people's good. And now, if my kingly bounty have been abused, and my grants turned to the hurt of my people, contrary to my will and meaning, or if any in authority under me have neglected or perverted what I have committed to them, I hope God will not lay their culps and offences to my charge; who though there were danger in repealing our grants, yet what danger would I not rather incur for your good than I would suffer them still to continue?

I know the title of a king is a glorious title. But assure yourself that the shining glory of princely authority hath not so dazzled the eyes of our understanding but that we well know and remember that we also are to yield an account of our actions before the great Judge.

To be a king and wear a crown is a thing more glorious to them that see it than it is pleasing to them that bear it. For myself, I was never so much enticed with the glorious name of a king, or royal authority of a queen, as delighted that God had made me His instrument to maintain His truth and glory, and to defend this kingdom (as I said) from peril, dishonor, tyranny and oppression.

There will never queen sit in my seat with more zeal to my country, care for my subjects, and that sooner with willingness will venture her life for your good and safety, than myself. For it is not my desire to live nor reign longer than my life and reign shall be for your good. And though you have had, and may have, many princes more mighty and wise sitting in this state, yet you never had, or shall have, any that will be more careful and loving.

Shall I ascribe anything to myself and my sexly weakness? I were not worthy to live then; and of all, most unworthy of the great mercies I have had from God, who hath ever yet given me a heart which never yet feared foreign or home enemy. I speak it to give God the praise, as a testimony before you, and not to attribute anything to myself. For I, O Lord, what am I, whom practices and perils past should not fear? Or, what can I do?

*These words she spake with a great emphasis. That I should speak for any glory, God forbid.*

This, Mr. Speaker, I pray you deliver to the House, to whom heartily commend me. And so, I commit you all to your best fortunes and further counsels. And I pray you, Mr. Comptroller, Mr. Secretary, and you of my council, that before these gentlemen depart into their countries, you bring them all to kiss my hand.

## *Francis Bacon's Advice to the Earl of Essex* ( 4 October, 1596 )

Francis Bacon (1561–1626) is best known as one of the fathers of modern science, and a selection from his *Novum Organum* can be read in the last chapter of this volume. Bacon, however, was also an important essayist, political analyst, and statesman. He knew his Elizabeth well and understood to perfection the political world in which she lived; possibly this is why he never rose to high office under the Queen and had to wait for political recognition until James I came to the throne. It is a pity that his astute, almost Machiavellian, advice to Robert Devereux, Earl of Essex, was not heeded by the young nobleman. Perhaps if Essex had listened, he would not have ended his life on the scaffold in 1601.

Whether I counsel you the best, or for the best, duty bindeth me to offer to you my wishes. I said to your L[ordship] last time, ... Win the Queen; if this be not the beginning, of any other course I can see no end. ... But how is it now [with you]? A man of a nature not to be ruled, that hath my affection and knoweth it, of an estate not grounded to his greatness, of a popular reputation, of a military dependence: I demand whether there can be a more dangerous image than this represented to any monarch living, much more to a lady, and of Her Majesty's apprehension? And is it not more evident than demonstration itself, that whilst this impression continueth in Her Majesty's breast, you can find no other condition than inventions to keep your estate bare and low; crossing and disgracing your actions, extenuating and blasting of your merit, carping with contempt at your nature and fashions; breeding, nourishing, and fortifying such instruments as are most factious against you, repulses and scorns of your friends and dependents that are true and stedfast, winning and inveigling away from you such as are flexible and wavering, thrusting you into odious employments and offices to supplant your reputation, abusing you, and feeding you with dalliances and demonstrations, to divert you from descending into the serious consideration of your own case; yea, and percase venturing you in perilous and desperate enterprizes. Herein it may please your L. to understand me; for I mean nothing less than that these things should be plotted and intended as in Her Majesty's royal mind towards you: I know the excellency of her nature too well. But I say, wheresoever the formerly described impression is taken in any king's

breast towards a subject, these other recited inconveniences must of necessity of politic consequence follow; in respect of such instruments as are never failing about princes, which spy into their humors and conceits, and second them; and not only second them, but in seconding increase them; yea, and many times, without their knowledge, pursue them further than themselves would.

For the removing of the impression of your nature to be opiniative and not rulable; first, [all past difficulties should be justified as efforts to protect the Queen and to enhance Essex's honor]. ... Next, whereas I have noted you to fly and avoid the resemblance or imitation of my Lord of Leicester, and my Lord Chancellor Hatton;[19] yet I am persuaded, — howsoever I wish your L. distant as you are from them in points of magnanimity and merit, favor and integrity, — that it will do you much good between the Queen and you to allege them, as often as you find occasion, for authors and patterns. Thirdly, when at any time your L., upon occasion, happen in speeches to do Her Majesty right, — for there is no such matter as flattery amongst you all, — [you should speak lightly without being overbearing]. ... Fourthly, your L. should never be without some particulars afoot, which you should seem to pursue with earnestness and affection; and then let them fall upon taking note of Her Majesty's opposition and dislike. Of which the weightiest sort may be if your L. offer to labor in the behalf of some that you favor, for some of the places[20] now void; choosing such a subject as you think Her Majesty is like to oppose unto; ... I say, commendation from so good a mouth doth not hurt a

SOURCE: From Walter B. Devereux, *Lives and Letters of the Devereux, Earls of Essex* ... *1540–1646*, 2 vols. (London: John Murray, 1853), Vol. I, pp. 395–400.

[19] the Queen's two favorites    [20] offices

man though you prevail not. A less weighty sort of particulars may be the pretence of some journies, which, at Her Majesty's request, your L. might relinquish; as if you would pretend a journey to see your living and estate in Wales; as for great foreign journies of employment and service it standeth not with your gravity to play or stratagem with them. And the lightest of particulars which yet are not to be neglected, are in your habits, apparel, wearings, gestures, and the like.

The impression of greatest prejudice next, is that of a military dependence, wherein, I cannot sufficiently wonder at your L. course, that you say, the wars are your occupation, and go in that course; . . . And here, my L., I pray mistake me not. I am not to play now the part of a gownman that would frame you best to mine own turn. I am infinitely glad of this last journey[21] now it is past; . . . There is none can of many years ascend near you in competition. Besides, the disposing of the places and affairs both, concerning the wars, will of themselves flow to you, which will preserve that dependence in full measure. But I say, keep it in substance, but abolish it in shows. For her Majesty loveth peace. Next, she loveth not charge.[22] Thirdly, that kind of dependence maketh a suspected greatness. Therefore, again, whereas I heard your L. designing

to yourself the Earl Marshal's place, or place of the Master of the Ordnance, I did not, in my own mind, so well like of either, because of their affinity with a martial greatness. But of the places now void I would name to you the place of Lord Privy Seal. For first, it is the third person of the great officers of the Crown. Next, it hath a kind of superintendence over the Secretary. It also hath an affinity with the Court of Wards, in regard of the fees from the liveries. And it is a fine honor, quiet place, and worth a thousand pounds by year. . . . And it fits a favourite to carry Her Majesty's image in seal,[23] . . . If you shall pretend to be as bookish and contemplative as ever you were; all these courses serve exceeding aptly to this purpose. . . .

The third impression is of a popular reputation, which, because it is a thing good in itself, being obtained as your L. obtained it, . . . is one of the flowers of your greatness, both present and to come; it should be handled tenderly. The only way is to quench it *verbis*[24] and not *rebus*;[25] and, therefore, to take all occasions to the Queen to speak against popularity and popular courses vehemently, and to tax it in all others; but, nevertheless, to go on in your honorable commonwealth courses as you do. . . .

## William Wentworth's Advice to His Son (1604)

William Wentworth was a country gentleman whose precepts for living and succeeding in the age of Elizabeth and James I ranged from how to select a wife and run a household to how to pick friends and handle the rich and powerful. Wentworth's words of advice to his twenty-two-year-old son may seem to the modern reader to be unnecessarily paranoid, but they are no more hard-nose and calculated than Bacon's words to Essex or other examples of a Tudor father's concern for a son's welfare in the world of hard knocks.

---

William Wentworth of Wentworth Woodhus esquire . . . being near the age of 45 years his advice and counsel to Thomas Went-

worth his son and heir . . . touching the managing of his private estate and affairs; all written with his own hand.

---

SOURCE: From J. P. Cooper, *Wentworth Papers 1397–1628* (London: Royal Historical Society, 1973), Camden 4th Series, Vol. 12, Doc. 1, pp. 9–24. By permission of the Royal Historical Society.

[21] the Cadiz expedition  [22] heavy expenses  [23] *carry* . . . i.e., be what the Queen desires  [24] by word
[25] by deed

Touching the good government of your person and affairs, albeit I verily hope that your own discretion guided from above, by the grace and power of a most merciful heavenly father, will give unto you the two inestimable benefits of a prosperous life and a happy ending. Yet, for that it pleaseth God many times to make the wise advice of some aged faithful friend the means of these blessings, by working in young men a sounder judgment than their small experience could otherways easily attain unto, I, your natural father, whose intents admit no guile and whose experience hath not been the least among others, have thought good, according to my small measure of wit, to deliver to you my best opinion and counsels touching the well ordering of yourself and your private estate.

GOD. First then fear God, love him and trust in him. Every night before you sleep and every morning before you rise, say prayers. . . . Bear a good conscience, be just, humble, charitable and merciful; be moderate in all things and frugal in expenses, for wasters and proud men be very fools. . . . Be very careful to govern your tongue and never speak in open places all you think; neither ever talk openly ill of any, for whatsoever you speak that way even in your own house most commonly is discovered and will certainly at some time do you harm. But to your wife, if she can keep counsel (as few women can), or to a private faithful friend, or some old servant that hath all his living and credit under you, you may be more open, yet ever talk thereof but to one. . . .

Touching the KING our Sovereign lord, pray for him and obey his laws; for in his safety consisteth the weale and prosperity of his subjects and the commonwealth is the ship we sail in. His greatest MAJESTRATE in the country as president or lieutenant, be you well known to them and deserve their favors by your discretion, humility and remembering your duty with presents in due time; yet ever take heed that no man living overreach you for great sums of money, neither ever lend to greater men than yourself more than you mean to lose. . . . If any

great man be to make an arbitrament betwixt you and your adversary wherein you mean to have favor, you must . . . deal with some favorite of that great man's and instruct him secretly and promise him a certain reward, if your desire be effected, but give little or nothing before hand; . . .

For NOBLE MEN in general it is dangerous to be familiar with them, or to depend upon them or to deal with or trust them too much. For their thoughts are bestowed upon their own weighty causes and their estates and actions are governed by policy. Again albeit they be most courtly in words, yet they could be contented that rich gentlemen were less able to live without depending on them, even as the gentleman looks with a discontented eye upon the stout rich yeoman. In any case never engage yourself for your superiors by bonds nor lend them more than you can be willing to give them. As it is no wisdom and many times danger to fawn and depend upon noblemen, so in any case be careful not to make them hate you. For their revenge by reason of the greatness of their mind and power at one time or other will do you displeasure; and against their displeasures you cannot defend yourself without great wit, much cost and peradventure danger of your life; therefore be provident and judicial that way. If the Sheriff or any Majestrate or Commissioner send you a letter from any great person directed to them and you for anything concerning you, which letter they will have returned after you have had notice of it, do you never fail but with all speed take a true copy of that letter before you send it back and, not resolving hastily, consult at leisure ripely what provident and discreet course to take therein. . . .

The Company of your EQUALS, whose estate is not declining and in whom there is a good conscience and a well governed tongue, is very fit for you; . . .

If you desire AUTHORITY or degree of HONOR, you must make means for it, otherways it will not be laid upon you, there be so many that make suit for it. For mine own particular humor I was ever well contented to be without them, having many children, a weak body, etc. Yet he that will be honored and feared in his country must bear countenance and authority; for people are servile, not generous and do reverence men for fear, not for love of their virtues which they apprehend not. . . .

To your PARENTS be humble, dutiful and patient. . . .

Of KINSFOLK esteem the company of them most that be rich, honest and discreet and use them in your cause before others. If they be poorer and yet of good conscience and humble, regard them well. Yet if any of all these have lands or goods joining with you in no case trust them too much, for such occasions breed suits and future enmities. Ever fear the worst, which discreet suspect is the surest means under God of your defence. . . .

Let your HOUSEKEEPING be frugal and so proportioned that at least the one half of your yearly rents and profits be yearly laid up towards uses of charity, profit and advancement of your house. Let there be good orders and peace in all your house and let the doors at night be surely shut up by some trusty innocent servant and your men so lodged as they may defend your house. . . .

In matters of great importance trust none, but either those that of long time have rejoiced in the prosperity of your house, or of whom your father or yourself have had a long and great experience. And if it be a matter of secrecy, talk thereof ever to one alone. Whosoever comes to speak with you, comes premediate for his advantage. Therefore presume not of your own wit (if the matter be worth anything) to make a sudden answer, but take a new day and after consultation give a constant and premeditate answer. Or if the answer do necessarily require haste, then walk by and debate thereof with some wise servant or friend, or for want thereof, debate the matter privately with yourself before such answer. In any case be suspicious of the conscience of any that seem more saintlike

than others and smooth like oil, having many times God and Conscience in their mouths, when their hearts are far from him; . . .

Now as you ought to have an inward hearty desire to live without [law] suits, so must you make show upon some occasions to be prone to them when you are wronged which show of contention appearing in two or three examples will make men fearful to do you wrong. For no man will willingly have suit with a powerful man that is taken to be contentious or apt to enter into suits. Though your cause be never so just, if it be of any importance, yet must you labor the judge for lawful favor and expedition and procure his good opinion by discretion and gifts. Then the undersheriff must in time have a brace of angels [ £ 12, 16s., 8d.] to return an indifferent jury and for a tales[26] of honest men. The same jury must be labored also and, after they have given a verdict with you, you must give them more than usual and either get them to your chamber and give them wine and sugar and many thanks, or if they will not come, let your servant do it for you in some other place to their liking. . . .

In any case have some insight in the laws, for it will be a great contentment, comfort and credit and quiet for you. . . .

LETTERS to friends and strangers write as few as you can and let these be penned with so good discretion as you need not care though they were proclaimed in any time to come. For it is a common custom of men to keep letters safely and sometimes many years after to produce them for evidence against the author of them, either in open court or otherwise. . . . . .

For your WIFE let her be well born and brought up but not too highly, of a healthful body, of a good complexion, humble and virtuous, some few years younger than yourself and many times not the prouder. . . . For her juncture[27] let it not be too large, lest your heir feel the smart and a second husband the sweet of that gross oversight.

---

[26] the pool from which jurors were selected  [27] settlement

After marriage and that she have born you some children you may, if you think she deserve and need it, enlarge her juncture, yet in any case for no longer time than she shall remain widow. Ever remembering that after your death, yea though she be wise and well given, she is most like to be the wife of a stranger and peradventure no friend to your house. . . .

It is very fit for men to make show of a revengeful mind and something inclining to contention where the contrary inwardly must be sought for. For nothing but fear of revenge or suits can hold back men from doing wrong. . . . Yet sometimes in honesty policy, you must seem something contentious and ready to sue men that do you wrong, of purpose to curb their beastly and base natures which otherwise will not care for you. . . .

Whensoever a reconcilement shall happen betwixt you and your enemy, be not so unwise as afterwards to trust him. For secret poison is like to lie invisible in his heart, what protestations or show soever to the contrary; and commonly those men that have most wit and can speak best for themselves are least to be trusted. . . .

## FURTHER DISCUSSION QUESTIONS

### Thomas Smith, The Commonwealth of England

1. What is Smith's definition of a knight and a gentleman? What, if anything, is the distinction between a nobleman and a gentleman?
2. What institution possessed the highest authority in England? Of what elements did that institution consist and whom did it represent?

### Thomas Starkey, England in the Reign of Henry the Eighth

1. What, according to the author, is the "true" commonwealth?
2. What is the goal of the well-organized commonwealth?
3. How do the author's assumptions about and approach to society differ from our own?

### An Exhortation Concerning Good Order and Obedience to Rulers and Magistrates

1. God created the universe in what kind of order and for what purpose? Why was order so necessary?
2. What were the consequences of rebellion and disobedience?

### William Lambarde, Eirenarcha

1. What, according to Lambarde, are the various kinds of punishment? What is the purpose of punishment?
2. What were the assumptions about crime that underlay Lambarde's statements?
3. Compare and contrast our modern attitudes toward crime and punishment with those presented by Lambarde.

### The Scaffold Speeches of Anne and George Boleyn

1. What view of the law and society is expressed in these speeches?
2. Are either of the speeches confessions? If not, what are they?
3. If Anne and George Boleyn were in fact innocent of the crimes for which they

were condemned to die, what possible explanation can be offered for their scaffold statements?

### The Privy Purse Expenses of Henry VII

1. On the basis of Henry VII's expenses, how would you describe the role of the king in government?
2. What were the most expensive aspects of early Tudor government? What do the accounts show about the efficiency of early Tudor government?
3. By modern standards what, if anything, is peculiar about these accounts?

### Henry VIII's Last Speech to Parliament

1. What did Henry VIII conceive his duty to be? What was his relationship to God and what was his definition of the "true" word of God?
2. Judging from his speech, how would you describe Henry's personality?

### Elizabeth's "Golden Speech" to Parliament

1. As an address that sought to deflect criticism and to defend the crown's economic policies, how successful would you judge Elizabeth's performance to have been?
2. Compare and contrast Henry's and Elizabeth's speeches in terms of their style, the concept of royalty presented, the two sovereign's relationship with God, their duty to their subjects, and the source of their authority.
3. Judging from her speech, how would you describe Elizabeth's personality?

### Francis Bacon's Advice to the Earl of Essex

1. What, according to Bacon, were the Earl's defects? Why were they so dangerous to a successful career at court?
2. What must Essex do to improve his standing with the Queen? How should he go about doing it? Why is a military reputation so dangerous?
3. What does Bacon show about the nature of Tudor politics and the difficulties of political life?

### William Wentworth's Advice to His Son

1. What attributes must a young man have to achieve success in Tudor England?
2. What view of women is expressed in Wentworth's advice?
3. What does Wentworth's advice show about the structure of Tudor Society and the relationship between the various ranks and levels?
4. What is the picture of Tudor society that you get from Wentworth's advice?
5. Is Wentworth's advice to his son still sound today?

# II

# *Renaissance England*

In the previous chapter it was suggested that every society has its own particular flavor. Nothing is more apparent or more difficult to explain than the Renaissance spirit that seems to have pervaded so much of Elizabethan England. This is not the place to offer explanations; it is baffling enough simply to describe that peculiar amalgam of optimism and discontent, dynamism and discord, restlessness and curiosity that characterized Gloriana's reign. Every textbook assures the student that these were the qualities that inspired Englishmen to go down to the sea in ships, defeat the Spanish colossus, acclaim the glory of a peculiarly militant and demanding Protestant God, and, finally, display their pride of country and faith in salvation in some of the most memorable literature ever written. As usual, however, the textbooks are only partly correct. Elizabethans were indeed inspired by God, glory and profit, but they were far from being devoid of fear or immune from doubt. The assortment of heroic descriptions, literary creations, private letters, and grim reminders collected in this chapter is designed to give a sense not only of the vitality, self-confidence, and impudence of Elizabeth's unruly subjects but also of the depth and the varity of their reflections upon life and death, heaven and hell, and power and its abuses. Elizabethans may have been addicted to life, but they were also desperately aware of the grave beyond.

The first document, by Richard Hakluyt (1552?–1616), is a jingoistic dedicatory letter, which prefaced his multivolumed collection of *Navigations, Voyages, Traffics and Discoveries of the English Nation* and was deliberately designed to charm Elizabethan society with the magic not only of the New World and its immeasurable riches but also of the colonization of those unknown lands and distant places. Hakluyt was a most improbable convert to English expansionism. He was a cleric and scholar who, while acting as chaplain to the English embassy in Paris in 1583, became incensed by the con-

tempt in which his countrymen were held for their maritime backwardness and "sluggish security." To rectify that image and educate his countrymen in the delights of "cosmographie," he compiled travel stories totaling 1,700,000 words. Originally published in 1589, the *Voyages* were enlarged to keep up with the prodigious pace of English seadogs and adventurers, and today the collection is regarded as the "prose epic of the modern English nation."

The next two selections — Sir Walter Raleigh's "Report on the trueth of the fight . . . betwixt the *Revenge* . . . and an Armada . . . of Spaine" and Jan Huigen Van Linschoten's account of Grenville's death and the sinking of the *Revenge* — are also from Hakluyt's *Voyages* and give two versions of one of the most extraordinary encounters in the annals of British naval tradition. In the summer of 1591 Sir Richard Grenville, vice-admiral on board the *Revenge*, grappled for fifteen hours with eight (Van Linschoten's estimate) or possibly fifteen (Raleigh's estimate) ships of the Spanish imperial navy. The *Revenge* was part of a small English fleet of six galleons and a number of smaller escorts and transports under the command of Lord Thomas Howard, which had been taking on water off the coast of Flores in the Azores when a much larger (possibly fifty-three sails) Spanish armada was sighted. Howard gave the order to cut cable and make a run for it. The English fleet escaped, but for reasons still unclear, Grenville elected to remain behind and to take on the entire Spanish fleet. The *Revenge* was eventually sunk, and Grenville was taken captive and died of his wounds. In fact, there is a legend that Sir Richard, when presented with a goblet of wine by his respectful captors, drank the wine and then proceeded to eat the glass, so as to insure his death and avoid the humiliation of captivity and defeat. Whatever the truth about the seadog's death, Grenville's actions in failing to follow Howard's orders are typical of Elizabethan military leaders, who were strong on heroics, but weak on common sense and discipline. Howard was not pleased by his subordinate's reckless performance, which resulted in the loss of a valuable vessel and permitted the Spanish to claim a victory. Sir Walter Raleigh wrote his report partly to answer Spanish bragging, partly to deflect Howard's criticism, and partly, since Grenville was his cousin, to defend the family name. Linschoten's version is no more a first-hand account than Raleigh's. He was a Dutchman in the service of Spain, who was in the Azores at the time of the encounter and received his information from Spanish sources.

Raleigh's pride of country is clearly jingoistic; in contrast, the next two selections, although filled with self-confidence, are very different in tone. Sir Henry Sidney (1528–1586) is less well known than the son to whom his letter of advice (1565) was written, for although the father was gentleman of the bedchamber under Edward VI and Lord Deputy of Ireland under Elizabeth, his son Philip (1554–1586) grew up to become the mirror of Elizabethan culture, learning, literature, and military tradition. If Sir Henry's letter presents the Tudor ideal in its most tempered and philosophical form, Gloriana's speech displayed it in its most theatrical terms. Delivered on August 18, 1589, at her military camp of Tilbury to soldiers brought together in anticipation of a successful Spanish landing in the wake of the Armada, Elizabeth's speech was a oratorical *tour de force*. Exactly in what form it was spoken is not known, but it is given here in blank verse in order to show that her words, like those of so many of her contemporaries, were sheer poetry. To enhance the effect, the Queen was dressed in a white velvet gown and hat with immense white plumes, was resplendent in a silver breast plate, and was mounted upon a white charger.

Poetry was the voice of Elizabethan England, but it was, as in the case of Christopher Marlowe's *The Tragical History of Dr. Faustus*, not always used to sing the praises of God, honor, conquest, and country. Without exception, the remaining documents in this chapter display a melancholy and ambivalence, fear and disenchantment that was the other side — one might say the medieval side — of Elizabeth England and the Renaissance spirit. Worldliness and power had their drawbacks, of which Elizabethans, no matter how highly placed, were well aware. Christopher Marlowe (1564–1593) was probably the most volatile and undisciplined but creative playwright of the century, and in his own life he displayed most of the strengths and weaknesses of his literary creations. Born the son of a Canterbury shoemaker and a clergyman's daughter, he rose by sheer intelligence and will to become the major playwright of his generation. Bad tempered but brilliant, iconoclastic, disorderly but immensely creative, Marlowe, who wrote four immensely successful plays, had a short but meteoric career. He was befriended by the great and the mighty, but at the same time he consorted with forgers, thieves, cutpurses, and political spies, and was suspected of religious unorthodoxy or, worse, atheism. He finally ended his life at the age of twenty-nine, murdered, in a tavern brawl. More than any other dramatist before Shakespeare, he was responsible for bringing to the Elizabethan stage that prototype of himself: the consumed and consuming individual whose passions for knowledge, power, riches, and the enjoyment of life leads to the overthrow of empires and the violation of the most cherished and sacred beliefs. *Dr. Faustus*, which was dashed off during the winter of 1588–1589, stands midway between the medieval and the modern worlds — between defiance and fear, magic and science, scepticism and faith.

The final documents — three letters by the Earl of Essex, two poems by Sir Walter Raleigh, and a description of the plague by Thomas Dekker — are grim reminders that Elizabethan England, its court, its spinster queen, its disease-ridden houses, and its stark fascination with death and dying, was not as the heroes and poets of Gloriana's reign would have us believe. Robert Devereux, Earl of Essex (1567–1601) has already been introduced in the previous chapter as one of Elizabeth's flaming favorites and beardless boys to whom Sir Francis Bacon gave excellent advice on how to succeed in Tudor politics. In his three letters dated 1591, 1598, and 1600, Essex appears as a figure out of one of Marlowe's plays and reveals why he was in such need of Bacon's counsel: unlike his sovereign queen, he could never do anything by half measures. The Earl's facile, if extravagant, style is also evidence of one of the most extraordinary aspects of the Renaissance in general and sixteenth-century England in particular. Soldiers and adventurers such as Essex and Raleigh were men of letters and philosophers, while poets, like Philip Sidney, were practical politicians and warriors.

Sir Walter Raleigh (1552?–1618) even more than Essex was the Renaissance man — poet, sailor, businessman, courtier, lover, historian, and politician. Yet Raleigh could also write the "Lie," one of the bitterest poems ever produced, and pen the tired, melancholic lines that concluded his restless, colorful life. Composed the evening before his execution for high treason in 1618, it is the perfect swan song to an Elizabethan age grown old and thoughtful. The final selection is a glimpse into the underside of the Renaissance mind, which was fascinated with death just as much as with life. Written by the playwright Thomas Dekker (1570?–1637?) in 1603, *The Wonderful Yeare* carries the subtitle "wherein is shewed the picture of London, lying sicke of the Plague; at the ende of all (like a mery Epilogue to a dull play) certaine Tales are cut out in sundry fashions, of purpose to shorten the lives of long winter nights, that lye watching in the darke for us."

## Richard Hakluyt's Dedicatory Letter to his English Voyages (1589)

Richard Hakluyt inspires his countrymen with the romance of "cosmography" and assures them that overseas discovery is pleasing to God.

*To the Right Honorable Sir Francis Walsingham Knight, Principal Secretary to her Majesty, Chancellor of the Duchy of Lancaster, and one of her Majesty's most honorable Privy Council.*

Right Honorable, I do remember that being a youth, and one of her Majesty's scholars at Westminster, that fruitful nursery, it was my hap to visit the chamber of M. Richard Hakluyt my cousin, a Gentleman of the Middle Temple, well known unto you, at a time when I found lying open upon his board certain books of cosmography, with an universal map. He seeing me somewhat curious in the view thereof, began to instruct my ignorance by showing me the division of the earth into three parts after the old account, and then according to the later, and better, distribution into more. He pointed with his wand to all the known seas, gulfs, bays, straits, capes, rivers, empires, kingdoms, dukedoms and territories of each part, with declaration also of their special commodities and particular wants, why by the benefit of traffic and intercourse of merchants are plentifully supplied. From the map he brought me to the Bible, and turning to the 107th psalm directed me to the twenty-third and twenty-fourth verses, where I read that they which go down to the sea in ships and occupy by the great waters, they see the works of the Lord and his wonders in the deep, etc. Which words of the prophet together with my cousin's discourse (things of high and rare delight to my young nature) took in me so deep an impression that I constantly resolved, if ever I were preferred to the university, where better time and more convenient place might be ministered for these studies, I would by God's assistance prosecute that knowledge and kind of literature, the doors whereof (after a sort) were so happily opened before me.

According to which my resolution, when, not long after, I was removed to Christchurch in Oxford, my exercises of duty first performed, I fell to my intended course, and by degree read over whatsoever printed or written discoveries and voyages I found extant either in the Greek, Latin, Italian, Spanish, Portuguese, French or English languages, and in my public lectures was the first that produced and showed both the old imperfectly composed and the new lately reformed maps, globes, spheres, and other instruments of this art for demonstration in the common schools, to the singular pleasure and general contentment of my audience. In continuance of time, and by reason principally of my insight in this study, I grew familiarly acquainted with the chiefest captains at sea, the greatest merchants and the best mariners of our nation; by which means, having gotten somewhat more than common knowledge, I passed at length the narrow seas into France with Sir Edward Stafford, her Majesty's careful and discreet ligier,[1] where during my five years abroad with him in his dangerous and chargeable residence in her Highness' service, I both heard in speech and read in books other nations miraculously extolled for their discoveries and notable enterprises by sea, but the English of all others for their sluggish security and continual neglect

SOURCE: From Richard Hakluyt, *The Principal Navigations Voyages Traffiques & Discoveries of the English Nation* (Glasgow: James MacLehose & Sons, 1903), Vol. I, pp. xvii–xxii.

[1] ambassador

of the like attempts, especially in so long and happy a time of peace, either ignominiously reported or exceedingly condemned. . . .

Thus both hearing and reading the obloquy[2] of our nation, and finding few or none of our own men able to reply herein; and further, not seeing any man to have care to recommend to the world the industrious labors and painful travels of our country men; for stopping the mouths of the reproachers, [I] determined, not withstanding all difficulties, to undertake the burden of that work wherein all others pretended either ignorance or lack of leisure, or want of sufficient argument, whereas (to speak truely), the huge toil and the small profit to ensue were the chief cause of the refusal. . . .

To harp no longer upon this string, and to speak a word of that just commendation which our nation does indeed deserve, it cannot be denied, but as in all former ages, there have been men full of activity, stirrers abroad, and searchers of the remote parts of the world, so in this most famous and peerless government of her most excellent Majesty, her subjects through the special assistance and blessing of God, in searching the most opposite corners and quarters of the world and, to speak plainly, in compassing the vast globe of the earth more than once, have excelled all the nations and people of the earth. For, which of the kings of this land before her Majesty had their banners ever seen in the Caspian Sea? Which of them hath ever dealt with the Emperor of Persia, as her Majesty hath done, and obtained for her merchants large and loving privileges? Who ever saw before this regiment an English ligier in the stately perch of the Grand Signor at Constantinople? Who ever found English conssuls and agents at Tripolis in Syria, at Aleppo, at Babylon, at Balsara, and which

is more, who ever heard of Englishmen at Goa before now? What English ships did heretofore ever anchor in the mighty river of Plate; pass and repass the unpassable (in former opinion) Strait of Magellan; range along the coast of Chili, Peru, and all the backside of New Spain, further than any Christian every passed; traverse the mighty breadth of the South Sea; land upon the Luzons in despite of the enemy; enter into alliance, anmity, and traffic with the princes of the Molluccas and the Isle of Java; double the famous Cape of Good Hope, arrive at the Isle of St. Helena; and last of all return home most richly laden with the commodities of China; as the subjects of this now flourishing monarchy have done? . . .

Now whereas I have always noted your wisdom to have had a special care of the honor of her Majesty, the good reputation of our country and the advancing of navigation, the very walls of our island, as the oracle is reported to have spoken of the sea forces of Athens, and whereas I acknowledge in all dutiful sort how honorably both by your letter and speech I have been animated in this and other my travels, I see myself, bound to make presentment of this work to yourself, as the fruits of your own encouragements and the manifestation both of my unfained[3] service to my prince and country, and my particular duty to your honor. . . .

And thus beseeching God, the giver of all true honor and wisdom, to increase both these blessings in you, with continuance of health, strength, happiness, and whatsoever good thing else yourself can wish, I humbly take my leave. London, the 17 of November.

> Your honors most humble always
>     to be commanded
> RICHARD HAKLUYT

---

2 disgrace   3 unfailing

## WALTER RALEIGH, *The Last Fight of the* Revenge (August, 1591)

Sir Walter Raleigh describes the loss of the English man-of-war *Revenge* and the circumstances of the death of its captain, Sir Richard Grenville. There is a legend that the indomitable sea dog, when taken captive and offered a glass of wine, seized the goblet, drank the wine, and, to the horror of his Spanish captors, chewed up and swallowed the glass, thereby ending his own life.

Because the rumors are diversely spread, as well in England as in the Low Countries and elsewhere, of this late encounter between her Majesty's ships and the Armada of Spain; and that the Spaniards, according to their usual manner, fill the world with their vain-glorious vaunts, making great appearance of victories, when on the contrary, themselves are most commonly and shamefully beaten and dishonoured; thereby hoping to possess the ignorant multitude by anticipating and forerunning false reports, it is agreeable with all good reason, for manifestation of the truth, to overcome falsehood and untruth; that the beginning, continuance and success of this late honorable encounter of Sir Richard Grenville, and other her Majesty's captains, with the Armada of Spain should be truly set down and published without partiality or false imaginations. . . .

The L[ord] Thomas Howard with six of her Majesty's ships, six victualers of London, the bark *Raleigh*, and two or three other pinnaces riding at anchor near unto Flores, one of the westerly islands of the Azores, the last of August in the afternoon, had intelligence by one Captain Middleton of the approach of the Spanish Armada. . . . Many of our ships companies were on shore in the island; some providing balast for their ships, others filling of water and refreshing themselves from the land with such things as they could either for money or by force recover. By reason whereof our ships being all pestered and romaging everything out

of order, very light for want of balast, and that which was most to our disadvantage: the one half part of the men of every ship sick and utterly unserviceable. . . .

The Spanish fleet, having shrouded their approach by reason of the island, were now so soon at hand as our ships had scarce time to weigh their anchors, but some of them were driven to let slip their cables and set sail. Sir Richard Grenville was the last that weighed [anchor], to recover the men that were upon the island, which otherwise had been lost. The Lord Thomas with the rest very hardly recovered the wind. . . . Sir Richard utterly refused to turn from the enemy, alledging that he would rather choose to die than to dishonor himself, his country and her Majesty's ship, persuading his company that he would pass through the two squadrons despite them, and force those of Saville to give him way. Which he performed upon divers of the foremost, who, as the mariners term it, sprang their luff[4] and fell under the lee of the *Revenge*. . . . In the meantime as he attended those which were nearest him, the great *San Philip*, being in the wind of him and coming towards him, becalmed his sails in such sort as the ship could neither make way nor feel the helm; so huge and high charged[5] was the Spanish ship, being of a thousand and five hundred tons. [The *San Philip*] laid the *Revenge* broadside. When he was thus bereft of his sails, the ships that were under his lee, luffing up, also laid him broadside: of which the next was the *Admiral*[6]

SOURCE: From Richard Hakluyt, *The Principal Navigations Voyages Traffiques & Discoveries of the English Nation* (Glasgow: James MacLehose & Sons, 1904), Vol. VII, pp. 38–53.

[4] *sprang* . . . brought the ship's bow closer to the wind    [5] armed    [6] flagship

of the Biscaines, a very mighty and puissance ship commanded by Brittandona. The said *Philip* carried three tier of ordinance on a side, and eleven pieces in every tier. . . .

After the *Revenge* was entangled with this *Philip*, four others boarded her; two on her larboard and two on her starboard. The fight thus beginning at three of the clock in the afternoon continued very terrible all that evening. But the great *San Philip* having received the lower tier of the *Revenge*, discharged with crossbarshot, shifted herself with all diligence from her sides, utterly misliking her first entertainment. Some say that the ship foundered but we cannot report it for truth, unless we were assured. The Spanish ships were filled with companies of soldiers, in some two hundred besides the mariners; in some five, in others eight hundred. In ours there were none at all besides the mariners, but the servants of the commanders and some few voluntary gentlemen only. After many exchanged volleys of great ordinance and small shot, the Spaniards deliberated[7] to enter the *Revenge*, and made divers attempts, hoping to force her by the multitudes of their armed soldiers and musketeers, but were still repulsed again and again, and at all times beaten back into their own ships or into the seas. . . .

After the fight had thus without intermission continued while the day lasted and some hours of the night, many of our men were slain and hurt, and one of the great galleons of the Armada and the *Admiral* of the Hulks[8] both sunk, and in many other of the Spanish ships great slaughter was made. Some write that Sir Richard was very dangerously hurt almost in the beginning of the fight and lay speechless for a time ere he recovered. But two of the *Revenge's* own company . . . affirmed that he was never so wounded as that he forsook the upper deck, till an hour before midnight, and then being shot into the body with a musket as he was dressing, was again

shot into the head and with all his surgeon wounded to death. . . .

But to return to the fight: the Spanish ships which attempted to board the *Revenge*, as they were wounded and beaten off, so always others came in their places; she [the *Revenge*] having never less than two mighty galleons by her side and broadside to her. So that ere the morning, from three of the clock the day before, there had [been] fifteen different armadas[9] [which] assailed her; and all so ill approved their entertainment as they were by the break of day far more willing to harken to a composition[10] than hastily to make any more assaults or entries. But as the day increased, so our men decreased; and as the light grew more and more, by so much more grew our discomforts. For none appeared in sight but enemies. . . .

All the powder of the *Revenge* to the last barrel was now spent, all her pikes broken, forty of her best men slain, and the most part of the rest hurt. In the beginning of the fight she had but one hundred free from sickness, and fourscore and ten sick, laid in [the] hold under the ballast — a small troop of men [for] such a ship, and a weak garrison to resist so mighty an army. By those hundred all was sustained: the volleys, boardings, and enterings of fifteen ships of war, besides those which beat her at large. On the contrary, the Spanish were always supplied with soldiers brought from every squadron: all manner of armies and powder at will. Unto ours there remained no comfort at all, no hope, no supply either of ships, men or weapons; the masts [of the *Revenge*] all beaten overboard, all her tackle cut asunder, her upper work altogether raised. . . .

Sir Richard finding himself in this distress, and unable any longer to make resistance, having endured in this fifteen-hour fight, the assault of fifteen different armadas . . . commanded the master gunner, whom he knew to be a most resolute man, to split

---

[7] determined   [8] transport ships   [9] galleons   [10] settlement

and sink the ship, [so] that thereby nothing might remain of glory or victory to the Spaniards, seeing in so many hours fight, and with so great a navy, they were not able to take her, having had fifteen hours time, above ten thousand men, and fifty and three sail of men of war to perform it withall. And [he] persuaded the company, or as many as he could induce, to yield themselves unto God, and to the mercy of none else; for as they had, like valiant resolute men, repulsed so many enemies, they should not now shorten the honor of their nation by prolonging their own lives for a few hours, or a few days. The master gunner readily condescended, and divers others, but the captain and the master were of another opinion and besought Sir Richard to have care of them, alledging that the Spaniard would be as ready to entertain a composition as they were willing to offer the same, and that there being divers sufficient and valient men yet living and whose wounds were not mortal, they might do their country and prince acceptable service hereafter. And whereas Sir Richard had alledged that the Spaniard should never glory to have taken one ship of her Majesty's, seeing they had so long and so notably defended themselves, they answered that the ship had six foot [of] water in [the] hold, three shot under water which were so weakly stopped as with the first working of the sea she must needs sink, and was besides so crushed and bruised as she could never be removed out of the place.

And as the matter was thus in dispute, and Sir Richard refusing to harken to any of those reasons, the master of the *Revenge* . . . was conveyed aboard the *General* [by] Don Alfonso Baçan, who (finding none over hasty to enter the *Revenge* again, doubting[11] lest Sir Richard would have blown them up and himself, . . .) yielded that all their lives should be saved, the company sent for England, and the better sort to pay such reasonable ransom as their estate would bear, and in the mean season to be free from galley or imprisonment. To this he so much the rather condescended as well, as I have said, for fear of further loss and mischief to themselves, as also for the desire he had to recover Sir Richard Grenville, whom for his notable valor he seemed greatly to honour and admire.

When this answer was returned, and that safety of life was promised, the common sort being now at the end of their peril, the most drew back from Sir Richard and the master gunner, being no hard matter to dissuade men from death to life. The master gunner, finding himself and Sir Richard thus prevented and mastered by the greater number, would have slain himself with a sword, had he not been by force withheld and locked into his cabin. Then the *General* sent many boats aboard the *Revenge*, and divers of our men, fearing Sir Richard's disposition, stole away aboard the *General* and other ships. Sir Richard thus overmatched was sent unto by Alfonso Baçan to remove out of the *Revenge*, the ship being marvelous[ly] unsavory, filled with blood and bodies of dead and wounded men, like a slaughter house. Sir Richard answered that he might do with his body what he list, for he esteemed it not, and as he was carried out of the ship, he swooned, and reviving again desired the company to pray for him. The [commander of the] *General* used Sir Richard with all humanity, and left nothing unattempted that tended to his recovery, highly commending his valour and worthiness, and greatly bewailing the danger wherein he was, being unto them a rare spectacle, and a resolution seldom approved, to see one ship turn toward so many enemies, to endure the charge and boarding of so many huge armadas, and to resist and repel the assaults and entries of so many soldiers. . . .

The *Admiral* of the Hulks and the *Ascension of Seville* were both sunk by the side of the *Revenge*; one other recovered

---

[11] fearing

the road[12] of Saint Michael and sunk also there; a fourth ran herself upon the shore to save her men. Sir Richard died, as it is said, the second or third day aboard the *General*, and was by them greatly bewailed. What became of his body — whether it were buried in the sea or on the land — we know not. The comfort that remaineth to his friends is that he hath ended his life honorably in respect of the reputation won to his nation and country, and of the same to his posterity, and that being dead, he hath not outlived his own honour. . . .

To conclude, it hath ever to this day

pleased God to prosper and defend her Majesty, to break the purposes of malicious enemies, of forsworn traitors, and of unjust practices and invasions. She hath ever been honored of the worthiest kings, served by faithful subjects, and shall, by the favour of God, resist, repel and confound all whatsoever attempts against her sacred person or kingdom. In the meantime let the Spaniard and traitor vaunt of his success, and we, her true and obedient vassals, guided by the shining light of her virtues, shall always love her, serve her and obey her to the end of our lives.

## *John Huighen van Linschoten's Account of the* Revenge (1591)

John Huighen van Linschoten gives his version of the sinking of the *Revenge* and the death of Grenville.

. . . The 13[th] of September the said Armada arrived at the Island of Corvo, where the Englishmen with about 16 ships as then lay, staying for the Spanish fleet, whereof some or the most part were come, and there the English were in good hope to have taken them. But when they perceived the King's army to be strong, the Admiral, being the Lord Thomas Howard, commanded his fleet not to fall upon them, nor any of them once to separate their ships from him, unless he gave commission so to do. Notwithstanding, the Vice Admiral Sir Richard Grenville, being in the ship called the *Revenge*, went into the Spanish fleet and shot among them, doing them great hurt, and thinking the rest of the company would have followed, which they did not, but left him there and sailed away; the cause why could not be known. Which the Spaniards perceiving, with 7 or 8 ships they boarded her, but she withstood them all, fighting with them at the least 12 hours together and sunk two of them, one being a new

double Flyboat of 600 tons, and *Admiral* of the Flyboats; the other a Biscaine. But in the end by reason of the number that came upon her, she was taken, but to their great loss; for they had lost in fighting and by drowning above 400 men, and of the English were slain about 100, Sir Richard Grenville himself being wounded in his brain, whereof afterwards he died. He was carried into the ship called *St. Paul*, wherein was the Admiral of the fleet, Don Alfonso de Baçan. There his wounds were dressed by the Spanish surgeons, but Don Alfonso himself would neither see him nor speak with him. All the rest of the captains and gentlemen went to visit him and to comfort him in his hard fortune, wondering at his courage and stout heart, for yet he showed not any sign of faintness nor changing of color; but feeling the hour of death to approach, he spoke these words in Spanish and said: "Here die I Richard Grenville with a joyfull and quiet mind, for that I have ended my life as a true soldier ought to do that hath

SOURCE: From Richard Hakluyt, *The Principal Navigations Voyages Traffiques & Discoveries of the English Nation* (Glasgow, James MacLehose & Sons, 1904), Vol. VII, pp. 79–81.

[12] straits

fought for his country, Queen, religion and honor; whereby my soul most joyful departeth out of this body, and shall always leave behind it an everlasting fame of a valient and true soldier that hath done his duty as he was bound to do." When he had finished these or such other like words, he gave up the Ghost, with great and stout courage, and no man could perceive any true sign of heaviness in him. . . .

## *Sir Henry Sidney's Letter to His Son Philip* (1565)

Sir Henry Sidney lists fifteen useful precepts for the benefit of his eleven-year-old son.

Son Philip,

I have received two letters from you, the one written in Latin, the other in French, which I take in good part, and will you to exercise that practice of learning often, for it will stand you in stead, in that profession of life which you are born to live in: and now, since that this is my first letter that ever I did write to you, I will not that it be all empty of some advices, which my natural care of you provoketh me to with you, to follow as documents to you in this tender age. Let your first action be the lifting up of your hands and mind to Almighty God, by hearty prayers, and feelingly digest the words you speak in prayer with continual meditations and thinking of him to whom you pray; and use this at an ordinary hour, whereby the time itself will put you in remembrance to do that thing which you are accustomed in that time.

2. Apply to your study such hours as your discreet master doth assign you earnestly, and the time, I know, he will so limit, as shall be both sufficient for your learning, and safe for your health; and mark the sense and matter of that you read, as well as the words; so shall you both inrich your tongue with words, and your wit with matter; and judgment will grow, as years grow on you.

3. Be humble and obedient to your master; for, unless you frame yourself to obey, yea, and to feel in yourself what obedience is, you shall never be able to teach others how to obey you hereafter.

4. Be courteous of gesture, and affable to all men with universality of reverence, according to the dignity of the person: there is nothing that winneth so much with so little cost.

5. Use moderate diet, so as after your meat, you may find your wit fresher, and not duller; and your body more lively, and not more heavy.

6. Seldom drink wines, and yet sometimes do; lest, being forced to drink upon the sudden, you should find yourself inflamed.

7. Use exercise of body, but such as is without peril of your bones or joints; it will much increase your force, and inlarge your breath.

8. Delight to be cleanly, as well in all parts of your body, as in your garments; it shall make you grateful in each company, and otherwise loathsome.

9. Give yourself to be merry; for you degenerate from your father, if you find not yourself most able in wit and body to do any thing, when you be most merry; but let your mirth be ever void of scurrillity and biting words to any man; for a wound given by a word, is harder to be cured, than that which is given by a sword.

10. Be you rather a hearer and bearer

SOURCE: From Walter Scott, *A Collection of Scarce and Valuable Tracts on the Most Interesting and Entertaining Subjects . . . selected from . . . particularly that of the Late Lord Somers* (London, 1809), Vol. I, pp. 492–493.

away of other men's talk, than a beginner, or procurer of speech, otherwise you will be accounted to delight to hear yourself speak.

11. Be modest in each assembly, and rather be rebuffed of light fellows for a maiden shamefacedness, than of your sober friends, for pert boldness.

12. Think upon every word you will speak before you utter it, and remember how nature hath, as it were, rampired up the tongue with teeth, lips, yea, and hair without the lips, and all betoken reins and bridles to the restraining the use of that member.

13. Above all things, tell no untruth, no not in trifles; the custom of it is naught: and let it not satisfy you, that the hearers, for a time, take it for a truth; for afterwards it will be known as it is to shame; and there cannot be a greater reproach to a gentleman, than to be accounted a liar.

14. Study, and endeavour yourself, to be virtuously occupied; so shall you make such a habit of well doing, as you shall not know how to do evil, though you would.

15. Remember, my son, the noble blood you are descended of by your mother's side, and think, that only by a virtuous life, and good actions, you may be an ornament to your illustrious family, and otherwise, through vice and sloth, you may be esteemed *Labes Generis*,[13] one of the greatest curses that can happen to a man. Well, my little Philip, this is enough for me, and I fear too much for you at this time; but yet, if I find that this light meat of digestion do nourish any thing the weak stomach of your young capacity, I will, as I find the same grow stronger, feed it with tougher food. Farewell; your mother and I send you our blessing, and Almighty God grant you his; nourish you with his fear, guide you with his grace, and make you a good servant to your prince and country.

Your loving Father,
HENRY SIDNEY

## *Elizabeth's Speech to her Troops at Tilbury* (July, 1588)

Elizabeth addresses her soldiers at the staging area of Tilbury during the Armada crisis.

My loving people,
We have been persuaded
By some that are careful of our safety,
To take heed
How we commit ourselves to armed
   multitudes,
For fear of treachery.
But I assure you,
I do not desire to live
To distrust my faithful and loving people.

Let tyrants fear.
I have always so behaved myself that,
   under God,

I have placed my chiefest strength and
   safeguard
In the loyal hearts and good will of my
   subjects;
And therefore I am come amongst you,
As you see, at this time,
Not for my recreation and disport,
But being resolved,
In the midst and heat of battle,
To live or die amongst you all,
To lay down for my God,
And for my kingdom,
And for my people,

SOURCE: From *Cabala, sive Serinia Sacra: Mysteries of State and Government in Letters of Illustrious Persons* ... (London, 1663), p. 373.

[13] a dishonor to your high birth or family

My honour and my blood,
Even in the dust.
I know I have the body of a weak and
  feeble woman,
But I have the heart and stomach
  of a king,
And of a king of England too,
And think foul scorn that Parma or Spain,
Or any prince of Europe
Should dare to invade the borders of
  my realm;

To which, rather than any dishonour shall
  grow by me,
I myself will take up arms,
I myself will be your general,
Judge, and rewarder of every one of your
  virtues in the field.
I know, already for your forwardness
You have deserved rewards and crowns;
And we do assure you,
In the word of a prince,
They shall be duly paid you.

---

CHRISTOPHER MARLOWE, *The Tragical History of Doctor Faustus*
(1589)

The scenes selected are from the beginning and the end of the play, in which
Marlowe introduces Doctor Faustus and his consuming desires, and then finally
reveals the price Faustus had to pay.

---

SCENE I

Faustus *discovered in his study.*

FAUSTUS: Settle thy studies, Faustus, and
  begin
To sound the depth of that thou wilt pro-
  fess:
Having commenc'd, be a divine in show,
Yet level at the end of every art,
And live and die in Aristotle's works.
Sweet Analytics, 'tis thou hast ravish'd me!
*Bene disserere est finis logices.*[14]
Is, to dispute well, logic's chiefest end?
Affords this art no greater miracle?
Then read no more; thou hast attain'd that
  end:
A greater subject fitteth Faustus' wit:
Bid Economy farewell, and Galen[15] come,
Seeing, *Ubi desinit philosophus, ibi incipit
  medicus.*[16]
Be a physician, Faustus; heap up gold,
And be eternis'd for some wondrous cure:
*Summum bonum medicinæ sanitas,*

"The end of physic is our body's health."
Why, Faustus, hast thou not attain'd that
  end?
Is not thy common talk found aphorisms?
Are not thy bills hung up as monuments,
Whereby whole cities have escap'd the
  plague,
And thousand desperate maladies been
  eas'd?
Yet art thou still but Faustus, and a man.
Couldst thou make men to live eternally,
Or, being dead, raise them to life again,
Then this profession were to be esteem'd.
Physic, farewell! Where is Justinian?[17]

  [*Reads*]

*Si una eademque res legatur duobus, alter
  rem, alter valorem rei, etc.*[18]
A pretty case of paltry legacies!

  [*Reads*]

*Exhæreditare filium non potest pater nisi,
  etc.*[19]

---

SOURCE: From John Gassner, *A Treasury of the Theatre* (New York: Simon & Schuster, 1951), pp.
  221–223, 236–237. Reprinted by permission of the publisher.

[14] "To argue well is the end of logic."   [15] 2nd-century Greek doctor   [16] "Where the philosopher
stops, the physician begins."   [17] Roman emperor   [18] "If one and the same thing is deeded to two
people, the one receives the thing, the other the value of the thing, etc."   [19] "A father cannot disinherit his son, unless, etc."

Such is the subject of the Institute,[20]
And universal body of the law:
This study fits a mercenary drudge,
Who aims at nothing but external trash;
Too servile and illiberal for me.
When all is done, divinity is best:
Jerome's Bible, Faustus; view it well.

[*Reads*]

*Stipendium peccati mors est.* Ha! *Stipendium, etc.*
"The reward of sin is death": that's hard.

[*Reads*]

*Si pecasse negamus, fallimur, et nulla est in nobis veritas;*
"If we say that we have no sin, we deceive
ourselves, and there's no truth in us."
Why, then, belike we must sin, and so consequently die:
Ay, we must die an everlasting death.
What doctrine call you this, *Che sera, sera,*
"What will be, shall be?" Divinity, adieu!
These metaphysics of magicians,
And necromatic books are heavenly;
Lines, circles, scenes, letters, and characters;
Ay, these are those that Faustus most desires.
O, what a world of profit and delight,
Of power, of honour, of omnipotence,
Is promis'd to the studious artisan!
All things that move between the quiet poles
Shall be at my command: emperors and kings
Are but obeyed in their several provinces,
Nor can they raise the wind, or rend the clouds;
But his dominion that exceeds in this,
Stretcheth as far as doth the mind of man;
Here, Faustus, tire thy brains to gain a deity.
A sound magician is a mighty god:

[*Enter* Wagner]

Wagner, commend me to my dearest friends,

The German Valdes and Cornelius;
Request them earnestly to visit me.
WAGNER:   I will, sir.

[*Exit*]

FAUSTUS:  Their conference will be a greater help to me
Than all my labours, plod I ne'er so fast,

[*Enter* Good Angel *and* Evil Angel]

GOOD ANGEL:  O, Faustus, lay thy damned book aside,
And gaze not on it, lest it tempt thy soul,
And heap God's heavy wrath upon they head!
Read, read the Scriptures: — that is blasphemy.
EVIL ANGEL:  Go forward, Faustus, in that famous art
Wherein all Nature's treasure is contain'd:
Be thou on earth as Jove is in the sky,
Lord and commander of these elements.

[*Exeunt* Angels]   • • •

SCENE III

*A grove.*

[*Enter* Faustus *to conjure*]

FAUSTUS:  Now that the gloomy shadow of the earth,
Longing to view Orion's drizzling look,
Leaps from th' antarctic world unto the sky,
And dims the welkin with her pitchy breath,
Faustus, begin thine incantations,
And try if devils will obey thy hest,
Seeing thou hast pray'd and sacrific'd to them.
Within this circle is Jehovah's name,
Forward and backward anagrammatis'd,
Th' abbreviated names of holy saints.
Figures of every adjunct to the heavens,
And characters of signs and erring stars,
By which the spirits are enforc'd to rise:
Then fear not, Faustus, but be resolute,
And try the uttermost magic can perform. — . . .

---

[20] Law code of Justinian

[*Enter* Mephistophilis]

I charge thee to return, and change thy
    shape;
Thou are too ugly to attend on me:
Go, and return an old Franciscan friar;
That holy shape becomes a devil best.

[*Exit* Mephistophilis]

I see there's virtue in my heavenly words:
Who would not be proficient in this art?
How pliant is this Mephistophilis,
Full of obedience and humility!
Such is the force of magic and my spells:
No, Faustus, thou art conjuror laureat,
That canst command great Mephistophilis.

[*Reenter* Mephistophilis *like a Franciscan
friar*]

MEPHISTOPHILIS: Now, Faustus, what
    wouldst thou have me do?
FAUSTUS: I charge thee wait upon me whilst
    I live,
To do whatever Faustus shall command,
Be it to make the moon drop from her
    sphere,
Or the ocean to overwhelm the world.
MEPHISTOPHILIS: I am a servant to great
    Lucifer,
And may not follow thee without his leave;
No more than he commands must we per-
    form.
FAUSTUS: Did not he charge thee to appear
    to me?
MEPHISTOPHILIS: No, I came hither of mine
    own accord.
FAUSTUS: Did not my conjuring speeches
    raise thee? speak.
MEPHISTOPHILIS: That was the cause, but
    yet *per accidens;*
For, when we hear one rack the name of
    God,
Abjure the Scriptures and his Saviour Christ,
We fly, in hope, to get his glorious soul;
Nor will we come, unless he use such means
Whereby he is in danger to be damn'd.
Therefore the shortest cut for conjuring
Is stoutly to abjure the Trinity,
And pray devoutly to the prince of hell.
FAUSTUS: So Faustus hath

Already done; and holds this principle,
There is no chief but only Belzebub;
To whom Faustus doth dedicate himself.
This word "damnation" terrifies not him,
For he confounds hell in Elysium:
His ghost be with the old philosophers!
But, leaving these vain trifles of men's souls,
Tell me what is that Lucifer thy lord?
MEPHISTOPHILIS: Arch-regent and com-
    mander of all spirits.
FAUSTUS: Was not that Lucifer an angel
    once?
MEPHISTOPHILIS: Yes, Faustus, and most
    dearly lov'd of God.
FAUSTUS: How comes it, then, that he is
    prince of devils?
MEPHISTOPHILIS: O, by aspiring pride and
    insolence;
For which God threw him from the face of
    heaven.
FAUSTUS: And what are you that live with
    Lucifer?
MEPHISTOPHILIS: Unhappy spirits that fell
    with Lucifer?
Conspir'd against our God with Lucifer,
And are for ever damn't with Lucifer.
FAUSTUS: Where are you damn'd?
MEPHISTOPHILIS: In hell.
FAUSTUS: How comes it, then, that thou art
    out of hell?
MEPHISTOPHILIS: Why, this is hell, nor am
    I out of it.
Think'st thou that I, who saw the face of
    God,
And tasted the eternal joys of heaven,
Am not tormented with ten thousand hells,
In being depriv'd of everlasting bliss?
O, Faustus, leave these frivolous demands,
Which strike a terror to my fainting soul!
FAUSTUS: What, is great Mephistophilis so
    passionate
For being deprived of the joys of heaven?
Learn thou of Faustus manly fortitude
And scorn those joys thou never shalt
    possess.
Go bear these tidings to great Lucifer:
Seeing Faustus hath incurr'd eternal death
By desperate thoughts against Jove's deity,
Say, he surrenders up to him his soul,
So he will spare him four-and-twenty years,

Letting him live in all voluptuousness;
Having thee ever to attend on me,
To give me whatsoever I shall ask,
To tell me whatsoever I demand,
To slay mine enemies, and aid my friends,
And always be obedient to my will.
Go and return to mighty Lucifer,
And meet me in my study at midnight,
And then resolve me of thy master's
mind.

MEPHISTOPHILIS: I will, Faustus.

[*Exit*]

FAUSTUS: Had I as many souls as there be
stars,
I'd give them all for Mephistophilis.
By him I'll be great emperor of the world,
And make a bridge through the moving
air,
To pass the ocean with a band of men;
I'll join the hills that bind the Afric shore,
And make that country continent to Spain,
And both contributory to my crown:
The Emperor shall not live but by my
leave,
Nor any potentate of Germany.
Now that I have obtained what I desir'd,
I'll live in speculation of this art,
Till Mephistophilis return again.

[*Exit*]

· · ·

SCENE XVI

*A room in the house of* Faustus.

[*Enter* Faustus, *with* Scholars]

FAUSTUS: Ah, gentlemen!

1ST SCHOLAR: What ails Faustus?

FAUSTUS: Ah, my sweet chamber-fellow,
had I lived with thee, then had I lived
still! but now I die eternally. Look, comes
he not? comes he not?

2ND SCHOLAR: What means Faustus?

3RD SCHOLAR: Belike he is grown into some
sickness by being over-solitary.

1ST SCHOLAR: If it be so, we'll have physicians to cure him — 'Tis but a surfeit;
never fear, man.

FAUSTUS: A surfeit of deadly sin, that hath
damned both body and soul.

2ND SCHOLAR: Yet, Faustus, look up to
heaven; remember God's mercies are infinite.

FAUSTUS: But Faustus' offence can ne'er be
pardoned: the serpent that tempted Eve
may be saved, but not Faustus. Ah, gentlemen, hear me with patience, and
tremble not at my speeches! Though my
heart pants and quivers to remember that
I have been a student here these thirty
years, O, would I had never seen Witten-
berg, never read book! and what wonders
I have done, all Germany can witness,
yea, all the world; for which Faustus
hath lost both Germany and the world,
yea, heaven itself, heaven, the seat of
God, the throne of the bessed, the kingdom of joy; and must remain in hell for
ever, hell, ah, hell, for ever! Sweet friends,
what shall become of Faustus, being in
hell for ever?

3RD SCHOLAR: Yet, Faustus, call on God.

FAUSTUS: On God, whom Faustus hath
abjured! on God, whom Faustus hath
blasphemed! Ah, my God, I would weep!
but the devil draws in my tears. Gush
forth blood, instead of tears! yea, life and
soul! O, he stays my tongue! I would lift
up my hands; but see, they hold them,
they hold them!

ALL: Who, Faustus?

FAUSTUS: Lucifer and Mephistophilis. Ah,
gentlemen, I gave them my soul for my
cunning!

ALL: God forbid!

FAUSTUS: God forbade it, indeed; but Faustus hath done it: for vain pleasure of
twenty-four years hath Faustus lost eternal joy and felicity. I writ them a bill
with mine own blood: the date is expired;
the time will come, and he will fetch
me.

1ST SCHOLAR: Why did not Faustus tell us
of this before, that divines might have
prayed for thee?

FAUSTUS: Oft have I thought to have done
so; but the devil threatened to tear me
in pieces, if I named God, to fetch both

body and soul, if I once gave ear to divinity: and now 'tis too late. Gentlemen, away, lest you perish with me.

2ND SCHOLARS: O, what shall we do to save Faustus?

FAUSTUS: Talk not of me, but save yourselves, and depart.

3RD SCHOLAR: God will strengthen me; I will stay with Faustus.

1ST SCHOLAR: Tempt not God, sweet friend; but let us into the next room, and there pray for him.

FAUSTUS: Ay, pray for me, pray for me; and what noise soever ye hear, come not unto me, for nothing can rescue me.

2ND SCHOLAR: Pray thou, and we will pray that God may have mercy upon thee.

FAUSTUS: Gentlemen, farewell: if I live till morning. I'll visit you; if not, Faustus is gone to hell.

ALL: Faustus, farewell.

[*Exeunt* Scholars. — *The clock strikes eleven*]

FAUSTUS: Ah, Faustus.
Now hast thou but one bare hour to live,
And then thou must be damn'd perpetually!
Stand still, you ever-moving spheres of heaven,
That time may cease, and midnight never come;
Fair Nature's eye, rise, rise again, and make
Perpetual day; or let this hour be but
A year, a month, a week, a natural day,
That Faustus may repent and save his soul!
*O lente, lente, currite noctis equi!*[21]
The stars move still, time runs, the clock will strike,
The devil will come, and Faustus must be damn'd.
O, I'll leap up to my God! — Who pulls me down? —
See, see, where Christ's blood streams in the firmament!
One drop would save my soul, half a drop: ah, my Christ! —
Ah, rend not my heart for naming of my Christ!

Yet will I call on him: O, spare me, Lucifer! —
Where is it now? 'tis gone: and see, where God
Stretcheth out his arm, and bends his ireful brows!
Mountains and hills, come, come, and fall on me,
And hide me from the heavy wrath of God!
No, no!
Then will I headlong run into the earth:
Earth, gape! O, no, it will not harbour me!
You stars that reign'd at my nativity,
Whose influence hath allotted death and hell,
Now draw up Faustus, like a foggy mist,
Into the entrails of yon labouring clouds,
That, when you vomit forth into the air,
My limbs may issue from your smoky mouths,
So that my soul may but ascend to heaven!

[*The clock strikes the half-hour*]

Ah, half the hour is past! 'twill all be past anon.
O God,
If thou wilt not have mercy on my soul,
Yet for Christ's sake, whose blood hath ransom'd me,
Impose some end to me incessant pain;
Let Faustus live in hell a thousand years,
A hundred thousand, and at last be sav'd!
O, no end is limited to damned souls!
Why wert thou not a creature wanting soul?
Or why is this immortal that thou hast?
Ah, Pythagoras' metempsychosis,[22] were that true,
This soul should fly from me, and I be chang'd
Unto some brutish beast! all beasts are happy,
For, when they die,
Their souls are soon dissolv'd in elements;
But mine must live still to be plagu'd in hell.
Curs'd be the parents that engender'd me!
No, Faustus, curse thyself, curse Lucifer

---

[21] "Oh, run softly, softly, horses of the night!"  [22] transmigration of souls

That hath depriv'd thee of the joys of heaven.

[*The clock strikes twelve*]

O, it strikes! Now, body, turn to air,
Or Lucifer will bear thee quick to hell!

[*Thunder and lightning*]

O soul, be chang'd into little water-drops,
And fall into the ocean, ne'er be found!

[*Enter* Devils]

My God, my God, look not so fierce on me!
Adders and serpents, let me breathe a while!
Ugly hell, gape not! come not, Lucifer!
I'll burn my books! — Ah, Mephistophilis!

[*Exeunt* Devils *with* Faustus]
[*Enter* Chorus]

CHORUS: Cut is the branch that might have grown full straight,
And burnèd is Apollo's laurel-bough,
That sometime grew within this learnèd man.
Faustus is gone: regard his hellish fall,
Whose fiendful fortune may exhort the wise,
Only to wonder at unlawful things,
Whose deepness doth entice such forward wits
To practise more than heavenly power permits.

[*Exit*]

## Three Letters of Robert Devereux, Earl of Essex (1591, 1598, 1600)

The following "love" letter was written to Queen Elizabeth while Essex was campaigning in France.

Most fair, most dear, and most excellent Sovereign, . . .

At my departure I had a restless desire honestly to disengage myself from this French action; in my absence I conceive an assured hope to do something which shall make me worthy of the name of your servant; at my return I will humbly beseech your Majesty that no cause but a great action of your own may draw me out of your sight, for the two windows of your privy chamber shall be the poles of my sphere, where, as long as your Majesty will please to have me, I am fixed and unmoveable. When your Majesty thinks that heaven too good for me, I will not fall like a star, but be consumed like a vapor by the same sun that drew me up to such a height. While your Majesty gives me leave to say I love you, my fortune is as my affection, unmatchable. If ever you deny me that liberty, you may end my life, but never shake my constancy, for were the sweetness of your nature turned into the greatest bitterness that could be, it is not in your power, as great a Queen as you are, to make me love you less. Therefore, for the honor of your sex, show yourself constant in kindness, for all your other virtues are confessed to be perfect; and so I beseech your Majesty receive all wishes of perfect happiness, from your Majesty's most humble, faithful and affectionate servant,

R. ESSEX

[*18 October, 1591*]

SOURCE: From Walter B. Devereux, *Lives and Letters of the Devereux, Earls of Essex . . . 1540–1646* (London: John Murray, 1853), 2 vols.: Vol. I, pp. 249–250, 499–502; Vol. II, pp. 98–99.

Essex had refused to listen to the Queen's advice. He turned his back on her, and she told him to "be hanged" and boxed his ears. The Earl then reached for his sword, stopped just in time, and walked out of the room. Lord Keeper Egerton wrote to give Essex a much needed warning, and the Earl answered, still very much the aggrieved party.

My very good Lord [Egerton], — Although there is not that man this day living whom I would sooner make a judge of any question that did concern me than yourself, yet must you give me leave to tell you that in such a case I must appeal from all earthly judges; and if in any, then surely in this, where the highest judge on earth has imposed on me, without trial or hearing, the most heavy judgment that ever hath been known.... Your Lordship should rather condole with me than expostulate about the same.... There is no tempest comparable to the passionate indignation of a prince; nor yet at any time is it so unseasonable, as when it lighteth upon those who might expect a harvest of their careful and painful labors. He that is once wounded must feel smart while his hurt be cured, or that the part be senseless; but no cure I expect, Her Majesty's heart being obdurate against me: and to be without sense I cannot, being made of flesh and blood....

As for the two last objections that I forsake my country when it hath most need of me, and fail in my indissoluable duty which I owe unto my sovereign, I answer that if my country had at this time any need of my public service, Her Majesty, that governs the same, would not have driven me into a private kind of life. I am tied unto my country by two bands: in public place, to discharge faithfully, carefully, and industriously the trust which is committed unto me; and the other private, to sacrifice for it my life and carcase which hath been nourished in it. Of the first I am freed, being dismissed, discharged and disabled by Her Majesty. Of the other, nothing can free me but death, and therefore no occasion of my performance shall offer itself, but I will meet it halfway.

The indissolvable duty which I owe to Her Majesty is only the duty of allegiance, which I never will, nor never can, fail in. The duty of attendance is no indissolvable duty. I owe to Her Majesty the duty of an Earl and Lord Marshal of England. I have been content to do Her Majesty the service of a clerk, but can never serve her as a villain or slave. But yet, you say, I must give way unto the time. So I do; for now I see the storm come, I put myself into the harbor. Seneca saith, we must give place unto fortune; I know that fortune is both blind and strong, and therefore I go as far out of her way as I can. You say the remedy is, not to strive; I neither strive, nor seek for remedy. But, say you, I must yield and submit; I can neither yield myself to be guilty, or this imputation laid upon me to be just. I owe so much to the author of all truth, as I can never yield falsehood to be truth, nor truth falsehood....

I patiently bear all, and sensibly feel all, that I then received when this scandal was given me. Nay more, when the vilest of all indignities are done unto me, doth religion enforce me to sue? Doth God require it? Is it impiety not to do it? What, cannot princes err? Cannot subjects receive wrong? Is an earthly power or authority infinite? Pardon me, pardon me, my good Lord, I can never subscribe to these principles....

As for me, I have received wrong, and feel it. My cause is good, I know it; and whatsoever come, all the powers on earth can never show more strength and constancy in oppressing than I can show in suffering whatsoever can or shall be imposed on me.

Your Lordship in the beginning made yourself a looker on, and me a player of my own game; so you can see more than I can, yet must you give me leave to tell you in the end of my answer, that since you do but see, and I suffer, I must of necessity feel more than you do. I must crave your

Lordship's patience to give him that hath a crabbed fortune, license to use a crabbed style; and yet whatsoever my style is, there is no heart more humble to his superiors,

nor any more affected to your Lordship, than that of your honor's poor friend,

ESSEX

[*18 October, 1598*]

The Earl was in serious trouble having defied the Queen's explicit order not to return to England from the Irish campaign. As a consequence, he was placed under house arrest, and, more serious, Elizabeth refused to renew his monopoly on the import of sweet wines, which was worth £3,000 a year and was absolutely essential to support Essex's aristocratic existence. Despite his ancient lineage and masculine pride, he was helpless without the Queen's financial support, and he knew it. In this letter he eats humble pie.

Before all letters written in this hand be banished, or he that sends this enjoin himself eternal silence, be pleased, I humbly beseech your Majesty to read over these humble lines. At sundry times and by sundry messengers I received these words as your Majesty's own, that you meant to correct and not to ruin; since which time, when I languished in four months sickness, forfeited almost all that I was able to engage, felt the very pangs of death upon me, and saw that poor reputation, whatsoever it was that I enjoyed hitherto, not suffered to die with me, but buried, and I alive, I yet kissed your Majesty's fair correcting hand and was confident in your royal word; for I said to myself, between my ruin and my Sovereign's favor there is no mean, and if she bestow favor again, she gives it with all things that in this world I either used or desire.

But now the length of my troubles, and the continuance, or rather increase, of your Majesty's indignation, have made all men so afraid of me, as mine own poor state is not only ruined but my kind friends and faithful servants are like to die in prison because I cannot help myself with mine own. Now, I do not only feel the weight of your Majesty's indignation, and am subject to their malicious insinuations that first envied me for my happiness in your favor, and now hate me out of custom; but as if I were thrown into a corner like a dead carcase, I am gnawed on and torn by the vilest and basest creatures upon earth. The prating tavern haunter speaks of me what he lists; the frantic libeller writes of me what he lists; already they print me and make me speak to the world; and shortly they will play me in what forms they list upon the stage. The least of these is a thousand times worse than death. But this is not the worst of my destiny, for your Majesty that hath mercy for all the world but me, that hath protected from scorn and infamy all to whom you ever avowed favor but Essex, and never repented you of any gracious assurance you had given till now; your Majesty, I say, hath now, in this eighth month of my close imprisonment, as if you thought mine infirmities beggary, and infamy too little punishment, rejected my letters and refused to hear of me, which to traitors you never did. What therefore remaineth for me? Only this: to beseech your Majesty, on the knees of my heart, to conclude my punishment, my misery, and my life all together, that I may go to my Savior, who hath paid himself a ransom for me and whom, methinks, I still hear calling me out of this unkind world, in which I have lived too long, and ever thought myself too happy.

From your Majesty's humblest vassal,
ESSEX

[*12 May, 1600*]

## Two Poems by Sir Walter Raleigh

"The Lie" is one of the most famous poems of the late sixteenth century. It is generally attributed to Raleigh, and it certainly fits his mood during the period of his imprisonment and prolonged disgrace after the scandal of his "shot-gun marriage" (November, 1591) to one of the Queen's maids-in-waiting.

### The Lie

Go, soul, the body's guest,
  Upon a thankless errand;
Fear not to touch the best;
  The truth shall be thy warrant.
    Go, since I needs must die,
    And give them all the lie.

Go, tell the court it glows,
  And shines like painted wood;
Go, tell the church it shews
  What's good, but does no good.
    If court and church reply,
    Give court and church the lie.

Tell potentates, they live
  Acting, but O their actions!
Not lov'd, unless they give;
  Nor strong, but by their factions.
    If potentates reply,
    Give potentates the lie.

Tell men of high condition,
  That rule affairs of state,
Their purpose is ambition;
  Their practice only hate:
    And if they do reply,
    Then give them all the lie.

Tell those that brave it most,
  They beg for more by spending;
Who in their greatest cost
  Seek nothing but commending.
    And if they make reply,
    Spare not to give the lie.

Tell zeal it lacks devotion;
  Tell love it is but lust;

Tell time it is but motion;
  Tell flesh it is but dust:
    And wish them not reply,
    For thou must give the lie.

Tell age it daily wasteth;
  Tell honour how it alters;
Tell beauty that it blasteth;
  Tell favour that she falters:
    And as they do reply,
    Give every one the lie.

Tell wit how much it wrangles
  In fickle points of niceness;
Tell wisdom she entangles
  Herself in over-wiseness:
    And if they do reply,
    Then give them both the lie.

Tell physic of her boldness;
  Tell skill it is pretension;
Tell charity of coldness;
  Tell law it is contention:
    And if they yield reply,
    Then give them still the lie.

Tell fortune of her blindness;
  Tell nature of decay;
Tell friendship of unkindness;
  Tell justice of delay:
    And if they do reply,
    Then give them all the lie.

Tell arts they have no soundness,
  But vary by esteeming;

SOURCE: From Walter Raleigh, *The Works of Walter Raleigh,* 8 vols. (London, 1829), Vol. VIII, pp. 725–729. Reprinted by Burt Franklin Co., New York.

Tell schools they lack profoundness,
  And stand too much on seeming.
    If arts and schools reply,
      Give arts and schools the lie.

Tell faith it's fled the city;
  Tell how the country erreth;
Tell manhood, shakes off pity;
  Tell virtue, least preferreth.

And if they do reply,
Spare not to give the lie.

So, when thou hast, as I
  Commanded thee, done blabbing;
Although to give the lie
  Deserves no less than stabbing
    Yet stab at thee who will,
    No stab the soul can kill!

The following poem was written by Raleigh the night before his execution on 29, October, 1618.

Even such is time, that takes on trust
  Our youth, our joys, our all we
    have,
And pays us but with age and dust;
  Who in the dark and silent grave,

When we have wandered all our ways,
Shuts up the story of our days!
But from this earth, this grave, this
  dust,
The Lord shall raise me up, I trust!

## Thomas Dekker's Description of the Plague (1603)

Thomas Dekker not only presents a grim picture of the Black Death, which struck London in a particularly virulent form during the last year of Elizabeth's reign, but he also introduces a favorite Elizabethan theme — the equality of death.

What an unmatchable torment were it for a man to be barred up every night in a vast silent Charnel-house, hung (to make it more hideous) with lamps dimly and slowly burning, in hollow and glimmering corners; where all the pavement should, instead of green rushs, be strewn with blasted rosemary, [where] withered hyacinth, fatal cyprus and ewe thickly mingled with heaps of dead men's bones; [where] the bare ribs of a father that begat him lying there; here the chapless[23] hollow scull of a mother that bore him; round about him a thousand corpses, some standing bolt upright in their winding sheets, others half molded in rotten coffins that should suddenly yawn wide open, filling his nostrils with noisome stench and his eyes with the sight of crawling worms. And to keep such a poor wretch waking, he should hear no noise but of toads croaking, screech-owls howling, mandrakes shrieking. Were not this an infernal prison? Would not the strongest-hearted man (beset with such a ghastly horror) look wild and run mad and die? And even such a formidable shape did the diseased city [of London] appear in. For he that darest (in the dead hour of gloomy midnight) have been so valient as to have walked through the still and melancholy streets, what think you would have been the music? Surely the loud groans of raving sick men, the struggling pangs of souls departing. In every house grief striking up an alarm: servants crying out for masters, wives for husbands, parents for children, children for their mothers. Here he would have met some [people] frantically running to knock

SOURCE: From Thomas Dekker, *The Wonderfull Yeare* (London, 1603), G. B. Harrison, ed. (London: The Bodley Head Ltd., 1924), pp. 38–42.

[23] bare

up sextons; there others fearfully sweating with coffins, to steal forth dead bodies, lest the fatal handwriting of death should seal up their doors. And to make this dismal consort more full, round about him bells heavily tolling in one place and ringing out in another. The dreadfulness of such an hour is unutterable: let us go further.

If some poor man, suddenly starting out of a sweet and golden slumber, should behold his house flaming about his ears, all his family destroyed in their sleep by the merciless fire, himself in the very midst of it, woefully and like a mad man calling for help, would not the misery of such a distressed soul appear the greater if the rich usurer dwelling next door to him should not stir (though he felt part of the danger) but suffer him to perish, when the thrusting out of an arm might have saved him? Oh, how many thousands of wretched people have acted this poor man's part? How often hath the amazed husband waking found the comfort of his bed lying breathless by his side! His children at the same instant gasping for life! And his servants mortally wounded at the heart by sickness! The distracted creature beats at death's doors, exclaims at windows; his cries are sharp enough to pierce heaven, but on earth no ear is opened to receive them.

And in this manner do the tedious minutes of the night stretch out the sorrows of ten thousand. It is now day, let us look forth and try what consolation rises with the sun. Not any, not any, for before the jewel of the morning be fully set in silver, [a] hundred hungry graves stand gaping, and everyone of them (as at a breakfast) hath swallowed down ten or eleven lifeless carcasses. Before dinner, in the same gulf are twice so many more devoured. And before the sun takes his rest, those numbers are doubled. Threescore that not many hours before had everyone several lodgings very delicately furnished are now thrust altogether into one close room: a little noisome room, not fully ten foot square. Doth not this strike coldly to the heart of a worldly miser? To some, the very sound of death's name is in stead of[24] a passing bell. What shall become of such a coward, being told that the self-same body of his, which now is so pampered with superfluous fare, so perfumed and bathed in odoriferous waters, and so gaily appareled in variety of fashions, must one day be thrown (like stinking carrion) into a rank and rotten grave, where his goodly eyes, which did once shoot forth such amorous glances, must be beaten out of his head; his locks that hang wantonly dangling trodden in dirt underfoot. This doubtless (like thunder) must needs strike him into the earth. But (wretched man!) when thou shalt see, and be assured (by tokens sent thee from heaven) that tomorrow thou must be tumbled into a muck-pit, and suffer thy body to be bruised and pressed with threescore dead men lying slovenly upon thee, and thou to be undermost of all — yea and half of that number were thine enemies (and see how they may be revenged, for the worms that breed out of their putrifying carcasses shall crawl in huge swarms from them and quite devour thee) — what agonies will this strange news drive thee into? If thou art in love with thyself, this cannot choose[25] but possess thee with frenzy. . . .

## FURTHER DISCUSSION QUESTIONS

### Richard Hakluyt's Dedicatory Letter

1. What were the motives for young Richard Hakluyt's interests in worlds to the east and west of Europe?
2. Why had the English suddenly taken to the high seas?

---

24 like    25 help

## Walter Raleigh, The Last Fight of the *Revenge*

1. By implication, what does Raleigh suggest would have happened had Howard not run from the Spanish?
2. How would you describe Grenville's actions? What were his motives throughout the encounter?
3. How might Lord Thomas Howard have reacted to Raleigh's description?
4. What do Raleigh's words show about the cult of Gloriana?

## John Huighen van Linschoten's Account of the *Revenge*

1. How does Linschoten's account differ from Raleigh's?
2. What explanations does Linschoten give for Grenville's decision to disobey Howard's command?

## Sir Henry Sidney's Letter to His Son Philip

1. Compare and contrast Sir Henry's advice with that given by William Wentworth to his son in the previous chapter.
2. What, according to Sir Henry, are the most important characteristics for a young man to develop?
3. Is it possible to reconcile Sir Henry's ideal for his son with Raleigh's idealized picture of Sir Richard Grenville?

## Elizabeth's Speech to Her Troops at Tilbury

1. What, in effect, was Elizabeth attempting to do in this speech? Compare this address with the one she presented to parliament in 1601 (see previous chapter).
2. What does the speech show about the relationship between Elizabeth and her subjects? On what sentiments was she deliberately playing?

## Christopher Marlowe, The Tragical History of Doctor Faustus

1. Why is Dr. Faustus attracted to magic above all other professions?
2. Why is "a sound magician like a mighty god"?
3. Why is magic regarded as being so dangerous? To whom is it dangerous?
4. What is the relationship between Mephistophilis and Dr. Faustus?
5. Why cannot Faustus be saved or save himself?

## Three Letters to the Earl of Essex

1. Is Essex's first letter to Elizabeth really a love letter?
2. In his letter to Lord Egerton, what is it that Essex is suggesting has been injured? Why were Essex's views so dangerous to the Tudor state in general and to Elizabeth in particular? Are his views about his relationship to the state modern or medieval?
3. Is it possible to reconcile Essex's words and the attitudes expressed in his 1591 letter with those in his letter to Lord Egerton?
4. What do these three letters show about the nature and position of the crown in sixteenth-century society? What do they show about surviving and getting along in Tudor politics?

### Two Poems by Walter Raleigh

1. What is the "lie"?
2. What, if anything, is Raleigh saying about his life in his final poem?

### Thomas Dekker's Description of the Plague

1. What can we learn about the behavior of the plague from Dekker's account? Why was the disease so terrifying?
2. What were the possible reactions to the plague?
3. What is the moral of Dekker's description?

# 12

## Protestant-Catholic
## Good Christian-Good Subject

Religion seeks to do many things: give understanding to the incomprehensibility of the universe, grant power in this world to true believers, bestow a sense of personal fulfillment and satisfaction on the individual, and most essential of all, give some answer and consolation to the horror pictured in Dekker's carnage house of death (see Chapter 11). Underlying the religious strife and commitment of the sixteenth century was this central issue: salvation in the midst of death. Regardless of labels — Protestant, Catholic, Antibaptist, Lutheran, Jesuit, etc. — there were four responses to the problems which religion sought to resolve: the emotional, the theological-doctrinal, the institutional-ceremonial, and the personal. The first six documents in this chapter have been organized around this four-fold division. The next three readings have less to do with religion *per se* than with religion as an instrument of social control. The final document sums up the religious dilemma of the sixteenth and early seventeenth centuries.

The first selection is by William Turner (d. 1568), an early religious reformer and polemical writer who applauded the break with Rome and hoped that Henry VIII would lead his subjects not only out of papal bondage but also into the light of a reformed and purified Christian church. Turner is best known for his prolonged debate with Stephen Gardiner, the formidable, conservative bishop of Winchester, whose views on the church and its political and social organization were anathema to the radical William Turner. In the *Rescuynge of the Romishe Foxe* (1545) Turner takes on Gardiner and the Bishop's "politic laws." What is interesting is not so much Turner's answer to Gardiner as his concept of society and the proper role of religion in life. Turner believed in a variety of religion that came from the heart, not from

doctrines or from institutions. One might well ask what it was that divided a Bishop Gardiner from a William Turner and what it was that Turner so feared and detested about Gardiner's "politic laws" and belly wisdom.

The next document is by Henry Barrow (1550–1593), who lived a generation after Turner but clearly belonged in the same camp. Barrow, however, was both more extreme in his religious ideas than Turner and less fortunate, for he was executed under Elizabeth in 1593 for his congregational and antiepiscopal views on church organization. He wrote *A Brief Discoverie of the False Church* while in prison awaiting trial, and he smuggled the pages out one by one. He was regarded by the Anglican Church as "a fantastical fellow" and "a hot brain," for he defined the true church as "a company of faithful people, separated from the unbelievers and heathens of the land, [and] gathered in the name of Christ," each congregation being organizationally independent and spiritually sustained solely by the Word of God revealed in the New Testament. The pages taken from *A Brief Discoverie* say nothing about church organization, but it is clear that Barrow and the supporters of the "false church" had completely different views of what religion, mankind, society and the meaning of existence were all about.

Religion, as has already been mentioned, is not simply a matter of heart; it is also a body of doctrine which seeks to link the human condition to God and the universe. Of all the beliefs that came under debate in the sixteenth century, that of the doctrine of the elect caused the most confusion and debate. The explanation of election given in this chapter was written by John

Foxe (1516–1587), the martyrologist who collected and immortalized in print the lives of the Protestant martyrs. His monumental work, *Acts and Monuments of these latter and perilous dayes touching matters of the Church* (popularly known as the "Book of Martyrs") was chained to the alters of all of the churches of England and had almost as great an impact on the Elizabethan mind and religious character as the Bible itself. The doctrine of the elect was central to the Protestant creed and became the wellspring for Puritan determination to reform both church and state, society and humankind.

The Thirty-Four Puritan Petitions of 1585 "to be humbly offered unto the Queen and parliament . . . for a learned ministry to preach the gospel . . . and for further regulation of the bishops, officers, and governors of the church" represent religion in its most extreme institutional form. The reforming and highly militant Puritan element of the Elizabethan church was endeavoring to remodel the government and organization of the Anglican Church in its own saintly image. Needless to say, the Queen, who was the Supreme Governor of the church, was unmoved by either the "humility" or the "reforms" proposed by her loyal Puritan subjects, and the Puritan Petitions and social ideal had to wait until her death and the revolutionary climate of the seventeenth century before they could again be seriously voiced.

Religion is ultimately neither a matter of organization nor creed but of personal and individual conviction: men and women must in the end decide on the extent and nature of their own commitment. And on both sides — Protestant and Catholic — the faithful paid with their lives for what they regarded as that Truth which encompasses all aspects of life and gives meaning to death. The Protestant Nicholas Sheterden's prayer and letter to his brother, which were both written immediately before his death at the stake in 1555 under Catholic Mary, and the Jesuit Robert Johnson's words as he stood on the scaffold in 1582, waiting to be hung, cut down while still living, castrated, disemboweled and quartered, are deeply moving examples of the intensity of faith that sustained both sides in the face of official persecution.

The choice that Turner, Barrow, Sheterden and Johnson made was that it was more important to be a good Christian than a good subject, although all four would have argued that it was impossible to divide the two roles. It was their passionate desire to improve and spiritualize the kingdom that led them into disobedience. The proponents of belly wisdom would have also argued that no choice was involved: good subjects were doing their Christian and godly duty when they obeyed the prince and the magistrate. The Stephen Gardiners of the sixteenth century viewed religion as part of the structure of society, which had been ordained by God so that men and women could live out their lives in peace and security. The emphasis for the conservatives was on the good, the obedient, and the Christian life here on earth, and not on the mysteries of the world to come. All of the authors of the next three selections — Bishop Stephen Gardiner (1483?–1555), Queen Elizabeth, and James I — saw religion from the political and social perspective. Gardiner's opinions come from two letters he wrote, one an open epistle dated December,

1545, and the other to Edward Vaughan in May, 1547, about Protestant disobedience in Portsmouth. Elizabeth's views come from a royal scolding that she delivered to the Lords and Commons of Parliament in March of 1585, and it should be read in the light of the Thirty-Four Puritan Petitions of that year. James' encounter with the Presbyterian Dr. Reynolds took place at Hampton Court in 1604, when there was an official debate between the representatives of the Puritan–Presbyterian position and the bishops of the established Anglican Church. It was described by William Barlow, Dean of Chester, and should be read with a touch of skepticism, since the Dean was violently biased in favor of the episcopal and Anglican point of view.

The final document sums up the religious controversy between the disciples of belly wisdom and those "fantastical fellows" who sought to spiritualize life, and at the same time it poses the ultimate Protestant dilemma. In this selection John Foxe presents a moving account of John Lambert's encounter with God's lieutenant on earth, Henry VIII, during the martyr's trial for heresy in 1538. Lambert had been accused of denying the miracle of the Mass and had to face the authority of a king who spoke for God. That confrontation and John Foxe's anger over the outcome stood at the core of the religious conflict of the century and would not be fully resolved for one hundred and fifty years.

## WILLIAM TURNER, *The Rescuynge of the Romishe Foxe* (1545)

William Turner attacks the conservative religious "politic law" on the veneration of images of saints as an invitation to idolatry and tantamount to popery.

---

What politic law is it to command all the people of a realm to kneel before a piece of molten or casten silver, to creep to it and to kiss it, and to sing *crucem tuam adoramus domine*, lord we worship thy cross? . . . What politic laws are these that . . . the water of the font shall be hallowed, as though the element took away original sin, and to hold stinking water half a year and more and to put on the coldest day of all winter a young tender infant in it, over both head and ears, whereby many children are lost? . . . What politic law is it to ordain that a man may eat so much fish at one meal as would serve for two and to call that fasting? . . . This is no new thing then that false prophets and maintainers of idolatry do call them, that labor to drive idolatry away, troublers and seducers of the commonwealth. . . .

And where as ye say that there hath been no man so mad as expelling a tyrant would cast away with him both that which was good and the bad also; whether ye mean of good profitable, or good pleasant, or good by creation, ye swerve far from the truth. For almighty God, the well of all wisdom, commanded the children of Israel when they should drive out the heathen kings with their folk of the land of promise — to drive and put away with them all their laws, ceremonies and traditions, even those that were laudful, were they never so profitable or pleasant for the commonwealth. . . .

What Jewish and dull Pharises are these

---

SOURCE: From William Turner [Willyan Wraghton], *The Rescuynge of the Romishe Foxe* (Zurich, 1545), pp. Biii–Biiii, Eiii, Giiii, Hiiii.

that either will not or cannot be content with the holy word of Christ and his sacraments to bring Christ to their memories that they may think on him, except they smell something to remember him and taste something also to remember him thereby? . . .

The finding out[1] of images is the beginning of fornication and the invention of the same is the destruction of life. Neither have they been from the beginning; neither shall they continue forever. Then the church cannot have images without jeopardy. And that we need no images in Christian church it is easy to prove, for the scripture teacheth the church all thing that is necessary for it. What thing can a blind block or stone do with jeopardy but a preacher of God's word can do the same? Can an image teach any example of faith, of hope, charity, humility, liberal patience, or of any other virtue, but a Christian preacher both can do the same and doth the same many times much better and without any peril of spiritual fornication.


HENRY BARROW, *A Brief Discoverie of the False Church* (1590)

The radical Puritan Henry Barrow refutes the Anglican position that the prince has the right to establish dietary regulations for Christians during fasting days and Lent, and that such laws touch only the political lives, not the tender consciences, of subjects.

Yet [there] remains two points of his [Dr. Some, *A Godly Treatise*, 1589] deep and pestilent divinity to be examined; the one, whether princes may set any permanent positive laws, set days and times, when, what time of the year, and how long to fast? The other [whether] the prince's lawful constitutions concerning outward things[2] bind the conscience. The first Robert Some affirmeth, and thereby ratifieth his Lent fast, embers, eve fasts, and Friday fasts. The other he saith toucheth not the conscience, making a subtle distinction between the external court and the court of conscience. . . .

And now further I would know of Mr. Doctor [Some] how he can prove by the law of God, that the prince may forbid his subjects to eat flesh upon such days and such times, etc. I demand not now any politic reasons, for then he would smite me down with these two; for the sparing of the young increase of beasts, and for the maintenance of the navy: but my conscience cannot rest upon them: I had rather have one rule or example out of the word of God, where I can find no such precedent. . . . I cannot see how upon any politic cause, such restraints may be made throughout, and from year to year.

My reasons are, first God hath created these creatures[3] and not man, and given to man sovereignty over them, to use them to food freely; therefore they which by law restrain the sober and free use of them: (1) both call back the Lord's liberal grant, and (2) deprive the Creator of honor and praise, in and for the use of them, and (3) make a law of that the Lord hath left in liberty. . . . For which reasons, I am (as yet) in conscience persuaded, that the civil magistrate ought not to make permanent laws of that the Lord hath left in our liberty, neither by way of law to restrain them one day, for any civil or politic causes whatsoever. I would not now be understood of ecclesiastical and religious fasts; we have both laws and plentiful examples in the

---

SOURCE: From Henry Barrow, *A Brief Discoverie of the False Church* (London, 1590), pp. 87–92, 96–97.

[1] supporting    [2] ceremonies, etc.    [3] cattle, sheep, pigs, etc.

Scriptures, that the prince and church may proclaim such general fasts, upon occasions, etc. Neither would I here be suspected to go about to diminish or pluck away the high sacred power and authoritie the Lord hath given to the civil magistrate, as to his lieutenant over both body, life, and goods; so much as to show that the prince's or magistrate's power is yet by God himself limited and circumscribed; for the transgression whereof, they shall (as any other men) account unto the Lord, in whom they are to command, as we also readily in the same Lord to obey . . .

The prince is to govern, oversee and provide for the commonwealth, administering and dispensing, gathering and dispersing the creatures and wealth thereof, as a father and a steward: yet still with this interim,[4] as the steward and servant of God according to their master's will as they that shall account.

But here it may be said, that the magistrate and not we shall answer for this sin, if it be any; that it is our duty to obey in these outward things without inquiry or questioning, because the reason, charge, nor account of the magistrate's office is not committed unto us; neither may we thus enquire into the same, being private men without apparent presumption and secret rebellion. God forbid that any of his servants should be stained with either of these faults: we honor, reverence and obey the office and person of the magistrate (I say not now worship and adore) as God himself. In that we seek to know the magistrate's duty, etc. We do not thereby either intermeddle or intrude into his office: unless we knew how to obey and how far, how should we obey? What is not of faith is sin: and where should we know either his or our own duty, but in the book of God? Whereby both he for commanding and making ungodly decrees, and we for obeying them, shall be judged. Obedience must always be in the Lord. If the prince demand or command my body or goods in his service, I am to

yield them both readily without further questioning of his intents, ends or purposes, those belong not unto me; only I am to look to the outward thing which I do, that it be lawful and warrantable by the word; as the prince commandeth me to make ready my weapons to serve in the war, I may not refuse, but if this war be apparently unlawful, as against God's servants, etc., I may not obey. The prince maketh me an officer or under magistrate; I am in this place to serve him, but not to execute any of his unlawful decrees, etc. The prince demandeth my goods; I am readily and willingly to depart with them all unto him, without inquiry; but if the prince command me to give my goods to such an idol, or after such a wicked manner, as by way of tithes to a minister, or by way of pension to an antichristian minister, I may not obey, but rather suffer his indignation, yea, death, because now I make myself a trespasser, in doing that which God forbiddeth, at the prince's commandment. So in like manner, if the prince should command all the goods, victuals or cattle I have, I most willingly would obey; knowing that for this he, and not I, should account. For I am commanded to pay tribute, and not to set the portion how much or when, myself. But if the prince make a law, that no man shall eat flesh during the Lent, but such as have special licence from him; I say this law is unjust, contrary to the bountiful liberality of God, who hath given all men at all times a free use of these creatures to food. It is contrary to the order of God's creation, who hath therefore created and ordained them. It is contrary to God's honor, who will have praise and thanks for the holy and pure use of them. It is contrary to God's wisdom, who hath seen no such law of restraint expedient. It is contrary to the liberty and freedom God hath given us in Christ: God having at all times put all his creatures for our sustenance in our choice and power, even as the green herbs of the field. . . . The Lord hath by his word given a blessing to

---

[4] qualification

all the creatures, that they should increase and multiply by virtue thereof to the use and sustenance of mankind even of every living soul that he bringeth into the world. Yea, before he made man, he provided food for him. This goodness he still extendeth to the good and bad generally to all. So that to make such politic laws for the restraint of this the Lord's bounty is not only to distrust the Lord's providence, and not to depend thereof for the future time, using the bread of the day with thankfulness in sobriety; but to ascribe to our own policy and counsel that, which is due to the Lord of life, the giver of increase. Famine and scarcity are not kept away with human policy; they are the messengers and punishments of God for sin. . . .

Now cometh to be considered that learned problem of Doctor Some, wherein he thinketh himself as safe, as if he had got a castle on his back . . . namely, that the conscience of man is not bound by this law, but the outward action: and he is a simple divine that cannot distinguish between the external court and the court of conscience.

A strange doctrine it is, to sever the conscience and the law; the conscience and the outward action; they may as well be here [in this world] while we live sever the body and the soul, which though they are distinct things, yet can they not be here separate. The body shall rue the thoughts of the soul; the soul shall rue the sins of the body; the body and soul together make a man, and the man both body and soul, are liable unto all God's laws, and shall be judged for the breach of the least. Hath God commanded it? We must obey and do his commandment with all our soul, and that with such circumstances and affections as the Lord requireth, be the action never so slight and bodily in our seeming, yet it must be done in singleness of heart as in the eyes and name of God; yea (saith the apostle), as unto God himself, to whom we shall account for all things done in this mortal flesh. Knowing then this terror of the Lord, it behooveth us to take heed what we put upon the file of that record against

that day, to examine our own hearts and consciences daily, lest they be hardened through the deceitfulness of sin; to judge ourselves here how we do the will of God in all things, and not to put off through security until we be judged of God. And sure if this doctrine were sincerely and soundly taught, it would stay the rage of sin, which now breaketh out (as the baker's oven while it is not tended) both in magistrates and people. The magistrate would be well advised what laws he maketh, the people how they obey; knowing that both shall answer unto the great Judge: whereas now by this deep learning of Doctor Some, the conscience not being bound by the prince's law, but the outward and temporal action only, the prince may make what laws he lust for civil policy; the people ought without all scruple to obey, seeing their laws bind not the conscience, etc. But if the prince's laws be contrary or divers to the laws of God, then is not our conscience or body bound by or unto them, then are we not to obey such laws, but stand for our Christian liberty and the maintenance of the faith in all patient manner, rather enduring the wrath of man, than procuring the wrath of God. The vain pretence of civil policy will neither excuse them nor us before God the Judge of all with whom we have to do. He will have his laws, statutes and judgments kept and not altered, innovate or neglected, according to human wisdom, the state and policies of times and humors of men, which vary and turn with the wind, making laws today and abrogating them tomorrow, one prince after one manner, another quite contrary. But the statutes and judgements of God, which are delivered and expounded unto us by his holy prophets, endure forever the pure wisdom, the upright justice, the true exposition and faithful execution of his moral law; . . . from which laws, it is not lawful in judgment to vary or decline, either to the one hand, or to the other. For what do we thereby, but control the wisdom and equity of God's ways, prefer and think our own more wise and equal, abrogate his, and set up our own instead thereof; frame God to the common- wealth, and not the commonwealth to the will of God. . . . These are the best fruits that are reaped by this doctor's deep di- vinity, whiles he severeth the conscience from the law, making the law to bind the outward action, but not the conscience. . .

## JOHN FOXE, *The Doctrine of Election* ( ca. 1555 )

John Foxe endeavors to explain the central tenet of the Puritan creed — the doctrine of election — and to define such terms as predestination, justification, glorification, and God's grace.

As touching the doctrine of election . . . three things must be considered.

1. First, What God's election is, and what is the cause thereof.
2. Secondly, How God's election pro- ceedeth in working our salvation.
3. Thirdly, To whom God's election per- taineth, and how a man may be cer- tain thereof.

Between predestination and election, this difference there is: predestination is as well to the reprobate, as to the elect; election pertaineth only to them that be saved.

Predestination, in that it respecteth the reprobate, is called reprobation: in that it respecteth the saved, is called election, and is thus defined:

Predestination is the eternal decreement of God, purposed before in himself, what shall befall on all men, either to salvation or damnation.

Election is the free mercy and grace of God in his own will, through faith in Christ his Son, choosing and preferring to life such as pleaseth him.

In this definition of election, first goeth before, "the mercy and grace of God," as the causes thereof, whereby are excluded all the works of the law, and merits of deserving, whether they go before faith, or come after. So was Jacob chosen, and Esau refused, before either of them began to work, etc.

Secondly, in that this mercy and grace of God in this definition is said to be "free," thereby is to be noted the proceeding and working of God not to be bounded to any ordinary place, or to any succession of chair, nor to state and dignity of person, nor to worthiness of blood, etc.; but all goeth by the mere will of his own purpose; as it is written, "The wind bloweth where it list- eth." . . . So was tall Saul refused, and little David accepted: the rich, the proud, the wise of this world rejected, and the word of salvation daily opened to the poor and miserable abjects; the high mountains cast under, and the low valleys exalted, etc.

Thirdly, where it is added "in his own will," by this falleth down the free will and purpose of man, with all his actions, coun- sels, and strength of nature; according as it is written, "It is not in him that willeth, nor in him that runneth, but in God that show- eth mercy:" so we see how Israel ran long, and yet got nothing. . . . Whereby we are to understand, how the matter goeth, not by the will of man, but by the will of God; as it pleaseth him to accept, according as it is written, "Which are born, not of the will of the flesh, nor yet of the will of man, but of God. Furthermore, as all then goeth by the will of God only, and not by the will of man: so again here is to be noted, that this will of God never goeth without faith in Christ Jesus his Son.

And therefore, fourthly, is this clause added in the definition, "Through faith in

SOURCE: From John Foxe, *Acts and Monuments,* George Townsend, ed. (London: Seeley, Burn- side & Seeley, 1847), Vol. VII, pp. 268–273.

Christ his Son:" which faith in Christ to us-ward[5] maketh all together. For first, it certifieth us of God's election; . . . for whosoever will be certain of election in God, let him first begin with his faith in Christ; which if he find in him to stand firm, he may be sure, and nothing doubt, but that he is one of the number of God's elect. Secondly, the said faith, and nothing else, is the only condition and means whereupon God's mercy, grace, election, vocation, and all God's promises to salvation, do stay, according to the words of St. Paul, "If ye abide in the faith." Thirdly, this faith also is the immediate and next cause of our justification simply, without any other condition annexed. For as the mercy of God, his grace, election, vocation, and other precedent causes, do save and justify us upon condition, if we believe in Christ: so this faith only in Christ, without condition, is the next and immediate cause, which, by God's promise, worketh our justification . . .

Now to the second consideration, let us see likewise, how and in what order this election of God proceedeth, in choosing and electing them which he ordaineth to salvation; which order is this. In them that be chosen to life, first, God's mercy and free grace bringeth forth election; election worketh vocation, or God's holy calling; which vocation, through hearing, bringeth knowledge and faith of Christ. Faith through promise, obtaineth justification; justification through hope, waiteth for glorification.

Election is before time. Vocation and faith come in time. Justification and glorification are without end.

Election, depending upon God's free grace and will, excludeth all man's will, blind fortune, chance, and all peradventures.

Vocation, standing upon God's election, excludeth all man's wisdom, cunning, learning, intention, power, and presumption.

Faith in Christ, proceeding by the gift of the Holy Ghost, and freely justifying man by God's promise, excludeth all other merits of men, all condition of deserving,

and all works of the law, both God's law and man's law, with all other outward means whatsoever.

Justification coming freely by faith, standeth sure by promise, without doubt, fear, or wavering in this life.

Glorification, pertaining only to the life to come, by hope is looked for.

Grace and mercy preventeth.

Election ordaineth.

Vocation prepareth and receiveth the word, whereby cometh faith.

Faith justifieth.

Justification bringeth glory.

Election is the immediate and next cause of vocation.

Vocation (which is the working of God's Spirit by the word) is the immediate and next cause of faith.

Faith is the immediate and next cause of justification.

And this order and connexion of causes is diligently to be observed, because of the papists, which have miserably confounded and inverted this doctrine, thus teaching, that Almighty God, so far forth as he foreseeth man's merits before to come, so doth he dispense his election. . . . That is, that the Lord recompenseth the grace of election, not to any merits preceding; but yet granteth the same to the merits which follow: as though we had our election by our holiness that followeth after, and not rather have our holiness by God's election going before. . . .

Wherefore, whosoever desireth to be assured that he is one of the elect number of God, let him not climb up to heaven to know, but let him descend into himself, and there search his faith in Christ the Son of God; which if he find in him not feigned, by the working of God's holy Spirit accordingly, thereupon let him stay, and so wrap himself wholly, both body and soul, under God's general promise, and cumber his head with no further speculations; knowing this, that "Whosoever believeth in him, shall not perish," "shall not be confounded,"

---

[5] toward us

"shall not see death," ... "shall have everlasting life," "shall be saved," "shall have remission of all his sins," "shall be justified," ...

Now then, forasmuch as we see faith to be the ground whereupon dependeth the whole condition of our justifying, let us discuss, in like manner, what is this faith whereof the Scripture so much speaketh, for the more plain understanding of the simple. For many kinds there be of faith: as a man may believe every thing that is true, yet not every truth doth save, neither doth the believing of every truth justify a man. He that believeth that God created all things of nought, believeth truly. He that believeth that God is a just God, that he is omnipotent, that he is merciful, that he is true of promise, believeth well, and holdeth the truth. So he that believeth that God hath his election from the beginning, and that he also is one of the same elect and predestinate, hath a good belief, and thinketh well: but yet this belief alone, except it be seasoned with another thing, will not serve to salvation ...

The only faith which availeth to salvation is that, whose object is the body and passion of Jesus Christ crucified. So that in the act of justifying, these two, faith and Christ, have a mutual relation, and must always concur together; faith as the action which apprehendeth, Christ as the object which is apprehended.

For neither doth the passion of Christ save without faith, neither doth faith help, except it be in Christ ... And as the sun, being the cause of all light, shineth not but to them only which have eyes to see; nor yet to them neither, unless they will open their eyes to receive the light: so the passion of Christ is the efficient cause of salvation, but faith is the condition whereby the said passion is to us effectual. ...

## The Thirty-Four Puritan Petitions (1585)

In 1585 the Puritan element in the House of Commons petitioned the Queen to reorganize her church along Presbyterian lines. Although never overtly raising the question of episcopal and priestly authority stemming from God and a divine-right queen, the Puritans called for a Presbyterian structure of ecclesiastical government, complete with elders and provincial and national synods.

IX. That every archbishop and bishop of this church of England and Ireland, ... shall, within the space of six weeks next after his or their consecration, (as it is called,) have assigned, nominated, and appointed unto him ... eight, ten, twelve, or more preaching pastors, doctors and deacons, such as are resident on their own parishes and charges, within his and their dioces, together with some other grave and godly men of worship, or justices of peace within that shire, in such a certain number, as shall be thought good to the queen and her council, which may be assistant to him, the said archbishop and bishop, in the government of all those causes ecclesiastical, which now the archbishop or bishop, with his chancellor or archdeacon, do use to hear and order alone. ...

x. And that it may be lawful for every pastor, resident on his charge, and that all and every such resident pastor, within six weeks next after that he be inducted into his benefice, shall, by the advice and direction of the bishop of the dioces, and of his associates, present to the said bishop and

SOURCE: From John Strype, *Annals of the Reformation and Establishment of Religion ... in the Church of England during Queen Elizabeth's Happy Reign,* 7 vols. (Oxford, England: Oxford University Press, 1824), Vol. III, Pt. ii, Doc. 39, pp. 278–302.

his associates, four, six, or eight inhabitants of his parish, such as shall be thought by their age, wisdom, godliness, and knowledge, to be meet to be the associates and seniors to and with the said pastor, to govern his said parish with him; to hear and order with him such quarels, offences, and disorders in life and manners, as should be among the same parishioners. And if the causes and quarels arising in his parish be such that the same pastor and his associates or seniors cannot determine the same among themselves in the parish, then shall the said pastor, and his associates and seniors, bring the said cause before the bishop of the dioces and the elders, which are to him associate, as is before said, that he and they may hear and determine the same.

xiii. That no one bishop do hereafter procede in admitting or depriving of any pastor by his sole authority; nor in excommunicating any faulty person; nor in absolving any person that is excommunicated; nor in the deciding and determining of any cause ecclesiastical, without the advice and consent of the aforesaid seniors and associates joyned with him. And that their consent may be testified by their own names in writing, set to every act and actes, which shall be determined and ordained by their common consent.

xiv. Moreover, that it be established, that it shall not be lawful for any man to appeal from the sentence and judgment of the bishop, given with the advice aforesaid, to any manner of person or persons, but only to the next provincial synod, which shal be kept in this church of England.

xv. And that it may be lawful for the provincial synod, . . . to admit every appeal so made; to hear, decide, and determine the causes; and to give sentence upon it by the word of God. From the which sentence of the provincial synod it shall not be lawful for any man to appeal in any respect, but only to a national and general council of the whole nation.

xvi. That such a provincial synod be called every year once, both in the province of Canterbury and also of York. And that the said synod may have full authority to call before them any disorder or controversy, which ariseth in any cause or matter ecclesiastical within that province; and to hear and determine the same according to the word of God and the laws of this realm. And that a national or general council, for the whole English and Irish nations, be called ever hereafter once in seven years, by the queen, her heirs and successors, in such place as she or they shall appoint. . . .

xvii. That it be commanded to the archbishops of England and Ireland, that neither the said archbishops within their provinces, nor the bishops within their dioceses, do hereafter, by their sole and private authority, make and publish any injunctions touching religion or church government; nor by their authority call and command the pastors, preachers, and clergy, subject to them, to subscribe to the same their devices, with such interpretations or qualifications as they shall think good to make, or to allow of the same: nor to compel men to yield to their devices by threats of suspension or deprivation. Neither that they, nor any of them, do set forth any other injunctions than such as have been beforehand consulted upon and concluded, according to the word of God, by common consent in a Christian and free synod, holden and approved by royal authority in this church of England.

xxiv. That at and in every synod hereafter to be called by the authority of the queen, her heirs and successors, the bishops, deans, archdeacons, clerks, and such as shall be called by order to the synod, do all sit together brotherly in one house. . . . That there may be also, by the appointment of the queen and her council, joyned to them, to sit with them in the synod or convocation, some other godly learned men which are not in the order of the ministry, to hear the causes in controversy, to reason with them, and to give their consent to the conclusions which shall be made in the said synod, as the rest of the ministers there do.

xxv. That it may also be lawful for the

said synod ... to call any cause or controversy ecclesiastical which now is or hereafter shall be in this church of England and Ireland, to their examination, which do touch any part of doctrine or ceremonies of the church, and namely, the Book of Common Prayer. ... That they of the synod may be commaunded to try and examine the same book, and every part of it, by the holy word of God; and both to cut off that which is doubtful or superfluous in it, and to add to it that which is necessary and wanting to it. So that the blockes that are in it, at which some godly men do now stumble, may be removed; and such a book of divine service be framed, commended and commaunded to the church of England, and to all the members of it, as is wholly founded upon true divinity, taught in the word of God; and so be commaunded to us subjects, by royal authority, as a thing commaunded first of God, and then of the prince. ...

xxix. That there may be some godly, learned, and zealous men appointed by the queens highness, with the advice of her honorable council, to visit the present state of all archbishops and bishops of England and Ireland. And first, to consider of such doings and actions as have passed by the authority of the said archbishops and bishops, and through the hands of their officers, under the name of the said archbishops and bishops, sithence[6] the beginning of her blessed and peaceful government: that so the queens highness may perfectly understand how the said archbishops and bishops have, sithence the beginning of her majesties happy reign, behaved themselves in their offices. And whether they have in all actions faithfully discharged their duty according to the trust which was reposed in them, served the church of God faithfully, or have done unfaithfully, and neglected

their duty to God, to his church, to her highness, or not. ...

Therefore may it please the queens highness, with the advice of her honorable council and authority of parliament, to take order for the removing of all that which shall be found to be abuse in the offices of the said archbishops and bishops of this church of England and Ireland; and provide that hereafter bishops may be pastors in humbleness, diligence, and sincerity, to feed the flock of Christ: and not be *stately bishops*, bearing lordship among politic lords; overlooking the flock of Christ more like stout prelates than fatherly pastors. And to the end that the said bishops may hereafter do that office which shall be committed to them the more sincerely, we desire that all they, and every one of them, may be delivered from the burden of all worldly pomp, honour, and charge; and not to be puft up any longer with the swelling titles and dignities of worldly honour and lordship: and that they also be set so free from the administration of all civil causes and offices, that they may wisely apply themselves to the labour of the gospel and ecclesiastical function, in diligence and sincerity. ...

xxx. That the Lord's day, even the sabbath day, which we do barbarously cal Sunday, may hereafter be kept so holily, that it be not abused, nor mispent, neither in open feasting, nor in making or using any public shews, plays, or pastimes. Nor that there be any fairs or markets kept upon any sabbath day hereafter. ... And that all games and pastimes of shooting, bowling, cocking, bearbaiting, dancing, prices of defence, wakes, Maygames, and all other such rude disports, be utterly forbidden to be used upon any sabbath day: and that upon great punishment to be laid upon the offenders. ...

---

[6] since

# Nicholas Sheterden's Prayer and Letter to His Brother (1555)

Nicholas Sheterden makes it clear in his prayer and letter to his brother shortly before his death at the stake exactly what it meant to be a true Protestant.

## The Christian Prayer of Nicholas Sheterden before his death.

O Lord my God and Saviour, which art Lord in heaven and earth, maker of all things visible and invisible, I am the creature and work of thy hands. Lord God, look upon me, and other thy people, which at this time are oppressed of the worldly minded for thy law's sake: yea Lord, thy law itself is now trodden under foot, and men's inventions exalted above it, and for that cause do I, and many thy creatures, refuse the glory, praise, and commodity of this life, and do choose to suffer adversity, and to be banished; yea to be burnt with the books of thy word, for the hope's sake that is laid up in store. For Lord thou knowest, if we would but seem to please men in things contrary to thy word, we might by thy permission enjoy these commodities that others do, as wife, children, goods, and friends, which all I acknowledge to be thy gifts, given to the end I should serve thee. And now, Lord, that the world will not suffer me to enjoy them, except I offend thy laws, behold I give unto thee my whole spirit, soul and body; and lo, I leave here all the pleasures of this life, and do now leave the use of them for the hope's sake of eternal life purchased in Christ's blood, and promised to all them that fight on his side, and are content to suffer with him for his truth, whensoever the world and the devil shall persecute the same.

O Father, I do not presume unto thee, in mine own righteousness; no, but only in the merits of thy dear Son my Saviour. For the which excellent gift of salvation I cannnot worthily praise thee, neither is any sacrifice worthy, or to be accepted with thee, in comparison of our bodies mortified, and obedient unto thy will. And now, Lord, whatsoever rebellion hath been, or is found in my members, against thy will, yet do I here give unto thee my body to the death, rather than I will use any strange worshipping, which I beseech thee accept at my hand for a pure sacrifice. Let this torment be to me the last enemy destroyed, even death, the end of misery, and the beginning of all joy, peace and solace; and when the time of resurrection cometh, then let me enjoy again these members then glorified, which now be spoiled and consumed by the fire. O Lord Jesus, receive my spirit into thy hands. AMEN.

## A Letter to his Brother, Walter Sheterden.

I wish you health in Christ, true knowledge of his word, and a faithful obedient heart unto the same. It is showed me, my brother, that ye willed me by a letter made to a friend of yours to persuade with me, that I should be ruled by mine uncle, which saith, he will bestow his goods very largely upon me, if I should not stand too high in mine own conceit. But, my good brother, I trust ye do not judge so evil of me, that I should have a faith to sell for money. For though he or you were able to give me the treasure of the whole country, yet, I thank my Lord God, I do judge it but a heap of dung, in respect of the treasure hid within; yet I do esteem a buckle of your shoe, if it come with good will. And for to be counselled and ruled by him or you, or any other my friends, I do not, neither have refused it, if they require no more of me

SOURCE: From John Foxe, *Acts and Monuments,* George Townsend, ed. (London: Seeley, Burnside & Seeley, 1847), Vol. VII, pp. 312–315.

than my power, and that which belongeth to mortal men. But, if they require of me any thing which pertaineth to God only, there is neither high nor low, friend nor foe (I trust in God), shall get it of me, nor yet the angels in heaven. . . . Pray for me as I do for you.

By your brother,
Nicholas Sheterden,
Prisoner for the truth in Westgate.

## The Scaffold Address of Robert Johnson (May, 1582)

The Jesuit priest Robert Johnson maintains his faith enroute to his execution for treason.

Being brought from the hurdle, he was commanded to look upon Mr. Shert, who was hanging, and then immediately cut down: and so being help'd into the cart, he was commanded again to look back towards Mr. Shert, who was then in quartering. And after he had turned and sign'd himself with the sign of the cross, saying, *In nomine patris, etc.* "Dispatch," quoth the sheriff, "and speak quietly." "I would be sorry," answered Mr. Johnson, "to trouble or offend your worship." "You shall not offend me," saith the sheriff, "so that you offend not God."

JOHNSON. "I am a Catholic, and am condemn'd for conspiring the queen's death at Rheims, with the other company who were condemn'd with me. I protest, that as for some of them with whom I was condemn'd to have conspired withal, I did never see them before we met at the barr, neither did I ever write unto them, or receive letters from them: and as for any treasons, I am not guilty in deed nor thought." . . .

SHERIFF. "Dost thou acknowledge the queen for lawful queen? Repent thee, and notwithstanding thy traitorous practices, we have authority from the queen to carry thee back."

JOHNSON. "I do acknowledge her as lawful as Queen Mary was. I can say no more; but pray to God to give her grace, and that she may now stay her hand from shedding of innocent blood."

SHERIFF. "Dost thou acknowledge her supreme head of the church in ecclesiastical matters?"

JOHNSON. "I acknowledge her to have as full and great authority as ever Queen Mary had; and more with safety and conscience I cannot give her."

SHERIFF. "Thou art a traitor most obstinate."

JOHNSON. "If I be a traitor for maintaining this faith, then all the kings and queens of this realm heretofore, and all our ancestors, were traitors, for they maintain'd the same."

SHERIFF. "What! You will preach treason also, if we suffer you!"

JOHNSON. "I teach but the Catholic religion."

Hereupon the rope was put about his neck, and he was willed to pray, which he did in Latin. They willed him to pray in English, that they might witness with him; he said, "I pray that prayer which Christ taught, in a tongue I well understand." A minister cried out, "Pray as Christ taught": to whom Mr. Johnson replied, "What! do you think Christ taught in English?" He went on, saying in Latin his *Pater, Ave,* and Creed, and *In manus tuas, etc.* And so the cart was drawn away, and he finish'd this life as the rest did. . . .

SOURCE: From Richard Challoner, *Memoirs of Missionary Priests and Other Catholics of Both Sexes That Have Suffered Death in England on Religious Accounts from the year 1577 to 1684* (Philadelphia: Michael Kelly, 1840), Vol. I, pp. 62–63.

## *Two Letters by Stephen Gardiner, Bishop of Winchester* (1545, 1547)

In an open letter, dated 1 December, 1545, Bishop Stephen Gardiner maintains that it is quite impossible for a sane and sensible person to debate with the religious radicals.

Reader, if you sincerely cherish goodness, consider the wretched condition of our times, when abandoned men, the very dregs of humanity, hurl themselves against the defenses of rectitude, and, putting on the semblance of virtue — as far as talk goes — and a theatrical mask of piety, want to appear to be vigorously banishing vices and renewing and restoring religion. To which baseness this also is added: that they do not hesitate in the least to despise others in comparison with themselves, and to push off the road, strike down, lay low, beat to the ground, with arms, fists, feet, everyone who stands in their way. . . .

Moreover, their pride of empty knowl-edge and their boasting of learning falsely so called, have made altogether impossible a courteous and temperate controversy with them, such as the nature of the matter handled demands. . . . Indeed, such is their disposition that they interpret gentleness, mildness, moderation, courteous speech in their opponents as cowardice and lack of confidence in the cause debated; and they persuade their followers to take nothing rightly, in the spirit in which it is done, but to constrain everything to contribute to a sorry victory, which they seek to effect by the overthrow of established [religious] practices. . . .

Bishop Gardiner, in a letter to Stephen Vaughan (May, 1547), laments the Protestant destruction of religious images in Plymouth and explains the social and political value of imagery.

. . . Now of late, within these two days, I have heard of a great and detestable (if it be true that is told me) innovation in the town of Portsmouth, where the images of Christ and his saints have been most contemptuously pulled down and spitefully handled. Herein I thought good both to write to you and to the mayor, the King's Majesty's chief ministers, as well to know the truth as to consult with you for the reformation of it . . . and whether ye think the matter so far gone with the multitude and whether the reproof and disproving of the deed might, without a further danger, be enterprised in the pulpit or not; minding, if it may so be, to send one thither for the purpose upon Sunday next coming.

I would use preaching as it should not be occasion of any further folly where a folly is begun; and to a multitude persuaded in that opinion of distruction of images I would never preach; for, as Scripture willeth us, we should cast no precious stones before hogs. Such as be infected with that opinion, they be hogs and worse than hogs, if there be any grosser beasts than hogs be, and have been ever so taken. And in England they are called Lollards, who, denying images, thought therewithall the crafts of painting and graving to be generally superfluous and naught, and against God's laws. . . .

For the destruction of images containeth an enterprise to subvert religion and the

SOURCE: Reprinted from *The Letters of Stephen Gardiner* by James A. Muller by permission of Cambridge University Press, London, 1933, pp. 206–207, 272–274.

state of the world with it; and especially the nobility, who, by images, set forth and spread abroad, to be read of all people, their lineage [and] parentage, with remembrance of their state and acts. And the pursivant[7] carryeth not on his breast the King's names written in such letters as a few can spell, but such as all can read, be they never so rude, being great known letters in images of three lions and three fleur-de-lis, and others beasts holding those arms. And he that cannot read the scripture written about the King's great seal, either because he cannot read at all, or because the wax doth not express it, yet he can read Saint George on horseback on the one side and the King sitting in his majesty on the other side; and readeth so much written in those images as, if he be an honest man, he will put off his cap. . . .

## Queen Elizabeth's Speech to Parliament (March, 1585)

Elizabeth scolds parliament and especially the Puritan element (see the Thirty-Four Articles) for interfering in religious matters. As far as the Queen was concerned, religion belonged to the royal prerogative and was no concern of parliament.

My Lords and ye of the lower house, my silence must not injure the owner so much as to suppose a substitute sufficient to render you the thanks that my heart yieldeth you — not so much for the safekeeping of my life (for which your care appeareth so manifest) as for the neglecting your private future peril, not regarding other way than my present state. No prince herein, I confess, can be surer tied or faster bound than I am, with the link of your good will; and can for that but yield a heart and head to seek forever all your best. Yet one matter toucheth me so near as I may not overskip: religion, the ground on which all other matters ought to take root, and being corrupted may mar all the tree. And that there be some fault finders with the order of the ·clergy, which so may make a slander to myself and the church, whose overruler God hath made me, whose negligence cannot be excused, if any schisms or errors heretical were suffered.

Thus much I must say, that some faults and negligences may grow and be (as in all other great charges it happeneth), and what vocation [is] without [its faults]? All which if you my lords of the clergy do not amend, I mean to depose you. Look you therefore well to your charges; this may be amended without heedless or open exclamation. I am supposed to have many studies, but most philosophical; I must yield this to be true, that I suppose few that be no professors have read more. And I need not tell you that I am so simple that I understand not, nor so forgetful that I remember not; and yet amongst my many volumes, I hope God's book hath not been my seldomest lectures, in which . . . by reason . . . we ought to believe. . . .

And so you see that you wrong me too much, if any such there be as doubt my coldness in that behalf. For if I were not persuaded that mine were the true way of God's will, God forbid I should live to prescribe it to you. . . . I see many over-bold with God Almighty, making too many subtle scannings of His blessed will, as lawyers do with human testaments. The presumption is so great as I may not suffer it. Yet mind I not hereby to animate Romanists — what adversaries they be to mine estate is sufficiently known — nor tolerate new fangled-

SOURCE: From Ralph Holinshed, *Chronicles of England, Scotland and Ireland*, 6 vols. (London, 1807–1808), Vol. IV, pp. 588–589.

[7] herald

ness.[8] I mean to guide them both by God's true rule. In both parts be perils, and of the latter I must pronounce them dangerous to a kingly rule, to have every man according to his own censure to make a doom of the validity and privity of his prince's government, with a common veil and cover of God's word, whose followers must not be judged but by private men's exposition. God defend you from such a ruler that so evil will guide you. . . .

## James I and the Hampton Court Conference (January, 1604)

Much to the delight of the Puritans, James I, early in his reign, called a religious conference at Hampton Court in order to listen to the opposing points of view. The Puritans were soon disappointed, however, in their expectation that James, having been brought up in Scotland among Presbyterians, would favor a religious compromise between Anglicans and English Puritan-Presbyterians. James made it clear in his answer to Dr. Reynolds how politically and socially dangerous he thought Puritanism was.

. . . Then he [Dr. Reynolds] desireth [1] that according to certain provincial constitutions, they of the clergy might have meetings once every three weeks; first in rural deaneries, and therein to have prophesying, according as the Reverend Father, Archbishop Grindal and other bishops desired of her late Majesty; (2) that such things as could not be resolved upon there might be referred to the archdeacon's visitation; and so (3) from thence to the episcopal synod, where the bishop with his presbytery should determine all such points as before could not be decided.

At which speech his Majesty was somewhat stirred; yet, which is admirable in him, without passion or show thereof, thinking that they aimed at a Scottish presbytery, "which," said he, "as well agreeth with a monarchy as God and the Devil. Then Jack and Tom and Will and Dick shall meet, and at their pleasures censure me and my Council and all our proceedings. Then Will shall stand up and say, it must be thus; then Dick shall reply and say, nay, marry, but we will have it thus. And therefore, here

I must once reiterate my former speech, *Le Roy S'auisera*:[9] Stay, I pray you, for one seven years before you demand that of me, and if then you find me purseye[10] and fat, and my wind-pipes stuffed, I will perhaps hearken to you, for let that government be once [set] up, I am sure, I shall be kept in breath. Then shall we all of us have work enough, both our hands full. But, Doctor Reynolds, till you find that I grow lazy, let that alone."

And here because Doctor Reynolds had twice before obtruded[11] the King's Supremacy . . . [and] his Majesty at those times said nothing, but now growing to an end, he said, "I shall speak of one matter more; yet somewhat out of order, but it skilleth not." "Doctor Reynolds," quoth the King, "you have often spoken for my Supremacy, and it is well, but know you any here, or any else where, who like of the present government ecclesiastical, that find fault or dislike my Supremacy?" Dr. Reynolds said, "No." "Why then," said his Majesty, "I will tell you a tale. After that the religion restored by King Edward VI

SOURCE: From William Barlow, *The Summe and Substance of the Conference which it pleased his Excellent Majesty to have with the Lords, Bishops, and other of his Clergie . . . at Hampton Court, January 14, 1603* (London, 1604), pp. 78–82.

[8] i.e., Calvinism   [9] The king will consider the matter further.   [10] shortwinded   [11] introduced

was soon overthrown by the succession of Queen Mary, here in England, we in Scotland felt the effect of it. Whereupon Master Knox[12] writes to the Queen Regent . . . telling her that she was supreme head of the church, and charged her, as she would answer it before God's tribunal, to take care of Christ his Angel, and of suppressing the popish prelates who withstood the same. But how long, think ye, did this continue? Even so long, till by her authority the popish bishops were repressed, he himself and his adherents were brought in and well settled, and by these means made strong enough to undertake the matters of reformation themselves. Then, lo, they began to make small account of her Supremacy, nor would longer rest upon her authority, but took the cause into their own hand. . . . And how they dealt with me, in my minority, you all know; it was done secretly, and though I would, I cannot conceal it. I will apply it thus." And then putting his hand to his hat, his Majesty said: "My Lords the Bishops, I may thank you, that these men do thus plead for my Supremacy. They think they cannot make their party good against you, but by appealing unto it, as if you, or some that adhere unto you, were not well affected towards it. But if once you were out, and they in place, I know what would become of my Supremacy. No Bishop, no King, as before I said." . . .

## John Foxe's Description of the Trial of John Lambert (1538)

John Foxe describes the heresy trial of John Lambert, at which Henry VIII himself presided. The gulf between the religious views of the King and Lambert is immense. Foxe has great difficulty in reconciling his duty to accept the decision of God's lieutenant on earth with his conviction that a terrible injustice has been committed.

By and by the godly servant of Christ, John Lambert, was brought from the prison with a guard of armed men (even as a lamb to fight with many lions), and placed right over against where the king's royal seat was, so that now they tarried but for the king's coming to that place.

At last the king himself did come as judge of that great controversy, with a great guard, clothed all in white, as covering, by that colour and dissembling, severity of all bloody judgment. On his right hand sat the bishops, and behind them the famous lawyers, clothed all in purple, according to the manner. On the left hand sat the peers of the realm, justices, and other nobles in their order; behind whom sat the gentlemen of the king's privy chamber. And this was the manner and form of the judgment, which, albeit it was terrible enough of itself to abash any innocent, yet the king's look, his cruel countenance, and his brows bent unto severity, did not a little augment this terror; plainly declaring a mind full of indignation far unworthy such a prince, especially in such a matter, and against so humble and obedient a subject. . . .

When the king was set in his throne, he beheld Lambert with a stern countenance; and then, turning himself unto his councillors, he called forth Dr. Day, bishop of Chichester, commanding him to declare unto the people the causes of this present assembly and judgment. The whole effect of his oration tended in a manner to this point:

SOURCE: From John Foxe, *Acts and Monuments*, George Townsend, ed. (London: Seeley, Burnside & Seeley, 1847), Vol. V, pp. 229–236.

[12] John Knox writes to Mary of Guise

That the king in this session would have all states, degrees, bishops, and all others to be admonished of his will and pleasure, that no man should conceive any sinster opinion of him, that now, the authority and name of the bishop of Rome being utterly abolished, he would also extinguish all religion, or give liberty unto heretics to perturb and trouble the churches of England, without punishment, whereof he is the head. . . .

When he had made an end of his oration, the king, standing up upon his feet, leaning upon a cushion of white cloth of tissue, turning himself toward Lambert with his brows bent, as it were threatening some grievous thing to him, said these words: "Ho! good fellow; what is thy name?" Then the humble lamb of Christ, humbly kneeling down upon his knee, said, "My name is John Nicholson, although of many I be called Lambert." "What," said the king, "have you two names? I would not trust you, having two names, although you were my brother."

LAMBERT. "O most noble prince! your bishops forced me of necessity to change my name." And after divers prefaces and much talk had in this manner, the king commanded him to go unto the matter, and to declare his mind and opinion, what he thought as touching the sacrament of the altar.

Then Lambert, beginning to speak for himself, gave God thanks, who had so inclined the heart of the king, that he himself would not disdain to hear and understand the controversies of religion: for that it happeneth oftentimes, through the cruelty of the bishops, that many good and innocent men, in many places, are privily murdered and put to death, without the king's knowledge. But now, forasmuch as that high and eternal King of kings, in whose hands are the hearts of all princes, hath inspired and stirred up the king's mind, that he himself will be present to understand the causes of his subjects, specially whom God of his divine goodness hath so abundantly endued with so great gifts of judgment and knowledge, he doth not mistrust but that God will bring some great thing to pass through him, to the setting forth of the glory of his name.

Then the king, with an angry voice, interrupting his oration: "I came not hither," said he, "to hear mine own praises thus painted out in my presence; but briefly go to the matter, without any more circumstance." . . . But Lambert, being abashed at the king's angry words, contrary to all men's expectation, stayed a while, considering whither he might turn himself in these great straits and extremities. But the king, being hasty, with anger and vehemency said, "Why standest thou still? Answer as touching the sacrament of the altar, whether dost thou say, that it is the body of Christ, or wilt deny it?" And with that word the king lifted up his cap.

LAMBERT. "I answer, with St. Augustine, that it is the body of Christ, after a certain manner."

THE KING. "Answer me neither out of St. Augustine, nor by the authority of any other; but tell me plainly, whether thou sayest it is the body of Christ, or no." . . .

LAMBERT. "Then I deny it to be the body of Christ."

THE KING. "Mark well! for now thou shalt be condemned even by Christ's own words, 'Hoc est corpus meum.' "

Then he commanded Thomas Cranmer, archbishop of Canterbury, to refute his assertion; who, first making a short preface unto the hearers, began his disputation with Lambert very modestly, saying, "Brother Lambert! let this matter be handled between us indifferently, that if I do convince this your argument to be false by the Scriptures, you will willingly refuse the same; but if you shall prove it true by the manifest testimonies of the Scripture, I do promise, I will willingly embrace the same." . . .

At last, when the day was passed, and torches began to be lighted, the king, minding to break up this pretensed disputation, said unto Lambert in this wise: "What sayest thou now," said he, "after all these great labours which thou hast taken upon thee, and all the reasons and instructions of these learned men? Art thou not yet satisfied? Wilt thou live or die? What sayest thou? Thou hast yet free choice."

Lambert answered, "I yield and submit myself wholly unto the will of your majesty." Then said the king, "Commit thyself unto the hands of God, and not unto mine."

LAMBERT. "I commend my soul unto the hands of God, but my body I wholly yield and submit unto your clemency." Then said the king, "If you do commit yourself unto my judgment, you must die, for I will not be a patron unto heretics." . . .

And in this manner was the condemnation of John Lambert; wherein great pity it was, and much to be lamented, to see the king's highness that day so to oppose, and set his power and strength so fiercely and vehemently, in assisting so many proud and furious adversaries against that one poor silly soul, to be devoured, whom his majesty, with more honour, might rather have aided and supported, being so on every side oppressed and compassed about without help or refuge, among so many wolves and vultures. . . .

But how much more commendable had it been for thee, O King Henry! (if that I may a little talk with thee, wheresoever thou art), if thou hadst aided and holpen the poor little sheep, being in so great perils and dangers, requiring thy aid and help against so many vultures and libardes;[13] and hadst granted him rather thy authority, to use the same for his safeguard, rather than unto the other, to abuse it unto slaughter. For they, even of themselves, were cruel enough, that thou shouldst not have needed to have given thy sword of authority unto those mad men, whose force and violence if you had that day broken, believe me! You should have committed a worthy spectacle unto all men, and have done a most commendable and praiseworthy

thing for yourself. For what hath that poor man Lambert offended against you, which never so much as once willed you evil, neither could resist against you. . . .

But, O King Henry! I know you did not follow your own nature therein, but the pernicious counsels of the bishop of Winchester: notwithstanding your wisdom should not have been ignorant of this . . . that the time shall once come, when as ye shall give account of all the offences which you have either committed by your own fault, or by the counsel or advice of others. What shall then happen, if these miserable heretics, which you here in this world do so afflict and torment, shall come with Christ and his apostles and martyrs, . . . with like severity, shall execute their power upon you — what then I say shall become of you? With what face will ye behold their majesty, which here in this world have showed no countenance of pity upon them? With what heart will ye implore their mercy, which so unmercifully rejected and cast them off, when they fled unto your pity and mercy? Wherefore, if that the ears of princes be so prompt and ready to hearken unto the counsels of others, being void of counsel themselves, why do they not rather set apart these flatterers, backbiters, and greedy blood-suckers, and hearken unto the wholesome counsel of the prophetical king, which, crying out in the Psalms, sayeth, "Now, ye kings, understand, and ye which judge the earth be wise and learned, serve the Lord in fear, and rejoice in him with trembling. . . ."

But thus was John Lambert, in this bloody session, by the king judged and condemned to death; whose judgment now remaineth with the Lord against that day, when as before the tribunal seat of that great Judge both princes and subjects shall stand and appear, not to judge, but to be judged, according as they have done and deserved.

---

[13] leopards

FURTHER DISCUSSION QUESTIONS

### William Turner, The Rescuynge of the Romishe Foxe

1. What "politic laws" does Turner object to and why?
2. Why is Turner so scornful of anyone who is not content solely with the "holy word of Christ"?
3. Why is the use of images "the beginning of fornication" and the "destruction of life"?
4. What for Turner is the only true authority? What kind of authority is he objecting to?

### Henry Barrow, A Brief Discoverie of the False Church

1. Why, according to Barrow, is Dr. Some wrong in arguing that princes may control the time and place of fasting and that "outward things" do not bind the consciences of true Christians?
2. What are the powers and proper function of a prince and magistrate? What are the implications of Barrow's arguments about the authority of princes and magistrates?
3. What is Barrow's view of society and his view of God?
4. Given Barrow's argument, is it possible for a good Christian to be a good subject?
5. What, according to Barrow, are the causes of famine? Can they be cured?
6. What, according to Barrow, should a good Christian do every day, and what must he always remember above all else? What would the consequences for society be if all men and women did as Barrow urged?

### John Foxe, The Doctrine of Election

1. What is God's election and how does it relate to salvation?
2. How can men or women know they are elected? Can election be earned?
3. How does God's election operate and how is it related to grace, vocation, faith, and glorification?
4. What is the psychological appeal of the doctrine of election?
5. Why would the doctrine produce a militant and crusading approach to religion and life?

### The Thirty-Four Puritan Petitions

1. Why would Elizabeth have opposed the Thirty-Four Petitions?
2. What concept of church government underlies the Petitions?
3. How humbly offered would you say the thirty-four articles were?

### Nicholas Sheterden's Prayer and Letter

1. What for Sheterden is the most important thing in life?
2. Would it be fair to describe Sheterden's decision to die as a form of suicide? What does he expect to gain from death?
3. Are there any people comparable to Sheterden today?

### The Scaffold Address of Robert Johnson

1. Why doesn't Johnson accept the offer to save his life made to him by the sheriff?
2. Why does the sheriff find Johnson's answer unacceptable?

### The Letters of Stephen Gardiner

1. Why is it impossible to carry out a "courteous" discussion with the reformers? Under what conditions do you think a "courteous" conversation would have been possible?
2. On what grounds does Gardiner defend the use of images?
3. Why can't Gardiner understand the ideas and actions of the religious reformers?

### Queen Elizabeth's Speech to Parliament

1. What does Elizabeth regard her relationship to God to be? Why does she regard religion to be so important?
2. On what grounds does she criticize and condemn the Presbyterians? Why are they so dangerous to her "kingly rule"?

### James I and the Hampton Court Conference

1. What, according to James, was wrong with the Presbyterian form of government? Why couldn't it agree with his concept of monarchy? What does he mean by "no bishop, no king"?
2. Is James' attitude towards and handling of the Presbyterians any different from those of Elizabeth's?

### John Foxe's Description of the Trial of John Lambert

1. How does Henry view his duty towards religion and the church?
2. Why is Henry so suspicious of Lambert?
3. Wherein lies the disagreement between Lambert and the king? How do their approaches to religion differ?
4. What is it about the king's actions that upsets Foxe? How does he seek to explain it?
5. What is Foxe's dilemma?

# 13

# *Political Styles*
# *and Constitutional Conflict*

The constitutional crisis that eventually led to Civil War and the destruction of the Tudor-Stuart monarchy involved far more than a dispute over concepts of society, religious fanaticism and hysteria, and the financial plight of the government. The events leading up to the outbreak of war in 1642 must also be studied in relationship to political styles and personalities. The selections in this chapter are concerned, directly or indirectly, with two themes that underlie the political events of the century following Elizabeth's succession in 1558 — the impact of personality on political events and institutions, and the economic, social, and political forces to which governmental leadership, parliamentary or monarchical, had to respond. The more theoretical aspects of the crisis are given in Chapter 15, "Changing Views of Society," while the assignment of causes and blame for the coming of war and the political revolution are presented in Chapter 14, "The Great Rebellion."

The documents are roughly in chronological order and begin with Sir John Hayward's descriptions of Elizabeth's coronation procession of January 14, 1559, and her first address to the House of Commons several months later. The new Queen's speech was in answer to what would become a chronic debate throughout the first half of her reign: When and whom should she marry in order to secure the succession in the Protestant line? John Hayward (1564–1627) was a lawyer and historian, whose literary and historical talents were never appreciated or approved by Elizabeth. In fact, Glorianna once ordered that Hayward be tortured on the rack in order to extract the truth behind his authorship of a book on the overthrow of Richard II. The Queen disliked the subject of successful usurpers to the throne, especially when the publication coincided with her troubles with the Earl of Essex during the last years

KING JAMES I DISPOSING OF BARONETCIES

of her life. Fortunately for Hayward, Sir Francis Bacon dissuaded his sovereign on the grounds that it was always safer and more effective to tear apart a writer's style than his body. Hayward's *Annals of the First Four Years of the Reign of Queen Elizabeth* were not written until at least a decade after Gloriana's death, and considering the Queen's treatment of the author, the *Annals* speak well both for Hayward's honesty and objectivity and for Elizabeth's magical reputation.

It has often been pointed out that most of the issues that tore the kingdom apart under the Stuarts were apparent under Elizabeth. The growing religious rift between crown and subject has already been discussed in Chapter 12. What made that controversy so politically dangerous was that it coincided with, and in many ways overlapped, two major and interrelated political disagreements that went to the root of Tudor-Stuart society and the role the monarchy was expected to play: the right of freedom of speech in the House of Commons and the nature and extent of the royal prerogative in government. Both issues surfaced in dramatic fashion during Elizabeth's reign.

The debate over freedom of speech was the opening salvo in the clash between crown and parliament over the double-edged question of initiative and advice: Did the crown alone have the right to initiate legislation, and was it obliged to listen to and act upon the advice offered by parliament? The issue, particularly in its early manifestations, was made more explosive because it was associated with Puritan demands that the Queen reform her church. The fact that the most outspoken advocate of parliamentary privilege, Peter Wentworth, was also an independent-minded Puritan was no accident.

He twice challenged the Queen and her government: once in 1576 over Elizabeth's order that the House of Commons not debate or attempt to legislate in the area of religion, and again in 1587. Fortunately for the Queen, his views were in the minority. In 1576 the House of Commons "out of reverent regard for her Majesty's honor" stopped him from continuing his disloyal and revolutionary words and sent him to the Tower of London. In 1586 his articles addressed to the Speaker of the House were "pocketed up," and Wentworth again found himself in the Tower. The incorrigible and unrepentant Mr. Wentworth learned neither parliamentary discretion nor obedience to the sovereign from his sojourns in the Tower, for in February of 1593 he petitioned the House of Lords to join the Commons in a "supplication" to the Queen to name her successor and insure the Protestant succession, yet another subject Elizabeth had expressly forbidden Parliament to discuss. The Queen was so offended that Wentworth was clapped into the Tower, where three years later he died, and Elizabeth scolded the House in no uncertain terms for its persistent efforts to debate matters that did not concern it. Both of Wentworth's appeals for freedom of speech, as well as the Queen's statement on the subject, deserve careful reading, for they represent two very different views about the relationship between crown and parliament and about the structure of Tudor politics and society.

The exact nature and historic origin of the royal prerogative, particularly the veto power of the sovereign, its right to dispense or suspend law, and the authority of the sovereign to issue grants and rule by proclamation, was a subject of chronic discussion and considerable concern to the crown throughout much of the sixteenth century. The royal prerogative emerged, however, as a major issue in November, 1601, when Mr. Laurence Hide introduced a bill into the House of Commons to limit and control the Queen's right to grant economic monopolies. Parliament had been called in order to provide financing for the interminable war in Ireland, but the Lower House proved to be rebellious, unruly, and uncooperative. Its members were particularly vexed by what they considered to be the government's favoritism in granting patents or monopolies for the manufacture, distribution, and sale of specific commodities. Almost everyone admitted the evil of the policy, but the House floundered on how to remedy the situation: to reform the entire system by parliamentary statute, to insist that each monopoly be approved or canceled by parliament, or to petition the Queen to exercise her prerogative rights and reform the operation herself. As the parliamentary debate indicates, no one knew exactly how to handle such a potentially explosive issue until the Queen dramatically resolved the problem. Recognizing that she faced a Commons largely united in its opposition to her administration of monopolies and that many members were beginning to ask embarrassing questions about her prerogative, she ordered the Speaker of the House to inform the members that "she herself would take present order of reformation." Then she called both houses of parliament into her presence and delivered her famous "Golden Speech," which can be reread in Chapter 11.

Elizabeth died before she could do her own reforming and before she had to face further defiance to her authority, but she had strong views about loyalty in action, which she did not hesitate to communicate to the man whom she had in her own obscure and circuitous fashion designated as her successor. Her letter to James VI of Scotland was written on the occasion of James' troubles with his Scottish nobility in 1592, and, as the reader can perceive, Elizabeth was very precise on the subject of proper princely behavior. As soon as James became the first Stuart king of England, the comparison between the two sovereigns was quickly made, and Sir Roger Wilbraham (1553–1616) wrote his comparative evaluation of his new master within months of his old mistress's death in 1603. He had served Elizabeth as Master of Requests and was promoted by James to the surveyorship of the Court of Wards. The characterization of the two royal personalities and their styles is worth studying with care, for it goes to the root of the controversy between those who see the Civil War and the collapse of divine kingship as the result of long-term social, economic, political, and ideological forces and those who argue that it was the product of accident and personality.

James I ascended the throne in March, 1603. Because the plague was raging in London at the time, his coronation was delayed and a new parliament did not meet until March of 1604, at which time James delivered himself of his first and longest oration, explaining what was obvious to all, especially to James: he was in 1604 "an old and experienced king." Though the age and experience differential is marked, a comparison between Elizabeth's initial address to parliament and her successor's is not out of place, for it gives a clear picture of the difference between their oratorical and princely styles.

James introduced himself to parliament in March; three months later the House of Commons responded with its Apology. It had been said that the Lower House chose to ignore James's wisdom and experience in government and "tried to sell him a bill of goods about the constitutional position." Whether it did or not may not be as important as the spirit in which the Apology was presented, the theory of parliamentary privilege it advanced, and the consequences of such a concept for the crown and the historic constitution. James did not answer the House of Common's claims until 1610, when he lectured parliament on the subject of kingship. Both the Apology and James's speech of 1610 should be read in light of Elizabeth's troubles with her parliament, along with her views about monarchy and its proper relationship to the two houses of parliament.

By 1610 the constitutional dispute between crown and parliament was of long standing. Whether or not the division within the body politic was irrevocable is a question of historical taste; that it continued to grow is a matter of historical fact, the culmination and consequences of which will be reviewed in the next chapter.

## John Hayward's Description of Elizabeth's Coronation (14 January, 1559)

John Hayward describes Elizabeth's masterful behavior during her passage through the city of London enroute to her coronation at Westminster Abbey.

Upon the fourteenth day of January, [1559] in the afternoon, she passed from the Tower through the City of London to Westminster, most royally furnished, both for her person and for her train, knowing right well that in pompous ceremonies a secret of government doth much consist, for that the people are naturally both taken and held with exterior shows. The nobility and gentlemen were very many, and no less honorably furnished. The rich attire, the ornaments, the beauty of ladies, did add particular graces to the solemnity, and held the eyes and hearts of men dazzled between contentment and admiration. When she took her coach within the Tower, she made a solemn thanksgiving to God, that He had delivered her no less mercifully, no less mightily from her imprisonment in that place, than He had delivered Daniel from the lions' den: that He had preserved her from those dangers wherewith she was both environed and overwhelmed, to bring her to the joy and honor of that day. As she passed through the City, nothing was omitted to do her the highest honors, which the citizens (who could procure good use both of purses and inventions) were able to perform. It were the part of an idle orator to describe the pageants, the arches, and other well devised honors done unto her; the order, the beauty, the majesty of this action, the high joy of some, the silence and reverence of others, the constant contentment of all; their untired patience never spent, either with long expecting (some of them from a good part of the night before) or with insatiable beholding the ceremonies of that day.

The Queen was not negligent on her part to descend to all pleasing behavior, which seemed to proceed from a natural gentleness of disposition, and not from any strained desire of popularity or insinuation. She gave due respect to all sorts of persons, wherein the quickness of her spirit did work more actively than did her eyes. When the people made the air ring with praying to God for her prosperity, she thanked them with exceeding liveliness both of countenance and voice, and wished neither prosperity nor safety to herself, which might not be for their common good. As she passed by the Companies of the City, standing in their liveries, she took particular knowledge of them, and graced them with many witty formalities of speech. She diligently both observed and commended such devices as were presented unto her, and to that end sometimes caused her coach to stand still, sometimes to be removed to places of best advantage for hearing and for sight; and in the meantime fairly entreated the people to be silent. And when she understood not the meaning of any representation, or could not perfectly hear some speeches that were made, she caused the same to be declared unto her. When the Recorder of the City presented to her a purse of crimson satin, very richly and curiously wrought, and therein a thousand marks in gold, with request that she would continue a gracious mistress to the City, she answered that she was bound in natural obligations so to do, not so much for their gold as for their good wills; that as they had been at great expense of treasure that day to honor her passage, so all the days of her life she would be

SOURCE: From John Hayward, *Annals, or The First Four Years of the Reign of Queen Elizabeth,* John Bruce, ed. (London: Camden Society, 1840), pp. 15–18.

ready to expend not only her treasure but the dearest drops of her blood to maintain and increase their flourishing estate. When she spied a pageant at the Little Conduite in Cheape,[1] she demanded (as it was her custom in the rest) what should be represented therein. Answer was made that Time did there attend for her. "Time?" (said she) "How is that possible, seeing it is time that hath brought me hither?" Here a Bible in English richly covered was let down unto her by a silk lace from a child that represented truth. She kissed both her hands, with both her hands she received it, then she kissed it; afterwards applied it to her breast; and lastly held it up, thanking the City especially for that gift, and promising to be a diligent reader thereof. When any good wishes were cast forth for her virtuous and religious government, she would lift up her hands toward heaven, and desire the people to answer "Amen." When it was told her that an ancient citizen turned his head back and wept: "I warrant you" (said she) "it is for joy"; and so in very deed it was. She cheerfully received not only rich gifts from persons of worth, but nosegays, flowers, rosemarie branchs, and such like presents, offered unto her from very mean persons, insomuch as it may truly be said, that there was neither courtesy nor cost cast away that day upon her. It is incredible how often she caused her coach to stay, when any made offer to approach unto her, whether to make petition or whether to manifest their loving affections.

Hereby the people, to whom no music is so sweet as the affability of their prince, were so strongly stirred to love and joy that all men contended how they might more effectually testify the same; some with plausible acclamations, some with sober prayers, and many with silent and true-hearted tears, which were then seen to melt from their eyes. And afterwards, departing home, they so stretched everything to the highest strain, that they inflamed the like affections in others. It is certain that these high humilities, joined to justice, are of greater power to win the hearts of people than any, than all other virtues beside. All other virtues are expedient for a prince, all are advised, but these are necessary, these are enjoined; without many others a prince may stand, but without these upon every occasion he stands in danger.

The day following, being Sunday, she was, with all accustomed ceremonies, crowned in the Abbey Church at Westminster; having made demonstration of so many princely virtues before, that all men were of opinion that one crown was not sufficient to adorn them.

## John Hayward's Description of Elizabeth's Speech to the House of Commons (1559)

The House of Commons asks Elizabeth to marry. In answer, the new Queen exhibits for the first time her oratorical skill and displays her mettle.

And, during the continuance of this parliament, the Knights and Burgesses of the Lower House (doubtful whether of themselves or set unto it by some lofty spirit) made suit to the Queen that they might have access to her presence, to move a matter unto her which they esteemed of great importance for the general state of all the realm. This was granted, and a certain time of audience appointed; upon which

SOURCE: From John Hayward, *Annals, or The First Four Years of the Reign of Queen Elizabeth*, John Bruce, ed. (London: Camden Society, 1840), pp. 30–33.

[1] Little Conduit Street in Cheapside in London

day she came forth into the great gallery at White Hall, richly furnished in attire, and honorably attend. And, when she was placed in her royal seat, the Commons of the parliament were brought before her. Here the Speaker delivered a set oration. . . . The sum and substance of that which he said contained a suit that she would be pleased to dispose herself to marriage, as well for her own comfort and contentment, as for the assurance to the realm by her royal issue; that, if succession to the Crown were by this means certainly known, not only those dangers should be prevented which, after her death, might fall upon the state, but those also which, in the meantime, did threaten herself; and that, thereby, as well the fears of her faithful subjects and friends, as the ambitious hopes of her enemies, should clean be cut off.

The Queen, after a sweet graced silence, with a princely countenance and voice, and with a gesture somewhat quick but not violent, returned answer, that she gave them great thanks (as she saw great cause) for the love and care which they did express as well towards her person as the whole state of the realm; "and first" (said she) "for the manner of your petition, I like it well, and take it in good part, because it is simple, without any limitation, either of person or place. If it had been otherwise; if you had taken upon you to confine, or rather to bind, my choice, to draw my love to your liking, to frame my affections according unto your fantasies, I must have disliked it very much; for as, generally, the will desireth not a larger liberty in any case than in this, so had it been a great presumption for you to direct, to limit, to command me herein, to whom you are bound in duty to obey.

"Concerning the substance of your suit, since my years of understanding, since I was first able to take consideration of myself, I have hitherto made choice of a single life, which hath best, I assure you, contented me, and, I trust, hath been most acceptable to God. . . . Nevertheless, if any of you suspect that, in case it shall please God hereafter to change my purpose, I will determine something to the prejudice of the realm, put the jealousy out of your heads, for I assure [you] . . . I will never conclude anything in that matter which shall be hurtful to the realm, for the preservation and prosperity whereof as a loving mother I will never spare to spend my life. And upon whomsoever my choice shall fall he shall be as careful for your preservation, — I will not say as myself, for I cannot undertake for another as for myself, — but my will and best endeavour shall not fail that he shall be as careful for you as myself. And, albeit it shall please God that I still persevere in a virgin's state, yet you must not fear but He will so work, both in my heart and in your wisdoms, that provision shall be made, in convenient time, whereby the realm shall not remain destitute of an heir who may be a fit governor, and peradventure, more beneficial than such offspring as I should bring forth, for, although I be careful of your well-doings, and ever purpose so to be, yet may my issue degenerate, and grow out of kind. The dangers which you fear are neither so certain, nor of such nature, but you may repose yourselves upon the providence of God, and the good provisions of the state. Wits curious in casting things to come are often hurtful, for that the affairs of this world are subject to so many accidents that seldom doth that happen which the wisdom of men doth seem to foresee. As for me, it shall be sufficient that a marble stone shall declare that a Queen, having lived and reigned so many years, died a virgin. And here I end, and take your coming in very good part, and again give hearty thanks to you all; yet more for your zeal and good meaning, than for the matter of your suit."

## Freedom of Speech: Two Speeches by Peter Wentworth, 1576, 1587, and the Queen's Statement of 1593

Wentworth addresses the House of Commons on 8 February, 1576, questioning the Queen's right to stifle debate, especially on matters of religion.

I was never of parliament but the last, and the last session, at both which times I saw the liberty of free speech, the which is the only salve to heal all the sores of this commonwealth, so much and so many ways infringed, and so many abuses offered to this honourable council, as hath much grieved me even of very conscience and love to my prince and state. Wherefore to avoid the like, I do think it expedient to open the commodities that grow to the prince and whole state by free speech used in this place . . . Amongst other, Mr. Speaker, two things do great hurt in this place, of the which I do mean to speak: the one is a rumour which runneth about the House, and this it is, "Take heed what you do, the Queen liketh not such a matter: whosoever preferreth it, she will be offended with him; or the contrary, her Majesty liketh of such a matter: whosoever speaketh against it, she will be much offended with him." The other: sometimes a message is brought into the house, either of commanding or inhibiting, very injurious to the freedom of speech and consultation. I would to God, Mr. Speaker, that these two were buried in hell, I mean rumours and messages . . .

This grievous rumour, What is it forsooth? Whatsoever thou art that pronouncest it, thou dost pronounce thy own discredit. Why so? for that thou dost what lieth in thee to pronounce the prince to be perjured . . . For the Queen's Majesty is the head of the law, and must of necessity maintain the law; for by the law her Majesty is made justly our Queen, and by it she is most chiefly main-

tained . . . The King ought not to be under man, but under God and under the law, because the law maketh him a King . . . I pray you mark the reason why my authority [Bracton] saith, "The King ought to be under the law," for, saith he, "He is God's vicegerent upon earth," that is, his lieutenant to execute and do his will, the which is law or justice; and thereunto was her Majesty sworn at her coronation, as I have heard learned men in this place sundry times affirm; unto the which I doubt not but her Majesty will, for her honour and conscience sake, have special regard, for free speech and conscience in this place are granted by a special law, as that without the which the prince and state cannot be preserved or maintained.

Now the other was a message [from the Queen], Mr. Speaker, brought the last session into the House that we should not deal in any matters of religion, but first to receive from the bishops. Surely this was a doleful message; for it was as much as to say, "Sirs, ye shall not deal in God's causes, no, ye shall in no wise seek to advance His glory" . . . Certain it is, Mr. Speaker, that none is without fault, no, not our noble Queen, since her Majesty hath committed great fault, yea dangerous faults to herself. Love, even perfect love, void of dissimulation, will not suffer me to hide them to her Majesty's peril, but to utter them to her Majesty's safety: and these they are. It is a dangerous thing in a prince unkindly to abuse his or her nobility and people, and it is a dangerous thing in a prince to oppose

SOURCE: From Sir Simond D'Ewes, *A Complete Journal of the Votes, Speeches, and Debates . . . Throughout the Whole Reign of Queen Elizabeth* (London, 1693), in G. W. Prothero, *Select Statutes and Other Constitutional Documents, Illustrative of the Reigns of Elizabeth and James I* (Oxford, England: Clarendon Press, 1913), pp. 120–125.

or bend herself against her nobility and people, yea against most loving and faithful nobility and people.

. . . I do surely think, before God I speak it, that the bishops were the cause of that doleful message; and I will show you what moveth me so to think. I was, amongst others, [during] the last parliament sent unto the bishop of Canterbury, for the Articles of Religion that then passed this House. He asked us, Why we did put out of the book the Articles for the Homilies, Consecrating of Bishops, and such like? Surely, sir, said I, because we were so occupied in other matters, that we had no time to examine them how they agreed with the Word of God. What, said he, surely you mistook the matter, you will refer yourselves wholly to us therein? No, by the faith I bear to God, said I, we will pass nothing before we understand what it is, for that were but to make you Popes; make you Popes who list, said I, for we will make you none . . .

Thus I have holden you long with my rude speech; the which, since it tendeth wholly with pure conscience to seek the advancement of God's glory, our honourable Sovereign's safety, and the sure defence of this noble isle of England, and all by maintaining of the liberties of this honourable council, the fountain from whence all these do spring; my humble and hearty suit unto you all is, to accept my good-will, and that this that I have here spoken out of conscience and great zeal unto my prince and state, may not be buried in the pit of oblivion, and so no good come thereof.

Wentworth defies the Speaker of the House of Commons on 1 March, 1587, again demanding that the House question the Queen's authority to limit freedom of speech.

Mr. Speaker, . . . I . . . do earnestly desire, by question, to be satisfied of a few questions to be moved by you, Mr. Speaker,[2] concerning the liberty of this honourable council. Wherefore I pray you, Mr. Speaker, eftsoons[3] to move these few articles, by question, whereby every one of this House may know how far he may proceed in this honourable council, in matters that concern the glory of God and our true and loyal service to our prince and state. . . .

Whether this council be not a place for any member of the same here assembled, freely and without controlment of any person, or danger of laws, by bill or speech, to utter any of the griefs of this commonwealth whatsoever, touching the service of God, the safety of the prince, and this noble realm? — Whether that great honour may be done unto God and benefit and service unto the prince and state without free speech in this council, which may be done with it? — Whether there by any council which can make, add to or diminish from the laws of the realm, but only this council of parliament? — Whether it be not against the orders of this council to make any secret or matter of weight, which is here in hand, known to the prince or any other, concerning the high service of God, prince or state, without the consent of the house? — Whether the Speaker or any other may interrupt any member of this council in his speech used in this House, tending to any of the forenamed high services? — Whether the Speaker may rise when he will, any matter being propounded, without consent of the House, or not? — Whether the Speaker may overrule the House in any matter or cause there in question; or whether he is to be ruled or overruled in any matter, or not? — Whether the prince and state can continue, stand and be maintained without this council of parliament, not altering the government of the state. [Wentworth was imprisoned for this speech by order of the Queen.]

---

2 The speaker was appointed by the Queen.   3 again

In this speech, delivered 19 February, 1593, the Lord Keeper presents the Queen's definition of free speech.

... To your three demands the Queen answereth; liberty of speech is granted you; but how far this is to be thought on, there be two things of most necessity, and those two do most harm, which are wit and speech: the one exercised in invention, and the other in uttering things invented. Privilege of speech is granted, but you must know what privilege you have; not to speak every one what he listeth, or what cometh in his brain to utter that; but your privilege is, *aye* or *no*. Wherefore, Mr. Speaker, her Majesty's pleasure is, That if you perceive any idle heads, which will not stick to hazard their own estates, which will meddle with reforming the Church and transforming the Commonwealth, and do exhibit any bills to such purpose, that you receive them not, until they be viewed and considered by those who it is fitter should consider of such things and can better judge of them. To your persons all privilege is granted, with this caveat, that under colour of this privilege, no man's ill-doings or not performing of duties be covered and protected. The last; free access is granted to her Majesty's person, so that it be upon urgent and weighty causes, and at times convenient, and when her Majesty may be at leisure from other important causes of the realm.

## The Debate in the House of Commons over Monopolies (November, 1601)

Mr. Lawrence Hide introduced a bill on 20 November, 1601, to limit the Queen's right to grant monopolies, i.e., trade and manufacturing licenses.

MR. FRANCIS BACON said: ... I confess the bill, as it is, is in few words, but yet ponderous and weighty. For the prerogative royal of the prince, for my own part I ever allowed of it, and it is such as I hope shall never be discussed. The Queen, as she is our sovereign, hath both an enlarging and restraining liberty of her prerogative; that is, she hath power by her patents to set at liberty things restrained by statute law or otherwise; and, by her prerogative she may restrain things that are at liberty. ... If any man out of his own wit, industry or endeavour find out anything beneficial for the commonwealth ... her Majesty is pleased perhaps to grant him a privilege to use the same only by himself or his deputies for a certain time: this is one kind of monopoly. Sometimes there is a glut of things when they be in excessive quantities, as of corn, and perhaps her Majesty gives licence to one man of transportation: this is another kind of monopoly. Sometimes there is a scarcity or small quantity: and the like is granted also. ... Mr. Speaker, (said he, pointing to the bill) this is no stranger in this place, but a stranger in this vestment: the use hath been ever by petition to humble ourselves unto her Majesty and by petition to desire to have our grievances redressed, especially when the remedy toucheth her so nigh in prerogative. All cannot be done at once, neither was it possible since the last parliament to repeal all. If her Majesty make a patent or a monopoly unto any of her servants, that we must go and cry out against: but if she grant it to a number of burgesses or a corporation, that must stand, and that forsooth is no monopoly. I say, and I say again, that we ought not to

SOURCE: From Townsend's *Journals*, in G. W. Prothero, *Select Statutes and other Constitutional Documents Illustrative of the Reigns of Elizabeth and James I* (Oxford, England: Clarendon Press, 1913), pp. 111–117.

deal or meddle with or judge of her Majesty's prerogative . . .

MR. LAWRENCE HIDE: I confess, Mr. Speaker, that I owe duty to God and loyalty to my prince. And for the bill itself I made it, and I think I understand it: and far be it from this heart of mine to think, this tongue to speak, or this hand to write anything, either in prejudice or derogation of her Majesty's prerogative royal and the state . . . And, Mr. Speaker, as I think it is no derogation to the omnipotency of God, to say he can do no ill, so I think, it is no derogation to the person or majesty of the Queen, to say so . . .

MR. FRANCIS MOORE: Mr. Speaker, I know the Queen's prerogative is a thing curious to be dealt withal, yet all grievances are not comparable. I cannot utter with my tongue or conceive with my heart the great grievances that the town and country, for which I serve, suffer by some of these monopolies. It bringeth the general profit into a private hand, and the end of all is beggary and bondage to the subjects. We have a law for the true and faithful currying of leather: there is a patent that sets all at liberty, notwithstanding that statute. And to what purpose is it to do anything by act of parliament, when the Queen will undo the same by her prerogative? Out of the spirit of humility, Mr. Speaker, I do speak it: there is no act of hers that hath been or is more derogatory to her own Majesty, or more odious to the subject, or more dangerous to the commonwealth than the granting of these monopolies . . .

SIR EDWARD STANHOPE informed the House of the great abuse by the patentee for salt in his country, that betwixt Michaelmas and St. Andrew's tide, where salt was wont (before the patent) to be sold for 16d, a bushel, it is now sold for 14s. and 15s. a bushel: but, after the Lord President had understood thereof, he committed the patentee, who caused it to be sold as before . . . To Lynn there is every year brought at least 3000 weight of salt; and every weight, since this patent, is enhanced 20s.; and where the bushel was wont to be 8d.

it is now 16d. And I dare boldly say it, if this patent were called in, there might well be £3000 a year saved in the ports of Lynn, Boston, and Hull. I speak this of white salt. . . .

SIR ROBERT WROTH: . . . There have been divers patents granted since the last parliament; these are now in being, viz. the patents for currants, iron, powder, cards, horns, ox shin bones, train-oil, transportation of leather, lists of cloth, ashes, bottles, glasses, bags, shreds of gloves, aniseed, vinegar, sea-coals, steel, aquavitæ, brushes, pots salt, salt-petre, lead, accedence, oil, calamint stone, oil of blubber, fumathoes, or dried pilchers in the smoke, and divers others.

Upon reading of the patents aforesaid, Mr. Hackwell of Lincoln's Inn stood up and asked thus: Is not bread there? Bread, quoth another; This voice seems strange, quoth a third. No, quoth Mr. Hackwell, but if order be not taken for these, bread will be there before the next parliament.

[On November 23, the debate was renewed.]

MR. SECRETARY CECIL: If there had not been some mistaking or confusion in the committee, I would not now have spoken. The question was, of the most convenient way to reform these grievances of monopolies: but after disputation, of that labour we have not received the expected fruit . . . This dispute draws two great things in question; first, the prince's power; secondly, the freedom of Englishmen. I am born an Englishman, and a fellow-member of this House; I would desire to live no day, in which I should detract from either. I am servant to the Queen; and before I would speak or give my consent to a case that should debase her prerogative or abridge it, I would wish my tongue cut out of my head. . . . And you, Mr. Speaker, should perform the charge her Majesty gave unto you at the beginning of this parliament not to receive bills of this nature; for her Majesty's ears be open to all grievances, and her hand stretched out to every man's petition. For the matter of access I like it well, so it be first moved and the way prepared. I had rather all the patents were burnt than her Majesty should lose the hearts of so many subjects as is pretended she will . . .

[On November 25, the Speaker brought the following message[4] to the house.]

. . . It pleased her Majesty to say unto me, That if she had an hundred tongues she could not express our hearty good-wills. And further she said, That as she had ever held our good most dear, so the last day of our or her life should witness it; and that if the least of her subjects were grieved, and herself not touched, she appealed to the throne of Almighty God, how careful she hath been, and will be, to defend her people from all oppressions. She said, That partly by intimation of her council, and partly by divers petitions that have been delivered unto her both going to chapel and also walking abroad, she understood that divers patents, that she had granted, were grievous to her subjects; and that the substitutes of the patentees had used great oppression. But, she said, she never assented to grant anything which was *malum in se*.[5] And if in the abuse of her grant there be

anything evil, which she took knowledge there was, she herself would take present order of reformation thereof. I cannot express unto you the apparent indignation of her Majesty towards these abuses. She said her kingly prerogative was tender; and therefore desireth us not to speak or doubt of her careful reformation; for, she said, her commandment given a little before the late troubles (meaning the Earl of Essex's matters) by the unfortunate event of them was not so hindered, but that since that time, even in the midst of her most great and weighty occasions, she thought upon them. And that this should not suffice, but that further order should be taken presently, and not *in futuro* (for that also was another word which I take it her Majesty used), and that some should be presently repealed, some suspended, and none put in execution but such as should first have a trial according to the law for the good of the people. Against the abuses her wrath was so incensed, that she said, that she neither could nor would suffer such to escape with impunity. So to my unspeakable comfort she hath made me the messenger of this her gracious thankfulness and care.

## Elizabeth's Letter to James VI of Scotland (11 September, 1592)

Elizabeth, having just heard of an attempted palace revolution against James of Scotland, writes to instruct him on how to behave as a proper and successful monarch.

The dear care, my dear Brother, that ever I carried, from your infancy, of your prosperous estate and quiet, could not permit [me to] hear of so many, yea so traitorous attempts, without unspeakable dolour and unexpressful woe. . . . To redouble crimes so oft, I say with your pardon, most to your charge, which never durst have been renewed if the first had received the condign[6]

reward; for slacking of due correction engenders the bold minds for new crimes. And if my counsels had as well been followed as they were truly meant, your subjects had now better known their King, and you no more need of further justice. You find by sour experience what this neglect hath bred you.

I hear of so uncouth a way taken by

SOURCE: From John Bruce, *Letters of Queen Elizabeth and James VI of Scotland* (London: Camden Society, 1849), Original Series, Vol. 46, pp. 75–76).

[4] from the Queen   [5] evil in itself   [6] deserving

some of your conventions, yea, agreed to by yourself, that I must [wonder] how you will be clerk to such lessons. Must a king be prescribed what councillors he will take as if you were their ward? Shall you be obliged to tie or undo what they list make or revoke? O Lord, what strange dreams hear I, that would God they were so, for then at my waking I should find them fables. If you mean, therefore, to reign, I exhort you to show you worthy the place, which never can be surely settled without a steady course held to make you loved and feared. I assure myself many have escaped your hands more for dread of your remissness than for love of the escaped; so oft they see you cherishing some men for open crimes, and so they mistrust more their revenge than your assurance. My affection for you best lies on this, my plainness, whose patience is too much moved with these like everlasting faults.

And since it so likes you to demand my counsel, I find so many ways your state so unjointed, that it needs a skilfuller bone-setter than I to join each part in his right place. But to fulfil your will, take, in short, these few words: For all whose you know the assailers of your courts, the shameful attempters of your sacred decree, if ever you pardon I will never be the suitor. Who to peril a king were inventors or actors, they should crack a halter if I were king. Such is my charity. Who under pretence of better your estate, endangers the king, or needs will be his schoolmasters, if I might appoint their university they should be assigned to learn first to obey; so should they better teach you next. I am not so unskilful of a kingly rule that I would wink at no fault, yet would be open-eyed at public indignity. Neither should all have the whip though some were scourged. But if, like a toy, of a king's life so oft endangered nought shall follow but a scorn, what sequel I may doubt of such contempt I dread to think and dare not name. The rest I bequeath to the trust of your faithful servant, and pray the Almighty God to inspire you in time, afore too late, to cut their combs whose crest may danger you. I am void of malice. God is judge. I know them not. Forgive this too too long a writing.

## Roger Wilbraham's Comparison of Elizabeth and James I ( 1603 )

Roger Wilbraham sets down "without flattery the nature and virtues with the apparent defects" of Elizabeth and her successor, James I.

... Because future ages will perhaps write either uncertainly or variably of our late Queen or her next successor, being both princes of highest renown for all external happiness that nature, art or fortune can afford, I, [who] have been Master of Requests in ordinary three years to the Queen and three months to the King, will according to the means of my apprehension without flattery set down the nature and virtues with the apparent defects in both the princes.

The Queen was of comely personage, sound in health till her last sickness, strong of constitution. Her only physician was her own observation and good diet: not tied to hours of eating or sleeping but following appetite; not delighted in belly cheer to please the taste but feeding always upon meats that sustain and strengthen nature. In all these habits the King's Majesty, her kinsman, hath similar disposition, respecting his age and difference of sex.

The King hath a magnanimous spirit,

SOURCE: From H. S. Scott, ed., *Journal of Sir Roger Wilbraham* (London: Camden Society, 1902), Miscellany X, pp. 58–60.

venturous to hazard his own body in hunting especially, and most patient of labor, cold and heat. So was the Queen far above all others of her sex and years.

Both of them most merciful in disposition. They soon anger yet without bitterness or stinging revenge. In prudence, justice and temperance they are both the admiration to princes in their several sexes.

The King most bountiful, seldom denying any suit; the Queen strict in giving, which age and her sex inclined her unto. The one often complained of for sparing; the other so benign that his people fear his over-readiness in giving.

The Queen slow to resolution and seldom to be retracted; His Majesty quick in concluding and more variable in subsisting.

The Queen solemn and ceremonious, and requiring decent and disparent[7] order to be kept convenient in each degree; and although she bare a greater majesty, yet would she labor to entertain strangers, suitors and her people with more courtly courtesy and favorable speechs than the King used, who although he be indeed of a more true benignity and ingenious nature, yet the neglect of those ordinary ceremonies — which his variable and quick wit cannot attend — makes common people judge otherwise of him. . . .

The Queen took delight and made profit in simulation and dissimulation, and thereby discovered fashions and pretences and favorers to suits, and the true meaning of her several councilors in matters of importance. The King seems to neglect that as baseness, thinking his own wit sufficient to exploit things pertinent by ordinary means, without such labor and insinuation.

The Queen was quick of apprehension, wise in counsel by reason of her great reading and overreaching experience. Of an admirable felicity of memory and albeit of great constancy, yet by continual labor, her benign nature was changed and in part depraved by years and jealousies and [those] ill affected about her, which she could hardly eschew, being in age as a recluse cloistered to hear only such tunes as her keepers sounded unto her. . . .

The King is of sharpest wit and invention, ready and pithy speech, an exceeding good memory, of the sweetest, pleasantest and best nature that ever I know, desiring nor affecting anything but true honor. As his learning and religious virtues hath extolled him above all princes in the world, so I pray unfainedly[8] that his most gracious disposition and heroic mind be not depraved with ill counsel, and that neither the wealth and peace of England make him forget God, nor the painted flattery of the Court cause him to forget himself.

## James I's First Speech to Parliament (March, 1604)

James informs Parliament, in a "plain and sincere" address to both houses, of "the blessings which God hath in my royal person bestowed upon you all."

It did not sooner please God to lighten His hand, and relent the violence of His devouring angel against the poor people of this city, but as soon did I resolve to call this parliament, and that for three chief and principal reasons: the first whereof is . . . that you who are here presently assembled to represent the body of this whole kingdom, and of all sorts of people within the same, may with your own ears hear, and

SOURCE: From Walter Scott, *A Collection of Scarce and Valuable Tracts, on the Most Interesting and Entertaining Subjects . . . Selected . . . That of the Late Lord Somers* (London, 1809), Vol. II, pp. 60–69.

7 distinct    8 unfailingly

that I out of mine own mouth may deliver unto you the assurance of my due thankfulness for your so joyful and general applause to the declaring and receiving of me in this seat (which God by my birthright and lineal descent had in the fulness of time provided for me).... Not that I am able to express by words, or utter by eloquence, the live image of mine inward thankfulness, but only that out of mine own mouth you may rest assured to expect that measure of thankfulness at my hands, which is according to the infiniteness of your deserts, and to my inclination and ability for requital of the same.... And therefore for expressing my thankfulness, I must resort unto the other two reasons for my convening of this parliament....

As to the first, it is the blessings which God hath in my person bestowed upon you all, wherein I protest, I do more glory at the same for your weale, then for any particular respect of mine own reputation or advantage therein.

The first then of these blessings, which God hath jointly with my person sent unto you is outward peace: that is, peace abroad with all foreign neighbors; for I thank God I may justly say that never since I was a king, I either received wrong of any other Christian prince or state, or did wrong to any. I have ever, I praise God, yet kept peace and amity with all, which hath been so far tied to my person as at my coming here you are witnesses I found the state embarked in a great and tedious war, and only by my arrival here and by the peace in my person is now amity kept, where war was before, which is no small blessing to a Christian commonwealth....

But although outward peace be a great blessing, yet is it as far inferior to peace within, as civil wars are more cruel and unnatural than wars abroad. And therefore the second great blessing that God hath with my person sent unto you is peace within, and that in a double form. First, by my descent lineally out of the loins of Henry the Seventh is reunited and confirmed in me the union of the two princely roses of the two houses of Lancaster and York, whereof that king of happy memory was the first uniter, as he was also the first groundlayer of the other peace. The lamentable and miserable events by the civil and bloody dissention betwixt these two houses was so great and so late as it need not be renewed unto your memories; which, as it was first settled and united in him, so is it now reunited and confirmed in me, being justly and lineally descended not only of that happy conjunction, but of both the branch thereof many time before. But the union of these two princely houses is nothing comparable to the union of the two ancient and famous kingdoms which is the other inward peace annexed to my person.

And here I must crave your patience for a little space, to give me leave to discourse more particularly of the benefits that do arise of that union which is made in my blood, being a matter that most properly belongeth to me to speak of, as the head wherein that great body is united.... Hath not God first united these two kingdoms both in language, religion and similitude of manners? Yea, hath He not made us all in one island, [en]compassed with one sea, and of itself by nature so indivisible as almost those that were Borderers themselves on the late borders cannot distinguish nor know [n]or discern their own limits?... What God hath conjoined then, let no man separate. I am the husband and all the whole isle is my lawful wife; I am the head and it is my body; I am the shepherd and it is my flock....

Now although these blessings before rehearsed of inward and outward peace be great, yet seeing that in all good things a great part of their goodness and estimation is lost, if they have not appearance of perpetuity or long continuance, so hath it pleased Almighty God to accompany my person also with that favor, having healthful and hopeful issue of my body, whereof some are here present, for continuance and propagation of the undoubted right which is in my person; under whom I doubt not but it will please God to prosper and continue for many years this union and all other blessings of inward and outward peace which I have brought with me.

But neither peace outward nor peace inward, nor any other blessings that can follow thereupon, nor appearance of the perpetuity thereof by propagation in the posterity, is but a weak pillar and a rotten reed to lean unto, if God do not strengthen and by the staff of His blessing make them durable. . . . For all worldly blessings are like swift passing shadows, fading flowers, or chaff blown before the wind if the profession of true religion, and works according thereunto, God be not moved to maintain and settle the thrones of princes. And although that since mine entry into this kingdom I have, both by meeting with divers of the ecclesiastical estate and likewise by divers proclamations, clearly declared my mind in points of religion, yet do I not think it amiss, in this so solemn an audience, I should now take occasion to discover somewhat of the secrets of my heart in that matter. . . . At my first coming, although I found but one religion, and that which by myself is professed, publicly allowed and by the law maintained; yet found I another sort of religion, besides a private sect, lurking within the bowels of this nation. The first is the true religion, which by me is professed and by the law is established; the second is the falsely called Catholics but truly papists; the third, which I call a sect rather than religion, is the puritans and novelists, who do not so far differ from us in points of religion as in their confused form of policy and parity, being ever discontented with the present government and impatient to suffer any superiority, which maketh their sect unable to be suffered in any well governed commonwealth. But as for my course toward them, I remit it to my proclamations made upon that subject. . . .

But of one thing would I have the papists of this land to be admonished, that they presume not so much upon my lenity (because I would be loth to be thought a persecutor) as thereupon to think it lawful

for them daily to increase their number and strength in this kingdom, whereby, if not in my time at least in the time of my posterity, they might be in hope to erect their religion again. No, let them assure themselves, that as I am a friend to their persons if they be good subjects, so am I a vowed enemy and do denounce mortal war to their errors. And that as I would be sorry to be driven by their ill behavior from the protection and conservation of their bodies and lives, so will I never cease, as far as I can, to tread down their errors and wrong opinions. For I could not permit the increase and growing of their religion without first betraying of myself and mine own conscience. . . .

I must here make a little apology for myself, in that I could not satisfy the particular humors of every persons that looked for some advancement on reward at my hand since my entry into this kingdom. Three kind[s] of things were craved of me: advancement to honor, preferment to place of credit about my person, and reward in matters of land or profit. If I had bestowed honor upon all, no man could have been advanced to honor, for the degrees of honor do consist in preferring some above their fellows. If every man had the like access to my privy or bedchamber, then no man could have it because it cannot contain all. And if I had bestowed lands and rewards upon every man, the fountain of my liberality would be so exhausted and dried [up] as I would lack means to be liberal to any man. And yet was I not so sparing but I may, without vaunting, affirm that I have enlarged my favor in all the three degrees towards as many, and more, than ever king of England did in so short a space. No, I rather crave your pardon that I have been so bountiful, for if the means of the crown be wasted, I behoved then to have recourse to you my subjects and be burdensome to you, which I would be lothest to be of any king alive. For as it is true that as I have already said it was a whole body which did deserve so well at my hand, and not every particular person of the people, yet were there some who, by reason of their office, credit with the people or otherwise, took occasion both before and at the time of my coming amongst you to give proof of their love and affection towards me. Not that I am any way in doubt that if other of my subjects had been in their places and had had the like occasion, but they would have uttered the like good effects (so general and so great were the love and affection of you all towards me). But yet this having been performed by some special persons, I could not, without unthankfulness, but requite them accordingly. And, therefore, had I just occasion to advance some in honor, some to places of service about me, and by rewarding, to enable some who had deserved well of me, and were not otherwise able to maintain the ranks I thought them capable of, and others who, although they had not particularly deserved before, yet I found them capable and worthy of place of preferment and credit and not able to sustain those places, for which I thought them fit, without my help. Two special causes moved me to be so open handed: whereof the one was reasonable and honorable, but the other, I will not be ashamed to confess unto you, proceeded of mine own infirmity. That which was just and honorable was: that being so far beholding to the body of the whole state, I thought I could not refuse to let run some small brooks out of the fountain of my thankfulness to the whole, for refreshing of particular persons that were members of that multitude. The other, which proceeded out of mine own infirmity was the multitude and importunity of suitors. But although reason come[s] by infusion in a manner, yet experience groweth with time and labor; and therefore do I not doubt but experience in time coming will both teach the particular subjects of this kingdom not to be so importune and indiscreet in craving, and me not to be so easily and lightly moved in granting that which may be harmful to my estate and consequently to the whole kingdom.

And thus having declared unto you my mind in all the points for which I called this parliament, my conclusion shall only now be to excuse myself, in case you have not found such eloquence in my speech as peradventure you might have looked for at my hands. I might, if I list, allege the great weight of my affairs and my continual business and distraction that I could never have leisure to think upon what I was to speak before I came to the place where I was to speak; and I might also allege that my first sight of this so famous and honorable an assembly might likewise breed some impediment. But, leaving these excuses, I will plainly and freely in my manner tell you the true cause of it, which is that it becometh a king, in my opinion, to use no other eloquence than plainness and sincerity; by plainness I mean that his speechs should be so clear and void of all ambiguity that they may not be thrown nor rent asunder in contrary senses like the old oracles of the pagan gods; and by sincerity I understand that uprightness and honesty which ought to be in a king's whole speechs and actions that, as far as a king is in honor erected above any of his subjects, so far should he strive in sincerity to be above them all, and that his tongue should be ever the true messenger of his heart; and this sort of eloquence may you ever assuredly look for at my hands.

## The Apology of the House of Commons ( 20 June, 1604 )

The House of Commons seeks to educate its new sovereign about the rights,
liberties, and privileges of the Lower House.

. . . No other help or redress appearing, and finding these misinformations to have been the first, yea, the chief and almost the sole cause of all the discontentful and troublesome proceedings so much blamed in this parliament, . . . we have been constrained to break our silence, and freely to disclose unto your Majesty the truth of such matters concerning your subjects the Commons, as hitherto by misinformation hath been suppressed or perverted. Wherein that we may more plainly proceed (which next unto truth we affect in this discourse), we shall reduce these misinformations to three principal heads; first, touching the cause of the joyful receiving of your Majesty into this your kingdom: secondly, concerning the rights and liberties of your subjects of England and the privileges of this House; thirdly, touching the several actions and speeches passed in the House.

. . . Now concerning the ancient rights of the subjects of this realm, chiefly consisting in the privileges of this house of parliament, the misinformation openly delivered to your Majesty hath been in three things: first, that we held not privileges of right, but of grace only, renewed every parliament by way of donature upon petition, and so to be limited. Secondly, that we are no Court of Record, nor yet a court that can command view of records; but that our proceedings here are only to acts and memorials, and that the attendance with the records is courtesy, not duty. Thirdly and lastly, that the examination of the return of writs for knights and burgesses is without our compass, and due to the chancery.

Against which assertions, most gracious Sovereign, tending directly and apparently to the utter overthrow of the very fundamental privileges of our House, and therein of the rights and liberties of the whole Commons of your realm of England, which they and their ancestors from time immemorial have undoubtedly enjoyed under your Majesty's most noble progenitors, we the knights, citizens and burgesses of the House of Commons assembled in parliament and in the name of the whole Commons of the realm of England, with uniform consent for ourselves and our posterity, do expressly protest, as being derogatory in the highest degree to the true dignity, liberty and authority of your Majesty's high court of parliament and consequently to the rights of all your Majesty's said subjects and the whole body of this your kingdom; and desire that this our protestation may be recorded to all posterity. And contrariwise, with all humble and due respect to your Majesty our sovereign lord and head, against these misinformations we most truly avouch, first, that our privileges and liberties are our right and due inheritance, no less than our very lands and goods. Secondly, that they cannot be withheld from us, denied or impaired, but with apparent wrong to the whole state of the realm. Thirdly, that our making of request in the entrance of parliament to enjoy our privilege is an act only of manners, and doth weaken our right no more than our suing to the King for our lands by petition, which form, though new and more decent than the old by *praecipe*, yet the subject's right is no less now than of old. Fourthly, we avouch also that our House is a court of record,

SOURCE: From William Petyt, *Jus Parliamentarium* (London, 1739), in G. W. Prothero, *Select Statutes and Other Constitutional Documents Illustrative of the Reigns of Elizabeth and James I* (Oxford, England: Clarendon Press, 1913), pp. 286–293.

and so ever esteemed. Fifthly, that there is not the highest standing court in this land that ought to enter into competency either for dignity or authority with this high court of parliament, which with your Majesty's royal assent gives laws to other courts, but from other courts receives neither laws nor orders. Sixthly and lastly, we avouch that the House of Commons is the sole proper judge of return of all such writs, and of the election of all such members as belong unto it, without which the freedom of election were not entire; and that the chancery, though a standing court under your Majesty, be to send out those writs and receive the returns and to preserve them, yet the same is done only for the use of the parliament; over which neither the chancery nor any other court ever had or ought to have any manner of jurisdiction. . . .

The rights and liberties of the Commons of England consisteth chiefly in these three things: first, that the shires, cities and boroughs of England, by representation to be present, have free choice of such persons as they shall put in trust to represent them: secondly, that the persons chosen, during the time of the parliament, as also of their access and recess, be free from restraint, arrest and imprisonment: thirdly, that in parliament they may speak freely their consciences without check and controlment, doing the same with due reverence to the sovereign court of parliament, that is, to your Majesty and both the Houses, who all in this case make but one politic body, whereof your Highness is the head.

⋅ . . . For matter of religion, it will appear, by examination of truth and right, that your Majesty should be misinformed, if any man should deliver that the kings of England have any absolute power in themselves, either to alter religion (which God defend should be in the power of any mortal man whatsoever) or to make any laws concerning the same, otherwise than as in temporal

causes by consent of parliament. We have and shall at all times by our oaths acknowledge, that your Majesty is sovereign lord and supreme governor in both. Touching our own desires and proceedings therein, they have not been a little misconceived and misreported. We have not come in any Puritan or Brownish spirit to introduce their parity, or to work the subversion of the state ecclesiastical, as now it standeth . . . Our desire hath also been to reform certain abuses crept into the ecclesiastical state, even as into the temporal: and lastly, that the land might be furnished with a learned, religious, and godly ministry, for the maintenance of whom we would have granted no small contributions, if in these (as we trust) just and religious desires we had found that correspondency from others which was expected . . .

There remaineth, dread Sovereign, yet one part of our duty at this present, which faithfulness of heart, not presumption, doth press: we stand not in place to speak or do things pleasing. Our care is, and must be, to confirm the love and tie the hearts of your subjects, the commons, most firmly to your Majesty. Herein lieth the means of our well deserving of both: there was never prince entered with greater love, with greater joy and applause of all his people. This love, this joy, let it flourish in their hearts for ever. Let no suspicion have access to their fearful thoughts, that their privileges, which they think by your Majesty should be protected, should now by sinister informations or counsel be violated or impaired; or that those, which with dutiful respects to your Majesty, speak freely for the right and good of their country, shall be oppressed or disgraced. Let your Majesty be pleased to receive public information from your Commons in parliament as to the civil estate and government; for private informations pass often by practice: the voice of the people, in the things of their knowledge, is said to be as the voice of God. . . .

## *James I's Speech to Parliament* ( 21 March, 1610 )

James I lectures parliament on its proper role in government and on the divine nature of monarchy.

. . . The state of monarchy is the supremest thing upon earth: for kings are not only God's lieutenants upon earth and sit upon God's throne, but even by God himself they are called gods. There be three principal similitudes that illustrate the state of monarchy: one taken out of the word of God, and the two other out of the grounds of policy and philosophy. In the Scriptures kings are called gods, and so their power after a certain relation compared to the Divine power. Kings are also compared to fathers of families: for a king is truly *parens patriae*, the politic father of his people. And lastly, kings are compared to the head of this microcosm of the body of man . . .

I conclude then this point touching the power of kings with this axiom of divinity, That as to dispute what God may do is blasphemy, . . . so is it sedition in subjects to dispute what a king may do in the height of his power. But just kings will ever be willing to declare what they will do, if they will not incur the curse of God. I will not be content that my power be disputed upon; but I shall ever be willing to make the reason appear of all my doings, and rule my actions according to my laws . . .

Now the second general ground whereof I am to speak concerns the matter of grievances. . . . First then, I am not to find fault that you inform yourselves of the particular just grievances of the people; nay I must tell you, ye can neither be just nor faithful to me or to your countries that trust and employ you, if you do it not . . . But I would wish you to be careful to avoid three things in the matter of grievances.

First, that you do not meddle with the main points of government: that is my craft: . . . I am now an old king. . . . I must not be taught my office.

Secondly, I would not have you meddle with such ancient rights of mine as I have received from my predecessors, possessing them *more majorum*: such things I would be sorry should be accounted for grievances. All novelties are dangerous as well in a politic as in a natural body: and therefore I would be loath to be quarrelled in my ancient rights and possessions: for that were to judge me unworthy of that which my predecessors had and left me. .

And lastly I pray you, beware to exhibit for grievance anything that is established by a settled law, and whereunto (as you have already had a proof) you know I will never give a plausible answer: for it is an undutiful part in subjects to press their king, wherein they know beforehand he will refuse them. Now if any law or statute be not convenient, let it be amended by Parliament, but in the meantime term it not a grievance; for to be grieved with the law is to be grieved with the king, who is sworn to be the patron and maintainer thereof. But as all men are flesh and may err in the execution of laws, so may ye justly make a grievance of any abuse of the law, distinguishing wisely between the faults of the person and the thing itself. As for example, complaints may be made unto you of the High Commissioners: if so be, try the abuse and spare not to complain upon it, but say not there shall be no Commission, for that were to abridge the power that is in me . . .

SOURCE: From *Works of James I* (London, 1616) in G. W. Prothero, *Select Statutes and other Constitutional Documents Illustrative of the Reigns of Elizabeth and James I* (Oxford, England: Clarendon Press, 1913), pp. 293–295.

FURTHER DISCUSSION QUESTIONS

### John Hayward's Description of Elizabeth's Coronation

1. According to the author, wherein did the secret of government reside? Does it still hold good today?
2. What attributes of leadership did Elizabeth display during her coronation procession that might have helped her throughout her reign?

### John Hayward's Description of Elizabeth's Speech to Parliament in 1559

1. What is the tenor of Elizabeth's message to parliament? How does she convey that message?
2. What is her view of royal authority and the proper role of parliament?
3. Why did Elizabeth like the "suit" of parliament? How did she answer that "suit"?

### Freedom of Speech: Peter Wentworth's Speechs of 1576 and 1587; and the Queen's Statement of 1593

1. Why, according to Wentworth, is the prince obliged to support and defend free speech in the House?
2. What happens to the doctrine of the divinity of kings in the hands of Wentworth?
3. What fault does Wentworth find in the Queen?
4. According to Wentworth, how is it possible to unite the glory of God and loyal service to the prince?
5. What are the consequences of Wentworth's questioning the authority of the Speaker of the House of Commons?
6. What is Elizabeth's definition of free speech, and how does it differ from Wentworth's?
7. What, according to the Queen, is the proper behavior of a member of the House of Commons? What is her opinion of the Lower House?

### The Debate in the House of Commons Over Monopolies

1. What is Francis Bacon's definition of the prerogative power? What is his defense of monopolies?
2. What are the constitutional implications of Laurence Hide's defense of his bill?
3. What is the basis of Francis Moore's attack on monopolies?
4. Why is Mr. Secretary Cecil opposed to the bill?

### Elizabeth's Letter to James VI of Scotland

1. What does Elizabeth suggest James should have done?
2. What is the view of kingship expressed in the letter?
3. What is the thing that kings should fear most? Do you agree?
4. Is there any evidence that Elizabeth in her own kingdom ever practiced what she preaches in this letter?

### Roger Wilbraham's Comparison of Elizabeth and James I

1. In what ways are James and Elizabeth similar or different?
2. What future problems does Wilbraham hint at in his comparison?
3. Who, according to Wilbraham, appears to be the better sovereign?

### James's First Speech to Parliament

1. What is James's apology? On what grounds does he excuse himself?
2. What kind of ruler would you anticipate James to be on the basis of his speech?
3. How effective as a first speech to parliament would you judge James's address to have been?

### The Apology of the House of Commons

1. How does the Apology differ from the claims made by Peter Wentworth and those suggested in the debate over monopolies?
2. What reasons does the House of Commons give for issuing the Apology?
3. What claims is the House of Commons making about religion and the king's authority as Supreme Governor of the church?
4. What does the Commons conceive its first duty to be?
5. How would Elizabeth have reacted to the Apology?

### James's Speech to Parliament in 1610

1. Why is it wrong to dispute with a king in "the height of his power"? What do you think James meant by the phrase?
2. What should parliament avoid in the matter of grievances and why?
3. How would Elizabeth have reacted to James's speech?

# 14

## The Great Rebellion

Serious as the political crisis had been under James I, both sides had exercised restraint and refrained from extreme claims; the ancient constitution of king in parliament still stood. By the time the first two documents in this chapter were written the polarization of thought and the spiral of mutual suspicion between king and parliament had reached revolutionary proportions, and the kingdom was on the brink of war. The first selection, the Nineteen Propositions, was penned in June of 1642, two months before Charles I raised his standard at Nottingham on August 22, 1642. The propositions were presented to the King as a basis for negotiation between the two elements of the constitution; they were rejected by Charles out-of-hand for reasons that will be clear to anyone who compares them to the Apology of the Commons of 1604. Charles's rejection was predictable, but not his arguments for doing so, and his Answer to the Nineteen Propositions should be read in the light both of what Elizabeth and James I had maintained and of the government that would eventually emerge after the Glorious Revolution of 1688–1689. Charles spoke his mind about the English constitution and the proper role of the crown on a second occasion, when he was being tried for his life in January, 1649. Seven years of violence and war had resulted in the total defeat of his army and the abolition of both the crown and the House of Lords. Nothing remained except the House of Commons, and it was a "rump" of its former self. Charles stood trial for his crimes against "the people of the Commonwealth of England," and his defiance of the authority of the court that had been established by the House of Commons to judge him goes to the core of the constitutional controversy and raises profound questions about the nature of law and the rule of force. Possibly no speech better sums up the lessons that were eventually learned and that became the rationale for the restoration of the monarchy in 1660 and for the political settlement of 1688–1689.

"Charles I was a Cavalier King and therefore had a small pointed head, long flowing curls, a large, flat, flowing hat and *gay attire*. The Roundheads, on the other hand, were clean-shaven and wore tall, comical hats, white ties and *somber garments*. In these circumstances, a Civil War was inevitable."

Civil war and rebellion were nothing new to England; nor was the violent death of kings — at least a half dozen had been murdered or killed in battle since the Norman Conquest in 1066. But the abolition of the monarchy and the legal execution of the sovereign in the name of law were unprecedented actions, and almost from the moment the fighting ceased, the agonizing analysis began. Why had the kingdom been led to such straits that Englishmen were induced to slaughter Englishmen and loyal subjects had ended by executing their king? To the victor belongs the right of interpretation, but unfortunately in the English Civil War it was never absolutely clear who were the victors. Indeed, it turned out that the longest, most thorough, and, in many ways, best account of the Great Rebellion was written by a parliamentarian turned royalist, Edward Hyde, who was created Earl of Clarendon in 1660. Born in 1609, Hyde was a member of the Long Parliament, and until 1641, he was an opponent of absolute monarchy and Charles's "eleven year tyranny." After the trial and execution of the Earl of Strafford, however, he became alarmed by the growing extremism in the House of Commons, and in defense of church and crown he swung over into the royalist camp. During the war he became one of Charles's counsellors and young Prince Charles's chief adviser. He went into exile with the prince and is often given credit for engineering the moderate terms of Charles II's restoration in 1660. He became Lord Chancellor, and until the fiasco of the first Dutch War in 1667 was Charles's chief minister. On his fall from power he went into exile where he began his multivolume history. Drawing from memory, notes, and personal correspondence, Hyde put together a masterful account of the war which, although not entirely free from self-justification, judiciously balanced class interest, political ambition, and human failing as the underlying forces that produced the war. Hyde's analysis of Charles I's character remains the most informed and penetrating account we possess of the man who was described by his opponents as "the grand delinquent of England" and by his supporters as a semidivine martyr to his cause. Either way, Charles's responsibility for the war is one of the central problems of English seventeenth-century historiography.

The second historian of the war, Lucy Hutchinson (1620–?), belonged on the winning side, and her account of the war years is taken from her *Memoirs* of her husband, John Hutchinson (1615–1664), who was a colonel in Cromwell's New Model Army and ended his days after the restoration in a royal prison. Lucy, as the daughter of the Lieutenant of the Tower of London, was brought up in the height of early Stuart fashion, thinking it no sin to "learn or hear witty songs and amorous sonnets." As the years went on, she became a more and more rigid and devout Puritan, and her interpretation of English history clearly reflects her religious bias. For Lucy, the blame for what happened was easily placed, and her understanding of historical causation was clear and straightforward.

The third interpretation was written by one of the most important political thinkers of the century, Thomas Hobbes (1588–1679). A clergyman's son and a graduate of Oxford, Hobbes was a schoolteacher who earned his living by tutoring the children of the aristocracy and accompanying them on their grand tours of Europe. He left England in 1641, predicting that the extremists in parliament would plunge the country into war. While in voluntary exile, he wrote his most enduring treatise, the *Leviathan*, extracts from which will appear in Chapters 15 and 16. In theory a defense of the monarchy, the *Leviathan* outraged almost every royalist for its brutally secular approach to the nature of power, justice, law, and society. Hobbes elected to return to England in 1651, where he remained, despite the vicissitudes of politics, until his death at the age of ninety-one, always protected by a handful of powerful patrons (including Charles II) who admired his intellect but who found it impolitic or morally reprehensible to advocate his political philosophy. Hobbes wrote his history of the events from 1640 to 1660, entitled *Behemoth or the Epitome of the Civil Wars of England*, in 1668, but no one cared to publish it until after his death. In it he systematically and ruthlessly analyzed by means of a dialogue exactly how a 600-year-old monarchy had been destroyed in a matter of decades.

The fourth writer, like Hobbes, is difficult to place politically, for if Hobbes was a monarchist detested by most royalists and Edward Hyde was a parliamentarian turned royalist, James Harrington (1611–1677) was a moderate republican who succeeded in combining a close friendship with Charles I with radical political ideas. As a consequence, he got into trouble with both sides, despite his efforts to remain out of politics. In *The Commonwealth of Oceana*, which he wrote in 1656, he developed the concept of the perfect state based on a balance between economic interests (property) and political power. His ideal republic was in effect a self-interested aristocracy limited by history and practicality, and his model was Venice of the seventeenth century. His analysis of the long-term social and economic causes underlying the Great

Rebellion has a very modern flavor, for he sought and found the sources of historic change and political stability, whether monarchical or republican, in the structure of society and the interrelationship of its parts.

The final document is both an interpretation of the Great Rebellion and a conclusion to the revolutionary era. Written in 1659 by an anomymous radical commentator, *A True State of the Case of the Commonwealth* makes rewarding reading, for the student can see the steady drift back to a more conservative and historic position, which culminated in the Restoration of 1660.

## The Nineteen Propositions ( 1642 )

The Nineteen Propositions were composed in June, 1642, two months before the Civil War broke out. Although the Propositions asserted the absolute supremacy of parliament in practice, like so many other important English constitutional documents, they did not claim that supremacy in theory. The language of the Propositions must have been particularly galling to King Charles.

Here follows the petition and propositions sent to the king, as they are agreed on by both houses of parliament: *videlicet,*

Your majesty's most humble and faithful subjects, the lords and commons in parliament, having nothing in their thoughts and desires more precious, and of higher esteem, next to the honor and immediate service of God, than the just and faithful performance of their duty to your majesty and this kingdom, ... do, in all humility and sincerity, present to your majesty their most dutiful petition and advice, that, out of your princely wisdom, for the establishing of your own honor and safety, and gracious tenderness of the welfare and security of your subjects and dominions, you will be pleased to grant and accept these their humble desires and propositions, as the most necessary and effectual means, through God's blessing, of removing those jealousies and differences, which have unhappily fallen betwixt you and your people, and procuring both your majesty and them a constant course of honor, peace, and happiness.

1. First, that the lords and others of your majesty's privy council, and such great officers and ministers of state either at home or beyond the seas, may be put from your privy council, and from those offices and employments, excepting such as shall be approved of by both houses of parliament; and that the persons put into the places and employments of those that are removed, may be approved of by both houses of parliament; and that all privy councillors shall take an oath for the due execution of their places, in such form as shall be agreed upon by both houses of parliament.

2. That the great affairs of the kingdom may not be concluded or transacted by the advice of private men, or by any unknown or unsworn councillors; but that such matters as concern the public, and are proper for the high court of parliament, which is your Majesty's great and Supreme Council, may be debated, resolved, and transacted, only in parliament, and not elsewhere; and such as shall presume to do anything to the contrary shall be reserved to the censure and judgment of Parliament; and such other matters of state as are proper for your majesty's privy council shall be debated and concluded by such of the nobility and others as shall, from time to time, be chosen for that place, by approbation of both houses

SOURCE: From *Journals of the House of Lords*, Vol. V, pp. 97–99.

of parliament; and that no public act, concerning the affairs of the kingdom, which are proper for your privy council, may be esteemed of any validity, as proceeding from the royal authority, unless it be done by the advice and consent of the major part of your council, attested under their hands; and that your council may be limited to a certain number, not exceeding twenty-five, nor under fifteen; and if any councillor's place happen to be void in the intervals of parliament, it shall not be supplied without the assent of the major part of the council, which choice shall be confirmed at the next sitting of the parliament, or else to be void.

3. That the lord high steward of England, lord high constable, lord chancellor, or lord keeper of the great seal, lord treasurer, lord privy seal, earl marshal, lord admiral, warden of the cinque ports, chief governor of Ireland, chancellor of the exchequer, master of the wards, secretaries of state, two chief justices, and chief baron, may always be chosen with the approbation of both houses of parliament; and, in the intervals of parliaments, by assent of the major part of the council. . . .

4. That he or they, unto whom the government and education of the king's children shall be committed, shall be approved of by both houses of parliament; . . . and that all such servants as are now about them, against whom both houses shall have any just exception, shall be removed.

5. That no marriage shall be concluded or treated, for any of the king's children, with any foreign prince, or other person whatsoever, abroad or at home, without the consent of parliament, . . . and that the said penalty shall not be pardoned, or dispensed with, but by the consent of both houses of parliament.

6. That the laws in force against Jesuits, priests, and popish recusants, be strictly put in execution without any toleration or dispensation to the contrary. . . .

7. That the votes of popish lords in the house of peers may be taken away, so long as they continue papists; and that his majesty would consent to such a bill as shall be drawn, for the education of the children of papists, by protestants, in the protestant religion.

8. That your majesty would be pleased to consent, that such a reformation be made of the church government and liturgy, as both houses of parliament shall advise; . . . and that your majesty will be pleased to give your consent to laws for the taking away of innovations and superstitions, and of pluralities, and against scandalous ministers.

9. That your majesty will be pleased to rest satisfied with that course that the lords and commons have appointed, for ordering the militia, until the same shall be further settled by a bill. . . .

10. That such members of either house of parliament as have, during this present parliament, been put out of any place and office, may either be restored to that place and office or otherwise have satisfaction for the same. . . .

11. That all privy councillors and judges may take an oath, the form whereof to be agreed on and settled by act of parliament, for the maintaining of the Petition of Right. . . .

12. That all the judges, and all officers placed by approbation of both houses of parliament, may hold their places *quamdiu bene se gesserint.*[1]

13. That the justice of parliament may pass upon all delinquents, whether they be within the kingdom, or fled out of it; and that all persons cited by either house of parliament may appear, and abide the censure of parliament.

14. That the general pardon offered by your majesty may be granted, with such exceptions as shall be advised by both houses of parliament.

15. That the forts and castles of this kingdom may be put under the command and custody of such persons as your maj-

---

[1] during good behavior

esty shall appoint, with the approbation of your parliament; and, in the intervals of parliament, with approbation of the major part of the council, . . .

16. That the extraordinary guards and military forces now attending your majesty may be removed and discharged; and that, for the future, you will raise no such guards or extraordinary forces, but, according to the law, in case of actual rebellion or invasion.

17. That your majesty will be pleased to enter into a more strict alliance with the States of the United Provinces, and other neighbor princes and states of the protestant religion. . . .

18. That your majesty will be pleased, by act of parliament, to clear the Lord Kimbolton, and the Five Members of the house of commons, . . .

19. That your majesty will be graciously pleased to pass a bill, for restraining peers made hereafter from sitting or voting in parliament, unless they be admitted thereunto with the consent of both houses of parliament.

And these our humble desires being granted by your majesty, we shall forthwith apply ourselves to regulate your present revenue, in such sort as may be for your best advantage; and likewise to settle such an ordinary and constant increase of it, as shall be sufficient to support your royal dignity in honor and plenty, beyond the proportion of any former grants of the subjects of this kingdom to your majesty's royal predecessors; . . . and cheerfully employ to the uttermost our power and endeavor, in the real expression and performance of our most dutiful and loyal affections, to the preserving and maintaining the royal honor, greatness, and safety of your majesty and your posterity.

## Charles I's Answer to the Nineteen Propositions (1642)

Charles's response to the Nineteen Propositions is much more theoretical in conception than parliament's challenge to royal authority, for his answer describes the nature of the "true" and historic constitution as the King perceived it.

There being three kinds of government among men, absolute monarchy, aristocracy and democracy, and all these having their particular conveniences and inconveniences. The experience and wisdom of your ancestors hath so moulded this [present government] out of a mixture of these, as to give to this kingdom (as far as human prudence can provide) the conveniences of all three, without the inconveniences of any one, as long as the balance hangs even between the three estates, and they run jointly on in their proper channel. . . .

In this kingdom the laws are jointly made by a king, by a house of peers, and by a house of commons chosen by the people, all having free votes and particular privileges. The government according to these laws is entrusted to the king: power of treaties of war and peace, of making peers, of choosing officers and counsellors for state, judges for law, commanders for forts and castles; giving commissions for raising men; to make war abroad, or to prevent or provide against invasions or insurrections at home; benefit of confiscations, power of pardoning, and some more of the like kind are placed in the king. And this kind of regulated monarchy, having this power to preserve that authority, without which it would be disabled to preserve the laws in their force and the subjects in their liberties

SOURCE: From John Rushworth, *Historical Collections* (London: 1680–1722), Vol. VII, pp. 1403–732.

and properties, is intended to draw to him such a respect and relation from the great ones as may hinder the ills of division and faction; and such a fear and reverence from the people as may hinder tumults, violence and licentiousness.

Again, that the prince may not make use of this high and perpetual power to the hurt of those for whose good he hath it, and make use of the name of public necessity for the gain of his private fortunes and followers, to the detriment of his people, the House of Commons (an excellent conserver of liberty, but never intended for any share in government or the choosing of them that should govern) is solely entrusted with the first propositions concerning the levies of moneys . . . and the impeaching of those, who for their own ends . . . have violated that law, which he[2] is bound (when he knows it) to protect. . . . And the Lords being trusted with a judicatory power are an excellent screen and blank between the prince and people, to assist each against any encroachments of the other, and by just judgments to preserve that law which ought to be the rule of every one of the three . . .

Since, therefore, the power legally placed in both houses is more than sufficient to prevent and restrain the power of tyranny; and [since] without the power which is now asked from us we shall not be able to discharge that trust which is the end of monarchy; since this would be a total subversion of the fundamental laws and that excellent constitution of this kingdom . . . ; since to the power of punishing (which is already in your hands according to law) if the power of preferring be added, we shall have nothing left to us but to look on; since the encroaching of one of these estates upon the power of the other is unhappy in the effects, . . . : for all these reasons to all these demands our answer is *nolumus leges Angliae mutari*.[3] . . .

## Charles I's Defiance of the Court Set Up by Parliament to Try Him (January, 1649)

By January, 1649, the constitutional crisis was reaching its climax. Commons had declared itself to "have the supreme power in this nation" and whatever it enacted had "the force of law . . . although the consent of the King or the House of Peers be not had thereunto." On the basis of that authority, 135 commissioners met on January 20 as a court to try a monarch whose royal office had already been outlawed as "unnecessary, burdensome and dangerous" to the Commonwealth of England. Consequently, when the trial began, the court insisted it was trying not a king but a private gentleman by the name of Charles Stuart, Esquire. In answering the authority of the court, Charles went to the root of the situation: He had law and history on his side; the court had power. In the end, Charles was found guilty of high treason against the "people of England" and was executed on Sunday, January 30, 1649.

Having already made my protestations, not only against the illegality of this pretended Court, but also, that no earthly power can justly call me (who am your King) in question as a delinquent, I would not any more open my mouth upon this occasion, more

SOURCE: From John Rushworth, *Historical Collections* (London: 1680–1722), Vol. IV, pp. 731–1404.

[2] the prince  [3] We do not wish the laws of England to be changed. . . .

than to refer myself to what I have spoken, were I in this case alone concerned: but the duty I owe to God in the preservation of the true liberty of my people will not suffer me at this time to be silent: for, how can any free-born subject of England call life or anything he possesseth his own, if power without right daily make new, and abrogate the old fundamental laws of the land which I now take to be the present case? Wherefore when I came hither, I expected that you would have endeavored to have satisfied me concerning these grounds which hinder me to answer to your pretended impeachment. But since I see that nothing I can say will move you to it (though negatives are not so naturally proved as affirmatives) yet I will show you the reason why I am confident you cannot judge me, nor indeed the meanest man in England: for I will not (like you) without showing a reason, seek to impose a belief upon my subjects.

There is no proceeding just against any man, but what is warranted, either by God's laws or the municipal laws of the country where he lives. Now I am most confident this day's proceeding cannot be warranted by God's laws; for, on the contrary, the authority of obedience unto Kings is clearly warranted, and strictly commanded in both the Old and New Testament, which, if denied, I am ready instantly to prove.

And for the question now in hand, there it is said, that "where the word of a King is, there is power; and who may. say unto him, what dost thou?" Eccles. viii. 4. Then for the law of this land, I am no less confident, that no learned lawyer will affirm that an impeachment can lie against the King, they all going in his name: and one of their maxims is, that the King can do no wrong. Besides, the law upon which you ground your proceedings, must either be old or new: if old, show it; if new, tell what authority, warranted by the fundamental laws of the land, hath made it, and when. But how the House of Commons can erect a Court of Judicature, which was never one itself (as is well known to all

lawyers) I leave to God and the world to judge. And it were full as strange, that they should pretend to make laws without King or Lords' House, to any that have heard speak of the laws of England.

And admitting, but not granting, that the people of England's commission could grant your pretended power, I see nothing you can show for that; for certainly you never asked the question of the tenth man in the kingdom, and in this way you manifestly wrong even the poorest ploughman, if you demand not his free consent; nor can you pretend any color for this your pretended commission, without the consent at least of the major part of every man in England of whatsoever quality or condition, which I am sure you never went about to seek, so far are you from having it. Thus you see that I speak not for my own right alone, as I am your King, but also for the true liberty of all my subjects, which consists not in the power of government, but in living under such laws, such a government, as may give themselves the best assurance of their lives, and property of their goods. . . . Then for anything I can see, the higher House is totally excluded; and for the House of Commons, it is too well known that the major part of them are detained or deterred from sitting; so as if I had no other, this were sufficient for me to protest against the lawfulness of your pretended Court. Besides all this, the peace of the kingdom is not the least in my thoughts; and what hope of settlement is there, so long as power reigns without rule or law, changing the whole frame of that government under which this kingdom hath flourished for many hundred years? (nor will I say what will fall out in case this lawless, unjust proceeding against me do go on) and believe it, the Commons of England will not thank you for this change; . . . and by this time it will be too sensibly evident, that the arms I took up were only to defend the fundamental laws of this kingdom against those who have supposed my power hath totally changed the ancient government.

Thus, having showed you briefly the

reasons why I cannot submit to your pretended authority, without violating the trust which I have from God for the welfare and liberty of my people, I expect from you either clear reasons to convince my judgment, showing me that I am in an error (and then truly I will answer) or that you will withdraw your proceedings. . . .

## Edward Hyde, Earl of Clarendon, Remembers Charles I (ca. 1669)

Edward Hyde, although partial to Charles and to the theory of kingship, gives a provocative analysis of the King's character.

But it will not be unnecessary to add a short character of his person, that posterity may know the inestimable loss which the nation then underwent, in being deprived of a prince, whose example would have had a greater influence upon the manners and piety of the nation, than the most strict laws can have. To speak first of his private qualifications as a man, before the mention of his princely and royal virtues; he was, if ever any, the most worthy of the title of an honest man; so great a lover of justice, that no temptation could dispose him to a wrongful action, except it was so disguised to him that he believed it to be just. He had a tenderness and compassion of nature, which restrained him from ever doing a hardhearted thing: and therefore he was so apt to grant pardon to malefactors, that the judges of the land represented to him the damage and insecurity to the public, that flowed from such his indulgence. And then he restrained himself from pardoning either murders or highway robberies, and quickly discerned the fruits of his severity by a wonderful reformation of those enormities. He was very punctual and regular in his devotions; he was never known to enter upon his recreations or sports, though never so early in the morning, before he had been at public prayers; so that on hunting days his chaplains were bound to a very early attendance. He was likewise very strict in observing the hours of his private cabinet devotions; and was so severe an exactor of gravity and reverence in all mention of religion, that he could never endure any light or profane word, with what sharpness of wit soever it was covered: and though he was well pleased and delighted with reading verses made upon any occasion, no man durst bring before him any thing that was profane or unclean. That kind of wit had never any countenance then. He was so great an example of conjugal affection, that they who did not imitate him in that particular durst not brag of their liberty: and he did not only permit, but direct his bishops to prosecute those scandalous vices, in the ecclesiastical courts, against persons of eminence, and near relation to his service.

His kingly virtues had some mixture and allay, that hindered them from shining in full lustre, and from producing those fruits they should have been attended with. He was not in his nature very bountiful, though he gave very much. This appeared more after the duke of Buckingham's death, after which those showers fell very rarely; and he paused too long in giving, which made those, to whom he gave, less sensible of the benefit. He kept state to the full, which made his court very orderly; no man presuming to be seen in a place where he had no pretence to be. He saw and observed men long, before he received them about his person; and did not love strangers; nor very confident men. He was a patient hearer of causes; which he frequently accustomed himself to at the council board; and judged

SOURCE: From Edward Hyde, Earl of Clarendon, *History of the Great Rebellion and Civil War in England* (Oxford, England: Clarendon Press, 1826), Vol. VI, pp. 236–241.

very well, and was dexterous in the mediating part: so that he often put an end to causes by persuasion, which the stubbornness of men's humours made dilatory in courts of justice.

He was very fearless in his person; but, in his riper years, not very enterprising. He had an excellent understanding, but was not confident enough of it; which made him oftentimes change his own opinion for a worse, and follow the advice of men that did not judge so well as himself. This made him more irresolute than the conjuncture of his affairs would admit: if he had been of a rougher and more imperious nature, he would have found more respect and duty. And his not applying some severe cures to approaching evils proceeded from the lenity of his nature, and the tenderness of his conscience, which, in all cases of blood, made him choose the softer way, and not hearken to severe counsels, how reasonably soever urged. This only restrained him from pursuing his advantage in the first Scottish expedition, when, humanly speaking, he might have reduced that nation to the most entire[4] obedience that could have been wished. But no man can say he had then many who advised him to it, but the contrary, by a wonderful indisposition all his council had to the war, or any other fatigue. He was always a great lover of the Scottish nation, having not only been born there, but educated by that people, and besieged by them always, having few English about him till he was king; and the major number of his servants being still of that nation, who he thought could never fail him. And among these, no man had such an ascendant over him, by the humblest insinuations, as duke Hamilton had.

As he excelled in all other virtues, so in temperance he was so strict, that he abhorred all debauchery to that degree, that, at a great festival solemnity, where he once was, when very many of the nobility of the English and Scots were entertained, being told by one who withdrew from thence, what vast draughts of wine they drank, and "that there was one earl, who had drank most of the rest down, and was not himself moved or altered," the king said, "that he deserved to be hanged;" and that earl coming shortly after into the room where his majesty was, in some gayety, to shew how unhurt he was from that battle, the king sent one to bid him withdraw from his majesty's presence; nor did he in some days after appear before him.

So many miraculous circumstances contributed to his ruin, that men might well think that heaven and earth conspired it. Though he was, from the first declension of his power, so much betrayed by his own servants, that there were very few who remained faithful to him, yet that treachery proceeded not always from any treasonable purpose to do him any harm, but from particular and personal animosities against other men. And, afterwards, the terror all men were under of the parliament, and the guilt they were conscious of themselves, made them watch all opportunities to make themselves gracious to those who could do them good; and so they became spies upon their master, and from one piece of knavery were hardened and confirmed to undertake another; till at last they had no hope of preservation but by the destruction of their master. And after all this, when a man might reasonably believe that less than a universal defection of three nations could not have reduced a great king to so ugly a fate, it is most certain, that, in that very hour when he was thus wickedly murdered in the sight of the sun, he had as great a share in the hearts and affections of his subjects in general, was as much beloved, esteemed, and longed for by the people in general of the three nations, as any of his predecessors had ever been. To conclude, he was the worthiest gentleman, the best master, the best friend, the best husband, the best father, and the best Christian, that the age in

---

[4] slavish

which he lived produced. And if he were not the greatest king, if he were without some parts and qualities which have made some kings great and happy, no other prince was ever unhappy who was possessed of half his virtues and endowments, and so much without any kind of vice.

---

LUCY HUTCHINSON, *Memoirs of the Life of Colonel Hutchinson* ( ca. 1664 )

Mrs. Hutchinson gives the historical background to the Civil War. Starting with the Reformation under Henry VIII, she traces the story through the religious and international crises of Elizabeth's reign, the growing corruption of government under James I, and the final persecution of the godly under Charles I.

---

When the dawn of the gospel began to break upon this isle, after the dark midnight of papacy, the morning was more cloudy here than in other places by reason of the state-interest, which was mixing and working itself into the interest of religion, and which in the end quite wrought it out. King Henry the Eighth, who, by his royal authority cast out the pope, did not intend the people of the land should have any ease of oppression; but only changed their foreign yoke for home-bred fetters, dividing the pope's spoils between himself and his bishops, who cared not for their father at Rome, so long as they enjoyed their patrimony and their honours here under another head: so that I cannot subscribe to those who entitle that king to the honour of the reformation. But even then there wanted not many who discerned the corruptions that were retained in the church and eagerly applied their endeavours to obtain a purer reformation; against whom, those — who saw no need of further reformation, either through excess of joy for that which was already brought forth, or else through a secret love of superstition rooted in their hearts thought this too much, — were bitterly incensed, and, hating that light which reproved their darkness, everywhere stirred up spirits of envy and persecution against them. Upon the great revolution which took place at the accession of Queen Elizabeth to the crown, the nation became divided into three great factions, the papists, the state protestants, and the more religious zealots, who afterwards were branded with the name of Puritans. In vain it was for these to address the queen and the parliament; for the bishops, under the specious pretences of uniformity and obedience, procured severe punishments to be inflicted on such as durst gainsay their determinations in all things concerning worship, whereupon some even in those godly days lost their lives.

England was not an idle spectator of the great contest between the papist and protestant, in which all Christendom seemed to be engaged. During the reign of Queen Elizabeth, the protestant interest, being her peculiar interest, that princess became not only glorious in the defence of her own realm, but in the protection she gave to the whole protestant cause in all the neighbouring kingdoms; wherefore, as if it had been devolved upon her person, the pope shot all his arrows at her head, and set on many desperate assassinations against her, which, by the good providence of God, were all frustrated, and she, not only miraculously delivered from those wretches, but re-

SOURCE: From Lucy Hutchinson, *Memoirs of the Life of Colonel Hutchinson* (London: George Bell & Sons, 1908), pp. 69–70, 75–81, 83–86, 88–90.

nowned at home and abroad for successes against her rebellious subjects in England and Ireland, and for the assistance of her distressed neighbours; but, above all, for the mercy which it pleased God to afford her and this realm in the year 1588, when the invading Spaniard had devoured us in his proud hopes, and by the mighty hand of God was scattered as a mist before the morning beams. That which kept alive the hopes of the papists, most part of her reign, was the expectation of the Queen of Scots, who, entering into confederacy with them, lost her head for the forfeit, wherein the duke of Norfolk suffered also for her the loss of his. The Queen of England was very loath to execute this necessary justice; but the true-hearted protestants of her council, foreseeing the sad effects that might be expected if ever she arrived to the crown, urged it on; and after the death of Queen Elizabeth, the wiser of them much opposed the admission of her son. But he, dissembling the resentment of his mother's death, by bribes and greater promises, managed a faction in the court of the declining queen, which prevailed on her dotage to destroy the Earl of Essex, the only person who would have had the courage to keep out him they thought it dangerous to let in. So subtlely brought they their purpose about, that wise counsel was in vain to a blinded and betrayed people. The anti-prelatical party hoping that, with a king bred up among the Calvinists, they should now be freed from the episcopal yoke, were greedy of entertaining him, but soon cured of their mistake; when, immediately after his entry into the kingdom, himself being moderator at a dispute between both parties, the nonconformists were cast out of doors, and the offensive ceremonies, instead of being removed, were more strictly imposed; the penalties against papists were relaxed, and many of them taken into favour; whilst those families who suffered for his mother were graced and restored as far as the times would bear, and those who consented any

way to the justice done upon her, disfavoured. A progress was made suitable to this beginning, the protestant interest abroad was deserted and betrayed, the prelates at home daily exalted in pride and pomp, and declining in virtue and godliness. . . .

The court of this king was a nursery of lust and intemperance; he had brought in with him a company of poor Scots, who, coming into this plentiful kingdom, were surfeited with riot and debaucheries, and got all the riches of the land only to cast away. The honour, wealth, and glory of the nation, wherein Queen Elizabeth left it, were soon prodigally wasted by this thriftless heir; and the nobility of the land was utterly debased by setting honours to public sale, and conferring them on persons that had neither blood nor merit fit to wear, nor estates to bear up their titles, but were fain to invent projects to pill[5] the people, and pick their purses for the maintenance of vice and lewdness. The generality of the gentry of the land soon learned the court fashion, and every great house in the country became a sty of uncleanness. To keep the people in their deplorable security, till vengeance overtook them, they were entertained with masks, stage plays, and various sorts of ruder sports. . . . The ministers warned the people of the approaching judgments of God, which could not be expected but to follow such high provocations; God in his mercy sent his prophets into all corners of the land, to preach repentance, and cry out against the ingratitude of England, who thus requited so many rich mercies that no nation could ever boast of more; and by these a few were every where converted and established in faith and holiness; but at court they were hated, disgraced, and reviled, and in scorn had the name of Puritan fixed upon them. . . .

The king had upon his heart the dealings both of England and Scotland with his mother, and harboured a secret desire of revenge upon the godly in both nations, yet

---

[5] plunder

had no courage enough to assert his resentment like a prince, but employed a wicked cunning he was master of, and called kingcraft, to undermine what he durst not openly oppose, — the true religion; this was fenced with the liberty of the people, and so linked together, that it was impossible to make them slaves, till they were brought to be idolaters of royalty and glorious lust; and as impossible to make them adore these gods, while they continued loyal to the government of Jesus Christ. The payment of civil obedience to the king and the laws of the land satisfied not; if any durst dispute his impositions in the worship of God, he was presently reckoned among the seditious and disturbers of the public peace, and accordingly persecuted; if any were grieved at the dishonour of the kingdom, or the griping of the poor, or the unjust oppressions of the subject, by a thousand ways, invented to maintain the riots of the courtiers, and the swarms of needy Scots the king had brought in to devour like locusts the plenty of this land, he was a puritan. . . . In short, all that crossed the views of the needy courtiers, the proud encroaching priests, the thievish projectors, the lewd nobility and gentry — whoever was zealous for God's glory or worship, could not endure blasphemous oaths, ribald conversation, profane scoffs, sabbath breaking, derision of the word of God, and the like — whoever could endure a sermon, modest habit or conversation, or anything good, — all these were puritans. . . . The king, grudging that his people should dare to gainsay his pleasure, and correct his misgovernment in his favourites, broke up parliaments, violated their privileges, imprisoned their members for things spoken in the house, and grew disaffected to them, and entertained projects of supply by other grievances of the people. The prelates, in the mean time, finding they lost ground, meditated reunion with the popish faction, who began to be at a pretty agreement with them; and now there was no more endeavour in their public

sermons to confute the errors of that church, but to reduce our doctrines and theirs to an accommodation. . . .

The face of the court was much changed in the change of the king, for King Charles was temperate, chaste, and serious; so that the fools and bawds, mimics and catamites,[6] of the former court, grew out of fashion; and the nobility and courtiers, who did not quite abandon their debaucheries, yet so reverenced the king as to retire into corners to practice them. Men of learning and ingenuity in all arts were in esteem, and received encouragement from the king, who was a most excellent judge and a great lover of paintings, carvings, gravings, and many other ingenuities, less offensive than the bawdry and profane abusive wit which was the only exercise of the other court. But, as in the primitive times, it is observed that the best emperors were some of them stirred up by Satan to be the bitterest persecutors of the church, so this king was a worse encroacher upon the civil and spiritual liberties of his people by far than his father. He married a papist, a French lady, of a haughty spirit, and a great wit and beauty, to whom he became a most uxorious husband. By this means the court was replenished with papists, and many who hoped to advance themselves by the change, turned to that religion. All the papists in the kingdom were favoured, and, by the king's example, matched into the best families; the puritans were more than ever discountenanced and persecuted. . . . The example of the French king was propounded to him, and he thought himself no monarch so long as his will was confined to the bounds of any law; but knowing that the people of England were not pliable to an arbitrary rule, he plotted to subdue them to his yoke by a foreign force, and till he could effect it, made no conscience of granting anything to the people, which he resolved should not oblige him longer than it served his turn; for he was a prince that had nothing of faith or truth, justice or

---

[6] boys kept for unnatural purposes

generosity, in him. He was the most obstinate person in his self-will that ever was, and so bent upon being an absolute, uncontrollable sovereign, that he was resolved either to be such a king or none. His firm adherence to prelacy was not for conscience of one religion more than another, for it was his principle that an honest man might be saved in any profession; but he had a mistaken principle that kingly government in the state could not stand without episcopal government in the church; and, therefore, as the bishops flattered him with preaching up his sovereign prerogative, and inveighing against the puritans as factious and disloyal, so he protected them in their pomp and pride, and insolent practises against all the godly and sober people of the land....

There were two above all the rest, who led the van of the king's evil counsellors, and these were Laud, archbishop of Canterbury, a fellow of mean extraction and arrogant pride, and the Earl of Strafford, who as much outstripped all the rest in favour as he did in abilities, being a man of deep policy, stern resolution, and ambitious zeal to keep up the glory of his own greatness.... But above all these the king had another instigator of his own violent purpose, more powerful than all the rest, and that was the queen, who, grown out of her childhood, began to turn her mind from those vain extravagancies she lived in at first, to that which did less become her, and was more fatal to the kingdom; which is never in any place happy where the hands which were made only for distaffs affect the management of sceptres. — If any one object the fresh example of Queen Elizabeth, let them remember that the felicity of her reign was the effect of her submission to her masculine and wise counsellors; but wherever male princes are so effeminate as to suffer women of foreign birth and different religions to intermeddle

with the affairs of state, it is always found to produce sad desolations; and it hath been observed that a French queen never brought any happiness to England. ... This lady being by her priests affected with the meritoriousness of advancing her own religion, whose principle it is to subvert all other, applied that way her great wit and parts, and the power her naughty spirit kept over her husband, who was enslaved in his affection only to her, though she had no more passion for him than what served to promote her designs. Those brought her into a very good correspondence with the archbishop and his prelatical crew, both joining in the cruel design of rooting the godly out of the land. The foolish protestants were meditating reconciliations with the church of Rome, who embraced them as far as they would go, carrying them in hand, as if there had been a possibility of bringing such a thing to pass; meanwhile they carried on their design by them, and had so ripened it, that nothing but the mercy of God prevented the utter subversion of protestantism in the three kingdoms. — But how much soever their designs were framed in the dark, God revealed them to his servants, and most miraculously ordered providences for their preservation. About the year 1639, the Scots, having the English service-book obtruded upon them violently, refused it, and took a national covenant against it, and entered England with a great army, to bring their complaints to the king, which his unfaithful ministers did, as they supposed, much misreport. The king himself levied an army against them, wherein he was assisted by the nobility and gentry, but most of all by the prelates, insomuch that the war got the name of *bellum episcopale*, or "bishops' war;" but the commonalty of the nation, being themselves under grievous bondage, were loath to oppose a people that came only to claim their just liberties. ...

## THOMAS HOBBES, *Behemoth*: (1668)

Thomas Hobbes explains how a monarchy, which had endured for six centuries, was destroyed from within by poison that spread out from the universities, undermining all sense of loyalty and social cohesion.

A. In the year 1640, the government of England was monarchical; and the King that reigned, Charles, the first of that name, holding the sovereignty by right of a descent continued above six hundred years, and from a much longer descent King of Scotland. . . .

B. How could he then miscarry, having in every county so many trained soldiers, as would, put together, have made an army of 60,000 men, and divers magazines of ammunition in places fortified?

A. If those soldiers had been, as they and all other of his subjects ought to have been, at his Majesty's command, the peace and happiness of the three kingdoms had continued as it was left by King James. But the people were corrupted generally, and disobedient persons esteemed the best patriot.

B. But sure there were men enough, besides those that were ill-affected, to have made an army sufficient to have kept the people from uniting into a body able to oppose him.

A. Truly, I think, if the King had had money, he might have had soldiers enough in England. For there were very few of the common people that cared much for either of the causes, but would have taken any side for pay or plunder. But the King's treasury was very low, and his enemies, that pretended the people's ease from taxes, and other specious things, had the command of the purses of the city of London, and of most cities and corporate towns in England, and of many particular persons besides.

B. But how came the people to be so corrupted: And what kind of people were they that did so seduce them?

A. The seducers were of divers sorts. One sort were ministers; ministers, as they called themselves, of Christ; and sometimes, in their sermons to the people, God's ambassadors; pretending to have a right from God to govern every one his parish, and their assembly the whole nation.

Secondly, there were a very great number, though not comparable to the other, which notwithstanding that the Pope's power in England, both temporal and ecclesiastical, had been by Act of Parliament abolished, did still retain a belief that we ought to be governed by the Pope, whom they pretended to be the vicar of Christ, and, in the right of Christ, to be the governor of all Christian people. And these were known by the name of Papists; as the ministers I mentioned before, were commonly called Presbyterians.

Thirdly, there were not a few, who in the beginning of the troubles were not discovered, but shortly after declared themselves for a liberty in religion, and those of different opinions one from another. Some of them, because they would have all congregations free and independent upon one another, were called Independents. Others that held baptism to infants, and such as understood not into what they are baptized, to be ineffectual, were called therefore Anabaptists. Others that held that Christ's kingdom was at this time to begin upon the earth, were called Fifth-monarchy-men; besides divers other sects, as Quakers,

SOURCE: From Thomas Hobbes, *Behemoth or the Epitome of the Civil Wars of England* in William Molesworth, ed., *The English Works* (London: John Bohn, 1840), Vol. VI, pp. 165–169, 212–213, 233, 236– 237.

Adamites, &c., . . . And these were the enemies which arose against his Majesty from the private interpretation of the Scripture, exposed to every man's scanning in his mother-tongue.

Fourthly, there were an exceeding great number of men of the better sort, that had been so educated, as that in their youth having read the books written by famous men of the ancient Grecian and Roman commonwealths concerning their polity and great actions; in which books the popular government was extolled by that glorious name of liberty, and monarchy disgraced by the name of tyranny; they became thereby in love with their forms of government. And out of these men were chosen the greatest part of the House of Commons, or if they were not the greatest part, yet by advantage of their eloquence, were always able to sway the rest.

Fifthly, the city of London and other great towns of trade, having in admiration the prosperity of the Low Countries after they had revolted from their monarch, the King of Spain, were inclined to think that the like change of government here, would to them produce the like prosperity.

Sixthly, there were a very great number that had either wasted their fortunes, or thought them too mean for the good parts they thought were in themselves; and more there were, that had able bodies, but saw no means how honestly to get their bread. These longed for a war, and hoped to maintain themselves hereafter by the lucky choosing of a party to side with, and consequently did for the most part serve under them that had greatest plenty of money.

Lastly, the people in general were so ignorant of their duty, as that not one perhaps of ten thousand knew what right any man had to command him, or what necessity there was of King or Commonwealth, for which he was to part with his money against his will; but thought himself to be so much master of whatsoever he possessed, that it could not be taken from him upon any pretence of common safety without his own consent. . . . And he was thought wisest and fittest to be chosen for a Parliament, that was most averse to the granting of subsidies or other public payments.

B. In such a constitution of people, methinks, the King is already ousted of his government, so as they need not have taken arms for it. For I cannot imagine how the King should come by any means to resist them.

A. There was indeed very great difficulty in the business. But of that point you will be better informed in the pursuit of this narration. . . .

A. Judge then, what kind of men such a multitude of ignorant people were like to elect for their burgesses and knights of shires.

B. I can make no other judgment, but that they who were then elected, were just such as had been elected for former Parliaments, and as are like to be elected for Parliaments to come. For the common people have been, and always will be, ignorant of their duty to the public, as never meditating any thing but their particular interest; in other things following their immediate leaders; which are either the preachers, or the most potent of the gentlemen that dwell amongst them. . . .

A. Why may not men be taught their duty, . . . and much more easily than any of those preachers and democratical gentlemen could teach rebellion and treason?

B. But who can teach what none have learned? . . .

A. . . . Many cannot read; many, though they can, have no leisure; and of them that have leisure, the greatest part have their minds wholly employed and taken up by their private businesses or pleasures. So that it is impossible that the multitude should ever learn their duty, but from the pulpit and upon holidays; but then, and from thence, it is, that they learned their disobedience. And, therefore, the light of that doctrine has been hitherto covered and kept under here by a cloud of adversaries, which no private man's reputation can break through, without the authority of the Universities. But out of the Universities, came all those preachers that taught the contrary. The Universities have been to this nation, as the wooden horse was to the Trojans. . . .

B. They must punish then the most of those that have had their breeding in the Universities. For such curious questions in divinity are first started in the Universities, and so are all those politic questions concerning the rights of civil and ecclesiastic government; and there they are furnished with arguments for liberty out of the works of Aristotle, Plato, Cicero, Seneca, and out of the histories of Rome and Greece, for their disputation against the necessary power of their sovereigns. Therefore I despair of any lasting peace amongst ourselves, till the Universities here shall bend and direct their studies to the settling of it, that is, to the teaching of absolute obedience to the laws of the King, and to his public edicts under the Great Seal of England. For I make no doubt, but that solid reason, backed with the authority of so many learned men, will more prevail for the keeping of us in peace within ourselves, than any victory can do over the rebels. But I am afraid that it is impossible to bring the Universities to such a compliance with the actions of state, as is necessary for the business.

A. . . . The core of rebellion, as you have seen by this, and read of other rebellions, are the Universities; which nevertheless are not to be cast away, but to be better disciplined: that is to say, that the politics there taught be made to be, as true politics should be, such as are fit to make men know, that it is their duty to obey all laws whatsoever that shall by the authority of the King be enacted, till by the same authority they shall be repealed; such as are fit to make men understand, that the civil laws are God's laws, as they that make them are by God appointed to make them and to make men know, that the people and the Church are one thing, and have but one head, the King; and that no man has title to govern under him, that has it not from him; that the King owes his crown to God only, and to no man, ecclesiastic or other; and that the religion they teach there, be a quiet waiting for the coming again of our blessed Saviour, and in the mean time a resolution to obey the King's laws, which also are God's laws. . . . When the Universities shall be thus disciplined, there will come out of them, from time to time, well-principled preachers, and they that are now ill-principled, from time to time fall away.

B. I think it a very good course, and perhaps the only one that can make our peace amongst ourselves constant. For if men know not their duty, what is there that can force them to obey the laws? An army, you will say. But what shall force the army? Were not the trained bands an army? Were they not the janissaries, that not very long ago slew Osman in his own palace at Constantinople? I am therefore of your opinion, both that men may be brought to a love of obedience by preachers and gentlemen that imbibe good principles in their youth at the Universities, and also that we never shall have a lasting peace, till the Universities themselves be in such manner, as you have said, reformed; and the ministers know they have no authority but what the supreme civil power gives them; and the nobility and gentry know that the liberty of a state is not an exemption from the laws of their own country, whether made by an assembly or by a monarch, but an exemption from the constraint and insolence of their neighbours.

## JAMES HARRINGTON, *The Commonwealth of Oceana* (1656)

James Harrington gives a very modern analysis of the social and economic instability that led to the collapse of the monarchy.

[Henry VII abased and impoverished the old nobility.] Henceforth the country-lives, and great tables of the nobility, which no longer nourished veins that would bleed for them, were fruitless and loathsome till they changed the air, and of princes became courtiers; where their revenues, never to have been exhausted by beef and mutton, were found narrow, whence followed racking rents, and at length sale of lands: the riddance through the statute of alienations being rendered far more quick and facile than formerly it had been through the new invention of entails.

To this it happened, that . . . the successor [Henry VIII] of that king, dissolving the abbeys, brought with the declining state of the nobility so vast a prey to the industry of the people, that the balance of the commonwealth was too apparently in the popular party, to be unseen by the wise council of queen Parthenia [Elizabeth], who converting her reign through the perpetual lovetricks that passed between her and her people into a kind of romance, wholly neglected the nobility. And by these degrees came the house of commons to raise that head, which since has been so high and formidable to their princes, that they have looked pale upon those assemblies. Nor was there any thing now wanting to the destruction of the throne, but that the people, not apt to see their own strength, should be put to feel it; when a prince, [Charles I] as stiff in disputes as the nerve of monarchy was grown slack, received that unhappy encouragement from his clergy which became his utter ruin. . . . It came to an irreparable breach; for the house of peers, which alone had stood in this gap, now sinking down between the king and the commons, showed that . . . the isthmus[7] broken. But a monarchy divested of its nobility, has no refuge under heaven but an army. Wherefore the dissolution of this government caused the war, not the war the dissolution of this government.

Of the king's success with his arms it is not necessary to give any further account, than that they proved as ineffectual as his nobility; but without a nobility or an army . . . there can be no monarchy. Wherefore what is there in nature that can arise out of these ashes, but a popular government, or a new monarchy to be erected by the victorious army?

To erect a monarchy, be it never so new . . . it must stand upon old principles; that is, upon a nobility or an army planted on a due balance of dominion; . . . and there is no standing for a monarchy unless it finds this balance, or makes it. If it finds it, the work's done to its hand: for, where there is inequality of estates, there must be inequality of power; and where there is inequality of power, there can be no commonwealth.[8] To make it, the sword must extirpate out of dominion all other roots of power, and plant an army upon that ground. . . . There must not only be confiscations, but confiscations to such a proportion as may answer to the work intended. . . .

To conclude, *Oceana*, or any other nation of no greater extent, must have a competent nobility, or is altogether incapable of monarchy: for where there is equality of estates, there must be equality of power: and where there is equality of power, there can be no monarchy. . . .

SOURCE: From John Harrington, *The Commonwealth of Oceana* in *The Oceana of James Harrington and His Other Works* . . . (London: John Toland, 1700), pp. 69–70, 72.

[7] the bridge between crown and commons   [8] republic

## A True State of the Case of the Commonwealth (1654)

The unknown author of the *Case of the Commonwealth* states clearly what many
Englishmen thought the Civil War was all about—not religion, not the conflict
of interest groups, not the corruption of government, but the desire for liberty.
He then explains why "the great Cause hitherto so happily upheld and maintained"
was lost and why it was necessary in December, 1653, to turn all "Power and
Authority" over to Oliver Cromwell.

Look over all the Declarations, Remonstrances, and Protestations made by either [King or parliament], and it will appear that we never fought against the King, as King; nor for the Parliament or Representative considered purely as such. . . . And therefore (we say) Government under this or that Form, was not the moving Cause of this great Controversy, but those common ends of safety and Freedom, for which all sorts of Governments were instituted and appointed. . . . This was the Soul that animated their whole Undertaking; which was not by them intended to quarrel at the Kingly Form then established, but to regulate the disorders and excesses of the King and his Government, and reduce him within the due bounds of Authority. . . . And seeing it was impossible to secure the Interest of Religion and Liberty, with respect had any longer to the King himself, he was utterly laid aside; the consideration of those great ends being superior to the dignity of his Person.

· · ·

As to the *Laws* and *Civil Rights* of the Nation; When the point of Law came into consideration in the House, the one Party was for pruning away its exuberances and superfluities; the other, for a hewing down of the main Body: The more sober Judgments were for a regulation of the Law, by making it more succinct, intelligible, and certain, as also to remedy the Abuses of it, and render it less tedious and chargeable to the People; yet nothing would serve the

other, but a total eradication of the old, and introduction of a new: And so the good old Laws of *England* (the Guardians of our lives and Fortunes) established with prudence, and confirmed by the experience of many ages and generations (the preservation whereof was a principal Ground of our late Quarrel with the King) having been once abolished, what could we have expected afterward, but an enthroning of arbitrary Power in the Seats of Judicature, and an exposing of our Lives, our Estates, our Liberties, and all that is dear unto us, as a Sacrifice to the boundless appetite of mere Will and Pleasure. For, it hath been said of old; *The Law is that which puts a difference between Good and Evil, between Just and Unjust: If you once take away the Law, all things will fall into a confusion; every man will become a Law unto himself.* . . . As for our parts, we in this Nation may easily perceive the event of such courses, having lived some years at the pleasure of a long-continued Parliament, who contrary to their Trust, and the nature of a Parliament (whose great work is to make Laws) took upon them ordinarily to administer Law and Justice, according to their own wills, and endeavored to perpetuate the Office of Administration in their own hands, against the will of the People: In which Acts of absolute and Lordly power, as they were followed to the heels by this last Assembly [Barebone's Parliament]; so these exceeded them in other dangerous attempts, which extended not only to the

SOURCE: From "A True State of the Case of the Commonwealth" from *The Puritan Revolution: A Documentary History* by Stuart E. Pratt. Copyright © 1968 by Stuart E. Pratt. Reprinted by permission of Doubleday & Company, Inc.

abolition of Law, but to the utter subversion of Civil Right and Property. For, there was a Party of men among them who assumed to themselves only the name of Saints, from which Title they excluded all others that were not of their Judgment and opinion, and therefore seeing it is a name that shall be had in everlasting honor; we are heartily sorry to have seen it so wretchedly abused in this Age of light and godliness, as that the pretense of it hath by some men been intended for a Rise to advantages of worldly Power and glory, above the rest of their brethren.

For what else could be the intention of those in the last House? who were no sooner met, but they would have waved the way of Call upon a human account, and generally made pretense to an extraordinary Call from *Christ* himself, and to take upon them to rule the Nation by virtue of a supposed Right of Saintship in themselves; and upon this principle would have laid the foundation of a new platform, which was to go under the name of a *Fifth Monarchy*, never to have an end, but to war with all other Powers, and break them in pieces. In order whereunto, that they might make way for this *Fifth Kingdom*, they said their party having wrested and fitted Scriptures for their turn, professed and declared abroad (and into this principle and persuasion they baptized all their Proselytes) that the Powers in being were all branches of the *Fourth Monarchy*, which must be rooted up and destroyed; whereupon they took the confidence not only to asperse and judge whole States and Governments, and prophesy their ruin, but did, as much as in them lay, devote them to destruction, and thereby prepare the spirits of the people to embrace any opportunity to follow them and put their designs in execution. So that if their design of setting up the *Fifth Monarchy* according to the dreams they had of it, had taken effect, wherein men could have had no other Right but what they must have derived from them and their Party; it is no hard matter to discern how the common Interest of this

Nation would have been swallowed up by a particular Faction. . . . And therefore seeing their design was of so high a nature, as it aimed at no less than the extirpation of Law, and Government itself, and of the main Rights and Interests of the People relating thereunto; it is the less needful to mention their intrenching upon other Rights which are of an inferior consideration, as in the matter of Tithes, and of Patronage and Presentation of Ministers to Livings: Concerning which we shall only say, that in this, as in all other things, nothing of moderation would content them. . . .

As concerning the *Army*, this being the great Impediment in the way of *their Monarchy*, they were not without their designs also upon it: which not being to be contended with by any open attempt, they proceeded towards it by other methods. For, when the necessary continuation of Assessments came to be debated in the House, they labored might and main (under specious pretenses) to have cast out the Bill, and so at once to have cut all the sinews of the Army and their subsistence, the only visible support of the Nation's security: the consequence whereof would have been an exposing of the Soldiery to Free-quarter and disorder, and thereby the Country to rapine; all supplies must have been cut off likewise from the Navy, and our Affairs and Friends left to sink or swim in *Ireland* and *Scotland*; yea, and all this at such a time of unusual danger and necessity, when *Scotland* was unquiet, the Commonwealth engaged with Enemies abroad, and forced to an extraordinary Charge for the maintenance of our Fleets at Sea, which are as the walls and bulwards of this Nation against Invasions of Foreigners. But the Bill of Assessments being past, and their intentions this way frustrated, their next method was to have altered the Government of the Army, and to have committed it to such hands as would have assisted them in their intended Transformations. . . . Nor did these men rest here: but not being able to serve their own wills and fantasies within the House, so easily as they desired; then they resolved to divide and separate themselves from the other Members, who followed them not in their excesses, and to constitute themselves into a Power distinct from them. To this end, they led off divers well-meaning Gentlemen of the House along with them, to private Meetings of their own appointment, upon pretense of seeking the Lord by prayer for direction. But, to the great dishonor of God, and profanation of his holy Ordinances, the use that was made of those Meetings by the Contrivers of them, was, only for the better carrying on of things that they had beforehand resolved to act. And in order thereto, they took liberty to arraign and condemn the persons and proceedings of their fellow Members, and provoked others to Remonstrate against them; saying, That if the House then sitting should send for them, they ought not to obey them. . . .

Things being at this pass, and the House (through these Proceedings) perfectly disjointed, and the two Parties wound up to such a height of animosity, that they were as much divided, as if they had been people of two distinct Nations, mutually contending for each other's Rights, it was in vain to look for a Settlement of this Nation from them thus constituted; but on the contrary, nothing else could be expected, but that the Commonwealth should sink under their hands, and the great Cause hitherto so happily upheld and maintained, be for ever lost, through their preposterous management of those Affairs wherewith they had been trusted. And therefore the major part of that Assembly being convinced, that they could sit no longer, without incurring the guilt of that destruction which was coming on the whole Land, did upon the 12th day of *December* 1653 by subscribing their Names to an Instrument in writing, resign up their Powers and Authorities to his now *Highness* (then Captain General of all the Forces of this Commonwealth) [Cromwell].

## FURTHER DISCUSSION QUESTIONS

### The Nineteen Propositions

1. How much of the royal prerogative is left by the Propositions?
2. What are the most "revolutionary" features of the Propositions?

### Charles I's Answer to the Nineteen Propositions

1. What, according to Charles, were the proper roles of the Lords and Commons?
2. Why does Charles argue the way he does? How might Henry VIII or Elizabeth have stated the case?

### Charles I's Defiance of the Court

1. How does Charles's argument differ from the case he presented against the Nineteen Propositions? Is he making a different claim?
2. Is there any truth in Charles's statement that his cause is the cause of all Englishmen?

### Edward Hyde Remembers Charles I

1. What qualities did Charles possess that may have helped cause the Civil War? Were they, in Hyde's estimation, good or bad characteristics?
2. How does Charles compare with Elizabeth and James as a human being and as a sovereign?
3. Whom does Hyde blame for the destruction of Charles?

### Lucy Hutchinson, Memoirs

1. What, according to Mrs. Hutchinson, were the forces at work that produced the Civil War and the destruction of the Stuart crown?
2. Does her explanation have anything in common with Hyde's?
3. How accurate is her history? What kind of history would you call it?
4. What is Mrs. Hutchinson's attitude toward women?

### Thomas Hobbes, Behemoth

1. To what does Hobbes attribute the fall of the monarchy? Who or what group was most to blame?
2. What, according to Hobbes, must be done to stop further rebellions?
3. Does Hobbes believe in the effectiveness of military force to keep a king on his throne?

### James Harrington, Oceana

1. To what does Harrington attribute the troubles of mid-seventeenth century England?
2. To what kind of modern historian is Harrington closest?
3. To what extent were the Tudor kings and queens themselves responsible, in Harrington's estimation, for the collapse of the monarchy under Charles?
4. What does Harrington mean when he says Charles had "no refuge under Heaven but an army"?
5. Compare and contrast Mrs. Hutchinson, Hobbes, and Harrington in their approach and explanation of what happened in the seventeenth century and in the Civil War.

### The Case of the Commonwealth

1. To what does the writer attribute the Great Rebellion and the overthrow of the monarchy?
2. What happened to the ideals of the rebellion as time went on?
3. Do the writer and Harrington have anything in common in their analyses of the situation?
4. What, according to the writer, is wrong about the advocates of the so-called "Fifth Monarchy"? Why are they dangerous, and why must Cromwell be given nearly absolute power?

# 15

# *Changing Perceptions of Society*

In the previous chapter contemporary historians agonized over the Great Rebellion, some seeing the hand of God, others, the consequences of evil men, and yet others hinting at, but never clearly articulating, the theme of the present chapter: upheavals in politics are produced by revolutions in perceptions about the nature of man, the role of God in society, and the purpose of government. Five political statements have been brought together; individually, each is the product of a particular historical situation; collectively, they are indicators of a fundamental revolution of the mind that had been taking place throughout the seventeenth century. The governmental-political aspects of the revolution are handled in this chapter, while the scientific, economic, and spiritual implications are reserved for the next and final chapter of the book.

The first document, *The True Law of Free Monarchies: or, the Reciprocall and Mutuall Dutie Betwixt a Free King and his Naturall Subjects*, is by James VI of Scotland (1566–1625). Written in 1598, five years before he succeeded Elizabeth on the English throne, it is the classic statement of the theory of the divine right of kings. James's views must be understood in terms of his experience as a sovereign of an exceedingly unruly feudal kingdom. The life expectancy of Scottish monarchs was not great, and James displayed his mettle by having survived for thirty-one years upon that unstable throne. Under the circumstances, it may not be surprising that he claimed God as his ally and proclaimed the freedom of monarchies.

The next statement is by a man who has already been introduced, Thomas Hobbes, the author of *Behemoth*. In 1651 Hobbes produced his most important and enduring work, the *Leviathan, or the Matter, Form and Power of a Commonwealth Ecclesiastical and Civil*. Like James, he wrote on the basis of personal experience, and the lesson of the Civil War seemed clear — the first requirement of any political institution is that it provide peace and security

to those over whom it possesses sovereignty. Hobbes was deeply influenced by the new science of Kepler and Galileo, and he endeavored to bring to political analysis the logic of mathematics and the theories of physical science. He sought to discover the nature and proper function of the commonwealth by breaking society down into its essential parts. Applying the scientific theory that matter is at all times in a state of motion, Hobbes argued that it is the nature of every human being to avoid the danger of collision (i.e., confrontation) with another individual and thereby to preserve himself from destruction. As he said, "the skill of making and maintaining commonwealths consists in certain rules, as doth arithmetic and geometry; not, as tennis-play, in practice." Here then is the birth of political science.

The third statement is an interesting example of radical political theorizing versus conservative "tennis-play." It consists of the Agreement of the People of October, 1647, and the ensuing debate among members of the military over the first article of the Agreement dealing with political representation. The kingdom in 1647 was without an effective sovereign because Charles was the captive of the parliamentary forces. The historic constitution was in shambles, a Presbyterian-dominated parliament was at loggerheads with a Congregationalist and radically-inclined army, and every political-religious group had its own notions about the proper government of the realm. The Agreement of the People was one of the more radical statments, expressing Leveller political opinion about the birthrights of Englishmen, the equality of representation, and the nature of sovereignty. It was supported by the rank and file and the lesser echelons of the New Model Army. The debates took place at Putney Church in the autumn of 1647, and the sides were clearly drawn as Oliver Cromwell, his son-in-law Henry Ireton, and the other grandees of the army, all men of property accustomed to ruling, were confronted by Major Rainborough and other regimental officers. The Agreement of the People, even in a modified form reissued in 1649, was never adopted by the military or by parliament. It does, however, reveal, along with the Putney debates, the gulf that had opened up between the historical ruling elite — be it military, parliamentary, Presbyterian, Anglican, or royalist — and those "fastastical fellows" who threatened property. The astute reader at this point might wish to turn back to the last document of the preceding chapter and reread *A True State of the Commonwealth.*

The most influential of the five political statements were John Locke's *Two Treatises of Government.* The second treatise, *An Essay Concerning the True Original, Extent and End of Civil-Government* (presented below in highly abbreviated form), became the key document for all liberal thought in the eighteenth and nineteenth centuries throughout the Western world. At one time the *Two Treatises* were regarded as a product and vindication of the Glorious Revolution, for they were published in 1690 and Locke wrote in his preface that he hoped his arguments would be "sufficient to establish the Throne of our great Restorer, our present King William; to make good his title, in the Consent of the People; . . . and to justify to the World the People of *England,* whose love of their just and natural Rights . . . saved the Nation when it was on the very birth of Slavery and Ruin." In fact, it is now known that the *Two Treatises* were written during the exclusion crisis of 1679–1681, when Locke was associated with the Earl of Shaftsbury and the Whig Party's efforts to abrogate Catholic James's rights to succeed to his brother's throne. What made Locke's work so enduring was its appeal to reason, common sense, and utility, which transcended the historical setting and politics of a particular society. The *Two Treatises* were immediately translated into French and then into Italian, German, and Swedish, and became the inspiration for the American Declaration of Independence.

The final selection is tennis playing in a particularly English style. Except for the change in royal personnel (which is a very large exception, indeed), the Glorious Revolution was embodied in a single, prosaic, and ambiguous document — An Act Declaring the Rights and Liberties of the Subject and Settling the Succession of the Crown (1689), better known as the Bill of Rights. It is clearly an historical document, looking backwards far more than it looks forwards, but it incorporates, if not openly states, those profound constitutional changes that set the stage for eighteenth-century England.

If the right questions are asked, the reader will be able to perceive in these five statements the immensity of the revolution in perception and in social-political orientation that had occurred during the seventeenth century. The questions that can be raised are endless, but for a start one might ponder the contrast between James, Hobbes, the Levellers, Locke, and the framers of the Bill of Rights in their views on human nature, the location and operation of sovereignty, the existence of a social contract, the nature of laws, and the existence of human rights. The reader might also compare their attitudes toward the unwashed multitude and what could be expected of the "common" people, their ideas about the role and necessity of God in the operation of society, and, finally, their assumptions in analyzing and framing the perfect society. One further comparison comes to mind: what would Sir Thomas More have thought of the ideas expressed in this chapter?

## James I on the Divinity of Kings (1598)

James I expounds on the theory of the divine right of kings. A monarch is responsible to God alone, and, therefore, subjects cannot rebel without breaking God's laws.

. . . In the coronation of our own kings, as well as of every Christian monarch, they give their oath, first to maintain the religion presently professed within their country, according to their laws, whereby it is established, and to punish all those that should press to alter or disturb the profession thereof. And next to maintain all the lovable and good laws made by their predecessors: to see them put in execution, and the breakers and violators thereof to be punished, according to the tenor of the same. And lasty, to maintain the whole country, and every state therein, in all their ancient priviledges and liberties, as well against all foreign enemies, as among themselves. And shortly to procure the weale and flourishing of his people, not only in maintaining and putting to execution the old lovable laws of the country, and by establishing of new (as necessity and evil manners will require) but by all other means possible to forsee and prevent all dangers that are likely to fall upon them, and to maintain concord, wealth, and civility among them, as a loving father and careful watchman, caring for them more than for himself, knowing himself to be ordained for them, and they not for him; and therefore countable to that great God who placed him as his lieutenant over them, upon the peril of his soul to procure the weale of both souls and bodies, as far as in him lieth, of all them that are committed to his charge. . . .

The King towards his people is rightly compared to a father of children, and to a head of a body composed of divers members, for as fathers, the good princes and magistrates of the people of God acknowledged themselves to their subjects. And for all other well ruled Commonwealths, the style of *pater patriae* was ever, and is commonly used to kings. And the proper office of a king towards his subjects agrees very well with the office of the head towards the body, and all members thereof; for from the head, being the seat of judgment, proceedeth the care and forsight of guiding and preventing all evil that may come to the body or any part thereof. The head cares for the body, so doeth the king for his people. As the discourse and direction flows from the head, and the execution according thereunto belongs to the rest of the members, everyone according to their office: so it is betwixt a wise prince and his people. . . .

And now first for the father's part (whose

SOURCE: From *A Trew Law of Free Monarchies; or The Reciprocall and Mutuall Dutie Betwixt a Free King and His Naturall Subjects* (London, 1642), pp. 4, 10, 14–16.

natural love to his children I described in the first part of this my discourse, speaking of the duty that kings owe to their subjects) consider, I pray you, what duty his children owe to him and whether upon any pretext whatsoever, it will not be thought monstrous and unnatural to his sons to rise up against him, to control him at their appetite, and when they think good to slew him or to cut him off and adopt to themselves any other they please in his room. . . .

[Are there, asks James, any good arguments for rebellion. He poses four possible arguments and demolishes each.] But the unhappy inequity of the time, which hath oft times given over good success to their treasonable attempts, furnisheth them the ground of their third objection. For, say they, the fortunate success that God hath so oft given to such enterprises proveth plainly by the practise that God favored the justness of their quarrel.

To the which I answer, that it is true indeed that all the success of battles, as well as other wor[l]dly things, lieth only in God's hand, and therefore it is that in the Scripture he takes to himself the style of God of Hosts. But upon that general to conclude that he ever gives victory to the just quarrel would prove the Philistines, and divers other neighbor enemies of the people of God, to have oft times had the just quarrel against the people of God, in respect of the many victories they obtained against them. . . . Therefore, as I said in the beginning, it is oft times a very deceivable argument, to judge of the cause by the event.

And the last objection is grounded upon the mutual paction[1] and adstipulation[2] (as they call it) betwixt the king and his people at the time of his coronation. For there, say they, there is a mutual paction and contract bound up and sworn betwixt the king and the people. Whereupon it followeth that if the one part of the contract or the indent be broken upon the king's side, the people are no longer bound to keep their part of it, but are thereby freed of their oath; for (say they) a contract betwixt two parties, of all law, frees the one party if the other break unto him.

As to this contract alledgedly made at the coronation of a king, although I deny any such contract to be made then, especially containing such a clause irritant as they alledge; yet I confess that a king at his coronation, or at the entry to his kingdom, willingly promiseth to his people to discharge honorably and truly the office given him by God over them. But presuming that thereafter he breaks his promise unto them never so inexcusable, the question is who should be judge of the break. . . . I think no man that hath but the smallest entrance into the civil law will doubt that of all law, either civil or municipal of any nation, a contract cannot be thought broken by the one party and so the other likewise to be freed therefore, except that first a lawful trial and cognition be had by the ordinary judge of the breakers thereof. Or else every man may be both party and judge in his own cause; which is absurd once to be thought. Now in this contract (I say) betwixt the king and his people, God is doubtless the only judge, both because to him only the king must make count of his administration (as is oft said before) as likewise by the oath in the coronation. . . . What justice then is it that the party shall be both judge and party, usurping upon himself the office of God, may by this argument easily appear. And shall it lie in the hands of headless multitude, when they please to weary of subjection, to cast off the yoke of government that God hath laid upon them, to judge and punish him whom by they should be judged and punished, and in that case, wherein by their violence they kythe[3] themselves to be most passionate parties, to use the office of an ungracious judge or arbiter? . . . And therefore since it is certain that a king, in case so it should fall out that his people in one body had rebelled against him, he should not in that

---

[1] to make a pact  [2] the addition of a second receiving party in a bargain  [3] show

case, as thinking himself free of his promise and oath, become an utter enemy and practice the wreak of his whole people and native country; although he ought justly to punish the principal authors and fellows of that universal rebellion. . . .

Not that by all this former discourse of mine, and apology for kings, I mean that whatsoever errors and intollerable abominations a sovereign prince commit, he ought to escape all punishment, as if thereby the world were only ordained for kings, and they without controlment to turn it upside down at their please; but by the contrary, by remitting them to God (who is their only ordinary judge) I remit them to the sorest and sharpest schoolmaster that can be devised for them. For the further a king is preferred by God above all other ranks and degrees of men, and the higher that his seat is above theirs, the greater is his obligation to his maker. . . .

## THOMAS HOBBES, *Leviathan* (1651)

Thomas Hobbes describes the condition of mankind in a state of nature and explains why the social contract is necessary to the creation of society and the maintenance of law and order.

### The Introduction

Nature, the art whereby God hath made and governs the world, is by the *art* of man, as in many other things, so in this also imitated, that it can make an artificial animal. For seeing life is but a motion of limbs, the beginning whereof is in some principal part within; why may we not say, that all *automata* (engines that move themselves by springs and wheels as doth a watch) have an artificial life? For what is the *heart*, but a *spring*; and the *nerves*, but so many *strings*; and the *joints*, but so many *wheels*, giving motion to the whole body, such as was intended by the artificer? *Art* goes yet further, imitating that rational and most excellent work of nature, *man*. For by art is created that great LEVIATHAN called a COMMONWEALTH, or STATE, in Latin CIVITAS, which is but an artificial man; though of greater stature and strength than the natural, for whose protection and defence it was intended; and in which the *sovereignty* is an artificial *soul*, as giving life and motion to the whole body; the *magistrates*, and other *officers* of judicature and execution, artificial *joints*; *reward* and *punishment*, by which fastened to the seat of the sovereignty every joint and member is moved to perform his duty, are the *nerves*, that do the same in the body natural; the *wealth* and *riches* of all the particular members, are the *strength*; *salus populi*, the people's safety, its *business*; *counsellors*, by whom all things needful for it to know are suggested unto it, are the *memory*; *equity*, and *laws*, an artificial *reason* and *will*; *concord*, health; *sedition*, *sickness*; and *civil war*, *death*. Lastly, the *pacts* and *covenants*, by which the parts of this body politic were at first made, set together, and united, resemble that *fiat*, or the *let us make man*, pronounced by God in the creation. . . .

### CHAPTER XIII

#### Of the Natural Condition of Mankind as Concerning their Felicity, and Misery

. . . So that in the nature of man, we find three principal causes of quarrel. First, competition; secondly, diffidence; thirdly, glory.

The first, maketh men invade for gain;

SOURCE: From Thomas Hobbes, *Leviathan or the Matter, Form, and Power of a Commonwealth Ecclesiastical and Civil* in *The English Works,* William Molesworth, ed. (London: John Bohn, 1839), Vol. III, pp. ix–x, 110–132, 146.

the second, for safety; and the third, for reputation. The first use violence, to make themselves masters of other men's persons, wives, children, and cattle; the second, to defend them; the third, for trifles, as a word, a smile, a different opinion, and any other sign of undervalue, either direct in their persons, or by reflection in their kindred, their friends, their nation, their profession, or their name.

Hereby it is manifest, that during the time men live without a common power to keep them all in awe, they are in that condition which is called war; and such a war, as is of every man, against every man. For WAR, consisteth not in battle only, or the act of fighting; but in a tract of time, wherein the will to contend by battle is sufficiently known: ... so the nature of war, consisteth not in actual fighting; but in the known disposition thereto, during all the time there is no assurance to the contrary. All other time is PEACE.

Whatsoever therefore is consequent to a time of war, where every man is enemy to every man; the same is consequent to the time, wherein men live without other security, than what their own strength, and their own invention shall furnish them withal. In such condition, there is no place for industry; because the fruit thereof is uncertain: and consequently no culture of the earth; no navigation, nor use of the commodities that may be imported by sea; no commodious building; no instruments of moving, and removing, such things as require much force; no knowledge of the face of the earth; no account of time; no arts; no letters; no society; and which is worst of all, continual fear, and danger of violent death; and the life of man, solitary, poor, nasty, brutish, and short. ...

The desires, and other passions of man, are in themselves no sin. No more are the actions, that proceed from those passions, till they know a law that forbids them: which till laws be made they cannot know: nor can any law be made, till they have agreed upon the person that shall make it. ...

But though there had never been any time, wherein particular men were in a condition of war one against another; yet in all times, kings, and persons of sovereign authority, because of their independency, are in continual jealousies, and in the state and posture of gladiators; having their weapons pointing, and their eyes fixed on one another; that is, their forts, garrisons, and guns upon the frontiers of their kingdoms; and continual spies upon their neighbours; which is a posture of war. ...

To this war of every man, against every man, this also is consequent; that nothing can be unjust. The notions of right and wrong, justice and injustice have there no place. Where there is no common power, there is no law: where no law, no injustice. Force, and fraud, are in war the two cardinal virtues. Justice, and injustice are none of the faculties neither of the body, nor mind. ... They are qualities, that relate to men in society, not in solitude. It is consequent also to the same condition, that there be no propriety, no dominion, no *mine* and *thine* distinct; but only that to be every man's, that he can get; and for so long, as he can keep it. And thus much for the ill condition, which man by mere nature is actually placed in; though with a possibility to come out of it, consisting partly in the passions, partly in his reason.

The passions that incline men to peace, are fear of death; desire of such things as are necessary to commodious living; and a hope by their industry to obtain them. And reason suggesteth convenient articles of peace, upon which men may be drawn to agreement. These articles, are they, which otherwise are called the Laws of Nature. ...

## CHAPTER XIV

### Of the First and Second Natural Laws, and of Contracts

The right of nature, which writers commonly call *jus naturale*, is the liberty each man hath, to use his own power, as he will himself, for the preservation of his own nature; that is to say, of his own life; and consequently, of doing any thing, which in his own judgment, and reason, he shall conceive to be the aptest means thereunto.

By LIBERTY, is understood, according to the proper signification of the word, the absence of external impediments: which impediments, may oft take away part of a man's power to do what he would; but cannot hinder him from using the power left him, according as his judgment, and reason shall dictate to him.

A LAW OF NATURE, *lex naturalis*, is a precept or general rule, found out by reason, by which a man is forbidden to do that, which is destructive of his life, or taketh away the means of preserving the same; and to omit that, by which he thinketh it may be best preserved. . . .

And because the condition of man, as hath been declared in the precedent chapter, is a condition of war of every one against every one: in which case every one is governed by his own reason; and there is nothing he can make use of, that may not be a help unto him, in preserving his life against his enemies; it followeth, that in such a condition, every man has a right to every thing; even to one another's body. And therefore, as long as this natural right of every man to every thing endureth, there can be no security to any man . . . and consequently it is a precept, or general rule of reason, *that every man, ought to endeavour peace, as far as he has hope of obtaining it; and when he cannot obtain it, that he may seek, and use, all helps, and advantages of war*. The first branch of which rule, containeth the first, and fundamental law of nature; which is, *to seek peace, and follow it*. The second, the sum of the right of nature; which is, *by all means we can, to defend ourselves*.

From this fundamental law of nature, by which men are commanded to endeavour peace, is derived this second law; *that a man be willing, when others are so too . . . for peace, and defence of himself he shall think it necessary, to lay down this right to*

*all things; and be contented with so much liberty against other men, as he would allow other men against himself*. For as long as every man holdeth this right, of doing any thing he liketh; so long are all men in the condition of war. But if other men will not lay down their right, as well as he; then there is no reason for any one, to divest himself of his: for that were to expose himself to prey, which no man is bound to. . . .

To *lay down* a man's *right* to any thing, is to *divest* himself of the *liberty*, of hindering another of the benefit of his own right to the same. For he that renounceth, or passeth away his right, giveth not to any other man a right which he had not before; because there is nothing to which every man had not right by nature: but only standeth out of his way, that he may enjoy his own original right, without hindrance from him; not without hindrance from another. So that the effect which redoundeth to one man, by another man's defect of right, is but so much diminution of impediments to the use of his own right original.

Right is laid aside, either by simply renouncing it; or by transferring it to another. By *simply* RENOUNCING; when he cares not to whom the benefit thereof redoundeth. By TRANSFERRING; when he intendeth the benefit thereof to some certain person, or persons. And when a man hath in either manner abandoned, or granted away his right; then he is said to be OBLIGED, or BOUND, not to hinder those, to whom such right is granted, or abandoned, from the benefit of it: and that he *ought*, and it is his DUTY, not to make void that voluntary act of his own: and that such hindrance is INJUSTICE, and INJURY. . . . The way by which a man either simply renounceth, or transferreth his right, is a declaration, or signification, by some voluntary and sufficient sign, or signs, that he doth so renounce, or transfer; or hath so renounced, or transferred the same, to him that accepteth it. And these signs are either words only, or actions only; or, as it happeneth most often, both words, and actions. And the same are the BONDS, by which men are bound, and obliged: bonds, that have their strength, not from their own nature, for nothing is more easily broken than a man's word, but from fear of some evil consequence upon that rupture.

Whensoever a man transferreth his right, or renounceth it; it is either in consideration of some right reciprocally transferred to himself; or for some other good he hopeth for thereby. For it is a voluntary act: and of the voluntary acts of every man, the object is some *good to himself*. And therefore there be some rights, which no man can be understood by any words, or other signs, to have abandoned, or transferred. As first a man cannot lay down the right of resisting them, that assault him by force, to take away his life; because he cannot be understood to aim thereby, at any good to himself. . . . And lastly the motive, and end for which this renouncing, and transferring of right is introduced, is nothing else but the security of a man's person, in his life, and in the means of so preserving life, as not to be weary of it. . . .

The mutual transferring of right, is that which men call CONTRACT. . . .

If a covenant be made, wherein neither of the parties perform presently, but trust one another; in the condition of mere nature, which is a condition of war of every man against every man, upon any reasonable suspicion, it is void: but if there be a common power set over them both, with right and force sufficient to compel performance, it is not void. For he that performeth first, has no assurance the other will perform after; because the bonds of words are too weak to bridle men's ambition, avarice, anger, and other passions, without the fear of some coercive power; which in the condition of mere nature, where all men are equal, and judges of the justness of their own fears, cannot possibly be supposed. And therefore he which performeth first, does but betray himself to his enemy; contrary to the right, he can never abandon, of defending his life, and means of living.

But in a civil estate, where there is a power set up to constrain those that would otherwise violate their faith, that fear is no more reasonable; and for that cause, he which by the covenant is to perform first, is obliged so to do. . . .

He that transferreth any right, transferreth the means of enjoying it, as far as lieth in his power. As he that selleth land, is understood to transfer the herbage, and whatsover grows upon it: nor can he that sells a mill turn away the stream that drives it. And they that give to a man the right of government in sovereignty, are understood to give him the right of levying money to maintain soldiers; and of appointing magistrates for the administration of justice. . . .

Men are freed of their covenants two ways; by performing; or by being forgiven. For performance, is the natural end of obligation; and forgiveness, the restitution of liberty; as being a retransferring of that right, in which the obligation consisted.

Covenants entered into by fear, in the condition of mere nature, are obligatory. For example, if I covenant to pay a ransom, or service for my life, to an enemy; I am bound by it: for it is a contract, wherein one receiveth the benefit of life; the other is to receive money, or service for it; and consequently, where no other law, as in the condition of mere nature, forbiddeth the performance, the covenant is valid. . . . And even in commonwealths, if I be forced to redeem myself from a thief by promising him money, I am bound to pay it, till the civil law discharge me. . . .

## CHAPTER XV

### Of Other Laws of Nature

From that law of nature, by which we are obliged to transfer to another, such rights, as being retained, hinder the peace of mankind, there followeth a third; which is this, *that men perform their covenants made*: without which, covenants are in vain, and but empty words; and the right of all men to all things remaining, we are still in the condition of war.

And in this law of nature, consisteth the fountain and original of JUSTICE. For where no covenant hath preceded, there hath no right been transferred, and every man has right to every thing; and consequently, no action can be unjust. But when a covenant is made, then to break it is *unjust*: and the definition of INJUSTICE, is no other than *the not performance of covenant*. And whatsoever is not unjust, is *just*. . . .

Therefore before the names of just, and unjust can have place, there must be some coercive power, to compel men equally to the performance of their covenants, by the terror of some punishment, greater than the benefit they expect by the breach of their covenant; and to make good that propriety, which by mutual contract men acquire, in recompense of the universal right they abandon: and such power there is none before the erection of a commonwealth. And this is also to be gathered out of the ordinary definition of justice in the Schools: for they say, that *justice is the constant will of giving to every man his own*. And therefore where there is no *own*, that is no propriety, there is no injustice; and where there is no coercive power erected, that is, where there is no commonwealth, there is no propriety; all men having right to all things: therefore where there is no commonwealth, there nothing is unjust. So that the nature of justice, consisteth in keeping of valid covenants: but the validity of covenants begins not but with the constitution of a civil power, sufficient to compel men to keep them: and then it is also that propriety begins. . . .

And the science of them, is the true and only moral philosophy. For moral philosophy is nothing else but the science of what is *good*, and *evil*, in the conversation, and society of mankind. *Good*, and *evil*, are names that signify our appetites, and aversions; which in different tempers, customs, and doctrines of men, are different: and divers men, differ not only in their judgment, on the senses of what is pleasant, and unpleasant to the taste, smell, hearing, touch, and sight; but also of what is conformable, or disagreeable to reason, in the actions of common life. Nay, the same man, in divers times, differs from himself; and one time praiseth, that is, called good, what another time he dispraiseth, and calleth evil: from whence arise disputes, controversies, and at last war. And therefore so long as a man is in the condition of mere nature, which is a condition of war, as private appetite is the measure of good, and evil: and consequently all men agree on this, that peace is good, and therefore also the way, or means of peace, which, as I have shewed before, are *justice*, *gratitude*, *modesty*, *equity*, *mercy*, and the rest of the laws of nature, are good; that is to say; *moral virtues*; and their contrary *vices*, evil. . . .

## The Agreement of the People and Putney Debates (October, 1647)

By October, 1647, the ancient constitution of king in parliament had collapsed. The monarch was a prisoner of parliament; the House of Commons had been twice purged — first of its cavalier members and then of its Presbyterian elements — and had been reduced to a rump of eighty-seven; and the House of Lords was a cipher. Change — republicanism and all varieties of political radicalism and idealism — was in the air. In the army, the Rump of the House of Commons, and the kingdom at large, there was debate and speculation, not to mention deep-seated disagreement, over the proper form of government for a commonwealth that had just been through the agony of civil war. The Agreement of the People was drawn up by the political radicals within the military. The debate over the first and most important article of the agreement, ignoring property qualifications for voting, went to the core of the growing dissension between the ruling propertied elite and the landless elements in society.

## The Agreement of the People

... We declare:

I. That the people of England, being at this day very unequally distributed by counties, cities, and boroughs, for the election of their deputies in Parliament, ought to be more indifferently proportioned, according to the number of the inhabitants; the circumstances whereof, for number, place, and manner, are to be set down before the end of this present Parliament.

II. That to prevent the many inconveniences apparently arising from the long continuance of the same persons in authority, this present Parliament be dissolved upon the last day of September, which shall be in the year of our Lord 1648.

III. That the people do of course choose themselves a Parliament once in two years. ...

IV. That the power of this, and all future Representatives of this nation is inferior only to theirs who choose them, and doth extend, without the consent or concurrence of any other person or persons, to the enacting, altering, and repealing of laws; to the erecting and abolishing of offices and courts; to the appointing, removing, and calling to account magistrates and officers of all degrees; to the making war and peace; to the treating with foreign states; and generally to whatsoever is not expressly or impliedly reserved by the represented to themselves.

Which are as followeth:

1. That matters of religion, and the ways of God's worship, are not at all entrusted by us to any human power, because therein we cannot remit or exceed a title of what our consciences dictate to be the mind of God, without wilful sin; nevertheless the public way of instructing the nation (so it be not compulsive) is referred to their discretion.

2. That the matter of impressing and constraining any of us to serve in the wars is against our freedom, and therefore we do not allow it in our representatives; the rather because money (the sinews of war) being always at their disposal, they can never want numbers of men apt enough to engage in any just cause.

3. That after the dissolution of this present Parliament, no person be at any time questioned for anything said or done in reference to the late public differences. ...

4. That in all laws made, or to be made, every person may be bound alike, and that no tenure, estate, charter, degree, birth or place, do confer any exemption from the ordinary course of legal proceedings, whereunto others are subjected.

5. That as the laws ought to be equal, so they must be good, and not evidently destructive to the safety and well-being of the people.

These things we declare to be our native rights. ...

## The Putney Debates

MAJOR RAINBOROUGH: I desire we may come to that end we all strive after. I humbly desire you will fall upon that which is the engagement of all, which is the rights and freedoms of the people, and let us see how far we have made sure to them a right and freedom. ...

SOURCE: From John Rushworth, *Historical Collections . . .*, London, 1659–1721, Vol. VII, pp. 859–860. Reprinted in C. H. Firth, *The Clarke Papers* (London: Camden Society, 1891), New Series, Vol. 49, pp. 299–327.

First Article of the Agreement was read.

IRETON: The exception that lies in it is this. It is said: "The people of England" etc., . . . they are to be distributed "according to the number of inhabitants"; and this doth make me think that the meaning is that every man that is an inhabitant is to be equally considered, and to have an equal voice in the election of the representatives. . . . [Does this statement mean] that all that had a former right of election [are to be electors], or [whether] those that had no right before are to come in? . . .

PETTY: We judge that all inhabitants that have not lost their birthright should have an equal voice in elections.

RAINBOROUGH: I desired that those that had engaged in it [should speak], for really I think that the poorest he that is in England hath a life to live, as the greatest he; and therefore truly, sir, I think it's clear that every man that is to live under a government ought first by his own consent to put himself under that government; and I do think that the poorest man in England is not at all bound in a strict sense to that government that he hath not had a voice to put himself under; . . .

IRETON: . . . I think that no person hath a right to an interest or share in the disposing or determing of the affairs of the kingdom, and in choosing those that shall determine what laws we shall be ruled by here . . . that hath not a permanent fixed interest in this kingdom; and those persons together are properly the represented of this kingdom, and consequently are to make up the representors of this kingdom, who taken together do comprehend whatsoever is of real or permanent interest in the kingdom. . . . We talk of birthright. Truly [by] birthright there is thus much claim. Men may justly have by birthright, by their very being born in England, that we should not seclude them out of England, that we should not refuse to give them air and place and ground, and the freedom of the highways and other things, to live amongst us. . . . That I think is due to a man by birth.

But that by a man's being born here he shall have a share in that power that shall dispose of the lands here, and all things here, I do not think it a sufficient ground. . . . Those that choose the representors for the making of laws by which this state and kingdom are to be governed, are the persons who, taken together, do comprehend the local interest of this kingdom; that is, the persons in whom all land lies, and those in corporations in whom all trading lies. This is the most fundamental constitution of this kingdom, which if you do not allow, you allow none at all. . . . If we shall go to take away this fundamental part of the civil constitution, we shall plainly go to take away all property and interest that any man hath, either in land by inheritance, or in estate by possession, or anything else. . . .

RAINBOROUGH: . . . I do hear nothing at all that can convince me, why any man that is born in England ought not to have his voice in election of burgessess. . . . Therefore I say, that either it must by the law of God or the law of man that must prohibit the meanest man in the kingdom to have this benefit as well as the greatest. I do not find anything in the law of God that [says that] a lord shall choose twenty burgesses, and a gentleman but two, or a poor man shall choose none. I find no such thing in the law of Nature, nor in the law of Nations. But I do find that all Englishmen must be subject to English laws, and I do verily believe that there is no man but will say that the foundation of all laws lies in the people, and if [it lie] in the people, I am to seek for this exemption. . . .

IRETON: . . . I think I agreed to this matter, that all should be equally distributed. But the question is, whether it should be distributed to all persons, or whether the same persons that are the electors [now] should be the electors still, and it [be] equally distributed amongst them. . . .

All the main thing that I speak for is because I would have an eye to property. I hope we do not come to contend for victory, but let every man consider with himself that he do not go that way to take away all property. . . . Now those people [that have freeholds] and those that are the freemen of corporations were looked upon by the former constitution to comprehend the permanent interest of the kingdom. . . . Now I wish we may all consider of what right you will challenge, that all the people should have right to elections. Is it by the right of nature? If you will hold forth that as your ground, then I think you must deny all property too, and this is my reason. For thus: by that same right of nature, whatever it be that you pretend, by which you can say, "one man hath an equal right with another to the choosing of him that shall govern him" — by the same right of nature, he hath an equal[4] right in any goods he sees: meat, drink, clothes, to take and use them for his sustenance. . . .

RAINBOROUGH: . . . And sir, to say because a man pleads that every man hath a voice [by the right of nature], that therefore it destroys, [by] the same [argument, all property] — [this is to forget the law of God]. . . . Else why [hath] God made that law, "Thou shalt not steal"? . . . For my part I am against any such thought, and, as for yourselves, I wish you would not make the world believe that we are for anarchy.

CROMWELL: . . . No man says that you have a mind to anarchy, but the consequence of this rule tends to anarchy, must end in anarchy; for where is there any bound or limit set if you take away this [limit], that men that have no interest but the interest of breathing [shall have no voices in elections]? . . .

RAINBOROUGH: . . . And I would fain know what we have fought for. [For our laws and liberties?] And this is the old law of England and that which enslaves the people of England that they should be bound by laws in which they have no voice at all! [So with respect to the law which says "Honour thy father and thy mother"], the great dispute is, who is a right father

and a right mother? . . . I take it in the same sense you do: I would have a distinction, a character whereby God commands me to honour [them]. And for my part I look upon the people of England so, that wherein they have not voices in the choosing of their [governors — their civil] fathers and mothers, they are not bound to that commandment.

PETTY: I desire to add one word concerning the word property. It is for something that anarchy is so much talked of. For my own part I cannot believe in the least that it can be clearly derived from that paper [the first article]. 'Tis true, that somewhat may be derived in the paper against the power of the King, and somewhat against the power of the Lords; and the truth is when I shall see God going about to throw down King and Lords and property, then I shall be contented. But I hope that they [who] may live to see the power of the King and the Lords thrown down, that yet may [they] live to see property, preserved. And for this of changing the Representative, making of them more full, taking more into the number than formerly, I had verily thought we had all agreed that more should have chosen, and that all had desired a more equal representation than we now have. For now those only choose who have forty shillings freehold. A man may have a lease for one hundred pounds a year, a man may have a lease for three lives [but he has no voice]. But [as] for this [argument] that it destroys all right [to property] that every Englishman that is an inhabitant of England should choose and have a choice in the representatives, I suppose it is [on the contrary] the only means to preserve all property. For I judge every man is naturally free; and I judge the reason why men when they were in so great numbers [chose representatives] was that every man could not give his voice [directly]; and therefore men agreed to come into some form of government that they who were chosen might preserve property. . . .

---

4 the same

IRETON: . . . I do not speak of not enlarging this [representation] at all, but of keeping this to the most fundamental constitution in this kingdom. That is, that no person that hath not a local and permanent interest in the kingdom should have an equal dependence in election [with those that have]. But if you go beyond this law, if you admit any man that hath a breath and being, I did show you how this will destroy property. It may come to destroy property thus: you may have such men chosen, or at least the major part of them [as have no local and permanent interest]. Why may not those men vote against all property? . . .

COLONEL [NATHANIEL] RICH: I confess [there is weight in] that objection that the Commissary-General [Ireton] last insisted upon; for you have five to one in this kingdom that have no permanent interest. Some men [have] ten, some twenty servants, some more, some less. If the master and servant shall be equal electors, then clearly those that have no interest in the kingdom will make it their interest to choose those that have no interest. It may happen, that the majority may by law, not in a confusion, destroy property; there may be a law enacted that there shall be an equality of goods and estate. . . . In the Roman Senate . . . the people's voices were bought and sold, and that by the poor; and thence it came that he that was the richest man, and [a man] of some considerable power among the soldiers, and one they resolved on, made himself a perpetual dictator. And if we strain too far to avoid monarchy in kings [let us take heed] that we do not call for emperors to deliver us from more than one tyrant. . . .

WILDMAN: Unless I be very much mistaken we are very much deviated from the first question. Instead of following the first proposition to inquire what is just, I conceive we look to prophecies, and look to what may be the event, and judge of the justness of the thing by the consequence. I desire we may recall [ourselves to the question] whether it be right or no. I con-

ceive all that hath been said against it will be reduced to this [question of consequences], and [to] another reason — that it is against a fundamental law, that every person [choosing] ought to have a permanent interest, because it is not fit that those should choose Parliaments that have no lands to be disposed of by Parliament. . . .

Our case is to be considered thus, that we have been under slavery. That's acknowledged by all. Our very laws were made by our conquerors; and whereas it's spoken much of chronicles, I conceive there is no credit to be given to any of them; and the reason is because those that were our lords, and made us their vassals, would suffer nothing else to be chronicled. We are now engaged for our freedom. That's the end of Parliaments: not to constitute what is already [established, but to act] according to the just rules of government. Every person in England hath as clear a right to elect his representative as the greatest person in England. I conceive that's the undeniable maxim of government: that all government is in the free consent of the people. If [so], then upon that account, there is no person that is under a just government, or hath justly his own, unless he by his own free consent be put under that government. . . . And therefore I should humbly move, that if the question be stated — which would soonest bring things to an issue — it might rather be this: Whether any person can justly be bound by law, who doth not give his consent that such persons shall make laws for him? . . .

IRETON: . . . A man ought to be subject to a law that did not give his consent, but with this reservation, that if this man do think himself unsatisfied to be subject to this law he may go into another kingdom. And so the same reason doth extend, in my understanding, to that man that hath no permanent interest in the kingdom. . . .

RAINBOROUGH: For my part, I think we cannot engage one way or other in the Army if we do not think of the people's liberties. If we can agree where the liberty and freedom of the people lies, that will do all.

IRETON: I cannot consent so far. As I said before: when I see the hand of God destroying King, and Lords, and Commons too, [or] any foundation of human constitution, when I see God hath done it, I shall, I hope, comfortably acquiesce in it. But . . . if the principle upon which you move this alteration, or the ground upon which you press that we should make this alteration, do ·destroy all kind of property or whatsoever a man hath by human constitution, [I cannot consent to it]. The law of God doth not give me property, nor the law of Nature, but property is of human constitution. I have a property and this I shall enjoy. Constitution founds property. If either the thing itself that you press or the consequence [of] that you press [do destroy property], though I shall acquiesce in having no property, yet I cannot give my heart or hand to it; because it is a thing evil in itself and scandalous to the world, and I desire this Army may be free from both.

SEXBY: I see that though it [liberty] were our end, there is a degeneration from it. We have engaged in this kingdom and ventured our lives, and it was all for this: to recover our birthrights and privileges as Englishmen; and by the arguments urged there is none. There are many thousands of us soldiers that have ventured our lives; we have had little propriety in the kingdom as to our estates, yet we have had a birthright. But it seems now, except a man hath a fixed estate in this kingdom, he hath no right in this kingdom. I wonder we were so much deceived. If we had not a right to the kingdom, we were mere mercenary soldiers. There are many in my condition that have as good a condition [as I have]; it may be little estate they have at present, and yet they have as much a [birth] right as those two [i.e., Cromwell and Ireton] who are their lawgivers, as any in this place. I shall tell you in a word my resolution. I am resolved to give my birthright to none. Whatsoever may come in the way, and [whatsoever may] be thought, I will give it to none. . . .

IRETON: Now let us consider where our

difference lies. We all agree that you should have a Representative to govern, [and] this Representative to be as equal as you can. But the question is, whether this distribution can be made to all persons equally, or whether equally amongst those equals that have the interest of England in them. . . . I do wish that they that talk of birthrights . . . would consider what really our birthright is.

If a man mean by birthright, whatsoever he can challenge by the law of Nature, (supose there were not constitution at all, . . . no civil law and civil constitution), [and] that I am to contend for against constitution; [then] you leave no property, nor no foundation for any man to enjoy anything. But if you call that your birthright which is the most fundamental part of your constitution, then let him perish that goes about to hinder you or any man of the least part of your birthright, or will [desire to] do it. But if you will lay aside the most fundamental constitution, which is as good for aught you can discern as anything you can propose — at least it is a constitution, and I will give you consequence for consequence of good upon [that] constitution as you [can give] upon your birthright — and if you merely upon pretence of a birthright, of the right of nature . . . ; if you will upon that ground pretend that this constitution, the most fundamental constitution, the thing that hath reason and equity in it, shall not stand in you way, [it] is the same principle to me, say I, [as if] but for your better satisfaction you shall take hold of anything that a man calls his own.

RAINBOROUGH: Sir, I see that it is impossible to have liberty but all property must be taken away. If it be laid down for a rule, and if you will say it, it must be so. But I would fain know what the soldier hath fought for all this while? He hath fought to enslave himself, to give power to men of riches, men of estates, to make him a perpetual slave. We do find in all presses that go forth none must be pressed that are freehold men. When these gentlemen fall out among themselves they shall press the poor scrubs to come and kill them. . . .

IRETON: . . . I shall tell you what the soldier of the kingdom hath fought for. First, the danger that we stood in was, that one man's will must be a law. The people of the kingdom must have this right at least, that they should not be concluded [but]

by the Representative of those that had the interest of the kingdom, . . . that is, that the will of one man should not be a law, but that the law of this kingdom should be by a choice of persons to represent, and that choice to be made by the generality of the kingdom. Here was a right that induced men to fight. . . .

## JOHN LOCKE, *Second Treatise of Government* (1690)

John Locke, in one of the most influential political tracts ever written, presents a theory of society that was completely in tune with the views and needs of the landed oligarchy. Like Hobbes, Locke starts off with a description of the state of nature and the need for a social contract, but he ends with a different definition of the contract and a very different picture of society.

### CHAPTER II

#### Of the State of Nature

To understand political power aright and derive it from its original, we must consider what state all men are naturally in, and that is, a state of perfect freedom to order their actions and dispose of their possessions and persons as they think fit, within the bounds of the law of nature, without asking leave, or depending upon the will of any other man.

[A state of nature is] a state also of equality, wherein all the power and jurisdiction is reciprocal, no one having more than another. . . .

But though this be a state of liberty, yet it is not a state of license; though man in that state have an uncontrolable liberty to dispose of his person or possessions, yet he has not liberty to destroy himself, or so much as any creature in his possession, but where some nobler use than its bare preservation calls for it. The state of nature has

a law of nature to govern it, which obliges everyone; and reason, which is that law, teaches all mankind who will but consult it that, being all equal and independent, no one ought to harm another in his life, health, liberty, or possessions; for men being all the workmanship of one omnipotent and infinitely wise maker — all the servants of one sovereign master, sent into the world by his order and about his business — they are his property whose workmanship they are, made to last during his, not one another's, please. . . .

And that all men may be restrained from invading others' rights and from doing hurt to one another, and the law of nature be observed, which wills the peace and preservation of all mankind, the execution of the law of nature is, in that state, put into every man's hands, whereby everyone has a right to punish the transgressors of that law to such a degree as may hinder its violation; for the law of nature would, as all other laws that concern men in this

SOURCE: From John Locke, *Two Treatises of Government: In the Former, the False Principles and Foundation of Sir Robert Filmer, and His Followers Are Detected and Overthrown. The Latter Is An Essay Concerning the True Original, Extent, and End of Civil-Government* (London, 1698), pp. 167–171, 173, 176, 185–191, 193, 195, 199–200, 229, 230–231, 238–239, 261–265, 330–332, 335–339, 342–344.

world, be in vain if there were nobody that in that state of nature had a power to execute that law and thereby preserve the innocent and restrain offenders. . . .

. . . In transgressing the law of nature, the offender declares himself to live by another rule than that of reason and common equity, which is that measure God has set to the actions of men for their mutual security; and so he becomes dangerous to mankind, the tie which is to secure them from injury and violence being slighted and broken by him. . . . And thus it is that every man in the state of nature has a power to kill a murderer, both to deter others from doing the like injury, which no reparation can compensate, by the example of the punishment that attends it from everybody, and also to secure men from the attempts of a criminal, who, having renounced reason — the common rule and measure God has given to mankind — has, by the unjust violence and slaughter he has committed upon one, declared war against all mankind, and therefore may be destroyed as a lion or a tiger, one of those wild savage beasts with whom men can have no society nor security. . . .

. . . The laws which have been hitherto mentioned[5] to bind men absolutely, even as they are men, although they have never any settled fellowship, never any solemn agreement amongst themselves what to do or not to do; but forasmuch as we are not by ourselves sufficient to furnish ourselves with competent store of things needful for such a life as our nature doth desire, a life fit for the dignity of man; therefore to supply those defects and imperfections which are in us, as living singly and solely by ourselves, we are naturally induced to seek communion and fellowship with others. This was the cause of men's uniting themselves at first in politic societies. But I, moreover, affirm that all men are naturally in that state and remain so till by their own consents they make themselves members of some politic society; and I doubt

not in the sequel of this discourse to make it very clear. . . .

CHAPTER V

**Of Property**

. . . God, who has given the world to men in common, has also given them reason to make use of it to the best advantage of life and convenience. The earth and all that is therein is given to men for the support and comfort of their being. . . .

Though the earth and all inferior creatures be common to all men, yet every man has a property in his own person; this nobody has any right to but himself. The labor of his body and the work of his hands, we may say, are properly his. Whatsoever then he removes out of the state that nature has provided and left it in, he has mixed his labor with, and joined to it something that is his own, and thereby makes it his property. It being by him removed from the common state nature has placed it in, it has by this labor something annexed to it that excludes the common right of other men. For this labor being the unquestionable property of the laborer, no man but he can have a right to what that is once joined to, at least where there is enough and as good left in common for others.

He that is nourished by the acorns he picked up under an oak, or the apples he gathered from the trees in the wood, has certainly appropriated them to himself. Nobody can deny but this nourishment is his. . . . And will anyone say he had no right to those acorns or apples he thus appropriated because he had not the consent of all mankind to make them his? Was it a robbery thus to assume to himself what belonged to all in common? If such a consent as that was necessary, man had starved, notwithstanding the plenty God had given him. We see in commons, which remain so by compact, that it is the taking any part of what is common and removing it out of

---

[5] i.e., the laws of nature

the state nature leaves it in which begins the property, without which the common is of no use. And the taking of this or that part does not depend on the express consent of all the commoners. Thus the grass my horse has bit, the turfs my servant has cut, and the ore I have digged in any place where I have a right to them in common with others, become my property without the assignation or consent of anybody.... 

It will perhaps be objected to this that "if gathering the acorns, or other fruits of the earth, etc., makes a right to them, then anyone may engross as much as he will." To which I answer: not so. The same law of nature that does by this means give us property does also bound that property too. "God has given us all things richly" (I Tim. vi. 17), is the voice of reason confirmed by inspiration. But how far has he given it us? To enjoy. As much as anyone can make use of to any advantage of life before it spoils, so much he may by his labor fix a property in; whatever is beyond this is more than his share and belongs to others. Nothing was made by God for man to spoil or destroy.... 

But the chief matter of property being now not the fruits of the earth and the beasts that subsist on it, but the earth itself, as that which takes in and carries with it all the rest, I think it is plain that property in that, too, is acquired as the former. As much land as a man tills, plants, improves, cultivates, and can use the product of, so much is his property. He by his labor does, as it were, enclose it from the common.... 

God gave the world to men in common; but since he gave it them for their benefit and the greatest conveniences of life they were capable to draw from it, it cannot be supposed he meant it should always remain common and uncultivated. He gave it to the use of the industrious and rational (and labor was to be his title to it).... Which measure[6] did confine every man's possession to a very modest proportion, and such as he

might appropriate to himself without injury to anybody.... 

This is certain, that in the beginning, before the desire of having more than man needed had altered the intrinsic value of things which depends only on their usefulness to the life of man, or had agreed that a little piece of yellow metal which would keep without wasting or decay should be worth a great piece of flesh or a whole heap of corn, though men had a right to appropriate, by their labor, each one to himself as much of the things of nature as he could use, yet this could not be much, nor to the prejudice of others, where the same plenty was still left to those who would use the same industry.... 

The same measures governed the possession of land, too: whatsoever he tilled and reaped, laid up and made use of before it spoiled, that was his peculiar right; whatsoever he enclosed and could feed and make use of, the cattle and product was also his. But if either the grass of his enclosure rotted on the ground, or the fruit of his planting perished without gathering and laying up, this part of the earth, notwithstanding his enclosure, was still to be looked on as waste and might be the possession of any other.... 

Nor is it so strange, as perhaps before consideration it may appear, that the property of labor should be able to overbalance the community of land; for it is labor indeed that put the difference of value on everything; and let anyone consider what the difference is between an acre of land planted with tobacco or sugar, sown with wheat or barley, and an acre of the same land lying in common without any husbandry upon it, and he will find that the improvement of labor makes the far greater part of the value. I think it will be but a very modest computation to say that of the products of the earth useful to the life of man, nine tenths are the effects of labor.... 

The greatest part of things really useful

---

[6] labor

to the life of man, and such as the necessity of subsisting made the first commoners of the world look after, as it does the Americans now, are generally things of short duration, such as, if they are not consumed by use, will decay and perish of themselves; gold, silver, and diamonds are things that fancy or agreement has put the value on, more than real use and the necessary support of life. Now of those good things which nature has provided in common, everyone had a right, as has been said, to as much as he could use, and property in all that he could effect with his labor; all that his industry could extend to, to alter from the state nature had put it in, was his. He that gathered a hundred bushels of acorns or apples had thereby a property in them; they were his goods as soon as gathered. He was only to look that he used them before they spoiled, else he took more than his share and robbed others. And indeed it was a foolish thing, as well as dishonest, to hoard up more than he could make use of. If he gave away a part to anybody else so that it perished not uselessly in his possession, these he also made use of. And if he also bartered away plums that would have rotted in a week for nuts that would last good for his eating a whole year, he did no injury; he wasted not the common stock, destroyed no part of the portion of the goods that belonged to others, so long as nothing perished uselessly in his hands. Again, if he would give his nuts for a piece of metal, pleased with its color, or exchange his sheep for shells, or wool for a sparkling pebble or a diamond, and keep those by him all his life, he invaded not the right of others; he might heap up as much of these durable things as he pleased; the exceeding of the bounds of his just property not lying in the largeness of his possession, but the perishing of anything uselessly in it.

And thus came in the use of money — some lasting thing that men might keep without spoiling, and that by mutual consent men would take in exchange for the truly useful but perishable supports of life. . . .

## CHAPTER VII

### Of Political and Civil Society

. . . Man, being born, as has been proved, with a title to perfect freedom and uncontrolled enjoyment of all the rights and privileges of the law of nature equally with any other man or number of men in the world, has by nature a power not only to preserve his property — that is, his life, liberty, and estate — against the injuries and attempts of other men, but to judge of and punish the breaches of that law in others as he is persuaded the offense deserves, even with death itself in crimes where the heinousness of the fact in his opinion requires it. But because no political society can be, nor subsist, without having in itself the power to preserve the property and, in order thereunto, punish the offenses of all those of that society, there and there only is political society where every one of the members has quitted his natural power, resigned it up into the hands of the community in all cases that exclude him from appealing for protection to the law established by it. And thus all private judgment of every particular member being excluded, the community comes to be umpire by settled standing rules, indifferent and the same to all parties, and by men having authority from the community for the execution of those rules decides all the differences that may happen between any members of that society concerning any matter of right, and punishes those offenses which any member has committed against the society with such penalties as the law has established; whereby it is easy to discern who are, and who are not, in political society together. . . .

And thus the commonwealth comes by a power to set down what punishment shall belong to the several transgressions which they think worthy of it committed amongst the members of that society — which is the power of making laws — as well as it has the power to punish any injury done unto any of its members by anyone that is not of it — which is the power of war and peace

— and all this for the preservation of the property of all the members of that society as far as is possible. But though every man who has entered into civil society and is become a member of any commonwealth has thereby quitted his power to punish offenses against the law of nature in prosecution of his own private judgment, yet, with the judgment of offenses which he has given up to the legislative in all cases where he can appeal to the magistrate, he has given a right to the commonwealth to employ his force for the execution of the judgments of the commonwealth, whenever he shall be called to it; which, indeed, are his own judgments, they being made by himself or his representative. And herein we have the original of the legislative and executive power of civil society, which is to judge by standing laws how far offenses are to be punished when committed within the commonwealth, and also to determine by occasional judgments founded on the present circumstances of the fact, how far injuries from without are to be vindicated; and in both these to employ all the force of all the members when there shall be need. . . .

## CHAPTER VIII

### Of the Beginning of Political Societies

Men being, as has been said, by nature all free, equal and independent, no one can be put out of this estate and subjected to the political power of another without his own consent. The only way whereby anyone divests himself of his natural liberty and puts on the bonds of civil society is by agreeing with other men to join and unite into a community for their comfortable, safe, and peaceable living one amongst another, in a secure enjoyment of their properties and a greater security against any that are not of it. . . .

And thus every man, by consenting with others to make one body politic under one government, puts himself under an obligation to every one of that society to submit to the determination of the majority and to be concluded by it; or else this original compact, whereby he with others incorporates into one society, would signify nothing, and be no compact, if he be left free and under no other ties than he was in before in the state of nature. For what appearance would there be of any compact? What new engagement if he were no further tied by any decrees of the society than he himself thought fit and did actually consent to? This would be still as great a liberty as he himself had before his compact, or any one else in the state of nature has who may submit himself and consent to any acts of it if he thinks fit. . . .

## CHAPTER IX

### Of the Ends of Political Society and Government

If man in the state of nature be so free, as has been said, if he be absolute lord of his own person and possessions, equal to the greatest, and subject to nobody, why will he part with his freedom, why will he give up his empire and subject himself to the dominion and control of any other power? To which it is obvious to answer that though in the state of nature he has such a right, yet the enjoyment of it is very uncertain and constantly exposed to the invasion of others; for all being kings as much as he, every man his equal, and the greater part no strict observers of equity and justice, the enjoyment of the property he has in this state is very unsafe, very unsecure. This makes him willing to quit a condition which, however free, is full of fears and continual dangers; and it is not without reason that he seeks out and is willing to join in society with others who are already united, or have a mind to unite, for the mutual preservation of their lives, liberties, and estates, which I call by the general name "property."

The great and chief end, therefore, of men's uniting into commonwealths and putting themselves under government is the preservation of their property. To which in the state of nature there are many things wanting:

First, there wants an established, settled, known law, received and allowed by common consent to be the standard of right and wrong and the common measure to decide all controversies between them; for though the law of nature be plain and intelligible to all rational creatures, yet men, being biased by their interest as well as ignorant for want of studying it, are not apt to allow of it as a law binding to them in the application of it to their particular cases.

Secondly, in the state of nature there wants a known and indifferent judge with authority to determine all differences according to the established law; for every one in that state being both judge and executioner of the law of nature, men being partial to themselves, passion and revenge is very apt to carry them too far and with too much heat in their own cases, as well as negligence and unconcernedness to make them too remiss in other men's.

Thirdly, in the state of nature there often wants power to back and support the sentence when right, and to give it due execution. They who by any injustice offend will seldom fail, where they are able, by force, to make good their injustice; such resistance many times makes the punishment dangerous and frequently destructive to those who attempt it. . . .

For in the state of nature, to omit the liberty he has of innocent delights, a man has two powers:

The first is to do whatsoever he thinks fit for the preservation of himself and others within the permission of the law of nature, by which law, common to them all, he and all the rest of mankind are one community, make up one society, distinct from all other creatures. And, were it not for the corruption and viciousness of degenerate men, there would be no need of any other, no necessity that men should separate from this great and natural community and associate into less combinations.

The other power a man has in the state of nature is the power to punish the crimes committed against that law. Both these he gives up when he joins in a private, if I may so call it, or particular politic society and incorporates into any commonwealth separate from the rest of mankind. . . .

But though men when they enter into society give up the equality, liberty, and executive power they had in the state of nature into the hands of the society, to be so far disposed of by the legislative as the good of the society shall require, yet it being only with an intention in every one the better to preserve himself, his liberty and property — for no rational creature can be supposed to change his condition with an intention to be worse — the power of the society, or legislative constituted by them, can never be supposed to extend farther than the common good, but is obliged to secure everyone's property by providing against those three defects abovementioned that made the state of nature so unsafe and uneasy. And so whoever has the legislative or supreme power of any commonwealth is bound to govern by established standing laws, promulgated and known to the people, and not by extemporary decrees; by indifferent and upright judges who are to decide controversies by those laws; and to employ the force of the community at home only in the execution of such laws, or abroad to prevent or redress foreign injuries, and secure the community from inroads and invasion. And all this to be directed to no other end but the peace, safety, and public good of the people. . . .

## CHAPTER XIX

### Of the Dissolution of Government

He that will with any clearness speak of the dissolution of government ought in the first place to distinguish between the dissolution of the society and the dissolution of the government. That which makes the community and brings men out of the loose state of nature into one politic society is the agreement which everybody has with the rest to incorporate and act as one body and so be one distinct commonwealth. The usual and almost only way whereby this union is dissolved is the inroad of foreign force making a conquest upon them; for in that case, not being able to maintain and support themselves as one entire and independent body, the union belonging to that body which consisted therein must necessarily cease, and so every one return to the state he was in before, with a liberty to shift for himself and provide for his own safety, as he thinks fit, in some other society. Whenever the society is dissolved, it is certain the government of that society cannot remain. . . .

Besides this overturning from without, governments are dissolved from within.

First, when the legislative is altered. Civil society being a state of peace amongst those who are of it, from whom the state of war is excluded by the umpirage which they have provided in their legislative for the ending all differences that may arise amongst any of them, it is in their legislative that the members of a commonwealth are united and combined together into one coherent living body. This is the soul that gives form, life, and unity to the commonwealth; from hence the several members have their mutual influence, sympathy, and connection; and, therefore, when the legislative is broken or dissolved, dissolution and death follows; for the essence and union of the society consisting in having one will, the legislative, when once established by the majority, has the declaring and, as it were, keeping of that will. The constitution of the legislative is the first and fundamental act of society, whereby provision is made for the continuation of their union under the direction of persons and bonds of laws made by persons authorized thereunto by the consent and appointment of the people, without which no one man or number of men amongst them can have authority of making laws that shall be binding to the rest. When any one or more shall

take upon them to make laws, whom the people have not appointed so to do, they make laws without authority, which the people are not therefore bound to obey; by which means they come again to be out of subjection and may constitute to themselves a new legislative as they think best, being in full liberty to resist the force of those who without authority would impose anything upon them. Everyone is at the disposure of his own will when those who had by the delegation of the society the declaring of the public will are excluded from it, and others usurp the place who have no such authority or delegation. . . .

There is one way more whereby such a government may be dissolved, and that is when he who has the supreme executive power neglects and abandons that charge, so that the laws already made can no longer be put in execution. This is demonstratively to reduce all to anarchy, and so effectually to dissolve the government; for laws not being made for themselves, but to be by their execution the bonds of the society, to keep every part of the body politic in its due place and function, when that totally cease, the government visibly ceases, and the people become a confused multitude, without order or connection. Where there is no longer the administration of justice for the security of men's rights, nor any remaining power within the community to direct the force to provide for the necessities of the public, there certainly is no government left. Where the laws cannot be executed, it is all one as if there were no laws; and a government without laws is, I suppose, a mystery in politics, inconceivable to human capacity and inconsistent with human society.

In these and the like cases, when the government is dissolved, the people are at liberty to provide for themselves by erecting a new legislative, differing from the other by the change of persons or form, or both, as they shall find it most for their safety and good. . . .

There is, therefore, secondly, another way whereby governments are dissolved, and that is when the legislative or the prince, either of them, act contrary to their trust.

First, the legislative acts against the trust reposed in them when they endeavor to invade the property of the subject, and to make themselves or any part of the community masters or arbitrary disposers of the lives, liberties, or fortunes of the people.

The reason why men enter into society is the preservation of their property; and the end why they choose and authorize a legislative is that there may be laws made and rules set as guards and fences to the properties of all the members of the society to limit the power and moderate the dominion of every part and member of the society; for since it can never be supposed to be the will of the society that the legislative should have a power to destroy that which every one designs to secure by entering into society, and for which the people submitted themselves to legislators of their own making. Whenever the legislators endeavor to take away and destroy the property of the people, or to reduce them to slavery under arbitrary power, they put themselves into a state of war with the people who are thereupon absolved from any further obedience, and are left to the common refuge which God has provided for all men against force and violence. Whensoever, therefore, the legislative shall transgress this fundamental rule of society, and either by ambition, fear, folly, or corruption, endeavor to grasp themselves, or put into the hands of any other, an absolute power over the lives, liberties, and estates of the people, by this breach of trust they forfeit the power the people had put into their hands for quite contrary ends, and it devolves to the people, who have a right to resume their original liberty and, by the establishment of a new legislative, such as they shall think fit, provide for their own safety and security, which is the end for which they are in society. What I have said here concerning the legislative in general holds true also concerning the supreme executor, who having a double trust put in him — both to have a part in the legislative and the supreme execution of the law — acts against both when he goes about to set up his own arbitrary will as the law of the society. He acts also contrary to his trust when he either employs the force, treasure, and offices of the society to corrupt the representatives and gain them to his purposes, or openly pre-engages the electors and prescribes to their choice such whom he has by solicitations, threats, promises, or otherwise won to his designs, and employs them to bring in such who have promised beforehand what to vote and what to enact. Thus to regulate candidates and electors, and new-model[7] the ways of election, what is it but to cut up the government by the roots, and poison the very fountain of public security? For the people, having reserved to themselves the choice of their representatives, as the fence to their properties, could do it for no other end but that they might always be freely chosen, and, so chosen, freely act and advise as the necessity of the commonwealth and the public good should upon examination and mature debate be judged to require. . . .

In both the forementioned cases, when either the legislative is changed or the legislators act contrary to the end for which they were constituted, those who are guilty are guilty of rebellion; for if any one by force takes away the established legislative of any society, and the laws of them made pursuant to their trust, he thereby takes away the umpirage which every one had consented to for a peaceable decision of all their controversies, and a bar to the state of war amongst them. They who remove or change the legislative take away this decisive power which nobody can have but by the appointment and consent of the people, and so destroying the authority which the people did, and nobody else can, set up, and introducing a power which the people has not authorized, they actually introduce a state of war which is that of

---

[7] remodel

force without authority; and thus by removing the legislative established by the society — in whose decisions the people acquiesced and united as to that of their own will — they untie the knot and expose the people anew to the state of war. And if those who by force take away the legislative are rebels, the legislators themselves, as has been shown, can be no less esteemed so, when they who were set up for the protection and preservation of the people, their liberties and properties, shall by force invade and endeavor to take them away; and so they putting themselves into a state of war with those who made them the protectors and guardians of their peace, are properly, and with the greatest aggravation, *rebellantes*, rebels. . . .

The end of government is the good of mankind. . . .

## The Bill of Rights (1689)

The Bill of Rights was the crowning piece of legislation to the Glorious Revolution, bringing William and Mary to the throne in February of 1689. It was enacted under the title An Act Declaring the Rights and Liberties of the Subject and Settling the Succession of the Crown. What Parliament passed, however, was less a statement of rights than a bill of limitations upon the new monarchs.

**An Act Declaring the Rights and Liberties of the Subject and Settling the Succession of the Crown**

Whereas the Lords Spiritual and Temporal and Commons assembled . . . did upon the thirteenth day of February in the year of our Lord one thousand six hundred eighty-eight[8] present unto their Majesties, then called and known by the names and style of William and Mary Prince and Princess of Orange, being present in their proper persons, a certain declaration in writing made by the said Lords and Commons in the words following viz:

Whereas the late King James the Second by the assistance of diverse evil councellors, judges and ministers employed by him did endeavor to subvert and extirpate the Protestant religion and the laws and liberties of this kingdom. . . .

And whereas the said late King James the Second having abdicated the government and the throne being thereby vacant, His [Highness] the Prince of Orange (whom it hath pleased Almighty God to make the glorious instrument of delivering this kingdom from popery and arbitrary power) did (by the advice of the Lords Spiritual and Temporal and diverse principal persons of the Commons) cause letters to be written to the Lord Spiritual and Temporal, being Protestants, and other letters to the several counties, cities, universities, boroughs and Cinque Ports for the choosing of such persons to represent them as were of right to be sent to Parliament to meet and sit at Westminster upon the two and twentieth day of January in this year one thousand six hundred eighty and eight[8] in order to such an establishment as that their religion, laws and liberties might not again be in danger of being subverted, upon which letters elections having been accordingly made.

And thereupon the said Lords Spiritual and Temporal and Commons pursuant to their respective letters and elections being now assembled in a full and free representative of this nation, taking into their most serious consideration the best means for attaining the ends aforesaid, do in the first place (as their ancestors in like case have usually done) for the vindicating and asserting their ancient rights and liberties, declare:

---

SOURCE: From *Statutes of the Realm* (London, 1810–1828), Vol. VI, pp. 142–144.

[8] Parliament seems to have deliberately confused the year.

That the pretended power of suspending of laws or the execution of laws by regal authority without consent of Parliament is illegal;

That the pretended power of dispensing with laws or the execution of laws by regal authority as it hath been assumed and exercised of late is illegal;

That the commission for erecting the late Court of Commissioners for Ecclesiastical Causes and all other commissions and courts of like nature are illegal and pernicious;

That levying money for or to the use of the crown by pretence of prerogative without grant of Parliament for longer time or in other manner then the same is or shall be granted is illegal;

That it is the right of the subjects to petition the King and all commitments and prosecutions for such petitioning are illegal;

That the raising or keeping a standing army within the kingdom in time of peace unless it be with consent of Parliament is against law;

That the subjects which are Protestants may have arms for their defence suitable to their conditions and as allowed by law;

That election of members of Parliament ought to be free;

That the freedom of speech and debates or proceedings in Parliament ought not to be impeached or questioned in any court or place out of Parliament;

That excessive bail ought not be required nor excessive fines imposed, nor cruel and unusual punishments inflicted;

That jurors ought to be duly impaneled and returned, and jurors which pass upon men in trials for high treason ought to be freeholders;

That all grants and promises of fines and forfeitures of particular persons before conviction are illegal and void;

And that for redress of all grievances and for the amending, strengthening and preserving of the laws, Parliaments ought to be held frequently.

And they do claim, demand and insist upon all and singular [of] the[se] premises as their undoubted rights and liberties. . . .

To which demand of their rights they are particularly encouraged by the declaration of his Highness the Prince of Orange as being the only means for obtaining a full redress and remedy therein. Having, therefore, an entire confidence that his said Highness the Prince of Orange will perfect the deliverance so far advanced by him and will still preserve them from the violation of their rights which they have here asserted and from all other attempts upon their religion, rights and liberties, the said Lords Spiritual and Temporal and Commons assembled at Westminster do resolve that William and Mary, Prince and Princess of Orange, be and be declared King and Queen of England, France and Ireland and the Dominions thereunto belonging, to hold the crown and royal dignity of the said kingdoms and dominions to them, the said Prince and Princess, during their lives and the life of the survivor of them. And that the sole and full exercise of the regal power to be only in and executed by the said Prince of Orange in the names of the said Prince and Princess during their joint lives, and after their deceases the said crown and royal dignity of the said kingdoms and dominions to be to the heirs of the body of the said Princess. And for default of such issue to the Princess Anne of Denmark and the heirs of her body; and for default of such issue to the heirs of the body of the said Prince of Orange. And the Lords Spiritual and Temporal and Commons do pray the said Prince and Princess to accept the same accordingly. . . . And whereas it hath been found by experience that it is inconsistent with the safety and welfare of this Protestant kingdom to be governed by a popish Prince or by any King or Queen marrying a papist, the said Lords Spiritual and Temporal do further pray that it may be enacted that all and every person and persons that is, are, or shall be reconciled to, or shall hold communion with, the see or Church of Rome, or shall profess the popish religion, or shall marry a papist, shall be excluded and be forever incapable to inherit, possess or enjoy the crown and government of this Realm and Ireland and the Dominions thereunto belonging, or any part of the same, or to have use or exercise any regal power, authority or jurisdiction within the same. . . .

## FURTHER DISCUSSION QUESTIONS

### James I, on the Divinity of Kings

1. To what extent is a "free" monarch possessed of absolute power?
2. To what extent is the relationship between a subject and a king a two-way street involving both rights and duties?
3. What, according to James, is the ultimate sanction for all governmental and social authority, and what, if anything, restrains the divine-right king?

### Thomas Hobbes, Leviathan

1. How would James have responded to Hobbes's definition of the commonwealth?
2. What is Hobbes's concept of war?
3. How is moral action determined by Hobbes?
4. What for Hobbes is the distinction between the laws of nature and the laws of society?
5. Why cannot rights, once given in the form of a contract, be taken back?
6. Why were Hobbes's theories an unacceptable defense for the royalist cause?
7. Do you agree with Hobbes?

### The Agreement of the People and Putney Debates

1. What articles of the agreement ran counter to prevailing religious, political, and social opinions?
2. Does the issue that divided General Ireton and Major Rainborough still exist today?
3. Who is more convincing, Rainborough et al. or Ireton and Cromwell?
4. Where would Hobbes and Charles I have stood in this debate?

### John Locke, Second Treatise of Government

1. Of the two, Ireton and Rainborough, who would have approved more of Locke? Why?
2. Compare and contrast the states of nature and rights of man as argued by Hobbes and Locke.
3. What is Locke's definition of property? Does it make sense?
4. Of the two, Hobbes and Locke, who makes the most sense? Who is the most logical? Who is the closest to modern society?

### The Bill of Rights

1. Compare and contrast our own Bill of Rights with the English bill. Consider the rights covered, the emphasis, the circumstances, and the format.

# 16

# *New Horizons*

This final chapter is a study in contrasts, for it seeks to lay bare the anatomy of the modern secular and statistical mind as it emerged out of its medieval-Christian past. The starting point is a sad spectacle of man's inhumanity to his own species and his ability to live a nightmare of unreason and misconception: the trial of nineteen and the execution of ten men and women for witchcraft in the city of Lancaster in August, 1612. It is doubtless unfair in a concluding chapter to associate the premodern mentality that could produce Aquinas' *Summa Theologica*, "Our Lady's Tumbler," Bishop Nigel's analysis of the Exchequer, Chaucer's Canterbury pilgrims, and the literary masterpieces of Elizabethan England with "The Wonderfull Discoverie of Witches." But the use of a priori logic and the assumptions about God, society, and the universe made by Isabel Robey and her persecutors are peculiarly dramatic symptoms of a way of thinking, of viewing the world, of marshalling evidence, and of relating causes to effects that stand in stark contrast to the three documents that follow.

The historical timing of witchcraft and its persecution remain something of a mystery. A question worthy of thought and speculation is why both appeared in England and the colonies in particularly virulent forms just as the religiously oriented, Aristotelian-based world of the sixteenth century was giving way to the secular mentality and probing minds of Galileo in astronomy, Boyle and Gilbert in chemistry and physics, Bacon in scientific logic, Hobbes in religion, Thomas Mun in economics, William Petty in statistics, and John Locke in epistomology. The chronology is significant. The Lancaster witch trials took place in 1612; Francis Bacon wrote *Novum Organum* in 1620, while Hobbes worked out his views on religion only a generation later during the 1640s. Sir Francis Bacon (1561–1626) has already been encountered as the political gray eminence advising the Earl of Essex (Chapter 10). He stands

Bacon, ye great Moral Philosopher.(From a remarkably scarce Print.)

almost alone in his generation as a man who was a major political figure, a political analyst, and an important scientific theorist. Indeed, he had one of the most eclectic, imaginative, and forceful, if not incisive, minds of the century. Born the youngest son of Gloriana's Lord Keeper, Nicholas Bacon, he moved naturally and easily into the world of Elizabethan society and politics, but it was not until the succession of James I that his talents and ambitions were fully rewarded. By 1613 Bacon was Attorney General; three years later he was appointed Lord Chancellor and Baron Verulam; and by the time of his disgrace and trial for having taken bribes as Lord Chancellor, he had been created Vicount St. Albans. Even before his enforced retirement from politics in 1622, Bacon had somehow found time to write the *Novum Organum*, from which his "Aphorisms concerning the Interpretation of Nature and the Kingdom of Man" are taken. In the field of science Bacon was more a prophet than an architect, a critic of the old than a builder of the new. As an effort to lay down a new set of principles for logic, the *Novum Organum* leaves much to be desired; as a clarion call for a new age, filled with hope for man—his capabilities, his control over nature, and God's expectations for him—it is a magnificent public relations' job. As such, it should be read with Christopher Marlowe's *Dr. Faustus* in mind (see Chapter 11).

The authors of the next two documents have already been quoted extensively in Chapters 14 and 15, which is evidence enough of the impact of their thought on contemporaries and succeeding generations. Thomas Hobbes's views on religion, taken from Chapter 12 of the *Leviathan*, were strong medicine for the mid-seventeenth century, and he was accused of being an atheist. The label was unjust, but his approach to religion was, nevertheless, devastatingly modern. The investigation by John Locke (1632–1704) into the genesis of ideas represents a small portion of his most important philosophical work, his 700-page *Essay Concerning Human Understanding*, which, as he confessed, was "begun by chance, continued by intreaty, written by incoherent parcels, and after long intervals of neglect" finally published in 1690. No minds stand further apart than those of Hobbes and Locke at one extreme and Isabel Robey and Sir Edward Bromley at the other. The former are squarely in the modern world; the latter belong in the medieval past, for their assumptions about God, man, heaven, hell and earthly society, and the interaction between the five—if not their silliness, blindness, and self-delusion—are alien to the twentieth century.

The remaining three documents involve a related but different area of contrast: how the seventeenth century viewed, measured, and controlled the economic life of the kingdom and its human and material resources. The first selection, "Reasons to be concerned for iustifieinge the undertakeres of the intended Plantation in New England," was penned by John Winthrop (1588–1649), the first governor of the Massachusetts Bay Colony. The tract was written in 1629, the year before he sailed for the New World. Winthrop was a country gentleman, lawyer, and devout Puritan. His efforts to publicize what was clearly a combined religious and commercial enterprise, as well as his reasons for urging his countrymen to forsake the comforts of the hearthside, deserve careful scrutiny. His reasoning contains a strange mixture of the religious and the profane. Although one might fruitfully speculate on the connection between Puritanism and expansionism, — capitalistic or territorial — Winthrop's reasons for leaving England are clear and stand in contrast to the approach of the next two writers.

Sir William Petty (1623–1687) is the embodiment of the perfect seventeenth-century success story. Born the son of a clothier, he became a seaman and ship designer, a medical student, a professor of anatomy as well as of music, an inventor, a surveyor, a member of parliament, an economic theorist, a statistician, a statesman, and a founding member of the Royal Society. By the end of his life, he had been knighted by his sovereign, had purchased the London townhouse of the Earl of Arundel, had acquired extensive landholdings in Ireland, and was worth some £15,000 per annum. He knew Thomas Hobbes well. And as Hobbes had attempted to apply the logic and theories of science to society, so Petty sought to apply political arithmetic or "the art of reasoning by figures" to economics. His goal was to express himself "in terms of number, weight, or measure; to use only arguments of sense, and to consider only such causes as have visable foundations in nature." Petty's introductory letter to an essay on "The Value and Encrease of People and Colonies," printed as a preface to his better-known essay "Concerning the Growth of the City of

London" and originally published in 1672, is something of a laundry list; but it reflects the spirit, breath, and limits of his mind and his approach to the subject.

Chronologically, the concluding selection should come before Petty's essay on the "Encrease of People," for Thomas Mun (1571–1641) was born an Elizabethan and died before the Great Rebellion broke out. The son and grandson of London commercialists, he made his own fortune in the Levant trade. In 1615 he was elected one of the directors of the newly founded East India Company. He became one of the fathers of mercantilistic economic theory, especially of the branch which insisted that a favorable balance of trade should be computed by including the profits from the carrier trade and invisible assets. His treatise, *England's Treasure by Forraign Trade*, published posthumously in 1664, became one of the gospels for state and mercantile policy until well into the nineteenth century. Dates are sometimes less significant than content, and Mun has been placed at the end of the chapter partly because *England's Treasure* is in some ways even further removed in spirit and approach from John Winthrop than is William Petty's "Encrease of People," and partly because Mun's introductory letter to his son and first chapter to his book stand as a signal that the elusive "middle class" was finally aware of its own existence. As a consequence, *England's Treasure* must be read as a separate entity, a final study in contrast that should be viewed in relationship to an earlier letter to a son, Sir Henry Sidney's exhortation to young Philip, dated 1565 and presented in Chapter 11.

## The Wonderfull Discoverie of Witches in the Countie of Lancaster (August, 1612)

Nineteen men and women were tried for witchcraft in the city of Lancaster in August, 1612. Ten were executed, including Isabel Robey, the record of whose trial and judgment follows.

---

*The Arraignment and Trial of* Isabel Robey, *in the County of Lancaster, for Witchcraft, upon Wednesday the nineteenth of August, 1612, at the Assizes and General Jail-Delivery, holden at Lancaster. Before* Sir Edward Bromley, *Knight, one of his Majesty's Justices of Assize at Lancaster.*

ISABEL ROBEY,

Thus at one time may you behold witches of all sorts, from many places in this county of Lancaster, which now may lawfully be said to abound as much in witches of divers kinds, as seminaries, Jesuits and Papists. Here then is the last that came to act her part in this lamentable and woeful tragedy, wherein his majesty hath lost so many subjects, mothers their children, fathers their friends and kinsfolk, the like whereof hath not been set forth in any age. What hath the King's majesty written and published in his *Demonology* by way of premonition and prevention, which hath not here by the

---

SOURCE: From Walter Scott, *A Collection of Scarce and Valuable Tracts on the Most Interesting and Entertaining Subjects . . . Selected from . . . Particularly That of the Late Lord Somers* (London, 1809), Vol. III, pp. 149–153.

first and last been executed, put in practice or discovered? What witches have ever, upon their arraignment and trial, made such open, liberal and voluntary declarations of their lives and such confessions of their offences; the manner of their offences; the manner of their attempts and their bloody practices, their meetings, consultations and what not? Therefore I shall now conclude with this Isabel Robey who is now come to her trial.

This Isabel Robey, prisoner in the castle at Lancaster, being brought to the bar before the great seat of justice, was there, according to the former order and course, indicted and arraigned, for that she felloniously had practised, exercised and used her devilish and wicked arts called witchcrafts, enchantments, charms and soceries.

Upon her arraignment to this indictment, she pleaded not guilty, and for the trial of her life put herself upon God and her country.

So as now the gentlemen of the jury of life and death stand charged with her as with others.

*The Evidence against* Isabel Robey, *Prisoner at the Bar The Examination of* Peter Chaddock *of Windle, in the County of Lancaster, taken at Windle aforesaid, the 12th day of July 1612. . . .*

The said examinate upon his oath saith that before his marriage he heard say that the said Isabel Robey was not pleased that he should marry his now wife; whereupon this examinate called the said Isabel witch and said that he did not care for her. Then, with two days next after, this examinate was sore pained in his bones. And this examinate having occasion to meet Master John Hawarden at Peaseley Cross, wished one Thomas Lyon to go thither with him, which they both did so; but as they came homewards, they both were in evil case. But within a short time after, this examinate and the said Thomas Lyon were both very well amended.

And this examinate further saith that about

four years last past his now wife was angry with the said Isabel, she then being in his house, and his said wife thereupon went out of the house, and presently after that the said Isabel went likewise out of the house, not well pleased, as this examinate then did think; and presently after, upon the same day, this examinate with his said wife, working in the hay, a pain and a starkness[1] fell into the neck of this examinate which grieved him very sore. Whereupon this examinate sent to one James, a glover, which then dwelt in Windle, and desired him to pray for him, and within four or five days next after this examinate did mend very well. Nevertheless, this examinate during the same time was very sore pained and so thirsty withall, and hot within his body, that he would have given anything he had to have slaked his thirst, having drunk enough in the house and yet could not drink until the time that the said James, the glover, came to him; and this examinate then said before the said glover, I would to God that I could drink; whereupon the said glover said to this examinate, take that drink and in the name of the Father, the Son and the Holy Ghost drink it, saying the devil and witches are not able to prevail against God and his word. Whereupon this examinate then took the glass of drink and did drink it all, and afterwards mended very well, and so did continue in good health until our Lady['s] day in Lent was twelve month[s] or thereabouts; since which time this examinate saith that he hath been sore pained with great warch[2] in his bones and all his limbs, and so yet continueth. And this examinate further saith that his said warch and pain came to him rather by means of the said Isabel Robey, than otherwise, as he verily thinketh.

*The Examination of* Jane Wilkinson, *Wife of* Francis Wilkinson *of Windle . . . the day and place aforesaid. . . .*

The said examinate upon her oath saith that upon a time the said Isabel Robey asked her [for] milk, and she denied to give her any;

---

[1] rigidity   [2] ache

and afterwards she met the said Isabel, whereupon this examinate waxed afraid of her and was then presently sick and so pained that she could not stand; and the next day after this examinate, going to Warrington, was suddenly pinched on her thigh, as she thought with four fingers and a thumb, twice together, and thereupon was sick, in so much as she could not get home but on horse-back. Yet soon after she did mend.

*The Examination of* Margaret Lyon, *Wife of* Thomas Lyon *the younger, of Windle aforesaid. Taken . . . the day and place aforesaid. . . .*

The said Margaret Lyon, upon her oath, saith that upon a time Isabel Robey came into her house and said that Peter Chaddock could never mend until he had asked her forgiveness, and that she knew he would never do; whereupon this examinate said: How do you know that, for he is a true Christian and he would ask all the world forgiveness? Then the said Isabel said: That is all one, for he will never ask me foregiveness; therefore he shall never mend. . . . And yet this examinate further saith that the said Peter Chaddock had very often told her that he was very afraid that the said Isabel had done him much hurt and that he being fearful to meet her, he hath turned back at such time as he did meet her alone, which the said Isabel hath since then affirmed to be true, saying that he, the said Peter, did turn again when he met her in the lane.

*The Examination of* Margaret Parre, *Wife of* Hugh Parre, *of Windle aforesaid. Taken . . . the day and place aforesaid. . . .*

The said examinate upon her oath saith that upon a time the said Isabel Robey came to her house, and this examinate asked her how Peter Chaddock did, and the said Isabel answered she knew not, for she went not to see. And then this examinate asked her how Jane Wilkinson did, for that she had been lately sick and suspected to have been bewitched; then the said Isabel said twice together: I have bewitched her

too. And then this examinate said that she trusted she could bless herself from all witches and defied them; and then the said Isabel said twice together: Would you defy me? And afterwards the said Isabel went away not well pleased.

Here the gentlemen of the last jury of life and death, having taken great pains, the time being far spent and the number of the prisoners great, returned into the court to deliver up their verdict against them as followeth. *Viz.*

### The Verdict of Life and Death

Who upon their oaths found the said Isabel Robey guilty of the fellony by witchcraft contained in the indictment against her. . . .

### The Prisoners being brought to the Bar

The court commanded three solemn proclamations for silence until judgment for life and death were given.

Whereupon I presented to his lordship the names of the prisoners in order, which were now to receive their judgment.

*The Names of the Prisoners at the Bar to receive their Judgment of Life and Death*

| | |
|---|---|
| Anne Whittle, | Katherine Hewet |
|   alias Chattox | John Bulcock |
| Elizabeth Device | Jane Bulcock |
| James Device | Alizon Device |
| Alice Redferne | Isabel Robey |
| Alice Nutter | |

*The Judgment of the Right Honourable* Sir Edward Bromley, *Knight, one of his Majesties Justices of Assize at Lancaster, upon the Witches convicted, as followeth*

There is no man alive more unwilling to pronounce this woefull and heavy judgement against you than myself; and if it were possible, I would to God this cup might pass from me. But since it is otherwise provided that after all proceedings of the law, there must be a judgment, and the execution of that judgment must succeed and follow in due time, I pray you have patience to receive that which the law doth lay upon you. You of all people have least cause to complain since in the trial of your lives there hath been great care and pains taken, and much time spent; and very few or none of you but stand convicted upon your own voluntary confessions and examinations, *Ex ore proprio.* Few witnesses examined against you but such as were present and parties in your assemblies. Nay, I may further affirm: What persons of your nature and condition ever were arraigned and tried with more solemnity, had more liberty given to plead or answer to every particular point of evidence against you? In conclusion, such hath been the general care of all that had to deal with you that you have neither cause to be offended in the proceedings of the justices, that first took pains in these businesses; nor with the court, that hath had great care to give nothing in evidence against you but matter of fact, sufficient matter upon record and not to induce or lead the jury to find any one of you guilty upon matter of suspicion or presumption; nor with the witnesses, who have been tried as it were in the fire. Nay, you cannot deny but must confess what extraordinary means hath been used to make trial of their evidence and to discover the least intended practice in any one of them to touch your lives unjustly.

As you stand simply (your offences and bloody practises not considered), your fall would rather move compassion than exasperate any man. For whom would not the ruin of so many poor creatures at one time touch, as in appearance simple and of little understanding?

But the blood of those innocent children, and others his majesty's subjects, whom cruelly and barbarously you have murdered and cut off, with all the rest of your offences,

hath cried out unto the Lord against you and sollicited for satisfaction and revenge, and that hath brought this heavy judgment upon you at this time. . . .

First, yield humble and hearty thanks to Almighty God for taking hold of you in your beginning and making stay of your intended bloody practises (although God knows there is too much done already) which would in time have cast so great a weight of judgment upon your souls.

Then praise God that it pleased Him not to surprise or strike you suddenly, even in the execution of your bloody murders, and in the midst of your wicked practises, but hath given you time and takes you away by a judicial course and trial of the law.

Last of all, crave pardon of the world, and especially of all such as you have justly offended either by tormenting themselves, children or friends, murder of their kinsfolk or loss of any of their goods. . . .

It only remains [that] I pronounce the judgment of the court against you by the king's authority, which is [that] you shall all go from hence to the castle, from whence you came; from thence you shall be carried to the place of execution for this county, where your bodies shall be hanged until you be dead. And God have mercy upon your souls. For your comfort in this world I shall commend a learned and worthy preacher to instruct you and prepare you for another world. All I can do for you is to pray for your repentance in this world, for the satisfaction of many, and forgiveness in the next world, for saving of your souls. And God grant you may make good use of the time you have in this world, to His glory and your own comfort.

FRANCIS BACON, *Aphorisms Concerning the Interpretation of Nature and the Kingdom of Man* ( 1620 )

Francis Bacon discusses the conditions for the advancement of science and suggests the wonders in store once "men's minds" are properly prepared.

## Aphorism

### I

Man, being the servant and interpreter of Nature, can do and understand so much and so much only as he has observed in fact or in thought of the course of nature: beyond this he neither knows anything nor can do anything.

### XIX

There are and can be only two ways of searching into and discovering truth. The one flies from the senses and particulars to the most general axioms, and from these principles, the truth of which it takes for settled and immoveable, proceeds to judgment and to the discovery of middle axioms. And this way is now in fashion. The other derives axioms from the senses and particulars, rising by a gradual and unbroken ascent, so that it arrives at the most general axioms last of all. This is the true way, but as yet untried.

### XXII

Both ways set out from the senses and particulars, and rest in the highest generalities; but the difference between them is infinite. For the one just glances at experiment and particulars in passing, the other dwells duly and orderly among them. The one, again, begins at once by establishing certain abstract and useless generalities, the other rises by gradual steps to that which is prior and better known in the order of nature.

### LXXXI

Again there is another great and powerful cause why the sciences have made but little progress; which is this. It is not possible to run a course aright when the goal itself has not been rightly placed. Now the true and lawful goal of the sciences is none other than this: that human life be endowed with new discoveries and powers. . . .

But by far the greatest obstacle to the progress of science and to the undertaking of new tasks and provinces therein, is found in this — that men despair and think things impossible. For wise and serious men are wont in these matters to be altogether distrustful; considering with themselves the obscurity of nature, the shortness of life, the deceitfulness of the senses, the weakness of the judgment, the difficulty of experiment and the like; and so supposing that in the revolution of time and of the ages of the world the sciences have their ebbs and flows; that at one season they grow and flourish, at another wither and decay, yet in such sort that when they have reached a certain point and condition they can advance no further. . . . I am now therefore to speak touching Hope; especially as I am not a dealer in promises, and wish neither to force nor to ensnare men's judgments, but to lead them by the hand with their good will. And though the strongest means of inspiring hope will be to bring men to particulars; especially to particulars digested and arranged. . . . I will proceed with my plan of preparing men's minds; of which preparation to give hope is no unimportant

SOURCE: From Francis Bacon, *Novum Organum*, Book I, Aphorisms 1, 19, 22, 81, 92, 109, 129 in James Spedding, Robert Ellis, and Douglas Heath, eds., *The Works of Francis Bacon* (London: Longman & Co., 1860), Vol. IV.

part. For without it the rest tends rather to make men sad (by giving them a worse and a meaner opinion of things as they are than they now have, and making them more fully to feel and know the unhappiness of their own condition) than to induce any alacrity or to whet their industry in making trial. And therefore it is fit that I publish and set forth those conjectures of mine which make hope in this matter reasonable; just as Columbus did, before that wonderful voyage of his across the Atlantic, when he gave the reasons for his conviction that new lands and continents might be discovered besides those which were known before; which reasons, though rejected at first, were afterwards made good by experience, and were the causes and beginnings of great events.

CIX

Another argument of hope may be drawn from this, — that some of the inventions already known are such as before they were discovered it could hardly have entered any man's head to think of; they would have been simply set aside as impossible. For in conjecturing what may be men set before them the example of what has been, and divine of the new with an imagination preoccupied and coloured by the old; which way of forming opinions is very fallacious; for streams that are drawn from the springheads of nature do not always run in the old channels.

If, for instance, before the invention of ordnance, a man had described the thing by its effects, and said that there was a new invention, by means of which the strongest towers and walls could be shaken and thrown down at a great distance; men would doubtless have begun to think over all the ways of multiplying the force of catapults and mechanical engines by weights and wheels and such machinery for ramming and projecting; but the notion of a fiery blast suddenly and violently expanding and exploding would hardly have entered into any man's imagination or fancy; being a thing to which nothing immediately analogous had been seen, except perhaps in an

earthquake or in lightning, which as *magnalia* or marvels of nature, and by man not imitable, would have been immediately rejected. . . .

There is therefore much ground for hoping that there are still laid up in the womb of nature many secrets of excellent use, having no affinity or parallelism with any thing that is now known, but lying entirely out of the beat of the imagination, which have not yet been found out. They too no doubt will some time or other, in the course and revolution of many ages, come to light of themselves, just as the others did; only by the method of which we are now treating they can be speedily and suddenly and simultaneously presented and anticipated.

CXXIX

. . . Further, it will not be amiss to distinguish the three kinds and as it were grades of ambition in mankind. The first is of those who desire to extend their own power in their native country; which kind is vulgar and degenerate. The second is of those who labour to extend the power of their country and its dominion among men. This certainly has more dignity, though not less covetousness. But if a man endeavour to establish and extend the power and dominion of the human race itself over the universe, his ambition (if ambition it can be called) is without doubt both a more wholesome thing and a more noble than the other two. Now the empire of man over things depends wholly on the arts and sciences. For we cannot command nature except by obeying her. . . .

Lastly, if the debasement of arts and sciences to purposes of wickedness, luxury, and the like, be made a ground of objection, let no one be moved thereby. For the same may be said of all earthly goods; of wit, courage, strength, beauty, wealth, light itself, and the rest. Only let the human race recover that right over nature which belongs to it by divine bequest, and let power be given it; the exercise thereof will be governed by sound reason and true religion.

## THOMAS HOBBES, *Of Religion* ( 1651 )

Thomas Hobbes exposes religion to the scrutiny of a highly rational and critical mind.

---

Seeing there are no signs, nor fruit of *religion*, but in man only; there is no cause to doubt, but that the seed of *religion*, is also in man; and consisteth in some peculiar quality, or at least in some eminent degree thereof, not to be found in any other living creatures.

And first, it is peculiar to the nature of man, to be inquisitive into the causes of the events they see, some more, some less; but all men so much, as to be curious in the search of the causes of their own good and evil fortune.

Secondly, upon the sight of anything that hath a beginning, to think it also had a cause, which determined the same to begin, then when it did, rather than sooner or later.

Thirdly, whereas there is no other felicity of beasts, but the enjoying of their quotidian food, ease, and lusts; as having little or no foresight of the time to come, for want of observation, and memory of the order, consequence, and dependence of the things they see; man observeth how one event hath been produced by another; and remembereth in them antecedence and consequence; and when he cannot assure himself of the true causes of things, (for the causes of good and evil fortune for the most part are invisible), he supposes causes of them, either such as his own fancy suggesteth; or trusteth the authority of other men, such as he thinks to be his friends, and wiser than himself.

The two first, make anxiety. For being assured that there be causes of all things that have arrived hitherto, or shall arrive hereafter; it is impossible for a man, who continually endeavoureth to secure himself against the evil he fears, and procure the good he desireth, not to be in a perpetual solicitude of the time to come; so that every man, especially those that are over provident, are in a state like to that of Prometheus. For as Prometheus, which interpreted, is, *the prudent man*, was bound to the hill Caucasus, a place of large prospect, where, an eagle feeding on his liver, devoured in the day, as much as was repaired in the night: so that man, which looks too far before him, in the care of future time, hath his heart all the day long, gnawed on by fear of death, poverty, or other calamity; and has no repose, nor pause of his anxiety, but in sleep.

This perpetual fear, always accompanying mankind in the ignorance of causes, as it were in the dark, must needs have for object something. And therefore when there is nothing to be seen, there is nothing to accuse, either of their good, or evil fortune, but some *power*, or agent *invisible*: in which sense perhaps it was, that some of the old poets said, that the gods were at first created by human fear: which spoken of the gods, that is to say, of the many gods of the Gentiles, is very true. But the acknowledging of one God, eternal, infinite, and omnipotent, may more easily be derived, from the desire men have to know the causes of natural bodies, and their several virtues, and operations; than from the fear of what was to befall them in time to come. For he that from any effect he seeth come to pass, should reason to the next and immediate cause thereof, and from thence to the cause of that cause, and plunge himself profoundly in the pursuit of causes; shall at last come

---

SOURCE: From Thomas Hobbes, *Leviathan or the Matter, Form, and Power of a Commonwealth Ecclesiastical and Civil*, in William Molesworth ed., *The English Works* (London: John Bohn, 1839), Vol. III, Chap. 12, "Of Religion," pp. 94–109.

to this, that there must be, as even the heathen philosophers confessed, one first mover; that is, a first, and an eternal cause of all things; which is that which men mean by the name of God: and all this without thought of their fortune; the solicitude whereof, both inclines to fear, and hinders them from the search of the causes of other things; and thereby gives occasion of feigning of as many gods, as there be men that feign them. . . .

The worship which naturally men exhibit to powers invisible, it can be no other, but such expressions of their reverence, as they would use towards men; gifts, petitions, thanks, submission of body, considerate addresses, sober behaviour, premeditated words, swearing, that is, assuring one another of their promises, by invoking them. Beyond that reason suggesteth nothing; but leaves them either to rest there; or for further ceremonies, to rely on those they believe to be wiser than themselves.

Lastly, concerning how these invisible powers declare to men the things which shall hereafter come to pass, especially concerning their good or evil fortune in general, or good or ill success in any particular undertaking, men are naturally at a stand; save that using to conjecture of the time to come, by the time past, they are very apt, not only to take casual things, after one or two encounters, for prognostics of the like encounter ever after, but also to believe the like prognostics from other men, of whom they have once conceived a good opinion.

And in these four things, opinion of ghosts, ignorance of second causes, devotion towards what men fear, and taking of things casual for prognostics, consisteth the natural seed of *religion*; which by reason of the different fancies, judgments, and passions of several men, hath grown up into ceremonies so different, that those which are used by one man, are for the most part ridiculous to another.

For these seeds have received culture from two sorts of men. One sort have been they, that have nourished, and ordered them, according to their own invention. The other have done it, by God's commandment, and direction: but both sorts have done it, with a purpose to make those men that relied on them, the more apt to obedience, laws, peace, charity, and civil society. So that the religion of the former sort, is a part of human politics; and teacheth part of the duty which earthly kings require of their subjects. And the religion of the latter sort is divine politics; and containeth precepts to those that have yielded themselves subjects in the kingdom of God. Of the former sort, were all the founders of commonwealths, and the lawgivers of the Gentiles: of the latter sort, were Abraham, Moses, and our blessed Saviour; by whom have been derived unto us the laws of the kingdom of God. . . .

And therefore the first founders, and legislators of commonwealths among the Gentiles, whose ends were only to keep the people in obedience, and peace, have in all places taken care, first, to imprint in their minds a belief, that those precepts which they gave concerning religion, might not be thought to proceed from their own device, but from the dictates of some god, or other spirit; or else that they themselves were of a higher nature than mere mortals, that their laws might the more easily be received. . . . Secondly, they have had a care, to make it believed, that the same things were displeasing to the gods, which were forbidden by the laws. Thirdly, to prescribe ceremonies, supplications, sacrifices, and festivals, by which they were to believe, the anger of the gods might be appeased; and that ill success in war, great contagions of sickness, earthquakes, and each man's private misery, came from the anger of the gods, and their anger from the neglect of their worship, or the forgetting, or mistaking some point of the ceremonies required. . . .

And by these, and such other institutions, they obtained in order to their end, which was the peace of the commonwealth, that the common people in their misfortunes, laying the fault on neglect, or error in their ceremonies, or on their own disobedience to the laws, were the less apt to mutiny against their governors; and being entertained with the pomp, and pastime of festivals; and public games, made in honour of the gods, needed nothing else but bread to keep them from discontent, murmuring, and commotion against the state.

JOHN LOCKE, *The Genesis of Ideas* ( 1690 )

John Locke raises the problem of the origin of ideas. Are they innate, or are they implanted upon the mind by observation and experience and developed by reflection?

. . . I know it is a received doctrine that men have native ideas and original characters stamped upon their minds in their very first being. This opinion I have at large examined already; and I suppose what I have said in the foregoing book will be much more easily admitted when I have shown whence the understanding may get all the ideas it has, and by what ways and degrees they may come into the mind, for which I shall appeal to everyone's own observation and experience.

Let us then suppose the mind to be, as we say, white paper, void of all characters, without any ideas. How comes it to be furnished? Whence comes it by that vast store which the busy and boundless fancy of man has painted on it with an almost endless variety? Whence has it all the materials of reason and knowledge? To this I answer, in one word, from experience. In that all our knowledge is founded; and from that it ultimately derives itself. Our observation, employed either about external sensible objects or about the internal operations of our minds perceived and reflected on by ourselves, is that which supplies our understandings with all the materials of thinking. These two are the fountains of knowledge, from whence all the ideas we have, or can naturally have, do spring.

First, our senses, conversant about particular sensible objects, do convey into the mind several distinct perceptions of things, according to those various ways wherein those objects do affect them. And thus we come by those ideas we have of yellow, white, heat, cold, soft, hard, bitter, sweet, and all those which we call sensible qualities — which, when I say the senses convey into the mind, I mean they from external objects convey into the mind what produces there those perceptions. This great source of most of the ideas we have, depending wholly upon our senses and derived by them to the understanding, I call Sensation.

Secondly, the other fountain from which experience furnisheth the understanding with ideas is the perception of the operations of our own mind within us as it is employed about the ideas it has got; which operations, when the soul comes to reflect on and consider, do furnish the understanding with another set of ideas which could not be had from things without. And such are perception, thinking, doubting, believing, reasoning, knowing, willing, and all the different actings of our own minds which we, being conscious of and observing in ourselves, do from these receive into our understandings as distinct ideas as we do from bodies affecting our senses. This source of ideas every man has wholly in himself, and though it be not sense, as having nothing to do with external objects, yet it is very like it and might properly enough be called internal sense. But as I call the other Sensation, so I call this Reflection, the ideas it

SOURCE: From John Locke, *An Essay Concerning Humane Understandings* 5th ed. (London, 1706), Book II, Chap. I, pp. 50–51, 61.

affords being such only as the mind gets by reflecting on its own operations within itself. By Reflection then, in the following part of this discourse, I would be understood to mean that notice which the mind takes of its own operations, and the manner of them, by reason whereof there come to be ideas of these operations in the understanding. These two, I say, *viz.*, external material things, as the objects of sensation, and the operations of our own minds within, as the objects of reflection, are to me the only originals from whence all our ideas take their beginnings. . . .

. . . The first capacity of human intellect is that the mind is fitted to receive the impressions made on it, either through the senses by outward objects or by its own operations when it reflects on them. This is the first step a man makes towards the discovery of anything and the groundwork whereon to build all those notions which ever he shall have naturally in this world. All those sublime thoughts which tower above the clouds and reach as high as heaven itself take their rise and footing here; in all that great extent wherein the mind wanders in those remote speculations it may seem to be elevated with, it stirs not one jot beyond those ideas which sense or reflection have offered for its contemplation. . . .

## JOHN WINTHROP, *Reasons to be considered for iustifieinge the undertakeres of the intended Plantation in New England* ( 1629 )

John Winthrop, partly to persuade himself to risk the long voyage to New England, partly to encourage others, lists the attractions of the New World and the disadvantages of the old.

1. It will be a service to the church of great consequence to carry the gospel into those parts of the world, to help on the coming of the fullness of the gentiles and to raise a bullwork against the kingdom of anti-Christ which the Jesuits labour to rear up in those parts.

2. All other churches of Europe are brought to desolation and sin, for which the Lord begins already to frown upon us and to cut us short, do threaten evil times to be coming upon us, and who knows, but that God hath provided this place to be a refuge for many whom he means to save out of the general calamity, and seeing the church hath no place left to fly into but the wilderness, what better work can there be than to go and provide tabernacles and food for her against [the time] she comes thither.[3]

3. This land grows weary of her inhabi-

tants, so as man, who is the most precious of all creatures, is here more vile and base than the earth we tread upon, and less prized among us than an horse or a sheep. Masters are forced by authority to entertain servants, parents to maintain their own children; all towns complain of the burden of their poor, though we have taken up many unnecessary — yea unlawful — trades to maintain them, and we use the authority of the law to hinder the increase of people, as by arguing the statute against cottages and in-mates, and thus it is come to pass that children, servants and neighbors, especially if they be poor, are counted the greatest burdens, which if things were right would be the chiefest earthly blessings.

4. The whole earth is the Lord's garden and he hath given it to the sons of men with a gentle commission: Gen: I:28: in-

SOURCE: From R. Winthrop, *Life and Letters of John Winthrop* (Boston, 1864), Vol. I, pp. 309–311.

[3] i.e., arrives

crease and multiply, and replenish the earth and subdue it, which was again renewed to Noah. The end is double and natural that man might enjoy the fruits of the earth, and God might have his due glory from the creature. Why then should we stand striving here for places of habitation, etc. (many men spending as much labor and cost to recover and keep sometimes an acre or two of land, as would procure them many and as good or better in another country), and in the meantime suffer a whole continent as fruitful and convenient for the use of man to lie waste without any improvement?

5. We are grown to that height of intemperance in all excess of riot, as no man's estate almost will suffice to keep sail with his equals, and he who fails herein must live in scorn and contempt. Hence it comes that all arts and trades are carried in that deceitful and unrighteous course, as it is almost impossible for a good and upright man to maintain his charge and live comfortably in any of them. . . .

7. What can be a better work, and more honorable and worthy a Christian than to help raise and support a particular church while it is in the infancy, and to join his forces with such a company of faithful people, as by a timely assistance may grow strong and prosper, and for want of it may be put to great hazard, if not wholly ruined.

8. If any such as are known to be godly and live in wealth and prosperity here shall forsake all this to join themselves with this church and to run an hazard with them of an hard and mean condition, it will be an example of great use both for removing the scandal of worldly and sinister respects which is cast upon the adventurers; to give more life to the faith of God's people, in their prayers for the plantation; and to encourage others to join the more willingly in it.

9. It appears to be a work of God for the good of his church, in that he hath disposed the hearts of so many of his wise and faithful servants, both ministers and others, not only to approve of the enterprise but to interest themselves in it, some in their persons and estates, others by their serious advice and help otherwise, and all by their prayers for the welfare of it. Amos 3: the Lord revealeth his secret to his servants the prophets, it is likely he hath some great work in hand which he hath revealed to his prophets among us, whom he hath stirred up to encourage his servants to this plantation, for he doth not use to seduce his people by his own prophets, but commit that office to the ministry of false prophets and lying spirits.

WILLIAM PETTY, *The Extract of a Letter . . . Concerning the Value and Encrease of People and Colonies* (1672)

In an introductory letter, William Petty outlines the fourteen propositions and questions he proposes to discuss.

The scope of this essay is concerning people and colonies, and to make way for another essay concerning the growth of the City of London. I desire in this first essay to give the world some light, concerning the numbers of people in England, with Wales, and in Ireland; as also, of the number of houses and families wherein they live and of acres they occupy.

2. How many live upon their lands, how many upon their personal estates and commerce, and how many upon art and labour; how many upon alms, how many upon offices and public employments, and how

SOURCE: From William Petty, *Several Essays in Political Arithmetick*, 4th ed. (London, 1755), pp. 4–6.

many as cheats and thieves; how many are impotents, children and decrepit old men.

3. How many upon the poll-taxes in England do pay extraordinary rates, and how many at the level.

4. How many men and women are prolific, and how many of each are married or unmarried.

5. What the value of people are in England, and what in Ireland, at a medium, both as members of the church or commonwealth, or as slaves and servants to one another; with a method how to estimate the same in any other country or colony.

6. How to compute the value of land in colonies, in comparison to England and Ireland.

7. How 10,000 people in a colony may be, and planted to the best advantage.

8. A conjecture in what number of years England and Ireland may be fully peopled, as also all America, and lastly the whole habitable earth.

9. What spot of the earth's globe were fittest for a general and universal emporium, whereby all the people thereof may best enjoy one another's labours and commodities.

10. Whether the speedy peopling of the earth would make *First*, for the good of mankind. *Secondly*, to fulfil the revealed will of God. *Thirdly*, to what prince or state the same would be most advantageous.

11. And exhortation to all thinking men to salve the Scriptures and other good histories, concerning the number of people in all ages of the world, in the great cities thereof, and elsewhere.

12. An appendix concerning the different number of sea-fish and wild-fowl at the end of every thousand years, since Noah's Flood.

13. An hypothesis of the use of those spaces (of about 8,000 miles through) within the globe of our earth, supposing a shell of 150 miles thick.

14. What may be the meaning of glorified bodies, in case the place of the Blessed shall be without the convex of the orb of the fixed stars, if that the whole system of the world was made for the use of our earth's men.

## THOMAS MUN, *England's Treasure by Forraign Trade* (1664)

Thomas Mun, in a work written for the benefit of his son, gives the qualities required in a "perfect merchant of foreign trade," and explains how overseas commerce increases the wealth of the kingdom.

### [Introduction]

My son, in a former discourse I have endeavoured after my manner briefly to teach thee two things: the first is piety, how to fear God aright, according to His works and Word; the second is policy, how to love and serve thy country, by instructing thee in the duties and proceedings of sundry vocations, which either order, or else act[4] the affairs of the commonwealth. In which, as some thing do especially tend to preserve and others are more apt to enlarge the same; so am I now to speak of money, which doth indifferently serve to both those happy ends. Wherein I will observe this order: first, to show the general means whereby a kingdom may be enriched; and then proceed to those particular courses by which princes are accustomed to be supplied with treasure. But first of all I will say something of the merchant, because he must be a principal agent in this great business.

SOURCE: From Thomas Mun, *England's Treasure by Forraign Trade* (London, 1664). Reprinted by Macmillan & Co. (New York, 1895).

[4] help

CHAPTER I

*The Qualities which are required in a*
*perfect Merchant of Foreign Trade*

The love and service of our country consisteth not so much in the knowledge of
those duties which are to be performed by
others as in the skillful practice of that
which is done by ourselves; and therefore
(my son) it is now fit that I say something
of the merchant, which I hope in due time
shall be thy vocation. Yet herein are my
thoughts free from all ambition, although I
rank thee in a place of so high estimation;
for the merchant is worthily called the
steward of the kingdom's stock by way of
commerce with other nations; a work of no
less reputation than trust, which ought to be
performed with great skill and conscience,
that so the private gain may ever accompany the public good. And because the
nobleness of this profession may the better
stir up thy desires and endeavours to obtain
those abilities which may effect it worthily,
I will briefly set down the excellent qualities
which are required in a perfect merchant.

1. He ought to be a good penman, a good
arithmetician, and a good accomptant,[5] by
that noble order of debtor and creditor,
which is used only amongst merchants; also
to be expert in the order and form of char-
ter-parties, bills of lading, invoices, contracts, bills of exchange and policies of
insurance.

2. He ought to know the measures,
weights and monies of all foreign countries. . . .

3. He ought to know the customs, tolls,
taxes, impositions, conducts and other
charges upon all manner of merchandise
exported or imported to and from the said
foreign countries.

4. He ought to know in what several
commodities each country abounds, and
what be the wares which they want, and
how and from whence they are furnished
with the same.

5. He ought to understand and to be a
diligent observer of the rates of exchanges
by bills, from one state to another. . . .

6. He ought to know what goods are
prohibited to be exported or imported in
the said foreign countries, lest otherwise he
should incur great danger and loss in the
ordering of his affairs.

7. He ought to know upon what rates and
conditions to freight his ships and ensure
his adventures from one country to another,
and to be well acquainted with the laws,
orders and customs of the insurance office
both here and beyond the seas. . . .

8. He ought to have knowledge in the
goodness and in the prices of all the several
materials which are required for the building and repairing of ships, and the divers
workmanships of the same, as also for the
masts, tackling, cordage, ordnance, victuals,
munition and provisions of many kinds; together with the ordinary wages of commanders, officers and mariners, all which concern the merchant as he is an owner of
ships.

9. He ought (by the divers occasions
which happen sometime in the buying and
selling of one commodity and sometimes in
another) to have indifferent if not perfect
knowledge in all manner of merchandise or
wares, which is to be as it were a man of
all occupations and trades.

10. He ought by his voyaging on the seas
to become skillful in the art of navivagation.

11. He ought, as he is a traveller and
sometimes abiding in foreign countries, to
attain to the speaking of divers languages,
and to be a diligent observer of the ordinary
revenues and expenses of foreign princes,
together with their strength both by sea and
land. . . .

12. Lastly, although there be no necessity that such a merchant should be a great
scholar; yet is it (at least) required that in
his youth he learn the Latin tongue, which
will the better enable him in all the rest of
his endeavours.

Thus have I briefly showed thee a pattern

---

[5] accountant

for thy diligence, the merchant in his qualities, which in truth are such and so many that I find no other profession that leadeth into more worldly knowledge. And it cannot be denied but that their sufficiency doth appear likewise in the excellent government of state at Venice, Luca, Genoa, Florence, the Low Countries, and divers other places of Christendom. . . . It is true indeed that many merchants here in England find less encouragement given to their profession than in other countries, and seeing themselves not so well esteemed as their noble vocation requireth, and according to the great consequence of the same, do not therefore labour to attain unto the excellence of their profession; neither is it practised by the nobility of this kingdom as it is in other states from the father to the son throughout their generations, to the great increase of their wealth and maintenance of their names and families. Whereas the memory of our richest merchants is suddenly extinguished; the son being left rich scorneth the profession of his father, conceiving more honor to be a gentleman (although but in name), to consume his estate in dark ignorance and excess, than to follow the steps of his father as an industrious merchant to maintain and advance his fortunes. . . .

## Chapter II

### The means to enrich the Kingdom, and to increase our Treasure

Although a kingdom may be enriched by gifts received, or by purchase taken from some other nations, yet these are things uncertain and of small consideration when they happen. The ordinary means therefore to increase our wealth and treasure is by foreign trade, wherein we must ever observe this rule: to sell more to strangers yearly than we consume of theirs in value. For suppose that when this kingdom is plentifully served with the cloth, lead, tin, iron, fish and other native commodities, we do yearly export the overplus to foreign countires to the value of twenty-two hundred

thousand pounds; by which means we are enabled beyond the seas to buy and bring in foreign wares for our use and consumptions, to the value of twenty hundred thousand pounds. By this order duly kept in our trading, we may rest assured that the kingdom shall be enriched yearly two hundred thousand pounds, which must be brought to us in so much treasure; because that part of our stock which is not returned to us in wares must necessarily be brought home in treasure.

For in this case it cometh to pass in the stock of a kingdom, as in the estate of a private man, who is supposed to have one thousand pounds yearly revenue and two thosand pounds of ready money in his chest. If such a man through excess shall spend one thousand five hundred pounds per annum, all his ready money will be gone in four years, and in the like time his said money will be doubled if he take a frugal course to spend but five hundred pounds per annum; which rule never faileth likewise in the commonwealth, but in some cases (of no great moment) which I will hereafter declare, when I shall show by whom and in what manner this balance of the kingdom's account ought to be drawn up yearly, or so often as it shall please the state to discover how much we gain or lose by trade with foreign nations. . . .

## Chapter IV

### The Exportation of our Moneys in Trade of Merchandise is a means to increase our Treasure

This position is so contrary to the common opinion that it will require many and strong arguments to prove it before it can be accepted of the multitude, who bitterly exclaim when they see any monies carried out of the realm, affirming thereupon that we have absolutely lost so much treasure. . . .

We have already supposed our yearly consumptions of foreign wares to be for the value of twenty hundred thousand pounds, and our exportations to exceed that two hundred thousand pounds, which sum we have thereupon affirmed is brought to us in treasure to balance the accompt.[6] But now if we add three hundred thousand pounds more in ready money unto our former exportations in wares, what profit can we have (will some men say) although by this means we should bring in so much ready money more than we did before, seeing that we have carried out the like value.

To this the answer is that when we have prepared our exportations of wares, and sent out as much of everything as we can spare or vent abroad, it is not therefore said that then we should add our money thereunto to fetch in the more money immediately, but rather first to inlarge our trade by enabling us to bring in more foreign wares, which being sent out again will in due time much increase our treasure.

For although in this manner we do yearly multiply our importations to the maintenance of more shipping and mariners, improvement of his Majesty's customs and other benefits, yet our consumption of those foreign wares is no more than it was before; so that all the said increase of commodities brought in by the means of our ready money sent out as is aforewritten, doth in the end become an exportation unto us of far greater value than our said monies were, which is proved by three several examples following.

1. For I suppose that £100,000 being sent in our shipping to the east countries will buy there one hundred thousand quarters of wheat clear abroad the ships, which after being brought into England and housed, to export the same at the best time for vent thereof in Spain or Italy, it cannot yield less in those parts than two hundred thousand pounds to make the merchant but a saver, yet by this reckoning we see the kingdom hath doubled that treasure.

2. Again this profit will be far greater when we trade thus in remote countries; as for example if we send one hundred thousand pounds into the East-Indies to buy pepper there, and bring it hither, and from hence send it for Italy or Turkey, it must yield seven hundred thousand pounds at least in those places, in regard of the excessive charge which the merchant disburseth in those long voyages in shipping, wages, victuals, insurance, interest, customs, imposts, and the like, all which notwithstanding the King and the Kingdom gets. . . .

But if any man will yet object that these returns come to us in wares and not really in money as they were issued out, the answer is (keeping our first ground) that if our consumption of foreign wares be no more yearly than is already supposed, and that our exportations be so mightily increased by this manner of trading with ready money as is before declared, it is not then possible but that all the over-balance or difference should return either in money or in such wares as we must export again, which, as is already plainly showed will be still a greater means to increase our treasure. . . .

Again, some men have alledged that those countries which permit money to be carried out, do it because they have few or no wares to trade withall, but we have great store of commodities, and therefore their action ought not to be our example.

To this the answer is briefly that if we have such a quantity of wares as doth fully provide us of all things needful from beyond the seas, why should we then doubt that our monies sent out in trade must not necessarily come back again in treasure, together with the great gains which it may procure in such manner as is before set down? And on the other side, if those nations which send out their monies do it because they have but few wares of their own, how come they then to have so much treasure as we ever see in those places which suffer it freely to be exported at all times and by whomsoever? I answer, Even by trading with their monies, for by what other means can they get it, having no mines of gold or silver?

Thus may we plainly see that when this

---

[6] account

weighty business is duly considered in His [God's] end, as all our humane actions ought well to be weighed, it is found much contrary to that which most men esteem thereof, be-

cause they search no further than the beginning of the work, which misinforms their judgments and leads them into error. . . .

### FURTHER DISCUSSION QUESTIONS

#### The Wonderfull Discoverie of Witches in the Countie of Lancaster: August, 1612

1. There are so-called "witch trials" today. Do they bare any resemblance to the Lancaster trials?
2. How was it possible for an educated man such as Sir Edward Bromley to have believed in witches and witchcraft?

#### Francis Bacon, Aphorisms

1. What, according to Bacon, is the goal of science? Why has it made so little progress?
2. In what ways is Bacon in tune with modern sentiments and attitudes? In what ways does he depart from them?
3. Would it have been possible for a man like Bacon to have written the "Aphorisms" and at the same time to have believed in witches and witchcraft?

#### Thomas Hobbes, Of Religion

1. What, according to Hobbes, are the causes of religion?
2. Why would the seventeenth century have been appalled by Hobbes's views?

#### John Locke, The Genesis of Ideas

1. What is new about Locke's approach to knowledge? Why would it have been extremely difficult for a medieval man to have conceived the question, stated the argument, or developed the kind of logic that Locke did?

#### John Winthrop, Reasons for iustifieinge the undertakeres of the intended Plantation in New England

1. It has been argued that capitalism and Puritanism have an affinity for one another. It there any evidence for this in Winthrop's statement?
2. What, according to Winthrop, is wrong with seventeenth-century England?

#### William Petty, The Value and Encrease of People and Colonies

1. Do Petty and Bacon have anything in common?
2. Is there anything strange about Petty's list of things to do? How long do you think it would have taken him to finish what he proposes?
3. Is Petty making assumptions that a modern demographer would not? Exactly how modern would you judge him to be?

### Thomas Mun, England's Treasure by Forraign Trade

1. How does Mun's merchant ideal differ from the aristocratic ideal?
2. Compare and contrast Mun's analysis of wealth, power, and economic life with that found in Richard Nigel's *Course of the Exchequer* (Chapter 4), Aquinas' "Of Cheating which is committed in Buying and Selling" (Chapter 6), and More's *Utopia* (Chapter 9).

3  4  5  6  7  8  9  0